THE SELF-HELP GROUP DIRECTORY

Twenty-First Edition
2006

A guide to self-help groups in New Jersey with national organizations, models, and online groups.

Edited by:
Nicole Klem
&
Wendy Rodenbaugh

New Jersey Self-Help Clearinghouse

Saint Clare's Health System
100 East Hanover Ave., Suite 202
Cedar Knolls, NJ 07927-2020

1-800-367-6274 or 973-326-6789
Website: www.selfhelpgroups.org

ISBN 1-930683-06-5

Twenty-First Edition
March 2006

ACKNOWLEDGEMENTS

We are grateful to the **NJ Department of Human Services** and the **Division of Mental Health Services** for their initial and continued funding and support that makes the Clearinghouse services possible. We appreciate too, the efforts of many dedicated **support group representatives** who regularly contribute information on their work that make our services possible.

We wish to express our deep appreciation to all of our wonderful and hardworking **volunteers** who have contributed their time and energy in helping callers and extending services at the Clearinghouse. Our heartfelt thanks go to:

Donna Ammiano	**Mary Ellen Kerin**	**Sekhar Subramani**
Lois Fallat	**Paul Riddleberger**	**Leah Dorman**
Baiba Ozols	**Diane Clarke**	**Pete Lodato**
Deanna Baum	**Sandy Lacher**	**Berit Wenner**
Leslie Johnson	**Harry Salle**	**Adrienne Rothblatt**
Pauravi Patel	**Pat de la Fuente**	**Janet Stone**
Barbara Blumenfeld	**Howard Lerner**	**Patricia Heller**

Much appreciation goes out to the rest of the Clearinghouse staff:

Jeanne Rohach for consistently providing an extra hand, ear and opinion in any situation when needed. Her contribution goes far beyond simply alleviating the share of daily work.

Barbara White for her unending guidance, explanations and assistance and for knowing when to say "It's up to you!", as well as vocal motivation for the directory at all stages of development.

Ed Madara for sharing respected insight on the daily workings of the Clearinghouse in addition to providing kindness, consideration and support to everyone he meets.

In addition, thank you to **Gary Martin & Claude Pain** for their assistance in designing our 25th Anniversary logo and cover.

TABLE OF CONTENTS

MENTAL HEALTH

MISCELLANEOUS

ABOUT THE CLEARINGHOUSE

The New Jersey Self-Help Group Clearinghouse was established in 1981 to promote the awareness, utilization, and development of mutual aid self-help groups. Sponsored by Saint Clare's Health Service and funded primarily by state government, the Clearinghouse provides information and referral, consultation services, and training to help people find and form self-help groups.

The Clearinghouse maintains a database of information on over 4,500 groups within the state and over 1,100 national organizations, one-of-a-kind group models, and online groups. Easy access to this information is assured through our toll-free phone lines.

An important component of our work is the development of new groups as needs arise. For example, if a caller inquires about a support group for any disorder, and our computer search yields nothing in the caller's area, we invite the person to consider starting a group. If they are interested, we can advise them on how they can join with others to develop a group, and include them in our database. Subsequent callers would then be referred to this contact person if they were interested in helping them to start that type of a group.

If the caller is not interested in starting a group, they can still leave their name and contact information and the Clearinghouse will let them know if we subsequently identify an appropriate group in their area.

The Clearinghouse also sponsors training conferences and workshops on starting groups, facilitation skills, publicizing your group, maintaining your group, and other issues of interest to group leaders.

Other services provided by the Clearinghouse include speaking engagements, a variety of guides and hand-outs on specific and general issues related to group development, research projects, facilitation workshops, speakers series, and a website on the Internet. We also work with the media to increase public awareness of groups and their value.

Various volunteer and student opportunities exist at the Clearinghouse. We offer a variety of rewarding volunteer positions, as well as opportunities for internships and applied research that supports self-help groups. Call for details.

HOW TO USE THIS DIRECTORY

For an overview of the variety of groups available, review the Table of Contents, which is a categorization of self-help groups according to the general problem or concern addressed. But to find a mutual aid self-help group for a particular concern, turn to the index at the end of the directory. The index will refer you to pages in the directory where listings of groups dealing with your concern may be found. Within each category, listings are arranged in a geographical order, with statewide groups shown first, local groups next in alphabetical order by county, and finally national organizations, model, and online groups.

In some categories, there are additional resources at the end of the listing. NOTE: Statewide listings include New Jersey groups that cover all, or a large portion of the state; local groups can either be autonomous groups or chapters of national organizations; national groups have chapters in several states and provide assistance to persons interested in starting local chapters; national networks usually don't have face-to-face meetings but link members together for mutual support; model one-of-a-kind groups usually have just one or two local groups, but are willing to help others start similar groups in their areas; and online groups and resources are included to supplement areas where few support groups have been identified.

Each group listing includes the group name, a brief description of the group, and meeting and contact information. If there are no dues or fees listed, it means that the group is free of charge, although many groups will "pass the hat" for contributions for refreshments, literature, and other group expenses.

Remember, when calling a group, please show your consideration for others. Many of the phone numbers given are home numbers, so several tries may be necessary, and contact persons may shift periodically from one member to another. With few exceptions, contact numbers are not hotlines. (See separate helpline listings beginning on page 587). We request that you not call them too early in the morning or too late at night. In our listings, we have tried to indicate whether the phone numbers are best reached during the day or evening.

If you leave a message on an answering machine, speak very clearly and slowly, and include your area code. Sometimes contact people are unable to return calls because they cannot understand the messages left. Also, please be thoughtful of the type of message you leave for the contact person (either on an answering machine or with another person), especially when it concerns sensitive issues. Leave discreet messages—you never know if the person answering the phone or listening to the messages on the answering machine knows that the contact person is a member of a certain group. When writing to a national or local group, it's good to enclose a self-addressed stamped envelope to help defer the expenses and make it easier for the group to respond quickly.

When you cannot find an appropriate group, or a group you wanted has disbanded, please call the Clearinghouse to see if there have been any additional groups identified since the directory was printed, or if there are any groups in the process of forming. Also, ask yourself if you or someone you know would be interested in joining with others to form a self-help group. If so, please call us to find out about our free consultation services.

Don't use this directory after one year has gone by! After a year, consider the directory to be out-of-date and ready for the recycling bin. If this directory is replacing an older edition, we request that you take this opportunity now to recycle your older directory. Consider passing the old directory on to a student or colleague to help educate them to the wide variety of groups available. Do tell them they need to call the Clearinghouse for the most current groups and contacts. Much of the information changes in that time. We are continually updating information and group contact persons and locations are often changing. We also identify new groups that are added to our database. Please call us for the most up-to-date information on referrals.

PLEASE NOTE: The Clearinghouse has made every effort to include as many different support groups as possible. However, The Clearinghouse reserves the right to include or exclude any names, groups, or telephone contacts at its absolute discretion. Omission of any organization does not signify disapproval; nor does inclusion of an organization signify approval. The use of any materials contained herein is entirely the responsibility of the reader. The Clearinghouse further disclaims any and all liability for any use or non-use of the information herein. There are no warranties implied or expressed in any of the information provided. The information provided is based upon that which is supplied by the groups themselves. The Clearinghouse is not responsible for printing, insertion, or deletion errors.

Finally, understand that the quality of individual groups will differ, sometimes even among those with the same name. Phone and visit the group to see if it is *for you*. The ultimate evaluation and very survival of any self-help group is determined by those who attend it and decide whether or not to continue as contributing members.

WHAT IS A SELF-HELP GROUP?

Most of the self-help groups listed on the following pages can better be described as mutual aid self-help groups because they derive their energy from members helping one another. Among the various organizations that deal with stressful life situations, we look for those that provide opportunities for mutual help. In addition, three other characteristics constitute a self-help group: the group is composed of peers, i.e. people who share a similar experience or situation; the group is primarily run by and for its members who have a sense of ownership of the group; and the group is voluntary and non-profit in that there are no fees for services, although the group may charge dues or request donations.

While the focus of the Clearinghouse is on the development of self-help groups that are run by members themselves, we include in our listings some support groups that are run by professionals (identified in their listing as "professionally-run"). While professionally-run support groups are not self-help groups, we include them in the directory if the meetings are free or have a nominal charge, the professional does not receive a fee from members for facilitating the group, and the purpose of the group is mutual support among peers.

Please understand that there are other types of self-help organizations that do indeed provide mutual aid and support. They include civic, ethnic, fraternal, housing, cultural, political, church, and the neighborhood groups — some of which spring up naturally without even a name or with little structure beyond mutual help discussions. However, groups in any one of these categories could, by their nature and sheer numbers, warrant a separate directory of their own, and are therefore not included here.

"However much we are affected by the things of the world, however deeply they may stir and stimulate us, they become human for us only when we can discuss them with our fellows... We humanize what is going on in the world and in ourselves only by speaking of it, and in the course of speaking of it we learn to be human."

-Hanna Arendt in "Confiding"

HOW SELF-HELP GROUPS HELP

Have you ever noticed that when you have a problem it helps to talk with someone who has had a similar problem? Simply finding others who have "been there" and realizing that "you are not alone" can in itself be a great relief. Providing the opportunity for this is one way mutual aid self-help groups help.

With time, some self-help groups resemble an extended family, providing a caring community that is often available 24 hours a day without forms, fees, or appointments. Yet the groups also emphasize self-reliance, as each member assumes responsibility for helping him or herself while helping others.

Within such groups, people who share similar problems and needs gather to help one another cope with the problem they face. The problem may be a disability, a chronic illness, loss of a loved one, an addiction, or any one of hundreds of other difficult life situations. Social support can make it easier to cope with a stressful situation, and this alleviation of stress can be directly related to the prevention of further illness and distress.

Another important way that self-help groups help is the way in which members not only receive help from their peers, but can also provide help to others. Helping someone else deal with a problem that you also experience builds self-confidence and reinforces the use of coping strategies that have worked for you and others. Those who have been able to cope with a particular problem can serve as valuable role models for those who are just beginning to reach out for encouragement and practical information.

Self-help groups are not meant to replace needed professional services, although they supplement and sometimes prevent the need for them. Many groups tap professionals as advisors, guest speakers, consultants, trainers, and referral resources. When pooling their personal experiences, coping skills, and insights group members will often come to recognize the specific agencies and therapists who best meet their needs. For literature and research study references on additional ways that self-help groups help, contact the Clearinghouse.

"Two are better than one, because they have a good reward for their labor. For if they fall, one will lift up his companion. But woe to him who is alone when he falls, for he has no one to help him up."

- Ecclesiastes 4: 9-10.

CHOOSING A SUPPORT GROUP

Whether you are a professional considering groups for your clients, or a person simply looking for a helpful group for yourself, you may wonder if a support group is right for you. Let's examine the choices from those two perspectives.

Professional Considerations

For caring professionals, who realize that they cannot be all things to their clients, support groups are welcome community resources that supplement your assistance, and in so doing, can help prevent professional burnout. Groups also provide support at times when professional offices are closed, whether it is the actual meetings or the phone support often available between meetings. Since the groups provide the unique support of "others who have been there," they can be especially helpful for clients who feel alone and isolated with the stressful situation they face. But groups provide a variety of other benefits: acceptance, positive role models, normalization, coping skills, practical information, education, community, sometimes a "program to work" as in 12-step groups, advocacy, and "helper therapy," the ability to help others in the group.

In providing a referral, a professional can point out the potential value of a group. In actually making the referral, it's helpful to suggest to the client that they check out the support group to see if it is "for you." It's often helpful to have the brochures of particular groups that are most often referred to, since the group's brochure explains what the group offers and takes away the fear of the unknown. Ideally these brochures should be available in the waiting area

For the Person Seeking a Group

When looking for a support group, first identify the source of your stress (e.g., the specific illness, addiction, loss, etc.) and any special situation (your being a caregiver, parent, or friend of the person with the problem). In addition to a group's problem focus, there are many other differences in the types of groups available. Some support groups are member-run, while others have professional facilitators; some have a very narrow focus while others are very broad; some are based upon either spiritual or religious beliefs, while many are not; some are very structured while others have little structure at all; some focus on emotional support, education, or advocacy, while others are more social. These differences may be important to you, so the more you learn about a group, the better you will be able to choose the right group for you.

Learn About A Group Before Attending a Meeting The best information about a group comes from the group itself. Most groups have a phone contact person who will answer any questions you have about the group before you attend a meeting. Also, many groups have a brochure or other literature that describes their group's purpose and activities.

Questions You Might Ask In addition to finding out the meeting time and place, there are other questions you may want to ask before attending. You might ask about the people in the group: do they understand what you are going through because they have had similar experiences? How many usually attend the meeting (more people means more interest and energy, but less time for each member to share concerns)? What is the ratio of men to women, or the age range of the members (if it makes a difference to you). You might inquire about any meeting formats, and any costs associated with joining the group.

The First Meeting You Attend Once you decide to attend a meeting, there are many aspects of the group you can learn about first hand. One of the first impressions you'll get about the group will be how welcome you feel. Do people welcome you and introduce themselves to you? Do they sit near you, smile at you, and in general make you feel like they are glad you're there? How much mutual help occurs within the group? Do people really help each other, or is it one or two people giving advice to everyone else? If the group is led by a professional, why is he or she leading the group, and what kind of leadership style does he or she exert?

If the members lead the group, how is leadership decided upon? Is it rotated, shared among group members, or limited to just one or two people? What other roles are assumed by group members? How many people help to run the group? Again, a good match between your needs and the group is what you're seeking.

Another observation you can make has to do with general group tone. Does it seem like the group is helpful to its members? Do people seem glad to see each other? Is there positive energy? Humor? Honesty? Do people listen to each other? Do they show concern, respect, understanding, and acceptance?

Sometimes you will find a group that's perfect for you on the first try. Other times you may have to try several types of groups or a different meeting of the same group before you've found the best match. The bottom line is whether you feel the group meets your needs. Finally, after you have chosen and benefited from a self-help group, please consider staying for a while to "give back" and help others. Self-help groups depend upon such volunteer efforts. Your volunteer efforts will not only help others, but will most probably benefit you in terms of your own physical and mental well-being.

Remember, if there is no group for you (or your client, if you are a professional), consider joining with others to start one – call the Clearinghouse for free help.

HOW THE CLEARINGHOUSE HELPS
PEOPLE START GROUPS

The New Jersey Self-Help Clearinghouse provides a variety of services — a vital one being the assistance given to people interested in starting groups. Whether you are a lay person or a supportive professional who recognizes the need for a group, we can help. Some callers contact the Clearinghouse already committed to the idea of starting a group. Others, when there is no local group available for their problem, respond affirmatively to the question, "Would you be interested in joining with others to start a group?" and are put in touch with a Clearinghouse group development consultant.

Assistance is available to help people develop self-help groups for a wide variety of life situations and transitions, medical or emotional problems, addictions—just about any issue which affects a person's daily life.

Literature: The Clearinghouse has a wide range of printed materials related to self-help which are available to people starting groups, including:

- General how-to's which explain the basic steps in getting a group started; from finding co-founders, to structuring a group meeting.
- Group development materials from specific groups explaining how to start that type of group.
- Many other related materials, such as how to write a press release or group maintenance strategies.

Networking with Other Groups: One way beginning groups can "learn the ropes" is by learning how others have done it. The Clearinghouse staff can put you in touch with representatives of similar groups. You can call or visit a local group to ask how they got their groups started: what they do to find members, what they do in their meetings, what problems they encounter in their groups and how they solve those problems. Contact with a nationally organized group can provide group development information, newsletters, pamphlets and brochures, and many other kinds of information and services. You can contact and learn from others who "have been there." Having a support network of such people can be very helpful for both the short and long run. This continuing dialogue models the support and concern that a self-help group provides its members.

Our referrals to persons interested in starting groups: The Clearinghouse will list a person interested in starting a group on its database so that we refer any callers interested in help you. This is just one of the ways you may find others who are similarly interested in working with you to help create a new group in your area.

Training Workshops: The Clearinghouse offers periodic workshops on issues related to self-help which may be useful to beginning groups (e.g. how to get groups started, how to deal with difficult people, listening skills, etc.). The Clearinghouse also periodically co-sponsors special interest conferences with self-help groups and other organizations.

Phone help: Once a person has decided to start a group and begins to work with a Clearinghouse trainer, this relationship usually continues until the group has started. On-going phone contact is available to discuss issues or problems that come up while the person is starting the group, such as: what kind of meeting place would be suitable and ways to locate such a space; how to enlist others to help you start the group; or how to do outreach for membership. Sometimes the consultant can suggest ways to locate speakers, or provide more specific printed materials for a particular problem or need. Sometimes it's simply a question of providing support and encouragement when things seem overwhelming and discouraging; at other times, the satisfaction of sharing a success.

Clearinghouse relationship to those starting groups: In the interest of maintaining the best climate possible for the development of an independent, member-run mutual aid self-help group, the Clearinghouse primarily provides telephone assistance and resource materials. Clearinghouse trainers are available to offer advice, suggestions, and guidelines on the development of your group, but you are under no obligation to follow through on those suggestions. We provide neither implied nor actual sponsorship nor co-sponsorship of any group developed.

"My years as a medical practitioner, as well as my own first-hand experience, have taught me how *important* self-help groups are in assisting their members in dealing with problems, stress, hardship and pain... the benefits of mutual aid are experienced by *millions of people* who turn to others with a similar problem to attempt to deal with their isolation, powerlessness, alienation, and the awful feeling that nobody understands."

- former **U.S. Surgeon General C. Everett Koop, MD**, who also served as a member of *Compassionate Friends*, an international self-help group for bereaved parents, following the sudden death of his own college age son (see pages 143-152 for local Compassionate Friends chapters).

IDEAS AND SUGGESTIONS FOR STARTING A MUTUAL AID SELF-HELP GROUP

Self-help groups offer people who face a common problem the opportunity to meet with others and share their experiences, knowledge, strengths and hopes. Run by and for their members, self-help groups can better be described as "mutual help" groups. Hundreds of these groups are started each week across the nation by ordinary people with a little bit of courage, a fair sense of commitment, and a good amount of caring. The following guidelines are based on our experience at the Clearinghouse helping hundreds of individuals to start groups. While there is no one recipe for developing a group (different national groups offer different model approaches), here is an overview of the basic steps and strategies. Call us for additional ideas and specific how-to's.

Don't Re-invent the Wheel. If you are interested in starting a group around a particular concern or problem, find out what groups already exist for it. Call our Clearinghouse to confirm that there are no existing local groups that may address your issue. Check first in this Directory for any national self-help groups that address your concern. Contact and ask them for what help and "how-to" starter packet information they can provide, and which of their groups might be closest to you. You can also speak to a Clearinghouse group consultant and ask for their help. In addition to free consultation, literature, and contacts, the consultant can also list your interest on our computer to network you with any callers interested in helping you.

Think "Mutual-Help" From the Start. Find a few others who share your interest in starting (not simply joining) a self-help group. Starting a group should not be on one person's shoulders alone. So, put out flyers or letters that specifically cite your interest in hearing from those who would be interested in "joining with others to help start" such a group. Include your first name and phone number. Make copies and post them at places you feel most appropriate, e.g., library, community center, or post office. Mail copies to key people whom you think would know others like yourself. Post it on any online message boards that deal with the issue or your local community. When, hopefully, you receive calls, discuss with the caller what their interests are, share your vision of what you would like to see the group do, and finally ask if they would be willing to work with you for a specific period of time to try to get the group off the ground. Suggest different possibilities: greeting people at the door and introducing new members; bringing refreshments; making coffee; or co-chairing the meeting, etc.

Once a couple of people have said yes, you have a "core group" or "steering committee" - and you won't have to do it alone. It's much easier to start a group if the work is shared. But most importantly, if several people are involved in the initial work at that first meeting (refreshments, publicity, name tags, greeting new people, etc.), you will model for newcomers what your self-help group is all about - not one person doing it all, but the volunteer efforts and the active participation of all the members.

Find a Suitable Meeting Place and Time. Try to obtain free meeting space at a local church, synagogue, library, community center, hospital or social service agency. If you anticipate a small group and feel comfortable with the idea, you could even consider initial meetings in members' homes. Would evening or day meetings be better for members? Many prefer weeknights. It is also easier for people to remember the meeting time if it's a fixed day of the week or month, like the second Thursday of the month, etc.

Publicize & Run your First Public Meeting. Reaching potential members is never easy. Depending upon the problem area, consider where potential members go. Would they be seen by particular doctors or agencies? Contacting physicians, clergy or other professionals can be one approach to try. Posting flyers in post offices, community centers, hospitals, and libraries is another. Free announcements in the community calendar sections of local newspapers can be especially fruitful. Consider simply calling the paper and asking to speak with an editor to suggest an article on the group and the issue. Editors are often grateful for the idea. The first meeting should be arranged so that there will be ample time for you to describe your interest and work, while allowing others the opportunity to share their feelings and concerns. Do those attending agree that such a group is needed? Will they attend another meeting, helping out as needed? What needs do they have in common that the group could address? Based on group consensus, you can make plans for your next meeting.

If your group intends to have guest speakers, another idea for a first meeting is to arrange for a good speaker and topic that can be publicized well in advance. But be sure to build in time for people to discuss the speaker's points in light of their own experiences, i.e., after questions and answers with the speaker, have a discussion group or (if a large turnout) break into smaller discussion groups. Then come together as a full group and present the idea of continuing discussions as an ongoing self-help group.

Identify and Respond to the Felt Needs of Your Members. If your group is new and doesn't follow a set program for helping members help one another, always remember to plan your groups' activities and goals based upon the expressed needs of your members. Share your vision. At the very first meeting, go "round-robin" permitting each member an opportunity to say what they would like to see the group do. Then discuss these needs and come to a consensus as to which ones you will address first. Don't make the same mistake that some professionals make in professionally-run groups--of thinking that you know the members' needs without ever asking them. Remember to regularly ask your new members about their needs, and what they think the group might do to meet those needs. Similarly, be sure to avoid the pitfall of the core group members possibly becoming a clique. The welcoming of new people into the group is a process that continues well beyond welcoming them at the door.

Future Meetings. Considerations for future meetings may be the following:

- *Define the purpose (mission) of the group in no more than two sentences.* Is it clear? You may want to add it to any flyer or brochure that you develop for the group. Some groups also include any guidelines that they have for their meetings right on their flyer or brochure.

- *Membership.* Who can attend meetings and who cannot? Do you want regular membership limited to those with the problem and an associate membership for spouses and family?

- *Meeting format.* What choice or combination of discussion time, education, business meeting, service planning, socializing, etc. best suits your group? What guidelines might you use to assure that discussions be non-judgmental, confidential and informative? Topics can be selected or guest speakers invited. A good discussion group size may be about 7 to 15. As your meeting grows larger, consider breaking down into smaller groups for discussion.

- *Ongoing use of professionals.* Consider using professionals as speakers, advisors, sources of needed space or services, educators, helpful gatekeepers, advocates, possible trainers, researchers, consultants to your group, or simply as sources of continued referrals. All you have to do is ask them.

- *Help between meetings.* Many groups encourage the exchange of telephone numbers or a telephone list to provide members with help over

- the phone when it is needed between meetings. Older groups have a buddy system that pairs newcomers with veteran members.

- *Projects.* Begin with small projects, e.g. developing a flyer, obtaining newspaper coverage by calling editors, beginning a newsletter, etc. Rejoice and pat yourselves on the back when you succeed with these first projects. Then, if the group desires, work your way up to more difficult tasks and projects, e.g. planning a conference, advocating the introduction of specific legislation, developing a visitation program, etc.

- *Sharing responsibilities and nurturing new leaders.* You will want to look for all the different, additional roles that people can play in helping other members and making the group work, e.g., group librarian, arranging for speakers, greeter of new members, group liaison with an agency, etc. In asking for volunteers, it's easier to first ask the group what specific tasks they think would be helpful. If you haven't yet experienced it, you'll come to know the special "helper's high" satisfaction of helping others. Don't be selfish. Remember to let your members feel the fine satisfaction of helping others in the group. By sharing responsibilities you help create opportunities for others to become key members and leaders in the group.

- *Lastly, expect your group to experience regular "ups and downs"* in terms of attendance and enthusiasm. It's natural and to be expected. You may want to consider joining or forming a coalition or state association of leaders from the same or similar types of self-help groups, for your own periodic mutual support and for sharing program ideas and successes.

!! PLEASE BE ADVISED !!

The Self-Help Clearinghouse publishes a directory of support groups *annually*. Information, contacts, locations, chapters and facilitators are always changing. New groups are added just as frequently as groups are disbanded. Therefore we strongly advise you **not** to depend upon entries in this Directory past one full year of its publication, since a significant portion of the group information becomes outdated.

So, this current volume will become ineffectual to your needs after the **Spring of 2007**. At or before that time please call us to inquire about the newest edition. Also, consider passing this Directory on to a student or staff member - browsing through the Directory pages can often provide helpful education as to the wide variety of groups available. At any time you may also call our helpline through which we distribute the most up-to-date information on support groups and hotlines.

1-800-367-6274

ABUSE

CHILD ABUSE (PHYSICAL / EMOTIONAL)
(see also sexual abuse, toll-free helplines)

STATEWIDE

Parents Anonymous *(BILINGUAL) Professionally-run.* Self-help for parents who are under stress and who want to improve their relationships with their children. Groups meet weekly and are facilitated by a volunteer professional. Many groups provide childcare. Groups meet in most counties throughout the state with some bilingual groups available. On-line parent support group available. P.A.C.T. (Parents and Adolescents Changing Together) is a 16 week program that addresses the needs of both incarcerated teens and their families. Write: Parents Anonymous, 127 Route 206, Suite 10, Hamilton, NJ 08610. Call 1-800-843-5437 (stressline) or 609-585-7666 (office). *Website:* http://www.pa-of-nj.org *Email:* panjstress@aol.com

ATLANTIC

Parents Anonymous *Professionally-run.* Self-help for parents who are under stress and who want to improve their relationships with their children. Meets Tues., 5-7pm, Interstate Reality Management, 925 Caspean Ave., Atlantic City. Before attending call Pamela Curtis 609-347-1791 or Parents Anonymous 1-800-843-5437.

BERGEN

H.O.P.E.S. (Healing Ourselves Physically, Emotionally and Spiritually) *Professionally-run.* Self-help for adult survivors of any form of child abuse. Meets Fri., 6:30-8pm, St. Mark's Episcopal Church, 118 Chadwick Rd., Teaneck. Call Sara 201-357-4490, Anne 201-287-0527 or Parents Anonymous 1-800-843-5437. *Website:* http://www.pa-of-nj.org

BURLINGTON

H.O.P.E.S. (Healing Ourselves Physically, Emotionally and Spiritually) *Professionally-run.* Self-help for adult survivors of any form of child abuse. Meets Thurs., 7-9pm, Family Service Center, 770 Woodlane Rd., Suite 23, Mt. Holly. Call Parents Anonymous 1-800-843-5437 or Charles Robinson 856-686-0600 (day). *Website:* http://www.pa-of-nj.org

Parents Anonymous *Professionally-run.* Self-help for parents who are under stress and who want to improve their relationships with their children. Call Parents Anonymous 1-800-843-5437.

> **Mt. Holly** Meets Wed., 11am-1pm, Human Service Facility, 795 Woodland Rd. Before attending call Shirley 609-261-2323.
>
> **West Hampton** Meets Thurs., 7-9pm, Family Service Center, 770 Woodlane Rd., Suite 15. Before attending call Charles 609-261-2323 ext. 249.

CAMDEN

Parents Anonymous *Professionally-run.* Self-help for parents who are under stress and who want to improve their relationships with their children. Call Parents Anonymous 1-800-843-5437.

> **Camden** Meets Mon., 5-7pm, Glover Substance Abuse Coalition, 1419 Baird Blvd. Before attending call Margaret 856-963-4722.
>
> **Sicklerville** Meets Wed., 6-7:30pm, St. James Church, 516 Church Rd. Before attending call Diedre 856-875-4483.

CUMBERLAND

H.O.P.E.S. (Healing Ourselves Physically, Emotionally and Spiritually) *Professionally-run.* Self-help for adult survivors of any form of child sexual abuse. Meets Wed., 7-8:30pm, Second United Methodist Church, 911 Church St., Millville. Call Claire Riley 856-825-6810 ext. 259 (day).

ESSEX

Parents Anonymous *Professionally-run.* Self-help for parents who are under stress and who want to improve their relationships with their children. Call Parents Anonymous 1-800-843-5437.

> **East Orange** Meets Thurs., 10am-noon, East Orange Child Development Center, 106 Washington St.
>
> **East Orange** *(GRANDPARENTS GROUP)* Meets Thurs., noon-2pm, East Orange Child Development Center, 42 Chestnut St. Before attending call Ms. Rutledge 973-676-1110.
>
> **Irvington** Meets Wed., 9-11am, Grove St. Elementary School, 602 Grove St. Before attending call Donna 973-399-6949.
>
> **Newark** Meets Thurs., 1-2:30pm, Choices Inc., 169 Roseville Ave. Child care available. Before attending call Juanita 973-481-1889 (day).

If you are using this book past Spring 2007, please call us for information about our most recent directory. 1-800-367-6274

P.O.S.S.E. Support group for men and male relatives to improve relationships within the family and to prevent child abuse. Offers rap sessions, mutual sharing and literature. Meets Mon., 7-9pm, Christian Love Baptist Church, Lower Level, 830 Lyons Ave., Irvington. Call Shabazz Abdallah or John Graham 973-414-6650 (day). *Website:* http://www.pa-of-nj.org

GLOUCESTER

Parents Anonymous *Professionally-run.* Self-help for parents who are under stress and who want to improve their relationships with their children. Meets Thurs., 6-7:30pm, Glassboro Housing Authority, Ellis Manor Community Center, 739 Lincoln Blvd., Glassboro. Before attending call Rafael 856-881-5480 or Parents Anonymous 1-800-843-5437.

HUDSON

Parents Anonymous *Professionally-run.* Self-help for parents who are under stress and who want to improve their relationships with their children. Call Parents Anonymous 1-800-843-5437.
> **Jersey City** Meets Wed., 6-7:30pm, HCCAP, 880 Bergen Ave., Room 302. Before attending call Jenissa or Peter 201-789-5588.
> **West New York** Meets Wed., 5:30-7pm, North Hudson Community Action Corp., 5701 Broadway. Before attending call Wanda 201-726-6491.

MERCER

Parents Anonymous *Professionally-run.* Self-help for parents who are under stress and who want to improve their relationships with their children. Call Parents Anonymous 1-800-843-5437.
> **Hamilton** *(PARENTS OF TEENS)* Meets Wed., 5:30-7:30pm, Parents Anonymous Office, 127 Rt. 206 South. Before attending call Orysia 609-243-9799.
> **Trenton** Meets Wed., 6-7:30pm, Reach-Out/Speak-Out, 121 North Broad St. Before attending call Rose 609-585-7666.

MIDDLESEX

Parents Anonymous *Professionally-run.* Self-help for parents who are under stress and want to improve their relationships with their children. Childcare available. Call Parents Anonymous 1-800-843-5437.

New Brunswick *(BILINGUAL)* Meets Thurs., 9-11am and 5:30-7:30pm, Puerto Rican Action Board, 18 Drift Ave. Before attending call Carmen 732-828-4572.

New Brunswick Meets Thurs., 11:30am-1:30pm, Ebenezer Baptist Church, 126 Lee Ave.

MONMOUTH

Parents Anonymous *Professionally-run.* Self-help for parents who are under stress and want to improve their relationships with their children. Call Parents Anonymous 1-800-843-5437.

Freehold Meets Tues., 10am-noon, Monmouth County Human Services Bldg., 3000 Kozloski Rd., First Floor. Childcare available. Before attending call Jackie 732-901-0522.

Keansburg *(KEANSBURG RESIDENTS ONLY)* Meets Wed., 9:30-11:30am, Port Monmouth School, 142 Port Monmouth Rd., Room 309. Before attending call Jeff 732-787-2007 ext. 5242.

MORRIS

H.O.P.E.S. (Healing Ourselves Physically, Emotionally and Spiritually) *Professionally-run.* Self-help for adult survivors of any form of child abuse. Meets Wed., 7:30-9:30pm, First Presbyterian Church, 35 Church St., Rockaway. Before attending call Janice Taitel 973-586-8979 or Parents Anonymous 1-800-843-5437. *Website:* http://www.pa-of-nj.org

OCEAN

Parents Anonymous *Professionally-run.* Self-help for parents who are under stress and who want to improve their relationships with their children. Child care available. Meets Thurs., 5:30-7:30pm, Center for Kids and Family, 591 Lakehurst Rd., Toms River. Before attending call Jackie 732-901-0522 or Parents Anonymous 1-800-843-5437.

SALEM

Parents Anonymous *Professionally-run.* Self-help for parents who are under stress and who want to improve their relationships with their children. Child care available. Meets Wed., 11am-12:30pm, Inter Agency Council, 98 Market St., Salem. Before attending call Utausha 856-935-7510 ext. 8312 or Parents Anonymous 1-800-843-5437.

UNION

Parents Anonymous *Professionally-run.* Self-help for parents who are under stress and who want to improve their relationships with their children. Child care and transportation provided. Call Parents Anonymous 1-800-843-5437.

>   **Cranford** Meets Wed., 10am-noon, Cranford United Methodist Church, Walnut and Lincoln Ave. Before attending call Joan 908-276-5894 (eve).
>   **Roselle** Meets 2nd and 4th Tues., 5:30-7:30pm, Abraham Clark High School, 122 E. Sixth Ave. Call Ayisha 908-298-7800.

NATIONAL

Adult Survivors of Child Abuse *International. 11 affiliated groups. Founded 1991.* Mutual support for adult survivors of physical, sexual and /or emotional child abuse or neglect. Encourages victims to become survivors, then thrivers. Online support group meetings, monthly newsletter, group starter manuals and general information. Offers assistance in starting groups. Write: Adult Survivors of Child Abuse, PO Box 14477, San Francisco, CA 94114-0038. Call 415-928-4576. *Website:* http://www.ascasupport.org *Email:* ascaoutreach@yahoo.com

Parents Anonymous, Inc. *National. Founded 1969.* Country's oldest child abuse prevention organization. Opportunity for parents to learn new skills, transform their attitudes and behaviors and create lasting changes in their lives. Group meetings offer structured children's programs. Helps to develop new community groups by providing training, technical assistance, materials and networking. Write: Parents Anonymous, Inc., 675 W. Foothill Blvd., Suite 220, Claremont, CA 91711-3475. Call 909-621-6184; *Website:* http://www.parentsanonymous.org *Email:* parentsanonymous@parentsanonymous.org

Shaken Baby Alliance *National. Founded 1998.* Promotes public awareness and education, victim and family support and victim advocacy. Offers networking and literature. Dues $30-50/yr. Provides assistance in starting groups. Provides case consultation services to professionals involved in diagnosing, investigating and prosecuting physical child abuse. Online listserv. Write: Shaken Baby Alliance, 4516 Boat Club Rd., Ste. 114, Fort Worth, TX 76135. Call 1-877-636-3727; Fax: 817-882-8687. *Website:* http://www.shakenbaby.com *Email:* Info@shakenbaby.com

ONLINE

Abused Survivors *Online* Offers an outstretched hand to adult survivors of abuse (physical, verbal, emotional or sexual). Open only to survivors. *Website:* http://health.groups.yahoo.com/group/AbusedSurvivors

Take Root *Online. Founded 2000.* Peer support for adult children (age 18+) who were abducted by a parent as a child. Offers literature, information, referrals, newsletter, peer support and advocacy. Write: Take Root, PO Box 930, Kalama, WA 98625. Call 1-800-766-8674. *Website:* http://www.takeroot.org

SEXUAL ABUSE / INCEST / RAPE

(see also child abuse, toll-free helplines)

STATEWIDE

12 Steps To Healing With A Christian Emphasis 12-Step. Mutual support for adult and youth survivors of sexual assault. Group meets for 12 weeks. Each week a different step is reviewed. Meeting location varies throughout Northern New Jersey. For information call Erin 973-398-2862 or 973-919-0703 (cell). *Email:* thadnerin@optonline.net

BERGEN

H.O.P.E.S. (Healing Ourselves Physically, Emotionally and Spiritually) *Professionally-run.* Self-help for adult survivors of any form of child abuse. Meets Fri., 6:30-8pm, St. Mark's Episcopal Church, 118 Chadwick Rd., Teaneck. Call Sara Accordino 201-357-4490 (day), Anne 201-287-0527 or Parents Anonymous 1-800-843-5437. *Website:* http://www.pa-of-nj.org

Men's Survivor Group *Professionally-run.* Mutual support for male survivors of child sexual abuse. Group runs for 12-16 sessions 2-3 times/yr. Meets Mon., YWCA of Bergen County, Rape Crisis Center, Hackensack. Before attending call Rachel 201-487-2227 (24 hr. hotline); TDD: 201-487-0916. *Website:* http://www.bergencountyrapecrisis.org *Email:* bcrcc@aol.com

Support for Significant Others *Professionally-run.* Mutual support for families, friends and significant others of sexual abuse survivors to understand about sexual victimization and learn how to be supportive. Also available to parents of a child who was molested. Meets for 12 week sessions twice/yr., 6-8:30pm, YWCA, 75 Essex St., Suite 108, Hackensack. Before attending call 201-487-2227. *Website:* http://www.bergencountyrapecrisis.org

Survivors of Rape *Professionally-run.* Support for adult female survivors of sexual assault. Meets Thurs., YWCA, 75 Essex St., Suite 108, Hackensack. Before attending call 201-487-2227 (24 hr); TTY: 201-487-0916. *Website:* http://www.bergencountyrapecrisis.org *Email:* bcrcc@aol.com

BURLINGTON

H.O.P.E.S. (Healing Ourselves Physically, Emotionally and Spiritually) *Professionally-run.* Self-help for adult survivors of any form of child abuse. Meets Tues., 7-9pm, Family Service Center, 770 Woodlane Rd., Suite 23, Mt. Holly. Call Parents Anonymous 1-800-843-5437 or Charles Robinson 856-686-0600 (day). *Website:* http://www.pa-of-nj.org

CAMDEN

Healing Hearts Ministry *Professionally-run.* Christian-based confidential support group for individuals who have been mishandled or sexually abused. Education, rap sessions, guest speakers and phone help. Meets 2nd & 4th Fri., 7-8pm, Bethany Baptist Church, 10 Foster Ave., Annex Building, Gibbsboro. Call Charlene Ransom 856-782-9540 (day) or Felisha Jones 856-581-7327 (day). *Website:* http://www.abundantharvest.com *E-mail:* healinghearts@abundantharvest.com

Survivors of Incest Anonymous 12-Step program for men and women, 18 yrs. or older, who have been victims of child sexual abuse, are not abusing any child and want to be survivors. Literature and newsletter. Meets Sat., 9:30-11am, The Starting Point, 215 Highland Ave., Suite C, Westmont. Call Natalie 856-858-5630 (eve) or Helen 856-768-1925 (day).

CUMBERLAND

H.O.P.E.S. (Healing Ourselves Physically, Emotionally and Spiritually) *Professionally-run.* Self-help for adult survivors of any form of child sexual abuse. Meets Wed., 7-8:30pm, Second United Methodist Church, 911 Church St., Millville. Call Claire Riley 856-825-6810 ext. 259 (day).

HUNTERDON

Women's Crisis Services *Professionally-run.* Mutual support for victims of domestic violence and sexual assault. Also provides shelters and other services. Groups meet various times and days, Women's Crisis Center, 47 E. Main St., Flemington. Call 908-788-7666 (day) or hotline 1-888-988-4033 (24 hr); TTY/TDD: 1-866-954-0100. *Website:* http://www.womenscrisisservices.org *Email:* agencyinfo@womenscrisisservices.org

This information is constantly changing. New groups are being started, others are ending. Please call for the most up-to-date information from our database, 1-800-367-6274.

MERCER

SASS (Sexual Abuse Survivor Support) *Professionally-run.* Mutual support, education and coping skills for female rape survivors age 13-26. Rap sessions. Meets Thurs., 7:30-9pm, HiTOPS, 21 Wiggins St., Princeton. Before attending call Elizabeth Walters 609-683-0179 ext. 18 (day). *Email:* elizabeth@hitops.org

MIDDLESEX

Adult Survivors of Sexual Assault *Professionally-run.* Provides a safe, confidential environment for female survivors to share and receive support. Rap sessions. Group runs for 19 weeks, twice a year, Edison. Pre-registration required. Call Michelle Montalto 1-877-665-7273 (day).

Male Survivors of Sexual Abuse/Assault *Professionally-run.* Provides a safe, confidential environment for male survivors of sexual abuse or assault to learn to cope with the effects of the abuse. Rap sessions. Runs for 10 weeks, 3 times a year in Edison. Call Jeanne Manchin 1-877-665-7273 (day).

Women in Conflict Support Group Mutual support for women, (primarily ages 20-50), who have been sexually assaulted. Goal is to help individuals gain control over their lives and move from being a victim to a survivor. Meetings vary, Robert Wood Johnson University Hospital, One Robert Wood Johnson Place, New Brunswick. Before attending call 732-418-8110 (day).

MONMOUTH

Parents United *Professionally-run.* Separate support groups for adult, teen and pre-adolescent incest victims, mothers of incest victims, non-offending parents. Slight fee required (sliding scale). Meets various days and times in Red Bank. Before attending call Judith Loder 732-758-0094 (day).

Women Survivors of Sexual Abuse / Incest *(FREEHOLD RESIDENTS ONLY) Professionally-run.* To aid in the empowerment of women who have been sexually victimized. Helps deal with the isolation, shame and powerlessness that can result. Members encouraged to be in therapy and must not be actively abusing substances. Meets Mon., 6-9pm, Freehold Community Counseling Service, 30 Jackson Mill Rd., Freehold. Call Patricia Ervin 732-409-6260 (day/eve).

While it's no substitution for talking to our staff, you can call evenings or weekends! Leave a message and we will get back to you the next workday.
1-800-367-6274

MORRIS

Adult Survivors Group *(BILINGUAL) (WOMEN ONLY) Professionally-run.* Mutual support for female survivors of sexual abuse. Helps survivors process their feelings and understand the pain. Education, guest speakers, rap sessions. Groups meet for 12 consecutive weeks in Denville. Call Sonia Reyes 973-299-5400.

H.O.P.E.S. (Healing Ourselves Physically, Emotionally and Spiritually) *Professionally-run.* Self-help for adult survivors of any form of child abuse. Meets Wed., 7:30-9:30pm, First Presbyterian Church, 35 Church St., Rockaway. Before attending call Janice Taitel 973-586-8979 or Parents Anonymous 1-800-843-5437. *Website:* http://www.pa-of-nj.org

PASSAIC

Passaic County Women's Center *(BILINGUAL) Professionally-run.* Support groups for survivors of domestic violence and/or sexual assault. Discussions include coping skills, legal issues and parenting skills. Groups meet weekly in Paterson. Call Sophie Robinson 973-881-0725 (day) or hotline 973-881-1450 (24 hr).

SALEM

Female Survivors of Childhood Sexual Abuse *Professionally-run.* Support, education and information for women survivors of childhood sexual abuse. Opportunity to share with other survivors. Group starts periodically and runs for 8-10 weeks in in Salem County. For information call 856-935-6655 (24 hr).

SOMERSET

Survivors of Sexual Violence *Professionally-run.* Supportive and confidential group for adult female survivors of sexual assault and abuse. Provides a therapeutic environment to aid in the healing of sexual trauma. Meets for 10 week sessions several times a year, Women's Health and Counseling Center, Somerville. To pre-register call Chrisula 908-526-2335 ext. 130. *Website:* http://www.womenandhealth.org *Email:* ctasiopoulos@womenandhealth.org

SUSSEX

Sexual Trauma Resource Center *Professionally-run.* Support groups for female and male survivors of sexual assault, sexual abuse and incest. Meetings vary, Newton. Call 973-300-5609; 973-875-1211 (24 hr. hotline); TTY: 973-875-1211. *Email:* strc@nac.net

WARREN

Women's Domestic Violence Support Groups *Professionally-run.* Supportive and confidential environment to help women victims of domestic violence work towards healing. Need prior screening to attend. Educational series meets in Phillipsburg and Belvedere. For information call 908-453-4181; TTY: 908-453-2553. *Website:* http://www.darcc.org

NATIONAL

Adult Survivors of Child Abuse *International. 11 affiliated groups. Founded 1991.* Mutual support for adult survivors of physical, sexual and /or emotional child abuse or neglect. Encourages victims to become survivors, then thrivers. Online support group meetings, monthly newsletter, group starter manuals and general information. Offers assistance in starting groups. Write: Adult Survivors, PO Box 14477, San Francisco, CA 94114-0038. Call 415-928-4576. *Website:* http://www.ascasupport.org *Email:* ascaoutreach@yahoo.com

Incest Resources, Inc. *Resource. Support groups in Boston, MA area. Founded 1980.* Provides educational and resource materials for female and male survivors of childhood sexual abuse and the professionals who work with them. International listing of survivor self-help groups, manual for starting survivor self-help group and many other resources. For complete information send self-addressed envelope with two 1st class stamps. Write: Incest Resources, Inc., 46 Pleasant St., Cambridge, MA 02139. *Website:* http://www.incestresourcesinc.org

Incest Survivors Anonymous *International. Founded 1980.* Uses 12-Step/12-traditions principles and tools of recovery. Fellowship of men, women and teens who meet to share their experience, strength and hope so that they may recover from their incest experiences and break free to freedom and a new peace of mind. Offers several packets of information, pen pals, email family letter and cassettes. Not open to initiators, pedophiles or Satanists. Provides assistance in starting I.S.A. groups. When writing send a self-addressed stamped envelope (2 stamps). Write: I.S.A., PO Box 17245, Long Beach, CA 90807-7245. Call 562-428-5599. *Website:* http://www.lafn.org/medical/isa *Email:* isa@lafn.org

LINKUP *International network of independent groups. Founded 1991.* Mutual support for survivors of clergy abuse. Aims to educate victims, clergy, professionals and the public. Newsletter, advocacy, conferences, assistance in starting independent groups. Dues $35. Write: LINKUP, PO Box 429, Pewee Valley, KY 40056. Call 502-241-5544 Fax: 502-241-0031. *Website:* http://www.thelinkup.org *Email:* linkupoffice@aol.com

Male Survivor: National Organization Against Male Sexual Victimization *National. Founded 1995.* Information and referrals for male survivors of sexual assault. Referrals to local resources. Newsletter. Online bulletin board and chat room. Write: NOMSV, PMB 103, 5505 Connecticut Ave., NW, Washington, DC 20015-2601. Call 1-800-738-4181 *Website:* http://www.malesurvivor.org

Molesters Anonymous *Model Founded 1985.* Provides support with anonymity & confidentiality for men who molest children. Use of "thought stoppage" technique & buddy system. Groups are initiated by a professional but become member-run. Group development manual ($9.95). Write: Dr. Jerry Goffman, PhD, 1040 S. Mt. Vernon Ave., G-306, Colton, CA 92324. Call Dr. Jerry Goffman 909-355-1100 Fax: 909-370-0438. *Email:* jerrygoffman@hotmail.com

Parents United International, Inc. *National. 42 chapters. Founded 1972.* Provides support for child sexual abuse. Includes individual therapy, group therapy and guided self-help. Also for adults molested as children. Chapter development guidelines & training available for professionals wishing to start groups. Write: Parents United Int'l, 615 15th St., Modesto, CA 95354. Call 209-572-3446 Fax: 209-524-7780. *Website:* http://members.tripod.com/~Parents_United

S.A.R.A. (Sexual Assault Recovery Anonymous) Society *National. 20 groups. Founded 1983.* Education and self-help for adults and teens who were sexually abused as children. Group development guidelines and assistance provided for starting groups. Literature for recovery and prevention available. Newsletter. Dues $10/yr. Write: SARA Soc., PO Box 16, Surrey, BC V3T 4W4 Canada. Call 604-584-2626 Fax: 604-584-2636. *Website:* http://www.sarasociety.ca *Email:* sarasociety@shaw.ca

SESAME (Survivors of Educator Sexual Abuse/Misconduct Emerge) *National network. Founded 1993.* Support network for victims, their families, academia and professionals who have been impacted by or work with cases of sexual abuse, sexual exploitation or harassment by teachers and other school staff. Aims to raise public awareness by providing information and referrals, email/phone support, literature, advocacy, newsletter. Write: SESAME, Inc., PO Box 94601, Las Vegas 89193-4601. Call 702-371-1290. *Website:* http://www.sesamenet.org *Email:* Babe4justice@aol.com

"If someone listens, or stretches out a hand, or whispers a word of encouragement, or attempts to understand a lonely person, extraordinary things begin to happen."

Loretta Girzartis

SNAP (Survivors Network of those Abused by Priests) *International. 50+ affiliated groups. Founded 1989.* Support for men and women who were sexually abused by any clergy person (priests brothers nuns deacons teachers etc.) Extensive phone network, newsletter, advocacy, conferences, information and referrals. Information on finding support groups. Dues $25 (optional). Write: SNAP, PO Box 6416, Chicago, IL 60680. Call 312-409-2720. *Website:* http://www.snapnetwork.org *Email:* SNAPBlaine@hotmail.com

Survivor Connections, Inc. *National network. Founded 1993.* Grassroots activist organization for non-offending survivors of sexual assault by family, ritual, youth leaders, counselors, doctors, clergy, etc. Newsletter, peer support groups. Referrals. Maintains database of perpetrators. Write: Survivor Connections, Inc., Frank Fitzpatrick, 52 Lyndon Rd., Cranston, RI 02905. Call 401-941-2548 Fax: 401-941-2335. *Website:* http://www.members.cox.net/survivorconnections

Survivors of Incest Anonymous *International. 300 groups. Founded 1982.* 12-Step program for men and women 18 yrs. or older who have been victims of child sexual abuse and are not abusing any child and want to be survivors. Newsletter ($15/yr.), literature ($25/19 pieces). Offers assistance in starting groups, volunteer information, referral line and speakers' bureau. Send self-addressed stamped envelope when writing (include $3 if possible). Write: SIA, PO Box 190, Benson, MD 21018-9998. Call 410-893-3322. *Website:* http://www.siawso.org *Email:* feedback@siawso.org

VOICES In Action, Inc. *International. Founded 1980.* Assists adult victims of incest/child sexual abuse in becoming survivors by helping them locate local support services and treatment. Provides public education on effects of incest. Newsletter. Guidelines on starting self-help groups. Special interest correspondence groups. Conferences, publications. Dues $35/yr. (newsletter, conference discounts). Write: VOICES in Action, Inc., 8041 Hosbrook Road, Suite 236, Cincinnati, OH, 45236. Call 1-800-786-4238. *Website:* http://www.voices-action.org

ONLINE

Abused Survivors *Online* support group that offers an outstretched hand to adult survivors of abuse (physical, verbal, emotional or sexual). Open only to survivors. *Website:* http://health.groups.yahoo.com/group/AbusedSurvivors

Positive Partners of Survivors *Online.* Offer mutual support and understanding to anyone who has a loved one who was sexually abused. Provides chat room, e-group, message board. *Website:* http://groups.yahoo.com/group/positivepartnersofsurvivors/

SPOUSE ABUSE / DOMESTIC VIOLENCE
(see also toll-free helplines)

ATLANTIC

Atlantic County Women's Center Mutual support and education for persons affected by spouse abuse. Goal is to end domestic violence through legal advocacy, information and group support. Also has "Alternatives to Violence" program for men for a slight fee. For information call Atlantic County Women's Center 1-800-286-4184 or 609-646-6767 (for men's program). *Website:* http://www.acwc.org *Email:* acwc@bellatlantic.net

BERGEN

Separated/ Divorced/ Victims of Domestic Violence *Professionally-run.* Support and education for persons going through a divorce, separation or are victims of domestic violence. Mutual sharing of emotional, legal and parenting concerns. Under 18 welcome. Meets Mon., 7:15-8pm, Christian Reformed Church, Godwin Ave., Midland Park. For meeting information call 201-445-4260 (day). *Email:* epurcell@bergen.edu

BURLINGTON

Providence House *Professionally-run.* Support, education and counseling for victims who are or have been, in battering situations. Group for children (age 3-17). Uses creative art therapy. Call 609-871-7551 (24 hr hotline).

CAMDEN

Domestic Violence Women's Support Group Support group for female victims and survivors of domestic violence. Group focuses on solutions that help end the abuse and increase education. Rap sessions, literature, phone help, buddy system and guest speakers. Meets Wed., Gloucester Township. For information call Michele Walsh 609-386-2220 (day).

Women's Domestic Violence Support Group *(BILINGUAL) Professionally-run.* Mutual support for female victims/survivors of domestic violence. Educational series and advocacy. Meets Tues., Collingswood; and Thurs., Camden. For meeting information call Sheila Lindsay 856-963-5668 (day). *Website:* http://www.ccwomenscenter.org

33

CAPE MAY

CARA Buddy System *Professionally-run.* Confidential support for battered women to discuss problems and share resources. Rap sessions, guest speakers, phone help and literature. Meets Wed., 7:30pm, CARA, Cape May Court House. Before attending call Juanita Battle 609-522-6489 (day) or CARA 1-877-294-2272 (Mon.-Fri., 8:30-4:30pm); TTY: 609-463-0818.

M.E.N.D. (Men Exploring New Directions) *Professionally-run.* To help men learn other ways of coping with anger and stop violence in families. Rap sessions, phone help, literature. Meets Thurs., 7-9pm, Burdette Tomlin Memorial Hospital, Cape May Court House. Register before attending. Call 609-522-6489 (day) or 1-877-294-2272; TTY: 609-463-0818.

CUMBERLAND

ACT (Abuse Ceases Today) *Professionally-run.* Mutual support for men to help deal with their anger. Educational series, rap sessions, literature. Meets Tues., 6-8pm, location confidential. For meeting information call 856-691-3713 (day); TTY: 856-691-6024.

ESSEX

Babyland Family Services, Inc. *Professionally-run.* Support for women who have been in abusive relationships. Aim is to educate, liberate and empower domestic violence victims and survivors. Shelter and hotline. Pre-requisite requirements. Also offers a men's PEACE group ($2 fee). Meets at various locations in Essex County. Call 973-484-4446 (24 hr). *Website:* http://www.babyland.org

HUNTERDON

Women's Crisis Services *Professionally-run.* Mutual support for victims of domestic violence and sexual assault. Provides other services including shelters. Offers a men's program for a fee. Groups meet various times and days, 47 E. Main St., Flemington. Call 908-788-7666 (day) or hotline 1-888-988-4033 (24 hr); TTY: 1-866-954-0100. *Website:* http://www.womenscrisisservices.org *Email:* agencyinfo@womenscrisisservices.org

We know this Directory is big and chances are we can probably find the group
you're looking for quicker than you paging through it.
Call us! (We're really friendly!)
1-800-367-6274

MIDDLESEX

Manavi Support Group *(SOUTH ASIAN)* Mutual support for any South Asian woman (Indian, Pakistan, Bangladeshi, Nepali, Sri Lankan) who has experienced spousal or partner abuse. Advocacy, guest speakers and literature. Child care provided. Meets 2nd and 4th Sat., 1:30-3:30pm, New Brunswick. Call Aisha 732-435-1414 (day). *Website:* http://www.manavi.org *Email:* manavi@manavi.org

Women Aware, Inc. *(BILINGUAL) Professionally-run.* Support groups, education and advocacy for battered women. Information on emergency shelter and other services. Call 732-249-4504 (Voice/TTY); for legal advocacy 732-937-9525 (day).

MORRIS

Jersey Battered Women's Service, Inc. *Professionally-run.* Provides support groups and emergency shelter for victims or survivors of domestic violence and/or abusive relationships. Children's services available. Legal advocacy. Call 973-267-4763 hotline; TDD: 973-285-9095 (24 hr). ACT (Abuse Ceases Today) also offers services to assist batterers in stopping abuse and in developing alternative behaviors. Call 973-539-7801 (for men's group). *Website:* http://www.jbws.org *Email:* info@jbws.org

PASSAIC

Domestic Violence Support Group *Professionally-run.* Provides emotional support and networking for women. Educational series, social group, advocacy and guest speakers. Meets Thurs., 6-7pm, Senior Citizen Center, 330A Passaic St., Passaic. Call Miriam Torres 973-365-5740 (day) or Tom Fischetti 973-365-5741 (day). *Email:* prevention@rcn.com

Passaic County Women's Center *(BILINGUAL) Professionally-run.* Support groups for survivors of domestic violence and/or sexual assault. Discussions include coping skills, legal issues and parenting skills. Various groups meet weekly in Paterson. Call Tracy Francese or Evelyn Murphy 973-881-0725 (day) or Hotline 973-881-1450 (24 hr).

SALEM

Female Victims and Survivors of Family Violence *Professionally-run.* Support, education and information for women to share with other victims. Meets bi-weekly in a confidential location in Salem County. Men's batterers program. Call 856-935-6655 (24 hr); TTY/TDD: 856-935-7118.

SOMERSET

Resource Center for Women and their Families *(BILINGUAL) (SOMERSET COUNTY RESIDENTS ONLY) Professionally-run.* Support groups for women who are survivors of domestic violence. Groups meet during the day and evening in Hillsborough area. Call Resource Center for Women 1-866-685-1122 or 908-685-1122 (24 hr hotline). *Website:* http://wwww.rcwtf.org *Email:* info@rcwtf.org

SUSSEX

Domestic Abuse Services, Inc. Mutual support for survivors of domestic violence and abuse. Meets in Newton. Call 973-579-2386; 973-875-1211 (24 hr hotline); TTY: 973-875-6369 (24 hr). *Website:* http://www.dasi.org *Email:* dasi@nac.net

UNION

Choices For Women *Professionally-run.* Support for women who are or have been, in an abusive situation. Mutual sharing and phone help. Meets Wed., 7pm, 23 North Ave. East, Cranford. Before attending call Elaine Hewins or Nancy Marie Bride 908-272-0300.

Project Protect *Professionally-run.* Provides support to victims of domestic violence. Also educational programs for men who are violent, abusive or over-controlling. Fee for men's group. Meets Thurs., various locations. Call 908-355-1500 (day).

WARREN

VIP (Violence Intervention Program) Support for women who are past or present victims of domestic violence. Teaches methods to eliminate violence from women's lives. Addresses other women's issues such as anger awareness, self-esteem, stress management, goal setting and healthy relationships. Meets Mon., 6:30-8pm, Phillipsburg. Call Donna Scrafano 908-453-4121 (10am-3pm) or 908-387-8330. *Website:* http://www.darcc.org

NATIONAL

Batterers Anonymous *National. 20 chapters. Founded 1980.* Self-help program for men who wish to control their anger & eliminate their abusive behavior toward women. Buddy system. Group development manual ($9.95) Write: B.A., Attn: Dr. Jarry Goffman, 1040 S. Mt. Vernon Ave., G-306, Colton, CA, 92324. Call 909-355-1100; Fax: 909-370-0438.

Pathways To Peace *International. 11 groups. Founded 1998.* Self-help program for anger management. Offers peer support, education, workbook ($17.95) and assists with starting groups. Write: Pathways To Peace, PO Box 259, Cassadaga, NY, 14718. Call 1-800-775-4212 or 716-595-3886; Fax: 716-595-3886. *Website:* http://www.pathwaystopeaceinc.com/index.htm#1 *Email:* transfrm@netsync.net

ONLINE

Abused Guys *Online.* Provides support for male victims of domestic violence. Offers online chat room and message forum. Must join the group to post. *Website:* http://groups.yahoo.com/group/abusedguys

Battered Husbands Support *Online.* Support for men who have been or who are currently, being battered by their female or male partner. Offers message boards, chat room and useful links. *Website:* http://health.groups.yahoo.com/group/batteredhusbandssupport

End Verbal Abuse *Online.* Informational, anti-abuse email support group for those who are dedicated to overcoming obstacles to leaving a verbal abuser in a healthy and safe manner, resolving abusive behavior, protecting children from abuse or recovery after leaving an abuser. *Website:* http://health.groups.yahoo.com/group/End_Verbal_Abuse

Woman's Emotional Abuse Support *Online. Founded 1999.* Offers support and understanding for victims of verbal and emotional abuse. Provides message boards, chat room, links and email list. *Website:* http://groups.yahoo.com/group/womansemotionalabusesupport

This information is constantly changing.
New groups are beginning, others are ending.
Please call us anytime for the most up-to-date information
from our database.
1-800-367-6274

"It's not enough to have lived.

We should be determined to live for something.

May I suggest that it be creating joy for others,

sharing what we have for the betterment of personkind,

bringing hope to the lost and love to the lonely."

Leo Buscaglia

ADDICTIONS

ALCOHOL ABUSE
(see also toll-free helplines)

STATEWIDE

Al-Anon's Adult Children 12-Step. Fellowship offering comfort, hope and friendship through shared experiences for adult children of alcoholics. Weekly meetings available throughout New Jersey. Write: Al-Anon's Adult Children, 73 S. Fullerton Ave., 2nd Floor, Montclair, NJ 07042. For local meeting information call Al-Anon Information Service North New Jersey 973-744-8686 (day) or South New Jersey 856-547-0855 (day). *Website:* http://www.northjerseyal-anon.org *Email:* northjerseyais@verizon.net

Al-Anon Family Groups Fellowship of families and friends of alcoholics, following the 12-Step program. Offers comfort, hope and friendship through shared experiences. Includes groups for parents, children and adult children, gays, men, women. Some groups offer babysitting services. Weekly meetings throughout NJ.

> **North Jersey Information Service** *(MULTILINGUAL)* (Covers Bergen, Essex, Hudson, Hunterdon, Middlesex, Monmouth, Morris, Passaic, Somerset, Sussex, Union and Warren counties). Write: Al-Anon Family Groups, North Jersey Information Service, 73 South Fullerton Ave., Montclair, NJ 07042. Call Al-Anon 973-744-8686 (day). *Website:* http://www.northjerseyal-anon.org *Email:* northjerseyais12@verizon.net
> **South Jersey Intergroup** (Covers Atlantic, Burlington, Camden, Cape May, Cumberland, Gloucester, Mercer, Ocean and Salem counties). Write: Al-Anon Family Groups, 116 White Horse Pike, Haddon Heights, NJ 08035. Call Al-Anon Information Service 856-547-0855 (10am-3pm).

Alcoholics Anonymous *(BILINGUAL)* 12-Step. Fellowship of men and women who share their experiences, strengths and hopes to help each other recover from alcoholism. Groups meet weekly throughout New Jersey.

> **Cape/Atlantic Intergroup** (Covers Atlantic and Cape May counties.) Write: A.A., 32 Blackhorse Pike, P.O. Box 905, Pleasantville, NJ 08232. Call 609-641-8855; Spanish-speaking 609-344-0202. *Website:* http://www.capeatlanticintergroup.org
> **Central Jersey Intergroup** (Covers Mercer County and parts of Ocean, Monmouth, Middlesex, Somerset and Hunterdon counties.) Write: A.A. Central Jersey Intergroup, P.O. Box 4096, Trenton, NJ 08610.

Call 609-656-8900 (24 hr. hotline); 609-656-8908 (day); Spanish-speaking call 973-824-0555. *Website:* http://www.centraljerseyintergroup.org

North Jersey Intergroup (Covers Bergen, Essex, Hudson, Hunterdon, Middlesex, Monmouth, Morris, Ocean, Passaic, Somerset, Sussex, Union and Warren counties.) Write: A.A., 2400 Morris Ave., Union, NJ 07083. Call 908-687-8566 (day) or 1-800-245-1377. Spanish speaking 973-824-0555 *Website:* http://www.nnjaa.org

South Jersey Intergroup (Covers Burlington, Camden, Cumberland, Gloucester and Salem Counties.) Write: A.A., P.O. Box 2514, Cherry Hill, NJ 08034. Call 856-486-4444 (hotline); Spanish-speaking 973-824-0555. *Website:* http://www.aasj.org

International Pharmacists Anonymous Network of pharmacists and pharmacy students recovering from any addiction. Members must belong to a 12-Step group. Conferences. Write: IPA, c/o Nan, 11 Dewey Lane, Glen Gardner, NJ 08826-3102. Call Nan 908-391-2673 (day). *Email:* nandrx@earthlink.net

Lawyers Concerned for Lawyers Statewide network of independent, self-help groups that support attorneys, judges and law students in recovery from alcoholism and drug dependence. Based on the 12-Steps but not affiliated with A.A. and is not meant to be a substitute for participation in A.A. or other fellowships. The NJ Lawyers Assistance Program performs an "intergroup function" for LCL. All services free and confidential. Write: NJLAP, NJ Law Center, One Constitution Square, New Brunswick, NJ 08901-1520. Call 1-800-246-5527 (day) or 732-937-7549 (day). For information about women's group, call Denise 732-937-7541. *Website:* http://wwww.LawyersAssistance.org *Email:* info@njlap.org or njlap@aol.com

Nurse Recovery Group *Professionally-run.* Mutual support and information for nurses who are recovering from addictions. Sharing of professional concerns and encouragement. Meets in most counties. Write: Peer Assistance Project, 1479 Pennington Rd., Trenton, NJ 08618. Call 1-800-662-0108 (day).

Professional Assistance Program of New Jersey *Professionally-run.* For physicians and other licensed professionals suffering from alcohol, chemical dependency, psychiatric or physical disabilities. Local groups are independently member-run and strictly confidential. Some are AA affiliated. Write: Prof. Asst. Prog. Of NJ, 742 Alexander Rd., Princeton, NJ, 08540. Call Linda Pleva, Executive Assistant 609-919-1660 (day). *Email:* Linda.Pleva@papnj.org

We can also refer callers to over 100 individuals who are seeking others to help start new support groups throughout NJ, if you don't see it, that doesn't mean it doesn't exist!
1-800-367-6274

Signs of Sobriety *Professionally-run.* Provides alcoholism and drug addiction services to persons who are deaf or hard-of-hearing. Makes referrals to deaf and sign interpreter-based 12-Step groups throughout NJ (alcohol or drug addiction, gambling, families of alcoholics, etc). Offers prevention awareness, education classes, SoberCamp annual summer retreat and Sober/Deaf activities for deaf or hard of hearing individuals in recovery. Newsletter. Write: SOS, 100 Scotch Road, 2nd Floor, Ewing, NJ 08628. Call TTY: 1-800-332-7677; Voice: 609-882-7677 (day); Fax: 609-882-6808. *Website:* http://www.signsofsobriety.org *Email:* info@signsofsobriety.org

ATLANTIC

Addictions Victorious of South Jersey, Inc. 12-Step. Group for both Christian and non-Christian men and women who, in their struggle with substance abuse and emotional problems, come together that they may solve their problems and help others as well. Guest speakers, rap sessions, phone help, literature, newsletter. Optional donation. Meets Tues., 7:30pm, Light of the World Church, 111 Route 50, Mays Landing. Call Bob 609-476-2075 or Pastor George Sanders 609-517-3776. *Website:* http://www.addvicinc.org

Alcoholics Anonymous *(BILINGUAL)* 12-Step. Fellowship of men and women who share their experience, strength and hope with each other that they may solve their common problem and help others to recover from alcoholism. Young people's groups also available. Call 609-641-8855. *Website:* http://www.capeatlanticintergroup.org

Dual Recovery Anonymous *Professionally-run.* 12-Step. Mutual support for alcoholics and drug abusers with psychiatric disorders. Meets Thurs., 1:30-3pm, C.O.D.I. Building, 901 Atlantic Ave., Egg Harbor City. For directions call Bill 609-965-6871 (day).

Family Support Group Mutual support for parents and families of persons diagnosed with both a mental illness and alcohol addiction. Sharing of emotional and practical coping skills. Guest speakers. Meets 2nd Thurs., 10am and 4th Thurs., 4:30pm, Mental Health Association, 611 Doughty Rd., Pleasantville. Call Christine Gromadzyn, MSW 609-272-1700 (day). *Website:* http://www.mhaac.org

Lawyers Concerned for Lawyers Self-help group that supports recovery from alcoholism and drug dependence for attorneys, judges, law students and others in the legal system. Based on the 12-Step program adapted from A.A. All inquiries are confidential. Meets Wed., 5:30pm, 1555 Zion Rd., Suite 201, Northfield. Call John 609-641-2266 (day) or NJ Lawyers Assistance Program 1-800-246-5527.

Nurse Recovery Group *Professionally-run.* Mutual support and information for nurses who are recovering from addictions. Sharing of professional concerns and encouragement. Meets in Pomona. Call 1-800-662-0108 (day).

BERGEN

Al-Anon's Adult Children 12-Step. Fellowship offering comfort, hope and friendship through shared experiences for adult children of alcoholics. Call Al-Anon 973-744-8686 (day).
> **Fort Lee** Meets Sat., 10:30am, First Reformed Church, 2420 Lemoine Ave.
> **Maywood** Meets Thurs., 7:30pm, Lutheran Redeemer Church, 401 Maywood and Taplin Ave.

Alateen 12-Step. Fellowship of young persons (age 10+) whose lives have been affected by someone else's drinking. An active adult member of Al-Anon serves as a sponsor. Meets Tues., 7:30pm, St. Mark's Episcopal Church, Chadwick and Grange Rd., Teaneck. Call Al-Anon Information Services 973-744-8686 (day). *Website:* http://www.nj-al-anon.org *Email:* northjerseyais@verizon.net

Alcoholics Anonymous *(BILINGUAL)* 12-Step. Fellowship of men and women who share their experience, strength and hope with each other that they may solve their common problem and help others to recover from alcoholism. Young people's groups also available. Call 908-687-8566 or 1-800-245-1377; Spanish-speaking 973-824-0555. *Website:* http://www.nnjaa.org

CARE (Christians, Addictions, Recovery and Education) 12-Step. Support ministry for substance abusers and their families to help find sobriety, solace and a way to a comfortable non-judgmental Christian walk. Meets Mon., 7:30pm, Church of the Nazarene, 285 E. Midland Ave., Paramus. Call 201-262-3323 (9:30am-4pm). *Website:* http://www.maranathanj.org

Families Anonymous 12-Step. For relatives and friends concerned about the use of drugs, alcohol or related behavioral problems.
> **Englewood** Meets Fri., 7:30pm, Englewood Hospital, Learning Center, Main Floor, 350 Engle St. Call Jesse 201-568-2922.
> **Tenafly** Meets Tues., 7:30pm, Trinity Lutheran Church, Basement, 430 Knickerbocker Rd. Call Judy or Gene 201-262-7758 (day) or Jesse 201-944-0256.

While it's no substitution for talking to our staff, you can call evenings or weekends!
Leave a message and we will get back to you the next workday. ***1-800-367-6274***

Families Anonymous 12-Step. Mutual support for parents and families of children and young adults with alcohol, drug abuse and/or emotional problems. Meets Wed., 7:30-8:30pm, Church of the Immaculate Conception, 900 Darlington Ave., Mahwah. Call Richard or Barbara 201-327-0748. *Website:* http://www.familiesanonymous *Email:* famahway@verizon.net

Nurse Recovery Group *Professionally-run.* Mutual support and information for nurses who are recovering from addictions. Sharing of professional concerns and encouragement. Meets in Teaneck. Call 1-800-662-0108 (day).

Parent Support Group - New Jersey, Inc. *Professionally-run.* Confidential support group for parents of chemically dependent children (ages 13-40+). Meets Mon., 6:30pm, Behavioral Health Center, Room E222, Bergen Pines Hospital, Paramus. Call Karol Sullivan or Adrienne Mellana 1-800-561-4299 or 973-736-3344 (day). *Website:* http://www.psgnjhomestead.com *Email:* psgnj1@aol.com

Psychiatrically Recovering Alcoholics 12-Step. Mutual support for psychiatrically recovering alcoholics who suffer from emotional and mental disorders to share experiences, strengths and hopes while recovering from alcoholism and psychiatric disorders. Meets Tues., 7-8pm, Bethany Presbyterian Church, Palisade Ave. and William St., Englewood. Call Ed 201-541-8452 (day/eve).

Seniors Count *Professionally-run.* 12-Step. Support for persons (age 60+) who are recovering from substance abuse or co-dependency. Meets Fri., 1:30-3pm, Presbyterian Church, 2nd Floor, 150 East Palisades Ave., Englewood. Call Anne Wennhold 201-569-6667. *Website:* http://www.vanostinstitute.org *Email:* vanost@msn.com

Women For Sobriety Self-help designed specifically to help women with addictions achieve sobriety. Helps develop self-esteem and coping skills. Donation $2. Meets Tues., noon-1pm and Thurs., 7pm (new members 6:45pm), YWCA, 112 Oak St., Ridgewood. Call Dee Waddington 201-487-2224 (day).

BURLINGTON

Addictions Victorious of South Jersey, Inc. 12-Step. Group for both Christian and non-Christian men and women who, in their struggle with substance abuse and emotional problems, come together that they may solve their problems and help others as well. Meets Thurs., 7pm, Lighthouse Tabernacle, 716 Main St., Lumberton. Call Wayne or Ronnie 609-267-2657. *Website:* http://www.addvicinc.org

Al-Anon Family Groups 12-Step. Fellowship of families and friends of alcoholics. Offers comfort, hope and friendship through shared experiences. Includes groups for children and adult children. Call Al-Anon Information Service 856-547-0855 (10am-3pm) or 973-744-8686 (day).

Alcoholics Anonymous 12-Step. Fellowship of men and women who share their experience, strength and hope with each other that they may solve their common problem and help others to recover from alcoholism. Young people's groups also available. Call 856-486-4444; Spanish 973-824-0555. *Website:* http://www.aasj.org

Double Trouble Mutual support for persons with a substance abuse problem who are also taking medication for psychiatric problems. Meets Sun., Mon. and Wed., 8:30pm, Hampton Hospital, Cafeteria, 650 Rancocas Rd., Westampton. Call Pam Sachs 609-267-7000 (day).

Nurse Recovery Group *Professionally-run.* Mutual support and information for nurses who are recovering from addictions. Sharing of professional concerns and encouragement. Meets in Moorestown. Call 1-800-662-0108 (day).

Rap Room Parent-to-Parent Coalition *Professionally-run.* Support and education for parents of teens and young adult children dealing with substance/alcohol addictions. Mutual sharing, advocacy, guest speakers, crisis intervention and referral. Meets 1st Tues., 7-9pm, Greentree Executive Campus, 1003 A Lincoln Drive West, Marlton. Call Louise 856-983-3328. *Website:* http://www.raproom.org *Email:* p2p@raproom.org

CAMDEN

Addictions Victorious of South Jersey, Inc. 12-Step. Group for both Christian and non-Christian men and women who, in their struggle with substance abuse and emotional problems, come together that they may solve their problems and help others as well. Guest speakers, rap sessions, phone help, literature, newsletter. Optional donation. *Website:* http://www.addvicinc.org

> **Barrington** Meets Mon., 7pm, Grace Bible Church, 887 Clements Bridge Rd. Call Ginny 856-232-0207.
> **Camden** Meets Tues., 6pm, Fellowship House, 1722 S. Broadway. Call Lucy 856-964-4545.
> **Sicklerville** Meets Fri., 6pm, Christ Care Unit Missionary Baptist Church, Sicklerville and Grimes Rd. Call Quinton and Pricilla 856-262-1833.
> **Somerdale** Meets Thurs., 8pm, Park Avenue Community Church, 431 Hilltop Ave. Call Pastor Glenn Marshall 856-435-0309.

Al-Anon Family Groups 12-Step. Fellowship of families and friends of alcoholics. Offers comfort, hope and friendship through shared experiences. Includes groups for children and adult children. Call Al-Anon Information Service 856-547-0855 (10am-3pm) or 973-744-8686 (day).

Alcoholics Anonymous *(BILINGUAL)* 12-Step. Fellowship of men and women who share their experience, strength and hope with each other that they may solve their common problem and help others to recover from alcoholism. Young people's groups also available. Call 856-486-4444; Spanish-speaking call 973-824-0555. *Website:* http://www.aasj.org

Camden County Parent-to-Parent Mutual support for parents of children of any age who have alcohol or drug-related problems. Guest speakers, literature and phone help. Meets 2nd and 4th Tues., 6:30-8:30pm, Bellmawr Library, Bellmawr Health Clinic, Browning Rd., Bellmawr. Call Kathleen Dobbs 856-968-2301 (day).

Dual Recovery Anonymous Mutual support for alcoholics/addicts who are taking medication for psychiatric problems. Meets Wed., 6-7pm, MICA Club, 498 Marlboro Ave., Cherry Hill. Call Freddy R. 856-662-0955 (voice/TDD) (day).

Lawyers Concerned for Lawyers Self-help group that supports recovery from alcoholism and drug dependence for attorneys, judges, law students and others in the legal system. Based on the 12-Step program adapted from AA. All inquiries are confidential. Meets 1st and 3rd Wed., 6pm, Steininger Center, Board Room, 19 E. Ormond Ave., Cherry Hill. Call John 609-261-3841 (day) or NJ Lawyers Assistance Program 1-800-246-5527.

Nurse Recovery Group *Professionally-run.* Mutual support and information for nurses who are recovering from addictions. Sharing of professional concerns and encouragement. Meets in Haddonfield. Call 1-800-662-0108 (day).

CAPE MAY

Addictions Victorious of South Jersey, Inc. 12-Step. Group for both Christian and non-Christian men and women who, in their struggle with substance abuse and emotional problems, come together that they may solve their problems and help others as well. Guest speakers, rap sessions, phone help, literature, newsletter. Optional donation. Meets Mon., 7pm, Seashore Community Church of Nazarene, 446 Seashore Rd., Cape May. Call Phil 609-408-1191, Marty 609-827-1517 or Church 609-886-6196. *Website:* http://www.addvicinc.org

Al-Anon Family Groups 12-Step fellowship of families and friends of alcoholics. Offers comfort, hope and friendship through shared experiences. Includes groups for children and adult children. Call Al-Anon Information Service 856-547-0855 (10am-3pm) or 973-744-8686 (day).

Alcoholics Anonymous 12-Step. Fellowship of men and women who share their experience, strength and hope with each other that they may solve their common problem and help others to recover from alcoholism. Young people's groups also available. Call 609-641-8855. *Website:* http://www.capeatlanticinterrgroup.org

CUMBERLAND

Al-Anon Family Groups 12-Step. Fellowship of families and friends of alcoholics. Offers comfort, hope and friendship through shared experiences. Includes groups for children and adult children. Call Al-Anon Information Service 856-547-0855 (10am-3pm) or 973-744-8686 (day).

Alcoholics Anonymous *(BILINGUAL)* 12-Step. Fellowship of men and women who share their experience, strength and hope with each other that they may solve their common problem and help others to recover from alcoholism. Young people's groups also available. Call 856-486-4444; Spanish-speaking 973-824-0555. *Website:* http://www.aasj.org

ESSEX

Al-Anon's Adult Children 12-Step. Fellowship offering comfort, hope and friendship through shared experiences for adult children of alcoholics. Meets Tues., 8pm, First Presbyterian Church, 10 Fairview Ave., Verona. Call Al-Anon 973-744-8686.

Al-Anon Family Groups 12-Step. Fellowship of families and friends of alcoholics. Offers comfort, hope and friendship through shared experiences. Includes groups for children and adult children. Call Al-Anon Information Service 973-744-8686 (day).

Alcoholics Anonymous *(BILINGUAL)* 12-Step. Fellowship of men and women who share their experience, strength and hope with each other that they may solve their common problem and help others to recover from alcoholism. Young people's groups also available. Call 908-687-8566 or 1-800-245-1377; Spanish-speaking 973-824-0555. *Website:* http://www.nnjaa.org

"Never look down on anybody unless you're helping them up"
- Jesse Jackson

BASA (Brothers And Sisters of Addicts) *Professionally-run.* Confidential support group for young adults (age 13 and older) living with a chemically dependent sibling. Meets at St. Cloud Presbyterian Church, Old Indian Rd. and Ridgeway Ave., West Orange. Call Karol Sullivan or Adrienne Mellana 1-800-561-4299 or 973-736-3344 (day).

Double Trouble Support for persons in dual recovery from a mental illness and a substance or alcohol addiction. Meets Mon., 5-6pm, Where Peaceful Waters Flow, 3-5 Vose Ave., 2nd Floor, South Orange. Call Jacqueline Bankston 973-762-7469.

Families Anonymous 12-Step. Support for families and friends concerned about the use of drugs or related behavioral problems. Sharing of experiences, strengths and hopes. Dues $1. Meets Wed., 7:30pm, First Episcopal Church of the Holy Spirit, 36 Gould St., Verona. Call Jim 973-338-6952 or Roxy 973-667-1067 (day).

Lawyers Concerned for Lawyers Self-help group that supports recovery from alcoholism and drug dependence for attorneys, judges, law students and others in the legal system. Based on the 12-Step program adapted from A.A. All inquiries are confidential. Meets Tues., 7:30pm, United Way, Room 211A, 60 South Fullerton Ave., Montclair. Call Kenneth 973-429-5588 (day) or 973-509-6062 (eve) or NJLAP 1-800-246-5527.

Parents Support Group - New Jersey Inc. *Professionally-run.* Confidential support group for parents of a chemically dependent child (age 13-40+). Meets Wed., 6pm and Thurs., 6:30pm; St. Cloud Presbyterian Church, Old Indian Rd. and Ridgeway Ave., West Orange. Call Karol Sullivan 973-736-3344 (9am-3pm) or 1-800-561-4299 (24 hr hotline).

GLOUCESTER

Addictions Victorious of South Jersey, Inc. 12-Step. Group for both Christian and non-Christian men and women who in their struggle with substance abuse and emotional problems come together that they may solve their problems and help others as well. Guest speakers, rap sessions, phone help, literature, newsletter. Optional donation. *Website:* http://www.addvicinc.org

> **Glassboro** Meets Tues., 7pm, Olivet Wesleyan Church, 711 Heston Rd. Call Chip 856-881-8241.
> **Pitman** Meets Wed., 7:30pm, Joy Community Fellowship, Florence and Long Rd. Call Charlie 856-881-2966.
> **Pitman** Meets Mon., 7:30pm, The Rock Church, 205 Esplanade Ave. Call 856-582-2277.

Al-Anon Family Groups 12-Step. Fellowship of families and friends of alcoholics. Offers comfort, hope and friendship through shared experiences. Includes groups for children and adult children. Call Al-Anon Information Service 856-547-0855 (10am-3pm) or 973-744-8686 (day).

Alcoholics Anonymous *(BILINGUAL)* 12-Step. Fellowship of men and women who share their experience, strength and hope with each other that they may solve their common problem and help others to recover from alcoholism. Young people's groups also available. Call 856-486-4444; Spanish-speaking 973-824-0555. *Website:* http://www.aasj.org

Dual Recovery Anonymous *Professionally-run.* Mutual support for alcoholics or drug addicts with psychiatric disorders. Meets Fri., 7pm, Old Medical Arts Building, 1st Floor, Suite 14, 52 West Redbank Ave., Woodbury. Call 856-845-0100 (day).

HUDSON

Al-Anon Family Groups 12-Step. Fellowship of families and friends of alcoholics. Offers comfort, hope and friendship through shared experiences. Includes groups for children and adult children. Call Al-Anon Information Service 973-744-8686 (day).

Alateen 12-Step. Fellowship of young persons (age 12+) whose lives have been affected by someone else's drinking. An active adult Al-Anon sponsor serves as a facilitator. Call Al-Anon 973-744-8686 (day).

Alcoholics Anonymous *(BILINGUAL)* 12-Step. Fellowship of men and women who share their experience, strength and hope with each other that they may solve their common problem and help others to recover from alcoholism. Young people's groups also available. Call 908-687-8566 or 1-800-245-1377; Spanish-speaking 973-824-0555. *Website:* http://www.nnjaa.org

HUNTERDON

Al-Anon Family Groups 12-Step. Fellowship of families and friends of alcoholics. Offers comfort, hope and friendship through shared experiences. Includes groups for children and adult children. Call Al-Anon Information Service 973-744-8686 (day).

Nurse Recovery Group *Professionally-run.* Mutual support and information for nurses who are recovering from addictions. Sharing of professional concerns and encouragement. Meets in Flemington. Call 1-800-662-0108 (day).

MERCER

Al-Anon Family Groups 12-Step. Fellowship of families and friends of alcoholics. Offers comfort, hope and friendship through shared experiences. Includes groups for children and adult children. Call Al-Anon Information Service 856-547-0855 (10am-3pm) or 973-744-8686 (day).

Alcoholics Anonymous 12-Step. Fellowship of men and women who share their experience, strength and hope with each other that they may solve their common problem and help others to recover from alcoholism. Young people's groups also available. Call 609-656-8900 (hotline) or 609-656-8908, Spanish-speaking 973-824-0555. *Website:* http://www.centraljerseyintergroup.org

Families Anonymous 12-Step. Program for families, especially parents of those with substance abuse or other disruptive behavioral problems. Meets Mon., 7:30pm, St. Lawrence Rehab Center, 2381 Lawrenceville Rd., Route 206 South, Lawrenceville. Call Joan 609-883-1403. *Website:* http://www.familiesanonymous.org *Email:* joan@brra.com

Lawyers Concerned for Lawyers 12-step self-help group that supports recovery from alcoholism and drug dependence for attorneys, judges, law students and others in the legal system. Meets Thurs., 6pm, 3490 Route 1, Bldg. 7B, Princeton. Call Michael 609-392-7734 (day) or NJLAP 1-800-246-5527.

Nurse Recovery Group *Professionally-run.* Mutual support and information for nurses who are recovering from addictions. Sharing of professional concerns and encouragement. Meets in Trenton. Call 1-800-662-0108 (day).

Princeton ACOA (Adult Children Of Alcoholics) 12-Step. Fellowship for adult children from alcoholic or dysfunctional families. Guest speakers, phone help, rap sessions and literature. Meets Thurs., 7:30-9pm, Unitarian Church of Princeton, 50 Cherry Hill Rd., Princeton. Call Audrey 609-716-8063.

MIDDLESEX

Al-Anon Adult Children 12-Step. Fellowship offering comfort, hope and friendship through shared experiences for adult children of alcoholics. Meets Fri., 8pm, St. Luke's Episcopal Church, 17 Oak Ave. and Route 27, Metuchen. Call Al-Anon 973-744-8686 (day).

Alateen 12-Step. Fellowship of young persons (age 12-19) whose lives have been affected by someone else's drinking. An active adult member of Al-Anon serves as a sponsor. Meets Fri., 8pm, St. Joseph's Parish Center, 80 High St., Carteret. Call Al-Anon Information Services 973-744-8686.

Alcoholics Anonymous 12-Step. Fellowship of men and women who share their experience, strength and hope with each other that they may solve their common problem and help others to recover from alcoholism. Young people's groups also available. Call 908-687-8566, 609-888-2662 or 609-888-3333 (hotline) or 1-800-245-1377; Spanish-speaking 973-824-0555. *Website:* http://www.nnjaa.org

Double Trouble Mutual support for alcoholics or drug addicts who are taking medication for psychiatric problems. Optional donation. Meets Thurs. (last Thurs. open mtg.), 7:30pm, UMDNJ - The Club, 189 New St., Room B, New Brunswick. Call Tim 732-235-6116 (day).

Lawyers Concerned for Lawyers *(WOMEN ONLY)* Self-help group that supports recovery from alcoholism and drug dependence for attorneys, judges, law students and others in the legal system. Based on the 12-Step program adapted from A.A. All inquiries are confidential. Meets one Sat. per month, New Brunswick. Call Denise at NJLAP 732-937-7541 or 1-800-246-5527 (day). *Email:* denise@njlap.org

Nurse Recovery Group *Professionally-run.* Mutual support and information for nurses who are recovering from addictions. Sharing of professional concerns and encouragement. Meets in Woodbridge. Call 1-800-662-0108 (day).

Overcomer's Outreach 12-Step. Christian fellowship to overcome any type of addiction or compulsive behavior, anxiety, depression or loneliness using God's word as a basis of recovery. Discussion, Bible study, prayer, phone help. Meets Mon., 7:30-9:15pm, Metuchen Assembly of God, Rose and Whitman St., Metuchen. Call Janet 732-388-2856 (eve).

Overcomer's Turning Point 12-Step. Group for alcoholism, drug addiction, codependency and adult children of alcoholics. Under 18 welcome. Meets Tues., 7:30pm, Highland Park Baptist Church, 2nd and Raritan St., Highland Park. Call Tony Labenski 732-613-1582 (day/eve). *Email:* tonylabens@aol.com

Parent Support Group - New Jersey, Inc. Confidential support group for parents of chemically dependent children (age 13-40+). Meets Thurs., 7pm, Cheesequake First Aid Squad, Route 34, Old Bridge. Call Karol Sullivan or Adrienne Mellana 1-800-561-4299 or 973-736-3344 (day). *Website:* http://www.psgnjhomestead.com *Email:* psgnj1@aol.com

S.M.A.R.T. Recovery (Self-Management And Recovery Training) *Professionally-run.* Self-help group for individuals wanting to gain their independence from addictive behaviors (drugs, including alcohol and nicotine and other compulsive behaviors including gambling, eating disorders). SMART is an abstinence program based on cognitive-behavioral education and principles, especially those of rational-emotive behavior therapy. Meets Mon., 6:30-7:45pm, Rutgers University, Busch Campus, Psychology Building, Room A224, Piscataway. Call Tom Morgan 732-445-0902. *Website:* http://www.smartrecovery.org

MONMOUTH

Al-Anon Adult Children 12-Step. Fellowship offering comfort, hope and friendship through shared experiences for adult children of alcoholics. Meets Sun., 8pm, First Baptist Church, Oakland and Maple Ave., Red Bank. Call Al-Anon 973-744-8686 (day).

Al-Anon Family Groups 12-Step. Fellowship of families and friends of alcoholics. Offers comfort, hope and friendship through shared experiences. Includes groups for children and adult children. Call Al-Anon Information Service 973-744-8686 (day).

Alcoholics Anonymous *(BILINGUAL)* 12-Step. Fellowship of men and women who share their experience, strength and hope with each other that they may solve their common problem and help others to recover from alcoholism. Young people's groups also available. Call 908-687-8566, 609-656-8900, 609-656-8908 (hotline) or 1-800-245-1377; Spanish-speaking 973-824-0555. *Website:* http://www.centraljerseyintergroup.org

Double Trouble Dual Recovery 12-Step. Support for those who have an emotional/psychiatric illness and are alcohol/chemically addicted. Meets Mon. and Thurs., 10:15-11am, Park Place Program, 1011 Bond St., Asbury Park. Call Mark 732-869-2781 (day) or Mike Rafter 732-869-2765 (day).

Dual Recovery Mutual support for alcoholics or drug abusers who are taking medication for psychiatric problems. Transportation available. Meets Tues., 7pm, Freehold Self-Help Center, 17 Bannard St., Freehold. Call CSP 1-800-227-3729 (day).

Dual Recovery Anonymous Mutual support for alcoholics/addicts who are taking medication for psychiatric problems. Meets 2nd and 4th Sat., 2-3pm, CARE Center, 700 Mattison Ave., Asbury Park. Transportation available. Call Brian or Carolyn 732-869-9141 (day).

Dual Recovery Anonymous 12-Step. Professionally co-facilitated. Mutual support for any person recovering from mental illness and substance abuse. Meets Tues. and Fri., 10:30-11:30am, CPC/Aberdeen Counseling Center, 1088 Highway 34, Aberdeen. Call Mark 732-290-1700 ext. 5307 (day).

Families Anonymous 12-Step. For relatives and friends concerned about the use of drugs, alcohol or related behavioral problems. *Website:* http://familiesanonymous.org

> **Holmdel** Meets Mon., 7:30pm, Bayshore Community Hospital, 723 N. Beers St. Call Mary Lou 732-583-2238 (eve) or Nancy 732-264-5948 (6-8pm).
> **Leonardo** Meets Mon., 7:30pm, Middletown Township Complex, Leonardville Rd. Call 732-291-1467 (eve).
> **Ocean Grove** Meets Mon., 7:30pm, St. Paul's United Methodist Church, 80 Embury Ave. Call Diana 732-988-3903.
> **Red Bank** Meets Thurs., 7:30-9pm, United Methodist Church, 247 Broad St. Call 732-462-7707. *Email:* higley@optonline.net

Nurse Recovery Group *Professionally-run.* Mutual support and information for nurses who are recovering from addictions. Sharing of professional concerns and encouragement. Meets in Red Bank and Neptune. Call 1-800-662-0108 (day).

Parent Support Group - New Jersey, Inc. Confidential support group for parents of chemically dependent children (age 13-40+). Meets Tues., 7pm, Church of the Nativity, Hance and Ridge Rd., Fair Haven. Call Karol Sullivan or Adrienne Mellana 1-800-561-4299 or 973-736-3344 (day). *Website:* http://www.psgnjhomestead.com *Email:* psgnj1@aol.com

MORRIS

A.A. for MICA Patients Alcoholics Anonymous meeting for persons who also have a mental illness. Meets Fri., 7:30pm, New Views, Greystone Park Hospital, Main Building, 1st Floor, North Tier, Morris Plains. Call Tom Wicks 973-292-4015 (9am-4pm). *Email:* newviews@nac.net

Al-Anon's Adult Children 12-Step. Fellowship offering comfort, hope and friendship through shared experiences for adult children of alcoholics. Call Al-Anon 973-744-8686 (day). *Website:* http://www.al-anon.org

> **Dover** Meets Tues., 7pm, First Memorial Presbyterian Church, 51 W. Blackwell St.
> **Parsippany** Meets Sat., 7:30pm, Presbyterian Church, 1675 Route 46 East.
> **Stirling** Meets Fri., 8:15pm, First Presbyterian Church, 158 Central Ave.

Al-Anon Family Groups 12-Step. Fellowship of families and friends of alcoholics. Offers comfort, hope and friendship through shared experiences. Includes groups for children and adult children. Call Al-Anon Information Service 973-744-8686 (day).

Alateen 12-Step. Fellowship of young persons (age 13-19) whose lives have been affected by someone else's drinking. An active adult member of Al-Anon serves as a sponsor. Meets Tues., 7:30pm, St. David's Episcopal Church, Kinnelon Rd., Kinnelon. Call Al-Anon Information Services 973-744-8686 (day).

Alcohol and Drug Family Education *Professionally-run.* Support for families facing the chemical dependency of a family member. Deals with co-dependency issues. Meets Thurs., 6:30-8pm, Morristown Memorial Hospital, Outpatient Behavioral Health, Morristown. For meeting information call 1-888-247-1400.

Alcoholics Anonymous *(BILINGUAL)* 12-Step. Fellowship of men and women who share their experience, strength and hope with each other that they may solve their common problem and help others to recover from alcoholism. Young people's groups also available. Call 908-687-8566 or 1-800-245-1377; Spanish-speaking 973-824-0555. *Website:* http://www.nnjaa.org

Calix Society Mutual support to promote the spiritual development of Catholic alcoholics. Members of other faiths welcome. Mass followed by group discussion. Meets last Sat., 10am, St. Lawrence Center, (rear of church parking lot), Chester. Call Thomas Gibbons 908-876-4343 (day/eve).

Dual Recovery Anonymous *Professionally-run.* Mutual support for alcoholics or drug addicts with psychiatric disorders. Meets Tues., noon-1pm, MICA Group Room; Fri., noon-1pm, IOP group room and Sun., 11am-noon, Executive Dining Room, Saint Clares Hospital, Boonton. Call Nikki R. 973-664-0596.

Families Anonymous 12-Step. Mutual support for parents, relatives and friends of persons with drug or alcohol problems. Peer-counseling. Meets Tues., 7:30-9pm, First Presbyterian Church, 35 Church St., Rockaway. Call 973-586-2440 (eve).

Lawyers Concerned for Lawyers Self-help group that supports recovery from alcoholism and drug dependence for attorneys, judges, law students and others in the legal system. Based on the 12-Step program adapted from A.A. All inquiries are confidential. Meets Wed., 7:30pm, Center for Behavioral Health, 95 Mt. Kemble Ave., Morristown. Call Albert 973-538-0280 (day/eve) or NJ Lawyers Assistance Program 1-800-246-5527.

Moderation Management Offers support for problem drinkers who want to moderate their drinking behavior and make other positive lifestyle changes. Offers a 9-step program which includes moderate drinking guidelines, goal setting techniques, self-management strategies and drink-monitoring exercises. Meets Tues., 7:30-8:30pm, St. Mark's Lutheran Church, 100 Harter Rd., Morris Twp. Call Dick or Elaine Ottaway 908-221-1314 (day/eve). *Website:* http://www.moderation.org *Email:* rottaway@att.net

Nurse Recovery Group *Professionally-run.* Mutual support and information for nurses who are recovering from addictions. Sharing of professional concerns and encouragement. Meets in Boonton. Call 1-800-662-0108 (day).

Psychiatrically Recovering 12-Step. Mutual support for psychiatrically recovering people who wish to refrain from using alcohol or drugs, abusing food or any other compulsive behavior. Call Richie S. 973-865-4851 (day/eve).
> **Cedar Knolls** Meets Mon. and Thurs., 10am, Saint Clare's Behavioral Health Center, 100 East Hanover Ave.
> **Denville** Meets Mon., 1pm, Saint Clare's Behavioral Health Center, 50 Morris Ave., Room B-1.
> **Pompton Plains** Meets Fri., 9am, New Bridge: Crossroads, (formerly Pequannock Valley Mental Health Center), 640 Newark-Pompton Turnpike.

S.M.A.R.T. Recovery (Self-Management And Recovery Training) Self-help group for individuals wanting to gain their independence from addictive behaviors (drugs, including alcohol and nicotine and other compulsive behaviors including gambling, eating disorders). SMART is an abstinence program based on cognitive-behavioral education and principles, especially those of rational-emotive behavior therapy. Meets Thurs., 7-8:30pm, Beginnings, 65 Spring St., Morristown. Call Rich 973-983-0217. *Website:* http://www.smartrecovery.org

OCEAN

Adult Children of Alcoholics Self-help group for adult children of alcoholics or dysfunctional families. Follows the 12-Step program adapted from AA. Meets Tues., 7:45-9pm, Toms River Church of Christ, 1126 Hooper Ave., Toms River. Call Stephanie 732-573-1535 (answering machine).

Al-Anon Family Groups 12-Step. Fellowship of families and friends of alcoholics. Offers comfort, hope and friendship through shared experiences. Includes groups for children and adult children. Call Al-Anon Information Service 856-547-0855 (10am-3pm).

Alateen 12-Step. Fellowship of young persons (age 7+) whose lives have been affected by someone else's drinking. An active adult member of Al-Anon serves as a sponsor. Meets Sat., 11am, Brick Hospital, Jack Martin Blvd., Brick. Call Al-Anon Services 856-547-0855.

Alcoholics Anonymous *(BILINGUAL)* 12-Step. Fellowship of men and women who share their experience, strength and hope with each other that they may solve their common problem and help others to recover from alcoholism. Young people's groups also available. Call 908-687-8566, 609-656-8900, 609-656-8908 (hotline), 1-800-245-1377 or 609-494-5130 (Long Beach Island/Southern Ocean City), Spanish-speaking 973-824-0555. *Website:* http://www.aasj.org

Families Anonymous 12-Step. For relatives and friends concerned about the use of drugs or related behavioral problems. Meets Tues., 7:30pm, St. Andrews United Methodist Church, 1528 Church Rd., Toms River. Call 732-864-0548. *Email:* FamAnonTR@Comcast.net

Lawyers Concerned for Lawyers Self-help group that supports recovery from alcoholism and drug dependence for attorneys, judges, law students and others in the legal system. Based on the 12-Step program adapted from A.A. All inquiries are confidential. Meets Tues., 7:15pm, St. Mary's By The Sea, Meeting Room, Forman and Bay Ave., Point Pleasant. Call Fred 732-785-6314 (pager number) (day) or NJ Lawyers Assistance Program 1-800-246-5527.

Overcomers In Christ Recovery program that deals with every aspect of addiction and dysfunction (spiritual, physical, mental, emotional and social). Uses Overcomers goals which are Christ-centered. Resources, information and referrals. Literature. Meets Mon., 7pm, America's Keswick, 601 Route 530, Whiting. Separate group for men and women. For women's group call Diane Hunt 732-350-1187 ext. 47. For men's group call Pastor Mike 732-350-1187 ext. 39. *Website:* http://www.OvercomersinChrist.org

Parents Group, Inc. Mutual support and referrals for parents in crisis from their teenage and adult children's substance/alcohol abuse. Works with and outreaches to community resources for prevention, awareness and intervention. Meets Tues., 7-9pm, Toms River. Call Mary and Michael Holland 732-929-4443 (day/eve). *Email:* starfishpg@comcast.net

Parent Support Group - New Jersey, Inc. Confidential support group for parents of chemically dependent children (age 13-40+). Meets Mon., 7pm, Presbyterian Church of Toms River, 1070 Hooper Ave., Toms River. Call Karol Sullivan or Adrienne Mellana 1-800-561-4299 or 973-736-3344 (day). *Website:* http://www.psgnjhomestead.com *Email:* psgnj1@aol.com

PASSAIC

Al-Anon's Adult Children 12-Step. Fellowship offering comfort, hope and friendship through shared experiences for adult children of alcoholics. Meets Tues., 8pm, (beginners 7pm), Preakness Reformed Church, 131 Church Lane, Wayne. Call Al-Anon 973-744-8686 (day).

Al-Anon Family Groups 12-Step. Fellowship of families and friends of alcoholics. Offers comfort, hope and friendship through shared experiences. Includes groups for children and adult children. Call Al-Anon Information Service 973-744-8686 (day).

Alcoholics Anonymous *(BILINGUAL)* 12-Step. Fellowship of men and women who share their experience, strength and hope with each other that they may solve their common problem and help others to recover from alcoholism. Young people's groups also available. For meeting information call 908-687-8566 or 1-800-245-1377; Spanish-speaking call 973-824-0555. *Website:* http://www.nnjaa.org

Nurse Recovery Group *Professionally-run.* Mutual support and information for nurses who are recovering from addictions. Sharing of professional concerns and encouragement. Meets in Passaic. Call 1-800-662-0108 (day).

Parent Support Group - New Jersey, Inc. *Professionally-run.* Confidential support group for parents of chemically dependent children (ages 13-40+). Meets Mon., 6:30pm, St. Joseph's Hospital, 224 Hamburg Turnpike, 7th Floor, Wayne. Call Karol Sullivan or Adrienne Mellana 1-800-561-4299 or 973-736-3344 (day). *Website:* http://www.psgnjhomestead.com *Email:* psgnj1@aol.com

Psychiatrically Recovering 12-Step. Mutual support for psychiatrically recovering people who wish to refrain from using alcohol or drugs, abusing food or any compulsive behavior. Meets Fri., 10:15am, New Bridge: Visions, 22 Riverview Dr., Wayne. Call Richie S. 973-865-4851 (day/eve).

SALEM

Al-Anon Family Groups 12-Step. Fellowship of families and friends of alcoholics. Offers comfort, hope and friendship through shared experiences. Includes groups for children and adult children. Call Al-Anon Information Service 856-547-0855 (10am-3pm).

We can also refer callers to over 100 individuals who are seeking others to help start new support groups throughout NJ, if you don't see it, that doesn't mean it doesn't exist! **1-800-367-6274**

Alcoholics Anonymous *(BILINGUAL)* 12-Step. Fellowship of men and women who share their experience, strength and hope with each other that they may solve their common problem and help others to recover from alcoholism. Young people's groups also available. Call 856-486-4444; Spanish-speaking 973-824-0555. *Website:* http://www.aasj.org

SOMERSET

Al-Anon Family Groups 12-Step. Fellowship of families and friends of alcoholics. Offers comfort, hope and friendship through shared experiences. Includes groups for children and adult children. Call Al-Anon Information Service 973-744-8686 (day).

Alateen 12-Step. Fellowship of young persons (age 8-18) whose lives have been affected by someone else's drinking. An active adult member of Al-Anon serves as a sponsor. Meets Fri., 8:30pm, Somerset Hospital, Rehill Ave., Somerville. Call Al-Anon Information Services 973-744-8686 (day).

Alcoholics Anonymous *(BILINGUAL)* 12-Step. Fellowship of men and women who share their experience, strength and hope with each other that they may solve their common problem and help others to recover from alcoholism. Young people's groups also available. Call 908-687-8566, 609-888-2662 or 609-888-3333 (hotline) or 1-800-245-1377; Spanish-speaking 973-824-0555. *Website:* http://www.nnjaa.org

Bright Futures for Kids *Professionally-run.* Provides support, education and counseling for children (age 4-12) who are affected by a family members alcohol and/or drug addiction. Children learn how to express their feelings, coping skills, a sense of responsibility and the ability to resist peer pressure. Meets Sun., 11am-1pm, Carrier Clinic, Atkinson Amphitheater, Classroom 3, 252 Route 601, Belle Mead. Call Community Relations Dept. 908-281-1513.

Lawyers Concerned for Lawyers Self-help group that supports recovery from alcoholism and drug dependence for attorneys, judges, law students and others in the legal system. Based on the 12-Step program adapted from A.A. All inquires are confidential. Meets Tues., 6pm, 70 Grove St., Somerville. Call NJ Lawyers Assistance Program 1-800-246-5527.

Nurse Recovery Group *Professionally-run.* Mutual support and information for nurses who are recovering from addictions. Sharing of professional concerns and encouragement. Meets in Belle Mead. Call 1-800-662-0108 (day).

Overcomer's Outreach 12-Step. Christian fellowship to overcome any type of addiction or compulsive behavior using God's word as a basis of recovery. Discussion, scripture readings, prayer, phone help. Meets Sat., 3:30-5pm, Reformed Church, Fellowship Hall, 113 Clinton St., South Bound Brook. Call Carol Mehlenbeck 732-885-1023 or 732-457-9304 (day/eve).

Parent Support Group - New Jersey, Inc. Confidential support group for parents of chemically dependent children (age 13-40+). Meets Mon., 7pm, Carrier Foundation, Admissions Building, Belle Mead. Call Karol Sullivan or Adrienne Mellana 1-800-561-4299 or 973-736-3344 (day). *Website:* http://www.psgnjhomestead.com *Email:* psgnj1@aol.com

Psychiatrically Recovering 12-Step. Mutual support for psychiatrically recovering people who wish to refrain from using alcohol or drugs, abusing food or any other compulsive behavior. Meets Thurs., 7:30pm, Richard Hall Community Mental Health Center, 500 N. Bridge St., Room 121, Bridgewater. Call Richie S. 973-865-4851. (day/eve).

S.M.A.R.T. Recovery (Self-Management And Recovery Training) *Professionally-run.* Self-help group for individuals wanting to gain their independence from addictive behaviors (drugs, including alcohol and nicotine and other compulsive behaviors including gambling, eating disorders). SMART is an abstinence program based on cognitive-behavioral education and principles, especially those of rational-emotive behavior therapy. Meets 1st and 3rd Thurs., 7:30-8:45pm, Richard Hall Community Mental Health Center, Vogt and North Bridge St., Bridgewater. Call Brian Diskin 732-266-9483. *Website:* http://www.smartrecovery.org *Email:* bridisk@aol.com

Weekend Codependency Program *Professionally-run.* Support and education for families and friends of alcohol/drug abusers or those dealing with persons with any addiction problems. Educational lectures, discussion groups and parents group. Meets Sat. and Sun., 9:30am-3pm, Carrier Clinic, Atkinson Amphitheater, 252 Route 601, Belle Mead. Call 908-281-1513 (day) or 908-281-1000 (eve/weekend). *Website:* http://www.carrier.org

SUSSEX

Al-Anon's Adult Children 12-Step. Fellowship offering comfort, hope and friendship through shared experiences for adult children of alcoholics. Meets Wed., 8pm, Holy Counselor Lutheran Church, Sandhill Rd., Vernon. Call Al-Anon 973-744-8686 (day).

Al-Anon Family Groups 12-Step. Fellowship of families and friends of alcoholics. Offers comfort, hope and friendship through shared experiences. Includes groups for children and adult children. Call Al-Anon Information Service 973-744-8686 (day).

Alateen 12 Step. Fellowship of young persons (age 13+) whose lives have been affected by someone else's drinking. An active adult member of Al-Anon serves as a sponsor. Meets Mon., 7:30pm, Westside United Methodist Church, 16 Maxim Dr., Hopatcong. Call Al-Anon Information Services 973-744-8686 (day).

Alcoholics Anonymous *(BILINGUAL)* 12-Step. Fellowship of men and women who share their experience, strength and hope with each other that they may solve their common problem and help others to recover from alcoholism. Young people's groups also available. Call 908-687-8566 or 1-800-245-1377; Spanish-speaking 973-824-0555. *Website:* http://www.nnjaa.org

Lawyers Concerned for Lawyers Self-help group that supports recovery from alcoholism and drug dependence for attorneys, judges, law students and others in the legal system. Based on the 12-Step program adapted from AA. All inquiries are confidential. Meets Sat., 9am, Newton. Call Mary Jean 973-729-1847 or NJ-LAP 1-800-246-5527.

UNION

Al-Anon Family Groups 12-Step. Fellowship of families and friends of alcoholics. Offers comfort, hope and friendship through shared experiences. Includes groups for children and adult children. Call Al-Anon Information Service 973-744-8686 (day).

Alcoholics Anonymous *(BILINGUAL)* 12-Step. Fellowship of men and women who share their experience, strength and hope with each other that they may solve their common problem and help others to recover from alcoholism. Young people's groups also available. Call 908-687-8566 or 1-800-245-1377; Spanish-speaking 973-824-0555. *Website:* http://www.nnjaa.org

Families of Addiction *Professionally-run.* Mutual support for families of persons with an alcohol or drug addiction. Meets Tues., 6:30-8pm, Overlook Hospital, 46-48 Beauvoir Ave, Summit. Before attending call Rosemary Walsh 908-522-4878.

Nurse Recovery Group *Professionally-run.* Mutual support and information for nurses who are recovering from addictions. Sharing of professional concerns and encouragement. Meets in Berkeley Heights. Call 1-800-662-0108 (day).

Parent Support Group - New Jersey, Inc. *Professionally-run.* Confidential support group for parents of chemically dependent children (age 13-40+). Meets Tues., 6:30pm, Central Presbyterian Church, Library Room, 70 Maple Ave., Summit. Call Karol Sullivan or Adrienne Mellana 1-800-561-4299 or 973-736-3344 (day). *Website:* http://wwwpsgnjhomestead.com *Email:* psgn1@aol.com

Psychiatrically Recovering 12-Step. Mutual support for psychiatrically recovering people who wish to refrain from using alcohol or drugs, abusing food or any other compulsive behavior. Meets Tues., 9:30am, Occupational Center of Union County, New Building, Activity Room, 291 Cox St., Roselle. Call Richie S. 973-865-4851 (day/eve).

WARREN

Al-Anon Family Groups 12-Step. Fellowship of families and friends of alcoholics. Offers comfort, hope and friendship through shared experiences. Includes groups for children and adult children. Call Al-Anon Information Service 973-744-8686 (day).

Alcoholics Anonymous *(BILINGUAL)* 12-Step. Fellowship of men and women who share their experience, strength and hope with each other that they may solve their common problem and help others to recover from alcoholism. Young people's groups also available. Call 908-687-8566 or 1-800-245-1377; Spanish-speaking 973-824-0555. *Website:* http://www.nnjaa.org

Dual Recovery Anonymous Mutual support for alcoholics or drug addicts who are taking medication for psychiatric problems. Dues $2/month. Meetings vary, Better Future Help Center, 21 West Washington Ave., Washington. Call Robin Wolak 908-835-1180.

NATIONAL

Adult Children of Alcoholics World Services Org., Inc. *International. 1500+ meetings. Founded 1977.* 12-Step program of recovery for individuals who were raised in an alcoholic or otherwise dysfunctional household. Group development guidelines. Newsletter, literature. Send a self-addressed stamped envelope when writing. Write: ACA, PO Box 3216, Torrance, CA 90510-3216. Call 310-534-1815. *Website:* http://www.adultchildren.org *Email:* info@adultchildren.org

Al-Anon Family Groups, Inc. World Services Headquarters *(MULTILINGUAL) International. 26,000 groups. Founded 1951.* 12-Step. Fellowship of men, women, adult children and children whose lives have been affected by the compulsive drinking of a family member or friend. Opportunity for personal recovery and growth. Guidelines for starting groups. Literature available in 30 languages. For meeting information call 1-888-425-2666 (Mon.-Fri., 8am-6pm). Write: Al-Anon Family Groups, Inc., 1600 Corporate Landing Parkway, Virginia Beach, VA 23454-5617 Call 757-563-1600; Fax: 757-563-1655. *Website:* http://www.al-anon.org *Email:* wso@al-anon.org

Alateen International. *(MUTILINGUAL) International. 2696 groups. Founded 1957.* 12-Step. Fellowship of young persons whose lives have been affected by someone else's drinking. An active adult member of Al-Anon serves as a sponsor for each group. Group development guidelines, newsletter. Literature available in 30 languages. Write: Alateen Al-Anon Family Group Headquarters Inc.,1600 Corporate Landing Parkway Virginia Beach, VA 23454-5617. Call 757-563-1600; for meeting information call 1-888-425-2666 (English/French/Spanish); Fax: 757-536-1655. *Website:* http://www.al-anon.alateen.org *Email:* wso@al-anon.org

Alcoholics Anonymous World Services, Inc. *(MULTILINGUAL) International. 98000 groups worldwide. Founded 1935.* 12-Step. Fellowship of women and men who have found a solution to their drinking problem. The only requirement for membership is a desire to stop drinking. Supported by voluntary contributions of its members and groups. A.A. neither seeks nor accepts outside funding. Members observe personal anonymity at the public level, thus emphasizing A.A. principles rather than personalities. For more information check your local phone directory or newspaper. Write: General Service Office, PO Box 459 Grand Central Station, New York, NY 10163. Call 212-870-3400; Fax: 212-870-3003. *Website:* http://www.aa.org

Alcoholics Victorious *International. 150 affiliated groups. Founded 1948.* 12-Step. Christian-oriented group for those recovering from alcohol or chemical dependency. Information and referrals, literature, phone support, conferences, support group meetings, newsletter. Assistance in starting groups. How-to materials. Write: Alcoholics Victorious, c/o Association of Gospel Rescue Missions, 1045 Swift St., Kansas City, MO 64116-4127. Call 1-800-624-5156; Fax: 816-471-3718. *Website:* http://www.alcoholicsvictorious.org *Email:* info@alcoholicsvictorious.org

Anesthetists in Recovery *National network. Founded 1984.* Network of recovering nurse anesthetists. Provides phone support, information and referrals to groups and treatment. Write: AIR, c/o Art, 8233 Brookside Rd., Elkins Park, PA 19027. Call 215-635-0183. *Email:* a.to.z@comcast.net

Calix Society *International. 27 chapters. Founded 1947.* Fellowship of Catholic alcoholics maintaining their sobriety through Alcoholics Anonymous. Concerned with total abstinence, spiritual development and sanctification of the whole personality of each member. Bimonthly newsletter. Assistance in chapter development. Write: Calix Society, 2555 Hazelwood Ave., St. Paul, MN 55109. Call 1-800-398-0524. *Website:* http://www.calixsociety.org *Email:* calix@usfamily.net

Chemically Dependent Anonymous *National. 65 affiliated groups. Founded 1980.* Purpose is to carry the message of recovery to the chemically dependent person. For those with a desire to abstain from drugs or alcohol. Information, referrals, phone support and conferences. Group development guidelines. Write: Chemically Dependent Anonymous, PO Box 423, Severna Park, MD 21146. Call 1-888-232-4673. *Website:* http://www.cdaweb.org *Email:* williebrennan@comcasst.com

Double Trouble in Recovery, Inc. *National. 800+ affiliated groups. Founded 1989.* Fellowship of men and women who share their experience, strength and hope with each other so that they may solve their common problems and help others to recover from their particular addiction(s) and mental disorders. For persons dually-diagnosed with an addiction as well as a mental disorder. Literature, information, referrals and conferences. D.T.R. Basic Guide Book. Assistance in starting new groups. Write: DTR Inc., PO Box 245055, Brooklyn, NY 11224. Call 718-373-2684. *Website:* http://www.doubletroubleinrecovery.org *Email:* information@doubletroubleinrecovery.org

Dual Disorders Anonymous *National. Founded 1982.* 12-Step. Fellowship who come together to help those members who still suffer from both a mental disorder and alcoholism and/or drug addiction. Group development guidelines. Write: Dual Disorders Anonymous, PO Box 681264, Schaumburg, IL 60168-1264. Call 847-490-9379. *Website:* http://www.msnusers.com/dualdisordersanonymous *Email:* dualdisordersanonymous@msnusers.com

---

"The truth is that our finest moments are most likely to occur when we are feeling deeply uncomfortable, unhappy, or unfulfilled. For it is only in such moments, propelled by our discomfort, that we are likely to step out of our ruts and start searching for different ways or truer answers."

M. SCOTT PECK

Dual Recovery Anonymous *International. Chapters worldwide. Founded 1989.* A self-help program for individuals who experience a dual disorder of chemical dependency and a psychiatric or emotional illness. Based on the principles of the 12-Steps and the personal experiences of individuals in dual recovery. Literature, newsletter, assistance in starting local groups. Write: DRA, PO Box 8107, Prairie Village, KS 66208. Call 1-877-883-2332. *Website:* http://www.draonline.com

Families Anonymous *International. 500+ groups. Founded 1971.* 12-Step. Fellowship for relatives and friends of persons with drug, alcohol or behavioral problems. Members learn to achieve their own serenity in spite of the turmoil which surrounds them. Besides many booklets, pamphlets and bookmarks, publications include daily thought book, "Today A Better Way" and a bi-monthly newsletter "The Twelve-Step Rag." Offers group development guidelines. Write: F.A. PO Box 3475, Culver City, CA 90231-3475. Call 1-800-736-9805; Fax: 310-815-9682. *Website:* http://www.FamiliesAnonymous.org *Email:* famanon@FamiliesAnonymous.org

Intercongregational Addictions Program *International. Founded 1979.* Network of recovering alcoholic women in religious orders. Helps Roman Catholic women who are or have been, members of religious orders and are alcoholic or chemically dependent, compulsive eaters, compulsive gamblers, etc. Information, referrals, assistance in meeting other members, phone support, conferences and newsletters. Write: ICAP, 7777 Lake Street, Suite 115, River Forest, IL 60305-1734. Call 708-488-9770; Fax: 708-488-9774. *Website:* http://www.2icap.org *Email:* icapsrs@aol.com

International Doctors in Alcoholics Anonymous *International network. 6000 members. 175 affiliated groups. Founded 1949.* Opportunity for doctoral level health care professionals to discuss common problems and find common solutions to drug and alcohol problems. Annual meetings (1st week Aug.), phone support, information and referrals, newsletter. Mutual help meetings at conferences of other organizations. Write: IDAA, c/o Gordon L. Hyde, MD, Exec. Director, 3311 Brookhill Circle, Lexington, KY 40502. Call 859-277-9379. *Website:* http://www.idaa.org

International Lawyers in Alcoholics Anonymous *International. 40+ affiliated groups.* Founded 1975. Serves as a clearinghouse for support groups for lawyers who are recovering alcoholics or have other chemical dependencies. Newsletter, annual conventions. Group development guidelines. Write: ILAA, c/o Eli Guana, 14123 Victory Blvd., Van Nuys, CA 91401. Call 818-785-6541; Fax: 818-785-3887. *Website:* http://www.ilaa.org

JACS (Jewish Alcoholics, Chemically Dependent Persons & Significant Others) *International. Founded 1980.* Mutual support for alcoholic & chemically dependent Jews, their families, friends, associates, & the community. Networking, community outreach, retreats, newsletter, literature, spiritual events and speakers' bureau. Write: JACS, 850 Seventh Ave., New York, NY 10019. Call 212-397-4197; Fax: 212-399-3525. *Website:* http://www.jacsweb.org *Email:* jacs@jacsweb.org

LifeRing Secular Recovery *International. Founded 1999.* Secular community of persons who are building lives free of dependency on alcohol and other drugs. Group activities are not associated with religion or spirituality. Members practice complete abstinence from alcohol and other addicting drugs. Peer support, literature, information, referrals and advocacy activities. Guidelines available for starting similar groups. Large online email support group and several smaller special interest groups (women, weight loss, stop smoking, etc). Online chats, forum. Publishes sobriety literature. Write: LifeRing Secular Recovery, 1440 Broadway, Suite 312, Oakland, CA 94612-2029. Call 510-763-0779. *Website:* http://www.unhooked.com *Email:* service@lifering.org

Men for Sobriety International. *4 affiliated groups. Founded 1976.* Purpose is to help all men recover from problem drinking through the discovery of self, gained by sharing experiences, hopes and encouragement with other men in similar circumstances. Recognizes men's complex role in today's society. Write: Men for Sobriety, PO Box 618, Quakertown, PA 18951-0618. Call 215-536-8026; Fax: 215-538-9026. *Email:* NewLife@nni.com

Moderation Management *National. 50 groups. Founded 1993.* Behavioral change program and support network for people concerned about their drinking and who desire to make positive lifestyle changes. Moderation management empowers individuals to accept personal responsibility for choosing and maintaining their own path, whether moderation or abstinence. Promotes early self-recognition of risky drinking behavior, when moderation is a more easily achievable goal. Write: Moderation Management Network, Inc., 22 West 27th St., New York, NY. Call 212-871-0974. *Website:* http://moderation.org *Email:* mm@moderation.org

Overcomers In Christ *International. Founded 1987.* Recovery program that deals with every aspect of addiction and dysfunction (spiritual, physical, mental, emotional and social). Uses Overcomers Goals which are Christ-centered. Resources, information and referrals. Assistance in starting new groups. Literature. Write: Overcomers In Christ, PO Box 34460, Omaha, NE 68134-04604. Call 402-573-0966; Fax: 402-573-0960. *Website:* http://www.OvercomersInChrist.org *Email:* OIC@OvercomersInChrist.org

Overcomers Outreach, Inc. *International. 700 affiliated groups. Founded 1985.* 12-Step. Christ-centered support group for persons with any compulsive behavior, as well as their families and friends. Uses the 12-Steps of A.A. and applies them to the Scriptures. Uses Jesus Christ as "higher power." Supplements involvement in other 12-Step groups. Newsletter, group development guidelines, conferences. Write: Overcomers Outreach, PO Box 2208, Oakhurst, CA 93644. Call -800-310-3001. *Website:* http://www.overcomersoutreach.org

Psychologists Helping Psychologists *National network. Founded 1980.* For doctoral-level psychologists or students who've had a personal experience with alcohol or drugs. Aim is to support each other in recovery and help others to recover. Regional/national get-togethers, newsletter. Write: Psychologists Helping Psychologists, 3484 S. Utah St., Arlington, VA 22206-1921. Call Ann Stone 703-243-4470; Fax: 703-243-7125. *Email:* AnnS@Erols.com

Secular Organizations for Sobriety (Save Ourselves) *International. 20000 members. Founded 1986.* Mutual help for alcoholics and addicts who want to acknowledge their addiction and maintain sobriety as a separate issue from religion or spirituality. Newsletter. Guidelines and assistance available for starting groups. Real-time online chats and e-groups available. Write: S.O.S., 4773 Hollywood Blvd., Hollywood, CA 90027. Call 323-666-4295; Fax: 323-666-4271. *Website:* http://www.cfiwest.org/sos *Email:* sos@cfiwest.org

SMART Recovery (r) (Self-Management And Recovery Training) *National. 125+ affiliated groups. Founded 1994.* Network of self-help groups for individuals wanting to gain their independence from addictive and compulsive behaviors. SMART Recovery is an abstinence program based on cognitive-behavioral principles, especially those of rational emotive behavior therapy. Newsletter, information, referrals, literature and assistance in starting local groups. Write: SMART Recovery (r), 7537 Mentor Ave., Suite 306, Mentor, OH 44060. Call 1-866-951-5357; Fax: 440-951-5358. *Website:* http://www.smartrecovery.org *Email:* srmail1@aol.com

Social Workers Helping Social Workers *National network. Founded 1980.* Supports recovery from alcohol or other chemical dependence, either their own or that of a significant other, among social workers (BSW/MSW) or MSW matriculating students. Social workers with other addictions are welcome to attend meetings. Newsletter, annual conferences and some regional retreats/meetings, continuing education, daily email digest, group development guidelines. Write: SWHSW, c/o Betty Check, 5228 South Kenwood Ave., Chicago, IL 60615. Call 773-493-6940. *Website:* http://www.socialworkershelping.org *Email:* SWHSWIL@aol.com

Therapists In Recovery *Model. Founded 1986.* Mutual support for licensed therapists in recovery from alcohol or drug addiction. Local group meetings, phone support, information and referrals. Assistance in starting similar groups. Write: T.I.R., 2963 Butler St., Oceanside, CA 92054. Call 760-433-9169. *Email:* pec2963@aol.com

Veterinarians in Recovery *National network. Founded 1990.* Support network for veterinarians in recovery from alcoholism and addiction. Provides information and referrals, phone support and newsletter. Online email listserv. Maintains database of members for support. Al-Anon members and recovering veterinarian staff welcome at meetings. Many VIR members also are members of Int'l Doctors in A.A. and meet during their annual conference. Write: VIR, c/o Jeff H., 104 Maple Trace, Birmingham, AL 35244. Call 205-982-2406. *Website:* http://www.crml.uab.edu/~jah *Email:* jeffhalldvm@charter.net

Women For Sobriety *International. 150 groups. Founded 1976.* Program designed specifically to help the woman alcoholic achieve sobriety. Addresses need to overcome depressed feelings and guilt. Monthly newsletter, information and referrals, phone support, group meetings, pen pals, conferences and group development guidelines. Write: Women for Sobriety, PO Box 618, Quakertown, PA 18951-0618. Call 215-536-8026; Fax: 215-538-9026. *Website:* http://www.womenforsobriety.org *Email:* NewLife@nni.com

CO-DEPENDENCY / DYSFUNCTIONAL FAMILIES

BERGEN

Co-DA (Co-Dependents Anonymous) 12-Step. Fellowship for persons who have an inability to maintain functional relationships. For those who have a desire for healthy, fulfilling relationships with themselves and others. Open beginner meeting. Donation $1-2. Meets Wed., 8-9:30pm, Lutheran Church of Redeemer Maywood and Taplin Ave., Maywood. Call Dorothy 973-546-9322.

Seniors Count 12-Step. Support for persons (age 60+) who are recovering from substance abuse or co-dependency. Meets Fri., 1:30-3pm, Van Ost Institute for Family Living, Presbyterian Church, 2nd Floor, 150 East Palisades Ave. Englewood. Call Anne Wennhold 201-569-6667. *Website* http://www.vanostinstitute.org *Email:* vanost@msn.com

While it's no substitution for talking to our staff, you can call evenings or weekends! Leave a message and we will get back to you the next workday. **1-800-367-6274**

BURLINGTON

COLEAH (Center Of Love, Enlightenment And Healing) Separate groups for men and women to help them live better lives and build better relationships with themselves and others. Meets Tues., 7-8pm, 50 Springside Rd., Westampton. For information call Joyce 609-880-1593.

Free To Be Me 12-Step. Mutual support for those who want to learn to develop healthy, fulfilling relationships with others and themselves. Rap sessions, literature and buddy system. Meets Sun., 2-3:30pm, 449 Club, 6 Pemberton St., Pemberton. Call Susan S. 609-284-6311.

CAMDEN

Co-DA (Co-Dependents Anonymous) 12-Step. Fellowship for persons who have an inability to maintain functional relationships. For those who want to learn to develop healthy, fulfilling relationships with others and themselves. Meets Fri., 7:30pm, The Starting Point, 215 Highland Ave., Suite C, Westmont. Call 856-854-3155. *Website:* http://www.startingpoint.org *Email:* info@startingpoint.org

CUMBERLAND

Co-D.A. (Co-Dependents Anonymous) 12-Step. Fellowship for people unable to maintain functional relationships. For those with a desire to help in learning to maintain healthy, fulfilling relationships with others and themselves. Meets 2nd Mon., 7:30-8:30pm, 811 Landis Ave., Bridgeton. Call Christianna 856-453-0888.

GLOUCESTER

Women's Co-Dependent/God-Dependent Safe place where women are free to talk, feel, trust God and one another for any dysfunction, past or present or co-dependent issues that effects them. Educational series. Meets Wed., (except Aug.), 7-8:30pm, St. John's United Methodist Church, 149 Ganttown Rd., Turnersville. Call Rosemary 856-869-0084 (eve). *Website:* http://www.addvicinc.org *Email:* AddVicInc.@aol.com

MERCER

Princeton ACOA 12-Step. Fellowship for adult children from alcoholic and dysfunctional families. Guest speakers, phone help, rap sessions and literature. Donations $1/wk. Meets Thurs., 7:30-9pm, Unitarian Church of Princeton, 50 Cherry Hill Rd., Princeton. Call Audrey 609-716-8063.

MIDDLESEX

Overcomer's Turning Point 12-Step. Group for alcoholism, drug addiction, codependency and adult children of alcoholics. Under 18 welcome. Open to families. Rap sessions, phone help, literature, sponsorship. Meets Tues., 7:30pm, Highland Baptist Church, 2nd and Raritan St., Highland Park. Call Tony Labenski 732-613-1582 (day/eve). *Email:* tonylabens@aol.com

MONMOUTH

Co-DA (Co-Dependents Anonymous) *(Sunday Night Wayside)* Support group to bring people together who have difficulty in maintaining healthy relationships. Phone help. Meets Sun., 7-8pm, St. Anselm Church, 1028 Wayside Rd., Wayside. Call Betsy 732-542-9050.

OCEAN

Adult Children of Alcoholics 12-Step. Self-help group for adult children of alcoholics or dysfunctional families. Meets Tues., 7:45-9pm, Toms River Church of Christ, 1126 Hooper Ave., Toms River. Call Stephanie 732-573-1535.

Overcomers In Christ Recovery program that deals with every aspect of addiction and dysfunction (spiritual, physical, mental, emotional and social). Uses Overcomers goals which are Christ-centered. Resources, information and referrals. Literature. Meets Mon., 7pm, America's Keswick, 601 Route 530, Whiting. Separate group for men and women. Women's group call Diane Hunt 732-350-1187 ext. 47. Men's group call Pastor Mike 732-350-1187 ext. 39. *Website:* http://www.OvercomersinChrist.org

SOMERSET

Co-DA (Co-Dependents Anonymous) 12-Step. For persons unable to maintain functional relationships. For those with a desire for healthy, fulfilling relationships with others and themselves. Meets Sat., 9-10:30am and Mon., 7-8:15pm, United Methodist Church, Church St., Kingston. Call the Church 609-921-6812 (day).

Weekend Codependency Program *Professionally-run.* Support and education for families and friends of alcohol/drug abusers or those dealing with persons with any addiction problems. Educational lectures, discussions groups and parents group. Meets Sat. and Sun., 9:30am-3pm, Carrier Clinic, Atkinson Amphitheater, 252 Route 601, Belle Mead. Call 908-281-1513 (day) or 908-281-1000 (eve/weekend). *Website:* http://www.carrier.org

UNION

Co-D.A. (Co-Dependents Anonymous) 12-Step. Fellowship of men and women whose common purpose is to develop healthy relationships. For those who have a desire to build and maintain fulfilling relationships with themselves and others. Meets Tues., 7:30-9pm, All Saints Episcopal Church, 559 Park Ave., Scotch Plains. Call Joe F. 908-272-1926 (before 10pm).

NATIONAL

Co-Dependents Anonymous *International. Founded 1986.* 12-Step. Program of recovery from co-dependence. Members share experience, strength and hope in an effort to find freedom and peace in relationships with themselves and others. Library of literature and audio tapes. Guidelines on starting a similar group available. Newsletter. Listing of local support groups online. Write: CoDA, PO Box 33577, Phoenix, AZ 85067-3577. Call 602-277-7991. *Website:* http://www.coda.org *Email:* outreach@coda.org

Overcomers In Christ *International. Founded 1987.* Recovery program that deals with every aspect of addiction and dysfunction (spiritual, physical, mental, emotional and social). Uses Overcomers Goals which are Christ-centered. Resources, information and referrals. Assistance in starting new groups. Literature. Write: Overcomers In Christ, PO Box 34460, Omaha, NE 68134-04604. Call 402-573-0966; Fax: 402-573-0960. *Website:* http://www.OvercomersInChrist.org *Email:* OIC@OvercomersInChrist.org

Recovering Couples Anonymous *National. 130 groups. Founded 1988.* 12-Step. Goal is to assist couples find freedom from dysfunctional patterns in their relationships. RCA is made up of couples committed to restoring healthy communication, caring and developing a functional relationship. Offers local support group information. Write: RCA, PO Box 11029, Oakland, CA 94611. Call 510-663-2312. *Website:* http//:www.recovering-couples.org *Email:* info@recovering-couples.org

> *"No man is an island, entire of itself;*
> *Every man is a piece of the continent,*
> *A part of the main."*
>
> ***John Donne***

69

DEBT / OVERSPENDING
(see also toll-free helplines)

BERGEN

Debtor's Anonymous 12-Step. Program for those who wish to stop incurring debt. Meets Fri., 7:30-9pm, St. Paul's Lutheran Church, Church St. and Longfellow Rd., Teaneck. Call 908-580-8200 or 1-877-717-3328. *Website:* http://www.njpada.org

BURLINGTON

Overcomers 12-Step. Recovery group for anyone suffering from any type of addiction, dependency or compulsive disorder. Meets Thurs., 7:30-9pm, Fellowship Alliance Chapel, 199 Church Rd., Medford. Call 609-953-7333 (day).

ESSEX

Debtors Anonymous 12-Step. Program for those who wish to stop incurring debt. Meets Mon., 8pm, (beginners 7:30pm), Watchung Presbyterian Church, 375 Watchung Ave., (GSP exit 151), Bloomfield. Call Jane 973-667-2404 (day), Jeanette 973-509-9236 (eve) or D.A. Intergroup 1-877-717-3328 (recorded message). *Website:* http://www.njpada.org

MIDDLESEX

Debtors Anonymous 12-Step. For people to share experiences and common problem of incurring debt. Our goal is to stay solvent and help other compulsive debtors achieve solvency. Meets Sun., 7pm, (beginners 6:30pm), St. Luke's Episcopal Church, Oak St. and Route 27 North, Metuchen. Call 1-877-717-3328. *Website:* http://www.njpada.org

Overcomer's Outreach 12-Step. Christian fellowship to overcome any type of addiction or compulsive behavior, anxiety, depression and loneliness using God's word as a basis of recovery. Discussion, Bible study, prayer, phone help. Meets Mon., 7:30-9:15pm, Metuchen Assembly of God, Rose and Whitman St., Metuchen. Call Janet 732-388-2856 (eve).

MORRIS

Debtors Anonymous 12-Step. Program for those who wish to stop incurring debt. Meets Wed., 8pm, Saint Clare's Hospital, Powerville Rd, Boonton. Call 1-877-717-3328 (recorded message). *Website:* http://www.njpada.org

SOMERSET

Debtors Anonymous 12-Step. Program for those who wish to stop incurring debt. Meets Tues., 7:30-8:30pm, Presbyterian Church of Basking Ridge, East Oak St., Basking Ridge. Call Diana D. 908-647-7659 (eve) or 1-877-717-3328 (recorded message). *Website:* http://www.njpada.org

Overcomer's Outreach 12-Step. Christian fellowship to overcome any type of addiction or compulsive behavior using God's word as a basis of recovery. Discussion, scripture readings, prayer, phone help. Meets Sat., 3:30-5pm, Reformed Church, Fellowship Hall, 113 Clinton St., South Bound Brook. Call Carol Mehlenbeck 732-885-1023 or 732-457-9304 (day/eve).

NATIONAL

Debtors Anonymous *International. 520 groups. Founded 1976.* 12-Step. Fellowship that provides mutual help in recovering from compulsive indebtedness. Primary purpose of members is to stay solvent and help other compulsive debtors achieve solvency. Write: DAGSB, PO Box 920888, Needham, MA 02492-0009. Call 781-453-2743; Fax: 781-453-2745. *Website:* http://www.debtorsanonymous.org *Email:* new@debtorsanonymous.org

I.C.A.P. (Intercongregational Addictions Program) *International. Founded 1979.* Network of recovering alcoholic women in religious orders. Helps Roman Catholic women who are or have been, members of religious orders and are alcoholic, chemically dependent, compulsive eaters, compulsive gamblers, etc. Information, referrals, assistance in meeting other members, phone support, conferences and newsletters. Write: ICAP, 7777 Lake Street, Suite 115, River Forest, IL 60305-1734. Call 708-488-9770; Fax: 708-488-9774. *Website:* http://www.2icap.org *Email:* icapsrs@aol.com

Overcomers In Christ *International. Founded 1987.* Recovery program that deals with every aspect of addiction and dysfunction (spiritual, physical, mental, emotional and social). Uses Overcomers Goals which are Christ-centered. Resources, information and referrals. Assistance in starting new groups. Literature. Write: Overcomers In Christ, PO Box 34460, Omaha, NE 68134-04604. Call 402-573-0966; Fax: 402-573-0960. *Website:* http://www.OvercomersInChrist.org *Email:* OIC@OvercomersInChrist.org

Overcomers Outreach, Inc. International. *700 affiliated groups. Founded 1985.* 12-Step. Christ-centered support group for persons with any compulsive behavior, as well as their families and friends. Uses the 12-Steps of A.A. and applies them to

71

the Scriptures. Uses Jesus Christ as "higher power." Supplements involvement in other 12-Step groups. Newsletter, group development guidelines, conferences. Write: Overcomers Outreach, PO Box 2208, Oakhurst, CA 93644. Call 1-800-310-3001. *Website:* http://www.overcomersoutreach.org *Email* info@overcomersoutreach.org

Spenders Anonymous *National.* Support for those who have problems spending compulsively using the 12-Step approach. Script for running a meeting is at their website. Write: Spenders Anonymous, PO Box 2405, Minneapolis, MN 55402. Call 651-649-4573. *Website:* http://www.spenders.org

ONLINE

Shopping Addicts Support *Online.* Mutual support for people who are, or think they may be, addicted to shopping. Provides help for anyone who is trying to overcome their problem with over spending. *Website:* http://health.groups.yahoo.com/group/shopping_addicts

DRUG ABUSE
(see also toll-free helplines)

STATEWIDE

Cocaine Anonymous 12-Step. Fellowship of men and women who share their experiences, strengths and hopes that they may solve their common problem and help others to recover from addiction. Call Dominick 732-360-2999 (day) or 212-262-2463 (recording).

Families Anonymous 12-Step. Program for relatives and friends concerned about the use of drugs, alcohol or related behavioral problems. Meetings throughout NJ. Call 732-291-1467.

International Pharmacists Anonymous Fellowship of pharmacists and pharmacy students recovering from any addiction. Members must belong to a 12-Step group. Write: IPA, c/o Nan, 11 Dewey Lane, Glen Gardner, NJ 08826-3102. Call Nan 908-391-2673 (day). *Email:* nandrx@earthlink.net

Lawyers Concerned for Lawyers Statewide network of independent, self-help groups that support attorneys, judges, law students and others in the legal system in recovery from alcoholism and drug dependence. Based on the 12-Steps but not affiliated with AA. The NJ Lawyers Assistance Program performs an "intergroup function" for LCL. All services free and confidential. Write: NJLAP, N

Law Center, One Constitution Square, New Brunswick, NJ 08901-1520. Call 1-800-246-5527 (day) or 732-937-7549 (day). *Website:* http://www.LawyersAssistance.org *Email:* info@njlap.org or njlap@aol.com

Nar-Anon Family Group/Narateen Provides help for family members and friends of drug abusers by offering comfort, hope and friendship through shared experiences. Meeting locations throughout New Jersey. For information call Nar-Anon Answering Service 1-800-484-7385 (security code 4257) (day/eve) or 609-587-7215. *Website:* http://www.naranonofnj.org

Narcotics Anonymous *(BILINGUAL)* 12-Step. Fellowship of men and women seeking recovery from drug addiction. The only requirement for membership is the desire to stop using drugs. Meeting locations statewide, including several bilingual groups. Northern New Jersey write: NA North Jersey, 71 Ackerman Ave., Box 134, Clifton, NJ 07011-1501; Southern New Jersey write: NJ Regional Service Conference, PO Box 1911, Atlantic City, NJ 08401. Call 1-800-992-0401 or 732-933-0462. *Website:* http://www.nanj.org

Nurse Recovery Group *Professionally-run.* Mutual support and information for nurses who are recovering from addictions. Sharing of professional concerns and encouragement. Meets in Atlantic, Bergen, Burlington, Camden, Hunterdon, Mercer, Middlesex, Monmouth, Morris, Passaic, Somerset and Union counties. Write: Peer Assistance Project, 1479 Pennington Rd., Trenton, NJ 08618. Call 800-662-0108 (day).

Professional Assistance Program of New Jersey *Professionally-run.* For physicians and other licensed professionals suffering from alcohol, chemical dependency, psychiatric or physical disabilities. Local groups are independently member-run and strictly confidential. Some are AA affiliated. Write: Prof. Asst. Prog. Of NJ, 742 Alexander Rd., Princeton, NJ, 08540. Call Linda Pleva, Executive Assistant 609-919-1660 (day). *Email:* Linda.Pleva@papnj.org

Signs of Sobriety *Professionally-run.* Provides alcoholism and drug addiction services to persons who are deaf or hard-of-hearing. Makes referrals to deaf and sign interpreted 12-Step groups throughout NJ (alcohol or drug addiction, gambling, families of alcoholics, etc). Offers prevention awareness, education classes, SoberCamp annual summer retreat and Sober/Deaf activities for deaf or hard of hearing individuals in recovery. Newsletter. Write: SOS, 100 Scotch Road, 2nd Floor, Ewing, NJ 08628. Call TTY: 1-800-332-7677; Voice: 609-882-7677 (day); Fax: 609-882-6808. *Email:* info@signsofsobriety.org *Website:* http://www.signsofsobriety.org

ATLANTIC

Addictions Victorious of South Jersey, Inc. 12-Step. Group for both Christian and non-Christian men and women who in their struggle with substance abuse and emotional problems come together that they may solve their problems and help others as well. Guest speakers, rap sessions, phone help, literature, newsletter. Optional donation. Meets Tues., 7:30pm, Light of the World Church, 111 Route 50, Mays Landing. Call Bob 609-476-2075 or Pastor George Sanders 609-517-3776. *Website:* http://www.addvicinc.org

Dual Recovery Anonymous *Professionally-run.* 12-Step. Mutual support for alcoholics or drug abusers with psychiatric disorders. Meets Thurs., 1:30-3pm, C.O.D.I. Building, 901 Atlantic Ave., Egg Harbor City. For directions call Bill 609-965-6871 (day).

Family Support Group *Professionally-run.* Mutual support for parents and families of persons diagnosed with both a mental illness and chemical addiction. Sharing of emotional and practical coping skills. Guest speakers. Meets 2nd Thurs., 10am and 4th Thurs., 4:30pm, Mental Health Association, 611 Doughty Rd., Pleasantville. Call Christine Gromadzyn, MSW 609-272-1700 (day). *Website:* http://www.mhaac.org

Lawyers Concerned for Lawyers Self-help group that supports recovery from alcoholism and drug dependence for attorneys, judges, law students and others in the legal system. Based on the 12-Step program adapted from A.A. All inquiries are confidential. Meets Wed., 5:30pm, 1555 Zion Rd., Suite 201, Northfield. Call John 609-641-2266 (day) or NJ Lawyers Assistance Program 1-800-246-5527.

Nar-Anon Family Group Provides help for family members and friends of drug abusers by offering comfort, hope and friendship through shared experiences. Meeting locations throughout New Jersey. For information call Nar-Anon Answering Service 1-800-484-7385 (security code 4257) (day/eve) or 609-587-7215. *Website:* http://www.naranonofnj.org

Narcotics Anonymous 12-Step. Fellowship of men and women seeking recovery from drug addiction. The only requirement for membership is the desire to stop using drugs. Call 1-800-992-0401 or 732-933-0462. *Website:* http://www.nanj.org

Nurse Recovery Group *Professionally-run.* Mutual support and information for nurses who are recovering from addictions. Sharing of professional concerns and encouragement. Meets in Pomona. Call 800-662-0108 (day).

BERGEN

CARE (Christians, Addictions, Recovery and Education) 12-Step. Support ministry for substance abusers and their families to help our brothers and sisters find sobriety, solace and a way to a comfortable non-judgmental Christian walk. Meets Mon., 7:30pm, Church of the Nazarene, 285 East Midland Ave., Paramus. Call 201-262-3323 (9:30am-4pm). *Website:* http://www.maranathanj.org

Double Jeopardy Peer Support Group *Professionally-run.* Emotional support and information for men and women who have HIV/HCV and substance abuse issues. Meets Thurs., 6:30-8pm, Buddies of New Jersey, 149 Hudson St., Hackensack. Call Susan 201-489-2900 (10am-6pm).

Families Anonymous 12-Step. For relatives and friends concerned about the use of drugs or related behavioral problems.

> **Englewood** Meets Fri., 7:30pm, Englewood Hospital, Learning Center, Main Floor, 350 Engle St. Call Jesse 201-944-0256 (day/eve).
> **Tenafly** Meets Tues., 7:30pm, Trinity Lutheran Church, 430 Knickerbocker Rd. Call Judy or Gene 201-262-7758 (day) or Jesse 201-944-0256.

Families Anonymous 12-Step. Mutual support for parents and families of children and young adults with alcohol, drug abuse and/or emotional problems. Meets Wed., 7:30-8:30pm, Church of the Immaculate Conception, 900 Darlington Ave., Mahwah. Call Richard or Barbara 201-327-0748. *Website:* http://www.familiesanonymous *Email:* famahway@verizon.net

Lawyers Concerned for Lawyers (LCL) Self-help group that supports recovery from alcoholism and drug dependence for attorneys, judges, law students and others in the legal system. Based on the 12-Step program adapted from A.A. All inquiries are confidential. Meets Mon., 6:30pm, Red Cross Building, Union and Berry St., Hackensack. Call NJLAP 1-800-246-5527.

Nar-Anon Family Group 12-Step. Provides help for family members and friends of drug abusers by offering comfort, hope and friendship through shared experiences. Call Nar-Anon Answering Service 1-800-484-7385 (security code 4257) (day/eve) or 609-587-7215. *Website:* http://www.naranonofnj.org

Narcotics Anonymous 12-Step. Fellowship of men and women seeking recovery from drug addiction. The only requirement for membership is the desire to stop using drugs. Call 1-800-992-0401 or 732-933-0462. *Website:* http://www.nanj.org

Nurse Recovery Group *Professionally-run.* Mutual support and information for nurses who are recovering from addictions. Sharing of professional concerns and encouragement. Meets in Teaneck. Call 1-800-662-0108 (day).

Parent Support Group - New Jersey, Inc. *Professionally-run.* Confidential support group for parents of chemically dependent children (age 13-40+). Meets Mon., 6:30pm, Behavioral Health Center, Room E 222, Bergen Pines Hospital, Paramus. Call Karol Sullivan or Adrienne Mellana 1-800-561-4299 or 973-736-3344 (day). *Website:* http://www.psgnjhomestead.com *Email:* psgnj1@aol.com

Seniors Count *Professionally-run.* 12-Step. For persons age (60+) recovering from substance abuse or co-dependency. Meets Fri., 1:30-3pm, Presbyterian Church, 2nd Floor, 150 East Palisades Ave., Englewood. Call Anne Wennhold 201-569-6667. *Website:* http://www.vanostinstitute.org *Email:* vanost@msn.com

Women For Sobriety Self-help designed specifically to help women with addictions achieve sobriety. Helps develop self-esteem and coping skills. Donation $2. Meets Tues., noon-1pm and Thurs., 7pm, (new members 6:45pm), YWCA, 112 Oak St., Ridgewood. Call Dee Waddington 201-487-2224 (day).

BURLINGTON

Addictions Victorious of South Jersey, Inc. 12-Step. Group for both Christian and non-Christian men and women who in their struggle with substance abuse and emotional problems come together that they may solve their problems and help others as well. Guest speakers, rap sessions, phone help, literature, newsletter. Optional donation. Meets Thurs., 7pm, Lighthouse Tabernacle, 716 Main St., Lumberton. Call Wayne or Ronnie 609-267-2657. *Website:* http://www.addvicinc.org

Double Trouble Mutual support for persons with a substance abuse problem who are also taking medication for psychiatric problems. Meets Sun., Mon. and Wed., 8:30pm, Hampton Hospital, Cafeteria, 650 Rancocas Rd., Westampton. Call Pam Sachs 609-267-7000 (day).

Nar-Anon Family Group 12-Step. Help for families and friends of drug abusers by offering comfort, hope and friendship through shared experiences. For meeting information call Nar-Anon Answering Service 1-800-484-7385 (security code 4257) or 609-587-7215. *Website:* http://www.naranonofnj.org

If you are using this book past Spring 2007, please call us for information about our most recent directory. 1-800-367-6274

Narcotics Anonymous 12-Step. Fellowship of men and women seeking recovery from drug addiction. The only requirement for membership is the desire to stop using drugs. Several meeting locations throughout the county. For meeting information call 1-800-992-0401 or 732-933-0462. *Website:* http://www.nanj.org

Nurse Recovery Group *Professionally-run.* Mutual support and information for nurses who are recovering from addictions. Sharing of professional concerns and encouragement. Meets in Moorestown. Call 1-800-662-0108 (day).

Overcomers 12-Step. Recovery group for anyone suffering from any type of addiction, dependency or compulsive disorder. Meets Thurs., 7:30-9pm, Fellowship Alliance Chapel, 199 Church Rd., Medford. Call 609-953-7333 (day).

Rap Room Parent-to-Parent Coalition *Professionally-run.* Support and education for parents of teens and young adult children dealing with substance/alcohol addictions. Mutual sharing, advocacy, guest speakers, crisis intervention and referrals. Meets 1st Tues., 7-9pm, Greentree Executive Campus, 1003 A Lincoln Drive West, Marlton. Call Louise 856-983-3328. *Website:* http://www.raproom.org *Email:* p2p@raproom.org

CAMDEN

Addictions Victorious of South Jersey, Inc. 12-Step. Group for both Christian and non-Christian men and women who in their struggle with substance abuse and emotional problems come together that they may solve their problems and help others as well. Guest speakers, rap sessions, phone help, literature, newsletter. Optional donation. *Website:* http://www.addvicinc.org

> **Barrington** Meets Mon., 7pm, Grace Bible Church, 887 Clements Bridge Rd. Call Ginny 856-232-0207.
> **Camden** Meets Tues., 6pm, Fellowship House, 1722 South Broadway. Call Lucy 856-964-4545.
> **Sicklerville** Meets Fri, 6pm, Christ Care Unit Missionary Baptist Church, Sicklerville and Grimes Rd. Call Quinton and Pricilla 856-262-1833.
> **Somerdale** Meets Thurs., 8pm, Park Avenue Community Church, 431 Hilltop Ave. Call Pastor Glenn Marshall 856-435-0309.

Camden County Parent-to-Parent Mutual support for parents of children (any age) who have alcohol or drug related problems. Guest speakers, literature and phone help. Meets 2nd and 4th Tues., 6:30-8:30pm, Bellmawr Library, Bellmawr Health Clinic, Browning Rd., Bellmawr. Call Kathleen Dobbs 856-968-2301 (day).

Dual Recovery Anonymous (DRA) 12-Step. Mutual support for alcoholics/addicts who are taking medication for psychiatric problems. Meets Wed., 6-7pm, MICA Club, 498 Marlboro Ave., Cherry Hill. Call Freddy R. 856-662-0955.

Lawyers Concerned for Lawyers (LCL) Self-help group that supports recovery from alcoholism and drug dependence for attorneys, judges, law students and others in the legal system. Based on the 12-Step program adapted from AA. All inquiries are confidential. Meets 1st and 3rd Wed., 6pm, Steininger Center, Board Room, 19 East Ormond Ave., Cherry Hill. Call John 609-261-3841 (day) or NJ Lawyers Assistance Program 1-800-246-5527.

Nar-Anon Family Group 12-Step. Provides help for family members and friends of drug abusers by offering comfort, hope and friendship through shared experiences. Call Nar-Anon Answering Service 1-800-484-7385 (security code 4257) (day/eve) or 609-587-7215. *Website:* http://www.naranonofnj.org

Narcotics Anonymous 12-Step. Fellowship of men and women seeking recovery from drug addiction. The only requirement for membership is the desire to stop using drugs. Call 1-800-992-0401 or 732-933-0462. *Website:* http://www.nanj.org

Nurse Recovery Group *Professionally-run.* Mutual support and information for nurses who are recovering from addictions. Sharing of professional concerns and encouragement. Meets in Haddonfield. Call 1-800-662-0108 (day).

CAPE MAY

Addictions Victorious of South Jersey, Inc. 12-Step. Group for both Christian and non-Christian men and women who in their struggle with substance abuse and emotional problems come together that they may solve their problems and help others as well. Guest speakers, rap sessions, phone help, literature, newsletter. Optional donation. Meets Mon., 7pm, Seashore Community Church of Nazarene, 446 Seashore Rd., Cape May. Call Phil 609-408-1191, Marty 609-827-1517 or Church 609-886-6196. *Website:* http://www.addvicinc.org

Nar-Anon Family Group 12-Step. Provides help for family members and friends of drug abusers by offering comfort, hope and friendship through shared experiences. Call Nar-Anon Answering Service 1-800-484-7385 (security code 4257) (day/eve) or 609-587-7215. *Website:* http://www.naranonofnj.org

Narcotics Anonymous 12-Step. Fellowship of men and women seeking recovery from drug addiction. The only requirement for membership is the desire to stop using drugs. Call 1-800-992-0401 or 732-933-0462. *Website:* http://www.nanj.org

CUMBERLAND

Nar-Anon Family Group 12-Step. Provides help for family members and friends of drug abusers by offering comfort, hope and friendship through shared experiences. Call Nar-Anon Answering Service 1-800-484-7385 (security code 4257) (day/eve) or 609-587-7215. *Website:* http://www.naranonofnj.org

Narcotics Anonymous 12-Step. Fellowship of men and women seeking recovery from drug addiction. The only requirement for membership is the desire to stop using drugs. Call 1-800-992-0401 or 732-933-0462. *Website:* http://www.nanj.org

ESSEX

BASA/Brothers and Sisters of Siblings Confidential support group for siblings with a chemically dependent sibling. Meets 2nd and 4th Wed., 7pm, St. Cloud Presbyterian Church, Old Indian Rd. and Ridgeway Ave., West Orange. Call Karol Sullivan or Adrienne Mellana 973-736-3344 (day) or 1-800-561-3299.

Double Trouble *Professionally-run.* Support for HIV+ persons who are also substance abusers. Meets Wed., noon-2pm, North Jersey Community Support Center, 393 Central Ave., 3rd Floor, Newark. Call 973-483-3444. *Website:* http://www.njcri.org

Families Anonymous 12-Step. Support for families and friends concerned about the use of drugs or related behavioral problems. Sharing of experiences, strengths and hopes. Meets Wed., 7:30pm, First Episcopal Church of the Holy Spirit, 36 Gould St., Verona. Call Jim 973-338-6952 or Roxy 973-667-1067 (day).

Lawyers Concerned for Lawyers (LCL) Self-help group that supports recovery from alcoholism and drug dependence for attorneys, judges, law students and others in the legal system. Based on the 12-Step program adapted from A.A. All inquiries are confidential. Meets Tues., 7:30pm, United Way, Room 211A, 60 S. Fullerton Ave., Montclair. Call Kenneth 973-429-5588 (day) or 973-509-6062 (eve) or NJLAP 1-800-246-5527.

Nar-Anon Family Group 12-Step. Provides help for family members and friends of drug abusers by offering comfort, hope and friendship through shared experiences. Call Nar-Anon Answering Service 1-800-484-7385 (security code 4257) (day/eve) or 609-587-7215. *Website:* http://www.naranonofnj.org

Narcotics Anonymous 12-Step. Fellowship of men and women seeking recovery from drug addiction. The only requirement for membership is the desire to stop using drugs. Call 1-800-992-0401 or 732-933-0462. *Website:* http://www.nanj.org

Parents Support Group - New Jersey Inc. *Professionally-run.* Confidential support group for parents of a chemically dependent child age (13-40+). Meets Wed., 6pm and Thurs., 6:30pm, St. Cloud Presbyterian Church, Old Indian Rd. and Ridgeway Ave., West Orange. Call Karol Sullivan 973-736-3344 (9am-3pm) or 1-800-561-4299 (24 hr hotline).

GLOUCESTER

Addictions Victorious of South Jersey, Inc. 12-Step. Group for both Christian and non-Christian men and women who in their struggle with substance abuse and emotional problems come together that they may solve their problems and help others as well. Guest speakers, rap sessions, phone help, literature, newsletter. Optional donation. *Website:* http://www.addvicinc.org

> **Glassboro** Meets Tues., 7pm, Olivet Wesleyan Church, 711 Heston Rd. Call Chip 856-881-8241
> **Pitman** Meets Wed., 7:30pm, Joy Community Fellowship, Florence and Long Rd. Call Charlie 856-881-2966.
> **Pitman** Meets Mon., 7:30pm, The Rock Church, 205 Esplanade Ave. Call 856-582-2277.

Dual Recovery Anonymous *Professionally-run.* Mutual support for alcoholics or drug addicts with psychiatric disorders. Meets Fri., 7pm, Old Medical Arts Building, 1st Floor, Suite 14, 52 West Red Bank Ave., Woodbury. Call 856-845-0100 (day).

Nar-Anon Family Group 12-Step. Provides help for family members and friends of drug abusers by offering comfort, hope and friendship through shared experiences. Call Nar-Anon Answering Service 1-800-484-7385 (security code 4257) (day/eve) or 609-587-7215. *Website:* http://www.naranonofnj.org

Narcotics Anonymous 12-Step. Fellowship of men and women seeking recovery from drug addiction. The only requirement for membership is the desire to stop using drugs. Call 1-800-992-0401 or 732-933-0462. *Website:* http://www.nanj.org

HUDSON

Nar-Anon Family Group 12-Step. Provides help for family members and friends of drug abusers by offering comfort, hope and friendship through shared experiences. Call Nar-Anon Answering Service 1-800-484-7385 (security code 4257) (day/eve) or 609-587-7215. *Website:* http://www.naranonofnj.org

Can't find an appropriate group in your area? The Clearinghouse helps people start groups. Give us a call at 1-800-367-6274.

Narcotics Anonymous 12-Step. Fellowship of men and women seeking recovery from drug addiction. The only requirement for membership is the desire to stop using drugs. Call 1-800-992-0401 or 732-933-0462. *Website:* http://www.nanj.org

HUNTERDON

Nar-Anon Family Group 12-Step. Provides help for family members and friends of drug abusers by offering comfort, hope and friendship through shared experiences. Call Nar-Anon Answering Service 1-800-484-7385 (security code 4257) (day/eve) or 609-587-7215. *Website:* http://www.naranonofnj.org

Narcotics Anonymous 12-Step. Fellowship of men and women seeking recovery from drug addiction. The only requirement for membership is the desire to stop using drugs. Call 732-933-0462. *Website:* http://www.nanj.org

Nurse Recovery Group *Professionally-run.* Mutual support and information for nurses who are recovering from addictions. Sharing of professional concerns and encouragement. Meets in Flemington. Call 1-800-662-0108 (day).

MERCER

Families Anonymous 12-Step. Program for families, especially parents of those with substance abuse or other disruptive, behavioral problems. Meets Mon., 7:30pm, St. Lawrence Rehabilitation Center, 2381 Lawrenceville Rd., (Route 206 South), Lawrenceville. Call Joan 609-883-1403 (eve). *Website:* http://www.familiesanonymous.org *Email:* joan@brra.com

Lawyers Concerned for Lawyers (LCL) Self-help group that supports recovery from alcoholism and drug dependence for attorneys, judges, law students and others in the legal system. Based on the 12-Step program adapted from A.A. All inquiries are confidential. Meets Thurs., 6pm, 3490 Route 1, Bldg. 7B, Princeton. Call Michael 609-392-7734 (day) or NJLAP 1-800-246-5527.

Nar-Anon Family Group 12-Step. Provides help for family members and friends of drug abusers by offering comfort, hope and friendship through shared experiences. Call Nar-Anon Answering Service 1-800-484-7385 (security code 4257) (day/eve) or 609-587-7215. *Website:* http://www.naranonofnj.org

Narcotics Anonymous 12-Step. Fellowship of men and women seeking recovery from drug addiction. The only requirement for membership is the desire to stop using drugs. Call 1-800-992-0401 or 732-933-0462. *Website:* http://www.nanj.org

Nurse Recovery Group *Professionally-run.* Mutual support and information for nurses who are recovering from addictions. Sharing of professional concerns and encouragement. Meets in Trenton. Call 1-800-662-0108 (day).

MIDDLESEX

Double Trouble Mutual support for alcoholics or drug addicts who are taking medication for psychiatric problems. Optional donation. Meets Thurs., (last Thurs. open mtg.), 7:30pm, UMDNJ - The Club, 189 New St., Room B, New Brunswick. Call Tim 732-235-6900 (day).

Lawyers Concerned for Lawyers (LCL) Self-help group that supports recovery from alcoholism and drug dependence for attorneys, judges, law students and others in the legal system. Based on the 12-Step program adapted from A.A. All inquiries are confidential. Meets one Sat. per month (by invitation only), New Brunswick. Call Denise at NJLAP 732-937-7541 or 1-800-246-5527 (day). *Email:* denise@njlap.org

Nar-Anon Family Group 12-Step. Provides help for family members and friends of drug abusers by offering comfort, hope and friendship through shared experiences. Call Nar-Anon Answering Service 1-800-484-7385 (security code 4257) (day/eve) or 609-587-7215. *Website:* http://www.naranonofnj.org

Narcotics Anonymous 12-Step. Fellowship of men and women seeking recovery from drug addiction. The only requirement for membership is the desire to stop using drugs. Call 1-800-992-0401 or 732-933-0462. *Website:* http://www.nanj.org

Nurse Recovery Group *Professionally-run.* Mutual support and information for nurses who are recovering from addictions. Sharing of professional concerns and encouragement. Meets in Woodbridge. Call 1-800-662-0108 (day).

Overcomer's Outreach 12-Step. Christian fellowship to overcome any type of addiction or compulsive behavior, anxiety, depression and loneliness using God's word as a basis of recovery. Discussion, Bible study, prayer, phone help. Meets Mon., 7:30-9:15pm, Metuchen Assembly of God, Rose and Whitman St., Metuchen. Call Janet 732-388-2856 (eve).

Overcomer's Turning Point 12-Step. Group for alcoholism, drug addiction, codependency and adult children of alcoholics. Under 18 welcome. Open to families. Rap sessions, phone help, literature, sponsorship. Meets Tues., 7:30pm, Highland Park Baptist Church, 2nd and Raritan St., Highland Park. Call Tony Labenski 732-613-1582 (day/eve). *Email:* tonylabens@aol.com

Parent Support Group - New Jersey, Inc. Confidential support group for parents of chemically dependent children (age 13-40+). Meets Thurs., 7pm, Cheesequake First Aid Building, Route 34, Old Bridge. Call Linda Leck, Karol Sullivan or Adrienne Mellana 1-800-561-4299 or 973-736-3344 (day). *Website:* http://www.psgnjhomestead.com *Email:* psgnj1@aol.com

SMART Recovery (Self-Management And Recovery Training) *Professionally-run.* Self-help group for individuals wanting to gain their independence from addictive behaviors (drugs, including alcohol and nicotine and other compulsive behaviors i.e. gambling, eating disorders). SMART is an abstinence program based on cognitive-behavioral education and principles, especially those of rational-emotive behavior therapy. Meets Mon., 6:30-7:45pm, Rutgers University, Busch Campus, Psychology Building, Room A224, Piscataway. Call Tom Morgan 732-445-0902. *Website:* http://www.smartrecovery.org

MONMOUTH

Double Trouble Dual Recovery 12-Step. Support for those who have an emotional/psychiatric illness and are alcohol/chemically addicted. Meets Mon. and Thurs., 10:15-11am, Park Place Program, 1011 Bond St., Asbury Park. Call Mark 732-869-2781 (day) or Mike Rafter 732-869-2765 (day).

Dual Recovery Mutual support for alcoholics or drug abusers who are taking medication for psychiatric problems. Transportation available. Meets Tues., 7pm, Freehold Self-Help Center, 17 Bannard St., Freehold. Call CSP 1-800-227-3729 (day).

Dual Recovery Anonymous 12-Step. Professionally co-facilitated. Mutual support for any person recovering from mental illness and substance abuse. Meets Tues. and Fri., 10:30-11:30am, CPC/Aberdeen Counseling Center, 1088 Highway 34, Aberdeen. Call Mark 732-290-1700 Ext. 5307 (day).

Dual Recovery Anonymous (DRA) Mutual support for alcoholics/addicts who are taking medication for psychiatric problems. Meets 2nd and 4th Sat., 2-3pm, CARE Center, 700 Mattison Ave., Asbury Park. Transportation available. Call Brian or Carolyn 732-869-9141 (day).

Families Anonymous 12-Step. Fellowship of families and friends concerned about the use of drugs, alcohol and /or related behavioral problems.
> **Holmdel** Meets Mon., 7:30pm, Bayshore Community Hospital, 723 North Beers St. Call Mary Lou 732-583-2238 (eve) or Nancy 732-264-5948 (6-8pm).

Leonardo Meets Mon., 7:30pm, Middletown Township Complex, Leonardville Rd. Call 732-291-1467 (eve).

Ocean Grove Meets Mon., 7:30pm, St. Paul's United Methodist Church, 80 Embury Ave. Call Diana 732-988-3903.

Red Bank Meets Thurs., 7:30-9pm, United Methodist Church, 247 Broad St. Call 732-462-7707 (day). *Email:* higley@optonline.net

Nar-Anon Family Group Provides help for family members and friends of drug abusers by offering comfort, hope and friendship through shared experiences. Meeting locations throughout New Jersey. For information call Nar-Anon Answering Service 1-800-484-7385 (security code 4257) (day/eve) or 609-587-7215. *Website:* http://www.naranonofnj.org

Narcotics Anonymous 12-Step. Fellowship of men and women seeking recovery from drug addiction. The only requirement for membership is the desire to stop using drugs. Call 1-800-992-0401 or 732-933-0462. *Website:* http://www.nanj.org

Parent Support Group - New Jersey, Inc. Confidential support group for parents of chemically dependent children (age 13-40+). Meets Tues., 7pm, Church of the Nativity, Hance and Ridge Rd., Fair Haven. Call Karol Sullivan or Adrienne Mellana 1-800-561-4299 or 973-736-3344 (day). *Website:* http://www.psgnjhomestead.com *Email:* psgnj1@aol.com

T.M.E.W. (The Most Excellent Way) Christian alternative to chemical dependency. Principles of recovery are based upon God's words. Open to anyone desiring freedom from addictive and compulsive behavior. For local meeting information call Frank 732-741-0048, Mike C. 917-304-9074, Frank C. 732-842-4749 or Jack C. 732-741-7807. *Website:* http://www.mostexcellentway.com

MORRIS

Alcohol and Drug Family Education *Professionally-run.* Support for families facing the chemical dependency of a family member. Deals with co-dependency issues. Meets Thurs., 6:30-8pm, Morristown Memorial Hospital, Outpatient Behavioral Health, Morristown. For meeting information call 1-888-247-1400.

Dual Recovery Anonymous *Professionally-run.* Mutual support for alcoholics or drug addicts with psychiatric disorders. Meets Tues., noon-1pm, MICA Group Room; Fri., noon-1pm, IOP Room; and Sun., 11am-noon, Executive Dining Room, Saint Clares Hospital, Boonton. Call Nikki R. 973-664-0596.

Families Anonymous 12-Step. Mutual support for parents, relatives and friends of persons with drug or alcohol problems. Peer-counseling. Meets Tues., 7:30-9pm, First Presbyterian Church, 35 Church St., Rockaway. Call 973-586-2440 (eve).

Lawyers Concerned for Lawyers (LCL) Self-help group that supports recovery from alcoholism and drug dependence for attorneys, judges, law students and others in the legal system. Based on the 12-Step program adapted from A.A. All inquiries are confidential. Meets Wed., 7:30pm, Center for Behavioral Health, 95 Mt. Kemble Ave., Morristown. Call Albert 973-538-0280 (day/eve) or NJ Lawyers Assistance Program 1-800-246-5527.

Moderation Management Offers support for problem drinkers who want to moderate their drinking behavior and make other positive lifestyle changes. Moderation Management offers a 9-step program which includes moderate drinking guidelines, goal setting techniques, self-management strategies and drink-monitoring exercises. Meets Tues., 7:30-8:30pm, St. Mark's Lutheran Church, 100 Harter Rd., Morris Twp. Call Dick or Elaine Ottaway 908-221-1314 (day/eve). *Website:* http://www.moderation.org. *Email:* ottaway@att.net

Nar-Anon Family Group 12-Step. Provides help for family members and friends of drug abusers by offering comfort, hope and friendship through shared experiences. Call Nar-Anon Answering Service 1-800-484-7385 (security code 4257) (day/eve) or 609-587-7215. *Website:* http://www.naranonofnj.org

Narcotics Anonymous 12-Step. Fellowship of men and women seeking recovery from drug addiction. The only requirement for membership is the desire to stop using drugs. Call 1-800-992-0401 or 732-933-0462. *Website:* http://www.nanj.org

Narcotics Anonymous for MICA Patients Narcotics Anonymous meeting for those who also have a mental illness. Meets Thurs., 7:30pm, New Views, Greystone Park Hospital, Main Building, 1st Floor, North Tier, Morris Plains. Call Tom Wicks 973-292-4015 (9-4pm). *Email:* newviews@nac.net

Nurse Recovery Group *Professionally-run.* Mutual support and information for nurses who are recovering from addictions. Sharing of professional concerns and encouragement. Meets in Boonton. Call 1-800-662-0108 (day).

Psychiatrically Recovering 12-Step. Mutual support for psychiatrically recovering people who wish to refrain from using alcohol or drugs, abusing food or any other compulsive behavior. Call Richie S. 973-865-4851 (day/eve).
> **Cedar Knolls** Meets Mon. and Thurs., 10am, Saint Clare's Behavioral Health Center, 100 East Hanover Ave., Group Room, First Floor.

Denville Meets Mon., 1pm, Saint Clare's Behavioral Health Center, 50 Morris Ave., Room B-1.

Pompton Plains Meets Fri., 9am, New Bridge: Crossroads, (formerly Pequannock Valley Mental Health Center), 640 Newark-Pompton Turnpike.

S.M.A.R.T. Recovery (Self-Management And Recovery Training) Self-help group for individuals wanting to gain their independence from addictive behaviors (drugs, including alcohol and nicotine and other compulsive behaviors i.e. gambling, eating disorders). SMART is an abstinence program based on cognitive-behavioral education and principles, especially those of rational-emotive behavior therapy. Meets Thurs., 7-8:30pm, Beginnings, 65 Spring St., Morristown. Call Rich 973-983-0217 *Website:* http://www.smartrecovery.org

OCEAN

Checkpoint Support to help overcome dependencies and addictions through accountability, encouragement and spiritual development. Meets Thurs., 7-8:30pm, Safe Harbor, 600 Atlantic City Blvd., Beechwood. Call 732-244-3888 (day).

Families Anonymous 12-Step. For relatives and friends concerned about the use of drugs or related behavioral problems. Meets Tues., 7:30pm, St. Andrews United Methodist Church, 1528 Church Rd., Toms River. Call 732-864-0548. *Email:* FamAnonTR@Comcast.net

Lawyers Concerned for Lawyers (LCL) Self-help group that supports recovery from alcoholism and drug dependence for attorneys, judges, law students and others in the legal system. Based on the 12-Step program adapted from A.A. All inquiries are confidential. Meets Tues., 7:15pm, St. Mary's By The Sea, Meeting Room, Forman and Bay Ave., Point Pleasant. Call Fred 732-785-6314 (pager number) (day) or NJ Lawyers Assistance Program 1-800-246-5527.

Narcotics Anonymous 12-Step. Fellowship of men and women seeking recovery from drug addiction. The only requirement for membership is the desire to stop using drugs. Call 1-800-992-0401 or 732-933-0462. *Website:* http://www.nanj.org

Overcomers In Christ Recovery program that deals with every aspect of addiction and dysfunction (spiritual, physical, mental, emotional and social). Uses Overcomers goals which are Christ-centered. Resources, information and referrals. Literature. Meets Mon., 7pm, America's Keswick, 601 Route 530, Whiting. Separate group for men and women. For women's group call Diane Hunt 732-350-1187 ext. 47. For men's group call Pastor Mike 732-350-1187 ext. 39. *Website:* http://www.OvercomersinChrist.org

Parents Group, Inc. Mutual support and referrals for parents in crisis due to their teenage or adult children's chemical/alcohol addiction. Works with and outreaches to community resources for prevention, awareness and intervention. Meets Tues., 7-9pm, Toms River. Call Mary and Michael Holland 732-929-4443. *Email:* starfishpg@aol.com

Parent Support Group - New Jersey, Inc. Confidential support group for parents of chemically dependent children (age 13-40+). Meets Mon., 7pm, Presbyterian Church of Toms River, 1070 Hooper Ave., Toms River. Call Karol Sullivan or Adrienne Mellana 1-800-561-4299 or 973-736-3344 (day). *Website:* http://www.psgnjhomestead.com *Email:* psgnj1@aol.com

PASSAIC

Nar-Anon Family Group 12-Step. Provides help for family members and friends of drug abusers by offering comfort, hope and friendship through shared experiences. Call Nar-Anon Answering Service 1-800-484-7385 (security code 4257) (day/eve) or 609-587-7215. *Website:* http://www.naranonofnj.org

Narcotics Anonymous 12-Step. Fellowship of men and women seeking recovery from drug addiction. The only requirement for membership is the desire to stop using drugs. Call 1-800-992-0401 or 732-933-0462. *Website:* http://www.nanj.org

Nurse Recovery Group *Professionally-run.* Mutual support and information for nurses who are recovering from addictions. Sharing of professional concerns and encouragement. Meets in Passaic. Call 1-800-662-0108 (day).

Parent Support Group - New Jersey, Inc. Confidential support group for parents of chemically dependent children age (13-40+). Meets Mon., 6:30pm, St. Josephs Hospital, 6th Floor, Room 7B, 224 Hamburg Turnpike, Wayne. Call Karol Sullivan or Adrienne Mellana 1-800-561-4299 or 973-736-3344 (day). *Website:* http://www.psgnjhomestead.com *Email:* psgnj1@aol.com

Psychiatrically Recovering 12-Step. Mutual support for psychiatrically recovering people who wish to refrain from using alcohol or drugs, abusing food or any other compulsive behavior. Meets Fri., 10:15am, New Bridge: Visions, 22 Riverview Dr., Wayne. Call Richie S. 973-865-4851 (day/eve).

"The greatest gift we can give one another is rapt attention to one another's existence."

--Sue Atchley Ebaugh

SALEM

Nar-Anon Family Group 12-Step. Provides help for family members and friends of drug abusers by offering comfort, hope and friendship through shared experiences. Call Nar-Anon Answering Service 1-800-484-7385 (security code 4257) (day/eve) or 609-587-7215. *Website:* http://www.naranonofnj.org

Narcotics Anonymous 12-Step. Fellowship of men and women seeking recovery from drug addiction. The only requirement for membership is the desire to stop using drugs. Call 1-800-992-0401 or 732-933-0462. *Website:* http://www.nanj.org

SOMERSET

Bright Futures for Kids *Professionally-run.* Provides support, education and counseling for children (age 4-12) who are affected by a family member's alcohol and/or drug addiction in learning how to express their feelings, coping skills, a sense of responsibility and the ability to resist peer pressure. Meets Sun., 11am-1pm, Carrier Clinic, Atkinson Amphitheater, Classroom 3, 252 Route 601, Belle Mead. Call Community Relations 908-281-1513.

Lawyers Concerned for Lawyers (LCL) Self-help group that supports recovery from alcoholism and drug dependence for attorneys, judges, law students and others in the legal system. Based on the 12-Step program adapted from A.A. All inquires are confidential. Meets Tues., 6pm, 70 Grove St., Somerville. Call NJ Lawyers Assistance Program 1-800-246-5527.

Nar-Anon Family Group 12-Step. Provides help for family members and friends of drug abusers by offering comfort, hope and friendship through shared experiences. Call Nar-Anon Answering Service 1-800-484-7385 (security code 4257) (day/eve) or 609-587-7215. *Website:* http://www.naranonofnj.org

Narcotics Anonymous 12-Step. Fellowship of men and women seeking recovery from drug addiction. The only requirement for membership is the desire to stop using drugs. Call 1-800-992-0401 or 732-933-0462. *Website:* http://www.nanj.org

Nurse Recovery Group *Professionally-run.* Mutual support and information for nurses who are recovering from addictions. Sharing of professional concerns and encouragement. Meets in Belle Mead. Call 1-800-662-0108 (day).

Overcomer's Outreach 12-Step. Christian fellowship to overcome any type of addiction or compulsive behavior using God's word as a basis of recovery. Discussion, scripture readings, prayer, phone help. Meets Sat., 3:30-5pm,

Reformed Church, Fellowship Hall, 113 Clinton St., South Bound Brook. Call Carol Mehlenbeck 732-885-1023 or 732-457-9304 (day/eve).

Parent Support Group - New Jersey, Inc. *Professionally-run.* Confidential support for parents of chemically dependent children (age 13-40+). Meets Mon., 7pm, Carrier Foundation, Admissions Building, Belle Mead. Call Karol Sullivan or Adrienne Mellana 1-800-561-4299 or 973-736-3344 (day). *Website:* http://www.psgnjhomestead.com *Email:* psgnj1@aol.com

Psychiatrically Recovering 12-Step. Mutual support for psychiatrically recovering people who wish to refrain from using alcohol or drugs, abusing food or any other compulsive behavior. Meets Thurs., 7:30pm, Richard Hall Community Mental Health Center, 500 North Bridge St., Room 121, Bridgewater. Call Richie S. 973-865-4851 (day/eve).

SMART Recovery (Self-Management And Recovery Training) *Professionally-run.* Self-help group for individuals wanting to gain their independence from addictive behaviors (drugs, including alcohol and nicotine and other compulsive behaviors i.e. gambling, eating disorders). SMART is an abstinence program based on cognitive-behavioral education and principles, especially those of rational-emotive behavior therapy. Meets 1st and 3rd Thurs., 7:30-8:45pm, Richard Hall Community Mental Health Center, Vogt and North Bridge St., Bridgewater. Call Brian Diskin 732-266-9483. *Website:* http://www.smartrecovery.org *Email:* bridisk@aol.com

Weekend Codependency Program *Professionally-run.* Support and education for families and friends of alcohol/drug abusers or those dealing with persons with addiction problems. Educational lectures, discussions groups and parents group. Meets Sat. and Sun., 9:30am-3pm, Atkinson Amphitheater, Carrier Clinic, 252 Route 601, Belle Mead. Call 908-281-1513 (day) or 908-281-1000 (eve/weekend). *Website:* http://www.carrier.org

SUSSEX

Lawyers Concerned for Lawyers (LCL) Self-help group that supports recovery from alcoholism and drug dependence for attorneys, judges, law students and others in the legal system. Based on the 12-Step program adapted from AA. All inquiries are confidential. Meets Sat., 9am, Newton. Call Mary Jean 973-729-1847 or NJ-LAP 1-800-246-5527.

Nar-Anon Family Group 12-Step. Provides help for family members and friends of drug abusers by offering comfort, hope and friendship through shared

Call Nar-Anon Answering Service 1-800-484-7385 (security code 4257) (day/eve) or 609-587-7215. *Website:* http://www.naranonofnj.org

Narcotics Anonymous 12-Step. Fellowship of men and women seeking recovery from drug addiction. The only requirement for membership is the desire to stop using drugs. Several meeting locations throughout the county. For meeting information call 1-800-992-0401 or 732-933-0462. *Website:* http://www.nanj.org

UNION

Alcohol and Drug Family Education *Professionally-run.* Support for families facing the chemical dependency of a family member. Deals with co-dependency issues. Meets Tues., 6:30-8pm, Overlook Hospital, Summit. Call 908-522-4800 (day).

Families of Addiction *Professionally-run.* Mutual support for families of persons with an alcohol or drug addiction. Meets Wed., 6:30-8pm, Overlook Hospital, 46-48 Beauvoir Ave, Summit. Before attending call Rosemary Walsh 908-522-4800.

Nar-Anon Family Group 12-Step. Provides help for family members and friends of drug abusers by offering comfort, hope and friendship through shared experiences. Call Nar-Anon Answering Service 1-800-484-7385 (security code 4257) (day/eve) or 609-587-7215. *Website:* http://www.naranonofnj.org

Nurse Recovery Group *Professionally-run.* Mutual support and information for nurses who are recovering from addictions. Sharing of professional concerns and encouragement. Meets in Berkeley Heights. Call 1-800-662-0108 (day).

Parent Support Group - New Jersey, Inc. Confidential support group for parents of chemically dependent children ages 13-40+. Meets Tues., 6:30pm, Central Presbyterian Church, Library Room, 70 Maple Ave., Summit. Call Karol Sullivan or Adrienne Mellana 1-800-561-4299 or 973-736-3344 (day). *Website:* http://www.psgnjhomestead.com *Email:* psgnj1@aol.com

Psychiatrically Recovering 12-Step. Mutual support for psychiatrically recovering people who wish to refrain from using alcohol or drugs, abusing food or any other compulsive behavior. Meets Tues., 9:30am, Occupational Center of Union County, New Building, Activity Room, 291 Cox St., Roselle. Call Richie S. 973-865-4851.

If you are using this book past Spring 2007, please call us for information about our most recent directory. 1-800-367-6274

WARREN

Dual Recovery Anonymous (DRA) Mutual support for alcoholics or drug addicts who are taking medication for psychiatric problems. Dues $2/month. Meetings vary, Better Future Help Center, 21 W. Washington Ave., Washington. Call Robin Wolak 908-835-1180.

Nar-Anon Family Group 12-Step. Provides help for family members and friends of drug abusers by offering comfort, hope and friendship through shared experiences. Call Nar-Anon Answering Service 1-800-484-7385 (security code 4257) (day/eve) or 609-587-7215. *Website:* http://www.naranonofnj.org

Narcotics Anonymous 12-Step. Fellowship of men and women seeking recovery from drug addiction. The only requirement for membership is the desire to stop using drugs. Call 1-800-992-0401 or 732-933-0462. *Website:* http://www.nanj.org

NATIONAL

Alcoholics Victorious *International. 150 affiliated groups. Founded 1948.* 12-Step Christian oriented group for those recovering from alcohol or chemical dependency. Information and referrals, literature, phone support, conferences, support group meetings, newsletter. Assistance in starting groups. How-to materials. Write: Alcoholics Victorious, Association of Gospel Rescue Missions, 1045 Swift St., Kansas City, MO 64116-4127. Call 1-800-624-5156 or 816-471-8020; Fax: 816-471-3718. *Website:* http://www.alcoholicsvictorious.org *Email:* info@alcoholicsvictorious.org

Anesthetists in Recovery *National network. Founded 1984.* Network of recovering nurse anesthetists. Provides phone support, information and referrals to groups and treatment. Write: AIR, c/o Art, 8233 Brookside Rd., Elkins Park, PA 19027. Call 215-635-0183; Fax: 215-829-8757. *Email:* a.to.z@comcast.net

Benzodiazepine Anonymous *Model. 5 affiliated groups. Founded 1989.* Mutual support for persons in recovery from an addiction to benzodiazepines (Xanax, Halcion, Valium, Ativan, Dalmane, Librium, etc) or any other addicting prescription drug. Uses B.A. 12-Steps and 12-goals. Open to families. Assistance in starting new groups. Write: B.A., c/o Jeff M., 11507 Cumpston St., North Hollywood, CA 91601. Call Jeff 818-667-1070 or Virginia 310-645-4080.

Chemically Dependent Anonymous *National. 65 affiliated groups. Founded 1980.* Purpose is recovery of the chemically dependent person. Information and referrals, phone support, conferences. Group development guidelines. Write: Chemically Dependent Anonymous, PO Box 423, Severna Park, MD 21146.

Call   1-888-232-4673.   *Website:*   http://www.cdaweb.org   *Email:*
williebrennan@comcast.com

Chapter Nine Group of Hollywood, MD *Model. Founded 1989.* 12-Step. Program of recovering couples (substance abuse) in which partners work together. Group name comes from chapter nine of the A.A. Big Book "The Family Afterward" based on the belief that members of the family or couples should meet upon the common ground of tolerance, understanding and love. Write: Chapter Nine, c/o Don J., 1168 White Sands Dr., Lusby, MD 20657. Call 410-586-1425. *Email:* justiced@chesapeake.net

Co-Anon Family Groups *International. 28 groups. Founded 1985.* 12-Step. Program for families and friends of cocaine, crack and other drug addicts, whether they are actively using or not. Online email and face-to-face meetings. Provides assistance in starting new groups. Write: Co-Anon, PO Box 12722, Tucson, AZ 85732-2722.   Call   1-800-898-9985   or   520-513-5028.   *Website:* http://www.co-anon.org *Email:* info@co-anon.org

Cocaine Anonymous, Inc. *International. 2000 chapters. Founded 1982.* 12-Step. Fellowship of men and women who share their experience, strength and hope that they may solve their common problem and help others to recover from addiction. Quarterly newsletter. Group starter kit available. Write: Cocaine Anonymous, 3740 Overland Ave., Suite C, Los Angeles, CA 90034-6337. Call 1-800-347-8998; Fax: 310-559-2554. *Website:* http://www.ca.org *Email:* cawso@ca.org

Crystal Meth Anonymous 12-Step. Fellowship for those in recovery from addiction to crystal meth. The only requirement for membership is the desire to stop using crystal meth and to stay clean. Open to families and friends. Information on starting a group available. Provides referrals to groups. Write: CMA, 8205 Santa Monica Blvd., PMB 1-114, West Hollywood, CA 90046-5977. Call 213-488-4455. *Website:* http://www.crystalmeth.org

Double Trouble in Recovery, Inc. *National. 800+ affiliated groups. Founded 1989.* Fellowship of men and women who share their experience, strength and hope with each other so that they may solve their common problems and help others to recover from their particular addiction(s) and mental disorders. For persons dually-diagnosed with an addiction as well as a mental disorder. Literature, information and referrals, conferences. D.T.R. Basic Guide Book. Assistance in starting new groups. Write: DTR, Inc., PO Box 245055, Brooklyn, NY 11224. Call 718-373-2684. *Website:* http://www.doubletroubleinrecovery.org *Email:* information@doubletroubleinrecovery.org

Dual Disorders Anonymous *National. Founded 1982.* 12-Step. Fellowship of men and women who come together to help those members who still suffer from both mental disorder and alcoholism and/or drug addiction. Group development guidelines. Write: DDA, PO Box 681264, Schaumburg, IL 60168-1264. Call 847-490-9379. *Website:* http://msnusers.com/dualdisordersanonymous *Email:* dualdisordersanonymous@msnusers.com

Dual Recovery Anonymous *International. Chapters worldwide. Founded 1989.* A self-help program for individuals who experience a dual disorder of chemical dependency and a psychiatric or emotional illness. Based on the principles of the 12-Steps and the personal experiences of individuals in dual recovery. Literature, newsletter, assistance in starting local groups. Write: DRA, PO Box 8107, Prairie Village, KS 66208. Call 1-877-883-2332 *Website:* http://www.draonline.org

Families Anonymous *International. 500+ groups. Founded 1971.* 12-Step. Fellowship for relatives and friends of persons with drug, alcohol or behavioral problems. Members learn to achieve their own serenity in spite of the turmoil which surrounds them. Many booklets, pamphlets, bookmarks, publications include daily thought book, "Today A Better Way," and a bimonthly newsletter "The Twelve-Step Rag." Offers group development guidelines. Write: F.A., PO Box 3475, Culver City, CA 90231-3475. Call 1-800-736-9805; Fax: 310-815-9682. *Website:* http://www.FamiliesAnonymous.org *Email:* famanon@FamiliesAnonymous.org

Free-N-One Recovery *National. 30 affiliated groups. Founded 1985.* Group teaches people to be free mentally and spiritually, as well as free of drugs and alcohol. Information and referrals, phone support, literature, conferences. Assistance in starting local chapters. Write: Free-N-One Recovery, 404 N. Rose St., Compton, CA 90221. Call 310-764-4400; Fax: 310-764-5439.

I.C.A.P. (Intercongregational Addictions Program) *International. Founded 1979.* Network of recovering alcoholic women in religious orders. Helps Roman Catholic women who are or have been, members of religious orders and are alcoholic, chemically dependent, compulsive eaters, compulsive gamblers, etc. Information, referrals, assistance in meeting other members, phone support, conferences and newsletters. Write: ICAP, 7777 Lake Street, Suite 115, River Forest, IL 60305-1734. Call 708-488-9770; Fax: 708-488-9774. *Website:* www.2icap.org *Email:* icapsrs@aol.com

International Doctors in Alcoholics Anonymous *International network. 6000 members. 175 affiliated groups. Founded 1949.* Opportunity for doctoral level health care professionals to discuss common problems and find common solutions to drug and alcohol problems. Annual meetings (1st week Aug.), phone support, information and referrals, newsletter. Mutual help meetings at conferences of other organizations. Write: IDAA, c/o Gordon L. Hyde, MD, Exec. Director, 3311 Brookhill Circle, Lexington, KY 40502. Call 859-277-9379. *Website:* http://www.idaa.org

International Lawyers in Alcoholics Anonymous *International. 40+ affiliated groups. Founded 1975.* Serves as a clearinghouse for support groups for lawyers who are recovering alcoholics or have other chemical dependencies. Newsletter, annual conventions. Group development guidelines. Write: ILAA, c/o Eli Gauna, 14123 Victory Blvd., Van Nuys, CA 91401. Call 818-785-6541; Fax: 818-785-3887. *Website:* http://www.ilaa.org

J.A.C.S. (Jewish Alcoholics, Chemically Dependent Persons & Significant Others) *International. Founded 1980.* For alcoholic & chemically dependent Jews, their families, friends, associates, & community. Networking, community outreach, retreats, newsletter, literature, spiritual events and speaker's bureau. Write: JACS, 850 Seventh Ave., New York, NY 10019. Call 212-397-4197; Fax: 212-399-3525. *Website:* http://www.jacsweb.org *Email:* jacs@jacsweb.org

LifeRing Secular Recovery *International. Founded 1999.* Secular community of persons who are building lives free of dependency on alcohol and other drugs. Members practice complete abstinence from alcohol and other addicting drugs. Peer support, literature, information, referrals and advocacy activities. Guidelines available for starting similar groups. Large online email support group and several smaller special interest groups (women, weight loss, stop smoking, etc). Online chats, forum. Publishes sobriety literature. Write: LifeRing Secular Recovery, 1440 Broadway, Suite 312 , Oakland, CA 94612-2029. Call 510-763-0779. *Website:* http://www.unhooked.com *Email:* service@lifering.org

Marijuana Anonymous World Services *International. 50+ groups.* Founded 1989. 12-Step fellowship of men and women who desire to stay clean of marijuana. Literature and starter packets. Various online meetings. Write: M.A., PO Box 2912, Van Nuys, CA 91404. Call 1-800-766-6779 (recorded message). *Website:* http://www.marijuana-anonymous.org *Email:* office@marijuana-anonymous.org

Nar-Anon World Service Organization *International. Founded 1967.* 12-Step. Fellowship offering self-help recovery to families & friends of addicts. Members share their experience, hope and strength with each other. Packet of information for starting new groups. Nar-Ateen and Nar-Atot programs available. Write: Nar-Anon Family World Service Organization, 22527 Crenshaw Blvd., Suite 200B, Torrance, CA 90505. Call 1-800-477-6291 or 310-534-8188; Fax: 310-534-8688. *Website:* http://www.nar-anon.org *Email:* naranonwso@hotmail.com

Narcotics Anonymous *International. 32,000 meetings per week in 113 countries. Founded 1953.* 12-Step. Group whose primary purpose is to help any individual stop using drugs. There are no dues, fees or registration. The only requirement for membership is the desire to stop using drugs. Information is available in several languages, on audio tape, CD and in Braille. Write: NAWS, PO Box 9999, Van Nuys, CA 91409. Call 818-773-9999; Fax: 818-700-0700. *Website:* http://www.na.org *Email:* fsmail@na.org

National Family Partnership *National. 58 affiliates. Founded 1980.* Drug prevention, education, information & networking for parents to address drug prevention. Legislative advocacy on federal level and information resource for state & local efforts. Annual Red Ribbon Campaign, resource center, drug prevention, anti-tobacco resource. Write: National Family Partnership, 2490 Coral Way, Suite 501, Miami, FL 33145. Call 1-800-705-8997; Fax: 305-856-4815. *Website:* http://www.nfp.org *Email:* mcruz-ledon@informedfamilies.org

Overcomers In Christ *International. Founded 1987.* Recovery program that deals with every aspect of addiction and dysfunction (spiritual, physical, mental, emotional and social). Uses Overcomers goals which are Christ-centered. Resources, information and referrals. Assistance in starting new groups. Literature. Write: Overcomers In Christ , PO Box 34460, Omaha, NE 68134-04604. Call 402-573-0966; Fax: 402-573-0960. *Website:* http://www.OvercomersInChrist.org *Email:* OIC@OvercomersInChrist.org

Overcomers Outreach, Inc. *International. 700 affiliated groups. Founded 1985.* 12-Step. Christ-centered support group for persons with any compulsive behavior, as well as their families and friends. Uses the 12-Steps of A.A. and applies them to the Scriptures. Uses Jesus Christ as "higher power." Supplements involvement in other 12-Step groups. Newsletter, group development guidelines, conferences. Write: Overcomers Outreach, PO Box 2208, Oakhurst, CA 93644. Call 1-800-310-3001. *Website:* http://www.overcomersoutreach.org *Email:* info@overcomersoutreach.org

Pills Anonymous *Model. 2 groups in New York City.* Self-help, self-supporting, anonymous 12-Step program, based on A.A., for those who want to help themselves & others recover from chemical addiction. Groups meet in New York City. Call 212-874-0700. *Website:* http://www.pillsanonymous.com/ *Email:* pillsanonymous@groups.msn.com

Prescriptions Anonymous *National. Founded 1998.* 12-Step. Fellowship helping those affected by prescription or over-the-counter addictions. Offers members and families group support, phone consultations and informational literature. Write: Prescriptions Anonymous, Inc., PO Box 10534, Gaithersburg, MD 20898-0534.

10534, Gaithersburg, MD 20898-0534. Call 301-641-6533. *Website:* http://www.prescriptionanonymous.org *Email:* Cindy@prescriptionanonymous.org

Psychologists Helping Psychologists *National network. Founded 1980.* For doctoral-level psychologists or students who've had a personal experience with alcohol or drugs. Aim is to support each other in recovery and help others to recover. Tries to educate psychology community. Regional/national get-togethers, newsletter. Write: Psychologists Helping Psychologists, 3484 S. Utah St., Arlington, VA 22206-1921. Call Ann Stone 703-243-4470; Fax: 703-243-7125. *Email:* AnnS@Erols.com

Rational Recovery *Founded 1986.* Independent self-recovery from addiction to alcohol and other drugs through planned, permanent abstinence using addictive voice recognition technique (AVRT). Monitor program for mandated programming. Online message/discussion forum. Write: Rational Recovery Systems, PO Box 800, Lotus, CA 95651. Call 530-621-4374 or 530-621-2667; Fax: 530-622-4296. *Website:* http://www.rational.org *Email:* info@rational.org

Secular Organizations for Sobriety (Save Ourselves) *International. 20000 members. Founded 1986.* Mutual help for alcoholics and addicts who want to acknowledge their addiction and maintain sobriety as a separate issue from religion or spirituality. Newsletter. Guidelines and assistance available for starting groups. Write: S.O.S., 4773 Hollywood Blvd., Hollywood, CA 90027. Call 323-664-4295; Fax: 323-664-4271. *Website:* http://www.cfiwest.org/sos/ *Email:* sos@cfiwest.org

SMART Recovery Self-Help Network (Self-Management And Recovery Training) *National. 275 affiliated groups. Founded 1994.* Network of self-help groups for individuals wanting to gain their independence from addictive and compulsive behaviors. SMART Recovery is an abstinence program based on cognitive behavioral principles, especially those of rational emotive behavior therapy. Newsletter, information, referrals, literature and assistance in starting local groups. Write: SMART Recovery, 7537 Mentor Ave., Suite 306, Mentor, OH 44060. Call 866-951-5357; Fax: 440-951-5358. *Website:* http://www.smartrecovery.org *Email:* info@smartrecovery.org

Social Workers Helping Social Workers *National network. Founded 1980.* Supports recovery from alcohol or other chemical dependence, either their own or that of a significant other, among social workers (BSW/MSW) or MSW matriculating students. Social workers with other addictions are welcome to attend meetings. Newsletter, annual conferences, some regional retreats/meetings, continuing education, daily email digest and group development guidelines. Write: SWHSW, 5228 S. Kenwood Ave., Chicago, IL 60615-4006. Call Betty Check,

LCSW 773-493-6940. *Website:* http://www.socialworkershelping.org *Email:* SWHSWIL@aol.com

Therapists In Recovery *Model. Founded 1986.* Mutual support for licensed therapists in recovery from alcohol or drug addiction. Local group meetings, phone support, information and referrals. Assistance in starting similar groups. Write: T.I.R., 2963 Butler St., Oceanside, CA 92054. Call Paul 760-433-9169. *Email:* pec2963@aol.com

Veterinarians in Recovery *National network. Founded 1990.* Support network for veterinarians in recovery from alcoholism and addiction. Provides information and referrals, phone support and newsletter. Online email listserv. Maintains database of members for support. Al-Anon members and recovering veterinarian staff welcome at meetings. Many VIR members also are members of Int'l Doctors in A.A. and meet during their annual conference. Write: VIR, c/o Jeff H., 104 Maple Trace, Birmingham, AL 35244. Call 205-982-2406. *Website:* http://www.crml/uab.edu/~jah *Email:* jeffhalldvm@charter.net

GAMBLING
(see also toll-free helplines)

STATEWIDE

Gam-Anon *North/Central NJ* Fellowship of family members and friends of compulsive gamblers. Follows the 12-Step program adapted from A.A. Various meeting locations throughout New Jersey. Write: Gam-Anon, P.O. Box 177, Lodi, NJ 07644. Call 973-815-0988. *Website:* http://www.njgamanon.org

Gamblers Anonymous *New Jersey Intergroup* Fellowship of men and women who share their experiences, strengths and hopes with each other in order to recover from their common problem of compulsive gambling. Various meeting locations throughout New Jersey. Write: G.A., P.O. Box 283, Kearny, NJ 07032. Call NJ Intergroup 1-877-994-2465 (24 hr). *Website:* http://www.ga4nj.com

Signs of Sobriety *Professionally-run.* Provides alcoholism and drug addiction services to persons who are deaf or hard-of-hearing. Makes referrals to deaf and sign interpreted 12-Step groups throughout NJ (alcohol or drug addiction, gambling, families of alcoholics and general 12-Step meetings). Provides prevention and education classes. Offers SoberCamp-annual summer retreat and Sober/Deaf activities for deaf and hard of hearing individuals in recovery. Newsletter. Write: SOS, 100 Scotch Rd., 2nd Floor, Ewing, NJ 08628. TTY: 1-800-332-7677; Voice: 609-882-7677 (day); Fax: 609-882-6808. *Website:* http://www.signsofsobriety.org *Email:* info@signsofsobriety.org

ATLANTIC

Gam-Anon 12-step. Fellowship of family members and friends of compulsive gamblers. Meets Thurs., 8-10pm, Our Lady of Sorrows Church, Wabash and Poplar Ave., Linwood. Call 609-266-3933. *Website:* http://www.njgamanon.org

Gamblers Anonymous 12-Step. Fellowship of men and women who share experiences, strengths and hopes with each other to recover from compulsive gambling. Call NJ Intergroup 1-877-994-2465 (24 hr). *Website:* http://www.ga4nj.com

> **Absecon** Meets Mon., 7-9pm and Fri, 10am-noon, St. Elizabeth Anne Seaton Church, Rectory, 591 New Jersey Ave.
>
> **Brigantine** Meets Sat., 10am-noon, Community Presbyterian Church, 1501 Brigantine Ave. and 15th St.
>
> **Egg Harbor Township** Meets Tues., 7:30-9pm, Atlantic Care Behavioral Health Center, 6010 Blackhorse Pike.
>
> **Linwood** Meets Thurs., 8-10pm, Our Lady of Sorrow Church, Wabash and Popular Ave.
>
> **Margate** Meets Sun., 10:30am-noon, Margate Library, 8100 Atlantic Ave.

BERGEN

Gam-Anon 12-Step. Fellowship of family members and friends of compulsive gamblers. Call Gamblers Anonymous 973-815-0988. *Website:* http://www.njgamanon.com

> **Fair Lawn** Meets Tues., 7pm and Fri., 8pm, Episcopal Church of Atonement, 1-36 30th St. and Rosalie Ave.
>
> **Paramus** Meets Tues., 8pm, Bergen Regional Medical Center, 230 East Ridgewood Ave.

Gamblers Anonymous 12-Step. Fellowship of men and women who share experiences, strengths and hopes with each other to recover from compulsive gambling. Call NJ Intergroup 1-877-994-2465 (24 hr). *Website:* http://www.ga4nj.com

> **Carlstadt** Meets Wed., 7:30-9:45pm, First Presbyterian Church, 457 Division Ave.
>
> **Fair Lawn** Meets Tues., 7-8:30pm; Wed., 8-10pm and Fri., 8-10pm, Episcopal Church of Atonement, 1-36 30th St.
>
> **Hasbrouck Heights** Meets Sat., 10-11:30am, St. John The Divine Episcopal Church, Terrace and Jefferson Ave.
>
> **Westwood** Meets Sun., 8-9:45pm, United Methodist Church, 105 Fairview Ave.

BURLINGTON

Gam-Anon 12-Step. Fellowship of family members and friends of compulsive gamblers. Meets Sun., 6pm, Hampton Behavioral Health Center, 650 Rancocas Rd., Westampton Township. Call 609-267-7000. *Website:* http://www.njgamanon.org

Gamblers Anonymous 12-Step. Fellowship of men and women who share experiences, strengths and hopes with each other to recover from compulsive gambling. Call NJ Intergroup 1-877-994-2465 (24 hr). *Website:* http://www.ga4nj.com

> **Moorestown** Meets Mon., 8-9:30pm, Trinity Church, Church and Main St.
> **Mt. Holly** Meets Sun., 5:30pm and Wed., 7:30-9pm, Hampton Hospital, Beverly and Rancocas Rd.

Overcomers 12-Step. Recovery group for anyone suffering from any type of addiction, dependency or compulsive disorder. Rap sessions, guest speakers, literature. Meets Thurs., 7:30-9pm, Fellowship Alliance Chapel, 199 Church Rd., Medford. Call 609-953-7333 (day).

CAPE MAY

Gamblers Anonymous 12-Step. Fellowship of men and women who share experiences, strengths and hopes with each other to recover from compulsive gambling. Meets Sun., 7-8pm, Holy Trinity Episcopal Church, 30th and Bay Ave., Ocean City. Call NJ Intergroup 1-877-994-2465 (24 hr). *Website:* http://www.ga4nj.com

ESSEX

Gam-Anon 12-Step. Fellowship of family members and friends of compulsive gamblers. Call Gamblers Anonymous 973-815-0988. *Website:* http://www.njgamanon.org

> **Bloomfield** Meets Tues., 8:30-10:30pm, Bethany United Presbyterian Church, 293 West Passaic St.
> **Nutley** Meets Mon., 8pm; and Fri., 8:30pm, St. Paul's Congregational Church, 10 St. Paul's Place.

Gamblers Anonymous 12-Step. Fellowship of men and women who share experiences, strengths and hopes with each other to recover from compulsive gambling. Call NJ Intergroup 1-877-994-2465 (24 hr). *Website:* http://www.ga4nj.com

Bloomfield Meets Tues. and Thurs., 8:30-10:30pm, Bethany United Presbyterian Church, Basement Level, 293 W. Passaic Ave.

East Orange Meets Thurs., 8-9:15pm, East Orange General Hospital, South Munn and Central Ave., Pride Bldg.

Nutley Meets Mon., 8-10pm; and Fri., 8:30-10:30pm, St. Paul's Congregational Church, (side entrance), 1st Floor, 10 St. Paul's Place.

West Orange Meets Tues., 8-10pm, St. Cloud Presbyterian Church, Lower Level, 5 Ridgeway Ave.

GLOUCESTER

Gamblers Anonymous 12-Step. Fellowship of men and women who share experiences, strengths and hopes with each other to recover from compulsive gambling. Call NJ Intergroup 1-877-994-2465 (24 hr). *Website:* http://www.ga4nj.com

Blackwood Meets Fri., 8-10pm, Blackwood Methodist Church, 35 East Church St.

Woodbury Meets Tues., 7-8:30pm, St. Stephens Lutheran Church, 230 North Evergreen Ave.

HUDSON

Gamblers Anonymous 12-Step. Fellowship of men and women who share their experiences, strengths and hopes with each other to recover from compulsive gambling. Meets Wed., 8-9:30pm, Old Bergen Church, Bergen and Highland Ave., Jersey City. Call NJ Intergroup 1-877-994-2465 (24 hr). *Website:* http://www.ga4nj.com

MERCER

Gamblers Anonymous 12-Step. Fellowship of men and women who share experiences, strengths and hopes with each other to recover from compulsive gambling. Meets Tues., 8:30-10pm, University Office Plaza, 3635 Quakerbridge Rd., Suite 7, Hamilton. Call NJ Intergroup 1-877-994-2465 (24 hr). *Website:* http://www.ga4nj.com

MIDDLESEX

Gam-Anon 12-Step. Fellowship of family members and friends of compulsive gamblers. Call Gamblers Anonymous 973-815-0988. *Website:* http://www.njgamanon.org

Metuchen Meets Tues., 7pm, St. Luke's Episcopal Church, 17 Oak St.

Parlin Meets Wed. and Thurs., 8pm, Messiah Lutheran Church, 3091 Bordentown Ave.

Gamblers Anonymous 12-Step. Fellowship of men and women who share experiences, strengths and hopes with each other to recover from compulsive gambling. Call NJ Intergroup 1-877-994-2465 (24 hr). *Website:* hhtp://www.ga4nj.com

> **Edison** Meets Sat., 10-11:30am, Oak Tree Presbyterian Church, 455 Plainfield Rd.

> **Metuchen** *(Young Gamblers)* Meets Tues., 7-9pm, St. Luke's Episcopal Church, 17 Oak St.

> **Parlin** *(Young Gamblers)* Meets Wed., 8-9:30pm and Thurs., 8-9:30pm, Messiah Lutheran Church, 3091 Bordentown Ave.

Overcomer's Outreach 12-Step. Christian fellowship to overcome any type of addiction or compulsive behavior, anxiety, depression and loneliness using God's word as a basis of recovery. Discussion, Bible study, prayer, phone help. Meets Mon., 7:30-9:15pm, Metuchen Assembly of God, Rose and Whitman St., Metuchen. Call Janet 732-388-2856 (eve).

S.M.A.R.T. Recovery (Self-Management And Recovery Training) *Professionally-run.* Self-help group for individuals wanting to gain their independence from addictive behaviors (drugs, including alcohol and nicotine and other compulsive behaviors including gambling, eating disorders). SMART is an abstinence program based on cognitive-behavioral education and principles, especially those of rational-emotive behavior therapy. Meets Mon., 6:30-7:45pm, Rutgers University, Busch Campus, Psychology Building, Room A224, Piscataway. Call Tom Morgan 732-445-0902. *Website:* http://www.smartrecovery.org

MONMOUTH

Gamblers Anonymous 12-Step. Fellowship of men and women who share experiences, strengths and hopes with each other to recover from compulsive gambling. Call NJ Intergroup 1-877-994-2465 (24 hr). *Website:* http://www.ga4nj.com

> **Colts Neck** Meets Tues., 8-9:30pm and Sun. 6:30-8pm, St. Mary's Church, Spiritual Center Building, Route 34 and Phalanx Rd.

> **Freehold** Meets Fri., 8-9:30pm, Hope Lutheran Church, 211 Elton and Adelphia Rd., Route 524.

> **Ocean Township** Meets Mon., 8-9:30pm, Church of St. Anselm, 1028 Wayside Rd.

MORRIS

Gam-Anon 12-Step. Fellowship of family members and friends of compulsive gamblers. Call Gamblers Anonymous 973-815-0988. *Website:* http://www.njgamanon.org

> **Boonton** Meets Tues., 8-9:30pm, Saint Clare's Behavioral Health Center, Powerville Rd.
> **Lyons** Meets Thurs., 7-9:30pm, Lyons VA Medical Center, Building 93.

Gamblers Anonymous 12-Step. Fellowship of men and women who share experiences, strengths and hopes with each other to recover from compulsive gambling. Meets Tues., 8-9:45pm, Saint Clare's Behavioral Health Center, Powerville Rd., Boonton. Call NJ Intergroup 1-877-994-2465 (24 hr). *Website:* http://www.ga4nj.com

OCEAN

Checkpoint Support to help overcome dependencies and addictions through accountability, encouragement and spiritual development. Meets Thurs., 7-8:30pm, Safe Harbor, 600 Atlantic City Blvd., Beechwood. Call 732-244-3888 (day).

Gam-Anon 12-Step. Fellowship of family members and friends of compulsive gamblers. Meets Thurs., 7-9pm and Sat., 9:30-11:30am, Presbyterian Church of Toms River, 1070 Hooper Ave., Toms River. Call Gam-Anon Hotline 973-815-0988. *Website:* http://www.njgamanon.org

Gamblers Anonymous 12-Step. Fellowship of men and women who share experiences, strengths and hopes with each other to recover from compulsive gambling. Spouses, family members and significant others welcome. Call NJ Intergroup 1-877-994-2465 (24 hr). *Website:* http://www.ga4nj.com

> **Pt. Pleasant** *(Open Meeting)* Meets Wed., 7:30-9:30pm, Central United Methodist Church, 729 Arnold Ave.
> **Toms River** Meets Thurs., 7-9pm and Sat. 9:30-11:30am, Presbyterian Church of Toms River, 1070 Hooper Ave.
> **Toms River** Meets Fri., 7:30-9pm, Holy Cross Lutheran Church, 1500 Hooper Ave.

SOMERSET

Gam-Anon 12-Step. Fellowship of family members and friends of compulsive gamblers. Meets Thurs., 7pm, Lyons Veterans Administration Medical Center, Building # 143, Lyons. Call Gamblers Anonymous 973-815-0988. *Website:* http://www.njgamanon.org

Gamblers Anonymous 12-Step. Fellowship of men and women who share their experiences, strengths and hopes with each other in order to recover from compulsive gambling. Call NJ Intergroup 1-877-994-2465 (24 hr). *Website:* http://www.ga4nj.com

> **Basking Ridge** Meets Sat., 10-11am, Church of Saint James Parish Community Center, 184 South Finley Ave., Room 4.
> **Lyons** Meets Thurs., 7:30-9:30pm, Lyons Veterans Administration Medical Center, Bldg. # 143, Multi-Purpose Room, 151 Knollcroft Rd.

Overcomer's Outreach 12-Step. Christian fellowship to overcome any type of addiction or compulsive behavior using God's word as a basis of recovery. Meets Sat., 3:30-5pm, Reformed Church, Fellowship Hall, 113 Clinton St., So. Bound Brook. Call Carol Mehlenbeck 732-885-1023 or 732-457-9304 (day/eve).

SUSSEX

Gamblers Anonymous 12-Step. Fellowship of men and women who share experiences, strengths and hopes with each other to recover from compulsive gambling. Meets Wed., 7-8:30pm, Sparta United Methodist Church, 71 Sparta Ave., Sparta. Call NJ Intergroup 1-877-994-2465 (24 hr). *Website:* http://www.ga4nj.com

UNION

Gam-Anon 12-Step. Fellowship of family members and friends of compulsive gamblers. Meets Mon., 7:45-10pm, Temple Israel of Union, 2372 Morris Ave., Union. Call Gamblers Anonymous 973-815-0988. *Website:* http://www.njgamanon.org

Gamblers Anonymous 12-Step. Fellowship of men and women who share experiences, strengths and hopes with each other to recover from compulsive gambling. Call NJ Intergroup 1-877-994-2465 (24 hr). *Website:* http://www.ga4nj.com

> **Union** Meets Sun., 7-9pm, Union Methodist Church, Berwyn St. and Overlook Terrace.
> **Union** Meets Mon., 7:45-10pm; Wed., 1-2pm; and Sun., 8-9:30pm, Temple Israel of Union, 2378 Morris Ave.

NATIONAL

Bettors Anonymous *Model. 5 groups in Massachusetts. Founded 1990.* 12-Step. Fellowship who shares their experience, hope and strength with each other in order to help themselves and others recover from compulsive gambling. The only requirement for membership is a desire to stop gambling. Literature, information and referrals and phone support. Provides assistance in starting local groups. Write: Bettors Anonymous, PO Box 304, Wilmington, MA 01887. Call 978-988-1777 (answering machine) or 781-662-5199. *Website:* http://www.bettorsanonymous.org *Email:* info@bettorsanonymous.org

Gam-Anon Family Groups *International. 500 groups. Founded 1960.* 12-Step. Fellowship for men and women who are husbands, wives, relatives or friends of compulsive gamblers, who have been affected by the gambling problem. A few groups have Gam-a-teen groups for children of gamblers. Write: Gam-Anon, PO Box 157, Whitestone, NY 11357. Call 718-352-1671 (Tues. & Thurs., 9am-5pm); Fax: 718-746-2571. *Website:* http://www.gam-anon.org

Gamblers Anonymous *International. Approximately 2400 chapters. Founded 1957.* 12-Step. Fellowship of men & women who share experience, strength, & hope with each other to recover from compulsive gambling. Monthly bulletin for members. Offers assistance in starting new groups. Write: G.A., PO Box 17173, Los Angeles, CA 90017. Call 213-386-8789; Fax: 213-386-0030. *Website:* http://www.gamblersanonymous.org *Email:* isomain@gamblersanonymous.org

I.C.A.P. (Intercongregational Addictions Program) *International. Founded 1979.* Network of recovering alcoholic women in religious orders. Helps Roman Catholic women who are or have been, members of religious orders and are alcoholic, chemically dependent, compulsive eaters, compulsive gamblers, etc. Write: ICAP, 7777 Lake Street, Suite 115, River Forest, IL 60305-1734. Call 708-488-9770; Fax: 708-488-9774. *Website:* http://www.2icap.org *Email:* icapsrs@aol.com

Overcomers In Christ *International. Founded 1987.* Recovery program that deals with every aspect of addiction and dysfunction (spiritual, physical, mental, emotional and social). Uses Overcomers Goals which are Christ-centered. Resources, information and referrals. Write: Overcomers In Christ, PO Box 34460, Omaha, NE 68134-04604. Call 402-573-0966; Fax: 402-573-0960. *Website:* http://www.OvercomersInChrist.org *Email:* OIC@OvercomersInChrist.org

Overcomers Outreach, Inc. *International. 12-step. 700 affiliated groups. Founded 1985.* 12-Step Christ-centered support group for persons with any compulsive behavior, as well as their families and friends. Uses Jesus Christ as "higher power." Supplements involvement in other 12-Step groups. Newsletter, group development guidelines, conferences. Write: Overcomers

Outreach, PO Box 2204, Oakhurst, CA 93664. Call 1-800-310-3001. *Website:* http://www.overcomersoutreach.org *Email:* info@overcomersoutreach.org

OVERWEIGHT / OVEREATING
(see also eating disorders, toll-free helplines)

STATEWIDE

Overeaters Anonymous Fellowship of men, women and children who meet to help one another understand and overcome their common problem of compulsive overeating. Follows the O.A. 12-Step program. Meetings throughout New Jersey.

> **Central Jersey Intergroup** Covers Hunterdon, Mercer, Middlesex, Monmouth, Somerset and Union counties. Write: CJIOA, PO Box 284, Woodbridge, NJ 07095. Call Kim B., 732-634-6695 *Website:* www.oa-centraljersey.org *Email:* cjioa@att.net
>
> **Jersey Shore Intergroup** Covers Atlantic, Cape May, Ocean counties)609-698-0244 (day/eve). Write: P.O. Box 571, Manahawkin, NJ 08050. *Website:* http://www.oa.org
>
> **North Jersey Intergroup** Covers Bergen, Essex, Hudson, Morris, Passaic, Sussex, Union and Warren counties. $2 donation. Write: PO Box 827, Fairlawn, NJ 07410-0827. Call 973-746-8787 (day/eve). *Website:* http://www.njioa.org *Email:* info@njioa.org
>
> **South Jersey Intergroup** Ccovers Atlantic, Burlington, Camden, Cumberland, Gloucester and Salem counties. Call 609-239-0022. *Website:* http://www.southjerseyoa.org

T.O.P.S. (Take Off Pounds Sensibly) Helps overweight persons lose weight through medical supervision, competition and group process. Also open to children 7 years and older. Phone network, buddy system, peer-counseling, newsletter. Dues $20/yr. Meetings throughout NJ. For information call Jane 973-875-7649. (leave message) Check website for local meetings. *Website:* http://www.tops.org

ATLANTIC

Overeaters Anonymous Fellowship who meet to help one another understand and overcome their common problem of compulsive overeating. For information on local meetings call Jersey Shore Intergroup 609-698-0244.

Consider passing this Directory on to a student or staff member - browsing through the Directory pages can often provide helpful education as to the wide variety of groups available.

BERGEN

Food Addicts in Recovery Anonymous Support for people addicted to sugar, flour and quantities of food. Guest speakers, literature and phone help. Meets Thurs., 6:30-8pm, Valley Hospital, Luckow Pavilion, 1 Valley Health Plaza, Paramus; or Sun., 8-9:30am, Pascack Valley Hospital, 250 Old Hook Rd., Westwood. Call Naomi 201-265-6917.

Gastric Bypass Support Group *Professionally-run.* Mutual support and education for persons who have had bariatric surgery (gastric stapling or lap band) within the last year or are considering the procedure. Education, guest speakers and phone help. Meets 3rd Tues., 5:30-7pm, Englewood Hospital, Learning Center, 350 Engle St., Conference Room A and B, Englewood. Call Devorah E. Goldberg, RN 201-227-5543 (day). *Email:* devorahbbc@yahoo.com

Gastric Bypass Support Group *Professionally-run.* Mutual support and education for persons who have had bariatric surgery (gastric stapling) over a year past surgery. Education, guest speakers and phone help. Meets 3rd Tues., 5:30pm, Englewood Hospital, 350 Engle St., Englewood. Before attending call Christine 201-227-5530 (day). *Email:* bergenbariatric@yahoo.com

Gastric Bypass Support Group *Professionally-run.* Mutual support and education for persons who have had bariatric surgery (gastric stapling or lap band) or are considering the procedure. Education, guest speakers and phone help. Meets 4th Tues., 5:30pm, Holy Name Hospital, 718 Teaneck Rd., Teaneck. Before attending call Christine 201-227-5530 (day). *Email:* bergenbariatric@yahoo.com

GreySheeters Anonymous Fellowship of men and women who share their experiences, strength and hope with each other that they may solve their common problem and help others to recover from compulsive overeating. Primary purpose is to stay abstinent and help other compulsive overeaters to achieve abstinence. Members eat three weighed and measured meals a day. Families welcome. Newsletter, phone help, buddy system and pen pals. Meets 1st and 3rd Wed., 10 am, Our Lady of Sorrow's Catholic Church, 4th and Prospect Ave., South Orange. Call 1-888-473-9743.

Lap Band Support Group *Professionally-run.* Mutual support and education for persons who have had lap band surgery or are considering the procedure. Meets 4th Tues., 5:30pm, Englewood Hospital, 350 Engle St., Englewood. Before attending call Christine or Devorah 201-227-5543 (day). *Email:* bergenbariatric@yahoo.com

Overeaters Anonymous Fellowship who meet to help one another understand and overcome their common problem of compulsive overeating. For local meeting information by day of week call 973-746-8787.

T.O.P.S. (Take Off Pounds Sensibly) Helps overweight persons lose weight through medical supervision, competition and group process. Open to children 7 years and older. Phone network, buddy system, peer-counseling, newsletter. Membership $20/yr. Dues $1/wk. For meeting information call Jane 973-875-7649 (leave message). Check website for local meetings. *Website:* http://www.tops.org

BURLINGTON

Overeaters Anonymous Fellowship who meet to help one another understand and overcome their common problem of compulsive overeating. For local meetings call the O.A. South Jersey Intergroup 609-239-0022.

Overcomers Recovery group for anyone suffering from any type of addiction, dependency or compulsive disorder. Meets Thurs., 7:30-9pm, Fellowship Alliance Chapel, 199 Church Rd., Medford. Call 609-953-7333 (day).

T.O.P.S. (Take Off Pounds Sensibly) Helps overweight persons lose weight through medical supervision, competition and group process. Open to children 7 years and older. Phone network, buddy system, peer-counseling, newsletter. Membership $20/yr. Dues $1/wk. For meeting information call Dave 609-724-9328 (eve). Check website for local meetings. *Website:* http://www.tops.org

CAMDEN

Overeaters Anonymous Fellowship who meet to help one another understand and overcome their common problem of compulsive overeating. For local meetings call the O.A. South Jersey Intergroup 609-239-0022.

T.O.P.S. (Take Off Pounds Sensibly) Helps overweight persons lose weight through medical supervision, competition and group process. Open to children 7 years and older. Phone network, buddy system, peer-counseling, newsletter. Membership $20/yr. Dues $1/wk. For meeting information call DJ 609-758-6471 (eve). Check website for local meetings. *Website:* http://www.tops.org

We know this Directory is big and chances are we can probably find the group you're looking for quicker than you paging through it. Call us! (We're really friendly!)
1-800-367-6274

CAPE MAY

Overeaters Anonymous Fellowship who meet to help one another understand and overcome their common problem of compulsive overeating. For local meetings call the O.A. Jersey Shore Intergroup at 609-698-0244.

T.O.P.S. (Take Off Pounds Sensibly) Helps overweight persons lose weight through medical supervision, competition and group process. Open to children 7 years and older. Phone network, buddy system, peer-counseling, newsletter. Membership $20/yr. Dues $1/wk. For meeting information call Jane 973-875-7649 (leave message). Check website for local meetings. *Website:* http://www.tops.org

CUMBERLAND

Gastric Bypass Support Group Mutual support for those who have or are planning to have gastric bypass surgery (under 18 welcome). Rap sessions. Meets 4th Wed., 7pm, South Jersey Healthcare, Fitness Connection, 1430 W. Sherman Ave., Vineland. For information call 856-451-7533 (day).

Overeaters Anonymous Fellowship who meet to help one another understand and overcome their common problem of compulsive overeating. For local meetings call the O.A. South Jersey Intergroup 609-239-0022.

T.O.P.S. (Take Off Pounds Sensibly) Helps overweight persons lose weight through medical supervision, competition and group process. Open to children 7 years and older. Phone network, buddy system, peer-counseling, newsletter. Membership $20/yr. Dues $1/wk. For meeting information call Jane 973-875-7649 (leave message). Check website for local meetings. *Website:* http://www.tops.org

ESSEX

Food Addicts Anonymous Fellowship to recover from food addiction. Primary purpose is to maintain abstinence from sugar, flour and wheat. Meets Sun. 7:30-8:30pm, St. Peter's Episcopal Church, 94 East Mount Pleasant Ave. Livingston. Call Roger 908-403-6535 (day/eve) or Lisa 973-403-0333 (day).

Overeaters Anonymous Fellowship who meet to help one another understand and overcome their common problem of compulsive overeating. For local meeting information by day of week call 973-746-8787.

T.O.P.S. (Take Off Pounds Sensibly) Helps overweight persons lose weight through medical supervision, competition and group process. Open to children years and older. Phone network, buddy system, peer-counseling, newsletter. Membership $20/yr. Dues $1/wk. For meeting information call Jane 973-875-7649 (leave message). Check website for local meetings. *Website:* http://www.tops.org

GLOUCESTER

Overeaters Anonymous Fellowship who meet to help one another understand and overcome their common problem of compulsive overeating. For information on local meetings call the O.A. South Jersey Intergroup 609-239-0022.

South Jersey Bariatric Support System Support for persons who have had gastric bypass or are considering the procedure. Families welcome. Rap sessions, online support, literature. Meets every other Fri., Church of the Nazarene, Broadway, Pitman. For meeting information call Chrissie 856-256-9066 (day/eve). *Website:* http://www.yahoogroups.com/sjbss *Email:* shihtzumom@snip.net

T.O.P.S. (Take Off Pounds Sensibly) Helps overweight persons lose weight through medical supervision, competition and group process. Open to children 7 years and older. Phone network, buddy system, peer-counseling, newsletter. Membership $20/yr. Dues $1/wk. For meeting information call DJ 609-758-6471 (eve). Check website for local meetings. *Website:* http://www.tops.org

HUDSON

Overeaters Anonymous 12-Step. Fellowship who meet to help one another understand and overcome their common problem of compulsive overeating. For local meeting information by day of week call 973-746-8787. (Note: There is one group in Hudson County, on Sun).

HUNTERDON

Overeaters Anonymous Fellowship who meet to help one another understand and overcome their common problem of compulsive overeating. For local meeting information call the O.A. Central Intergroup at 908-253-3464.

T.O.P.S. (Take Off Pounds Sensibly) Helps overweight persons lose weight through medical supervision, competition and group process. Open to children 7 years and older. Phone network, buddy system, peer-counseling, newsletter. Membership $20/yr. Dues $1/wk. For meeting information call Jane 973-875-7649 (leave message). Check website for local meetings. *Website:* http://www.tops.org

MERCER

Lighter Reflections Mutual support and education for persons who have had bariatric surgery (gastric stapling or lap band) or are considering the procedure. Education, guest speakers, literature and phone help. Meets 1st Mon., 7-9pm, N.J. Bariatrics, 4250 US Route 1 North, Suite 1, Monmouth Junction. Before attending call Dena Zucker 732-257-2099 (day) or N.J. Bariatrics 732-274-3434 (day). *Email:* demusique@aol.com

Overeaters Anonymous Fellowship who meet to help one another understand and overcome their common problem of compulsive overeating. For local meetings call the O.A. Central Intergroup 908-253-3464.

T.O.P.S. (Take Off Pounds Sensibly) Helps overweight persons lose weight through medical supervision, competition and group process. Open to children 7 years and older. Phone network, buddy system, peer-counseling, newsletter. Membership $20/yr. Dues $1/wk. For meeting information call DJ 609-758-6471 (eve). Check website for local meetings. *Website:* http://www.tops.org

MIDDLESEX

Bariatric Angels *Professionally-run.* Mutual support for bariatric surgery patients using a 12-Step program. Education, advocacy, rap sessions, buddy system, social, newsletter and phone help. Meets Sat., 10:30am, (surgery less than 3 months) and 11am, (surgery more than 3 months), Bayshore Wellness Center, Conference Room, 1044 US Highway 9, Parlin. Registration required. Before attending call Kate Fenimore, RN 908-685-2200 ext. 3167 (day) or 732-203-2322 (eve).

Healthy Weighs Program, The *Professionally-run.* For people of all ages with any type of weight concern. Provides a forum to share challenges and disappointments while discussing ways to overcome specific problems. Meets 2nd and 4th Wed., 1:30-3pm or 7-8:30pm, Diabetes Center of NJ, Talmadge Rd., Edison. Call 1-800-991-6668.

Overeaters Anonymous Fellowship who meet to help one another understand and overcome their common problem of compulsive overeating. For local meeting information call the O.A. Central Intergroup 908-253-3464.

S.M.A.R.T. Recovery (Self-Management And Recovery Training *Professionally-run.* Self-help group for individuals wanting to gain their independence from addictive behaviors SMART is an abstinence program based on cognitive-behavioral education and principles, especially those of rational-emotive behavior therapy. Meets Mon., 6:30-7:45pm, Rutgers

University, Busch Campus, Psychology Building, Room A224, Piscataway. Call Tom Morgan 732-445-0902. *Website:* http://www.smartrecovery.org

T.O.P.S. (Take Off Pounds Sensibly) Helps overweight persons lose weight through medical supervision, competition and group process. Open to children 7 years and older. Phone network, buddy system, peer-counseling, newsletter. Membership $20/yr. Dues $1/wk. For meeting information call Dave 609-724-9328 (eve). Check website for local meetings. *Website:* http://www.tops.org

MONMOUTH

Bariatric Angels *Professionally-run.* Mutual support for bariatric surgery patients using a 12-Step program. Education, advocacy, rap sessions, buddy system, social, newsletter and phone help. Meets Fri. 7:30 pm at Angels Cove Retreat, 164 West Front St., Keyport. Registration required. Before attending call Kate Fenimore, RN 908-685-2200 ext. 3167 (day) or 732-203-2322

Gastric Bypass Support Group *Professionally-run.* Support group for individuals who have undergone gastric bypass surgery or to those considering surgery. Meets 4th Thurs., 7-9pm, Monmouth Medical Center, Long Branch. Registration required. Call 1-888-724-7123.

Overeaters Anonymous Fellowship who meet to help one another understand and overcome their common problem of compulsive overeating. For local meeting information call the Central Jersey Intergroup 908-253-3464.

T.O.P.S. (Take Off Pounds Sensibly) Helps overweight persons lose weight through medical supervision, competition and group process. Open to children 7 years and older. Phone network, buddy system, peer-counseling, newsletter. Membership $20/yr. Dues $1/wk. For meeting information call Dave 609-724-9328 (eve). Check website for local meetings. *Website:* http://www.tops.org

MORRIS

Food Addicts in Recovery Anonymous Fellowship of men and women who share experiences and support with each other to recover from the disease of food addiction. Open to persons under 18. Phone help, guest speakers and literature. Newsletter $10/yr. Meets Sat., 10-11:30am, Saint Clares Health System, 400 West Blackwell St., Conference Room C, Dover. Call Barbara Niziol 973-600-4449 (day). *Website:* http://www.foodaddicts.org

Gastric Bypass Support Group *Professionally-run.* For those who have undergone, or are considering, the surgery. Literature and phone help. Meets 4th Wed., 5:30-6:30pm, Hilton Garden Inn, 375 Mount Hope Ave., Rockaway. Call Patti Smith 973-989-3644 (day).

Lap Band Support Group *Professionally-run.* For those who have undergone, or are considering, the surgery. Literature and phone help. Meets 4th Wed., 7-8pm, St. Clares Hospital, Cafeteria, Dover. Call Patti Smith 973-989-3644.

Overeaters Anonymous Fellowship who meet to help one another understand and overcome their common problem of compulsive overeating. For local meeting information by day of week call 973-746-8787.

T.O.P.S. (Take Off Pounds Sensibly) Helps overweight persons lose weight through medical supervision, competition and group process. Open to children 7 and older. Phone network, buddy system, peer-counseling, newsletter. Membership $20/yr. Dues $1/wk. For meeting information call Jane 973-875-7649 (leave message). Check website for local meetings. *Website:* http://www.tops.org

OCEAN

Bariatric Angels *Professionally-run.* Mutual support for post-bariatric surgery patients using a 12-Step program. Education, advocacy, rap sessions, buddy system, social, newsletter and phone help. Meets Thurs., 7pm, (surgery less than 3 months) and 8pm, (surgery more than 3 months), Community Medical Center, Conference Room B, 99 Route 37 West, Toms River. Registration required. Before attending call Kate Fenimore, RN 908-685-2200 ext. 3167 (day) or 732-203-2322 (eve).

Checkpoint Support to help overcome dependencies and addictions through accountability, encouragement and spiritual development. Meets Thurs., 7-8:30pm, Safe Harbor, 600 Atlantic City Blvd., Beechwood. Call 732-244-3888 (day).

Overeaters Anonymous Fellowship who meet to help one another understand and overcome their common problem of compulsive overeating. For information on local meetings call Jersey Shore Intergroup 609-698-0244.

T.O.P.S. (Take Off Pounds Sensibly) Helps overweight persons lose weight through medical supervision, competition and group process. Open to children 7 years and older. Phone network, buddy system, peer-counseling, newsletter. Membership $20/yr. Dues $1/wk. For meeting information call DJ

609-758-6471 (eve). Check website for local meetings. *Website:* http://www.tops.org

PASSAIC

Overeaters Anonymous Fellowship who meet to help one another understand and overcome their common problem of compulsive overeating. For local meeting information by day of week call 973-746-8787.

T.O.P.S. (Take Off Pounds Sensibly) Helps overweight persons lose weight through medical supervision, competition and group process. Open to children 7 years and older. Phone network, buddy system, peer-counseling, newsletter. Membership $20/yr. Dues $1/wk. For meeting information call Jane 973-875-7649 (leave message). Check website for local meetings. *Website:* http:http://www.tops.org

SALEM

Overeaters Anonymous Fellowship who meet to help one another understand and overcome their common problem of compulsive overeating. For information on local meetings call the O.A. South Jersey Intergroup 609-239-0022 or Bobbie S. 856-346-2336 (day/eve).

T.O.P.S. (Take Off Pounds Sensibly) Helps overweight persons lose weight through medical supervision, competition and group process. Also open to children 7 years and older. Phone network, buddy system, peer-counseling, newsletter. Membership $20/yr. Dues $1/wk. For meeting information call Jane 973-875-7649 (leave message). Check website for local meetings. *Website:* http://www.tops.org

SOMERSET

Bariatric Angels *Professionally-run.* Mutual support for post-bariatric surgery patients using a 12-Step program. Education, advocacy, rap sessions, buddy system, social, newsletter and phone help. Meets Tues., 7pm, (surgery less than 3 months) and 8pm, (surgery more than 3 months), Presbyterian Church of Bound Brook, 950 Mountain Ave. and Route 28 (Union Ave.), Bound Brook. Registration required. Before attending call Kate Fenimore, RN 908-685-2200 ext. 3167 (day) or 732-203-2322 (eve).

Overeaters Anonymous Fellowship who meet to help one another understand and overcome their common problem of compulsive overeating. For local meeting information call O.A. Central Intergroup 908-253-3464.

SUSSEX

Overeaters Anonymous Fellowship who meet to help one another understand and overcome their common problem of compulsive overeating. For local meeting information by day of week call 973-746-8787.

T.O.P.S. (Take Off Pounds Sensibly) Helps overweight persons lose weight through medical supervision, competition and group process. Open to children 7 years and older. Phone network, buddy system, peer-counseling, newsletter. Membership $20/yr. Dues $1/wk. For meeting information call Jane 973-875-7649 (leave message). Check website for local meetings. *Website:* http://www.tops.org

UNION

Food Addicts Anonymous 12-Step meetings for recovery from food addiction. Primary purpose is to maintain abstinence from sugar, flour and wheat. *Website:* http://www.foodaddictsanonymous.org
> **Summit** Meets Fri., 8pm, St. Johns Lutheran Church, 587 Springfield Ave. Call Dorene 908-377-7939.
> **Union** Meets Mon., 8pm, Temple Israel, 2372 Morris Ave. Call Phyllis 732-574-1550.

GreySheeters Anonymous Fellowship of men and women who share their experience, strength and hope with each other that they may solve their common problem and help others to recover from compulsive overeating. Primary purpose is to stay abstinent and help other compulsive overeaters to achieve abstinence. Members eat three weighed and measured meals a day. Families welcome. Newsletter, phone help, buddy system and pen pals. Meets 2nd and 4th Sat., 9am and Tues., 7-8pm, United Methodist Church, 17 Kent Place, Summit. Before attending call Nena 908-522-3081.

Overeaters Anonymous 12-Step. Fellowship who meet to help one another understand and overcome their common problem of compulsive overeating. For local meeting information by day of week call 973-746-8787.

WARREN

Overeaters Anonymous Fellowship who meet to help one another understand and overcome their common problem of compulsive overeating. For local meeting information by day of week call 973-746-8787. (Note: There is only one group in Warren County on Sun.)

T.O.P.S. (Take Off Pounds Sensibly) Helps overweight persons lose weight through medical supervision, competition and group process. Open to children 7 years and older. Phone network, buddy system, peer-counseling, newsletter. Membership $20/yr. Dues $1/wk. For meeting information call Jane 973-875-7649 (leave message). Check website for local meetings. *Website:* http://www.tops.org

NATIONAL

Compulsive Eaters Anonymous - H.O.W. *International. 500 affiliated groups. Founded 1985.* 12-step fellowship to share experience, strength, and hope in order to help themselves and others who suffer from the self destruction of compulsive eating. H.O.W. (Honesty, Open-mindedness and Willingness) groups use a food plan which includes an abstinence of sugar and flour, and allows only three weighed and measured meals per day. Write: CEA-HOW, 5500 E. Atherton St., Suite 227 B, Long Beach, CA 90815-4017. Call 562-342-9344 (day); Fax: 562-342-9346. Website: http://www.ceahow.org E-mail: gso@ceahow.org

T.O.P.S. (Take Off Pounds Sensibly) *International. 10,000 chapters. Founded 1948.* Chapter members use professionally prepared materials on menu planning, food exchanges, motivation, and exercise. Promotes a sensible approach to managing weight as a life choice. Weekly meetings emphasize recognition and support. Newsletter. Tools for weight management and chapter development. New chapters may be started by a minimum of four people. Support group locations available online. Dues $24/USA; $30/Canada. Write: TOPS, P.O. Box 070360, 4575 South 5th St., Milwaukee, WI 53207. Call 1-800-932-8677. Website: http://www.tops.org E-mail: ctrinastic@tops.org

Overeaters Anonymous *International. 6,500 groups. Founded 1960.* A 12-step fellowship of men and women who meet to help one another understand and overcome compulsive eating. Also groups & literature for young persons and teens. Monthly magazine, literature, group development guidelines. Write: O.A., P.O. Box 44020, Rio Rancho, New Mexico 87174-4020. Call 505-891-2664 or look in white pages for local number. Fax: 505-891-4320. Website: http://www.oa.org E-mail: info@oa.org

Food Addicts In Recovery Anonymous *International. Founded 1998.* A 12-step fellowship addressing all forms of food addiction, e.g. undereating, overeating, and bulimia through purging and/or exercise. Literature, phone support, assistance in starting new groups, on-line listing of meetings. Write: Food Addicts Anonymous, 6 Pleasant St., Room 402, Malden, MA 02148. Call 781-321-9118; Fax: 781-321-9223. Website: http://www.foodaddicts.org E-mail: famail@aol.com

O-Anon *International. 6 affiliated groups. Founded 1979.* 12-step fellowship of friends and relatives of compulsive overeaters. Group development guidelines. Write: O-Anon, P.O. Box 44020, Rio Rancho, NM, 87174-4020. Call 505-891-2664; Fax: 505-891-4320. Email:info@oa.org Website: http://www.oa.org

National Association to Advance Fat Acceptance (NAAFA) *National. 50 chapters. Founded 1969.* Fights size discrimination and provides fat people with the tools for self-empowerment. Public education regarding obesity. Provides a forum for peer support and activism. Dues $35 (includes newsletter). Special interest groups include: youth, families, gays, diabetics, men, women, sleep apnea, military, mental health professionals, and couples. Write: NAAFA, P.O. Box 188620, Sacramento, CA 95818. Call 916-558-6880. Website: http://www.naafa.org

SEX / LOVE ADDICTION

STATEWIDE

New Jersey/Delaware Valley Sexaholics Anonymous Intergroup Mutual support for those who want to stop their sexually self-destructive thinking and behavior to become sexually sober. Several meeting locations throughout NJ. Call 1-800-739-2465 or 732-886-2142. *Website:* http://www.sa.org

S.L.A.A. (Sex and Love Addicts Anonymous) 12-Step. Fellowship for those who desire to stop living out a pattern of sex and love addiction, compulsive sexual behavior or emotional attachment. Meets in several locations throughout New Jersey. Write: Greater Delaware Valley Intergroup, The Augustine Fellowship (SLAA), PO Box 7437, Philadelphia, PA 19101. Call the Delaware Valley Intergroup 215-731-9760; Inspirational Line 215-574-2120 (day).

ATLANTIC

S.L.A.A. (Sex and Love Addicts Anonymous) 12-Step. Fellowship for those who desire to stop living out a pattern of sex and love addiction, compulsive sexual behavior or emotional attachment. Meets Tues., 7:30pm, First Presbyterian Church, 6001 Main St., Mays Landing. Call J.C. 609-625-6620 or Delaware Valley Intergroup 215-731-9760.

BERGEN

S-Anon 12-Step. Offers support for family members and the loved ones of those who are sexually addicted. Literature, phone help and newsletter Donation $2. Meets Tues., 7:30-8:30pm, First Presbyterian Church, Passaic and Union St., Hackensack. Call Tricia H. 201-651-9458 (eve).

Sexaholics Anonymous Mutual support for those who want to stop their sexually self-destructive thinking and behavior to become sexually sober. For information call Tom A. 908-351-3870, NJ Intergroup 1-800-739-2465 or 732-886-2142.
> **Ridgewood** Meets Thurs., 7:30-8:30pm.
> **Teaneck** Meets Tues. and Fri., 7-8am, St. Anatasias Church, 1095 Teaneck Rd.

BURLINGTON

S-Anon 12-Step. Offers support for family members and the loved ones of those who are sexually addicted. Literature. Meets Mon., 7:30-8:30pm, Prince of Peace Lutheran Church, 61 Route 70 East Marlton. Call Phyllis 609-239-7690 (day). *Website:* http://www.sanon.org

CAMDEN

Sexaholics Anonymous Mutual support for those who want to stop their sexually self-destructive thinking and behavior to become sexually sober. For information call Tom A. 908-351-3870, NJ Intergroup 1-800-739-2465 or 732-886-2142.
> **Stratford** Meets Wed., 7-8pm, Kennedy Gerontology Center.
> **Westmont** Meets Sat., 9-10am, Starting Point Inc., 215 Highland Ave.

S.L.A.A. (Sex and Love Addicts Anonymous) 12-Step. Fellowship for those who desire to stop living out a pattern of sex and love addiction, compulsive sexual behavior or emotional attachment. Meets Fri., 8pm, Conference Center of JFK Hospital, Gerontology Center, Laurel Rd., Stratford. Call Dana 856-566-1340 (day) or Delaware Valley Intergroup 215-731-9760.

ESSEX

Sexaholics Anonymous Mutual support for those who want to stop their sexually self-destructive thinking and behavior to become sexually sober. Meets Thurs., 8-9pm, (Tues., 8-9pm, July/Aug.), Unitarian Church, 67 Church St., Montclair. For meeting information call Tom A. 908-351-3870, NJ Intergroup 1-800-739-2465 or 732-886-2142.

S.L.A.A. (Sex and Love Addicts Anonymous) 12-Step. Fellowship for those who desire to stop living out a pattern of sex and love addiction, compulsive sexual behavior or emotional attachment. Call Delaware Valley Intergroup 215-731-9760.

Montclair Meets Mon., 7:30pm (members) and Fri., 7:30pm (beginners), 8:30pm (members), United Methodist Church, Chapel Room, 1st Floor, 24 North Fullerton St. Call George 973-481-5267 (Friday group), Mitch 201-445-6362 (Monday group).

Montclair *(WOMEN ONLY)* Meets Wed., 7:15-8:30pm, Evangelical Lutheran Church, 153 Park St. Call Randi 917-561-5326 (cell), or the church 973-744-6043.

HUDSON

Hoboken S.A.A. (Serenity Acceptance Affirmation) 12-Step. Support group for anyone concerned about their own addictive or compulsive sexual behavior. Meets Sun., 7-8:30pm, Hoboken Evangelical Free Church, 9th and Clinton St., Hoboken. Call Dave 201-459-8858. *Website:* http://www.saa-recovery.org

Sexaholics Anonymous Mutual support for those who want to stop their sexually self-destructive thinking and behavior to become sexually sober. Meets Tues., 7:30-8:30pm, Mt. Carmel Guild Catholic Services, 249 Virginia Ave., Jersey City. For information call Tom A. 908-351-3870, NJ Intergroup 1-800-739-2465 or 732-886-2142.

MIDDLESEX

S-Anon For family members and friends of those who are sexually addicted. Literature and phone help. Meets Tues., 7:30-9pm, Centenary United Methodist Church, Dellwood and Huxley Ave., Metuchen. Call Bari 908-303-9275 (eve). When calling please mention you are looking for information on "the Tuesday night meeting."

S-Anon Couples in Recovery Joint meeting for those who desire to work on their relationships, using the 12 steps of SA and S-Anon. Meets 3rd Sat., Centenary United Methodist Church, Metuchen. Call Lynne or Bob 732-698-1295.

Sexaholics Anonymous Mutual support for those who want to stop their sexually self-destructive thinking and behavior to become sexually sober. Meets Sun. 5-6:15pm and Wed., 7:30-8:30pm, St. Luke's Episcopal Church, Oak Ave. Metuchen. Call Tom A. 908-351-3870, NJ Intergroup 1-800-739-2465 or 732-886-2142.

MONMOUTH

S-Anon Offers support for family members and the loved ones of those who are sexually addicted.

Neptune Meets Fri., 7:30-8:30pm, Jersey Shore Medical Center, Route 33West. Call Pam 609-737-2452, Mary 732-681-2113 or Missy 732-899-9241.

Red Bank Meets Mon., 7:30pm, First United Methodist Church, Broad St. Before attending call Dianne 732-657-7442.

Sexaholics Anonymous Mutual support for those who want to stop their sexually self-destructive thinking and behavior to become sexually sober. For meeting information call Tom A. 908-351-3870, NJ Intergroup 1-800-739-2465 or 732-886-2142.

Lincroft Meets Mon., 7:30-8:30pm, St. Leo's Church, Hurley's Lane,

Neptune Meets Fri, 7:30-8:30pm, Jersey Shore Medical Center, Route 33 West.

Red Bank Meets Sun., 8:30-9:30am, Riverview Medical Center, Blazedale Bldg., 5th Floor Auditorium, Riverview Plaza.

Red Bank Meets Wed., noon-1pm, 1st Baptist Church, Oakland and Maple Ave.

MORRIS

S-Anon For family members and loved ones of those who are sexually addicted. Meets Mon., 8-9pm, St. John's Episcopal Church, South Bergen and Blackwell St., Dover. Donation $2/mtg. Call Barbara 973-659-0901.

Sexaholics Anonymous Mutual support for those who want to stop their sexually self-destructive thinking and behavior to become sexually sober. Call Tom A. 908-351-3870 (day), NJ Intergroup 1-800-739-2465 or 732-886-2142.

Dover Meets Mon., 8-9:15pm, St. John's Episcopal Church, 111 South Bergen St.

Morris Plains Meets Tues., 1pm; Thurs., noon-1pm and Fri., noon-12:45pm, St. Paul's Episcopal Church, Hillview Ave.

S.L.A.A. (Sex and Love Addictions Anonymous) 12-Step. Fellowship for those who desire to stop living out a pattern of sex and love addiction, compulsive sexual behavior or emotional attachment. Meets Tues., 7:30pm, Morristown Memorial Hospital, 100 Madison Ave., Franklin Wing, Room F571, Morristown. Call Lee 908-876-4081 or Delaware Valley Intergroup 215-731-9760.

OCEAN

S-Anon Offers support for family members and the loved ones of those who are sexually addicted. Meets Tues., 7:30pm, Manchester. Before attending call Dianne 732-657-7442. *Website:* http://www.sanon.org

Sexaholics Anonymous Mutual support for those who want to stop their sexually self-destructive thinking and behavior to become sexually sober. Call Tom A. 908-351-3870 (day), NJ Intergroup 1-800-739-2465 or 732-886-2142.

> **Beachwood** Meets Tues., 8-9pm, St. Paul Lutheran Church, 130 Cable Ave.

> **Toms River** Meets Sat., 9:30-10:30am, Presbyterian Church of Toms River, 1070 Hooper Ave.

PASSAIC

Sexaholics Anonymous Mutual support for those who want to stop their sexually self-destructive thinking and behavior to become sexually sober. Meets Mon., 7:30-9pm and Sat., 7:30-8:30am, United Methodist Church, 139 Church St., Little Falls. For information call Tom A. 908-351-3870, NJ Intergroup 1-800-739-2465 or 732-886-2142.

SOMERSET

Freedom Group 12-Step. Christ-based support group for men wanting freedom from being sexually driven. Confidential. Rap sessions, phone help, literature, guest speakers. Call Millington Baptist Church 908-647-0594 and ask for "Freedom Group" or Paul 908-705-3265.

Sexaholics Anonymous Mutual support for those who want to stop their sexually self-destructive thinking and behavior to become sexually sober. Meets Tues., 7-8pm and Thurs., 7:45-8:45pm, Wilson Memorial Union Church, Hillcrest Rd., Watchung. Call Tom A. 908-351-3870 (day), NJ Intergroup 1-800-739-2465 or 732-886-2142.

S.L.A.A. (Sex and Love Addicts Anonymous) 12-Step. Fellowship for those who desire to stop living out a pattern of sex and love addiction, compulsive sexual behavior or emotional attachment. Meets Sun. and Thurs., 8pm, Bound Brook Presbyterian Church, 409 Mountain Ave. and E. Union Ave., Bound Brook. Call Steve 908-413-2470 or Delaware Valley Intergroup 215-731-9760.

UNION

Sexaholics Anonymous Mutual support for those who want to stop their sexually self-destructive thinking and behavior to become sexually sober. For meeting information call Tom A. 908-351-3870, NJ Intergroup 1-800-739-2465 or 732-886-2142.

> **Cranford** Meets Mon.-Fri., 7:15-8:15am; Mon.-Fri., noon-1pm; Fri. 8-9:15pm; Sat., 7:30-8:30pm and Sun., 1:30-2:30pm, Cranford United Methodist Church, 201 Lincoln Ave.,

Elizabeth Meets Sat., noon-1pm, St. Mary's of the Assumption.

Elizabeth *(WOMEN ONLY)* Meets Thurs., 7-8pm, St. Paul's Evangelical Lutheran Church, 81 Galloping Hill Rd.

NATIONAL

Augustine Fellowship, Sex & Love Addicts Anonymous *International. 1234 affiliated groups. Founded 1976.* 12-Step. Fellowship based on A.A. for those who desire to stop living out a pattern of sex and love addiction, obsessive-compulsive sexual behavior or emotional attachment. Newsletter, journal, information and referrals, conferences, phone support. Write: Augustine Fellowship, PO Box 338, Norwood, MA 02062-0338. Call 781-255-8825 (voice mail); Fax: 781-255-9190. *Website:* http://www.slaafws.org *Email:* slaafws@slaafws.org

COSA (Codependents Of Sex Addicts) National Service Organization *National. 50+ affiliated groups. Founded 1980.* A self-help program of recovery using the 12-steps adapted from A.A. & Al-Anon, for those involved in relationships with people who have compulsive sexual behavior. Assistance in starting new groups. Newsletter ($12). Write: COSA NSO Inc., PO Box 14537, Minneapolis, MN 55414. Call 763-537-6904 (answering service - leave message). *Website:* http://www.cosa-recovery.org *Email:* info@cosa-recovery.org

Love-N-Addiction *International. 73 chapters. Founded 1986.* Explores how loving can become an addiction. Builds a healthy support system to aid in recovery from addictive love into healthy love. Uses ideas from book "Women Who Love Too Much" by Robin Norwood. Chapter development guidelines ($15). Write: Love-N-Addiction, PO Box 759, Willimantic, CT 06226. Call Carolyn Meister 860-423-2344 (will return call collect or leave mailing address).

Overcomers In Christ *International. Founded 1987.* Recovery program that deals with every aspect of addiction and dysfunction (spiritual, physical, mental, emotional and social). Uses Overcomers goals which are Christ-centered. Resources, information and referrals. Assistance in starting new groups. Literature. Write: Overcomers In Christ , PO Box 34460, Omaha, NE 68134-04604. Call 402-573-0966; Fax: 402-573-0960. *Website:* http://www.OvercomersInChrist.org *Email:* OIC@OvercomersInChrist.org

S-Anon *International. 200 affiliated groups. Founded 1984.* 12-Step. Group for persons who have a friend or family member with a sexual addiction. Assistance available for starting groups. Conferences. Quarterly newsletter ($10). Write: S-Anon, PO Box 111242, Nashville, TN 37222. Call 615-833-3152. *Website:* http://www.sanon.org *Email:* sanon@sanon.org

Sex Addicts Anonymous *International. 736 groups. Founded 1977.* 12-Step. Fellowship of men and women whose primary purpose is to stop addictive sexual behavior and to help others recover from sexual addiction. Bi-monthly newsletter. Write: ISO of SAA, PO Box 70949, Houston, TX 77270. Call 713-869-4902 or 1-800-477-8191. *Website:* http://www.saa-recovery.org *Email:* info@saa-recovery.org

Sexaholics Anonymous *International. 700 chapters. Founded 1979.* Program of recovery for those who want to stop sexually self-destructive thinking and behavior. Mutual support to achieve and maintain sexual sobriety. Phone network, quarterly newsletter, literature and books. Guidelines to help start a similar group. Write: S.A., PO Box 3565, Brentwood, TN 37024-3565. Call 615-370-6062 or 1-866-424-8777; Fax: 615-370-0882. *Website:* http://www.sa.org *Email:* saico@sa.org

Sexual Compulsives Anonymous *(BILINGUAL) International. 118+ groups. Founded 1982.* Fellowship of men and women who share their experience, strength and hope that they may solve their common problem and help others to recover from sexual compulsion. Based on the 12-Step model of recovery. Newsletter, information and referrals, phone support, conferences. Guidelines for starting similar groups. Write: SCA, PO Box 1585 Old Chelsea Station, New York, NY 10011. Call 1-800-977-4325. *Website:* http://www.sca-recovery.org *Email:* info@sca-recovery.org

Sexual Recovery Anonymous *International. 32 affiliated groups. Founded 1990.* 12-Step. Fellowship of men and women who share their experience, strength and hope with each other that they may solve their common problem and help others to recover. Online referrals, literature and support also available. For those with a desire to stop compulsive sexual behavior. Write: SRA, PO Box 1296, Redondo Beach, CA, 90278. Call 212-340-4650 (recorded information); 323-850-8565 (Los Angeles area); or 604-290-9382 (BC, Canada). *Website:* http://www.sexualrecovery.org *Email:* info@sexualrecovery.org

---

Groups are constantly changing. Starting, ending, moving. Call us for the most up-to-date information from our database.
1-800-367-6274

SMOKING
(see also toll-free helplines)

STATEWIDE

Nicotine Anonymous 12-Step program of recovery for people who want to help themselves and others recover from nicotine addiction and live free of nicotine in all forms. For meeting information call Bill C. 201-947-3305 or 631-665-0527 (NJ/NY/PA Intergroup). *Website:* http://www.nicotine-anonymous.org

New Jersey Quitnet *Online.* Free service provides access to peer support groups where one can learn from others who are quitting, and get advice from those who have successfully quit. Once registered, members get a Quitting Guide to help them develop their individually tailored plan for quitting. *Website:* http://www.nj.quitnet.com

ATLANTIC

Nicotine Anonymous 12-Step. Mutual support for persons wishing to stop smoking and their use of nicotine. Meets Mon., 7pm, Shore Memorial Hospital, Shore Rd., Conference Center, Somers Point. Call Beth B. 609-652-2514.

BERGEN

Nicotine Anonymous 12-Step. Mutual support for persons wishing to stop smoking and their use of nicotine. Call Bill C. 201-947-3305.
> **Paramus** Meets Wed., 7pm, Valley Hospital, Luckow Pavilion, One Valley Health Plaza.
> **Teaneck** Meets Sat., 7pm, St. Mark's Episcopal Church, Chadwick and Grange Rd.
> **Teaneck** Meets Tues., 7am, St. Paul's Lutheran Church, 61 Church St.

BURLINGTON

Nicotine Anonymous 12-Step. Mutual support for persons wishing to stop smoking and their use of nicotine. Meets Tues., 6pm, Divine Word Missionaries, Gym, 2nd Floor, 101 Park St., Bordentown. Call Tom D. 609-298-1866.

CAMDEN

Nicotine Anonymous 12-Step. Fellowship of men and women who want to achieve and maintain a nicotine-free life. Meets Mon., 7pm, Kennedy Hospital, 5th Floor, Chapel Ave., Cherry Hill. Call Ellie G. 856-354-0887.

Nicotine Anonymous 12-Step. Fellowship of men and women who want to achieve and maintain a nicotine-free life. Meets Wed., 6-7pm, Starting Point, 215 Highland Ave., Westmont. Call Carol 856-354-0431 (day/eve), Sharon 856-933-7918 (day/eve) or Roger 856-931-0273 (day/eve).

CAPE MAY

Nicotine Anonymous 12-Step. Fellowship of men and women who want to achieve and maintain a nicotine-free life. Call Joseph P. 609-729-9145.

<u>Wildwood</u> Meets Wed., 7pm, The Cape Self-Help, 4410 Pacific Ave.

<u>Wildwood</u> Meets Sat., 3:30-4:30pm, The Hut, 113 West Oak Ave.

MERCER

Nicotine Anonymous 12-Step. Fellowship of men and women who want to achieve and maintain a nicotine-free life. Meets Fri., 7pm, Hamilton Hospital, Library near Gift Shop, Whitehorse and Klockner Rd., Hamilton. Call Josephine 609-890-9176.

MIDDLESEX

Nicotine Anonymous 12-Step. Fellowship of men and women who want to achieve and maintain a nicotine-free life.

<u>Edison</u> Meets Tues., 7:30-8:30pm, Mortgage Money Mart, Tano Mall, 1st Bldg., 1st Floor, 1199 Amboy Ave. Call Frank N. 732-548-9423 (day).

<u>Metuchen</u> Meets Mon., 7:30pm, Centenary United Methodist Church, Room 20, 200 Hillside Ave. Call Jane G. 732-549-5955.

S.M.A.R.T. Recovery (Self-Management And Recovery Training) *Professionally-run.* Self-help group for individuals wanting to gain their independence from addictive behaviors (drugs, including alcohol and nicotine and other compulsive behaviors including gambling, eating disorders). SMART is an abstinence program based on cognitive-behavioral education and principles, especially those of rational-emotive behavior therapy. Meets Mon., 6:30-7:45pm, Rutgers University, Busch Campus, Psychology Building, Room A224, Piscataway. Call Tom Morgan 732-445-0902. *Website:* http://www.smartrecovery.org

MONMOUTH

Smoke Free Support Group *Professionally-run.* Offer support and education for those who are thinking about quitting, recently quit or are struggling to quit smoking. Meets 4th Tues., (except June, July, Aug.), 7-9pm, Monmouth Medical Center, 300 Second Ave., Long Branch. Call 732-923-6990 (8:30am-5pm).

MORRIS

Nicotine Anonymous 12-Step. Fellowship of men and women who want to achieve and maintain a nicotine-free life.

> **Boonton** Meets Thurs., 6:30pm, Saint Clare's Behavioral Health Center, Powerville Rd. Call Goran P. 973-586-3359.
> **Butler** Meets Tues., 7:30pm, Church of Nazarene, 188 Kiel Ave., (off Route 23 North), Downstairs Room. Call Debbie P. 973-208-2325.

PASSAIC

Nicotine Anonymous 12-Step. Fellowship of men and women who want to achieve and maintain a nicotine-free life. Meets Tues., 9pm, Eva's Recovery Center, 393 Main St., Paterson. Call Samuel B. 973-851-7469.

INTERNATIONAL

Nicotine Anonymous World Services *International. 500+ groups. Founded 1985.* 12-Step. Program for people who want to recover from nicotine addiction and live free of nicotine in all forms. Welcomes all, including persons using cessation programs and nicotine withdrawal aids. Write: NAWS, 419 Main St. PMB #370, Huntington Beach, CA 92648. Call 714-536-4539. *Website:* http://www.nicotine-anonymous.org *Email:* info@nicotine-anonymous.org

---

**"The isolated individual is not a real person.
A real person is one who lives in and for others.
And the more personal relationships we form with
others, the more we truly realize ourselves as persons.**

**It has even been said that there can be no true person
unless there are two, entering into communication with
one another."**

--Kallistos Ware

THE 12-STEPS OF ALCOHOLICS ANONYMOUS

Many self-help programs adapt the 12-steps of Alcoholics Anonymous for their particular problem. This material can be reprinted and adapted with permission form Alcoholics Anonymous World Services.

1. We admitted we were powerless over alcohol--that our lives had become unmanageable.

2. We came to believe that a Power greater than ourselves could restore us to sanity.

3. Made a decision to turn our will and our lives over to the care of God as we understood Him.

4. Made a searching and fearless moral inventory of ourselves.

5. Admitted to God, to ourselves, and to another human being the exact nature of our wrongs.

6. Were entirely ready to have God remove all these defects of character.

7. Humbly asked Him to remove our shortcomings.

8. Made a list of all persons we had harmed, and became willing to make amends to them all.

9. Made direct amends to such people wherever possible, except when to do so would injure them or others.

10. Continued to take personal inventory and when we were wrong promptly admitted it.

11. Sought through prayer and meditation to improve our conscious contact with God as we understood Him, praying only for knowledge of His will for us and the power to carry that out.

12. Having had a spiritual awakening as a result of these steps, we tried to carry this message to alcoholics, and to practice these principles in all our affairs.

The 12-steps are reprinted with permission of Alcoholics Anonymous World Services, Inc. Permission to reprint the 12-steps does not mean that A.A. is affiliated with this program. A.A. is a program of recovery from alcoholism - use of the 12-steps in connection with programs and activities which are patterned after A.A. but which address other problems, does not imply otherwise.

BEREAVEMENT

BEREAVEMENT (GENERAL)

STATEWIDE

COPS (Concerns Of Police Surviving, Inc. *(Garden State Chapter)* Peer support for families and co-workers of police officers who have died in the line of duty. Mutual sharing, phone help, rap sessions and social events. For information call 908-389-9559 *Website:* http://www.gardenstatecops.com *Email:* gssnjcops@gardenstatecops.com

Iraq/Afghanistan War Family Bereavement Groups *Professionally-run.* Veteran centers in New Jersey have support groups and related services for families of military killed in the war. Meetings vary. Write: Ann Talmage, Newark Vet Center, 45 Academy St., Suite 303, Newark, NJ 07102. For information contact the nearest center: Newark (Essex) 973-645-5954; Jersey City (Hudson) 201-748-4467; Trenton (Mercer) 609-989-2260; Ventnor (Atlantic) 609-487-8387. *Website:* http://www.va.gov/rcs *Email:* ann.talmage@med.va.gov

Rainbows, Inc. *Professionally-run.* Peer support for children and teens who are grieving the loss of a parent due to death, divorce or abandonment. Meets various locations throughout NJ. Helps to implement programs throughout the state. Call 908-608-0888 (day). *Website:* www.rainbowsnj.org *Email:* info@rainbowsnj.org

ATLANTIC

Coping With Loss *Professionally-run.* Mutual support and education for persons grieving the death of a loved one. Group runs for 6 week sessions, 4 times per year. Meeting location varies throughout Atlantic County. Call 609-272-2424 (day).

BERGEN

Bereavement Support Group *Professionally-run.* Mutual support and education for persons who have suffered the loss of a loved one. Literature. Groups run for 5-8 week sessions, 2-3 times per year, Emerson Public Library, 20 Palisades Ave., Emerson. Call Elizabeth Steel, Frances Castello or Wendy Megerman 201-358-2900 (day).

Bereavement Support Group Mutual support for persons (age 55+) to discuss issues, feelings and experiences due to the loss of a loved one. Rap sessions, literature and phone help. Meets Thurs., 1:30-2:30pm, Southeast Senior Center, 228 Grand Ave., Englewood. Call Gail Farina or Frieda Wells 201-569-4080.

Bereavement Support Group Support for adults who have lost a loved one due to cancer. Meets Tues., 6:30-8:30pm, Gilda's Club Northern NJ, 575 Main St., Hackensack. Call 201-457-1670 (day).

Bereavement Support Group *Professionally-run.* Support for newly bereaved, (2 years or less), who are experiencing normal grief. Urban Plaza Building, 25 E. Salem St., 3rd Floor, Hackensack. Pre-registration required. Call 201-342-7766 (day).

Bereavement Support Group *Professionally-run.* Mutual support and education for bereaved experiencing the grief and loss of a loved one. Groups run for approximately 8 sessions, periodically throughout the year. Meets at Englewood Hospital & Medical Center, 74 Demarest Ave, Englewood, NJ, 07631. Pre-registration is required. Call Nicholas J. Biancola, Jr. 201-541-2677 (day) or 201-894-3333 (day/eve)

Bereavement Support Group *Professionally-run.* Support and comfort for those grieving the loss of a loved one. Meets for 8 week sessions, several times a year, Wallington Presbyterian Church, 9 Bond St., Wallington. Call Rev. Peter Carey 973-779-2640.

Bereavement Support Group *Professionally-run.* Mutual support and education for persons who have suffered the loss of a loved one. Groups run for 8 sessions, 3 times year. Meets Mon., 6:30-8pm, Bergen Community Health Care, 400 Old Hook Rd., Suite G 3, Westwood. Call Frances Castello or Elizabeth Steel 201-358-2900 (day).

Bereavement Support Group *Professionally-run.* Mutual support and education for persons who are coping with the loss of a loved one. Meets 3rd Tues., 6:30-8pm, Bergen Community Health Care, 400 Old Hook Rd., Hospice Conference Room, Westwood. Call Elizabeth Steel 201-358-2900 (day).

New Start Bereavement Groups Offers emotional support and education for grief and its impact on the bereaved. Meets 2nd and 4th Wed., 11:30am-1pm or 1st and 3rd Tues., 7-8:30pm, Dorothy Kraft Building, 15 Essex Rd., Paramus. Before attending call Mary Maguire Reddy 201-291-6243.

Pathways Bereavement Support Group *Professionally-run.* Support group with educational components for people bereaved 4 or more months. Group runs for 8 sessions various times per year. Meets at Valley Hospice, 15 Essex Rd., Paramus. Pre-registration required. Call Mary Maguire Reddy 201-291-6243.

Rainbows, Inc. *Professionally-run.* Peer support for children, (age 4 - teens), who have experienced a family loss because of death, separation, divorce or abandonment. Goals are to: provide peer support, furnish an understanding of the grief experience, assist in building a stronger sense of self-esteem and teach appropriate coping mechanisms. Meets Tues., (Sept.-Dec.) and Wed., (Jan.-Apr.), Ridgewood YMCA, 112 Oak St., Ridgewood. Registration required. Call Kathy Meding 201-444-5600 ext. 332 (day). *Email:* kmeding@ridgewoodym.org

Safe Space Support for bereaved high school teens that have lost a loved one through death. Education, mutual sharing and literature. Meets for 8 week sessions, Creative Living Center, 37E Allendale Ave., Allendale. Call Dan Bottorff 201-327-2424 ext. 253 or Penny Gadzini ext. 254. *Website:* www.creativelivingresource.org

Separated, Divorced, Widowed and Bereaved Catholics Referrals to groups for emotional, spiritual support and social activities for separated, divorced, bereaved, men and women. Groups are sponsored by various churches throughout the counties and are open to people of any faith. Call Family Life Ministries, Archdiocese of Newark 973-497-4327.

BURLINGTON

Bereavement Support Group Mutual support for those suffering the loss a loved one. Various meeting locations and times. See group listings and contacts online at: http://www.dioceseoftrenton.org/church/consolation.asp (scroll down to "Support Groups for Bereavement") or call Office of Family Life, Trenton Diocese 609-406-7400 ext. 5557 (day).

Bereavement Support Group for Friends and Family *Professionally-run.* Support for friends and family grieving the death of a loved one to help cope with the loss. Meets 3rd Wed., (except July/Aug.), 7-8:30pm, Dougherty's Funeral Home, 2200 Trenton Rd., Levittown, PA. Call Deborah Gawthrop or Lisa Collier 215-624-8190 (day).

Big Hurts, Little Tears *Professionally-run.* Support group for 3-5 year-olds who have been affected by a loss. Meetings vary, Samaritan Hospice, Marlton. Pre-registration required. Before attending call The Samaritan Center for Grief Support 1-800-596-8550. *Website:* http://www.samaritanhospice.org

Daughters Without Mothers *Professionally-run.* Support group for women who have experienced the death of a mom. Education, discussions and an opportunity to share stories. Meetings vary, Samaritan Hospice, Marlton. Pre-registration required. Before attending call The Samaritan Center for Grief Support 856-596-8550. *Website:* http://www.samaritanhospice.org

Grief For The Loss Of A Pet *Professionally-run.* Offers grief support for persons coping with the loss of a companion animal. Meetings vary, Samaritan Hospice, Marlton. Pre-registration required. Before attending call The Samaritan Hospice 856-596-8550. *Website:* http://www.samaritanhospice.org

Helping Hand Grief Support Group Support for someone bereaving the loss of a loved one (including death of a child, loss to homicide or suicide) through education, encouragement, counseling and understanding. Families welcome. Meets 1st and 3rd Mon., 7-9pm, for 10 week sessions, Fellowship Alliance Chapel, (Log house in back of church), 199 Church Rd., Medford. Call Wanda and George Stein 609-953-7333 ext. 309 (day/eve).

Just the Guys *Professionally-run.* Mutual support for adult men grieving the loss of a family member or friend. Meetings vary, Samaritan Hospice, Marlton. Pre-registration required. Before attending call 856-596-8550 (day). *Website:* http://www.samaritanhospice.org

SIGH (Sharing in Grief and Hope) *Professionally-run.* Mutual support for anyone who has experienced the death of a loved one. Meets various days and locations. Pre-registration required. Before attending call The Samaritan Center for Grief Support 1-800-596-8550. *Website:* http://www.samaritanhospice.org

CAMDEN

Bereavement Support Group Support and comfort for newly bereaved adults grieving the loss of a loved one. Open to those who lost someone within the past year. Families welcome. Phone help and literature. Runs for 8 week sessions, 2 times per year, in various locations and times. Call Bereavement Coordinator 856-414-1155 (day).

Bereavement Support Group for Family and Friends *Professionally-run.* Emotional and educational grief support for family and friends grieving the death of a loved one. Meets 1st Wed., (except July/Aug./Sept.), 7-8:30pm, Lambie Funeral Home, Rhawn and Rowland St., NE Philadelphia, PA. Call Debbie Gawthrop 215-624-8190 (day).

Breath of Life Bereavement Support Group *Professionally-run.* Support for anyone grieving the loss of a loved one. Education, rap sessions, guest speakers and phone help. Meets 1st & 3rd Fri., 7-8pm, Bethany Baptist Church, 1115 Gibbsboro Rd., Lindenwald. Call Charlene Ransom 856-782-9540 (day) or Miki Brown 856-782-6749 (day). *Website:* http://www.abundantharvest.com *E-mail:* healinghearts@abundantharvest.com

Grief Management of St. Rose of Lima Mutual support for anyone grieving the loss of a significant person in their life due to death, separation or divorce. Families welcome. Meets Thurs., (for 12 week sessions), 7:30-9:30pm, St. Rose of Lima, Parish Lounge, 300 Kings Highway, Haddon Heights. Before attending call Sister Eucharista Johnson 856-310-1770. *Website:* http://www.strosenj.com

ESSEX

Adult Bereavement Group Offers mutual support for adults bereaving the death of a loved one. Newly bereaved group meets twice per month for eight weeks. Also offers an ongoing group for persons who have already attended a professionally-run bereavement group or had professional counseling. Meets 7-8pm, Hospice of NJ, 400 Broadacres Dr., 4th Floor, Bloomfield. For information call Michael Teague 973-893-0818 ext. 213 or Jason Coveleski 973-893-0818 ext. 206.

Adult Bereavement Support Group *Professionally-run.* Mutual support for any adult who has experienced a significant loss. Meets for 6-8 week sessions, (Fall/Spring), St. Barnabas Hospice and Palliative Care Center, 187 Millburn Ave., Millburn. Call St. Barnabas 973-322-4800 (day).

Daughter's Bereavement Mutual support for adult women who have experienced the loss of their mother. Meets for 7 week sessions, St. Barnabas Hospice and Palliative Care Center, 95 Old Short Hills Rd., West Orange. For meeting information call Henry de Mena 973-322-4800.

Family Bereavement Group *Professionally-run.* Group for spouses who lost spouses with young children (age 5-18) at home. Separate groups for children run concurrently. Meets 6:30-8pm, Saint Barnabas Corporate Building, 95 Old Short Hills Rd., West Orange. For meeting day call Henry de Mena 973-322-4858 (day).

Growing Through Loss Bereavement Group Offers a caring and supportive environment for persons grieving the loss of a loved one. Meets for 6-8 sessions twice a year, (Spring and Fall), St. Barnabas Medical Center, Old Short Hills Rd., Livingston. Registration required. Call Pastoral Care 973-322-5015 (day). Fax: 973-322-2410.

Our Lady of The Lake Bethany Support Group *Professionally-run.* Provides mutual support for persons affected by the loss of a loved one. Offers mutual sharing, education, literature and guest speakers. Meets twice a month, 7:30-9pm, Our Lady of The Lake Church, 32 Lakeside Ave., Verona. For meeting information call JoAnn 973-585-7278 (eve).

Rainbows, Inc. *Professionally-run.* Peer support for children and adolescents (kindergarten-eighth grade) who are grieving the loss of a parent due to death, divorce or abandonment. Meets Mon., (Spring/Fall), 7 week sessions, First Presbyterian Church, 10 Fairview Ave., Verona. Call Rev. Julia Dawson 973-239-3561 (day).

Separated, Divorced, Widowed and Bereaved Catholics Referrals to groups for emotional, spiritual support and social activities for separated, divorced, widowed or bereaved, men and women. Groups are sponsored by various churches throughout the county and are open to people of any faith. For information call Family Life Ministry, Newark Diocese 973-497-4327.

GLOUCESTER

Center for People in Transition *Professionally-run.* Assists displaced homemakers to become emotionally and economically self-sufficient through life skills training, career decision making, education or vocational training and supportive services. Evening divorce and bereavement support groups for men and women. Call 856-415-2222 (day). *Email:* peopleintransition@gccnj.edu

Grief and Loss Support Group *Professionally-run.* Mutual support for men and women grieving the loss of a loved one. Guest speakers, educational series, phone help and literature. Meets 3rd Wed., 7-9pm, Gloucester County Library, Bridgeton Pike, (Route 45), Mullica Hill. Call Joyce Tucker 856-223-1803.

SIGH (Sharing In Grief and Hope) *Professionally-run.* Mutual support for persons who have experienced the death of a loved one. Meets various days and locations. Pre-registration required. Before attending call The Samaritan Center for Grief Support 1-800-596-8550. *Website:* http://www.samaritanhospice.org

S.O.S. (Survivors Offering Support) Mutual support and encouragement for persons (ages 35-55) who have lost a family member (spouse, child or other family member) through death. Provides emotional support and education on the grieving process. Meets alternate Mon., 7pm, Gloucester County Community Church, Sewell. Before attending call Glenn 856-296-5262.

HUDSON

Bereavement Support *Professionally-run.* Support through pastoral care. Open to anyone feeling the loss of a loved one. Meets Thurs., 6:30pm, Christ Hospital, Chapel, Palisades Ave., Jersey City. Before attending call Pastoral Care Dept. 201-795-8397.

Hudson Hospice Bereavement Group *Professionally-run.* Provides a supportive environment for those grieving the recent death of someone close. The overall goal of the group is to help move toward the reconciliation of grief. Meets 1st and 2nd Wed., in Bayonne. For meeting information call Hospice 201-433-6225 (day). *Email:* OLS9395@comcast.net

Hudson Hospice Children's Bereavement Support Group *Professionally-run.* Program to help grieving families. Children (age 4-17) attend a weekly art therapy group while the parents participate in a companion parent group. Groups meet for 10 week sessions in Bayonne. Call Sharon or Sister Alice McCoy 201-433-6225 (day). *Email:* ols9395@comcast.net

Rainbows, Inc. *Professionally-run.* Peer support for children and adolescents (kindergarten - eighth grade) who are grieving the loss of a parent due to death, divorce or abandonment. Parent group meets concurrently. Meets Mon., 7-8pm, (Oct.-Dec.), St. Anne's School, Parish Center, Jersey City. Call Sister Alberta 201-656-2490 (day) or 201-963-0998 (eve).

Separated, Divorced, Widowed and Bereaved Catholics Referrals to groups for emotional, spiritual support and social activities for separated, divorced, widowed and bereaved, men and women. Groups are sponsored by various churches throughout the county and are open to people of any faith. For information call Family Life Ministry, Newark Diocese 973-497-4327.

HUNTERDON

Bereavement Support Group Mutual support for persons who have experienced the death of a loved one. Sessions run for 6-8 weeks, 2 times per year. Meets various locations throughout the county. For meeting information call Family Life Office 732-562-1990 ext. 1624.

Grieving and Growing Through Loss *Professionally-run.* Mutual support for persons going through the grief process. Meets 2nd and 4th Thurs., 7-8:30pm, Hunterdon Hospice Office, Hunterdon Regional Community Health Care, 5 Bartles Corner Rd., Flemington. Call 908-788-6600 (day).

MERCER

Bereavement Support Group *Professionally-run.* Mutual support for individuals whose loss has occurred at least 2 or more months ago. Meets 2nd and 4th Tues., 5-6:30pm, Cancer Institute of NJ at Hamilton, 2575 Klockner Rd., Hamilton. Before attending call Elsje Reiss, MSW, LCSW 609-584-2818 (day).

Bereavement Support Group Mutual support for those suffering the loss of a loved one. See group listings and contacts online at: http://www.dioceseoftrenton.org/church/consolation.asp (scroll down to "Support Groups for Bereavement") or call Trenton Diocese 609-406-7400 ext. 5557 (day).

Caring and Sharing Mutual support for anyone suffering the loss of a loved one. Meets 1st Wed., 7-9pm, Saul Colonial Home, 3795 Nottingham Way, Hamilton Square. Call Mary Lou Pizzullo 609-587-7072.

Coping with Bereavement *Professionally-run.* Support for those who have lost a family member or friend. Educational series. Meets 3rd Mon., 1-2:30pm, Princeton Senior Resource Center, Suzanne Patterson Building, (behind Borough Hall), 45 Stockton St., Princeton. Call Joann Laveman, LCSW or Cheryl Regis 609-497-4900 (day).

SIGH (Sharing In Grief and Hope) *Professionally-run.* Mutual support for any person who has experienced the death of a loved one. Meeting days vary, Hamilton Township. Pre-registration required. Before attending call The Samaritan Center for Grief Support 1-800-596-8550. *Website:* www.samaritanhospice.org

MIDDLESEX

Journey Through Grief Bereavement Support Group A non-denominational support group for the recently bereaved. Phone help. Meets 2nd Mon., 7:30-9pm, Queenship of Mary Church, Dey Rd. and Scudders Mill Rd., Plainsboro. Call Lorrie Quinlan 732-821-8447 (day).

St. James Bereavement Support Group On-going emotional support for those who have lost a loved one through death. Meets in Woodbridge. Call Sister Marie Pierson 732-634-0500 ext. 14 (day).

MONMOUTH

Art Therapy for Bereaved Children *Professionally-run.* Bereavement program for children who have lost a loved one. Uses art therapy to help children address their feelings. Meets periodically for 7 week sessions, Riverview Medical Center, 1 Riverview Plaza, Red Bank. Call 732-530-2382.

Bereavement Support Group *Professionally-run.* Mutual support for adults dealing with the death of a loved one. Meets 2nd and 4th Tues., 7:30pm, Bayshore Community Hospital, TCU Activity Room, 727 N. Beers St., (main lobby to 2 East Floor), Holmdel. Call Chaplain Anna Esposito 732-739-5888.

Bereavement Support Group *Professionally-run.* Mutual support for the loss of a spouse and adult children bereaving the death of a parent. Meets for 6 weeks, several times per year, Riverview Medical Center, Cancer Center, 1 Riverview Plaza, Red Bank. Call Sister Vida O'Leary 732-530-2382.

Bereavement Support Group Mutual support for those suffering the loss of a loved one. Various meeting locations and times. See group listings and contacts online at: http://www.dioceseoftrenton.org/church/consolation.asp (scroll down to "Support Groups for Bereavement") or call Office of Family Life, Trenton Diocese 609-406-7400 ext. 5557 (day).

HUGS (Help Us Grieve Someone) Confidential non-denominational bereavement group where those who have lost loved ones can share their feelings with others who truly understand what they are going through. Literature. Meets twice a month, 7:30pm, Old Tennent Presbyterian Church, Old Scott's Hall, 452 Tennent Rd., Tennent. For information call Rose Olson 732-845-9475 (day/eve). *Website:* http://www.hugsonline.net

Living With Loss *Professionally-run.* Mutual support for persons who have experienced the loss of a loved one. Meets Mon., 11:30am-1pm, CentraState Medical Center, Route 537, Freehold. Call Bunny Salomon 732-617-2221 (day/eve).

Mourning After, The *Professionally-run.* Support for people who are grieving the loss of a loved one. Group uses a wide range of interactive and creative interventions to assist in the grieving process. Meets Fri., 11:30am-1pm, Center Playhouse, 35 South St., (downtown) Freehold. Call Bernice Garfield or Bob Szita 732-577-1076. *Website:* http://www.actionartz.com *Email:* griefcounseling@actionartz.com

St. Rose Bereavement Support Group *Professionally-run.* Support for those who are experiencing grief due to the death of a loved one. Offers support to members while working through the changes in their lives by sharing their stories in a faith community. Guest speakers, phone help, literature, prayer and music. Meets 1st and 3rd Thurs., 7:30-8:30pm, (June/Aug. meetings are held only on 1st Thurs.), St.

Rose Rectory, 603 7th Ave., Belmar. Call Deacon Normand or Marie Bailey 732-774-0515 (day/eve) or Rosemarie Reilly 732-681-4745 (day/eve).

MORRIS

Adult Bereavement Support Group *Professionally-run.* Support for newly bereaved adults due to the loss of a loved one to cancer. Meets Wed., 5:30-6:30pm, Saint Clare's Hospital, Pocono Rd., Denville. Call 973-625-6176 (voice mail). *Email:* bjohnson@saintclares.org

Children's Bereavement Group *Professionally-run.* Provides support to children (age 6-13) who have experienced a recent loss due to cancer. Runs for 8 week sessions. For information call Brandy Johnson, MSW 973-625-6176 (day).

Compassionate Care Hospice Support Group *Professionally-run.* Support for anyone grieving the loss of a loved one. Rap sessions. Meets 1st and 3rd Thurs., 7-8:30pm, Compassionate Care Hospice, 140 Littleton Rd., Suite 200, Parsippany. Call Lisa Morrow 973-402-4712 (day).

Living Through Grief *Professionally-run.* Mutual support for persons who have recently experienced the death of a loved one. Group runs for 8 week, various times per year. Meets various times and locations. Call Atlantic Hospice 973-379-8440.

Pet Loss Support Group *Professionally-run.* Helps individuals cope with the loss or impending loss of their companion animal to work through feelings of grief and mourning. Under 18 welcome. Meets 1st and 3rd Tues., 7:30pm, St. Hubert's Giralda, Woodland Ave., Madison. For information or directions call 973-377-7094 (day).

Rainbows and Prism Peer support for children and adolescents (kindergarten - eighth grade) who are grieving the loss of a parent due to death or divorce. Parent group meets concurrently. Meets Tues., 7:15-8pm, (Sept.-Jan.), Our Lady of Magnificat, 2 Miller Rd., Kinnelon. Call Claudette Meehan 973-492-9406 (eve) or Peggy Tana 973-838-7265.

Rainbows, Inc. *Professionally-run.* Peer support for children and adolescents (kindergarten - eighth grade) who are grieving the loss of a parent due to death divorce or abandonment. Meets Tues., 7:15pm, (Summer/Winter), for 7-14 weeks Mt. Tabor Church, 5 Simpson Ave., Mt. Tabor. Must call to pre-register. Call Diane 973-627-2134 (day/eve).

OCEAN

Bereavement for Adults Mutual support for adults bereaving the loss of a loved one. Educational series, rap sessions and guest speakers. Meetings vary, Hospice of NJ-Toms River, 40 Bey Lea Rd., Toms River. For meeting information call Jeremy Lees 732-818-3460 (day).

Bereavement Support Group *Professionally-run.* Support for anyone bereaving the loss of a loved one. Meets Wed., 9:30-11am, Jewish Family and Children's Services, 301 Madison Ave., Lakewood. Call Rita Sason or Carol Powell 732-363-8010 (day).

Bereavement Support Group Mutual support for those suffering the loss a loved one. Various meeting locations and times. See group listings and contacts online at: http://www.dioceseoftrenton.org/church/consolation.asp (scroll down to "Support Groups for Bereavement") or call Office of Family Life, Trenton Diocese 609-406-7400 ext. 5557 (day).

Better Bereavement Support for anyone bereaving the loss of a loved one. Meets 1st and 3rd Tues., 7:30-9pm, (schedule varies June/Aug.), Ocean Medical Center, 425 Jack Martin Blvd., Brick. Pre-registration required. Before attending call Judy Willbergh 732-206-8340 (day).

Grief Share Support and sharing for persons grieving the loss of someone close to them. Meets Wed., 7-8:30pm, Safe Harbor, 600 Atlantic City Blvd., Beachwood. Call 732-244-3888.

Journey Through Grief *Professionally-run.* Support for men and women of all ages to work through the normal stages of grief with education and group support. Focuses on situations which frequently occur after the loss of a loved one. Meets at St. Francis Center, 4700 Long Beach Blvd., Brant Beach. Before attending call 609-494-1554 (day).

Kids Bereavement Support Group *Professionally-run.* Support for children (age 7-14) who are bereaving the loss of a parent, grandparent, sibling or friend. Rap sessions. Meets 1st and 3rd Thurs., 5-6pm, Center for Kids and Family, 591 Lakehurst Rd., Toms River. Call Michele 732-505-5437 (day).

PASSAIC

Lighted Path, The *Professionally-run.* Mutual support for persons who have suffered the loss of a loved one. Meets for 6 week sessions, 2-3 times a year,

Pathways Counseling Center, Kennedy Bldg., 31 Pompton Ave., Pompton Lakes. Call Peg Buczek 973-835-6337 (day).

Passaic Valley Hospice Bereavement Support Group *Professionally-run.* Offers mutual support and education for anyone who has experienced the death of a loved one. Sharing of feelings and experiences in a safe supportive environment. Literature and guest speakers. Meets for 6 week sessions, 4 times per year, Passaic Valley Hospice, 783 Riverview Dr., Totowa. Call Al Jousset, Hospice Chaplain 973-785-7406 (day).

SALEM

Bereavement Support Group *Professionally-run.* Mutual support to help facilitate an individual's grief process within a safe and confidential environment. Under 18 welcome. Group runs for 8 week sessions, Mon., 7-8:30pm, Memorial Hospital of Salem County, 310 Salem-Woodstown Rd., Salem. Call Rev. Walt Kellen 856-678-8500 ext. 315 (day).

SOMERSET

JANUS Bereavement Group *Professionally-run.* Support and education for anyone who has experienced a loss such as a death, separation/divorce, retirement, loss of a job, health or relocation. Helps individuals accept and adjust to the loss. Meets 2nd Tues., 7:30-9pm, Bridgewater Baptist Church, 324 Milltown Rd., Bridgewater. Call Barbara Ronca, LCSW 908-218-9062 (Mon.-Fri., 9am-3pm).

Rainbows, Inc. *Professionally-run.* Peer support for children and adolescents (kindergarten - eighth grade) who are grieving a loss due to death, divorce or abandonment. Single parent group meets concurrently. Meets Mon., 6:30-7:30pm. Call for location. Call Alyson Meyer 908-766-4755 ext. 35.

VNA of Somerset Hills Bereavement Support Group *Professionally-run.* Mutual support for family and friends bereaving the loss of a loved one. Meets 2nd and 4th Tues., 11am-12:30pm, Somerset Medical Center, 110 Rehill Ave., Somerville. Call Mary Lou Daley, LCSW 908-766-0180 (day). *Email:* mldaley@visitingnurse.org

SUSSEX

Bereavement Support Group Support for those grieving the loss of a loved one. Families and friends welcome. Guest speakers, education and literature. Meets for 2 sessions, 2 times year, Blessed Kateri Tekakwitha Roman Catholic Church, Sparta. Call Laura 973-726-8978 (eve) or Janice 973-729-9348 (eve).

Coping with Loss Support for those grieving the loss of a loved one through death. Phone help, literature, rap sessions and mutual sharing. Meets 4th Tues., 10-11:30am, United Methodist Church, West Ann St., Milford, PA. Call Lorri Opitz 973-383-0115 or Diana Sebzda 908-852-8730.

Coping with Loss Support Group *Professionally-run.* Provides a safe and supportive environment, for those who have lost a loved one, where they can share experiences and feelings. Meets 2nd Mon., 7-8:30pm, Karen Ann Quinlan Hospice, 99 Sparta Ave., Newton. Call Diana Sebzda 973-383-0115 or 1-800-882-1117. *Email:* bereavement@karenannquinlanhospice.org

UNION

Bereavement Support Group *Professionally-run.* Support for families and friends who have lost a loved one to cancer. Meets every other Mon., 5:30-6:30pm, Overlook Hospital, 99 Beauvoir Ave., Conference Room 1, Summit. Before attending call Kristen Scarlett, LPC, NCC 908-522-5255 (day).

Bereavement Support Groups *Professionally-run.* Series of 8 week meetings with separate groups for spouses and other family members. Registration fee $10 (adult fee can be waived). Meets various times, United Methodist Church, 1441 Springfield Ave., New Providence. Call Bereavement Coordinator 973-379-8440 (day).

Center For Hope Hospice Bereavement Support Group *Professionally-run.* Separate support groups for adults, teens and children (age 5+) who have experienced the death of a loved one. Donations accepted. Groups meet various times, Center for Hope Hospice, Acadia House, 175 Glenside Ave., Scotch Plains. For information call Donna Dandrilli 908-654-3103 (day). *Website:* http://www.centerforhope.com *Email:* ddandrilli@centerforhope.com

Donor Family Support Group *Professionally-run.* Bereavement support for families of organ and tissue donors. Information about transplantation and donation process. Meetings vary, Sharing Network, 841 Mountain Ave., Springfield. For meeting information call Mary Ellen McGlynn 973-379-4535 (day). *Website:* http://www.sharenj.org *Email:* mmcglynn@sharenj.org

Lazarus Ministry *Professionally-run.* Support group for adults experiencing the loss of a loved one or friend through death. Meets 1st Wed., 7:30pm, 321 South Broad St., Elizabeth. Call Sister Elaine Maguire 908-352-5154 (day).

Rainbows, Inc. *Professionally-run.* Peer support for children and adolescents (kindergarten - eighth grade) who are grieving the loss of a parent due to death, divorce or abandonment. Meets Thurs., 7-8pm, for 6 week sessions, St. Teresa's Parish, 306 Morris Ave., Summit. Before attending call Mary Ann Visocchi 908-273-2729 (eve).

Separated, Divorced, Widowed and Bereaved Catholics Referrals to groups for emotional, spiritual support and social activities for separated, divorced, widowed or bereaved, men and women. Groups are sponsored by various churches throughout the county and are open to people of any faith. Call Family Life Ministry, Newark Diocese 973-497-4327.

WARREN

Coping with Loss Support Group *Professionally-run.* Provides a safe and supportive environment, for those who lost a loved one, where they can share experiences and feelings. Call Diana Sebzda 973-383-0115 or 1-800-882-1117. *Email:* bereavement@karenannquinlanhospice.org
> **Milford, PA** Meets 4th Tues., 10-11:30am, United Methodist Church, Ann St.
> **Washington** Meets 4th Mon., 7-8:30pm, First Presbyterian Church, Church St..

Grief Recovery Program *Professionally-run.* Provides comfort, support and healing to persons (age 18+) who have suffered the loss of a loved one. Groups run for 4 weeks, (April and October), 7-9pm, Hackettstown Regional Medical Center, 651 Willow Grove St., Hackettstown. Call Carl Bannister 908-850-7757 (day).

Grief Support Group *Professionally-run.* Provides support for those coping with the loss of a partner, child, parent or friend. Meets for 6 week sessions, 3 times per year, Warren Hospital, Chapel, 185 Roseberry St., Phillipsburg. Call 908-859-6700 ext. 2048 (day).

NATIONAL

COPS (Concerns Of Police Survivors, Inc.) *National. 48 chapters. Founded 1984.* Provides resources for the surviving families of law enforcement officers killed in the line of duty according to Federal criteria. Also offers law enforcement training. Quarterly newsletter, departmental guidelines and peer support. Special hands-on programs for survivors. Summer camp for children (age 6-14) and their parent/guardian, parents' retreats, spouses getaways. Outward Bound experiences for young adults (age 15-20), siblings retreat, adult children's and in-laws retreat. Write: COPS, 3096 S. State Hwy 5, PO Box 3199, Camdenton, MO 65020. Call

573-346-4911; Fax: 573-346-1414. *Website:* http://www.nationalcops.org *Email:* cops@nationalcops.org

National Donor Family Council *National. 52 affiliated groups. Founded 1992.* Mutual support for families who donated the organs/tissues of a loved one who died. Provides literature, programs and local resources. Newsletter, pen pals, conferences, advocacy. Write: National Donor Family Council , 30 E. 33rd St. , New York, NY 10016. Call 1-800-622-9010 or 212-889-2210; Fax: 212-689-9261. *Website:* http://www.donorfamily.org *Email:* donorfamily@kidney.org

National Fallen Firefighters Foundation Survivors Support Network *National network. Founded 1992.* Provides emotional support to spouses, families and friends of firefighters who have died in the line of duty. Members are matched with survivors of similar experiences to help them cope during the difficult months following the death. Write: National Fallen Firefighters Foundation, PO Drawer 498, Emmitsburg, MD 21727 . Call 301-447-1365 Fax: 301-447-1645. *Website:* http://www.firehero.org *Email:* firehero@firehero.org

National Organization of Parents of Murdered Children *National. Over 235 chapters in US, Canada, Costa Rica. Founded 1978.* Self help support organization for the family and friends of those who have died by violence. Newsletter published 3 times a year. Court accompaniment also provided by many chapters. Parole Block Program and Second Opinion Service also available. Offers assistance in starting local chapters. Write: POMC , 100 E. 8th St., B-41 , Cincinnati, OH 45202. Call 1-888-818-7662 or 513-721-5683 (office); Fax: 513-345-4489. *Website:* http://www.pomc.com *Email:* POMC@aol.com

RAINBOWS *International. 8600 affiliated groups. Founded 1983.* Establishes peer support groups in churches, schools or social agencies for children and adults who are grieving a death, divorce or other painful transition in their family. Groups are led by trained adults. Online newsletter, information and referrals. Write: RAINBOWS, 2100 Golf Rd., Suite 370, Rolling Meadows, IL 60008-4231. Call 1-800-266-3206 or 847-952-1770; Fax: 847-952-1774. *Website:* http://www.rainbows.org *Email:* info@rainbows.org

TAPS (Tragedy Assistance Program for Survivors) *National network.* Provides support for persons who have lost a loved one while serving in the armed forces (Army, Air Force, Navy, Marine Corps, National Guard, Reserves, Service Academies or Coast Guard). Offers networking, crisis information, problem solving assistance and liaison with military agencies. Also TAPS youth programs. Annual seminar. Write: TAPS, 1621 Connecticut Ave., NW Suite 300,

141

20009. Call 1-800-959-8277 or 202-588-8277; Fax: 202-588-0784. *Website:* http://www.taps.org *Email:* info@taps.org

Twinless Twin Support Group *International network. 12 regional directors. Founded 1986.* Mutual support for twins and other multiples that have lost their twin or multiple(s). Information, phone support, local meetings, annual conference. Parents of infant/child age survivor twins welcome. Publishes "Twinless Times." Dues $50/yr. Write: Twinless Twin Support Group, PO Box 980481, Ypsilanti, MI 4819. Call 1-888-205-8962. *Website:* http://www.twinlesstwins.org *Email:* contact@twinlesstwins.org

Wings of Light, Inc. *National. 3 support networks. Founded 1995.* Support & information network for individuals whose lives have been touched by aviation accidents. Separate networks for airplane accident survivors; families & friends of persons killed in airplane accidents; and persons involved in rescue, recovery and investigation of crashes. Information and referrals, phone support. Write: Wings of Light, Inc.,16845 N. 29th Ave., Suite 1, PMB 448, Phoenix, AZ 85053. Call 623-516-1115. *Website:* http://www.wingsoflight.org

ONLINE

Adult Sibling Grief *Online.* Support for those who have suffered the devastating loss of an adult sibling. Chat rooms, message board and resources. *Website:* http://www.adultsiblinggrief.com

Autoerotic Asphyxiation Support *Online.* Supportive message board for family and friends of those who have died by autoerotic asphyxiation. *Website:* http://groups.yahoo.com/group/autoeroticasphyxiationsupport *Email:* dltsdad@yahoo.com

Compassionate Friends Internet Sibling Resources *Online.* Chat room for adults and teens who have lost a sibling. Sibling forum provides an opportunity for members to share concerns and feelings. Also offers pen pal program for members to network with other siblings with similar interests. Click on "sibling resources" at the website. *Website:* http://www.compassionatefriends.org *Email:* TCFsiblingrep@compassionatefriends.org

Delta Society *Online.* Maintains a database of pet bereavement support groups and pet loss resource persons. Call 425-226-7357; Fax: 425-235-1076. *Website:* http://www.deltasociety.org *Email:* info@deltasociety.org

If you are using this book past Spring 2007, please call us for information about our most recent directory. 1-800-367-6274

Drowning Support Network *Online. Founded 2002.* Offers support for people who have lost loved ones by drowning or in other water accidents, especially those in which no remains were found or in which the recovery process has been lengthy or difficult. *Website:* http://health.groups.yahoo.com/group/drowningsupportnetwork

GROWW (Grief Recovery Online by Widows and Widowers) *Online.* Support groups for persons bereaving the loss of a loved one. Offers a large variety of chat rooms, run by volunteers, dealing with specific issues (loss due to long-term illness, sudden death, violent losses, gays and lesbians, men and more). *Website:* http://www.groww.org

Pet Loss Grief Support Website *Online. (MULTILINGUAL)* Moderated board that offers support and understanding for persons grieving the loss of their pet or who have a pet that is ill. Provides personal support and thoughtful advice. Also offers "Monday Pet Loss Candle Ceremony," a chat room, tribute pages and other resources. *Website:* http://www.petloss.com

DEATH OF A CHILD / FETAL LOSS

(see also bereavement, suicide, crime)

ATLANTIC

Compassionate Friends Support for parents, grandparents and siblings bereaving the death of a child. Meets 2nd Wed., 7:30-9pm, Grace Lutheran Church, Shore Rd. and Dawes Ave., Somers Point. Call Gail Katten 609-653-8451 (day/eve), Patty Semprevivo 609-296-1298 (day) or Compassionate Friends 1-877-969-0010. *Website:* http://www.compassionatefriends.org *Email:* tcfnj@comcast.net

BERGEN

Compassionate Friends Support for parents grieving the death of a child. Grandparents and siblings are welcomed. Speakers' bureau. Meets 4th Tues., 7:30-9:30pm, (beginners 7:15pm), Christian Healthcare Center, Mountain Ave., Wyckoff. Call Compassionate Friends 201-567-0089 (day/eve). *Website:* http://www.compassionatefriends.org

Healing Hearts *Professionally-run.* Self-help support group for parents who have lost children to congenital heart defects. Mutual sharing, phone help, literature. Meets 4th Thurs., 7:30-10pm, Don Imus Pediatric Center, Hackensack Medical Center, 30 Prospect Ave., Hackensack. Call Scott and Diane Hosmer 201-641-4580 (eve) or Scott 973-575-4550 ext. 2516 (day).

Parents Who Have Lost A Child Support Group Mutual support, education and spirituality for parents who have lost a child. Meets 3rd Mon., 7:30pm, St. Peter the Apostle Church, 445 Fifth Ave., Rectory Basement, River Edge. Call Mary Davis 201-261-5400 (day) or 201-265-3688 (eve).

Perinatal Bereavement - Healing Hearts *Professionally-run.* Provides support for parents who have experienced a miscarriage, ectopic pregnancy, stillbirth or infant death to help with the grieving process. Meets 3rd Thurs., 7:30-9pm, Valley Hospital, 233 N. Van Dien Ave., Cheel Conference Room # 2, Ridgewood. Before attending call Karen Olaya 201-447-8278 (day) or Trudy Heerema, LCSW 201-447-8539 (day).

Perinatal Bereavement Support Group *Professionally-run.* For parents and significant others who have experienced the loss of a pregnancy or infant death. Meets 3rd Wed., 7:30pm, Englewood Hospital, Englewood. Call Sue Dziemian 201-384-8258 (day/eve).

Pregnancy and Newborn Loss Support Group *Professionally-run.* An opportunity for parents who have experienced the loss of an infant, miscarriage or still birth, to share their experiences with other parents. Provides information and resources for parents, families and friends on perinatal grief. Guest speakers. Meets 1st Tues., 7:30-9pm, Holy Name Hospital, 718 Teaneck Rd., Teaneck. Call Perinatal Bereavement Hotline 201-833-3058. *Email:* jgorab.holyname.org

Turning Point A Women's Resource Center *Professionally-run.* Confidential post-abortion support group using God's word as a basis for inner healing. Group meets for 8-12 weeks as needed. Call Bev Frutchey 973-584-8884 (day/eve) or Turning Point 201-501-8876. *Email:* TurnptResource@aol.com or Frutchey1@Juno.com

BURLINGTON

Bereaved Parents *Professionally-run.* Support for parents bereaving the loss of a child. Meetings vary, Samaritan Hospice, Marlton. Pre-registration required. Before attending call The Samaritan Center for Grief Support 1-800-596-8550. *Website: http://www.samaritanhospice.org*

Helping Hand Grief Support Group Support for someone bereaving the loss of a loved one (including death of a child, loss to homicide or suicide) through education, encouragement, counseling and understanding. Families welcome. Meets 1st and 3rd Mon., 7-9pm, for 10 week sessions, Fellowship Alliance Chapel, (Log house in back of church), 199 Church Rd., Medford. Call Wanda and George Stein 609-953-7333 ext. 309 (day/eve).

CAMDEN

Angels Lost To Addiction (ALTA) Mutual support for families affected by the loss of a child to addiction. Rap sessions, buddy system and pen pals. Meets 1st Wed., 7-9pm, Christ The King, School Library, 3252 Chesterfield Rd., Philadelphia, PA. Call Celeste Dale 215-824-3626 (eve) or Barbara Fitzgerald 215-637-2228 (eve). *Email:* alta0203@yahoo.com

Compassionate Friends Support for parents bereaving the death of a child. Grandparents and relatives welcome. Rap sessions and newsletter. Meets 3rd Fri., 8-9:30pm, Senior Center, Oak and Oakland Ave., Audubon. Call Lynne 856-401-8967 or Compassionate Friends 1-877-969-0010. *Website:* http://www.compassionatefriends.org *Email:* ketih_22_2000@msn.com

SIDS/Infant Loss Support Group Support for parents who have lost a child to a sudden infant death. Meeting days and time varies, West Jersey Hospital, Voorhees. Before attending call 1-800-545-7437.

UNITE Grief Support *Professionally-run.* Mutual support for parents who have experienced the loss of a child, either during pregnancy, at birth or up to the first year of life. Discussion of experiences and feelings in an atmosphere of support and respect. Meets 1st and 3rd Mon., 7-9pm, Virtua Health's Barry Brown Health Education Center, 106 Carnie Blvd., Voorhees. Call 1-888-847-8823.

CUMBERLAND

Helping Hands *Professionally-run.* Provides emotional support for parents who have lost a child to miscarriage, stillbirth or infant death. Open to grandparents as well. Meets 2nd Mon., 7pm, South Jersey Health Care, Vineland. Before attending call Judy Ford, RN BSN 856-507-2768 (day).

ESSEX

Compassionate Friends Offers friendship and understanding for parents bereaving the death of a child. Meets in Nutley area. For meeting information call Pat Gerges 201-420-3107 (day) or 973-535-9022 (eve). *Website:* http://www.compassionatefriends.org

HOPE (Helping Other Parents Endure) Mutual support, education and spirituality for parents who have lost a child. Meets 1st Wed., 7:30-9:30pm, St. Thomas of the Apostle, 60 Byrd Ave., Parish Center, Bloomfield. Call Mary Margaret or Bob Corriston 201-288-6886 (eve) or 1-877-633-2629 ext. 5442 (day). *Email:* bmmc917@optonline.net

SIDS/Infant Loss Support Group *(BILINGUAL) Professionally-run.* Support for parents who have lost a child to a sudden infant death. Families welcome. Meetings vary, 10am-noon, University Hospital, Campus, Newark. Before attending call 1-800-545-7437.

Perinatal Bereavement Group *Professionally-run.* Mutual support for parents who have experienced a miscarriage, infant death or stillbirth. Meets 1st Wed., 7:30pm, St. Barnabas Medical Center, Livingston. Call Dorothy Kurzweil, LCSW 973-322-5745 (day) or Social Services 973-322-5855 (day).

GLOUCESTER

Bereaved Parents *Professionally-run.* Support for parents to help deal with the long-term grief of the loss of a child. Meets 3 times per yr., Woodbury. For starting dates and times call The Samaritan Center for Grief Support 1-800-596-8550.

HOPING (Helping Other Parents In Normal Grief) *Professionally-run.* Support for parents who have experienced miscarriage, stillbirth, ectopic pregnancy or newborn death. Meets 4 times per year, Underwood Memorial Hospital, 509 N. Broad St., Woodbury. Before attending call 856-853-2063 (day).

S.O.S. (Survivors Offering Support) Mutual support and encouragement for persons (ages 35-55) who have lost a family member (spouse, child or other family member) through death. Provides emotional support and education on the grieving process. Meets alternate Mon., 7pm, Gloucester County Community Church, Sewell. Before attending call Glenn 856-296-5262.

HUNTERDON

Compassionate Friends Support for parents bereaving the death of a child. Rap sessions, literature, phone help. Meets monthly in High Bridge. For meeting information call Jay and Roselee Persinko 908-638-8717 or Compassionate Friends 1-877-969-0010. *Website:* http://www.compassionatefriends.org *Email:* compassionatefriends-hunterdon@earthlink.net

MERCER

Compassionate Friends Mutual support for parents, grandparents or adult siblings bereaving the death of a child. Guest speakers and phone help. Newsletter. Meets 1st Mon., 7:30-9pm, Robert Wood Johnson University Hospital at Hamilton, One Hamilton Health Place, Building # 2, Hamilton. Call Chaplain Jeff Pierfy 609-631-6980 (day). *Website:* http://www.compassionatefriends.org *Email:* jpierfy@rwjuhh.net

Time for Healing *Professionally-run.* A confidential support group for parents who have ended a pregnancy after abnormal prenatal test results. Adult family members welcome. Phone help available. Meets one Sun. per month, Capital Health System, 446 Bellevue Ave., Trenton. Before attending call Carolee Watkins 609-394-4072 ext. 2 (day). *Email:* cwatkins@chsnj.org

MIDDLESEX

Compassionate Friends – *(Central Jersey Chapter)* Mutual support for parents, grandparents or siblings grieving the death of a child. Phone help, guest speakers, rap sessions, literature and newsletter. Meets 2nd Sun., 2-4pm, St. Peter's Episcopal Church, 505 Main St., Parish Hall, Spotswood. Call Dick Quaintance 732-548-1419 (eve), Kathy Dopart 732-549-3807 (eve) or Compassionate Friends 1-877-969-0010. *Website:* http://www.compassionatefriends.org

Parent-to-Parent SIDS Support Group *Professionally-run.* Support for parents who have lost a child to a sudden infant death. Meetings vary, noon-2pm, UMDNJ, Clinical Academic Building, New Brunswick. Before attending call 1-800-545-7437.

SHARE *Professionally-run.* Provides support for parents, their families and friends who have experienced miscarriage, stillbirth or neonatal death. Offers phone help and literature. Meets 2nd Thurs., 7-9pm, St. Peter's University Hospital, 254 Easton Ave., New Brunswick. Call Dawn Brady 732-745-8600 ext. 5214 (day).

MONMOUTH

C.H.I.L.D. (Caring Help In Lost Dreams) *Professionally-run.* Bereavement group for parents and surviving siblings who have lost a child of any age. Offers emotional support to help cope with the unnatural loss of a deeply loved child. Meets 1st Thurs., 7:30-9pm, CentraState Medical Center, Route 537, Freehold. Call Bunny Salomon 732-617-2221.

S.H.A.R.E. *Professionally-run.* For parents grieving the loss of an infant through miscarriage, ectopic pregnancy, stillbirth or death of a newborn. Newsletter, phone help, guest speakers and literature. Meets 2nd Tues., 7:30-9:30pm, Riverview Medical Center, 1 River Plaza, Booker Conference Room, Red Bank. Call Pam Rossano 732-530-2315 (day), Kathy De Fazio 732-450-2871 or 1-800-560-9990 (day).

MORRIS

Compassionate Friends Mutual support for parents, grandparents and siblings bereaving the death of a child. Newsletter. Phone help, newsletter. Call Pegeen Lanahan 973-927-7078 or 201-213-6725 and Compassionate Friends 1-877-969-0010. *Website:* http://www.compassionatefriends.org *Email:* tcf_nj@yahoo.com

> **Chatham** Meets 3rd Sun., 7:00-9:30pm, (2nd Sun., June and Dec.), Chatham Township Presbyterian Church, 240 Southern Blvd. Call Cindy Cutcliff 908-306-1542.
> **Parsippany** Meets 2nd Thurs., 7:30-10pm, St. Christopher's Church, 1050 Littleton Rd., Room 101. Call Lynn Bain 973-334-5532 (eve).

M.I.D.S. (Miscarriage, Infant Death, Stillbirth) Mutual support and information for bereaved parents who have experienced stillbirth, miscarriage, infant death or ectopic pregnancy. Meets 2nd Wed., 8pm, Parsippany. Call Janet Tischler 973-884-1016 or Kathy O'Dowd-Allen 973-625-0486. *Website:* MIDSinc.org *Email:* MIDS1982@yahoo.com

RTS Perinatal Bereavement Services *Professionally-run.* For families who have experienced the loss of a baby through miscarriage, ectopic pregnancy, stillbirth or newborn death. Meets 3rd Wed., 7:30-9pm, Morristown Memorial Hospital, Patient Education Center, Morristown. Call Labor and Delivery 973-971-5748 (day/eve).

SHARE - Pregnancy and Infant Loss Support Group *Professionally-run.* Mutual support for parents who have lost a baby through neonatal death, miscarriage, ectopic pregnancy or stillbirth. Pen pals, monthly meetings, guest speakers, lending library and phone help available. Meets 3rd Tues., 7:30-9pm, 28 Drake Rd., Mendham. To confirm meeting date call Lucy 973-543-2495 (day). *Website:* www.shareatlanta.org *Email:* SHARENONJ@msn.com

OCEAN

Compassionate Friends Mutual self-help support for parents and siblings grieving the death of a child. Includes parents of stillbirth or fetal death. Monthly newsletter, occasional speakers, library. Meets 1st Tues., 7:30pm, Ocean County Administration Building, 129 Hooper Ave., 3rd Level Cafeteria, Toms River. Call Compassionate Friends 732-244-6439 (day/eve). *Website:* http://www.oceantcf.com *Email:* oceantcf@yahoo.com

"To live in the hearts we leave behind is not to die." Thomas Campbell

SOMERSET

Compassionate Friends Provides mutual support for parents bereaving the death of a child. Rap sessions, guest speakers, newsletter. Meets 4th Sun., 7:30pm, Temple Sholom, Bridgewater. Call ·Dossie Weissbein 908-725-7736 (day/eve), Marilyn and Fred Mountjoy 908-722-6199 (day/eve) or Compassionate Friends 1-877-969-0010. *Website:* http://www.freewebs.com/cfbridgewater *Email:* cfbridgewater@patmedia.net

UNION

F.A.T.E. (Feelings After Termination Experience) *Professionally-run.* Support for couples or individuals who have terminated a pregnancy due to fetal abnormalities. Meets monthly, Overlook Hospital, Summit. Call Gisela Rodriquez 973-972-3302 (day).

NATIONAL

AGAST, *International. Founded 1989.* Dedicated to assisting grandparents in the death of a grandchild. Offers support, literature and bimonthly newsletter. Also provides online message board, contact information and newsletter., Write: AGAST, 12200 E. State Route 69, Lot 382, Dewey, AZ 86327. Call 1-888-774-7437. *Website:* http://www.agast.org *Email:* reachout@agast.org

Alive Alone, Inc., *National network. Founded 1988.* Self-help network of parents who have lost an only child or all of their children. Provides education and publications to promote communication and healing, to assist in resolving grief and to develop means to reinvest lives for a positive future. Bimonthly newsletter. Write: Alive Alone, c/o Kay Bevington, 11115 Dull Robinson Rd., Van Wert, OH 45891. Call 419-238-7879. *Website:* http://www.alivealone.org *Email:* alivalon@bright.net

AMEND (Aiding Mothers and Fathers Experiencing Neonatal Death), *National network. Founded 1974.* Offers support and encouragement to parents having a normal grief reaction to the loss of their baby. Provides one-to-one peer counseling with trained volunteers. Write: AMEND, 4324 Berrywick Terrace, St. Louis, MO 63128. Call 314-487-7582. *Website:* http://www.amendgroup.com *Email:* martha@amendgroup.com

Bereaved Parents of the USA, *National. 60+ affiliated groups. Founded 1995.* Designed to aid and support bereaved parents and their families who are struggling to survive their grief after the death of a child. Assistance and guidelines in starting groups. Write: Bereaved Parents of the USA, PO Box 95, Park Forest, IL

149

60466. Call 708-748-7866. *Website:* http://www.bereavedparentsusa.org *Email:* PatLMoser@aol.com

CLIMB, Inc. (Center for Loss In Multiple Birth), *International network. Founded 1987.* Support by and for parents who have experienced the death of one or more of their twins or higher multiples during pregnancy, birth, in infancy or childhood. Newsletter, information on specialized topics, pen pals, phone support. Write: CLIMB, PO Box 91377, Anchorage, AK 99509. Call 907-222-5321. *Website:* http://www.climb-support.org, *Email:* climb@pobox.alaska.net

Compassionate Friends *National. 600 chapters. Founded 1969.* Offers mutual support, friendship and understanding to families following the death of a child of any age. Provides information on the grieving process, referrals to local chapter meetings and publishes quarterly magazine ($20/yr). Write: The Compassionate Friends, PO Box 3696, Oak Brook, IL 60522-3696. Call 1-877-969-0010; Fax: 630-990-0246. *Website:* http://www.compassionatefriends.org *Email:* nationaloffice@compassionatefriends.org

First Candle/SIDS Alliance National. *50 chapters. Founded 1987.* (Bilingual) Provides education, advocacy, research and support for families of babies who have died from SIDS (sudden infant death syndrome), stillbirth and miscarriages. Bilingual grief counselors available 24 hrs. Newsletter, conferences, chapter development guidelines. Write: First Candle/SIDS Alliance, 1314 Bedford Ave., Suite 210, Baltimore, MD 21208. Call 1-800-221-7437 or 410-653-8226; Fax: 410-653-8709. *Website:* http://www.firstcandle.org *Email:* info@firstcandle.org

Grief Recovery After Substance Passing (GRASP), *Model. 1 group in California. Founded 2002.* Support and advocacy group for parents who have suffered the death of a child due to substance abuse. Provides opportunity for parents to share their grief and experiences without shame or recrimination. Provides information and suggestions for those wanting to start a similar group elsewhere., Write: GRASP, c/o Patricia Wittberger, 1088 Torrey Pines Rd., Chula Vista, CA 91915. Call 619-656-8414; Fax: 619-397-3493. *Website:* http://www.grasphelp.org, *Email:* Mom@JennysJourney.org

M.I.S.S. Foundation, The *International. 20 affiliated groups. Founded 1995.* Offers emergency and on-going support for families suffering from the loss a child. Provides information, referrals, phone support, newsletter, pen pals, literature, advocacy and online chat room support. Information on local group development. Local support group listings online. Write: M.I.S.S., PO Box 5333, Peoria, AZ 85385-5333. Call 623-979-1000; Fax: 623-979-1001. *Website:* http://www.missfoundation.org, *Email:* joanne@missfoundation.org

National Organization of Parents of Murdered Children, *National. Over 235 chapters in the U.S., Canada and Costa Rica. Founded 1978.* Self-help support organization for the family and friends of those who have died by violence. Newsletter 3 times a year. Court accompaniment also provided by many chapters. Parole Block Program and Second Opinion Service also available. Offers assistance in starting local chapters., Write: NOPMC,, 100 E. 8th St., B-41, Cincinnati, OH 45202. Call 1-888-818-7662 or 513-721-5683 (office); Fax: 513-345-4489. *Website:* http://www.pomc.com *Email:* POMC@aol.com

SHARE: Pregnancy and Infant Loss Support, Inc., *National. 105 chapters. Founded 1977.* Mutual support for bereaved parents & families whose lives have been touched by the tragic death of a baby through early pregnancy loss, stillbirth or in the first few months of life. Provides support toward positive resolution of grief experienced following the death of a baby. Information, education and resources on the needs and rights of bereaved parents and siblings. Provides newsletter, pen pals, information re: professionals, & pastoral care. Chapter development guidelines. Online message board and weekly chat rooms. Write: National SHARE Office, c/o St. Joseph Health Center, 300 First Capital Dr., St. Charles, MO 63301. Call 1-800-821-6819 or 636-947-6164; Fax: 636-947-7486. *Website:* http://www.nationalshareoffice.com *Email:* share@nationalshareoffice.com

Tender Hearts, *International.* Sponsored by Triplet Connection. Founded 1983. Network of parents who have lost one or more children in multiple births. Information on selection reduction. Newsletter, information, referrals, phone support and networking., Write: Tender Hearts, c/o Triplet Connection, PO Box 429, Spring City, UT 84662. Call 435-851-1105; Fax: 435-462-7466. *Website:* http://www.tripletconnection.org *Email:* tc@tripletconnection.org

UNITE, Inc., *National. 14 groups. Founded 1975.* Support for parents grieving a miscarriage, stillbirth or infant death. Also provides support for parents through subsequent pregnancies. Group meetings, phone help, newsletter, annual conference. Offers guidelines for starting and facilitating groups. Grief counselor training programs. Professionals in advisory roles. Online referrals to local support groups., Write: UNITE, Inc., c/o Jeanes Hospital, 7600 Central Ave., Philadelphia, PA 19111-2499. Call 215-728-3777. *Website:* http://www.unitegriefsupport.org, *Email:* administrator@unitegriefsupport.org

ONLINE

A Heartbreaking Choice *Online.* Resource for parents who have had to terminate a wanted pregnancy due to prenatal news such as birth defects or risk

151

to the wellbeing of the mother. Listserv email list, discussion forum and grandparents forum. *Website:* http://www.aheartbreakingchoice.com

MyMolarPregnancy.com, *Online. Founded 2001.* Information, links, references and a number of interactive web features for women who have had a molar pregnancy. Support group, message board and chat room. *Website:* http://www.mymolarpregnancy.com,

Our Angels *Online.* Support for mothers and grandmothers of toddlers and young children who have drowned. Oriented towards the faith and belief that their children are in a better place. *Website:* http://health.groups.yahoo.com/group/OurAngels/

SUICIDE SURVIVORS
(see also bereavement, death of a child, widows)

ATLANTIC

Heartbreak to Healing Support for those who have lost a loved one to suicide. Literature. Meets last Tues., 7:30pm, Grace Lutheran Church 11 East Dawes Ave., (Shore Rd.), Somers Point. Call 609-345-1010.

BERGEN

Survivors After Suicide *Professionally-run.* Provides support for family members and friends of people who died by suicide. Open to all. Meets 1st and 3rd Wed., 7:15-8:45pm, Vantage Health System, 2 Park Ave., Dumont. Call 201-385-4400 (day) or Lynne Nierenberg 201-837-6321 (day/eve).

BURLINGTON

Helping Hand Grief Support Group Support for someone bereaving the loss of a loved one (including death of a child, loss to homicide or suicide) through education, encouragement, counseling and understanding. Families welcome. Meets 1st and 3rd Mon., 7-9pm, for 10 week sessions, Fellowship Alliance Chapel, 199 Church Rd., Medford. Call Wanda and George Stein 609-953-7333 ext. 309.

Sharing Suicide's Sorrows *Professionally-run.* Support for family and friends grieving a death from suicide. Meets 3 times per year, The Center for Grief Support, 5 Eves Dr., Suite 180, Marlton. Call 1-800-596-8550.

CAMDEN

Friends and Families of Suicide For those who have lost a loved one to suicide. Meets 2nd Tues., 7:45pm, Our Lady of Grace Church, 35 North White Horse Pike, Somerdale. Call Barbara 856-307-0331 or Gail 856-858-7044. *Email:* survivingsuicidenj@yahoo.com

MERCER

Surviving After Suicide *Professionally-run.* For those who have lost a loved one to suicide. Meets 2nd Wed., 7:30pm, Robert Wood Johnson University Hospital, 1 Hamilton Health Place, Hamilton. Call Peggy Farrell 732-462-5267 or Jeff Pierfy 609-631-6980.

MIDDLESEX

Surviving After Suicide *Professionally-run.* Group for survivors after the suicide of a family member or friend. Meets 3rd Mon., 7:30-9:30pm, University of Medicine and Dentistry of NJ, University Behavioral Health Care, 671 Hoes Lane, Piscataway. Call Peggy Farrell 732-462-5267. *Email:* farrmarg@aol.com

MORRIS

Survivors of Suicide Mutual support and discussion for people who have had someone close to them commit suicide. Meets 2nd and 4th Wed., 7:30-9pm, Grace Episcopal Church, Madison. Call Jane Cole 973-786-5178.

OCEAN

Survivors After Suicide For those who have lost a loved one to suicide. Meets 2nd Thurs., 7:30pm, Father Steve Kluge, St. Francis Center, Long Beach Blvd., Brant Beach. Call Jo and Roger 609-361-7608.

Survivors of Suicide For those who have lost a loved one to suicide. Meets 3rd Tues., 7-9pm, Kimball Medical Center, 619 River Ave., Lakewood. Call Jim Romer 732-886-4475 (day).

NATIONAL

American Association of Suicidology *Resource. 350 affiliated groups.* Referrals to local support groups for survivors of suicide nationwide. Directory of groups ($15). Book available on starting self-help groups ($30). Write: American Association of Suicidology, 5221 Wisconsin Ave., NW, Second Floor,

Washington, DC 20015. Call 202-237-2280; Fax: 202-237-2282. *Website:* http://www.suicidology.org *Email:* info@suicidology.org

American Foundation for Suicide Prevention Resource. *Founded 1987.* Provides state-by-state directories of survivor support groups for families and friends who have lost someone to suicide. Also provides information regarding suicide statistics, prevention and surviving. Guidelines available to help start similar groups. Write: American Foundation For Suicide Prevention, 120 Wall St., 22nd Floor, New York, NY 10005. Call 1-888-333-2377 or 212-363-3500; Fax: 212-363-6237. *Website:* http://www.afsp.org *Email:* inquiry@afsp.org

Heartbeat *National. 30 chapters. Founded 1980.* Mutual support for those who have lost a loved one through suicide. Information, referrals, phone support and chapter development guidelines online. Speakers on suicide bereavement. Write: Heartbeat, 2015 Devon St., Colorado Springs, CO 80909. Call 719-596-2575. *Website:* http://www.heartbeatsurvivorsaftersuicide.org *Email:* archlj@msn.com

SOLES (Survivors Of Law Enforcement Suicide) *Online. Founded 1995.* Provides emotional support to the families of police officers who died by suicide. Information and referrals on national and local resources including support groups, conferences, grief workshops. Email discussion list and weekly online chat. Quarterly newsletter. Write: SOLES, 2708 SW 48 Terrace, Cape Coral, FL 33914. Call 239-541-1151. *Website:* http://www.tearsofacop.com *Email:* AskT8@aol.com

Suicide Anonymous *Model. 2 groups in Tennessee. Founded 1996.* 12-Step fellowship of men and women who share their experience, strength and hope with each other in order to solve their common problem of suicidal ideation and behavior. Provides a safe environment for people to share their struggles with suicide, to prevent suicides and develop strategies for support and healing from the devastating effects of suicidal preoccupation and behavior. Networking, literature, advocacy. Write: Suicide Anonymous, 1037 Cresthaven, Memphis, TN 38119. Call 901-763-3693; Fax: 901-763-1876. *Website:* http://www.geocities.com/samemphis *Email:* samemphis@aol.com

ONLINE

Friends and Family of Suicide *Online. Founded 1998.* Provides online support to survivors of suicide. Offers moderated email mailing list. *Website:* http://www.friendsandfamiliesofsuicide.com *Email:* arlynsmom@cs.com

Parents of Suicide *Online. Founded 1998.* Support for parents whose sons and daughters have died due to suicide. Annual retreat. Offers private chat room, email discussion group, listserv. Write: Parents of Suicide, c/o Karyl Chastain Beal, PO

Box 417, Pavo, GA 31778. Call 229-859-2976. *Website:* http://www.parentsofsuicide.com *Email:* arlynsmom@cs.com

SOLOS (Survivors Of Loved One's Suicides) *Online.* Offers various email support groups for persons affected by suicide. Groups include survivors of a loved one's suicide, parents of attempters, medical/crisis response professionals, parents, spouses, siblings, gays/lesbians, men, grandparents, teens and children who have lost someone to suicide. Also groups for persons affected by murder-suicides, post-partum depression suicides and facilitators of suicide support groups. *Website:* http://www.1000deaths.com

WIDOWS / WIDOWERS
(see also bereavement, suicide, single parenting)

BERGEN

Partners Bereavement Support Group *Professionally-run.* Support for spouses/partners bereaving the loss of a loved one to cancer in the past year. Group meets for 8 week sessions, various days, Cancer Care, 141 Dayton St., Ridgewood. For information call 201-444-6630 (day). *Website:* http://www.cancercare.org *Email:* njino@cancercare.org

Separated, Divorced, Widowed and Bereaved Catholics Referrals to groups for emotional, spiritual support and social activities for separated, divorced, widowed or bereaved, men and women. Groups are sponsored by various churches throughout the county and are open to people of any faith. For information call Family Life Ministry, Newark Diocese 973-497-4327.

BURLINGTON

Bereavement Support Group for Widows and Widowers *Professionally-run.* Provides mutual support for widows and widowers. Meets 3rd Wed., (except July/Aug.), 7-8:30pm and 2nd and 4th Wed., 1:30-2:45pm, Dougherty's Funeral Home, 2200 Trenton Rd., Levittown, PA. Call Deborah Gawthrop 215-624-8190 (day). *Email:* Dgawthropcnit@cs.com

Early Endings *Professionally-run.* Support for young widow and widowers. Mutual support for persons who have lost a spouse or companion early in their lives. Meetings vary, Samaritan Hospice, Marlton. Pre-registration required. Before attending call 1-800-596-8550. *Website: http://www.samaritanhospice.org*

H.O.P.E. (Helping Other People Evolve, Inc.) Support and information for recently (up to 2 yrs) widowed men and women of all ages. Group runs for 10

155

week sessions, 4 times per year. Meets in various locations. Registration f ee $20. Call H.O.P.E. 1-888-920-2201 (Mon., Wed., Fri., 10am-1pm). *Email:* hopesnj@juno.com

Widows and Widowers Support Support for anyone feeling the loss of their spouse. Meets 1st Sat., 7pm, Lourdes Medical Center of Burlington County Hospital, 218A Sunset Rd., Cafeteria, Willingboro. Before attending call Helen Tellern 609-871-0783.

CAMDEN

Early Endings *Professionally-run.* Support for young widow and widowers. Mutual support for persons who have lost a spouse or companion early in their lives. Meetings vary. Pre-registration required. Before attending call The Samaritan Center for Grief Support 1-800-596-8550. *Website:* http://www.samaritanhospice.org

H.O.P.E. (Helping Other People Evolve, Inc.) Helps the recently widowed to cope with their loss and to move forward to become self-reliant persons. Group runs for 10 week sessions, 4 times per year. Meets in various locations. Registration fee $20. Call H.O.P.E. 1-888-920-2201. (Mon., Wed., Fri., 10am-1pm). *Email:* hopesnj@juno.com

To Live Again Support and encouragement for widows and widowers (age 45+). Newly widowed meets Tues., 7pm, Queen of Heaven Church, Cherry Hill. General group meets 2nd Mon., 7:30pm, St. Peter's Celestine School, Cafeteria, Cherry Hill. Dues $15/yr. Call Rita 856-779-9438 (day) or Stanley 856-662-6754 (eve).

Widow/Widower Bereavement Group *Professionally-run.* Support and recovery from grief for widows and widowers. Meets 6 week sessions, (Spring/Fall), John F. Fluehr and Sons Funeral Home, 3301 Cottman Ave., Meeting Room, Philadelphia, PA. Call Debbie Gawthrop 215-624-8190 (day). *Email:* Dgawthropcnit@cs.com

Young Widow/Widower Support Group *Professionally-run.* Support for widowed persons (under age 50) or those with young children. Meets 1st and 3rd Thurs., (except July and Aug.), 7:30-9pm, Elkins Park Hospital, Elkins Park Campus, 60 East Township Line Rd., Elkins Park, PA. Call Debbie Gawthrop 215-624-8190 (day). *Email:* Dgawthropcnlt@cs.com

CAPE MAY

H.O.P.E. (Helping Other People Evolve, Inc.) Support and information for recently (up to 2 yrs) widowed men and women of all ages. Group runs for 10

week sessions, 4 times per year. Meets in various locations. Registration fee $20. Call H.O.P.E. 1-888-920-2201 (Mon., Wed., Fri., 10am-1pm). *Email:* hopesnj@juno.com

ESSEX

Family Bereavement Group *Professionally-run.* Group for spouses who lost spouses with young children (age 5-18) at home. Separate groups for children run concurrently. Meets 6:30-8pm, Saint Barnabas Corporate Building, 95 Old Short Hills Rd., West Orange. For meeting day call Henry de Mena 973-322-4858 (day).

Separated, Divorced, Widowed and Bereaved Catholics Referrals to groups for emotional and spiritual support for separated, divorced, widowed or bereaved, men and women. Groups are sponsored by various churches throughout the county and are open to people of any faith. For information call Family Life Ministry, Newark Diocese 973-497-4327.

Widows Moving On For widows that have dealt with the bereavement phase and now want to meet other widows to talk about getting on with their lives. Groups start periodically and run for 6 weeks. Registration fee $45. Meets 7:30-9pm, Linda and Rudy Slucker NCJW Center for Women, 513 West Mt. Pleasant Ave., Livingston. Call Center for Women 973-994-4994 (day). *Website:* http://www.centerforwomennj.org *Email:* centerforwomen@ncjwessex.org

Widows Support Groups Mutual support for widows of all ages. Groups start periodically and run for 6 weeks. Registration fee $45. Meets at Linda and Rudy Slucker NCJW Center for Women, Livingston. Call Project GRO 973-994-4994. *Website:* http://www.centerforwomennj.org *Email:* centerforwomen@ncjwessex.org

Young Widows Support Group Mutual support for widows under the age of 40. Groups start periodically and run for 6 weeks. Registration fee $45. Meets at Linda and Rudy Slucker NCJW Center for Women, Livingston. Call Project GRO 973-994-4994. *Website:* http://www.centerforwomennj.org *Email:* centerforwomen@ncjwessex.org

GLOUCESTER

Early Endings *Professionally-run.* Support for young widows and widowers. Mutual support for people who have experienced the death of a spouse or companion early in their lives. Meetings vary. Pre-registration required. Before attending call The Samaritan Center for Grief Support 1-800-596-8550. *Website:* http://www.samaritanhospice.org

H.O.P.E. (Helping Other People Evolve, Inc.) Helps the recently widowed to cope with their loss, move forward and become self-reliant. Group runs for 10 week sessions, 4 times per year. Registration fee $20. Meets Thurs., 7pm, Mantua Methodist Church, Mantua. Call H.O.P.E. 1-888-920-2201 (Mon., Wed., Fri., 10am-1pm). *Email:* hopesnj@juno.com

S.O.S. (Survivors Offering Support) Mutual support and encouragement for persons (ages 35-55) who have lost a family member (spouse, child or other family member) through death. Provides emotional support and education on the grieving process. Meets alternate Mon., 7pm, Gloucester County Community Church, Sewell. Before attending call Glenn 856-296-5262.

HUDSON

Separated, Divorced, Widowed and Bereaved Catholics Referrals to groups for emotional and spiritual support for separated, divorced, widowed or bereaved, men and women. Groups are sponsored by various churches throughout the county and are open to people of any faith. Call Family Life Ministry, Newark Diocese 973-497-4327.

HUNTERDON

Catholic Widows and Widowers Mutual support for widowed persons of any faith. Groups for the recently bereaved as well as for those further along. Various meeting locations and times. Call Family Life Office 732-562-1990 ext. 1624 (day).

MERCER

Early Endings *Professionally-run.* Support for young widow and widowers. Mutual support for people who have experienced the death of a spouse or companion early in their lives. Meetings vary. Call 856-596-8550.

H.O.P.E. (Helping Other People Evolve, Inc.) Support and information for recently (up to 2 yrs) widowed men and women of all ages. Group runs for 10 week sessions, 4 times per year. Meets in various locations. Registration fee $20. Call H.O.P.E. 1-888-920-2201 (Mon., Wed., Fri., 10am-1pm). *Email:* hopesnj@juno.com

Starting Over *Professionally-run.* Support for widows and widowers under the age of 50 or those with dependent children. Meets 1st and 3rd Tues., 7-9pm, Saul Colonial Home, 3795 Nottingham Way, Hamilton Square. Before attending call Mary Lou Pizzullo or Deborah Myslinski 609-587-7072.

MIDDLESEX

Catholic Widows and Widowers Mutual support for widowed persons of any faith. Groups for the recently bereaved as well as for those further along. Various meeting locations and times. For information call the Family Life Office, Metuchen Diocese 732-562-1990 ext. 1624 (day).

Spousal Bereavement Group *Professionally-run.* Helps persons who have lost their spouse within the last two years to understand the grieving process and share feelings, while adjusting to new roles. Young widows/widowers (under age 55), meets 2nd Tues., 7-8:15pm and widows/widowers (age 55+), meets 3rd Tues., 7-8:30pm, JFK Medical Center, 65 James St., Edison. Pre-registration required. Before attending call 732-321-7769 (day).

St. Thomas WOW'S (Widows Or Widowers) Mutual support for widows and widowers. Open to persons of any faith. Rap sessions, education, social and guest speakers. Annual dues $8 per year, $1 per meeting. Meets 1st Tues., (except July/Aug.), 7pm, St. Thomas the Apostle Church, One St. Thomas Plaza, Pastoral Center, Old Bridge. Call Deacon John J. Fitzsimmons 732-251-4000 (day) or Irene Sutton 732-251-1458 (eve).

MONMOUTH

Bereavement Support Group *Professionally-run.* Mutual support for the loss of a spouse and adult children bereaving the death of a parent. Meets for 6 weeks, several times per year, Riverview Medical Center, Cancer Center, 1 Riverview Plaza, Red Bank. Call Sister Vida O'Leary 732-530-2382.

Growing Through Loss *Professionally-run.* Mutual bereavement support for "younger" widows and widowers (ages 30-60, plus or minus). Non-sectarian. Opportunity to share thoughts. Meets 1st and 3rd Mon., 7:30-9pm, (meets once a month Jan., Feb., Mar.), Temple Shaari Emeth, 400 Craig Rd., Manalapan. For meeting information call Temple Shaari Emeth 732-462-7744.

Separated / Divorced / Widows and Widowers Support Group Support for persons who have lost their spouse due to separation, divorce or death (past bereavement stage) to help members get on with their lives. NOT for crisis situations. Not intended as a social group. Meets Tues., 7:30pm, St. Veronica's Rectory Cellar, Route 9 North, Howell. Call Ree 732-431-0446 or Cookie 732-577-6964 (day). *Website:* http://www.divorceheadquarters.com *Email:* Reegroup@aol.com

Women's Support Group Helps women who are displaced homemakers (facing the loss of their primary source of income due to separation, divorce, disability or death of spouse). Issues addressed include: self-sufficiency, career development, assertiveness, self-esteem, divorce, separation, widowhood and other related topics. Groups are set-up as needed in Asbury Park, Long Branch, Bayshore and Lincroft. Call Robin Vogel 732-495-4496 (day) or Mary Ann O'Brien 732-229-8675.

MORRIS

Begin Again Mutual support for widows or widowers bereaving the death of a spouse. Rap sessions, phone help and guest speakers. Meets 2nd and 4th Fri., 6-8:45pm, Convent at St. Peter's Church, 189 Baldwin Road, Parsippany. Call Lucille 973-334-7924 (day).

Circle of Life Offers support for anyone feeling the loss of their spouse. Meets 2nd and 4th Sun., 6:30pm, First Church of Hanover, Mt. Pleasant Ave. and Hanover Rd., Parish House, East Hanover. Dues $35/yr. Before attending call for meeting topic and future schedule. Call Susana 973-887-0591 or Jan 973-884-8989. *Email:* njcircle@yahoo.com

Living with Loss of Spouse Mutual support for those who have lost a spouse and have completed a professionally led bereavement group or had professional counseling. Rap sessions and phone help. Meets 2nd and 4th Wed., 7-8:30pm, St. Clare's Hospital, 25 Pocono Rd., Urban 1 Conference Room, Denville. Call John Evans 973-895-3444. *Email:* jevans66@optonline.net

Widowed Early Support and social group for widows and widowers who have lost their spouse before the age of 65. Must be past the bereavement stage. Guest speakers, social activities, newsletter. Annual membership $25/yr. Meets 2nd Sat., 7:30-9:30pm, Resurrection Parish, Community Room, Randolph. Call Chris Ippolito 973-398-9068.

Widow/Widower Support Group *Professionally-run.* Opportunity for widows and widowers to share experiences and feelings with other newly bereaved who are living through similar circumstances. Rap sessions. Meets 4th Tues., 1-2:30pm, Chilton Memorial Hospital, 97 West Parkway, Pompton Plains. Call Joan Beloff 973-831-5167 (day).

Widows and Widowers Support Group *Professionally-run.* Provides support, education and mutual sharing for widows and widowers. Literature. Runs for 8 week sessions, 4 times year, Morristown Memorial Hospital, 100 Madison Ave., Morristown. Before attending call Zsuzsa 973-971-5402 (day) or Chris Anderson 973-971-7911 (day).

OCEAN

Community Medical Center Bereavement Support Group *Professionally-run.* For adults who have experienced the recent loss of a spouse. Meets Mon., 10-11:30am, Community Medical Center, Hooper Ave., Toms River. Pre-registration required. Before attending call Bereavement Coordinator 732-818-6826 (day).

Young Widows' Support Group Provides support and information for young women, (age 20-55), who have lost their husband. Meets monthly, Church of St. Luke, 1674 Old Freehold Rd., Toms River. For meeting information call church 732-286-2222.

PASSAIC

Widow/Widower Support Group *Professionally-run.* Support and sharing of experiences for newly widowed persons. Meets for 6 week sessions, 2-3 times year, Pathways Counseling Center, 31 Pompton Avenue, Kennedy Building, Pompton Lakes. Registration required. Call Peg Buczek 973-835-6337 (day).

Widows/Widowers Support Group Mutual support for all widowed persons. Provides guest speakers, group discussions, phone help, peer-counseling, visitation and refreshments. Newly bereaved persons meet 1st and 3rd Wed., 7:30pm; persons past bereavement stage meet 2nd and 4th Mon., 7:30pm, St. Philip the Apostle Church, Valley Rd., Clifton. Call John Cerullo 973-472-4494 (day/eve).

SALEM

Widows and Widowers Support Group *Professionally-run.* Opportunity for widows and widowers to share experiences and feelings with other newly bereaved who are living through similar circumstances. Guest speakers, educational series and literature. Meets 3rd Wed., 7pm, Elmer Presbyterian Church, Route 40, Elmer. Call Bob 856-769-2710 or Vicki 856-358-1402.

SOMERSET

Catholic Widows and Widowers Mutual support for widowed persons of any faith. Groups for the recently bereaved as well as for those further along. Various meeting locations and times. Call Family Life Office, Metuchen Diocese 732-562-1990 ext. 1624 (day).

While it's no substitution for talking to our staff, you can call evenings or weekends! Leave a message and we will get back to you the next workday. ***1-800-367-6274***

Single Senior Women Support for women (age 60+) who are divorced, separated and widowed. Meets 2nd and 4th Thurs., 10am-noon, Office on Aging, 92 East Main St., 1st Floor, Conference Room, Somerville. Call Erin 908-704-6339 (day).

UNION

Bereavement Support Groups *Professionally-run.* Series of 8 weekly meetings with separate groups for spouses and other family members. Registration fee $10 (adults fee can be waived). Meets various times, United Methodist Church, 1441 Springfield Ave., New Providence. Call Bereavement Coordinator 973-379-8440 (day).

Hospice Bereavement Support Group *Professionally-run.* Mutual support for persons bereaving the death of spouse. Rap sessions, literature, guest speakers. Group runs for 8 weeks (Spring/Fall). Meets Thurs., 1:30-3pm, Robert Wood Johnson University Hospital at Rahway, 865 Stone St., Rahway. For information call Shannon Wiese 732-499-6169 (day). *Email:* swiese@rwjuhr.com

Separated, Divorced, Widowed and Bereaved Catholics Referrals to groups for emotional and spiritual support for separated, divorced, widowed or bereaved, men and women. Groups are sponsored by various churches throughout the county and are open to people of any faith. Call Family Life Ministry 973-497-4327.

WARREN

Catholic Widows and Widowers Mutual support for widowed persons of any faith. Groups for the recently bereaved as well as for those further along. Various meeting locations and times. Call the Family Life Office, Metuchen 732-562-1990 ext. 1624 (day).

NATIONAL

Beginning Experience, The *International. 140 teams. Founded 1974.* Support programs for divorced, widowed and separated adults, & their children enabling them to work through the grief of a lost marriage. Write: The Beginning Experience, c/o International Ministry Center, 1657 Commerce Dr., South Bend, IN 46628. Call 574-283-0279 or 1-866-610-8877; Fax: 574-283-0287. *Website:* http://www.beginningexperience.org *Email:* imc@beginningexperience.org

We know this Directory is big and chances are we can probably find the group you're looking for quicker than you paging through it. Call us! (We're really friendly!)
1-800-367-6274

COPS (Concerns Of Police Survivors, Inc.) *National. 48 chapters. Founded 1984.* Provides resources for the surviving families of law enforcement officers killed in the line of duty according to Federal criteria. Also offers law enforcement training. Quarterly newsletter, departmental guidelines, peer support, Special hands-on programs for survivors. Summer camp for children (age 6-14) and their parent/guardian. Parents' retreats, spouse get-away, Outward Bound experiences for young adults (age 15-20), siblings retreat, adult children's and in-laws retreats. Write: COPS, PO Box 3199, 3096 S. State Hwy 5, Camdenton, MO 65020. Call 573-346-4911; Fax: 573-346-1414. *Website:* http://www.nationalcops.org *Email:* cops@nationalcops.org

North American Conference of Separated and Divorced Catholics *International. 3000+ groups. Founded 1974.* Religious, educational, and emotional aspects of separation, divorce, remarriage and widowhood are addressed through self-help groups, conferences and training programs. Families of all faiths are welcome. Group development guidelines. Newsletter. Membership dues starting at $35 (includes newsletter, discounts, & resources). Write: NACSDC, PO Box 10, Hancock, MI 49930. Call 906-482-0494; Fax: 906-482-7470. *Website:* http://www.nacsdc.org *Email:* office@nacsdc.org

Society of Military Widows *National. 24 chapters. Founded 1968.* Support & assistance for widows/widowers of members of all U.S. uniformed services. Helps people in coping with adjustment to life on their own. Promotes public awareness. Bimonthly magazine/journal. Dues $12. Chapter development guidelines. Online listing on local chapters. Write: Soc. of Military Widows, 5535 Hempstead Way, Springfield, VA 22151. Call 253-750-1342 or 1-800-842-3451 (press 5). *Website:* http://www.militarywidows.org *Email:* h.grant@naus.org

ONLINE

Young Widow *Online.* Mutual support group for young widows and widowers, who share experiences and strengths through an interactive message board. Also provides a listing of local face-to-face support groups, links to other related online email discussion groups and websites for young widowed persons. *Website:* http://www.youngwidow.com *Email:* contact@ywbb.org

GROWW (Grief Recovery Online (found by) Widows and Widowers *Online.* Support groups for persons bereaving the loss of a loved one. Offers a large variety of chat rooms, run by volunteers, dealing with specific issues (loss of someone to drugs, a child, sibling, parent, loss due to long term illness, sudden death, violent losses, gays and lesbians, men and many more). *Website:* http://www.groww.org

"The majority of us lead quiet,
unheralded lives as we pass through this world.
There will most likely be no ticker-tape parades for us, no
monuments created in our honor.

But that does not lessen our possible impact, for there are
scores of people waiting for someone just like us to come
along; people who will appreciate our compassion, our
unique talents.

Someone who will live a happier life merely because we
took the time to share what we had to give.

Too often we underestimate the power of a touch, a smile, a
kind word, a listening ear, an honest compliment, or the
smallest act of caring, all of which have a potential to turn a
life around.

It's overwhelming to consider the continuous opportunities
there are to make our love felt."

Leo Buscaglia

DISABILITIES

AMPUTATION / LIMB DEFICIENCY
(see also general disabilities)

BERGEN

Kessler Leg Amputee Support Group *Professionally-run.* Provides mutual support for both trans-tibial (below knee) and trans-femoral (above knee) amputees. Families welcome. Rap sessions, guest speakers, literature and buddy system. Meets 3rd Thurs., 6-7:30pm, Kessler Institute, 300 Market St., Saddle Brook. Call Cynthia Macaluso 201-368-6087 (day).

BURLINGTON

Amputee Support Group Provides physical, emotional and social support to amputees and their families. Rap sessions and guest speakers. Meets 3rd Wed., 7-8:30pm, Marlton Rehab Hospital, 92 Brick Rd., Marlton. Call Andrea Varone 856-988-8778 ext. 2030.

ESSEX

S.H.A.G. (Self-Help Amputee Group) Mutual support for amputees and their families (under 18 welcome). Phone support. Dues $10/yr. Meets 1st Sat., 10am, Kessler Institute, West Orange. Call Ann Silvestrini 973-759-4142 (day/eve).

OCEAN

James F. Gorman Amputee Support Group of NJ Mutual support, encouragement and education for amputees, their families, friends, caregivers or anyone who has involvement with an amputee. Rap sessions, guest speakers, literature, social, phone help and buddy system. Dues $5. Meets 1st Wed., noon-1:30pm, Health South Rehabilitation Hospital of Toms River, 14 Hospital Dr., Toms River. Call Larry 732-255-5480 (day/eve), Sue 732-286-5663 (day) or Randi 732-363-1636. *Email:* lszczepan@aol.com

---

If you are using this book past Spring 2007, please call us for information about our most recent directory. 1-800-367-6274

NATIONAL

American Amputee Foundation, Inc. *National. Founded 1975.* Provides self-help and educational information, referrals and peer support for amputees. Offers hospital visitation and counseling. Group development guidelines. Resource directory. Write: American Amputee Foundation, PO Box 250218, Little Rock, AR 72225. Call 501-666-2523. *Website:* http://www.americanamputee.org

Amputee Coalition of America *National.* Mission is to reach out to people with limb loss and to empower them through education, support and advocacy. Maintains the National Limb Loss Information Center. Offers a full listing of support groups. Provides referrals to peer visitors. Publishes "Starting a Support Group" information packet and "inMotion" and "First Step: A Guide for Adapting to Limb Loss" magazines. Write: Amputee Coalition of America, 900 East Hill Ave, Suite 285, Knoxville, TN 37915. Call 1-888-267-5669; Fax: 865-525-7917. *Website:* http://www.amputee-coalition.org *Email:* mgoins@amputee-coalition.org

National Amputation Foundation, Inc. *National. Founded 1919.* Self-help group for amputees of all ages. "Amp to Amp" program links individuals with others with similar amputations. Newsletter, information and referrals. Dues $25/yr. Write: National Amputation Foundation, 40 Church St., Malverne, NY 11565. Call 516-887-3600; Fax: 516-887-3667. *Website:* http://www.nationalamputation.org *Email:* amps76@aol.com

ONLINE

I-CAN (International Child Amputee Network) *Online.* Mailing list for parents of children with either acquired or congenital limb loss. Opportunity to share experiences with other parents. *Website:* http://www.amp-info.net/childamp.htm

LimbDifferences.org *Online.* A comprehensive resource to the families and friends of children with limb differences. Helps members establish contact with other families of children with limb differences through its forum. *Website:* http://www.limbdifferences.org

---

"All of us are, to some extent, victims of what we are. We are not limited by our imaginations, but by our ability to do what we imagine. We are not too often limited by our abilities as much as by circumstances. And we are not as often limited by our circumstances as much as by the lack of the will to respond."
--Dee Bowman

AUTISM / ASPERGER'S SYNDROME
(see also parents of the disabled)

STATEWIDE

ASPEN (Asperger Syndrome Parents Education Network) Information and support for parents of children with Asperger syndrome, pervasive developmental disorder and high functioning autism. Discussion groups, guest speakers and statewide workshops. Dues $25/yr. Write: ASPEN, 9 Aspen Circle, Edison, NJ, 08820. Call Lori Shery 732-321-0880 (9am-2pm). *Website:* http://www.aspennj.org *Email:* aspenorg@aol.com

COSAC (Center for Outreach and Services for the Autism Community) *Professionally-run.* Helps families, individuals, teachers and agencies concerned about the welfare and treatment of children and adults with autism. Pen pals for siblings, guest speakers, information, referral, advocacy assistance and workshops. Eleven support groups statewide. Newsletter. Write: COSAC, 1450 Parkside Ave., Suite 22, Ewing, NJ 08638. Call 1-800-428-8476 (day) or 609-883-8100 ext. 28. *Website:* http://www.njcosac.org *Email:* information@njcosac.org

ATLANTIC

ASPEN (Asperger Syndrome Parents Education Network) Atlantic/Cape May Counties Information and support for parents of children with Asperger syndrome/PDD-NOS and high functioning autism. Discussion groups and guest speakers. Meets 1st Tues., 7-8:30pm, Atlantic County Library, 40 Farragant Ave., Mays Landing. Call Florence Castro 609-625-2142 or Library 609-625-2776. *Website:* http://www.aspennj.org

BERGEN

ASPEN (Asperger Syndrome Parents Education Network) Provides resource information, education, caring, sharing and understanding to parents of children with Asperger syndrome. Phone help, literature, newsletter. Dues $25/yr. Meets 2nd Mon., Glen Rock. Call 201-391-0758. *Website:* http://www.aspennj.org *Email:* PIYT@x3@aol.com

COSAC (Center for Outreach and Services for the Autism Community) *Professionally-run.* Mutual support for parents of children with autism. Families welcome. Guest speakers, literature and phone help. Meets 1st Fri., 8-10pm, Mt. Carmel Church, Passaic St., Ridgewood. Call Gary 201-503-9476.

Spectrum Support Group Mutual support and education for families of children with autism and other pervasive developmental disorders. Aims to promote awareness and acceptance in order to help the children become more part of the community. Guest speakers, periodic workshops for children. Meets 3rd Mon., (except Dec., July, Aug.), 7:30pm, First Presbyterian Church, Carlstadt. Call Rev. Donald Pitches 201-438-5526 or Kathy Cromelin 201-438-4098 (day).

BURLINGTON

P.A.C.T (Parents of Autistic Children Together) Support and sharing of information by parents of autistic children. Outside activities with siblings and families. Newsletter. Meets 2nd Tues., (Sept.-May), 7:30-10pm, Christ Presbyterian Church, Main St., Marlton. Call 856-722-8518 (day). *Website:* http://www.solvingthepuzzle.com

CAMDEN

GRASP (Global & Regional Asperger Syndrome Partnership) Support network for adults diagnosed with high functioning autism or Asperger syndrome. Meets 2nd Sat., 2-4pm, Easttown Library, 720 First Ave., Berwyn, PA. Call Robert 610-993-8096.   *Website:* http://health.groups.yahoo.com/group/GRASP_Philadelphia_PA/

ESSEX

ADD Action Group Information about alternative solutions for attention deficit disorder, learning disabilities, hyperactivity, dyslexia and autism. Educational series, guest speakers, literature, phone help. Usually meets 3rd Thurs., 7-8:45pm, Millburn Public Library, 200 Glen Ave., Millburn. Call Lynne Berke 973-731-2189 (day/eve). *Email:* LTBerke@aol.com

ASPEN (Asperger Syndrome Parents Education Network) Support for parents and families of children whose lives are affected by Asperger syndrome/PDD-NOS and high functioning autism. Guest speakers and literature. Dues $25/yr. Meets 2nd Mon., 7:30-9:30pm, JCC of Metrowest, 760 Northfield Ave., West Orange. Call Anita 973-669-5757 (day). *Website:* http://www.aspennj.org

COSAC (Center for Outreach and Services for the Autism Community) *Professionally-run.* Mutual support for parents of children with autism. Families welcome. Guest speakers, literature and phone help.

> **Union City** *(SPANISH SPEAKING)* Meets 1st Thurs., 7-9pm, St. Augustine's Church, 3900 New York Ave. Call Susana 201-864-7262.

Verona Meets 1st Mon., 7-9pm, Temple/Congregation Beth Ahm, 56 Grove Ave. Call Michele Havens 201-486-5607 (day/eve). *Email:* mhavens523@aol.com

HUNTERDON

ASPEN (Asperger Syndrome Parents Education Network) *(Hunterdon County Adult Issues)* Young adults group for ages 18 and up who have Asperger syndrome, high functioning autism or PDD. Discussion, social and guest speakers. Parent group runs concurrently. Meets 3rd Sun., Health Quest, 310 Highway 31 North, Flemington. Call Matt and Carolyn 908-236-6153 (day). *Website:* http://www.aspergersfriends.com

Sharing and Caring of Bucks County Information and support for parents of children with autism, Asperger syndrome, mental retardation and related disorders. Discussion groups, guest speakers, sib-shop sibling support group, social and recreational activities. Suggested donation $15/yr. Meets 2nd Thurs., 7-9pm, St. Vincent DePaul Church, Education Building, Hatboro Rd., Richboro, PA. Call Holly Druckman 215-321-3202 (Mon.-Fri., 10am-6pm).

MERCER

ASPEN (Asperger Syndrome Parents Education Network) *(Central NJ Chapter)* Information and support for parents of children with Asperger syndrome/PDD-NOS and high functioning autism. Discussion groups and guest speakers. Dues $25/yr. Meets 3rd Tues., 7-9pm, West Windsor Library, Princeton Junction. Call Beth 609-275-5922 (day). *Website:* http://www.aspennj.org *Email:* Blondedawg@aol.com

COSAC (Center for Outreach and Services for the Autism Community) *Professionally-run.* Mutual support for parents of children with autism. Families welcome. Meets 3rd Fri., 7-9pm, Hamilton YMCA, Whitehorse-Mercerville Rd., Hamilton. Call Kelly 609-584-8825 (eve).

MIDDLESEX

ASPEN (Asperger Syndrome Parents Education Network) Information and support for parents of children with Asperger syndrome, PPD-NOS and high functioning autism. Discussion groups and guest speakers. Dues $25/yr. Meets monthly, Wed., 7:30-9:30pm, Community Campus-JCC, 1775 Oak Tree Rd., Edison. Call Lori Shery 732-321-0880 (day). *Website:* http://www.aspennj.org *Email:* aspenorg@aol.com

MONMOUTH

ASPEN (Asperger Syndrome Parents Education Network) Information and support for parents of children with Asperger syndrome/PDD-NOS and high functioning autism. Discussion groups and guest speakers. Meets 3rd Wed., 7-9pm, Monmouth County Library, Headquarters, Symmes Dr., Manalapan. Call Ann Hiller 732-446-7610 (eve). *Website:* http://www.aspennj.org *Email:* ann0912@aol.com

ASPEN Adult Issues Support for families of adults with high functioning autism and Asperger syndrome. Offers socialization opportunities, advocacy, literature, rap sessions, phone help, mutual sharing and education. Dues $25/yr. Meets Mon., 7-8:30pm, Monmouth County Library Headquarters, 125 Symmes Dr., Manalapan. Call Mary Laresch 609-409-1007.

MORRIS

ASPEN (Asperger Syndrome Parents Education Network) For parents and families of children with Asperger syndrome, high functioning autism and other pervasive developmental disorders to provide support, education, advocacy and sharing of resources. Guest speakers, literature. Dues $25/yr. Meets last Wed., 7:30-9:30pm, Saint Clare's Hospital, Conference Room D, 400 West Blackwell St., Dover. Call Janice 973-541-0178. *Website:* http://www.aspennj.org *Email:* janmlem1@hotmail.com

OCEAN

ASPEN (Asperger Syndrome Parents Education Network) Support for parents and families of children whose lives are affected by Asperger syndrome/PDD-NOS. Guest speakers. Dues $25/yr. Meetings vary, Temple Beth Shalom, Whitty & Old Freehold Rd., Toms River. Before attending call Eileen 732-473-9630 (day).

Autism Support Group Support and education for families affected by autism and their communities. Guest speakers, literature and phone help. Meets last Fri., 6:30-8:30pm, SOCH Resource Center, Ocean Club, 700 Route 9 South, Manahawkin. Call Jackie and Ed Seeger 609-294-0443. *Email:* facesgroup@comcast.net

Can't find an appropriate group in your area? The Clearinghouse helps people start groups. Give us a call at 1-800-367-6274.

PASSAIC

Autism/Asperger Support Group Support and education for parents of children with autism and Asperger syndrome. Rap sessions, buddy system, newsletter and phone help. Meets last Wed., 7-9pm, Hillcrest Community Center, 1810 Macopin Rd., Room 25, West Milford. Call Julie Rikon or Angela Abdul 973-728-8744 (day).

SALEM

Salem County Autism Support Group Mutual support and education for anyone concerned about the treatment of children and adults with autism. Guest speakers, literature and newsletter. Meets 2nd Wed., 7:30-9:30pm, Small Wonders Pre-School, 3 Ferry Rd., Pennsville. Call Diane Hitchner 856-351-6666 (day/eve) or Nancy Gayle 856-678-5741 (day).

SOMERSET

ASPEN (Asperger Syndrome Parents Education Network) Provides resource information, education, caring, sharing and understanding to parents of children with Asperger syndrome. Phone help, literature, newsletter. Dues $25/yr. Meets 2nd Thurs., 7:30pm, (Sept.-May), Hillsborough Presbyterian Church, Route 206 South and Homestead Rd., Hillsborough. Call Inez 908-904-1610.

WARREN

COSAC (Center for Outreach and Services for the Autism Community) *Professionally-run.* Mutual support for parents of children with autism. Families welcome. Guest speakers, literature and phone help. Meets 4th Mon., 7:30-9pm, Hackettstown Hospital, Willow Grove St., Hackettstown. Call Jodi 973-663-2505 (day).

NATIONAL

Autism Network for Hearing & Visually Impaired Persons *International network. Founded 1992.* Provides communication, education, research and advocacy for persons with autism combined with a hearing or visual disability, their families and professionals. Sharing of educational materials, phone help, support groups, referrals and conferences. Write: Autism Network for Hearing & Visually Impaired Persons, 7510 Ocean Front Ave., Virginia Beach, VA 23451. Call 757-428-9036. *Email:* d.bartel@cox.net

Autism Network International *International. Founded 1992.* Organization run by and for autistic people. Provides peer support and tips for coping and problem-solving. Information and referrals. Advocacy, education, retreats/conferences. Online listserv. Write: ANI, PO Box 35448, Syracuse, NY 13235-5448. Call 315-476-2462 (long-distance calls will be returned collect); TTY/TDD: 315-425-1978. *Website:* http://www.ani.ac *Email:* jisincla@mailbox.syc.edu

Autism Society of America *National. 200+ chapters. Founded 1965.* Organization of parents, professionals & citizens working together via education, advocacy and research for children & adults with autism. Newsletter and annual conference. Write: ASA, 7910 Woodmont Ave., Suite 300 Bethesda, MD 20814. Call 301-657-0881 or 1-800-328-8476 (information & referral only); Fax: 301-657-0869. *Website:* http://www.autism-society.org/ *Email:* jmellow@autism-society.org

GRASP - The Global and Regional Asperger Syndrome Partnership *National. Founded 2003.* Support network for adults diagnosed with high functioning autism, Asperger syndrome or pervasive developmental disorder. Newsletter, literature, advocacy, information and referrals and assistance in starting local chapters. Write: GRASP, 35 E. 15th St., New York, NY, 10003. Call 646-242-4003; Fax: 212-529-9996. *Website:* http://www.grasp.org *Email:* info@grasp.org

Parent Link *Model. 1 group in New York. Founded 1996.* Support and education for parents of children with higher functioning autism, Asperger syndrome or other pervasive developmental disorders. Develops activities and educates professionals. Provides information and referrals, newsletter and literature. Assistance in starting groups. Write: Parent Link, c/o Kay Grisar, 62 W. Orchard Rd., Chappaqua, NY 10514. Call Susan 914-763-0971 or Kay 914-666-2099. *Website:* http://www.westchesterparentlink.org *Email:* Kay@WestchesterParentLink.org

ONLINE

ASpar *Online.* Mutual support and advocacy for non-autistic persons who were raised by a parent with autistic traits. Opportunity to communicate with others from similar backgrounds. Also open to families of adults with autism. *Website:* http://www.aspar.klattu.com.du/aspmem.htm

Families of Adults Afflicted with Asperger's Syndrome *Online* Offers support to the family members of adult individuals with Asperger's Syndrome. Bulletin board, email list and resources. *Website:* http://www.faaas.org

OASIS (Online Asperger Syndrome Information and Support) *Online.* Interactive webpage providing information and support for Asperger syndrome and related disorders. Referrals to local, national and international support groups. Message boards and chat rooms. Forums for families affected by Asperger syndrome and the professionals working with them. Message board: http://forums.delphiforums.com/aspergeroasis *Website:* http://www.aspergersyndrome.org *Email:* bkirby@udel.edu

BLIND / VISUALLY IMPAIRED
(see also specific disorder, toll-free helplines)

STATEWIDE

American Council of the Blind of Central New Jersey Consumer organization for visually impaired persons age 16+. Information, referrals, advocacy and fundraising. Dues $10/yr. Meets 5 times per year, Sat., central NJ. Write: ACBC-NJ, 66 Fox Rd., Apt. 7B, Edison, NJ, 08817. Call David M. Zulli 732-985-3175.

DOROT/University Without Walls Telephone Support Teleconference support groups for persons age 59+ who are coping with vision loss, care giving, aging issues, etc. Registration fee $10 and $15 tuition per support group. Scholarships are available. Write: DOROT, 171 W. 85th St., NY, NY, 10024. For more information call DOROT 1-877-819-9147. *Website:* http://www.dorotusa.org

National Federation of the Blind of New Jersey Advocacy, self-help, education and support for blind persons, their families and friends. Under 18 welcome. Visitation, phone help, guest speakers. Annual state conference. Quarterly newsletter, "Sounding Board" available in print and cassette. Dues $5/yr. Write: NFBNJ, 254 Spruce St., Bloomfield, NJ 07003. Call Joe Ruffalo 973-743-0075 (9am-5pm). *Website:* http://www.nfb.org

New Jersey Association of the Deaf-Blind, Inc. *Professionally-run.* Purpose of group is to meet the needs of the deaf-blind, deaf or blind, communication impaired and their families in NJ. Provides advocacy, case management, education, information and referrals. Residential, community, support, employment, family support and training services available. Write: NJADB, Inc., 24 K Worlds Fair Dr., Somerset, NJ 08873. Call 732-805-1912 (voice/TTY).

Parents of Blind Children - NJ Support, information, training and advocacy for parents of blind and visually impaired children. Dues $10/yr. Write: POBC, 23 Alexander Ave., Madison, NJ, 07940. Call Carol Castellano 973-377-0976 (day). *Website:* http://www.blindchildren.org *Email:* center@webspan.net

ATLANTIC

VIP Flyers Mutual support for individuals who are blind or visually impaired. Families welcome. Rap sessions, guest speakers, literature, phone help, buddy system and speakers' bureau. Meets 4th Tues., 11am-1pm, John D. Young Blind Center, 100 Crestview Ave., Absecon. Call Ann Burns 609-677-1199 (day).

BERGEN

Adjustment to Vision Loss Support Support for persons dealing with vision loss to exchange helpful information, offer and obtain emotional support while learning practical solutions for dealing with vision loss.
> **Teaneck** Meets 3rd Fri., 10:30am-12:30pm, St. Luke's Church, 118 Chadwick Rd. Call Dorothy Barrow 201-837-5197 (after 3pm).
> **Westwood** Meets 4th Mon., 1-3pm, Pascack Valley Hospital, 250 Old Hook Rd. Call Paul Ingram 201-666-0833.

Focus on Eyes Support Group for the Visually-Impaired Mutual support for blind and visually impaired persons. Meets 1st Tues., 10am-noon, Fair Lawn Municipal Building, Fair Lawn Ave., Fair Lawn. Call Marion 201-797-6937 or Helen Markowitz 201-797-8839. *Email:* m.slacke@att.net

BURLINGTON

Choice Mutual support for blind and visually impaired persons, their families and friends. Rap sessions, phone help, guest speakers, literature, buddy system and speakers bureau. Meets 4th Tues., 10am-1pm, Resources for Independent Living, 126 Franklin St., Riverside. Call Joe Zesski 609-747-7745; TTY: 856-461-3482. *Email:* info@rilnj.org

V.I.P. Leisuretown Low Vision Support Group *Professionally-run.* Mutual aid self-help for blind and visually impaired persons. Emotional support, sharing of experiences and information. Meets 2nd Tues., 1:30-3pm, Touch House, Leisuretown, 202 North Plymouth Court, South Hampton. Call 609-859-2980.

CAMDEN

National Federation of the Blind of New Jersey Mutual support, information and advocacy for blind persons, their families and friends (under 18 welcome). Visitation, phone help, guest speakers. Dues $1.50/month. Meets 3rd Sat., Kennedy Memorial Hospital, 5th Floor, Conference Room A, Cherry Hill. Call Ryan Stevens 856-858-3518.

PILOTS (People Interested in Lending Others Their Support) Offers mutual support and education for blind and visually-impaired persons (age 35-65). Meets 2nd Fri., 11:30am-2pm, (except Nov., 3rd Fri.) R-Mac's Restaurant, 427 West Crystal Lake Ave., Haddon Township. Call Annemarie Del Sordo 856-629-7219 (day) or Linda Bernadino 856-764-7014.

ESSEX

Foresighters *(WEST ORANGE RESIDENTS ONLY)* Support for blind and visually impaired persons. Meets 4th Thurs., 1-3pm, West Orange. Call Helen Gromann 973-731-4650 (day).

National Federation of the Blind of New Jersey *Northern NJ Chapter* Advocacy, self-help, education and support for blind persons, their families and friends. Visitation, phone help, guest speakers. Dues $5/yr. Meets 3rd Sat., 10:30am, Hilton Hotel, Gateway Center Chapel, Newark. Call Ed Lewinson 973-374-1223.

S.C.I.L.S. (Senior Community Independent Living Services) *Professionally-run.* Support for seniors (age 55+) who are visually impaired/blind. Family and friends are welcome. Offers rap sessions, social group, literature, educational materials, mutual sharing and guest speakers. Transportation provided. Meets 3rd Wed., 1:30-2:45pm, (except June, July, Aug.), Bloomfield Civic Center, Bloomfield. Call Lauri Matera 201-656-6001 ext. 152.

GLOUCESTER

S.C.I.L.S. (Senior Community Independent Living Services) *(BILINGUAL) Professionally-run.* Support for interpersonal sharing, support and personal growth for blind and visually impaired persons (age 55+). Several small informal groups meet in various locations. Spanish-speaking group available. Call 201-656-6001 (day).

SHADES, INC. Mutual aid self-help for blind and visually impaired persons. Emotional support, sharing of experiences, guest speakers and information. Meets 4th Thurs., 11am-2pm, Gloucester County Library, Route 45, Mullica Hill. Call Kathryn 856-589-5438.

> *"Expect to have hope rekindled. Expect your prayers to be answered in wondrous ways. The dry seasons in life do not last.*
> *The spring rains will come again."*
> *--Sarah Ban Breathnach*

HUNTERDON

Hunterdon Eye Openers Support for persons dealing with vision loss to exchange helpful information, offer and obtain emotional support while learning practical solutions for dealing with vision loss. Dues $5/meeting. Meets 1st Thurs., 11:30am, Extension Building, Gauntt Pl., Flemington. Call Millie 908-236-6966 or Harriet Schwartz 908-806-7968.

MERCER

Adjustment to Vision Loss Support Support for persons dealing with vision loss to exchange helpful information, offer and obtain emotional support while learning practical solutions for dealing with vision loss. Dues $10/yr. Meets 3rd Thurs., 7:30-9:30pm, 1985 Pennington Rd., Ewing. Call Ottilie Lucas 609-882-2446. *Email:* ottilie@verizon.net

National Federation of the Blind Support and advocacy for the blind community. Family and friends are welcome to attend. Dues $10/yr. Meets 3rd Sat., 10am-noon, Lawrence Library, 2751 Brunswick Pike, Lawrenceville. Call Mary Jo 609-588-2145 (day) or 609-888-5459 (eve). *Email:* choir.nsb@verizon.net

MIDDLESEX

Adjustment to Vision Loss Support Support for persons dealing with vision loss to exchange helpful information, offer and obtain emotional support while learning practical solutions for dealing with vision loss.

> **Metuchen** Meets 4th Thurs., 7-9pm, (Mar.-Oct.), Metuchen Public Library, (rear entrance), 480 Middlesex Ave. Call Phyllis Boeddinghaus 732-548-1391; TTY/TDD: 732-738-9644.
> **Monroe Twp** Meets 3rd Thurs., 10:30am-12:15pm, Monroe Twp. Senior Center, 1 Municipal Plaza. Call Judy Kalman 732-521-6111.
> **Monroe Twp** Meetings vary, Monroe Village. Call Ted Alter 732-521-6418. *Email:* talter@phsnet.org
> **Perth Amboy** Dues $10 yr. Meets 3rd Mon., 7-9pm, Grace Lutheran Church, 600 New Brunswick Ave. Call Kelly Leary 732-388-1322. *Email:* kaklleary@aol.com

Eye Openers Of Central New Jersey Mutual aid self-help for blind and visually impaired persons. Emotional support, sharing of experience and information. Meets 1st Thurs., 7:15-9:15pm, at local restaurants. Call Bernard Zuckerman 732-494-0753 (day/eve).

MONMOUTH

Middletown Area Visually Challenged Group Support for persons dealing with vision loss to exchange helpful information, offer and obtain emotional support while learning practical solutions for dealing with vision loss. Meets 2nd Tues., 11am-noon, N.J.B.C.A., Camp Happiness, 18 Burlington Ave., Leonardo. Call Charles Blood 732-671-9371.

V.I.P. (Visually Impaired Persons) Support Group *(NEPTUNE RESIDENTS ONLY) Professionally-run.* Mutual support and information for blind and visually impaired persons (age 60+). Educational series, advocacy, rap sessions, guest speakers, phone help. Meets last Wed., 10-11:30am, Neptune Senior Center, 1825 Corlies Ave., Neptune. Call Ellen 732-988-8855.

MORRIS

North Jersey Retinitis Pigmentosa Support Group Mutual support for persons with retinitis pigmentosa, macular degeneration, Usher's syndrome or related disorders and their families. Provides education, referrals, phone help, rap sessions and guest speakers. Meetings vary, 1:30-4pm, Morristown. Before attending call Jean and Don Perlman 973-584-6471 (day/eve), Susan Strechay 973-267-2419 (eve) or Glorie Isakower 609-409-7985 (Usher's syndrome).

V.I.P. (Visually Impaired Persons) Mutual aid self-help for blind and visually impaired persons. Emotional support, sharing of experiences and information. Meets 2nd Wed., (except July/Aug.), 11am-1:30pm, Diamond Spring Lodge, 230 Diamond Spring Rd., Denville. Call Mary Ann Speenburgh 973-884-0039.

OCEAN

Adjustment to Vision Loss Support Support for persons dealing with vision loss to exchange helpful information, offer and obtain emotional support while learning practical solutions for dealing with vision loss. Meets 2nd Tues., 11am-noon, Leisure Village East, 1015 B Aberdeen Dr., Lakewood. Call Betty Gumanow 732-920-1522.

Eye Openers Mutual aid self-help for blind and visually impaired persons. Emotional support, sharing of experiences and information.

> **Point Pleasant** Meets 2nd and 4th Tues., 10am-noon, Pt. Pleasant Presbyterian Church, Education Annex, Bay and Forman Aves. Call George 732-892-5117.
>
> **Toms River** Meets 3rd Tues., 12:30-2:30pm, Dover Township Municipal

Bldg., Washington St. Call Jim Fox 732-244-7057 (day). *Email:* Jim2447057@comcast.net

Low Vision Support Group Support for persons afflicted with low vision, their families and friends. Guest speakers, mutual sharing and educational programs. Meets 1st Wed., 1pm, Ocean Club, 700 Route 9 South, Stafford Township. Call Betty 609-978-3559.

Visionares Emotional support, fun and information for blind and visually impaired persons. Meets 3rd Thurs., 1:30-3pm, (except July/Aug.), Holiday City South, Clubhouse, Toms River. Call Doris Frederick 732-244-1689.

UNION

Macular Degeneration Informational Support Group Mutual support and information for persons with macular degeneration, their families and friends. Guest speakers, rap sessions, educational series, literature. Usually meets the 2nd Sat., (except July-Sept.), 11am-12:30pm, Overlook Hospital, Conference Room 2, 99 Beauvoir Ave., Summit. For information Call J.P. Doyle 908-273-3633 (6:30-7:30pm). *Email:* JDoyle2000@verizon.net

Self-Help Group for the Visually-Impaired Provides mutual support and education for those that are blind or visually-impaired. Meets 1st Thurs., noon-2pm, (except July/Aug.), Senior Citizen Center, Bonnel Court, Union. Call Agnes 908-790-9336 (eve).

NATIONAL

American Council of the Blind National. *National 70 affiliates. Founded 1961.* Aims to improve the well-being of all blind & visually impaired people & their families through education, support, & advocacy. National conference, information & referrals, phone support, state and special interest affiliates (e.g. guide dog users, blind lawyers, teachers and students), magazine published eights times per year (available in Braille, half speed cassette, large print, diskette and online or via Email). Scholarships. Online job bank. Chapter development guidelines. Write: American Council of the Blind, 1155 15th St. NW, #1004, Washington, DC 20005. Call 1-800-424-8666 or 202-467-5081; Fax: 202-467-5085. *Website:* http://www.acb.org *Email:* info@acb.org

Association for Macular Diseases, Inc. *National. Local support groups. Founded 1978.* Support for persons suffering from macular diseases and their families. Distributes information on vision equipment. Supports national eye bank donor projects devoted solely to macular disease research. Quarterly newsletter, phone support network, participates in seminars, group development guidelines. Dues $20/year. Write: Association for Macular Diseases, 210 E. 64th St., New York, NY 10021. Call 212-605-3719; Fax: 212-605-3795. *Website:* http://www.macula.org

Autism Network for Hearing & Visually Impaired Persons *International network. Founded 1992.* Provides communication, education, research and advocacy for persons with autism combined with a hearing or visual disability, their families and professionals. Sharing of educational materials, phone help, support groups, referrals and conferences. Write: Autism Network for Hearing & Visually Impaired Persons, 7510 Ocean Front Ave., Virginia Beach, VA 23451. Call 757-428-9036; Fax: 757-428-0019.

Blinded Veterans Association *National. 55 regional groups. Founded 1945.* Information, support and outreach to blinded veterans including those who were blinded in combat and those suffering from age-related macular degeneration and other eye diseases. Help in obtaining prosthetic devices and accessing the latest technological advances to assist the blind. Information on benefits and rehabilitation programs. Quarterly newsletter. Regional meetings. Write: BVA, 477 H St., NW, Washington, DC 20001. Call 202-371-8880 or 1-800-669-7079; Fax: 202-371-8258. *Website:* http://www.bva.org *Email:* bva@bva.org

Council of Citizens with Low Vision International *International. Founded 1979.* Encourages low vision people to make full use of vision through use of equipment, technology, & services. Education and advocacy. Newsletter, information & referrals, group development guidelines, scholarships and conferences. Write: CCLVI, 1155 15th St. NW, Suite 1004, Washington, DC 20005. Call 1-800-733-2258. *Website:* http://www.cclvi.org

Foundation Fighting Blindness, The *National. Founded 1971.* Offers information and referral services for affected individuals and their families, as well as doctors and eye care professionals. Provides comprehensive information kits on retinitis pigmentosa, macular degeneration and Usher syndrome. Newsletter presents articles on coping, research updates and Foundation news. Supports research into the causes, treatments, preventive methods and cures for the entire spectrum of retinal degenerative diseases. National conferences. Write: Fdn. Fighting Blindness, 11435 Cronhill Dr., Owings Mill, MD 21117-2220. Call 1-800-683-5555 or 410-568-0150; TDD: 1-800-683-5551 or 410-363-7139; Fax: 410-363-2393. *Website:* http://www.FightBlindness.org *Email:* info@blindness.org

We can also refer callers to over 100 individuals who are seeking others to help start new support groups throughout NJ, if you don't see it, that doesn't mean it doesn't exist!
1-800-367-6274

Lighthouse International *Resource* Mission is to overcome vision impairment for people of all ages through rehabilitation services, education, research and advocacy. Free literature on eye diseases (macular degeneration, glaucoma, cataracts, diabetes and more) and various resource lists (reading options, adaptive computer technology, financial aid, etc.) Provides contact information for support groups, low vision services, rehabilitation agencies, state agencies and advocacy groups. Write: Lighthouse International, 111 East 59th St., New York, NY 10022. Call 1-800-829-0500 or 212-821-9200 Fax: 212-821-9705 or 1-212-821-9713. *Website:* http://www.lighthouse.org *Email:* info@lighthouse.org

MAB Community Services *National. 35 groups. Founded 1903.* Support network for persons coping with sight loss. Sponsors support groups for elders and mixed ages. Outreach services, phone support, community volunteers, Braille transcriptions, recording studio, large print literature, cassettes and newsletter. Assistive devices for a fee. Write: MAB Comm. Services, 23A Elm St., Watertown, MA 02472 Call 617-926-4232 or 1-800-852-3029 (MA only); Fax: 617-926-1412. *Website:* http://www.mabcommunity.org *Email:* fweisse@mabcommunity.org

National Association for Parents of Children with Visual Impairments *National. 21 groups. Founded 1980.* Outreach and support for parents of children with visual impairments. Promotes formation of local parent support groups. Increases public awareness. Quarterly newsletter. Dues $25/family. Group development guidelines. Write: NAPVI, Inc., PO Box 317, Watertown, MA 02471-0317. Call 1-800-562-6265; Fax: 617-972-7444. *Website:* http://www.napvi.org *Email:* napvi@perkins.org

National Association for Visually Handicapped *(MULTILINGUAL) National. 2 regional offices. Founded 1954.* Support groups for partially-seeing persons. Newsletter, phone support, information and referrals. Guide to starting groups for elders losing sight. Free large print loan library by mail, optical library. Large print informational materials available in English, some in Russian, Spanish and Chinese. Write: NAVH, c/o C. Gomez, 22 West 21st St., 6th Floor, New York, NY 10010. Call 212-889-3141; Fax: 212-727-2931. *Website:* http://www.navh.org *Email:* staff@navh.org

National Federation of the Blind *National. 52 affiliates. Founded 1940.* Serves as both an advocacy and a public information vehicle. Contacts newly blind persons to help with adjustment. Provides information on services & applicable laws. Student scholarships. Assists blind persons who are victims of discrimination. Literature, monthly meetings & magazine. Assistance in starting new groups. Write: National Federation of the Blind, 1800 Johnson St., Baltimore, MD 21230-4998. Call 410-659-9314; Fax: 410-685-5653. *Website:* http://www.nfb.org

National Keratoconus Foundation *National network. Founded 1986.* Provides information and support to persons with keratoconus, an eye condition where the cornea progressively thins causing a cone-like bulge. Newsletter, phone support, information and referrals. Online support group. Encourages research into cause and treatment. Write: NKCF, 8733 Beverly Blvd., Suite 201, Los Angeles, CA 90048. Call 1-800-521-2524. *Website:* http://www.nkcf.org *Email:* info@nkcf.org

National Organization of Parents of Blind Children *National. Founded 1983.* Support for parents of blind children. Serves as both an advocacy and public information vehicle. Provides information on services available. Offers positive philosophy and insights into blindness and practical guidance in raising a blind child. Newsletter, parent seminars, free parents' information packet, meetings and conventions. Dues $8. Write: NOPBC, c/o Barbara Cheadle, National Federation of the Blind, 1800 Johnson St., Baltimore, MD 21230. Call 410-659-9314; Fax: 410-685-5653. *Website:* http://www.nfb.org *Email:* bcheadle@nfb.org

USA Aniridia Network *National. Founded 2002.* Support and education to the public, medical community and members. Offers information, referrals, literature, newsletter, phone support, pen pals and conferences. Online Email support and chat rooms. Write: USA Aniridia Network, 1138 North Germantown Parkway, Suite 101, PMB #109, Cordova, TN 38016. Call 901-752-8835. *Website:* http://www.aniridia.net *Email:* info@aniridia.net

Vision Northwest *Regional model. 42 groups. Founded 1983.* Mission is to reach out with compassion, encouragement and understanding to those coping with vision loss, their families and friends. Helps persons with vision loss to become more independent through a network of peer support groups and individual peer counseling. Information and referral, membership newsletter, community newsletter. Loan-lending optical aids network. Write: Vision Northwest, 9225 SW Hall Blvd., Suite G, Tigard or 97223. Call 503-684-8389; Fax: 503-684-9359. *Website:* http://www.visionnw.com *Email:* kevin@visionnw.com

ONLINE

Aniridia Network *Online. Founded 1998.* International network that aims to bring people with aniridia (missing one or both irises) together for support. Provides practical information. Offers chat room and e-group. Write: Aniridia Network, 17 Sandmartin Crescent, Colchester Essex, CO4 3XU UK. *Website:* http://www.aniridia.org *Email:* hannah@aniridia.org

Association for Retinopathy Of Prematurity And Related Diseases *Online.* Mailing list that provides a source of information and support for persons with retinopathy of prematurity and their families. Opportunity to share feelings and experiences with those who have been through the same experiences. Call 1-800-788-2020. *Website:* http://www.ropard.org *Email:* ropard@yahoo.com

Leber's Congenital Amaurosis e-Group *Online.* Provides a listserv for persons who are interested in sharing support and information relating to Leber's congenital amaurosis, a genetic disorder. *Website:* http://groups.yahoo.com/group/LCA

BURN SURVIVORS
(see also facial disfigurement)

ESSEX

Burn Peer Support Group Education and support for burn patients and their families. Visitations, phone help. Meets monthly, St. Barnabas Medical Center, Old Short Hills Rd., Livingston. Call Susan Fischer 973-322-5276 (day).

NATIONAL

Burns United Support Groups *National. 4 affiliated groups. Founded 1986.* Mutual support for children and adults who have survived being burned, no matter how major or minor the burn. Also for the family and friends of the survivor. Outreach visitation, newsletter, pen pals, phone support and assistance in starting groups. Write: Burns United Support Groups, c/o Donna Schneck, PO Box 36416, Detroit, MI 48226. Call 313-881-5577 or 313-717-7277

Phoenix Society for Burn Survivors Inc., The, *International. Founded 1977.* Mission is to uplift and inspire anyone affected by burns through peer support, collaboration, education and advocacy. Services include referrals, quarterly newsletter "Burn Support News," SOAR Peer Support Program, annual World Burn
Congress, family services, informational website with online chat sessions, toll-free information and referral line, advocacy and educational programs. Write: The Phoenix Society, 1835 RW Berends Dr. SW, Grand Rapids, MI, 49519. Call 1-800-888-2876 or 616-458-2773; Fax: 616-458-2831. *Website:* http://www.phoenix-society.org *Email:* info@phoenix-society.org

ONLINE

Burn Survivors Online *Online.* Information and support for burn survivors and their families throughout the world. Offers burn survivor profiles, burn statistics, peer support scheduled chats, outreach to newly burned patients and families. List of books, articles, question and answer forum. *Website:* http://www.burnsurvivorsonline.com

CEREBRAL PALSY
(see also general disabilities, parents of disabled, toll-free helplines)

STATEWIDE

Cerebral Palsy of New Jersey Provides services statewide to advance the independence of children and adults with all types of disabilities. Programs include advocacy, employment services, family support, respite, assistive technology, substance abuse prevention, information and referral, personal assistance services and a technology lending center. Call 609-392-4004 or 1-888-322-1918. TTY: 609-392-7044. *Website:* http://www.cpofnj.org *Email:* info@cpofnj.org

NATIONAL

United Cerebral Palsy Associations, Inc. *National. 140 affiliates. Founded 1949.* Supports local affiliates that run programs for individuals with cerebral palsy and other disabilities. Local programs include support groups for parents and adults with cerebral palsy. Write: UCP, 1660 L St., NW, Suite 700, Washington, DC 20036-5603. Write: CP of NJ, 304 S. Broad St., Trenton, NJ, 08608. Call 1-800-872-5827 or 202-973-7197; Fax: 202-766-0414. *Website:* http://www.ucp.org

DEAF / HEARING IMPAIRED / TINNITUS / MENIERE'S DISEASE
(see also vestibular, toll-free helplines)

STATEWIDE

ALDA (Association of Late-Deafened Adults) Garden State Support, education and advocacy on behalf of all people with hearing loss. Accessible education workshops, guest speakers, advocacy, social events, newsletter. Yearly dues: $15/individual; $20/family. Free newsletters will be sent if requested. Meeting in various locations. All meetings equipped with interpreters and computer read-outs. Call Elinore Bullock 908-832-5056 (TTY); 908-832-5082 (Voice). *Website:* http://www.alda-gs.org *Email:* john.bullock@mindspring.com

ALDA-NJ (Association of Late Deafened Adults) Self-help group for persons who were raised in the hearing community, became deaf after learning to talk and are now unable to understand speech without visual cues. Meets in various homes. Write: ALDA-NJ, PO Box 423, Tenafly, NJ 07670. Call Nancy Kingsley 201-768-2552 (TTY); Fax: 201-767-5460. *Email:* Kingsnan@aol.com

183

New Jersey Association of the Deaf-Blind, Inc. *Professionally-run.* Purpose of group is to meet the needs of the deaf-blind, deaf or blind, communication impaired and their families in NJ. Provides advocacy, case management, education, information and referrals. Residential, community, family, employment support and training services. Write: NJ Association of Deaf-Blind, Inc., 24 K Worlds Fair Drive, Somerset, NJ 08873. Call 732-805-1912 (voice/TTY).

Signs of Sobriety Provides alcoholism and drug addiction services to persons who are deaf or hard-of-hearing. Makes referrals to deaf and sign interpreted 12-Step programs. Provides prevention and education classes. Offers S.T.E.P.S. Program, a weekly peer support group for recovering individuals. Sponsors sober/deaf activities. Newsletter. Write: SOS, 100 Scotch Rd., # 2, Ewing, NJ 08628-2507. Call TTY: 1-800-332-7677; Voice: 609-852-7677 (day); Fax: 609-882-6808. *Website:* http://www.signsofsobriety.org *Email:* info@signsofsobriety.org

BERGEN

HLA (Hearing Loss Association of America) *Bergen County Chapter* Mutual support and information for people who are hard-of-hearing. Guest speakers. Meets 2nd Wed., (Dec., Mar., June, Sept.), 1:30-3pm, Classic Residence, 655 Pomander Walk, Teaneck. Call Arlene Romoff 201-995-9594 or TTY 201-768-2552. *Email:* rdkoif@verizon.net

CAMDEN

South Jersey Tinnitus Support Group Information and support for tinnitus sufferers and family members. Meets 1st Thurs., (except July/Aug.), 7:30pm, Virtua Hospital, Barry Brown Education Building, Voorhees. Call Linda Beach 856-346-0200, Lynn Wolf 609-859-3260 or Mary Ann Halladay 609-429-5055; TDD: 856-346-0623. *Website:* http://www.pro-oto.com *Email:* lbeach@pro-oto.com

MERCER

Tinnitus Association of New Jersey *Professionally-run.* Mutual support for persons afflicted with tinnitus, their families and friends. Rap sessions, guest speakers, coping skills, literature, newsletter. Meets 1st Sat., 10-11:30am, First Presbyterian Church, Ewing. Call Dhyan Cassie 856-983-8981 (day).

We can also refer callers to over 100 individuals who are seeking others to help start new support groups throughout NJ, if you don't see it, that doesn't mean it doesn't exist!
1-800-367-6274

MIDDLESEX

HLA (Hearing Loss Association of America) *Middlesex County Chapter* Mutual support and information for people who are hard-of-hearing. Rap sessions, guest speakers. Dues $10/yr includes monthly newsletter. Meets 3rd Tues., (except July and Aug.), 7:30-9pm, First Baptist Church of South Plainfield, 201 Hamilton Blvd., South Plainfield. Call Marie Nordling 732-721-4183. *Email:* mcnord@yahoo.com

New Jersey CODA - (Children Of Deaf Adults) Provides mutual support for hearing adult children (age 18+) of deaf parents. Also open to deaf parents with children under 18. Promotes family awareness and individual growth in hearing children of deaf parents. Speakers' bureau, discussion sessions and phone assistance. Call Mariann Linfante Jacobson 732-548-2571. *Email:* jac2003@prodigy.net

MONMOUTH

HLA (Hearing Loss Association of America) *Ocean/Monmouth Chapter* Mutual support and information for people who cannot hear well. Guest speakers, rap sessions and literature. Families welcome. Meets 1st Sun., 1:30-4pm, (Oct.-June, except Jan.), Allaire Senior Center, Wall Circle Park, 1983 Route 34 South, Wall Township. Call Mary Ellen McSorley 732-773-6400 or 732-477-5306. *Email:* mernnj@aol.com (if possible prefers contact through Email)

MORRIS

Deaf Senior Citizens of Northwest Jersey *(SIGN LANGUAGE)* Support for deaf senior citizens, non-seniors and interpreter students. Provides mutual sharing social, lecture series and discusses health issues associated with being deaf. Group conducted in American Sign Language. Meets 1st Fri., 1-4pm, St. Peter's Episcopal Church, Parish Hall, Boulevard, Mountain Lakes. Call Lila Taylor 973-361-6032 (TDD) or Beverly 973-361-5666. *Website:* http://www.dawninc.org *Email:* info@dawninc.org

NATIONAL

American Society for Deaf Children *National. 120 affiliates. Founded 1967.* Information and support for parents and families with children who are deaf or hard–of-hearing. Quarterly magazine, biennial conventions, information and referral. Guidelines for starting similar groups. Dues $40/yr. Write: American Society for Deaf Children, PO Box 3355, Gettysburg, PA 17325. Call 1-800-942-2732. *Website:* http://www.deafchildren.org *Email:* asdc1@aol.com

American Tinnitus Association *National. 50 groups. Founded 1971.* Provides information, education, advocacy, hearing healthcare providers, tinnitus research and treatments to persons affected by tinnitus. Funds research. Dues $35/yr. includes quarterly magazine. Must be an active member to access online support. Write: American Tinnitus Association, PO Box 5, Portland or 97207. Call 1-800-634-8978. *Website:* http://www.ata.org *Email:* Tinnitus@ata.org

Auditory-Verbal International, Inc. *International network. Founded 1987.* Aim is to advance listening and speaking by children and adults who are deaf or hard-of-hearing through quality auditory-verbal practices worldwide. Newsmagazine, networking, literature, phone support, information and referrals. Email addresses and links for parents of deaf children. Conferences. Referrals to certified auditory-verbal therapists. Dues $50/US; $55/Canada/Mexico; $60/Int'l. Write: Auditory-Verbal Int'l, 1390 Chain Bridge Rd., # 100, McLean, VA 22101. Call 703-739-1049 (day/eve); Fax: 703-739-0395. *Website:* http://www.auditory-verbal.org *Email:* info@auditory-verbal.org

Autism Network for Hearing & Visually Impaired Persons *International network. Founded 1992.* Provides communication, education, research and advocacy for persons with autism combined with a hearing or visual disability, their families and professionals. Sharing of educational materials, phone help, support groups, referrals and conferences. Write: Autism Network for Hearing & Visually Impaired Persons, 7510 Ocean Front Ave., Virginia Beach, VA 23451. Call 757-428-9036; Fax: 757-428-0019.

CODA (Children Of Deaf Adults) *International. 12 affiliated groups. Founded 1983.* Provides mutual support for hearing children of deaf parents. Promotes family awareness and individual growth through self-help groups, educational programs, advocacy and resource development. Newsletter, information and referral, assistance in starting groups. Dues $25/yr. Write: CODA, Box 30715, Santa Barbara, CA 93130. Call 805-682-0997. *Website:* http://www.coda-international.org

Ear Foundation, The. *National. 35 groups. Founded 1971.* Support and information for persons with Meniere's disease. Education regarding the condition, treatment and coping strategies. Newsletter. Group development guidelines, phone buddies, pen pals. Dues $25/yr. Write: The Ear Foundation, 955 Woodland Ave, Nashville, TN 37206. Call 1-800-545-4327; Fax: 615-627-2724. *Website:* http://www.earfoundation.org *Email:* amy@earfoundation.org

HLA (Hearing Loss Association) *International. 250 chapters and groups. Founded 1979.* Aim is to open the world of communication to people with hearing loss by providing information, education, support, referrals and advocacy. Bi-monthly journal, online local group and chapter listings. Assistance in starting groups. Write: HLA, 7910 Woodmont Ave., Suite 1200, Bethesda, MD 20814. Call 301-657-2248; Fax: 301-913-9413. *Website:* http://www.hearingloss.org *Email:* info@hearingloss.org

National Association of the Deaf *National. 51 chapters. Founded 1880.* Advocates for the civil rights of deaf and hard-of-hearing. As a national federation of state association, organizational and business affiliates, offers grassroots and youth leadership development and legal expertise across a broad spectrum of areas including, but not limited to, accessibility, education, employment, healthcare, mental health, rehabilitation, technology, telecommunications and transportation. Write: NAD, 814 Thayer Ave., Suite 250, Silver Spring, MD 20910-4500. Call 301-587-1788; Fax: 301-587-1791, *Website:* http://www.nad.org *Email:* nadinfo@nad.org

Parents Section A.G. Bell Association for Deaf & Hard of Hearing *International. Founded 1958.* Network of parents whose members promote advocating independence through listening and talking. Concerned with early diagnosis and auditory, language and speech training for children who are deaf or hard-of-hearing. Works to preserve parents' and children's rights by advocating auditory-oral and auditory-verbal education. Serves as clearinghouse to dispense information and exchange ideas. Write: Parents Section, AG Bell Association, 3417 Volta Pl., NW, Suite 310, Washington, DC 20007. Call 202-337-5220 or 202-337-5221; Fax: 202-337-8314. *Website:* http://www.agbell.org *Email:* info@agbell.org

Rainbow Alliance of the Deaf *National. 23 affiliated chapters. Founded 1977.* Promotes the educational, economical and social welfare of deaf and hard-of-hearing gay, lesbian, bisexual and transgendered persons and their friends. Discussion of practical problems and solutions. Advocacy, conferences, newsletter, assistance in starting groups. Online information on contacting a local chapter. Write: RAD, c/o Bob Donaldson, 309 Millside Dr., Columbus, OH 43230. *Website:* http://www.rad.org *Email:* president@rad.org

HEAD INJURY / BRAIN INJURY / COMA
(see also general disabilities, specific disorder, toll-free helplines)

STATEWIDE

Brain Injury Association of NJ Provides information, education, outreach, prevention, advocacy and support services to all persons affected by brain injury. Write: Brain Injury Assn. of NJ, c/o Rene Hurley, 1090 King George Post Rd.

#708, Edison, NJ, 08837. Call 732-738-1002 (day) or 1-800-669-4323 (day); Fax: 732-738-1132 *Website:* http://www.bianj.org *Email:* info@bianj.org

ATLANTIC

Brain Injury Association of NJ *Professionally-run.* Emotional support and education for persons with head injuries, their families and friends. Meets 2nd Thurs., 7pm, Bacharach Institute for Rehabilitation, 61 W. Jimmie Leeds Rd., Pomona. Call Nutan Ravani 856-589-5797 (day) or Helpline 1-800-669-4323. *Website:* http://www.bianj.org *Email:* info@bianj.org

BERGEN

Brain Injury Association of NJ *Professionally-run.* Emotional support and education for persons with head injuries, their families and friends. Meets 3rd Mon., 6:30pm, Pascack Valley Hospital, Conference Rooms 1 and 2, Old Hook Rd., Westwood. Call Beth 845-358-4815 or Helpline 1-800-669-4323.

BURLINGTON

Brain Injury Association of NJ *Professionally-run.* Emotional support and education for persons with brain injuries and their families. Meets 2nd and 4th Wed., 7pm, Marlton Rehabilitation Hospital, 92 Brick Rd., Marlton. Call Mark Rader, PhD 856-988-4124 (day).

CAMDEN

Brain Injury Association of NJ *Professionally-run.* Emotional support and education for persons with brain injuries and their families. Meets 3rd Mon (except July/Aug.), 7-9pm, Bancroft School, Farrington Hall, Hopkins Lane Haddonfield. Call Bill 609-877-8464.

CUMBERLAND

Brain Injury Association of NJ *Professionally-run.* Emotional support and education for persons with brain injuries and their families. Meets 1st Tues., 7pm, Rehabilitation Hospital of South Jersey, 1237 West Sherman Ave., Vineland. Call Dr. Chris Wolf 856-696-7100 ext. 224.

ESSEX

Acoustic Neuroma Association *Northern NJ* Mutual support to assist those diagnosed with or receiving post-treatment for acoustic neuroma. Rap sessions guest speakers, literature and phone help. Meets 4 times/yr., Montclair. Call Jon Bonesteel 973-783-8723 (day/eve). *Email:* bonestee@verizon.net

Brain Injury Association of NJ *(MULTILINGUAL) Professionally-run.* Emotional support and education for persons with brain injuries, their families and friends. Meets last Tues., 6:30pm, Kessler Institute for Rehabilitation, 240 Central Ave., East Orange. Call Betty Collins 973-414-4743 (English) or Dr. Juan Arango 973-324-3558 (Spanish).

GLOUCESTER

Brain Injury Association of NJ *Professionally-run.* Emotional support and education for persons with brain injuries and their families. Meets 4th Mon., 6pm, Moss Rehab/Drucker Brain Injury Center, 135 South Broad Ave., Woodbury. Call Cynthia Abbott-Gaffney 856-853-9900 ext. 102.

Brain Injury Support Group Mutual support, friendship, networking and social activities for individuals who have sustained a brain injury. Meets Wed., 7-9:30pm, Apostles' Lutheran Church, 4401 Black Horse Pike, Turnersville. Call Teresa May 856-629-8487 or the church 856-629-4228.

HUNTERDON

Brain Injury Association of NJ *Professionally-run.* Emotional support and education for persons with brain injuries, their families and friends. Meets 3rd Wed., 6pm, Warren Hospital Health Education Department, 185 Roseberry St., Phillipsburg. Call Evelyn Dart 908-782-5344 (day) or Helpline 1-800-669-4323.

Brain Injury Support Group *Professionally-run.* Support group for people who have brain injury due to AVM's, aneurysm, tumors or stroke. Families welcome. Guest speakers and literature. Meets 2nd Thurs., 7-9pm, Hunterdon Medical Center, 2100 Wescott Dr., Flemington. Call Gwen Bartlett-Palmer 908-246-9648.

MERCER

Brain Injury Association of NJ *Professionally-run.* Emotional support and education for persons with brain injuries, their families and friends. Meets 1st Wed., 6:30pm, St. Lawrence Rehab Hospital, Room 117, 2381 Lawrenceville Rd., Lawrenceville. Call David Searles 609-896-9500 ext. 2303 or Helpline 1-800-669-4323.

MIDDLESEX

Brain Injury Association of NJ *Professionally-run.* Emotional support and education for persons with head injuries and their families. Meets 2nd Tues., 6pm, Hartwyck at Oak Tree, 2048 Oak Tree Rd., Edison. Call David DiPaolo 732-906-2640 ext. 42885 (day).

TBI Support Group Mutual support sharing of concerns and frustrations for persons with traumatic brain injuries. Families welcome. Meets 1st Tues., 10am, Edison Library, Meeting Room, 777 Grove St., Edison. Call Kathleen Orsett 732-738-4388 (day); TDD: 732-738-9644. *Website:* http://www.adacil.org *Email.* peersupport@adacil.org

MONMOUTH

Brain Injury Association of NJ *Professionally-run.* Emotional support and education for persons with head injuries and their families. Meets 1st Tues., 7pm, Dorbrook Park Recreation Area, Route 537, Colts Neck. Call Peggy DiTommaso 609-538-8464.

MORRIS

Adults with Brain Injury *Professionally-run.* Mutual support for adults (age 16+) with acquired brain injury and their families. Opportunity for patients with similar experiences to exchange information, coping skills and understanding. Meets 1st Wed., 6pm, Kessler Institute for Rehabiliation/Welkind Facility, Inpatient Conference Room, 201 Pleasant Hill Rd., Chester. Call Dr. Joyce Echo 973-252-6224.

OCEAN

Brain Injury Association of NJ *Professionally-run.* Emotional support and education for persons with head injuries, their families and friends.
> **Howell** Meets 2nd Wed., 7pm, Office Plus at Ideal Plaza, 2226 Highway 9 South, Howell. Call Olivia 732-408-9666 (eve).
> **Toms River** Meets 3rd Tues., 6pm, Community Medical Center, 99 Highway 37 West, Toms River. Call Vicki Hardy 732-557-8000 ext 10226 or Pam Lightfoot 732-557-8000 ext. 11547.

We know this Directory is big and chances are we can probably find the group you're looking for quicker than you paging through it. Call us! (We're really friendly!)
1-800-367-6274

PASSAIC

Brain Injury Association Family Support Group *Professionally-run.* Support for family members and caregivers of neurologically impaired people (brain injury, aneurysm, stroke, etc). Sharing sessions, guest speakers, literature. Meets 4th Thurs., 6pm, Haledon. Call Cindy Clawson 973-427-2600 ext. 19 (day).

Voices that Count *Professionally-run.* Encouragement, emotional support and socializing for head injured adults. Meets 4th Thurs., 6:30pm, Rehab Specialists, 401 Haledon Ave., Haledon. Before attending call Heidi Lewis 973-427-2600 ext. 25.

SOMERSET

Somerset/Hunterdon County Brain Injury Support Group Emotional support for persons with illnesses and injuries affecting the brain, their families and friends. Information, socialization, educational series and guest speakers. Meets 3rd Thurs., 6:30pm, Neurobehavioral Institute of NJ, 626 N. Thompson St., Raritan. Call Mary Liz McNamara 908-725-8877 (day). *Email:* mlmcnamara@verizonmail.com

SUSSEX

Brain Injury Association of NJ *Professionally-run.* Emotional support and education for persons with brain injuries, their families and friends. Meets 2nd Wed., 8pm, Redeemer Lutheran Church, 37 Newton-Sparta Rd., Newton. Call Angel McLaughlin 732-627-9890 ext. 202 or Helpline 1-800-669-4323.

WARREN

Brain Injury Association of NJ *Professionally-run.* Emotional support and education for persons with head injuries, their families and friends. Meets 3rd Wed., 7pm, Warren Hospital, Health Education Department, 185 Roseberry St., Phillipsburg. Call Evelyn Dart 908-782-5344 (day) or Helpline 1-800-669-4323.

NATIONAL

Brain Injury Association, Inc. *National. 47 state associations. 600 affiliated groups. Founded 1980.* Advocacy organization providing services to persons with brain injuries, their families and professionals. Increases public awareness through state associations, support groups, information and resource network, seminars, conferences, literature and prevention programs. Guidelines for starting similar groups. Write: Brain Injury Association, 8201 Greensboro Dr., Suite 611,

McLean, VA 22102. Call 1-800-444-6443 (family helpline) or 703-761-0750; Fax: 703-761-0755. *Website:* http://www.biausa.org

Coma Recovery Association *National network. Founded 1980.* Support & advocacy for families of coma and traumatic brain injury survivors. Provides information & referrals and support group for family members and survivors. Quarterly newsletter and yearly conferences for families, brain injury professionals and survivors. Write: Coma Recovery Assn., 807 Carman Ave., Westbury, NY, 11590. Call 516-997-1826. *Website:* http://www.comarecovery.org *Email:* inquiry@comarecovery.org

ONLINE

Brain Injury Information NETwork, The (TBINET) *Online* Various support group email lists for brain injury, stroke and other "medical" related issues. Has lists for caregivers and family and friends. *Website:* http://www.tbinet.org

LEARNING DISABILITY / ATTENTION DEFICIT DISORDER
(see also toll-free helplines)

BERGEN

CHADD Support and education for adults and parents of children with attention deficit disorder. Membership $45/yr. Meets 3rd Wed., 7:30pm, (Oct.-June), Valley Hospital, Auditorium, Ridgewood. Call CHADD 201-664-1313. *Website:* http://www.chaddbc.org

CAMDEN

ADDventure for Adults To lend an attentive ear and helping hand to all who have adult ADD or a connection with someone who has adult ADD. Rap sessions, guest speakers, literature and speakers bureau. Dues $5/mtg. Meets 2nd Thurs., 7:30-9pm, Barry D. Brown Health Education Center, Voorhees. Call 856-596-5520 (day/eve). *Website:* http://www.addventureforadults.org

CHADD of Southern NJ *Professionally-run.* Support for adults and parents of children with attention deficit hyperactivity disorder. Meetings vary, 7:30-9pm, (except Dec., July, Aug.), Barry D. Brown Health Education Center, Virtua West Jersey Hospital, 106 Carnie Blvd., Voorhees. Call Mary Fagnani or Linda Karanzalis 856-482-0756 (day).

ESSEX

ADD Action Group Information about alternative solutions for attention deficit disorder, learning disabilities, hyperactivity, dyslexia and autism. Educational series, guest speakers, literature, phone help. Usually meets 3rd Thurs., 7-8:45pm, Millburn Public Library, 200 Glen Ave., Millburn. Before attending call Lynne Berke 973-731-2189 (day/eve). *Email:* LTBerke@aol.com

MONMOUTH

Adult ADD Self-Help Support Group *Professionally-run.* For adults who have attention deficit disorder or those who suspect that they may. Significant others welcome. Meets 4th Thurs., (except Aug.), (3rd Thurs. in Nov./Dec.), 7:30-9:30pm, Monmouth Medical Center, 300 2nd Ave., Long Branch. Pre-registration required. Before attending call Dr. Robert LoPresti 732-842-4553 (day). *Website:* http://www.drlopresti.com

Parents and Children with ADHD Mutual support for children with attention deficit hyperactivity disorder. Parents meet concurrently. Social activities. Meets Thurs., 7pm, Family Based Services, 11 White St., Eatontown. Call 732-380-1300 (day).

MORRIS

Crossroads Community Satellite of CHADD Education and support for parents, teachers and friends of children and teens with attention deficit disorder and/or hyperactivity disorder. Guest speakers. Dues $1/mtg. Meets 2nd Fri., (except July, Aug, Dec.) 7:30–9pm, Crossroads Community Church, downstairs, 104 Bartley Rd., Flanders. Call Rev. Paul Ingeneri, 973-584-7149. Email: revpaul@optononline.net

Learning Disabilities Association Support and information for families of children with learning disabilities. Conferences, newsletters, literature. Dues $30/yr. Meets at various locations and times. Call Terry Cavanaugh 973-265-4303 (voice mail). *Email:* tccavanaugh@optonline.net

PASSAIC

Learning Disabilities Association *Professionally-run.* Emotional support, resources and information for parents of children and young adults with any type of learning disability. Support groups, parenting classes, advocacy, social activities, library, phone help and guest speakers. Dues $35/yr. Call Angela Abdul 973-728-8744.

SOMERSET

CHADD Provides education and support to families, friends, schools and other community agencies about attention deficit disorder and/or hyperactivity disorder. Guest speakers, literature, phone support. Meetings vary, Bernards Township Library, 32 South Maple Ave., Basking Ridge. Call Vicki Roche 908-647-9325. *Website:* http://www.chaddofsomerset.com *Email:* somersetchadd@aol.com

SUSSEX

Learning Disabilities Association *Professionally-run.* Emotional support, resources and information for parents of children and young adults with any type of learning disability. Support groups, parenting classes, advocacy, social activities, library, phone help and guest speakers. Meeting times and locations vary. Dues $35/yr. Call Angela Abdul 973-728-8744.

UNION

Parents of ADD Children Support and casual discussion about the challenges and joys associated with raising a child with attention deficit disorder. Sharing of coping of skills and resources. Meets 1st Mon., 7:30pm, Rustic Mill Diner, Cranford. Call Debbie Hargiss 908-272-2362 (eve). *Email:* dfhargiss@comcast.net

NATIONAL

ADDA (Attention Deficit Disorder Association) *National network. Founded 1989.* Mission is to provide information, resources and networking to adults with attention deficit hyperactivity disorder and to the professionals working with them. Aims to generate hope, awareness, empowerment and connections worldwide in the field of ADHD through bringing together science and the human experience. The information and resources provided to individual and families affected with ADHD focus on diagnoses, treatment, strategies and techniques for helping adults with ADHD lead better lives. Write: ADDA, PO Box 543, Pottstown, PA 19464. Call 484-945-2101; Fax: 610-970-7520. *Website:* http://www.add.org *Email:* mail@add.org

CHADD (Children and Adults with Attention-Deficit/Hyperactivity Disorder) *International. 250+ affiliated groups. Founded 1987.* Support network for parents and caregivers of children with attention deficit/hyperactivity disorder. Provides information for parents, adults, teachers and professionals. Bimonthly magazine, annual conference. Guidelines and assistance on starting self-help groups. Dues $45/ind; $35/student; $100/health care. Online listing of local support groups.

Write: CHADD, 8181 Professional Pl., Suite 150, Landover, MD 20785. Call 1-800-233-4050 or 301-306-7070; Fax: 301-306-7090. *Website:* http://www.chadd.org/

Feingold Association of the U.S. *National. Founded 1976.* Help for families of children with learning or behavior problems, including attention deficit disorder. Supports members in implementing the Feingold program. Generates public awareness about food & synthetic additives. Newsletter. Phone support network. Write: Feingold Association of the US, 554 East Main St. Suite 301, Riverhead, NY 11901. Call 631-369-9340 or 1-800-321-3287 (US only). *Website:* http://www.feingold.org *Email:* help@feingold.org

GT/LD Network *National network. Founded 1984.* Mutual support and information for parents of gifted children who are also learning disabled. Open to students and educators. Newsletter, library information and referrals, advocacy, literature, conferences, online discussion support group and local meetings in Maryland. Dues $30. Write: GT/LD Network, PO Box 30239, Bethesda, MD 20824. Fax: 301-681-4884. *Website:* http://www.gtldnetwork.org

ONLINE

Conduct Disorders Parent Message Board *Online.* Support for parents living with a child with one of the many behavior disorders including attention deficit hyperactivity disorder, oppositional defiance disorder, conduct disorder, depression and substance abuse. Parents with children of all ages welcome. *Website:* http://www.conductdisorders.com

Dyslexia Talk *Online.* Support for anyone affected by dyslexia. Offers message board, open discussions and separate support group for parents. *Website:* http://www.dyslexiatalk.com

NLDA-In-Common *Online.* Opportunity for loved ones of people with non-verbal learning disabilities (NLD), adults with NLD and certain professionals to come together to communicate. Provides listserv support and information. Membership subject to approval. *Website:* http://www.groups.yahoo.com/group/NLD-In-Common/

Premature Baby - Premature Child *Online. Founded 1997.* Offers support for parents of premature babies. For any of their special needs including mental, physical, emotional or learning disability. Provides support, discussion listserv, prematurity forums, advocacy and educational links. Special children's show-and-tell section. *Website:* http://www.prematurity.org

MENTAL RETARDATION / DOWN SYNDROME
(see also parents of disabled, specific syndrome, toll-free helplines)

STATEWIDE

ARC of NJ, The *Professionally-run.* Services and advocacy for the mentally retarded and their families. Parent support groups available at the chapter offices in each county. Membership dues vary for each chapter. Write: The Arc of NJ, 985 Livingston Ave., North Brunswick, NJ, 08902. Call 732-246-2525 (day). *Website:* http://www.arcnj.org

New Jersey Self-Advocacy Project Provides information on groups statewide. Helps people with developmental disabilities set up their own self-help groups. Groups have elected officers and a volunteer advisor. Members learn skills such as assertiveness, decision making and effective communication. Write: NJ Self-Advocacy Project, 44 Stelton Rd., Suite 110, Piscataway, NJ, 08854. Call Takeena Thomas 732-926-8010 (day). *Website:* http://www.arcnj.org

ATLANTIC

21 Down - Down Syndrome Awareness Group Inc. Support for families of a loved one with a developmental disability. Guest speakers. Meets 4 times a year. Call Susan 609-625-8141 (day). *Website:* http://www.21down.org *Email:* info@21down.org

CAPE MAY

Down Syndrome Awareness Group, Inc. Support for families of a loved one with a developmental disability. Discusses educational, recreational and medical issues. Guest speakers and visitation. Under 18 welcome. Meets 4 times/yr. Call Susan 609-625-8141 (day). *Website:* http://www.21down.org *Email:* info@21down.org

ESSEX

Down Syndrome Parent-To-Parent Support and current information to new parents and families of children with Down syndrome. Visitation, peer counseling, referrals. Meeting location rotates. Call 973-992-9830 (day). *Website:* http://www.arcessex.org

Consider passing this Directory on to a student or staff member - browsing through the Directory pages can often provide helpful education as to the wide variety of groups available.

HUDSON

Family Support Group *(BILINGUAL)* Support for family and friends of people with developmental disabilities. Mutual sharing, socialization, education, lectures and advocacy for parents and others concerned about people with developmental disabilities. Meets 2nd Fri., 6-8pm, 405-09 36th St., Union City. Call Sandra Vasquez 201-319-9229 (day). *Website:* http://www.arcnj.org *Email:* svasquez@arcnj.org

HUNTERDON

Sharing and Caring of Bucks County Information and support for parents of children with autism, Asperger syndrome, mental retardation and related disorders. Discussion groups, guest speakers, sib-shop sibling support group, social and recreational activities. Suggested donation $15/yr. Meets 2nd Thurs., 7-9pm, St. Vincent DePaul Church, Education Building, Hatboro Rd., Richboro, PA. Call Holly Druckman 215-321-3202 (Mon.-Fri., 10am-6pm).

MIDDLESEX

Down Syndrome Family Support Group *Professionally-run.* Support group for parents of children with Down syndrome. Meets in Edison. Call Children's Center 732-548-3356 (day). *Email:* anne.clark@cpamc.org

MONMOUTH

Down Syndrome Parent Support Group *Professionally-run.* Mutual support for parents of children with Down syndrome. Meets quarterly, 8-11pm in members' homes. Call Susan Levine 732-747-5310 (day). *Website:* http://www.familyresourceassociates.org

OCEAN

21 Down - Down Syndrome Awareness Group Inc. Support for families of a loved one with a developmental disability. Guest speakers. Meets 4 times a year. Call Susan 609-625-8141 (day). *Website:* http://www.21down.org *Email:* info@21down.org

SUSSEX

Self-Advocacy Group *Professionally-run.* Fosters independence and responsibility in developmentally disabled adults. Education on advocating for

197

one's own rights. Meets the last Tues., 11am, 112 Phil Hardin Rd., Fredon. Call 973-383-8574.

UNION

Adult Social Group *Professionally-run.* Social activities club for developmentally disabled adults over 18. Discussions, films, recreation. Meets Wed., (except Jan., May, June, July, Aug.), 7pm, Kean University, University Center, Morris Ave., Union. Call Ina White 908-737-3857 (day).

WARREN

Down Syndrome Group of Northwest New Jersey, The Opportunity for parents of children with Down syndrome to share information, experiences and provide education to new parents. Phone help, literature. Dues $20/yr. Meetings vary, Washington. Call Melissa Ehrhardt 908-859-2747 or Isabel Maginnis 908-537-6277 (day). *Website:* http://www.dsgnwnj.org

Go-Getters *Professionally-run.* Self-advocacy group for persons with developmental disabilities. Peer counseling, guest speakers. Sponsored by the ARC. Meets in Washington. Call Bonnie Hill 908-689-7525 (day). *Website:* http://www.arcwarren.org

NATIONAL

Arc, The *National. 1100 chapters. Founded 1950.* Provides support for people with mental retardation and their families. Advocacy groups and direct services. Quarterly newspaper. Chapter development guidelines. Local group information on website. Write: The Arc, 1010 Wayne Ave., Suite 650, Silver Spring, MD 20910. Call 301-565-3842 (day); Fax: 301-565-5342. *Website:* http://thearc.org *Email:* info@thearc.org

National Down Syndrome Congress *National. 400+ chapters. Founded 1974.* Support, information, & advocacy for families affected by Down syndrome. Serves as clearinghouse & network for parent groups. Newsletter ($25/yr). Annual convention, phone support, chapter development guidelines. Write: NDSC, 1370 Center Dr., Suite 102, Atlanta, GA 30338. Call 1-800-232-6372 or 770-604-9500; Fax: 770-604-9898. *Website:* http://www.NDSCcenter.org *Email:* info@NDSCcenter.org

People First *Model. 33 groups in Washington. Founded 1977.* Self-help advocacy organization created by & for people with developmental disabilities. Provides help in starting new chapters. Quarterly newsletter. Write: People First, PO Box 648,

Clarkston, WA 99403. Call 509-758-1123; Fax: 509-758-1289; TDD/TTY: 509-758-1123. *Email:* pfow@clarkston.com

Speaking For Ourselves *Model 12 groups. Founded 1982.* Self-help advocacy for people with developmental disabilities. Monthly chapter meetings. Members help each other resolve problems, gain self-confidence and learn leadership skills. Chapter development guidelines. Newsletter. Write: Speaking For Ourselves, 502 W. Germantown Pike, Suite 105, Plymouth Meeting, PA 19462. Call 610-825-4592; Fax: 610-825-4595. *Website:* http://www.speaking.org *Email:* info@speaking.org

Voice of the Retarded *National. 160 affiliated groups. Founded 1983.* Works to empower families of persons with mental retardation through information and advocacy. Weekly Email updates and quarterly newsletter for members. Annual dues $25. Write: VOR, 5005 Newport Dr., Suite 108, Rolling Meadows, IL 60008. Call 847-253-6020 (day); Fax: 847-253-6054. *Website:* http://www.vor.net *Email:* vor@vor.net

ONLINE

Trisomy 21 *Online* Offers support and information to those who have been touched by Trisomy 21 (Down syndrome). Chat group and several forums. *Website:* http://www.trisomy21online.com

DISABILITIES (General) /
SPINAL CORD INJURY
(see also parents of the disabled, specific disability, toll-free helpline)

STATEWIDE

Cerebral Palsy of New Jersey Provides services statewide to advance the independence of children and adults with all types of disabilities. Programs include advocacy, employment services, family support, assistive technology, substance abuse prevention, information and referral, Write: CP of New Jersey, 354 S. Broad St., Trenton, NJ 08608. Call 609-392-4004 or 1-888-322-1918; TDD: 609-392-7044. *Website:* http://www.cpofnj.org *Email:* info@cpofnj.org

C.U.S.A. Correspondence support group for persons of all faiths with any type of disability or chronic illness. Catholic in founding but open to all. Emphasis on spiritual values and mutual support. Through "group letters" members find close relationships, understanding and courage. Dues $20/yr. (can be waived). Write: CUSA, 176 West 8th St., Bayonne, NJ 07002. *Website:* http://www.cusan.org *Email:* ams4@juno.com

199

DOROT/University Without Walls Telephone Support Teleconference support groups for persons age 59+ who are coping with vision loss, care giving, aging issues, etc. Registration fee $10 and $15 tuition per support group. Scholarships are available. Write: DOROT, 171 W. 85th St., NY, NY, 10024. For more information call DOROT 1-877-819-9147. *Website:* http://www.dorotusa.org

Monday Morning Project, The Grassroots movement of people with disabilities their families, friends and neighbors. Made up of advocacy networks in each county, it brings together ordinary citizens to work with local, state and federal officials on public policy issues important to people with disabilities. Some of the groups will help a new member with a personal advocacy issue. Meetings are held monthly in Bergen, Burlington, Camden, Cumberland, Essex, Gloucester, Hudson Hunterdon, Mercer, Middlesex, Monmouth, Morris, Ocean, Passaic, Salem Somerset, Union and Warren counties. For information on your local county network call Carole Tonks 609-292-3453 (day) or Luke Koppisch 609-777-329? (day); TDD: 609-777-3228 or Monday Morning Hotline 1-800-216-1199. *Website* http://www.njddc.org

BERGEN

Big Wheels Mutual support for persons with physical disabilities to improve quality of life and enjoy outside activities. Group interacts with other state and Bergen County agencies. Monthly newsletters. Meets 2nd Thurs., 7:30pm, Pascack Valley Hospital, Old Hook Rd., Westwood. Call 201-358-3000, Tom Bengas 201-722-9537 (day) or Beverly Jensen 201-664-3581 (mornings).

Heightened Independence and Progress Support groups, information, referrals advocacy, peer counseling, recreational and other services for people of all types of disabilities, their families and advocates. Home modifications, assistance with equipment and assistive devices. Meets various times, Heightened Independence and Progress, 131 Main St., Suite 120, Hackensack. Call Paula Walsh 201-996-9100 or TDD: 201-996-9424.

Post Stroke and Disabled Adult Program *(BERGEN COUNTY RESIDENT. ONLY) Professionally-run.* Mutual support for post-stroke patients and disabled adults. Program functions include group discussions, various activities that promote physical fitness, arts and crafts, games, exercises and occasional recreational events. Meets various times/days, East Rutherford, Englewood, Oakland, Paramus River Vale and Maywood. Call Leo DePinto 201-336-6502 (day); TTY 201-336-6505.

While it's no substitution for talking to our staff, you can call evenings or weekends! Leave a message and we will get back to you the next workday. **1-800-367-6274**

Women With Disabilities Support Group Discussion and education for disabled women. Meets 1st and 3rd Mon., 11am-1pm, Heightened Independence and Progress, 131 Main St., Suite 120, Hackensack. Call Paula Walsh 201-996-9100 (day) or TDD: 201-996-9424. *Website:* http://www.hipcil.org

BURLINGTON

Go Getters, The Support group for physically disabled adults. Socialization, awareness, recreation, phone help and rap sessions. Dues $20/yr. (can be waived). Meets 3rd Wed., 7pm, 315 Green St., Edgewater Park. Call Tammi Gauntt 609-261-2267 or Sharon Wilkins 609-877-9264.

ESSEX

Monday Morning Network of Essex County Advocacy support group organized by and for people with disabilities. Purpose is to provide and improve the quality of life for persons with disabilities by having a voice in government policy making and legislation. Helps members with individual advocacy issues. Family and friends welcome. Newsletter. Meets 2nd Thurs., 10am-noon, Opportunity Project, 60 East Willow St., Millburn. Call Rob Fornoff 973-228-8230 (day), Frances Grant 973-470-8090 or Opportunity Project 973-921-1000 (day).

NJ Coalition on Women and Disabilities *(Essex County Chapter)* Support to empower, educate and motivate women with disabilities. Advocacy and guest speakers. Dues $12/yr. Meets 3rd Mon., 6:30-8:30pm, Pope John Paul Pavillion, 135 S. Center St., Orange. Call Cynthia De Souza 973-610-3394. *Email:* njcwd_essexchapter@verizon.net

HUNTERDON

Brain Injury Support Group *Professionally-run.* Support group for people who have brain injury due to AVM's, aneurysm, tumors or stroke. Families welcome. Guest speakers and literature. Meets 2nd Thurs., 7-9pm, Hunterdon Medical Center, 2100 Wescott Dr., Flemington. Call Gwen Bartlett-Palmer 908-246-9648.

Teen Activity Group *Professionally-run.* Recreation and support group for physically and developmentally handicapped teenagers. For meeting information Call Cindy Iarussi 908-788-6401 (day).

"I have found that sitting in a place where you have never sat before can be inspiring."--Dodie Smith

MERCER

Disability Support Group *Professionally-run.* Support for persons with any disability to share feelings, thoughts and resources. Under 18 welcome. Phone help and newsletter. Meets monthly, Progressive Center for Independent Living, 1262 Whitehorse-Hamilton Square Rd., Suite 102, Hamilton. Before attending call Susan Jacobsen 609-530-0006 (day) or TDD: 609-530-1234. *Website:* http://www.pcil.org *Email:* info@pcil.org

MIDDLESEX

Alliance For Disabled in Action Inc. Support for persons with any disability. Family members are welcome. Information, advocacy, education, referrals for housing, employment, transportation and assistive technology. Promotes barrier-free environments. Meets 3rd Thurs., 7pm, Brunswick Municipal Complex, 710 Hermann Rd., North Brunswick. Call Kathleen Orsetti 732-738-4388; TDD: 732-738-9644 *Website:* http://www.adacil.org *Email:* peersupport@adacil.org

MONMOUTH

NJ Coalition on Women and Disabilities (*Monmouth County Chapter*) Support to empower, educate and motivate women with disabilities. Rap sessions, advocacy and guest speakers. Dues $10/yr. Meetings vary, 1-5pm, Community Room, 384 2nd Ave., Long Branch. For meeting information call Evelyn Wilson 732-229-2027 (day).

P.O.W.E.R. (People On Wheels for Education and Rehabilitation) Social activities and advocacy for disabled persons and concerned others. Dues $4. Transportation provided in Monmouth County. Phone help. Meets 3rd Wed., 6:30pm; social 7pm, Ocean Township Firehouse, Ocean Township. Call Margie Pryor 732-571-0348 (day); TTY/TDD: 1-800-852-7897. *Email:* pryormargie@aol.com

PASSAIC

DIAL, Inc. Center for Independent Living Provides people with disabilities with information and referral, peer counseling, advocacy and independent living skills program. Deaf and hard-of-hearing outreach services. Dues $15/individual, $25/family. Meets last Tues., 6:30-9:30pm, Clifton Center for Seniors and Citizens with Disabilities, Clifton. Call 973-470-8090 (day); TTY: 973-470-2521. *Website:* http://www.dial-cil.org *Email:* info@dial-cil.org

Monday Morning Project Support and advocacy for persons with a disability. Meets monthly, Wayne Public Library, 461 Valley Rd., Wayne. Call 973-694-4272 ext. 5401.

SOMERSET

Alliance For Disabled in Action Inc. Support for persons with any disability. Family members are welcome. Information, advocacy, education, referrals for housing, employment, transportation and assistive technology. Promotes barrier-free environments. Meets 3rd Mon., 6:00pm, Bridgewater Library, 1 Vogt Dr., Bridgewater. Call Kathleen Orsetti 732-738-4388; TDD: 732-738-9644. *Website:* http://www.adacil.org *Email:* peersupport@adacil.org

UNION

Alliance For Disabled in Action, Inc. Support for persons with any disability. Family members are welcome. Information, advocacy, education, referrals for housing, employment, transportation and assistive technology. Promotes barrier-free environments. Meets last Thurs., 3:30pm, Runnells Specialized Hospital, 40 Watchung Way, Berkeley Heights. Call Kathleen Orsetti 732-738-4388; TDD: 732-738-9644. *Website:* http://www.adacil.org *Email:* peersupport@adacil.org

FOCAS Peer Support Group Mutual support for those with disabilities to enhance their daily living. Rap sessions and guest speakers. Meets 2nd Thurs., 7-9pm, Union Hospital, Galloping Hill Rd. and Clinton St., Classroom B, First Floor, Union. Call 908-355-3299 (day). *Email:* susysnowflake2002@yahoo.com

WARREN

Totally Kids Network Support for siblings age (5-10) that have a sibling with a disability. Children are given the opportunity to share feelings in a relaxing, recreational atmosphere. Meets monthly on Sat., Phillipsburg and Columbia. For meeting information call 908-689-7525 ext. 209. *Website:* http://www.arcwarren.org

NATIONAL

Ability Online Support Network *Online. Founded 1992.* A family friendly monitored electronic message system that enables children and adolescents with disabilities or chronic illness (also parents/caregivers/siblings) to share experiences, information, encouragement, support and hope through messages. Write: Ability

Online Support Network, 104-1120 Finch Ave. W., Toronto ON M3J 3H7 Canada. Call 416-650-6207; Fax: 416-650-5073. *Website:* http://www.abilityonline.org *Email:* information@ablelink.org

National Spinal Cord Injury Association *National. 35 chapters & support groups. Founded 1948.* Provides information & referrals on many topics to persons with spinal cord injuries and diseases, their families & interested professionals. Group development guidelines, monthly newsletter, support groups, peer counseling. Online listing of local chapters. Write: NSCIA, 6701 Democracy Blvd., Suite 300-9, Bethesda, MD 20817. Call 1-800-962-9629 or 301-214-4006; Fax: 301-881-9817. *Website:* http://www.spinalcord.org *Email:* info@spinalcord.org

Paralyzed Veterans of America *National. Chapters nationwide. Founded 1946.* Ensures that spinal cord injured or diseased veterans achieve the highest quality of life possible. Membership is available solely to individuals who are American citizens who suffer from spinal cord dysfunction as a result of trauma or disease. Must have served on active duty and had anything other than dishonorable discharge. Information & referrals, magazine. Write: PVA, 801 18th St. NW, Washington, DC 20006. Call 202-872-1300. *Website:* http://www.pva.org *Email:* info@pva.org

Project DOCC (Delivery Of Chronic Care) *International. 26 chapters. Founded 1994.* Provides education regarding the impact of chronic illness and/or disability on a family. Information, referrals, phone support, Email correspondence and "how-to" guides on developing a local group. Write: Project DOCC, One South Rd., Oyster Bay Cove, NY 11771. Call 1-877-773-8747; Fax: 516-498-1899. *Website:* http://projectdocc.org *Email:* projdocc@aol.com

Sibling Support Project of the Arc of the United States *National. 200+ affiliated groups. Founded 1994.* Opportunity for school-age brothers and sisters of children with special health and developmental needs to obtain peer support and education within a recreational context. Write: Donald Meyer, 6512 23rd Ave. NW, #213, Seattle, WA 98117. Call 206-297-6368; Fax: 509-752-6789. *Website:* http://www.thearc.org/siblingsupport/ *Email:* donmeyer@siblingsupport.org

ONLINE

Family Village *Online.* A global community that integrates information, resources and communication opportunities for persons with cognitive and other disabilities, their families and professionals. Broad range of discussion boards. *Email:* familyvillage@waisman.wisc.edu *Website:* http://www.familyvillage.wisc.edu/

FAMILY/PARENTING

ADOPTION
(see also parenting, toll-free helplines)

STATEWIDE

Foster and Adoptive Family Services Provides comprehensive information, education, training and support services to foster and adoptive parents. Advocates on behalf of foster and adoptive parents and their children for improved foster care and adoption services. Information for persons wishing to become foster parents. Write: Foster and Adoptive Family Services, 4301 Rt. 1 S., PO Box 518, Monmouth Junction, NJ, 08852. Call 1-800-222-0047. *Website:* http://www.FAFSonline.org

NJ Families For Russian Ukrainian Adoptions Support Group Support for people who have adopted or plan to adopt from Eastern Europe. Guest speakers, phone help, literature and newsletter. Dues $35/yr. Call Mirna Rucci 908-431-0318. *Website:* http://www.orgsites.com/nj/nj-frua/

BERGEN

Adoptive Parents Committee, Inc. Support and education for adoptive parents and those interested in adoption. Advocacy, social group, guest speakers, phone help, newsletter and annual conference. Dues $65/1st yr., $30/thereafter. Meets bi-monthly, Sat. (Sept.-May), 7:30-10:30pm, Temple Beth Orr, Ridgewood Rd., Washington Township. Call Barbara Kalish 201-689-0995 (day/eve). *Website:* http://www.adoptiveparents.org *Email:* apcconf2003@msn.com

Post Adoption Support Group of Northern NJ Mutual support and education for adoptees, adoptive and birth parents. Meets 2nd Wed., 7:30pm, Midland Park. For meeting information call Cindi Addesso 973-427-4521.

BURLINGTON

Birthmothers Support Group Support for mothers who lost a child to adoption recently or decades ago. Adoptees welcome. Rap sessions. Meets 1st Thurs., 6:30-8:30pm, Pemberton Library, 16 Broadway Ave., Browns Mills. Call Irene Gendron 609-893-6086. *Email:* Eastwestig@aol.com

HUNTERDON

Adoptive Families Group NJ/PA Support, child and adult socialization and education on various adoption issues for all adoptive families, including those considering adoption. Also open to adult adoptees, birthmothers who have made adoption plans for their children and any others who share an adoption connection. Rap sessions, guest speakers, literature, phone help and buddy system. Call Patricia Blum 908-475-8944 (day) or Barbara Hurte 908-213-0184 (day). *Email:* pblum@netcarrier.com

MIDDLESEX

Adoptive Family Support Mutual support for families who have adopted a child, particularly from Eastern Europe. Meets 4th Thurs., 7pm, Robert Wood Johnson University Hospital, Board Room, One Robert Wood Place, New Brunswick. Before attending call Mirna 908-431-0318 or RWJ Community Education 732-418-8110 (day).

MONMOUTH

Adoptive Parents Committee, Inc. Support, education and advocacy for adoptive parents and those interested in adopting. Social group, guest speakers, rap sessions, Dues $65/1st yr., $35/thereafter. Meets every other month, (Sept.-June), St. Anselm's Church, 1028 Wayside Rd., Wayside. For meeting days and times call Susan 201-689-0995. *Website:* http://www.adoptiveparents.org *Email:* susanadoptioninfo@earthlink.net

Monmouth/Ocean County Adoptive Parents Support Group Provides education, support and a network for all members of the adoption triad, (pre and post-adoption), especially those adopting transracially. Literature, guest speakers, phone help and buddy system. Dues $25/yr. Meets 3rd Fri., 7:30-9:30pm, St. Mary's Church, Spiritual Center, Phalanx Rd. and Route 34 North, Colts Neck. Call Danielle 732-845-0791 (day/eve) or Liz 732-473-9113 (day/eve). *Email:* webbymisha@hotmail.com or lgrudus@comcast.net

MORRIS

Concerned Persons for Adoption Information and support for those who have adopted or want to adopt. Newsletter, phone network. Dues $25. Meets 1st Mon., 8pm, First Presbyterian Church, Whippany. Call Joan Walsh 973-625-8440 (day/eve) or Janet O'Neill 973-659-9772. *Website:* http://www.cpfanj.org

NJ Coalition for Adoption Reform and Education Grassroots organization that supports honesty in adoption through educational outreach and legislative advocacy. Workshops. Links to statewide search/support groups. Meets Tues., 12:30pm, Presbyterian Church, Parish House, 65 South St., Morristown. Call Jane Nast 973-267-8698 (day/eve), Judy Foster 973-455-1268 or Betsy Forrest 201-891-4234 (eve). *Website:* http://www.nj-care.org *Email:* janenast@compuserve.com

Post-Adoption Support Group Support and education for adoptees, adoptive and birth parents, professionals (under 18 welcome). Donation $3. Guest speakers, advocacy, speakers bureau and search assistance. Meets 1st Sat., 1pm, Presbyterian Church Parish House, 65 South St., Morristown. Call Jane Nast 973-267-8698 or Judy Foster 973-455-1268. *Website:* http://www.nj-care.org *Email:* janenast@compuserve.com

SOMERSET

Adoption Support Group of Central New Jersey Support and search help for adoptees, adoptive parents, birthparents and significant others. Meets every other month, 7:30pm, Hillsboro Presbyterian Church, Basement, Route 206 and Homestead Rd., Hillsboro. Call Randi 609-683-3839 (day).

CHATS (Connected Hearts Adoption Triad Support) Seeks to involve and serve all members of the adoption triad i.e. adoptees, birthparents and adoptive parents as well as others interested in adoption. Phone help, guest speakers, educational series, sharing stories. Meets 4th Mon., 7:15-9:15pm, Watchung Avenue Presbyterian Church, 170 Watchung Ave., North Plainfield. Call Alyce 732-227-0607 (day), Dot 908-755-6978 (eve) or Susan 908-561-9654 (eve). *Website:* http://www.chatsnj.com *Email:* alycemj@aol.com

WARREN

Adoptive Families Group NJ/PA Support, child and adult socialization and education on various adoption issues for all adoptive families, including those considering adoption. Also open to adult adoptees, birthmothers who have made adoption plans for their children and any others who share an adoption connection. Rap sessions, guest speakers, literature, phone help and buddy system. Call Patricia Blum 908-475-8944 (day) or Barbara Hurte 908-213-0184 (day). *Email:* pblum@netcarrier.com

"Be kind, for everyone you meet is fighting a hard battle." —Plato

NATIONAL

Adoption Crossroads *International. 475 affiliated groups. Founded 1990.* Mutual support for persons separated by adoption. Referrals to adoption search and support groups. Newsletter, phone support, conferences. Provides information and referrals to support group meetings. Assistance in starting groups. Write: Adoption Crossroads, c/o Joe Soll, 74 Lakewood Dr., Congers, NY 10920. Call 845-268-0283 (day/eve); Fax: 845-267-2736. *Website:* http://www.adoptioncrossroads.org *Email:* info@adoptioncrossroads.org

ALMA Society (Adoptees' Liberty Movement Association) *International network. Founded 1971.* Provides moral support and guidance for adopted children in finding their birth parents and/or siblings. Also helps parents find the children they gave up for adoption. Open to foster children (age 18+). International reunion registry. One-time tax-deductible contribution of $50. Write: ALMA Society, PO Box 85, Denville, NJ 07834. Call 973-586-1358; Fax: 973-586-1358. *Website:* http://www.almasociety.org

Concerned United Birthparents, Inc. *National. 11 branches. Founded 1976.* Support for adoption-affected people in coping with adoption. Aims to prevent unnecessary separations. Quarterly newsletter. Dues $40/yr. Pen pals, phone network. Provides assistance in starting local groups. Online chat room. Write: CUB, PO Box 503475, San Diego, CA 92150-3475. Call 1-800-822-2777; Fax: 858-435-4863. *Website:* http://www.Cubirthparents.org *Email:* info@CUBirthparents.org

Korean American Adoptee Adoptive Family Network *International.* Mission is to network groups or individuals related to Korean adoption. Offers support, Email newsletter and lists, resources, adoptee services, birth family search, etc. Write: KAAN, PO Box 5585, El Dorado Hills, CA 95762. Call 916-933-1447. *Website:* http://www.kaanet.com *Email:* KAANet@aol.com

North American Council on Adoptable Children *International (US/Canada). Founded 1974.* Focuses on special needs adoption. Provides referrals and maintains current listing of adoptive parent support groups which conduct a wide range of activities. Helps new groups get started. Sponsors an annual adoption conference which features workshops for adoptive parents, prospective parents, foster parents, child welfare professionals and other child advocates. Newsletter. Membership $45/US and $60/Canada. Parent group manual ($10). Write: NACAC, 970 Raymond Ave., Suite 106, St. Paul, MN 55114-1149. Call 651-644-3036 (day); Fax: 651-644-9848. *Website:* http://www.nacac.org *Email:* info@nacac.org

Stars of David, Inc. *International. 32+ chapters.* Support and advocacy group for Jewish or interfaith adoptive families, extended families, interested clergy, social service agencies and adoption professionals. Socials, phone help, literature, education, online listserv and newsletter. Online directory of local groups. Dues $50/family; $125/professional. Write: Stars of David, 3175 Commercial Ave., Suite 100, Norbrook, IL 60062-1915. Call 1-800-782-7349 or 847-274-1527. *Website:* http://www.starsofdavid.org *Email:* info@starsofdavid.org

CESAREAN BIRTH
(see also childbirth, premature/high risk infants)

BURLINGTON

ICAN of Burlington County Support for women healing from Cesarean birth. Encouragement and information for those wanting vaginal birth after previous cesarean. Aims to lower the high cesarean rate through prevention and education. Dues $35/yr. Guest speakers, literature and phone help. Meets 2nd and 3rd Thurs., 7-8:30pm, Evesham Library, Tuckerton Rd., Marlton. Call Janet Cappetta 856-810-9509 (day). *Email:* icanofburlington@aol.com

NATIONAL

ICAN (International Cesarean Awareness Network) Inc. *International. 60 chapters. Founded 1982.* Support for women healing from Cesarean birth. Encouragement and information for those wanting vaginal birth after previous Cesarean. Aims to lower the high Cesarean rate through prevention and education. Newsletter. Chapter development guidebook. Write: ICAN, 1304 Kingsdale Ave., Redondo Beach, CA 90278. Call 1-800-686-4226 or 310-542-6400; Fax: 310-697-3056. *Website:* http://www.ICAN-online.org *Email:* info@ICAN-online.org

CHILDBIRTH / BREASTFEEDING
(see also parenting, toll-free help lines)

BERGEN

La Leche League of Teaneck Education and support for pregnant and breastfeeding women. Discussion group, educational, mutual sharing, phone help and literature. Dues $36/yr. Meetings and locations vary, Teaneck. Call Carmen Clark 201-837-7646, Susan Esserman 201-385-2377 (day) or Julie Rosen 201-837-5910. *Website:* http://www.lalecheleaguenj.org

CAMDEN

Breastfeeding Support Group *Professionally-run.* Support and education for nursing mothers regardless of the age of the child. Meets every other Fri., 10:30-11:30am, Virtua Health's Barry D. Brown Health Education Center, 106 Carnie Blvd., Voorhees. Call 1-888-847-8823 (day).

HUNTERDON

Breastfeeding Support Group Mutual support and education for women who are breastfeeding their infants. Moms welcome to bring lunch. Babies welcome. Meets 1st Thurs., noon-1pm, Hunterdon Medical Center, 2100 Westcott Dr., Flemington. Before attending call Jean Jamele, RN 908-788-6634 (day).

MERCER

Pregnancy and Postpartum Support Group *Professionally-run.* Support for pregnant and new mothers adjusting to emotional issues such as blues, depression and anxiety. Meets 3rd Sat., 10:30am-noon, 60 Mt. Lucas Rd., Princeton. Pre-registration required. Before attending call Joyce 609-683-1000.

MIDDLESEX

Breastfeeding Support Group Mutual support and education for women who are breastfeeding their infants. Moms welcome to bring bag lunch. Beverages provided. Babies are welcome. Expectant mothers can attend. Meets 1st and 3rd Wed., 12:15pm, Robert Wood Johnson University Hospital, Clinical Academic Building, Room 3405, New Brunswick. Call Community Education 732-418-8110.

Pregnant Again *Professionally-run.* Mutual support for anyone who has lost a child by miscarriage, stillbirth or infant death and are pregnant again. Literature and phone help. Meets 2nd Mon., 6-8pm, St. Peter's University Hospital, 254 Easton Ave., Conference Room 5, New Brunswick. Call Dawn Brady 732-745-8600 ext. 5214 (day).

NATIONAL

La Leche League *International. 1269 chapters. Founded 1956.* Support and education for breastfeeding mothers. Group discussions, personal help, classes and conferences. Phone support network. Assistance with starting new groups. Write: La Leche League, 1400 N. Meacham Rd., PO Box 4079, Schaumburg, IL 60168-4079. Call 1-800-525-3243 (day) or 847-519-7730; Fax: 847-519-0035. *Website:* http://www.lalecheleague.org *Email:* LLLI@llli.org

Lamaze International *International. Founded 1960.* Dedicated to promoting normal, natural, healthy and fulfilling childbearing, breastfeeding and early parenting experiences through education, advocacy and reform. Newsletter and publications. Write: Lamaze Int'l, 2025 M St. NW, Suite 800, Washington, DC 20036-3309. Call 1-800-368-4404; Fax: 202-367-2128. *Website:* http://www.lamaze.org *Email:* info@lamaze.org

NAPSAC (National Association of Parents & Professionals for Safe Alternatives in Childbirth) *National. 35 affiliated groups. Founded 1975.* Information and support about homebirth, family centered maternity care and midwifery. Latest scientific research on safety of homebirth vs. hospital birth. Childbirth activist handbook. Literature on starting an affiliate group available. Write: NAPSAC, Route 4, Box 646, Marble Hill, MO 63764. Call 573-238-2010 (Voice/Fax) *Website:* http://www.napsac.org *Email:* napsac@clas.net

National Association of Mothers' Centers *National. 40 sites. Founded 1975.* Discussion groups and other activities regarding parenting, pregnancy, childbirth and childrearing. National and some local newsletters, conference, advocacy. Up-to-date information on contacting local Mothers' Center programs, starting a center and how employers in NY/NJ/CT can offer a program for working parents. Write: NAMC, 64 Division Ave., Levittown, NY 11756. Call 1-800-645-3828 or 516-520-2929; Fax: 516-520-1639. *Website:* http://www.motherscenter.org *Email:* info@motherscenter.org

ONLINE

A Heartbreaking Choice *Online* Resource for parents who have had to terminate a wanted pregnancy due to prenatal news such as birth defects or risk to the well-being of the mother. List serve email list, discussion forum and grandparents forum. *Website:* http://www.aheartbreakingchoice.com

Diabetic Mommies *Online.* Support for women who are pregnant and diabetic. Support for dealing with complications of pregnancy and childbirth. Offers information, message boards, surveys, networking, online magazine and newsletter. *Website:* http://www.diabeticmommy.com

Postpartum Hemorrhage Survivors *Online* Email list for women who are supporting each other after a postpartum hemorrhage and hysterectomy. *Website:* http://health.groups.yahoo.com/group/pph-survivors/

Pregnant Teen Support *Online* Email list for teens (12-20 years) who are facing an unplanned, unexpected or unwanted pregnancy. *Website:* http://health.groups.yahoo.com/group/Pregnant_Teen_Support

FOSTER PARENTS / CHILDREN
(see also toll-free helplines)

STATEWIDE

Foster and Adoptive Family Services Provides comprehensive information, education, training and support services to foster and adoptive parents. Advocates on behalf of foster and adoptive parents and their children for improved foster care and adoption services. Information for persons wishing to become foster parents. Call 1-800-222-0047. *Website:* http://www.FAFSonline.org

MORRIS

Morris County Foster Parents Association Self-help for foster parents and their children to provide social and emotional support. Dues $20/yr. Meets 3rd Wed., (except Dec.), 7pm, DYFS Morris Local Office, 855 Route 10 East, Randolph. Write: Foster and Adoptive Services, 4301 Rt. 1 South, PO Box 518, Monmouth Junction, NJ, 08852. Call Michele Cannaveno 908-850-8303 (day). *Website:* http://www.morrisfpa.org *Email:* morrisfpa@yahoo.com

NATIONAL

National Foster Parent Association, Inc. *National. 50 affiliated groups. Founded 1972.* Support, education and advocacy for foster parents and their children. Resource center for foster care information. Quarterly newsletter. Annual national conference, workshops. Chapter development guidelines. Write: Nat'l Foster Parent Assn., 7512 Stanich Ave., #6, Gig Harbor, WA 98335. Call 1-800-557-5238 or 253-853-4000. *Website:* http://www.nfpainc.org *Email:* info@nfpainc.org

FACT (Fostered Adult Children Together) *Model. 1 group in MI. Founded 1999.* Provides mutual support for former foster children. Literature. Provides assistance in starting similar groups. Write: FACT c/o Carol Lucas, 226 S. Burkhart Rd., Howell, MI 48843. Call 517-546-7818 (voice/fax) *Website:* http://www.factsupportgroup.com

---

> **"Deep listening is miraculous for both listener and speaker. When someone receives us with open-hearted, non-judging, intensely interested listening, our spirits expand." --Sue Patton Thoele**

GRAND PARENTING

STATEWIDE

AtlantiCare Grandparents and Kin Support Group *(BILINGUAL)* *Professionally-run.* Provides information, advocacy and economic assistance to grandparents and kin raising other family members children. Families welcome. Rap sessions, guest speakers, literature, educational series and phone help. Meets 3rd Tues., 6-8pm, Uptown School Complex, 323 Madison Ave., Atlantic City. Call 609-345-1994 (day).

BURLINGTON

BCCAP Headstart Grandparent Support Group Support for grandparents, great-grandparents, great-aunts/uncles, etc. who are raising grandchildren. Meets monthly, (except July/Aug), 7-9pm, Human Services Building, 795 Woodlane Rd., Mt. Holly. Call Sue Dietz 609-261-2323 (day).

Live Your Best Life Mutual support for women of all ages, backgrounds and situations who are raising children on their own (divorced, widowed, grandmothers raising grandchildren, single moms, etc). Groups meet various times in Mount Holly. For information call Joyce Knox 609-880-1593.

CAMDEN

Camden County OEO Grandparents Support Group Support for grandparents who are raising grandchildren or seeking assistance in obtaining custody of grandchildren. Group shares experiences and information on resources regarding food, clothing, etc. Lecture series, educational series, advocacy, rap sessions, guest speakers and phone help. Dues $5/month. Meets 2nd Mon., 10am, CCOEO/CUI Bldg., 538 Broadway, Camden. Call Mattie Parker 856-964-6887 (before 2pm).

KidCor (Kids in the Care Of Relatives) *Professionally-run.* A self-help peer support and resource group for kinship caregivers. Rap sessions, guest speakers, literature and newsletter. Free parking available in attached garage. Meets 3rd Tuesday, noon-2pm, Cooper University Hospital, 3 Cooper Plaza, Suite 518, Camden. Registration is required. Call Jana Nelson 856-751-8923 ext. 1219 (day). *Email:* nelson-jana@cooperhealth.edu

Can't find an appropriate group in your area? The Clearinghouse helps people start groups. Give us a call at 1-800-367-6274.

CAPE MAY

Grandparents Raising Grandchildren *Professionally-run.* Support and educational workshops for grandparents raising their grandchildren. Members share ideas and challenges and learn new skills. Newsletter. Meets monthly, Rutgers Cooperative Research and Extension, 355 Court House, South Dennis Rd., Cape May Court House. For specific dates and times, call Marilou Rochford 609-465-5115.

ESSEX

Grandfamily Program *Professionally-run.* Mutual support for any family member and caregiver raising children. Rap sessions, literature, guest speakers, advocacy and phone help. Meets various days and times in Newark. Call 973-623-5959 ext. 207 (day).

MERCER

Grand-Parent Support Group *(MERCER COUNTY RESIDENTS ONLY) Professionally-run.* Provides support and education for grandparents who provide full-time or part-time care for grandchildren. On-going and short term groups. For meeting day, time and location call Barbara Stender 609-396-6788 ext. 241 (day). Email: bstender@gtbhc.org.

Grandparents Need More Than Hugs Emotional support for grandparents raising their grandchildren. Meetings vary, 6pm, Greenwood Ave., Trenton. Before attending Call Harriet Jones 609-695-4260 (5-9pm). *Email:* GrandforGrands@aol.com

MIDDLESEX

Grandparents Raising Grandchildren Coalition Support for grandparents responsible for raising grandchildren. Information, education, advocacy and mutual support. Dues $5. Meets 2nd Mon., 7-9pm, Edison Senior Center, 2963 Woodbridge Ave., Edison. Call Jill Williams 732-248-8255. *Email:* DMWJAS@aol.com.

NATIONAL

AARP Grandparent Information Center *National. Founded 1993.* Provides information and referrals for grandparents raising their grandchildren. Referrals to support groups nationwide. Free publications on a variety of issues related to raising grandchildren, financial assistance and advocacy. Write: AARP

Grandparent Information Center, 601 E St. NW, Washington, DC 20049. Call 1-888-687-2277; Fax: 202-434-6474. *Website:* http://www.aarp.org/grandparents *Email:* gic@aarp.org

GAP (Grandparents As Parents) *Model. 7 groups. Founded 1987.* Support network. Sharing of experiences and feelings between grandparents who are raising their grandchildren for various reasons. Information & referrals, emergency services, phone support network and group member listings. Assistance in starting similar groups. Write: GAP, PO Box 964, Lakewood, CA 90714. Call 818-727-9160 ext. 3003; Fax: 818-727-9132. *Email:* LaurenceGordon@sbcglobal.net

MARRIAGE / FAMILY

BERGEN

Family Issues *Professionally-run.* Self-help group designed to support seniors with interpersonal relationship problems. Opportunity for members to share feelings and experiences. Meets Tues., 1:15pm, Southeast Senior Center for Independent Living, 228 Grand Ave., Englewood. Call Gail Farina, Social Worker 201-569-4080 (Tues. or Thurs.).

S.O.U.R.C.E., The *Professionally-run.* Support, information, networking and referrals for all family concerns. Drop-in center, guest speakers, groups for parents and kids, phone help. Meets various times, The Source Building, #1 West Plaza, Glen Rock. Call Jean Baker Wunder 201-670-4673 (day).

ESSEX

G.I.F.T. (Getting Interracial/Cultural Families Together) Support for biracial individuals, interracial/cultural couples, families, dating teens, transracial adoptive families and extended families of these groups. Also includes anyone supportive of interracial/cultural issues. Meets periodically, various times. For information call Irene Rottenberg 973-783-0083 (eve). *Website:* http://groups.yahoo.com/group/NJGIFT *Email:* njgift@aol.com

MORRIS

BAN (Beyond Affairs Network) Support for men and women who are dealing with a partner's affair. Opportunity to come together for strength, insight and mutual support. Not open to persons who have had affairs. Meets Thurs. evenings in area library. For meeting information check website. *Website:* http://www.dearpeggy.com *Email:* randolphnjBAN@yahoo.com

NATIONAL

ACME (Association for Couples in Marriage Enrichment) *National network. Founded 1973.* Network of couples who want to enhance their own relationship as well as help strengthen marriages of other couples. Local chapters sponsor support groups, retreats, workshops. Write: ACME, PO Box 21374, Winston-Salem, NC 27120. Call 1-800-634-8325 or 336-724-1526; Fax: 336-721-4746. *Website:* http://www.bettermarriages.org *Email:* acme@bettermarriages.org

No Kidding! *International. 103 chapters in six countries. Founded 1984.* Mutual support and social activities for married and single people who either have decided not to have children, are postponing parenthood, are undecided or are unable to have children. Chapter development guidelines. Write: No Kidding!, Box 2802, Vancouver, BC, Canada V6B 3X2. Call 604-538-7736 (24 hr). *Website:* http://www.nokidding.net *Email:* info@nokidding.net

Recovering Couples Anonymous *National. 130 groups. Founded 1988.* 12 Step. Goal is to assist couples find freedom from dysfunctional patterns in their relationships. RCA is made up of couples committed to restoring healthy communication, caring and developing a functional relationship. Offers local support group information. Write: RCA, PO Box 11029, Oakland CA 94611. Call 510-663-2312. *Website:* http://www.recovering-couples.org *Email:* info@recovering-couples.org

ONLINE

After the Affair *Online.* Discussion forum to help persons recover after an extra-marital affair. Includes posts from those who have had an affair or those who have been involved with someone who has. Children whose parents have had an affair are welcome. *Website:* http://members3.boardhost.com/affair

PARENTING
(see also parents of adolescents, childbirth and toll-free helplines)

STATEWIDE

MOMS Club Support for stay-at-home moms. There are 46 groups that meet in NJ. For information on a local group log on to website: http://www.momsclub.org, click on support, then on to chapter links. Email: momsclub@aol.com

MOPS (Mothers Of Preschoolers) *30 Chapters.* Provides non-denominational Christian support for mothers of preschoolers. For information about a local chapter call 1-800-929-1287. *Website:* http://www.mops.org

Mothers and More Support groups for women who have altered their career paths to care for their children at home. 11 groups in NJ. Listing of these chapters is at http://www.mothersandmore.org or call the national office in Illinois 630-941-3553.

New Jersey Parents Against D.Y.F.S. Provides advocacy, education and support for families who feel they have been unjustifiably victimized by the NJ Division of Youth and Family Services. Buddy system, literature and newsletter. Dues $30/yr. Assistance provided in starting local support groups. Pre-screening required. Meetings in Monmouth County. Write: New Jersey Parents Against D.Y.F.S., PO Box 726, Oakhurst, NJ 07755. Call Mindy Anastasia 732-988-1115 (day).

Unschoolers Network Information and encouragement for families who educate their children at home. Guest speakers, literature, phone help. Quarterly newsletter $16 (optional). Annual conference. For local group information Call Nancy Plent 732-938-2473. *Email:* UnNet@aol.com

ATLANTIC

MOPS (Mothers Of Pre-Schoolers) Support and encouragement for mothers of pre-schoolers. Program includes fellowship, lectures on Christian womanhood, discussion groups and crafts. Suggested $5/mtg. Meets 1st and 3rd Mon., 9:30-11:30am, Trinity Baptist Church, 1049 Ocean Heights Ave., Egg Harbor Township. Call Jennifer Christiansen 609-909-9702 or Trinity Baptist Church 609-646-4693 (day).

BERGEN

Attachment Parenting International (API) of Bergen County A group open to parents and all others interested in learning about the principles of attachment parenting. Guest speakers, literature, newsletter and phone help. Dues $35/yr. Meets 4th Thurs., 10am-noon, Haworth. Call Susan Esserman 201-385-2377 (day) or Carole Blane 201-244-6758 (day).

Holistic Moms Network Mutual support for moms with an interest in natural health, alternative therapies and mindful parenting. Families welcome. Rap sessions and guest speakers. Dues $35/yr. Meets in Ridgewood. For information call 1-877-465-6667. *Website:* http://www.holisticmoms.org *Email:* info@holisticmoms.org

Groups are constantly changing. Starting, ending, moving. Call us for the most updated information from our database. 1-800-367-6274

BURLINGTON

Baby And Me Morning Support for moms of newborns to toddlers. Guest speakers, sharing, education and socialization. Meetings vary, Virtua Memorial Hospital, 175 Madison Ave., Mt. Holly. Before attending call 1-888-847-8823.

Holistic Moms Network Mutual support for moms with an interest in natural health, alternative therapies and mindful parenting. Families welcome. Rap sessions and guest speakers. Dues $35/yr. Meets in Roebling. For information call 1-877-465-6667. *Website:* http://www.holisticmoms.org *Email:* info@holisticmoms.org

I Can Problem Solve Support Group *Professionally-run.* Mutual support for parents of children (age 13 years and under) to learn conflict resolution and problem solving skills. Advocacy, social, guest speakers and newsletter. Meets 1st Wed., 6-8pm, Family Support Organization, 774 Eayrestown Rd., Lumberton. Call Michelle Tyler 609-265-8838 (day).

Live Your Best Life Mutual support for women of all ages, backgrounds and situations who are raising children on their own (divorced, widowed, grandmothers raising grandchildren, single moms, etc). Groups meet various times in Mount Holly. For information Call Joyce Knox 609-880-1593.

CAMDEN

Baby And Me Morning Voorhees Support for parents of newborns to toddlers. Guest speakers, sharing, education and socialization. Dues $4/mtg. Meets Fri., 9:30-11:30am, Virtua Health, Barry D. Brown Health Education Center, 106 Carnie Blvd., Voorhees. Call 1-888-847-8823 (day).

Holistic Moms Network Mutual support for moms with an interest in natural health, alternative therapies and mindful parenting. Families welcome. Rap sessions and guest speakers. Dues $35/yr. Meets in Cherry Hill. For information call 1-877-465-6667. *Website:* http://www.holisticmoms.org *Email:* info@holisticmoms.org

KidCor (Kids in the Care Of Relatives) *Professionally-run.* A self-help peer support and resource group for kinship caregivers. Free parking available in attached garage. Meets 3rd Tuesday., noon-2pm, Cooper University Hospital, 3 Cooper Plaza, Suite 518, Camden. Registration is required. Call Jana Nelson 856-751-8923 ext. 1219 (day). *Email:* nelson-jana@cooperhealth.edu

Toddler Time Support for caregivers and their toddlers (steady walkers) for support, fun and education. Dues $5/mtg. Snack and craft provided. Meets Mon., 10-11:30am, Virtua Health, Barry D. Brown Health Education Center,

218

106 Carnie Blvd., Voorhees. Before attending call 1-888-847-8823 (day).

ESSEX

G.I.F.T. (Getting Inter-racial/Cultural Families Together) Support for bi-racial individuals, inter-racial/cultural couples, families, dating teens, transracial adoptive families; extended families of these groups and anyone supportive of inter-racial/cultural issues. Meets periodically, various times, usually in Montclair. For information call Irene Rottenberg 973-783-0083 (eve). *Website:* http://www.groups.yahoo.com/group/NJGIFT *Email:* njgift@aol.com

Holistic Moms Network Mutual support for moms with an interest in natural health, alternative therapies and mindful parenting. Families welcome. Rap sessions and guest speakers. Dues $35/yr. Meets 3rd Thurs., 7-9:30pm, Unitarian Church of Montclair, 67 Church St., Montclair. Call 973-228-2110 (day). *Website:* http://www.holisticmoms.org *Email:* info@holisticmoms.org

M.O.M.S. Club of Bloomfield-Montclair *(ESSEX COUNTY RESIDENTS ONLY)* Support group for women who've chosen to stay home, at least part-time, with their children. Literature and guest speakers. Dues $25/yr. Meets 2nd Wed., 10am, Bloomfield Presbyterian Church on the Green, Parish House, Broad and Beach St., Bloomfield. Call Diane 973-406-4124 (day).

MOPS (Mothers Of Preschoolers) Provides non-denominational Christian support for mothers with children under school age. Education, group discussions, socials, guest speakers and crafts. For women with the desire to be the best mother they can be. Donation $5 (can be waived). Meets 4th Thurs., 9:30am-noon, (except July/Aug.), Montclair Community Church, 143 Watchung Ave., Upper Montclair. Before attending Call Rhonda 973-338-6053. *Website:* http://www.mops.org

Parenting Insights Support for new mothers. Opportunity for new mothers to share ideas and discuss parenting topics. Meeting times and locations vary. Before attending call 973-322-5360 (day).

GLOUCESTER

Gloucester County Parent To Parent Coalition *Professionally-run.* Confidential meetings that focus on providing parents with support, information, resources and referrals for dealing with substance abuse and related problems. Guest speakers, educational series, literature. Meets 2nd and 4th Mon., 7:30-9:30pm, Washington Township Municipal Building, Meeting Room C, 523 Egg Harbor Rd., Turnersville. Call 856-589-6446 (day).

219

Holistic Moms Network Mutual support for moms with an interest in natural health, alternative therapies and mindful parenting. Families welcome. Rap sessions and guest speakers. Dues $35/yr. Meets in Pitman. Call 1-877-465-6667. *Website:* http://www.holisticmoms.org *Email:* info@holisticmoms.org

HUDSON

Family Enrichment Program *Professionally-run* Educational series to strengthen families through support groups and recreational activities. Childcare available. Must sign up for six month program. Meets Thurs., 4:30-6:30pm, Women Rising Inc., 270 Fairmount Ave., Jersey City. Before attending call Jasmine Soto 201-333-5700 ext. 548 (day).

Women's Project Groups *Professionally-run.* Education, support, workshops and groups to help women on topics such as assertiveness, separation/divorce, self-esteem, parenting, along with stress management. Meets various days and times, Christ Hospital, 176 Palisade Ave., Jersey City. Call Michele Bernstein 201-795-8375 ext. 8416 (day).

HUNTERDON

Holistic Moms Network Mutual support for moms with an interest in natural health, alternative therapies and mindful parenting. Families welcome. Dues $35/yr. Meets in Lebanon. Call 1-877-465-6667. *Website:* http://www.holisticmoms.org *Email:* info@holisticmoms.org

MERCER

Hispanic Parenting Support Group *(SPANISH SPEAKING) Professionally-run.* Provides mutual support and education to Spanish-speaking parents. Rap sessions, guest speakers, literature. Life skills and parenting workshops. Also offers bilingual and multi-cultural parenting skills. Meets Fri., 10am-1pm, Latinas Unidas, YWCA, 140 E. Hanover St., Trenton. Call Cecy Weast 609-396-3040 (day).

Holistic Moms Network Mutual support for moms with an interest in natural health, alternative therapies and mindful parenting. Families welcome. Rap sessions and guest speakers. Dues $35/yr. Meets in Robbinsville. Call 1-877-465-6667. *Website:* http://www.holisticmoms.org *Email:* info@holisticmoms.org

New Moms Group Support designed for moms with an infant from birth to one year. Offers mutual support discussing the ups and downs of a new baby on the family. Meets for 8 week sessions, 2-3 times year, Jewish Center of Princeton, 435 Nassau St., Princeton. For dates and times call Debra Levenstein 609-987-8100 (eve).

MIDDLESEX

Holistic Moms Network Mutual support for moms with an interest in natural health, alternative therapies and mindful parenting. Families welcome. Rap sessions and guest speakers. Dues $35/yr. Meets in Piscataway. Call 1-877-465-6667. *Website:* http://www.holisticmoms.org *Email:* info@holisticmoms.org

MONMOUTH

Holistic Moms Network Mutual support for moms with an interest in natural health, alternative therapies and mindful parenting. Families welcome. Rap sessions and guest speakers. Dues $35/yr. Meets in Wall. Call 1-877-465-6667. *Website:* http://www.holisticmoms.org *Email:* info@holisticmoms.org

MOPS (Mothers Of Pre-Schoolers) Support and encouragement to mothers of preschoolers. Program includes fellowship, lectures on Christian womanhood, discussion groups and crafts. Suggested $4/mtg. Meets 2nd and 4th Thurs. (Sept.-May), 9:30-11am, First Presbyterian Church at Red Bank, 255 Harding Rd., Red Bank. Call the church 732-747-1348 (day) or Carol Andrews 732-671-0553 (day) to confirm meeting days.

Mother to Mother Support Group *Professionally-run.* Provides support and education to new mothers to help with topics such as feeding, sleeping, crying, as well as recovery from childbirth and postpartum depression. Newborns welcome. Meets Thurs., 10-11:30am, Monmouth Medical Center, Regional Newborn Center, Greenwall Pavilion, 3rd Floor, Room 305, Long Branch. Before attending call Jean Bonn or Carol Logan 732-923-6990 (day).

New Moms Network at Jersey Shore University Medical Center *Professionally-run.* Information and support for mothers of infants age birth to 12 months. Rap sessions, guest speakers and phone help. Meets Thurs., 1-3pm, Jersey Shore Medical Center, Lance B 104, 1945 Route 33, Neptune. Call Linda Carroll 732-776-4281 (day). *Email:* lcarroll@meridianhealth.com

Parent Linking Project Opportunity for parents to discuss parenting skills, child development and parent-child interaction. Some groups welcome young fathers and grandparents. Various meeting locations. For information call Jill Brown 732-246-8060. *Website:* http://www.preventchildabusenj.org

MORRIS

Holistic Moms Network Mutual support for moms with an interest in natural health, alternative therapies and mindful parenting. Families welcome. Rap sessions and guest speakers. Dues $35/yr. Meets in Boonton. Call 1-877-465-6667. *Website:* http://www.holisticmoms.org *Email:* info@holisticmoms.org

OCEAN

Holistic Moms Network Mutual support for moms with an interest in natural health, alternative therapies and mindful parenting. Families welcome. Rap sessions and guest speakers. Dues $35/yr. Meets in Toms River. Call 1-877-465-6667. *Website:* http://www.holisticmoms.org *Email:* info@holisticmoms.org

Mother's Center Offers information, social and education for mothers. Play groups for children. Meetings vary in northern Ocean County. Dues $30/yr. Call 732-449-3936. *Website:* http://www.mcjs.org

PASSAIC

Holistic Moms Network Mutual support for moms with an interest in natural health, alternative therapies and mindful parenting. Families welcome. Rap sessions and guest speakers. Dues $35/yr. Meets in Clifton. Call 1-877-465-6667. *Website:* http://www.holisticmoms.org *Email:* info@holisticmoms.org

Parent Linking Project Opportunity for parents to discuss parenting skills, child development and parent-child interaction. Some groups welcome young fathers and grandparents. Various meeting locations. For information call Tamara Brown 973-754-7400.

SOMERSET

Holistic Moms Network Mutual support for moms with an interest in natural health, alternative therapies and mindful parenting. Families welcome. Rap sessions and guest speakers. Dues $35/yr. Meets in Bridgewater. Call 1-877-465-6667. *Website:* http://www.holisticmoms.org *Email:* info@holisticmoms.org

Jersey Dads Online. Support for stay-at-home dads to discuss parenting and household skills. *Website:* http://www.JerseyDads.com *Email:* NJDads@hotmail.com

If you are using this book past Spring 2007, please call us for information about our most recent directory. 1-800-367-6274

222

SUSSEX

Project Self-Sufficiency *Professionally-run.* Support for single parents, teen parents and displaced homemakers. Offers mutual sharing, advocacy, social groups, literature, rap sessions, guest speakers and speakers' bureau. Meeting vary. Call Deborah Berry-Toon 973-383-5129 (day).

UNION

Holistic Moms Network Mutual support for moms with an interest in natural health, alternative therapies and mindful parenting. Families welcome. Rap sessions and guest speakers. Dues $35/yr. Meets in Mountainside. Call 1-877-465-6667. *Website:* http://www.holisticmoms.org *Email:* info@holisticmoms.org

Mother's Center of Central New Jersey, Inc. Support and discussion groups for mothers. Education, information and referrals, workshops, newsletter. Semi-annual kids' toys/clothes exchange. Babysitting available. Dues $50/yr. Meets in Cranford. Call 908-561-1751 (taped message). *Website:* http://www.westfieldnj.com/mccnj *Email:* mccnj@westfieldnj.com

WARREN

Holistic Moms Network Mutual support for moms with an interest in natural health, alternative therapies and mindful parenting. Families welcome. Rap sessions and guest speakers. Dues $35/yr. Meets in Hackettstown. Call 1-877-465-6667. *Website:* http://www.holisticmoms.org *Email:* info@holisticmoms.org

Mother's Center of Northwest New Jersey An opportunity for moms and dads to learn, share parenting experiences and make friends for self and family. Discussions, guest speakers, family activities. Non-sectarian. Dues $15/yr. Reservations required for optional child care $4/mtg/child. Meets 1st and 3rd Fri., 9:30-11:30am, Panther Valley Ecumenical Ministry, 1490 Route 517, Allamuchy. Call Marge Bidgood 973-347-5433 (day/eve) or Jennifer Braun 973-691-7611 (day/eve).

NATIONAL

Attachment Parenting International *International. Founded 1994.* Offers parenting methods to create strong, healthy emotional bonds between parents and their child. Dues $35/yr. Offers support group referrals, newsletter, advocacy, literature, information and referrals. Write: Attachment Parenting Int'l, 2906 Berry Hill Dr., Nashville, TN 37204. Call 615-298-4334; Fax: 615-298-9723. *Website:* http://www.attachmentparenting.org *Email:* info@attachmentparenting.org

Family Pride Coalition *National. 160+ local groups. Founded 1979.* Support, education and advocacy for gay/lesbian/transgendered parents and prospective parents. Families welcome. Information and referrals, phone support, family events, literature. Newsletter. Assistance in starting groups. Write: Family Pride Coalition, PO Box 65327, Washington, DC 20035-5327. Call 202-331-5015; Fax: 202-331-0080. *Website:* http://www.familypride.org *Email:* info@familypride.org

Fathers' Network, The *Model. 1 group in Oregon. Founded 1979.* Aims to increase involvement of fathers in parenting. Encourages mutually fulfilling relationships between fathers & their children. Challenges traditional "provider" role regardless of marital/custodial status. National men's resources on website. Not a divorce resource. Write: The Fathers' Network, 1080-SH, Brookings or 97415-0024. *Website:* http://www.menstuff.org

Holistic Moms Network *International. Chapters in 21 States and Canada. Founded 2002.* Purpose is to provide awareness, education and support for holistic parenting and provide a nurturing, open-minded and respectful community for parents to share these ideals. Encourages moms and dads to parent naturally and educate themselves about alternative health, mindful parenting and natural healing. Assists persons in starting new chapters. Write: Holistic Moms Network, PO Box 408, Caldwell, NJ 07006. Call 1-877-465-6667. *Website:* http://www.holisticmoms.org *Email:* info@holisticmoms.org

MAD DADS, Inc. (Men Against Destruction Defending Against Drugs and Social-disorder) *National. 60 affiliated groups in 16 states. Founded 1989.* Grassroots organization of fathers aimed at fighting gang and drug-related violence. Provides family activities, community education, speaking engagements and "surrogate fathers" who listen to and care about street teens. Provides assistance in starting groups. Also groups for kids, mothers, grandparents. Write: MAD DADS, Inc., 555 Stockton St., Jacksonville, FL 32204. Call 904-388-8171. *Website:* http://www.maddads.com *Email:* national@maddads.com

MELD *National. 65+ affiliated programs. Founded 1973.* Provides supportive, peer-based learning environments and knowledge about parenting at critical stages of child development. Programs serve families who can benefit from strong support and parenting knowledge and strategies, including adolescent parents, low-income families, culturally-diverse families or families who have children with disabilities or chronic illnesses. Also provides staff development training and comprehensive parent education materials. Offers over 250 publications that provide hands-on help or parents and professionals. Write: MELD, 219 North Second St., Suite 200 Minneapolis, MN 55401. Call 612-332-7563; Fax: 612-332-7563. *Website* http://www.meld.org *Email:* info@meld.org

Mocha Moms, Inc. *National. 100+ affiliated groups. Founded 1997.* Provides support for at-home mothers of color. Sponsors weekly support group meetings, monthly moms-only events and on-going community service and volunteer opportunities. Fee $20/year. Bulletins, information, assistance with starting local chapters and referrals to existing groups. Write: Mocha Moms, Inc., PO Box 829, Bowie, MD 20718. Fax: 301-805-8147. *Website:* http://www.mochamoms.org *Email:* nationaloffice@mochamoms.org

MOMS Club *International. 1900+ affiliated groups. Founded 1983.* Mutual support for mothers-at-home. Groups provide at-home mothers of children of all ages emotional and moral support, as well as a wide variety of activities. Provides assistance in starting and maintaining or locating chapters through local coordinators (enclose $2 to cover postage). Write: MOMS Club, 1464 Madera Road, N 191, Simi Valley, CA 93065. Call 805-526-2725. *Website:* http://www.momsclub.org *Email:* momsclub@aol.com

MOPS, International (Mothers Of Pre-Schoolers) *International. 3200 affiliated groups. Founded 1973.* Offers a non-denominational Christian support group for mothers with children under school age. MOPS groups meet in churches throughout the U.S., Canada and 15 other countries. Assistance in starting local groups. Write: MOPS, International, 2370 South Trenton Way, Denver, CO 80231. Call 1-800-929-1287 or 303-733-5353 (group referrals), 1-888-910-6677 (to start a MOPS group); Fax: 303-733-5770. *Website:* http://www.mops.org *Email:* info@mops.org

Mothers and More *National. 180 chapters. Founded 1987.* Support and advocacy for women who have altered their career paths to care for their children at home. It is not about opposing mothers who work outside the home; rather it is about respecting, supporting and advocating for choice in how one combines working and parenting. Provides ongoing support for women's personal needs and interests with regard to active parenting and advocates for public and employment policies that accommodate stay-at-home mothers. Newsletter, chapter development guidelines. Write: Mothers & More, PO Box 31, Elmhurst, IL 60126. Call 630-941-3553; Fax: 630-941-3551. *Website:* http://www.mothersandmore.org *Email:* nationaloffice@mothersandmore.org

NATHHAN (National Challenged Homeschoolers Association Network) *National network. Founded 1990.* Christian, non-profit organization encouraging families with special needs, particularly those who home educate. Bi-annual magazine, lending library, family phone book, phone support, information and referrals. Dues $25. Write: NATHHAN, PO Box 3. Porthill, ID 83853. Call 208-267-6246. *Website:* http://www.nathhan.org *Email:* nathanews@aol.com

National Association of Mothers' Centers *National. 40 sites. Founded 1975.* Offers discussion groups and other activities regarding parenting, pregnancy, childbirth and childrearing. NAMC has up-to-date information on contacting local Mothers' Center programs, starting a center and how employers in NY/NJ/CT can offer a program for working parents. Write: National Association of Mothers' Centers, 64 Division Ave., Levittown, NY 11756. Call 1-800-645-3828 or 516-520-2929; Fax: 516-520-1639. *Website:* http://www.motherscenter.org *Email:* info@motherscenter.org

PEP (Postpartum Education for Parents) *Model. 1 group in California. Founded 1977.* Volunteer-run group that provides emotional peer support for parents. Helps parents adjust to the changes in their lives that a baby brings. Education on basic infant care and parent adjustment. Monthly newsletter. Online support group. Phone help. Group development guidelines. Write: PEP, PO Box 6154, Santa Barbara, CA 93160. Call 805-564-3888. *Website:* http://www.sbpep.org *Email:* pepmail@cox.net

ONLINE

Conduct Disorders Parent Message Board *Online.* Support for parents living with a child with one of the many behavior disorders including attention deficit hyperactivity disorder, oppositional defiance disorder, conduct disorder, depression and substance abuse. Parents with children of all ages welcome. *Website:* http://www.conductdisorders.com

Expecting Parents Meet up Groups *Online.* Opportunity for new or expecting parents to exchange advice, support and laughs. Message boards. *Website:* http://newparents.meetup.com/

Parent Empowerment Network *Online. Founded 1996.* Email listserv for parents with disabilities. *Website:* http//www.disabledparents.net *Email:* trish@disabledparents.net

Parent Soup Message Boards *Online.* Offers a large variety of message boards which deal with parenting issues including infertility, pregnancy, parenting challenges, parents of disabled, pregnancy loss, newborn babies, toddlers, equipment, adoption, family issues, etc. *Website:* http://www.parentsoup.com/boards

Slow Lane *Online. Founded 1997.* Resources for stay-at-home fathers. Regionally-based discussion groups, online forums and chat, information and events. Write: Slow Lane, 1216 East Lee St., Pensacola, FL, 32503. Call 850-434-2626. *Website:* http://www.slowlane.com

PARENTS OF ADOLESCENTS / ADULT CHILDREN

(see also drugs, alcohol, parenting and toll-free helplines)

STATEWIDE

Toughlove America Mutual support for parents disturbed by their children's unacceptable behavior. Helps parents take a firm stand with their kids. Dues $5/wk. Membership $30/yr. Call Mary Cooke 609-883-1989.

ATLANTIC

Atlantic Cape Support Organization Provides education and social support to parents/caregivers who have children struggling with emotional and/or behavioral difficulties. Guest speakers and literature. Meets 1st and 3rd Wed., 6:30-8:30pm, Atlantic County Family Support Organization, 2312 New Rd., Northfield. Call Andrea Burleigh 609-485-0575 ext. 105 (day).

Toughlove America Support for parents and grandparents dealing with their children's unacceptable behavior. ($5/wk, $30/yr membership). Phone help and guest speakers. Meets Mon., 7:30pm, Zion Methodist Church, Zion Rd., Bargaintown. Call Mary 609-883-1989 (day/eve).

BERGEN

Parents in Crisis Mutual support for parents disturbed by their children's unacceptable behavior. Helps parents take firm stand with their kids. Meets Wed., 7:30pm, Community Church, 354 Rock Rd., Glen Rock. Call Jean Baker Wunder 201-652-8332 or The Source 201-670-4673.

BURLINGTON

B.I.L.Y. (Because I Love You) Mutual support to help parents with children, of any age, who have behavioral challenges. Guest speakers. Meets 2nd and 4th Wed., 6:30-8:30pm, Nesbit Community Center at Sunbury Village, 1 Anderson Rd., Pemberton. Call Deborah or Russ 609-265-8838 (day). *Email:* familyvoices@fsoburlco.org

Toughlove America Mutual support for parents disturbed by their children's unacceptable behavior. Helps parents take a firm stand with their children. Meets Tues., 7pm, 774 Eayrestown Rd., Lumberton. Call Russ H. 609-265-8838 (day).

While it's no substitution for talking to our staff, you can call evenings or weekends! Leave a message and we will get back to you the next workday. **1-800-367-6274**

227

CAMDEN

B.I.L.Y. (Because I Love You) Mutual support to help parents with children, of any age, who have behavioral challenges. Guest speakers, rap sessions, literature and phone help. Meets 1st and 3rd Wed., 7-9pm, Camden County Family Support Organization, 23 West Park Ave., Suite 103-104, Merchantville. Call Susan A. Doherty-Funke 856-662-2600 (day) or 856-261-0233 (eve). *Email:* kbirmingham@camdenfso.org

Grandparents Raising Grandchildren Support and education for women and men who are caring for their grandchildren struggling with emotional, behavioral and mental challenges. Guest speakers, literature, social, advocacy and buddy system. Meets 2nd and 4th Mon., 6:30-8:30pm, Holy Trinity Lutheran Church, 325 South Whitehorse Pike, Audubon. Call Marge Varneke 856-547-1620 (eve) or Susan A. Doherty-Funke 856-662-2600 (day).

CAPE MAY

Atlantic Cape Support Organization Provides education and social support to parents/caregivers who have children struggling with emotional and/or behavioral difficulties. Guest speakers and literature. Meets 1st and 3rd Wed., 6:30-8:30pm, Atlantic County Family Support Organization, 2312 New Rd., Northfield. Call Andrea Burleigh 609-485-0575 ext. 105 (day).

ESSEX

Parents Self-Help Group Mutual support for parents disturbed by their children's unacceptable behavior. Helps parents take a firm stand with their kids. Meets Tues., 7:30pm, Senior Community Center, Livingston. Call Debbie 973-533-1319 (day/eve), Helene and Jerry 973-994-4034 (day/eve) or Paul and Nancy 908-464-1590.

MERCER

Parent Support Group *Professionally-run.* Support and information for parents of adolescents. Opportunity to share ideas, concerns, strategies, learn helpful parenting skills and techniques. Meets Wed., 6-7pm, Anchor House, 482 Centre St., Trenton. Call 609-396-8329 (day/eve).

Toughlove America Mutual support for parents disturbed by their children's unacceptable behavior. Dues $5 week per family. Meets Mon., 7:30pm, Unitarian Universalist Church, Cherry Hill Rd., Princeton. Call Mary 609-883-1989.

MIDDLESEX

Family Support Organization of Middlesex County Support for parents raising a child with emotional and behavioral challenges. Guest speakers, literature, newsletter, phone help, buddy system and speakers bureau. Meets Mon., 6:30-8:30pm, (for parents of children 13 and older) and Thurs., 6-8pm (for parents of children 12 and under). Call Bobbie Locke, Bryan Schain or Lirie Mulaj 732-940-2837 (day). *Website:* http://www.njfamily.org

MONMOUTH

Toughlove America Mutual support for parents disturbed by their children's unacceptable behavior. Dues $5/mtg - $30/yr. Meets Tues. 7:30pm, Church of the Master, 110 Salem Hill Rd., Howell. Call Susan Walters 732-431-1740 or Ruth 732-536-9324.

PASSAIC

Family Support Organization of Passaic County *(BILINGUAL)* Support for parents raising a child with emotional and behavioral challenges. Group will begin in April, 2006. Meets at Family Support Organization of Passaic County, 1 Ottillo Terrace, Totowa. For meeting information call 973-720-0010.

Toughlove America Mutual support for parents disturbed by their children's unacceptable behavior. Helps parents take a firm stand with their kids. Donation $5/week. Meets Thurs., 7:15-9:45pm, Pompton Reformed Church, Hamburg Turnpike, Pompton Lakes. Call Carol 973-962-2234.

UNION

Family Support Organization of Union County Support for persons raising a child with emotional and behavioral challenges. Meets 3rd Tues., 6:30-8:30pm, (also separate youth group meets 2nd and 4th Wed.). Family Support Organization of Union County, 137 Elmer St., Westfield. Before attending call 908-789-7625. *Website:* http://www.fso-union.org

NATIONAL

Because I Love You: The Parent Support Group *National. 47 affiliated groups. Founded 1982.* Self-help groups for parents who have children of all ages with behavioral problems such as truancy, substance abuse or other forms of defiance of authority. Focus is on parents getting back their self-esteem and control of their

229

home. Write: Because I Love You, PO Box 2062, Winnetka, CA 91396-2062. Call 818-884-8242; Fax: 805-493-2714. *Website:* http://www.becauseiloveyou.org *Email:* BILY1982@aol.com

StandUp Parenting *National.* Offers mutual support, education, alternative strategies and practical solutions to family problems related to a child's out-of-control behavior. Local self-help groups in ten states. Call 1-800-972-0416. Website: http://www.standupp.org

Toughlove International *International. 43 affiliated groups. Founded 1979.* Self-help program for parents, kids and communities dealing with the out-of-control behavior of a family member. Parent support groups help parents to take a firm stand to help kids take responsibility for their behavior. Groups listed at website. 127 Manhattan Ave., Hermosa Beach, CA 90254. *Website:* http://www.toughlove.org

ONLINE

Conduct Disorders Parent Message Board *Online.* Support for parents living with a child with one of the many behavior disorders including attention deficit hyperactivity disorder, oppositional defiance disorder, conduct disorder, depression and substance abuse. Parents with children of all ages welcome. *Website:* http://www.conductdisorders.com

PARENTS OF DISABLED / ILL CHILDREN
(see also specific disability and toll-free helplines)

STATEWIDE

S.P.A.N. (Statewide Parent Advocacy Network) *(BILINGUAL) Professionally-run.* Training, information, technical assistance, leadership development and support for parents concerning education and health care issues for their children from birth to age 21. Special focus on children at risk due to disabilities, special health care or emotional needs, poverty, language or race. Workshops to increase knowledge of laws, effective education practices and advocacy strategies. Assist parents of children with special health needs in medical and insurance advocacy. Newsletter, phone help, networking of parents. Bilingual materials. Call 1-800-654-7726 (within NJ) (voice/TDD) or 973-642-8100; Fax: 973-642-8080 (day). Specialized services include: Parent-to-Parent at 1-800-372-6510 that matches families of children on a one-to-one basis, with similar disabilities, developmental delays or other special health needs; and the START Project which helps parents of children who have special needs and are in public schools to form their own support groups. *Website:* http://www.spannj.org *Email:* span@spannj.org

CAMDEN

Father's Group *Professionally-run.* Mutual support for fathers of children of any age who have a developmental delay or disability. A great opportunity for dads to informally meet to discuss issues affecting themselves and their families. Meets 1st Sat., (except July/Aug) 10am-noon, Virtua Memorial Hospital Burlington County, Conference Center,175 Madison Ave., Mt. Holly. Before attending call Virtua 1-888-847-8823 (day).

ESSEX

Determined To Achieve Parent Network Support for parents advocating for special needs children and their families. Goal is to assist families in development and self-empowerment. Also offers phone help, advocacy, socials, literature and mutual self-help. Dues $2 monthly. Meets Tues., 6-8pm, The Servicemen's Clubhouse, 1113 Springfield Ave., Irvington. Call Darlene 973-373-9904.

HUNTERDON

Sharing and Caring of Bucks County Information and support for parents of children with autism, Asperger syndrome, mental retardation and related disorders. Discussion groups, guest speakers, sib-shop sibling support group, social and recreational activities. Suggested donation $15/yr. Meets 2nd Thurs., 7-9pm, St. Vincent DePaul Church, Education Building, Hatboro Rd., Richboro, PA. Call Holly Druckman 215-321-3202 (Mon.-Fri., 10am-6pm).

MIDDLESEX

High Expectations Parents and Friends Support Group Mutual sharing, socializing and advocacy for parents, friends and relatives of children with disabilities. Meets monthly in Iselin. Call Diane Heitmeyer 732-283-0925 (eve). *Email:* DianeHeit@aol.com

Parents of Children with Disabilities Mutual support and encouragement for parents of children ages 14-21 with any type of disability. Information and referrals. Rap sessions and guest speakers. Meetings vary, Alliance for Disabled in Action, 629 Amboy Ave., Edison. Call Kathleen Orsetti 732-738-4388 (day); TDD: 732-738-9644. *Website:* http://www.adacil.org *Email:* peersupport@adacil.org

"The greatest motivational act one person can do for another is to listen."
--Roy E. Moody

MONMOUTH

Mothers Social Mutual support and information sharing in a relaxed social environment for parents of young children with delays and disabilities. Mom's social. Meets monthly in members' homes. Call Susan Levine 732-747-5310 (day).

Organization for Children with Profound Disabilities Mutual support for parents, grandparents and other caregivers of children of any age with severe multiple handicaps or who are medically fragile. Rap sessions, advocacy. Group meets various times and locations. For information call Jane 732-866-9217. *Email:* janeye@optonline.net

Parents Of Children With Multiple Impairments *Professionally-run.* Support for parents of children with multiple impairments. Meets monthly, 7:30-9pm, Family Resource Associates, 35 Haddon Ave., Shrewsbury. Call Susan Levine 732-747-5310 (day).

PASSAIC

Parents Place/Club de Padres Catholic Family and Community Services *(BILINGUAL)* Support for parents and families of children with disabilities. Information and referrals, translation/interpretation services available, technical assistance, immigration assistance, advocacy, recreation, training, employment. Meets in Paterson. Local transportation provided. Child care available. For meeting information call 973-523-8404 ext. 41 or 45 (day). *Email:* parentsplace26@aol.com

SOMERSET

Special Needs Parents Support Network Support, education and information sharing for parent of children with special needs. Meets twice a month in Peapack. For meeting information call Amy 908-704-8226 or Jessica 908-874-0927.

SUSSEX

The Center for Families with Special Needs Parent-run organization that provides emotional support, information and literature for families of children with special needs. Referrals to local services, phone help, guest speakers. Newsletter $10/yr. Parent Support Network meets various Fri., 7:30-9:30pm, St. Thomas Church, Route 94, Vernon. Call Sheila McNally 973-827-4419 (Tues and Thurs, 9-1pm). *Email:* thecenter@nac.net

WARREN

North Warren Special Needs Advocacy Support and advocacy to parents/guardians of children with special needs. Rap sessions, guest speakers and phone help. Dues $10/yr. Meetings vary, Catherine Dickson Hofman Library, Blairstown. Call Margaret Scocozza 908-362-9066.

NATIONAL

Birth Defect Research for Children *National network. Founded 1982.* Provides information about birth defects, as well as services and resources that may be helpful to families. Links parents of children with similar birth defects for mutual sharing and support. Sponsors national birth defect registry. Maintains database on medical/scientific literature and research. Monthly electronic newsletter. Write: Birth Defect Research for Children, 930 Woodcock Rd., Suite 225, Orlando, FL 32803. Call 407-895-0802; Fax: 407-895-0824. *Website:* http://www.birthdefects.org *Email:* abdc@birthdefects.org

Family Voices *National. 50 affiliated groups. Founded 1995. (BILINGUAL)* Grassroots organization that speaks on behalf of children with special health care needs at the national, state and local levels. Encourages and supports families who want to play a role in their child's health care. Advocacy. Literature (Spanish and English). Write: Family Voices, 2340 Alamo SE, Suite 102, Albuquerque, NM 87106. Call 1-888-835-5669 or 505-872-4774; Fax: 505-872-4780. *Website:* http://www.familyvoices.org *Email:* kidshealth@familyvoices.org

MELD *National. 65+ affiliated programs. Founded 1973.* On behalf of children, aims to enhance the capacity of those who parent to raise nurtured, competent children. Provides supportive, peer-based learning environments and knowledge about parenting at critical stages of child development. Programs serve families who can benefit from strong support and parenting knowledge and strategies, including adolescent parents, low-income families, culturally-diverse families or families who have children with disabilities or chronic illnesses. Provides staff development training and comprehensive parent education materials. Write: MELD, 219 N. Second St., Suite 200, Minneapolis, MN 55401. Call 612-332-7563; Fax: 612-344-1959. *Website:* http://www.meld.org *Email:* info@meld.org

Mothers From Hell 2 *Nationa.4 chapters. Founded 1992.* Support and advocacy for families of children with any type of disability. Mission is to improve the quality of the lives and education of persons with developmental and other disabilities. Seeks to promote understanding and acceptance of people with disabilities. Dues $10/yr. Newsletter, referral network, training packets. Assistance in starting local groups. Website and e-groups online. Write: Mothers From Hell 2, PO Box 19, German Valley, IL 61039. Call 815-362-5303; Fax: 303-374-3151. *Website:* http://www.mothersfromhell2.org *Email:* beth@mothersfromhell2.org

MUMS National Parent-to-Parent Network *National. 61 affiliated groups. Founded 1979.* Mutual support and networking for parents or care providers of children with any disability, rare disorder, chromosomal abnormality or health condition using a database of over 19,000 families from 60 countries, covering 3400 disorders, very rare syndromes or undiagnosed conditions. Referrals to support groups and provides assistance in starting groups. Newsletter ($15/parents, $25/ professionals). Matching services $5. Other literature available. Write: MUMS Nat'l Parent-to-Parent Network, 150 Custer Ct., Green Bay, WI 54301-1243. Call 1-877-336-5333 (parents only) or 920-336-5333 (day); Fax: 920-339-0995. *Website:* http://www.netnet.net/mums/ *Email:* mums@netnet.net

NATHHAN (National Challenged Homeschoolers Association Network) *National network. Founded 1990.* Christian, non-profit organization encouraging families with special needs, particularly those who home educate. Bi-annual magazine, lending library, family phone book, phone support, information and referrals. Dues $25. Write: NATHHAN, PO Box 39, Porthill, ID 83853. Call 208-267-6246. *Website:* http://www.nathhan.org *Email:* nathanews@aol.com

Parents Helping Parents *Model. 30 groups. Founded 1976. (MULTILINGUAL)* Parent-directed family resource center serving children with special needs (due to illness, accident, conditions of birth, learning differences or family stress), their families and the professionals who serve them. Information and referral, specialty programs, family support groups, peer counseling, training, library. Newsletter, group development guidelines. National resource directory online. Outreach in Spanish, Japanese, & Vietnamese. Write: PHP, 3041 Olcott St., Santa Clara, CA 95054-3222. Call 408-727-5775; Fax: 408-727-8339. *Website:* http://www.php.com *Email:* info@php.com

Sibling Support Project of The Arc of the United States *National. 200+ affiliated groups. Founded 1994.* Opportunity for school-age brothers and sisters of children with special health and developmental needs to obtain peer support and education within a recreational context. Groups are sponsored by local agencies and may be ongoing, weekly or time-limited. Assistance in starting groups. Write: Sibling Support Project, c/o Donald Meyer, 6512 23rd Ave. NW, #213, Seattle, WA 98117. Call 206-297-6368; Fax: 509-752-6789. *Website:* http://www.thearc.org/siblingsupport/ *Email:* donmeyer@siblingsupport.org

Washington PAVE *Model. 1 group in Washington. Founded 1979.* Parent-directed organization to increase independence, empowerment and opportunities for special needs children and their families through training, information, referrals and support. Newsletter, phone support and conferences on special education issues. Write: Washington PAVE, 6316 S. 12th, Tacoma, WA 98465. Call 253-565-2266 (Voice/TTY) or 1-800-5-PARENT (Voice/TTY); Fax: 253-566-8052. *Website:* http://www.washingtonpave.org *Email:* wapave9@washingtonpave.com

Washington State Fathers Network *Model. 15 groups in Washington. Founded 1986.* Provides mutual support and resources for fathers and families raising children with special needs and developmental disabilities. Print newsletters, e-newsletter, web page with extensive links, photo album of men and children, articles by dads and materials for providers regarding family-centered, culturally competent care. Statewide and regional conferences. Write: WSFN, 16120 N.E. Eighth St., Bellevue, WA 98008. Call Chris Morris 425-747-4004 ext. 4286. *Website:* http://www.fathersnetwork.org *Email:* cmorris@fathersnetwork.org

ONLINE

Premature Baby - Premature Child *Online. Founded 1997.* Offers support for parents of premature babies that are 4+ years old. Offers support for any of their special needs including mental, physical, emotional or learning disability. Provides support, discussion listserv, prematurity forums, advocacy and educational links. Special children's show and tell section. *Website:* http://www.prematurity.org

PARENTS OF PREMATURE / HIGH RISK INFANTS
(see also parents of twins and triplets, toll-free helplines)

NATIONAL

Sidelines High Risk Pregnancy Support *National network. Founded 1991.* Trained former high-risk pregnancy moms provide support to current high-risk patients & their families. Provides educational resources, advocacy and emotional support via phone and Email. Write: Sidelines Nat'l Support Network, PO Box 1808, Laguna Beach, CA 92652. Call 1-888-447-4754; Fax: 949-497-5598. *Email:* sidelines@sidelines.org *Website:* http://www.sidelines.org

ONLINE

Preemie-List *Online.* Mutual support and discussion forum for parents with children born six weeks or more before due date. Families and friends are welcome to join discussion. *Website:* http://groups.yahoo.com/group/preemie-list

Premature Baby - Premature Child *Online. Founded 1997.* Offers support for parents of premature babies that are 4+ years old. Offers support for any of their special needs including mental, physical and emotional or learning disability. Provides support, discussion listserv, prematurity forums, advocacy and educational links. *Website:* http://www.prematurity.org

PARENTS OF TWINS AND TRIPLETS

BERGEN

Twins Mothers Club of Bergen County Provides support, advice and camaraderie for mothers of multiples. Dues $35/year. Meets 4th Wed., 7:15-10pm, (except June, July, Aug., Dec.), American Legion Hall, 33 West Passaic St., Rochelle Park. Call Patty Walshe 201-599-2508 (day).

CAMDEN

South Jersey Mothers of Multiples Moral support for mothers of multiple births. Hospital visits, clothing sales, childrens' activities, speakers and newsletters. Dues $30/yr. Meets 1st Wed., 7:30pm, Voorhees Community Center, Voorhees. Call Lisa 856-797-9863 (day).

MIDDLESEX

Twin Mothers Club of the Greater Plainfield Area Help and information for mothers of older multiples (20 years and older). Phone help, guest speakers, visitation and peer counseling. Dues $25/yr. Meets 2nd Wed., 8:30pm, Italian-American Club, Garibaldi Ave., South Plainfield. Call Carmela Ford 908-755-1546 (day/eve) or Kathy Gangemi 732-968-4351.

MONMOUTH

Mid-Jersey Mothers of Multiples Mothers of multiples share information and advice on dealing with their unique problems and joys. Guest speakers and activities for adults and children. Dues $35/yr. Meets 4th Tues., 8pm, Jackson St. Firehouse, Matawan. Call Hilary 732-294-1329 (day) or Lisa 732-238-7682 (day). *Website:* http://www.midjerseymoms.org

MORRIS

Twins and Triplet Mothers of Morris County Mothers of multiples share information and advice on dealing with their unique problems and joys. Newsletter. Dues $30/yr. Meets 2nd Thurs., (except summer), 7:30pm, Morristown Memorial

Hospital, Auditorium A, Jefferson B, Madison Ave., Morristown. Call Cris Parente 973-257-0069 or Michelle Lawton 973-663-6554. *Email:* craftycrissy@aol.com

OCEAN

Mothers of Twins Club Support and education for mothers of multiples. Monthly local newsletter. Dues $25/yr. Meets 1st Thurs., 8pm (except July/Aug.), Knights of Columbus, Tennyson Ave., Toms River. Call Eileen Weiderspan 732-730-0573 (day) or Chris Church 732-364-2790 (eve). *Email:* oceancountymothersoftwins.org

SOMERSET

Mothers and More Central Jersey Triplets And More Support for mothers of triplets and more. Offers mutual sharing, exchanging of experiences and helpful hints. Meets 2nd Tues., 7:30-10pm, Somerset Medical Center, Cafeteria, 110 Rehill Ave, Somerset. Call 908-685-2814 (day).

Raritan Valley M.O.M.S. Support for moms of multiples. Friendship, guest speakers and newsletter. Dues $25/yr. Meets 4th Mon. (except summer), 7:30pm, Somerset Medical Center, Cafeteria, 110 Rehill Ave., Somerville. Call Liz Pollard 908-575-9385 (day) or Medical Center 1-800-443-4605. *Website:* http://www.rvmom.net

NATIONAL

Conjoined Twins International *International network. Founded 1996.* Support for conjoined twins, their families and professionals. Offers peer support, professional counseling, crisis intervention, telephone helpline, pen pal network, videos. Information and referrals. Peer counseling, speakers bureau. Registry of affected families. Membership directory. Write: Conjoined Twins International, PO Box 10895, Prescott, AZ 86304-0895. Call 928-445-2777. *Website:* http://www.conjoinedtwinsint.com *Email:* dwdegeraty@myexcel.org

M.O.S.T. (Mothers Of SuperTwins) *National. 50+ affiliated groups. Founded 1987.* Support network of families who are expecting or already are the parents of, triplets or more. Provides information, support, resources & empathy during pregnancy, infancy, toddler hood and school age. Magazine, networking, phone and online support, catalogue. Specific resource persons for individual challenges. Help in starting groups. Write: MOST, PO Box 306, East Islip, NY 11730-0306. Call Maureen Boyle 631-859-1110; Fax: 631-859-3580. *Website:* http://www.MOSTonline.org *Email:* info@mostonline.org

National Organization of Mothers of Twins Clubs *National. 475 clubs. Founded 1960.* Opportunity for parents of multiple birth children (twins, triplets, quads) to share information, concerns and advice on dealing with their unique challenges. Literature, quarterly newspaper ($15/yr.), group development guidelines, educational materials, special needs and bereavement support, pen pal program. Membership through local chapters or as individual affiliate members. Write: NOMOTC, PO Box 700860, Plymouth, MI 48170-0955. Call 1-877-540-2200 (referrals) or 248-231-4480. *Website:* http://www.nomotc.org/ *Email:* nomotc@aol.com

Triplet Connection *International network. Founded 1983.* Network of caring and sharing for families with multiple births. Emphasis is on providing quality information regarding pregnancy management and preterm birth prevention for high risk multiple pregnancies. Expectant parent's packet, quarterly newsletter, phone support and resources. Write: Triplet Connection, PO Box 429, Spring City, UT 84662. Call 435-851-1105; Fax: 435-462-7466. *Website:* http://www.tripletconnection.org *Email:* tc@tripletconnection.org

SEPARATION / DIVORCE

(see also men, women, single parenting and toll-free helplines)

STATEWIDE

F.A.C.E. (Father's And Children's Equality) Support group for non-custodial mothers or fathers and their families. Concerned with gaining equal rights for mothers and fathers in parental separation. Networking, emergency housing referrals and advocacy for equal access to children regardless of parents marital status. Restores children's rights to two equal parents. Dues $75/yr. Call Hotline 856-786-3223. Write: F.A.C.E., P.O. Box 2471, Cinnaminson, NJ 08077. *Website:* http://www.facenj.org *Email:* faceinfo@facenj.org

North American Conference of Separated and Divorced Catholics Network of support groups for separated and divorced Catholics. Leadership training, conferences, resource materials, social activities. Quarterly newsletter. Rap sessions, guest speakers, phone help. Membership $35/yr. Referrals to self-help groups statewide. Call Chuck Pender 908-883-1843. *Website:* http://www.nacsdc.org (click into Region 3)

Rainbows, Inc. *Professionally-run.* Peer support for children and teens who are grieving the loss of a parent due to death, divorce or abandonment. Meets various locations throughout NJ. Helps to implement programs throughout the state. Call

908-608-0888   (day).   *Website:*   http://www.rainbowsnj.org   *Email:*
info@rainbowsnj.org

BERGEN

Healing Hope Support with a spiritual emphasis on helping those who suffer catastrophic loss including death, divorce, serious illness, etc. Meets 1st and 3rd Tues., 7:30 – 9pm, Cornerstone Christian Church, 495 Wycoff Ave., Wycoff. Call Kris Pepper 201-847-8107 (eve).

New Beginnings *Professionally-run.* Support group for separated or divorced persons. Meets Tues., 7:30pm, Montvale Evangelical Free Church, Grand and Ackers Ave., Montvale. Call Dr. Brian Cistola 845-353-1433 (day) or 201-391-6233 (day).

Rainbows, Inc. *Professionally-run.* Peer support for children, (age 4 - teens), who experienced a family loss because of separation, divorce, death or abandonment. Provides peer support, an understanding of the grief experience, assistance in building a stronger sense of self-esteem. Meets Tues., 7-8pm, (Sept.-Dec.) and Wed., (Jan.-Apr.), Ridgewood YMCA, 112 Oak St., Ridgewood. Call Kathy Meding 201-444-5600 ext. 332 (day). *Email:* kmeding@ridgewoodym.org

Separated, Divorced, Widowed and Bereaved Catholics Referrals to groups for emotional, spiritual support and social activities for separated, divorced, widowed and bereaved men and women. Groups are open to people of any faith. For information call Family Life Ministry, Newark Archdiocese 973-497-4327.

BURLINGTON

Separated and Divorced Catholics Mutual support for separated or divorced men and women. Open to people of any faith. Various meeting locations and times. See group   listings   and   contacts   online   at: http://www.dioceseoftrenton.org/church/consolation.asp (scroll down to "Support Groups for Separated and Divorced") or call Office of Family Life, Trenton Diocese 609-406-7400 ext. 5557 (day).

CAMDEN

Grief Management of St. Rose of Lima Mutual support for anyone grieving the loss of a significant person in their life due to death, separation or divorce. Families welcome. Meets Thurs., (for 12 week sessions), 7:30pm, St. Rose of Lima, Parish Lounge, 300 Kings Highway, Haddon Heights. Before attending Call Sister Eucharista Johnson 856-310-1770. *Website:* http://www.strosenj.como

CUMBERLAND

Divorce Care Helps people heal and recover from separation and divorce by providing mutual support. Sharing of experiences, education, guest speakers, videos and phone help. Meets Thurs., 6:30-7:45pm, Vineland Nazarene Church, 2725 North Delsea Dr., Vineland. Call Sandy Bohren 856-697-3384. *Website:* http://www.vinelandnaz.com

ESSEX

Divorced and Separated Women Support for women coping with separation and divorce. Groups start periodically and run for 6 weeks. Registration fee $45. Meets at Linda and Rudy Slucker NCJW Center for Women, Livingston. Call Project GRO 973-994-4994 (day). *Website:* http://www.centerforwomennj.org *Email:* centerforwomen@ncjwessex.org

Rainbows, Inc. *Professionally-run.* Peer support for children and adolescents (kindergarten - eighth grade) who are grieving the loss of a parent due to death, divorce or abandonment. Meets Mon., (Spring and Fall), 7 week sessions, First Presbyterian Church, 10 Fairview Ave., Verona. Call Rev. Julia Dawson 973-239-3561 (day).

Separated, Divorced, Widowed and Bereaved Catholics *Professionally-run.* Emotional and spiritual support for separated, divorced, widowed and bereaved, men and women. Groups are held at various churches throughout the diocese and are open to people of any faith. For information call Family Life Ministry, Newark Archdiocese 973-497-4327.

Women Re-examining Their Marriage Mutual support and discussions for women who are living in a difficult marriage and are thinking of a separation. Meets various days, 7:30-9pm, Livingston. Registration fee $45. Call NCJW Center for Women 973-994-4994. *Website:* http://www.centerforwomennj.org *Email:* centerforwomen@ncjwessex.org

GLOUCESTER

Center for People in Transition *Professionally-run.* Assists displaced homemakers to become emotionally and economically self-sufficient through life skills training, career decision making, education or vocational training and supportive services. Evening divorce and bereavement support groups open to men and women. For information call 856-415-2222 (Mon.-Fri.). *Email:* peopleintransition@gccnj.edu

Single Again Support and Recovery Group *Professionally-run.* Christian support, encouragement and healing for those separated, in the process of divorce, and/or trying to transition from being part of a couple to single life. Families and friends welcome. Education and buddy system. Meets Thurs., 7-8:30pm, St. John's United Methodist Church, 147 Ganttown Rd., Room 202, Turnersville. Call Nancy Trowbridge 856-589-2208 (eve) or Joe Mango 856-728-3304.

HUDSON

Rainbows, Inc. *Professionally-run.* Peer support for children and adolescents (kindergarten - eighth grade) who are grieving the loss of a parent due to death, divorce or abandonment. Parent of attending child meets concurrently. Meets Mon., 7-8pm, (Oct.-Dec.), St. Anne's School, Parish Center, Jersey City. Call Sister Alberta 201-656-2490.

Separated, Divorced, Widowed and Bereaved Catholics *Professionally-run.* Emotional and spiritual support for separated, divorced, widowed and bereaved, men and women. Groups are sponsored by various churches throughout the county and are open to people of any faith. For information call Family Life Ministry, Newark Archdiocese 973-497-4327.

HUNTERDON

Separated and Divorced Catholics Mutual support and social events for separated or divorced men and women. Open to people of any faith. Various meeting times and locations. For information call the Office of Family Life, Metuchen Diocese 732-562-1990 ext. 1624.

MERCER

Divorce Recovery Program *Professionally-run.* Support and education seminar for separated or divorced persons. Support group meets 1st and 4th Fri., 7:30pm; seminar meets 2nd Fri., 7:30pm, Princeton Church of Christ, 33 River Rd., Princeton. Call Phyllis Rich 609-581-3889. *Website:* divorcerecovery@softhome.net

Separated and Divorced Catholics Mutual support for separated or divorced men and women. Open to people of any faith. Various meeting locations and times. See group listings and contacts online at: http://www.dioceseoftrenton.org/church/consolation.asp (scroll down to "Support Groups for Separated and Divorced") or call Office of Family Life 609-406-7400 ext. 5557 (day).

Separated and Divorced Support Group Aim is to help people through the pain and trauma of separation and divorce grow into well-adjusted, self-sufficient, whole single people. To encourage sharing and support among members with an end towards friendship (not for singles seeking dates). Meets Thurs., 7:30-9:30pm, Hopewell Presbyterian Church, Louellen and Broad St., Hopewell. Call 609-466-0758 ext. 1 (day).

MIDDLESEX

CONCORDS Mutual support for divorced and separated people. Literature. Meets 2nd Wed., (except July/Aug), 8pm, Our Lady of Fatima R.C. Church, Rectory Meeting Room # 2, 501 New Market Rd., Piscataway. Call Lucy 732-968-4093 (after 6pm) or Mel 732-926-1963 (day/eve).

Passages Support for separated or divorced persons to help them regain self-esteem, confidence and the ability to go on with their lives. Donation $3 per mtg. Meets Tues., 7:30-9:30pm, St. Peter's Episcopal Church, 505 Main St., Spotswood. Call Robin 732-238-7822 (eve) or Alan 732-828-5880 (eve). *Website:* http://www.passagesnj.com *Email:* passages@excite.com

Separated and Divorced Catholics Mutual support for recently separated or divorced men and women. Open to people of any faith. Various meeting times and locations. For information Call the Family Life Office, Metuchen Diocese 732-562-1990 ext. 1624 (day).

MONMOUTH

Divorce and Separation Support Group 12-Step. Support for persons affected by divorce and separation. Purpose is to help people overcome the pain of divorce. Meets Thurs., 6:30-7:30pm, United Methodist Church, 2nd Floor, Church St., Manasquan. Call Maria 551-208-2688 (cell).

Separated and Divorced Catholics Mutual support for separated or divorced men and women. Open to people of any faith. Various meeting locations and times. See group listings and contacts online at: http://www.dioceseoftrenton.org/church/consolation.asp (scroll down to "Support Groups for Separated and Divorced") or call Office of Family Life, Trenton Diocese 609-406-7400 ext. 5557 (day).

Separated / Divorced / Widows and Widowers Support Group Support for persons who have lost their spouse due to separation, divorce or death (past bereavement stage) to help members get on with their lives. NOT for crisis situations. Not intended as a social group. Meets Tues., 7:30pm, St. Veronica's Rectory Cellar, Route 9 North, Howell. Call Ree 732-431-0446 or Cookie 732-577-6964 (day). *Website:* http://www.divorceheadquarters.com *Email:* Reegroup@aol.com

Transitions Support for persons in all stages of separation and divorce to provide comfort, support and recovery. Rap sessions. Meets Tues., 7:30-8:45pm, Monmouth County Library, 125 Symmes Dr., Manalapan. Call David Nasoff 732-888-4440.

Women's Support Group Helps women who are displaced homemakers (facing the loss of their primary source of income due to separation, divorce, disability or death of spouse). Issues addressed include: self-sufficiency, career development, assertiveness, self-esteem, divorce, separation, widowhood and other related topics. Groups are set-up as needed in Asbury Park, Long Branch, Bayshore and Lincroft. Call Robin Vogel 732-495-4496 (day) or Mary Ann O'Brien 732-229-8675.

MORRIS

Crossroads Support for separated and divorced persons. Open to anyone who has experienced the pain of a broken marriage. Meets Sun., 7-8:30pm, St. Peter the Apostle Church, Convent, 189 Baldwin Rd., Parsippany. Call Nick DelMedico 973-334-8373 (eve). *Email:* ndmedico@yahoo.com

Rainbows, Inc. *Professionally-run* Peer support for children and adolescents (kindergarten - eighth grade) who are grieving the loss of a parent due to death or divorce. Parent group meets concurrently.

    Kinnelon Meets Tues., 7:15-8pm, (Sept.-Jan.), Our Lady of Magnificent, 2 Miller Rd.. Call Claudette Meehan 973-492-9406 (eve) or Peggy Tana 973-838-7265.

    Mt. Tabor Meets Tues., 7:15pm, (Summer and Winter), for 7-14 weeks, Mt. Tabor Church, 5 Simpson Ave.. Must Call to pre-register. Call Diane 973-627-2134 (day/eve).

Separated and Divorced Support Group Emotional and spiritual support for men and women in all stages of separation and divorce. Phone help, pen pals and buddy system. Meets Thurs., 7:30pm, St. Rose of Lima Church, Messina Hall, 312 Ridgedale Ave., East Hanover. Call Laura 973-581-1636 (day/eve) or Paul 973-428-4710 (day/eve).

"If we had no winter, the spring would not be so pleasant: if we did not sometimes taste of adversity, prosperity would not be so welcome."
--Anne Bradstreet

OCEAN

Divorce Care Support Group Mutual support for those going through separation or divorce. Video tapes. Meets Mon., 7-9pm, (13 week sessions, 2 times a year), Safe Harbor, 600 Atlantic City Blvd., Beachwood. Call 732-244-3888. *Email:* shorevineyard@comcast.net

Kids and Divorce Support Group *Professionally-run.* Support for children age (6-12) who have experienced a separation or divorce in their family. Rap sessions. Meets 2nd and 4th Thurs., 5-6pm, Center for Kids and Family, 591 Lakehurst Rd., Toms River. Call Michele 732-505-5437 (day).

Separated and Divorced Catholics Mutual support for separated or divorced men and women. Open to people of any faith. Various meeting locations and times. See group listings and contacts online at: http://www.dioceseoftrenton.org/church/consolation.asp (scroll down to "Support Groups for Separated and Divorced") or Call 609-406-7400 ext. 5557 (day).

St. Barnabas Ministry to Separated / Divorced and Remarried Catholics Provides a safe haven for people who are separated, divorced. Meets Thurs., 7:15-8:45pm, St. Barnabas Church, Annex, Room 5A, Woodland Rd., Bayville. Call Mary Alice Laird 732-269-2020 (eve) or Deacon Michael Taylor 732-269-2208 (day). *Email:* deaconmike@stbarnabasbayville.com or marala2020@aol.com

PASSAIC

Circle of Friendship Mutual support for those who are separated and divorced. Phone help, socials and guest speakers. Support group meets 2nd and 4th Thurs.; Topic and discussion group meets 1st, 3rd, 5th Thurs., 7:30pm, St. Mary's School, Conference Room, 17 Pompton Ave., Pompton Lakes. Call Christine Scott 973-335-9880, Donna White 973-831-8825 or church 973-835-0374.

Separation and Divorce Support Group Mutual support and education to help women through the emotional, legal, financial and family issues which arise during the divorce process. Meets Wed., 1-2:30pm, Women In Transition, 1022 Hamburg Turnpike, Wayne. Call Kate McAteer 973-694-9215 (day).

SOMERSET

JANUS Bereavement Group *Professionally-run.* Support and education for anyone who has experienced a loss such as a separation, divorce, death,

244

retirement, loss of a job, health or relocation). Helps individuals accept and adjust to the loss. Meets 2nd Tues., 7:30-9pm, Bridgewater Baptist Church, 324 Milltown Rd., Bridgewater. Call Barbara Ronca, LCSW 908-218-9062 (Mon.-Fri., 9am-3pm).

M.A.S.H. Group for Separated and Divorced Men and Women Support, education and discussion. Social activities between meetings. Donation $3/mtg. Meets Mon., 7:30-9pm, St. Luke's Roman Catholic Church, 300 Clinton Ave., North Plainfield. Call 908-889-7243 or 732-548-6580. *Email:* passages@excite.com

Rainbows, Inc. *Professionally-run.* Peer support for children and adolescents (kindergarten - eighth grade) who are grieving a loss due to death, divorce or abandonment. Single parent group meets concurrently. Meets various locations and times. Call Alyson Meyer 908-766-4755 ext. 35.

Separated and Divorced Catholics Mutual support and social events for separated or divorced men and women. Open to people of any faith. Various meeting times and locations. For information call the Office of Family Life, Metuchen Diocese 732-562-1990 ext. 1624 (day).

Single Senior Women Support for women (age 60+) who are divorced, separated, widowed, never married or who have a spouse who is ill. Recreational activities. Meets 2nd and 4th Thurs., 10am-noon, Office on Aging, 92 East Main St., 1st Floor, Conference Room, Somerville. Call Erin 908-704-6339 (day).

SUSSEX

Separated and Divorced Support Group *Professionally-run.* Support, discussion and encouragement for separated and divorced people. Meets Wed., 7:30-9:30pm, Partnership for Social Services, 48 Wyker Rd., Franklin. Call Greta Lochen 973-827-4702.

UNION

Divorce Care *Professionally-run.* Support for persons recovering from a separation or divorce. Offers mutual sharing. Meets Tues., 7:30-9pm, 11 week sessions, several times a year, Presbyterian Church, New Providence. Call Colleen 908-665-0050. *Email:* fletcher@pcnp.org

Separated, Divorced, Widowed and Bereaved Catholics *Professionally-run.* Emotional and spiritual support for separated, divorced, widowed and bereaved, men and women. Groups are sponsored by various churches throughout the county and are open to people of any faith. For information call Family Life Ministry, Newark Archdiocese 973-497-4327.

Rainbows, Inc. *Professionally-run.* Peer support for children and adolescents (kindergarten - eighth grade) who are grieving the loss of a parent due to death, divorce or abandonment. Meets Thurs., 7-8pm, for 6 week sessions, St. Teresa's Parish, 306 Morris Ave., Summit. Before attending call Mary Ann Visocchi 908-273-2729 (eve).

WARREN

Separated and Divorced Catholics Mutual support and social events for separated or divorced men and women. Open to people of any faith. Various meeting times and locations. For information call the Office of Family Life, Metuchen Diocese 732-562-1990 ext. 1624 (day).

NATIONAL

ACES (Association for Children for Enforcement of Support)*National. 400 affiliated groups. Founded 1984.* Information and support for parents who have custody of their children and have difficulty collecting child support payments. Location service on non-payers. Newsletter, information and referrals, assistance in starting local support groups. Write: ACES, PO Box 7842, Fredericksburg, VA 22404. Call 1-800-738-ACES (2237); Fax: 540-899-3330. *Website:* http://www.childsupport-aces.org *Email:* nataces@childsupport-aces.org

Beginning Experience, The *International. 135 teams. Founded 1974.* Support programs for divorced, widowed & separated adults, & their children enabling them to work through the grief of a lost marriage. Write: The Beginning Experience, c/o Int'l Ministry Center, 1657 Commerce Dr., South Bend, IN 46628. Call 574-283-0279 or 1-866-610-8877; Fax: 574-283-0287. *Website:* http://www.beginningexperience.org *Email:* imc@beginningexperience.org

Children's Rights Council *International. Chapters in 32 states, Japan, Sierra Leone & England. Founded 1985.* Concerned parents provide education and advocacy for reform of the legal system regarding child custody. Offers help with visitation, mediation, custody and support groups. Newsletter, information and referrals, directory of parenting organizations, neutral drop-off and pick-up sites for children and supervised visitation in various states, catalog of resources, conferences, group development guidelines. Write: CRC, c/o David L. Levy, Pres., 6200 Editors Park Drive, Hyattsville, MD 20782-4900. Call 301-559-3120; Fax: 301-559-3124. *Website:* http://www.gocrc.com *Email:* crcdc@erols.com

DivorceCare *International. 8000+ affiliated groups. Founded 1993.* Network of support groups to help people recover from separation or divorce. Information and referrals, support group meetings, literature. Provides online assistance to find a local group. Assistance in starting new groups. Write: DivorceCare, 250 S. Allen Rd., PO Box 1739, Wake Forest, NC 27588. Call 1-800-489-7778; Fax: 919-562-2114. *Website:* http://www.divorcecare.org *Email:* info@divorcecare.org

EX-POSE (Ex-Partners Of Servicemembers for Equality) *National membership. Founded 1981.* Disseminates information concerning military divorce. Lawyer referral. Quarterly newsletter. Membership dues $20. Offers list of questions to ask an attorney during the attorney selection process. Write: EX-POSE, PO Box 11191, Alexandria, VA 22312. Call 703-941-5844 (Mon.-Fri., 11am-3pm). *Website:* http://www.ex-pose.org *Email:* ex-pose@juno.com

Grandparents Rights Organization *National. Founded 1984.* Advocates and educates on behalf of grandparent-grandchild relationships primarily with respect to grandparent visits. Assists in the formation of local support groups dealing with the denial of grandparent visitation by custodial parent or guardian. Newsletter, information and referrals, conferences. Donations $40/yr. Write: Grandparents Rights Org., 100 W. Long Lake Rd., Suite 250, Bloomfield Hills, MI 48304. Call 248-646-7191; Fax: 248-646-9722. *Website:* http://www.grandparentsrights.org *Email:* RSVlaw@aol.com

Joint Custody Association *International network. Founded 1979.* Assists divorcing parents and their families to achieve joint custody. Disseminates information concerning family law research & judicial decisions. Advocates for legislative improvement of family law in state capitols. Referrals to local self-help groups. Write: Joint Custody Assn., c/o James A. Cook, 10606 Wilkins Ave., Los Angeles, CA 90024. Call 310-475-5352; Fax: 310-475-6541. *Website:* http://www.jointcustody.org

North American Conference of Separated & Divorced Catholics *International. 3000+ groups. Founded 1974.* Religious, educational & emotional aspects of separation, divorce, remarriage and widowhood are addressed through self-help groups, conferences and training programs. Families of all faiths are welcome. Group development guidelines. Newsletter. Membership dues starting at $35 (includes newsletter, discounts, & resources). Write: NACSDC, PO Box 10, Hancock, MI 49930. Call 906-482-0494; Fax: 906-482-7470. *Website:* http://www.nacsdc.org *Email:* office@nacsdc.org

RAINBOWS *International. 8300 affiliated groups. Founded 1983.* Establishes peer support groups in churches, schools or social agencies for children and adults who are grieving a death, divorce or other painful transition in their family. Groups

247

are led by trained adults. Online newsletter, information and referrals. Write: RAINBOWS, 2100 Golf Rd., Suite 370, Rolling Meadows, IL 60008-4231. Call 1-800-266-3206 or 847-952-1770; Fax: 847-952-1774. *Website:* http://www.rainbows.org *Email:* info@rainbows.org

SINGLE PARENTING
(see also parenting, divorce/separation and widows/widowers)

STATEWIDE

Parents Without Partners Devoted to the interests and welfare of single parents over 18 and their children. Provides recreational, educational and social activities. Rap sessions. Membership dues $25-40/yr. 18 chapters throughout NJ. Call 1-800-637-7974 (day). *Website:* http://www.parentswithoutpartners.org

ATLANTIC

Parents Without Partners Devoted to the interests and welfare of single parents over 18 and their children. Provides recreational, educational and social activities. Rap sessions, guest speakers, phone help. Membership dues $40/yr. Meets 2nd and 4th Fri., 8:30pm, VFW, Bethel Rd., Somers Point. Call PWP 609-653-7000 (day/eve). *Website:* http://www.pwp181.00go.com/homepage.htm

BERGEN

Parents Without Partners Mutual support for single parents and their children. Provides educational, social and recreational activities for children and adults.
> **Oakland** Membership dues $33/yr. Meets $7/members; $10/guests. Meets 2nd and 4th Sat., 8pm (orientation 7:30pm), American Legion Hall, Oak St.. Call Betty McKenzie 973-831-1535 (9am-8pm).
> **Pascack Valley Chapter** Dues $30/yr. Meets Sun., 7pm, Park Ridge Elks Club, Sulak Lane, Park Ridge. Call 201-573-9510.
> **Paramus (Chapter #962)** Rap sessions, guest speakers, phone help. Dues - $30/yr. Meets Thurs., 8pm, Elks Club, Route 17 North. Call 201-265-2446. *Website:* http://www.pwp962.org

Single Parents Group Mutual support and friendship for single parents. Rap sessions and guest speakers focusing on parenting skills. Dues $50/yr. Meets 2nd Tues., 7-8:15pm, YWCA, 112 Oak St., Ridgewood. Call Dee Waddington 201-487-2224 (day).

BURLINGTON

Live Your Best Life Mutual support for women of all ages, backgrounds and situations who are raising children on their own. Groups meet various times in Mount Holly. For information call Joyce Knox 609-880-1593.

ESSEX

Women Parenting Alone Mutual support for single mothers. Group starts periodically and runs for 6 weeks. Registration fee $45. Meets at Linda and Rudy Slucker NCJW Center for Women, 513 W. Mount Pleasant Ave., Suite 325, Livingston. Call Project GRO 973-994-4994. *Website:* http://www.centerforwomennj.org *Email:* centerforwomen@ncjwessex.org

GLOUCESTER

Single Parents Society Devoted to the interests and welfare of single parents and their children. Various events scheduled throughout the year. Open to parents who are separated, divorced, widowed or never married. Dues $25/yr. Meetings $7/members, $8/guests. Newsletter. Meets Fri., 8:30pm, American Legion Post, Clayton. Call Fran 856-845-6810. *Website:* http://www.singleparentsoc.com

MORRIS

Parents Without Partners Mutual support and education for single parents. Provides recreational, educational and social activities for single parents and their children. Dues $40/yr. (all children's activities are subsidized). Meets 2nd and 4th Sat., various meeting locations and times. For more information call Parents Without Partners 973-539-5523. *Website:* http://www.parentswithoutpartners.org

OCEAN

Women of Purpose Mutual support for women raising children on their own (including single mothers, wives of prison inmates and spouses of addicts). Aim is to help women and children at risk in the community. Also provides educational workshops on literacy, child care and health. Various groups meet at 19 North County Line Rd., Jackson. For information call Rev. Sarah Reed 732-901-4243.

NATIONAL

National Organization of Single Mothers *National. 3 affiliated groups. Founded 1991.* Networking system helping single mothers meet the challenges of daily life with wisdom, dignity, confidence and courage. Information and referrals. Dues

$15/yr. Assistance in starting new groups. Write: NOSM, PO Box 68, Midland, NC 28107. Call 704-888-5437. *Website:* http://www.singlemothers.org *Email:* info@singlemothers.org

Parents Without Partners *National. 225+ chapters/5 affiliates. Founded 1957.* Educational organization of single parents (either divorced, separated, widowed or never married). Online chat room. Activities both with and without children. Membership dues $30-50. Write: PWP, 1650 S. Dixie Highway, Suite 510, Boca Raton, FL 33432. Call 1-800-637-7974 or 561-391-8833; Fax: 561-395-8557. *Website:* http://www.parentswithoutpartners.org *Email:* pwpchapters@parentswithoutpartners.org

Single Mothers By Choice *National. 25 chapters. Founded 1981.* Support and information to mature, single women who have chosen or who are considering, single motherhood. "Thinkers" workshops. Quarterly newsletter. Brochure and list of back issues of newsletter available. Write: SMC, PO Box 1642 Gracie Square Station, New York, NY 10028. Call 212-988-0993. *Website:* http://www.singlemothersbychoice.com *Email:* mattes@pipeline.com

Single Parent Resource Center *Int'l. 7 affiliated groups. Founded 1975.* Network of single parent self-help groups. Information and referral, seminars, consultation, resource library. Separate group for men and coed groups and also groups for homeless single parents. Newsletter. Guidelines & materials for starting parenting & teen groups. Write: Single Parent Resource Ctr., 31 E. 28th St., New York, NY 10016. Call 212-951-7030; Fax: 212-951-7037. *Email:* SJones532@aol.com

Unwed Parents Anonymous - The Whole Parent *Model. 1 group in Arizona. Founded 1979.* Offers support and parenting guidance to anyone affected by an out-of-wedlock pregnancy. Encourages pre-marital sexual abstinence. Publishes "The Whole Parent: Book One." Write: Unwed Parents Anonymous, PO Box 15466, Phoenix, AZ 85060-5466. Call 602-794-1114; Fax: 602-257-9520. *Website:* http://www.thewholeparent.org *Email:* upawhole@yahoo.com

STEPPARENTING

NATIONAL

Stepfamily Association of America, Inc. *National. 57 affiliated chapters. Founded 1979.* Information and advocacy for stepfamilies. Educational resources. Online magazine. Guidelines available to start a similar group. Online chat room. Write: Stepfamily Association of America, 650 J St., Suite 205, Lincoln, NE 68508. Call 1-800-735-0329; Fax: 402-477-8317. *Website:* http://www.saafamilies.org or http://www.stepfam.org *Email:* saa@saafamilies.org

HEALTH

AIDS / HIV

(see also infectious disease, toll-free helplines)

STATEWIDE

AIDS Coalition of Southern New Jersey *Professionally-run.* To ensure the quality of care and continuity of vital resources for persons affected by AIDS/HIV. Provides support groups, direct services and education. Newsletter, speaker's bureau, phone help, guest speakers. Serves Burlington, Camden, Gloucester and Salem counties. Write: AIDS Coalition of Southern NJ, 100 Essex Ave., Suite 300, Bellmawr, NJ 08031. Call 856-933-9500 (day). *Website:* http://www.acsnj.org

Hyacinth AIDS Foundation Support groups and information for anyone affected by AIDS or HIV+ (patients, families, partners, friends). Provides buddies, advocacy, legal services, public education and training, short-term emergency services and hotline. All services are confidential. Serves Northern and Central NJ. Write: Hyacinth AIDS Foundation, 317 George St., Suite 203, New Brunswick, NJ 08901. For information call 800-433-0254 (9am-7pm) or Admin. 732-246-0204. *Website:* http://www.hyacinth.org *Email:* info@hyacinth.org

ATLANTIC

HIV Support Group *Professionally-run.* Support for persons with HIV. Families and friends welcome. Social group, literature and buddy system. Meets 3rd Tues., 6-8pm, 730 Shore Rd., Somers Point. Call Michele Keenan 609-927-6662 ext. 14 (day). *Email:* HIVaccess@aol.com

South Jersey A.I.D.S. Alliance *Professionally-run.* Support, education and information for anyone affected by AIDS (patients, families, partners, friends). Buddy system. Support centers in Atlantic City 609-347-1085, Bridgeton 856-455-5125, Cape May County 609-523-0024 and Hotline: 1-800-281-AIDS. *Website:* http://www.southjerseyaidsalliance.org

BERGEN

AIDS Interfaith Network Networking and support for clergy and laypersons of any age on the issue of AIDS. Meetings vary, Ridgewood. Call Rev. Jan Philips 201-670-1610 (day).

Double Jeopardy Peer Support Group *Professionally-run.* Emotional support and information for men and women who have HIV/HCV and substance abuse issues. Meets Thurs., 6:30-8pm, Buddies of New Jersey, 149 Hudson St., Hackensack. Call Susan 201-489-2900 (10am-6pm).

New Jersey Buddies *Professionally-run.* Provides support and education to people infected with or affected by HIV/AIDS. Support groups for HIV positive women, gay men, men and women and substance abusers, as well as a group for those who have engaged in risky activities, but have not been tested. Meetings held at Buddies of New Jersey, 149 Hudson St., Hackensack. Call 201-489-2900 (9am-5pm). *Website:* http://www.njbuddies.org *Email:* njbuddies@aol.com

S.E.L.F. (Support, Education, Learning, Friendship) Mutual support and education for HIV+ gay men. Rap sessions and guest speakers. Meets Mon., 7-8:30pm, Buddies of New Jersey, Inc., 151 B Hudson St., Hackensack. Call Steve Scheuermann (day). *Email:* njbuddies@aol.com

Step Sisters (Women with a Common Bond) *Professionally-run.* Emotional support and information for HIV+ women. Meets Tues., 1-2pm, Buddies of New Jersey, 149 Hudson St., Hackensack. Call Susan 201-489-2900 (10am-6pm).

CAPE MAY

South Jersey A.I.D.S. Alliance *Professionally-run.* Support, education and information for anyone affected by AIDS (patients, families, partners, friends) and prevention case management. Buddy system. Support centers in Atlantic City 609-347-1085, Bridgeton 856-455-5125, Cape May County 609-523-0024 and Hotline: 1-800-281-AIDS. *Website:* http://www.southjerseyaidsalliance.org

CUMBERLAND

Martin Luther King Outreach and Development, Inc. *(CUMBERLAND COUNTY RESIDENTS) (BILINGUAL) Professionally-run.* Provides support and education to persons with HIV+ or AIDS. Meets 3rd Tues., 6:30pm, Martin Luther King Outreach and Development, Inc., 726 Wood St., Vineland. Call Tina McCory 856-692-6012 (day).

South Jersey A.I.D.S. Alliance *Professionally-run.* Support, education and information for anyone affected by AIDS (patients, families, partners, friends) and prevention case management. Buddy system. Support center in Atlantic City 609-347-1085, Bridgeton 856-455-5125, Cape May County 609-523-0024 and Hotline 1-800-281-2437.

ESSEX

Double Trouble *Professionally-run.* Support for HIV+ persons who are also substance abusers. Group meets Wed., noon-2pm, North Jersey Community Support Center, 393 Central Ave., 3rd Floor, Newark. Call 973-483-3444. *Website:* http://www.njcri.org

Gay Men's HIV+ Support Group *Professionally-run.* Support group for gay men who are HIV+. Provides support, information and newsletter. Meets Wed., noon, Community Support Center, 393 Central Ave, 3rd Floor, Newark. Call 973-483-3444.

Men's HIV+ Support Group *Professionally-run.* Offers support for men who are HIV+. Meets Tues., noon-2pm, (lunch provided), Newark. Call Michael Bailey 973-483-3444 ext. 102 (day).

New Hope Baptist Church HIV/AIDS Support Ministry *Professionally-run.* Mutual support for persons diagnosed with AIDS, their caregivers, families and friends. Rap sessions, guest speakers. Provides information on new medications. Meetings vary, New Hope Baptist Church, 144 Norman St., East Orange. Call Sister Mary Frazier 973-675-5174, Church 973-678-6710 or Gary Haith 973-375-2768 (eve).

Our Other Place *Professionally-run.* Offers support for persons infected and affected by HIV/AIDS in a safe, confidential environment. Under 18 welcome. Meets Thurs., 7-9pm, Verona. Before attending call Ilene Palent, COPE Center 973-783-6655.

Our Place *Professionally-run.* Provides a safe and confidential environment to offer support for persons infected with the HIV virus, their loved ones and caregivers. Meets Tues. evenings in Montclair. For meeting information call Ilene Palent, COPE Center 973-783-6655. *Email:* info@copecenter.net

Women's HIV+ Support Group *Professionally-run.* Support for women who are HIV+. Meets Fri., noon-2pm (lunch provided), Newark. Guests welcome. Before attending call Sidsel Venger, LCSW 973-483-3444 ext. 119 (day).

HUDSON

Caregivers Support Group *(BILINGUAL)* Mutual support for caregivers of persons infected or affected by HIV/AIDS. Educational series, rap sessions, guest speakers, literature, respite and phone help. Transportation and childcare provided. English group meets Fri., 11am-1pm, educational group meets Thurs., 11am-1pm,

St. Clare's Program and Childcare, 15 Clifton Place, (side entrance), Jersey City. Spanish group also available. Before attending call Carol Jackson 201-435-4850 (day).

Hyacinth Foundation Support Group Mutual support for anyone infected/affected by AIDS or HIV+. Patients, families, friends and partners welcome. Call 201-432-1134 or the Hyacinth Foundation 1-800-433-0254 (10am-6pm). *Website:* http://www.hyacinth.org

> **Jersey City** Meets Thurs., 6:30-7:30pm, Hyacinth AIDS Foundation, 880 Bergen Ave., Suite 802.
> **Jersey City** Wellness community meets Wed. and Thurs., 1-3pm, treatment support group meets Tues., 4-7pm, and men's wellness group meets 2nd and 4th Thurs., 4-6pm, 82 Summit Ave.

Living Beyond HIV *(HUDSON COUNTY RESIDENTS ONLY) Professionally-run.* Mutual support for gay men who are HIV+. Rap sessions, guest speakers, literature and buddy system. Meets Thurs., 6:30-8:30pm, Jersey City. Call Kenny 201-963-4779.

Project HUGS, Inc. Support for those infected and affected by HIV/AIDS. Families welcome. Rap sessions, guest speakers, literature and speakers bureau. Meets Mon., (except holidays), 7-9pm, Grace Lutheran Church, Basement, 982 Summit Ave., Jersey City. Call 201-653-5311 (day).

MIDDLESEX

Comfort Zone *Professionally-run.* Support for HIV- partners who are coupled with partners who are HIV+/AIDS. Rap sessions and literature. Meets 2nd Tues., 6:30-8:30pm, E.B. Chandler Health Center, 277 George St., New Brunswick. Call Fran Hoey 732-235-6716 (day).

HIV Infected/Affected Group *Professionally-run.* Mutual support and education for persons infected or affected by HIV. Rap sessions, literature. Meets Mon., 6-8pm, Raritan Bay Medical Center, 530 New Brunswick Ave., Perth Amboy. Call Sandra Nilsson, ACRN 732-324-5022.

HIV Support Group *Professionally-run.* Support for men and women who have HIV. Rap sessions and literature. Meets Mon., 7-8:30pm, E.B. Chandler Health Center, 277 George St., New Brunswick. Call Fran Hoey 732-235-6716 (day).

Consider passing this Directory on to a student or staff member - browsing through the Directory pages can often provide helpful education as to the wide variety of groups available.

Project L.I.G.H.T. (Living In Good Health Together) *Professionally-run.* Mutual support and education for women who are infected with HIV/AIDS. Rap sessions, guest speakers, literature, phone help and buddy system. Meets Tues., 12:30-2:30pm, E.B. Chandler Health Center, 277 George St., New Brunswick. Call Fran Hoey 732-235-6716 (day).

Support Group for HIV+ Gay Men *Professionally-run.* Support for gay men who are HIV+. Rap sessions. Meets 3rd Tues., 6-7:30pm, E.B. Chandler Health Center, 277 George St., New Brunswick. Call Chas White 908-595-2674 (day).

MONMOUTH

HIV Support Group Mutual support for individuals infected/affected by HIV/AIDS. Family and friends welcome. Guest speakers. Meets Thurs., 6-8pm, Project Paul Annex, 79 Myrtle Avenue, Keansburg. Call Elise Millea 732-450-2863.

Positive and Beautiful *Professionally-run.* Support for women diagnosed HIV positive. Meets 1st and 3rd Tues., 11am, Monmouth Medical Center, Alexander Pavilion, Long Branch. Call Xiomara Pino, CSW 732-923-7138.

MORRIS

Gay Men's Support Group *Professionally-run.* Provides emotional support for gay men who are HIV+ or have AIDS. Under 18 welcome. Meets Wed., 7-8:30pm, Hope House, 19-21 Belmont Ave., Dover. Call Madeline 973-361-5565 ext. 158 (day). *Website:* http://www.hopehousenj.org

New Life Support Group *(BILINGUAL) Professionally-run.* Offers several support groups for HIV infected persons (HIV+/AIDS) at any stage of their illness. Groups also for adolescents, substance users and Spanish speaking group. Meetings vary, Hope House, 19-21 Belmont Ave., Dover. Call 973-361-5565 (day).

OCEAN

HIV/AIDS Infected/Affected Group *Professionally-run.* Support to persons who are infected and affected by HIV/AIDS. Members build a support network and share knowledge. Guest speakers, literature. Meets Tues., 7-8pm, Ocean County Department of Health, 175 Sunset Ave., Toms River. Call Patricia Brown 732-341-9700 ext. 7603, Anne McBride 732-341-9700 ext.7633 (day) or TDD 1-800-852-7899. *Email:* amcbride@ochd.org

PASSAIC

Barnert Hospital HIV/ AIDS Support Group Support group open to any person infected or affected by HIV/AIDS. Meets 4th Thurs., Barnert Hospital, 680 Broadway, Tap Office, 3rd Floor, Paterson. Before attending call Lakeshia Evans Fields, MPA 973-977-6657.

HIV / AIDS Support Group *(BILINGUAL) Professionally-run.* Mutual support and education for adults with HIV/AIDS and their families. Meetings vary, Paterson Division of Health, 176 Broadway, Paterson. Call Robert or Paul 973-321-1277 ext. 2732 (day).

SOMERSET

Healing Vibrations Mutual support for any HIV infected individual. Offers stress reduction, holistic venues, educational series, guest speakers, phone help and socials. Meetings vary, 6-7:30pm, Somerset. Pre-registration required. Before attending call Chas White 908-595-2674 (day).

Somerset Treatment Services Activity Group Mutual support for anyone living with HIV/AIDS. Dinner discussion group with hot meal provided. Meets Wed., 5:30-8pm, Somerset Treatment Services, 118 W. End Ave., Somerville. Call Grace Wosu 908-722-1232 ext. 3015 (day).

NATIONAL

Body Positive *(BILINGUAL) Model. Founded 1987.* Support and education for people affected by HIV. Information and referrals, public forums, support groups, social activities. Publishes monthly magazine in English and Spanish. Write: Body Positive of NY, 19 Fulton St., Suite 308 B, New York, NY 10038. Call 212-566-7333 or 1-800-566-6599 (helpline); Fax: 212-566-4539. *Website:* http://www.bodypos.org *Email:* info@bodypos.org

National Association of People With AIDS *National. Founded 1986.* Network of persons with AIDS. Sharing of information and collective voice for health, social, and political concerns. Write: NAPWA, 8401 Colesville Rd., Suite 750, Silver Spring, MD 20910. Call 240-247-0880 (day); Fax: 240-247-0574. *Website:* http://www.napwa.org *Email:* info@napwa.org

One Day At a Time *Model. 10 affiliated groups in Pennsylvania. Founded 1987.* To help people with HIV infection become aware of and make use of, services provided. To encourage self-empowerment by providing a source of support given by other HIV+ people. Also provides drug & alcohol addiction and homeless shelter services, community outreach, prevention and education. Newsletter, group development assistance. Write: One Day At A Time, 2532 North Broad St., Philadelphia, PA 19132. Call 215-226-7860; Fax: 215-226-7869. *Website:* http://www.odaat.us *Email:* info@odaat.us

ALLERGY

BERGEN

Families Of Children With Asthma And Allergies Support for parents of children with food allergies. Provides knowledge and confidence needed to manage food allergies and asthma in a relaxed non-threatening manner. Shared life experiences, guest speakers, educational series and literature. Meets 4th Tues., 7:30-9pm, Valley Home Care, 15 Essex Rd., Paramus. Call Maria Caroll 201-291-6335 (day).

NATIONAL

Asthma and Allergy Foundation of America *National. 100+ affiliated groups and 11 chapters. Founded 1953.* Serves persons with asthma and allergic diseases through the support of research, patient and public education and advocacy. Newsletter, support/education groups. Assistance in starting and maintaining groups. Books, videos and other educational resources. Write: AAFA, 1233 20th St. NW, Suite 402, Washington, DC 20036. Call 1-800-727-8462 or 202-466-7643. *Website:* http://www.aafa.org *Email:* info@aafa.org

Food Allergy & Anaphylaxis Network *National network. Founded 1991.* Mission is to increase public awareness about food allergies and anaphylaxis (a serious reaction to an allergen), provide education and advance research on behalf of all those affected by food allergies. Information and referrals, conferences, literature, phone support, booklets and newsletters. Guidelines available for starting similar groups. Write: FAAN, 11781 Lee Jackson Highway, Suite 160, Fairfax, VA 22033. Call 1-800-929-4040 or 703-691-3179; Fax: 703-691-2713. *Website:* http://www.foodallergy.org *Email:* faan@foodallergy.org

ALZHEIMER'S DISEASE / DEMENTIA
(see also caregivers, toll-free helplines)

ATLANTIC

Alzheimer's Caregivers Support Group *Professionally-run.* Offers support to families and caregivers coping with Alzheimer's disease. Guest speakers, literature. Meets 3rd Mon., 2pm, Herman Pogachefsky Senior Services Pavilion,

257

1102 Atlantic Ave., Atlantic City. Call Adrienne Epstein 609-345-5555 (day).

Alzheimer's Support Group *Professionally-run.* Support for anyone affected by someone with Alzheimer's. Rap sessions, guest speakers, literature and mutual sharing. Meets last Wed., 3:45pm, Brandall Estates, 432 Central Avenue, Linwood. Call Shannon Datig 609-926-5635 (day) or Eileen Bennett 609-926-4663 (day). *Email:* datigs@brandycare.com

BERGEN

Alzheimer's Association Family Support Group Support for caregivers and family members of Alzheimer's and related disorders. Provides opportunity to share practical information, exchange community resources, solve problems and learn new coping skills. *Website:* http://www.alznj.org

> **Dumont** Meets 3rd Wed., 7-8:30pm, Northern Valley Adult Day Health Center, 2 Park Ave. Call Rose Marie Dudas or Nancy Bortinger 201-384-7734.
>
> **Paramus** Meets 1st Wed., 7-9pm, Bergen Regional Medical Center, Bldg. 14, Room E 007, 230 East Ridgewood Ave. Before attending call Fred Meyer 201-797-3421.
>
> **Ramsey** Meets 3rd Tues., 8pm, St. John's Episcopal Church, Main St. and Franklin Turnpike. Call Caregiver Helpline 1-800-883-1180.
>
> **Rockleigh** Meets 1st Wed., 10am and 3rd Tues., 7pm, Gallen Adult Day Care Center, 10 Link Dr. Call Shelley Steiner 201-784-1414 ext. 5340.
>
> **Rutherford** Meets 2nd Thurs., 1pm, 55 KIP Center, 55 KIP Ave. Call Gertrude Cathey 201-438-8461 (day).
>
> **Tenafly** Meets 2nd Wed., 7:30pm and 4th Thurs., 11am, Adult Reach Center, 411 E. Clinton Ave. Call Vivian Green Korner 201-569-7900 ext.461.
>
> **Westwood** Meets 1st Wed., 7pm, Pascack Valley Hospital, 250 Old Hook Rd. Call Karen Angrist 201-358-3092.

Alzheimer's Support Group *Professionally-run.* Support and education for caregivers of Alzheimer's patients. Family and friends welcome. Guest speakers, literature, social, newsletter and phone help. Meets 1st Wed., 7-9pm, Pascack Valley Hospital, 250 Old Hook Rd., Harrington Park. Call Karen Angrist 201-358-3092 (day).

Caregivers Family Support Group *Professionally-run.* Support for caregivers and family members of persons with Alzheimer's or related disorders. Meets 3rd Thurs., 1:30-3pm, Bergen County Department of Health, Senior Care Center, Room 208, 327 E. Ridgewood Ave., Paramus. Call first if requesting professional supervision on frail family member. Call Diana Shapiro 201-634-2822 (day).

BURLINGTON

Living With Memory Loss Support Group *Professionally-run.* Early stage dementia intervention group for newly diagnosed dementia patients and their caregivers. Caregivers and dementia diagnosed participants meet separately for 1 hour, then share concerns for the final one-half hour. Meets 2 times/yr for a 6 week series, Marlton area. For information call 856-797-1212.

CAMDEN

Alzheimer's Support Group *Professionally-run.* Offers support to families and caregivers of dementia patients. Guest speakers, literature, phone help. Meets 1st Thurs., 7pm, Voorhees Center, 3001 Evesham Rd., Voorhees. Call Joan Cunningham or Mary Marcinowitz 856-751-1600 (day).

Alzheimer's Support Group - South Jersey *Professionally-run.* Support and information for families and friends of persons with Alzheimer's disease and related disorders. Meets 2nd Tues., 7:30-9:30pm, Cadbury Retirement Center, 2150 Route 38, Cherry Hill. Call 856-797-1212 (day). *Website:* http://www.alz-delawarevalley.org *Email:* mary.washart@alz.org

Promise Alternative Care Support and information to Alzheimer's patients and their families. Guest speakers, literature, newsletter. Meets last Mon., (except July Aug. Dec.), 7:30-9pm, Promise Alternative Care, 1149 Marlkress Rd., Cherry Hill. Call Kathy Licardo 856-751-4884 (day).

Senior Care of Haddon Heights *Professionally-run.* Offers support for persons caring for someone with Alzheimer's. Guest speakers, education, advocacy and literature. Meets 3rd Tues., 6:30-7:30pm, Senior Care of Haddon Heights, 607 South Whitehorse Pike, Audubon. Call Kim Lahr 856-546-0005 (day).

CAPE MAY

Alzheimer's Caregiver Support Group of Cape May County Offers support for caregivers of those with Alzheimer's disease. Meets 2nd Tues., 10am-noon, Chapin House, 1042 Route 47, Rio Grande. Call Marie Giansante 609-884-7670 (day/eve).

We know this Directory is big and chances are we can probably find the group you're looking for quicker than you paging through it. Call us! (We're really friendly!)
1-800-367-6274

CUMBERLAND

Cumberland County Alzheimer's Support Group Information, discussions and guest speakers for families and friends of persons with Alzheimer's disease and related disorders. Meets 3rd Thurs., 7pm, Genesis Elder Care, 54 Sharp St., Millville. Call Ray Gage 856-451-8383 (day).

ESSEX

Alzheimer's Association Family Support Group Support for caregivers of persons with Alzheimer's disease. Provides opportunity to share practical information, exchange community resources, solve problems and learn new ways of coping.

> **East Orange** Meets 4th Wed., 5pm, Good Life Adult Day Center, The Great Room, 515 North Arlington Ave. Call Grace Ann Kelly 973-674-2700 ext. 2276.
>
> **East Orange** Meets 1st Tues., 7pm, St. Mark AME Church, 587 Springdale Ave. Call church office 973-674-5859.
>
> **Montclair** *Professionally-run.* Meets 1st Tues., 2-3pm and 1st Mon., 7-9pm, Senior Care Activities Center, 46 Park St. Call Fran Moravick or Colleen Beach 973-783-5589 (day). *Website:* http://www.Sencare.org
>
> **Newark** Meets 3rd Tues., 4:30pm, Newark Beth Israel, 156 Lyons Ave. Call Sara Thompson 973-926-7489 or 973-926-3004.
>
> **West Caldwell** Meets 3rd Tues., 7pm, Crane's Mill Assisted Living Center, 459 Passaic Ave. Call Chaplain George Lofmark 973-276-6700 ext. 3008.

Alzheimer's Caregiver Support Group *Professionally-run.* Support for persons caring for someone with Alzheimer's or related memory impairment. Group sessions, guest speakers, literature, educational series. Meets 3rd Wed., 7:30pm, Arden Courts-Manorcare Health Services, 510 Prospect Ave., West Orange. Call Gail Kuchavik or Bill Milianes 973-736-3100 ext. 205 (day). *Website:* http://www.hcrmanorcare.com

GLOUCESTER

Alzheimer's Support Group Mutual support for family or friends caring for persons afflicted with Alzheimer's or dementia. Meets 3rd Mon., 7-9pm, Underwood Memorial Hospital, Medical Arts Building, Suite 14, 509 N. Broad St., Woodbury. Call Karen Rodemer 856-853-2114 (day).

HUDSON

Alzheimer's Association Family Support Group *Professionally-run*. Support for caregivers and family members of Alzheimer's and related disorders. Meets 4th Thurs., 2pm, Meadowlands Hospital Medical Center, Meadowlands Pkwy., Secaucus. Call Edna Mondadori 201-865-8542 (day).

HUNTERDON

Alzheimer's Association Family Support Group *Professionally-run*. Support for caregivers and family members of Alzheimer's and related disorders. Occasional educational programs with guest speakers. Meets 2nd Wed., 7-9pm, Hunterdon Medical Center, 4th Floor Conference Room, Flemington. Call Chris Stevens 908-788-6401.

MERCER

Alzheimer's Association Family Support Group *Professionally-run*. Support and information for caregivers. Meets 3rd Thurs., 6:30pm, St. Mark United Methodist Church, 465 Paxson Ave., Room 303, Hamilton Square. Call Kathy Wooley or Karin Rentschler 609-514-1180 (day). *Website:* http://www.alznj.org

Princeton Support Groups *Professionally-run*. Separate support groups for caregivers and family members of Alzheimer's patients and persons with early diagnosis. Meet 3rd Sat., 2pm, Woodlands Professional Building, Suite 6, 256 Bunn Dr., Princeton. Call Eileen 609-514-1180 (day). *Website:* http://www.alznj.org

MIDDLESEX

Alzheimer's Association Family Support Group Support for caregivers and family members of Alzheimer's and related disorders. Occasional educational programs with guest speakers.

> **Edison** Meets 1st Wed., 7pm, Jewish Family and Vocational Service of Middlesex County, 515 Plainfield Ave., Suite 201. Call Fran Starr 732-777-1940.
>
> **Iselin** *(BILINGUAL) Professionally-run*. Meets 3rd Tues., 6:30pm, Woodbridge Public Library, 1081 Green St. Call Rosemary Oarlsey or Joan Fuhr 732-324-6005.
>
> **Monroe Township** *Professionally-run*. Meets 1st Thurs., 7pm, Cranbury Center, 292 Applegarth Rd.. Call Linda Silverstein or Marilyn Magan 609-860-2500.

Old Bridge *Professionally-run.* Meets 1st Mon., 6:30pm, Old Bridge Medical Center, Route 9 and Route 18 on Ferry Rd., One Hospital Plaza. Call Linda Bullock 732-324-6005.

Perth Amboy *(BILINGUAL) Professionally-run.* Meets 2nd Mon., 7pm, Perth Amboy Adult School, 178 Barracks St., 2nd Floor Conference Room. Call Linda Bullock 732-324-6005 (English); Ana Cruz or Aurea Vasques 732-376-6240 ext 31410 (Spanish).

Piscataway *Professionally-run.* Meets 1st Mon., 9am, COPSA Institute for Alzheimer's Disease, UMDNJ, University Behavioral Health Care, 667 Hoes Lane. Call Mary Catherine Lundquist 732-235-2858 (day). *Website:* http://vbhcweb/ (then go to Aging-COPSA)

Piscataway Meets 1st Tues., 4:30-6pm, United Behavioral Health Center, UMDNJ, 667 Hoes Lane. Call Sandy Egan 732-235-4919.

Piscataway *Professionally-run.* Meets 2nd Thurs., 7-9pm, Piscataway Senior Center. Call Mildred Potenza 732-235-8400.

Alzheimer's Support Group Support for those who have a loved one afflicted with dementia and Alzheimer's. Mutual support, literature. Meets 1st Sat., 10:30am, JFK Hartwyck Adult Medical Day Center, Lifestyle Building, 2050 Oak Tree Rd., Edison. Call Mary Buglio or Michelle Charme 732-548-9770.

MONMOUTH

Alzheimer's Association Family Support Group Support for caregivers and family members of Alzheimer's and related disorders. Occasional educational programs with guest speakers. *Website:* http://www.alznj.org

Atlantic Highlands *Professionally-run.* Meets 1st Wed. 6:30pm, Royal Senior Care, 1041 State Highway 36. Call Rita Torres 732-291-0710 ext 14.

Freehold Meets 3rd Tues., 7pm, First United Methodist Church, 91 West Main St. Call Eileen Doremus or Lucinda Seares Monica 609-514-1180.

Freehold *Professionally-run* Meets 2nd Thurs., 2-3pm, Applewood Estates, Gully Rd. Call Winnie Kearns or Heleyne Gladstein 732-363-5150.

Holmdel *Professionally-run.* Meets 3rd Tues., 7-9pm, Bayshore Hospital, Conference Room B. Call Carol Auletto 732-914-9306.

Middletown Meets 4th Thurs., 7pm, Brighton Gardens, 620 Highway 35 South. Call Pearl Kaufman 732-275-0790.

Tinton Falls Meets 2nd Tues., 7pm, Kensington Court, 864 Shrewsbury Ave. Call Kathleen Geren, Betty Racioppi or Fran Lewis 732-784-2406.

Wall Meets last Mon., 6pm, Allaire Center Senior Day Care, Wall Circle Park, Route 34 South. Call Cheryl Fenwick 732-974-7666 or Phyllis Noviello 732-918-1960.

Alzheimer's Caregivers Support Group Offers emotional support and educational information to family members caring for loved ones with Alzheimer's at home or in a nursing home. Meets 2nd Thurs., 2-3:30pm, Day Break Adult Day Services, 816 Beaver Dam Rd., Point Pleasant. Call Megan Chopp 732-892-1717 (day). *Email:* mchopp@meridianhealth.com

MORRIS

Alzheimer's Association Family Support Group *Professionally-run* Support and education for caregivers and friends of individuals afflicted with Alzheimer's. Support, guest speakers, educational materials.

> **Chatham** Meets 3rd Thurs., 7:30pm, Chatham United Methodist Church, Route 24. Call Rita Dyer 973-635-6074 (eve).
>
> **Dover** Meets 1st Thurs., 2pm, St. Clare's Hospital, 400 West Blackwell St. Call Diane Wood 973-989-3228.
>
> **Pompton Plains** Meets 2nd Wed., 7-8:30pm, Chilton Memorial Hospital, Collins Pavilion, Classroom B, 2nd Floor, 97 West Parkway. Call Joan Beloff 973-831-5167 (day). *Email:* joan.beloff@chiltonmemorial.org

Alzheimer's Association Support Group / Northern NJ Chapter Support and education for caregivers and friends of individuals afflicted with Alzheimer's. Support, guest speakers, educational materials. Call Alzheimer's Association 1-800-883-1180

> **Chester** Meets 1st Thurs., 7pm, St. Lawrence Church Hall, Main St., (Route 24).
>
> **Denville** Meets 4th Mon., 10am, Alzheimer's Association, 400 Morris Ave. or Eudie Schachter 908-276-1740.

OCEAN

Alzheimer's Association Family Support Group *Professionally-run.* Support for those coping with a family member afflicted with Alzheimer's. Guest speakers, literature, mutual sharing.

> **Jackson** Meets last Tues., 10am, Bella Terra Assisted Living, 2 Kathleen Dr. Call Paula Douglass 732-730-9500.
>
> **Lakewood** Meets 4th Tues., 10am, Wellsprings Adult Day Program, 515 Route 70. Call Dawn Matthews or Rita Sason 732-942-1610.
>
> **Lakewood** Meets 2nd Thurs., 7-9pm, Kimball Medical Center, Center for Healthy Living, 198 Prospect St. Call Eileen Doremus, Irene Barrett or Dolores Rosen 609-514-1180 (day).
>
> **Manahawkin** Meets 2nd Mon., 2pm, (Feb., May, Aug. and Nov.), Southern Ocean County Hospital, Wellness Center, 1140 Route 72 West. Call Robyn Ciangetti 609-978-3559.

Point Pleasant Meets 2nd Thurs., 2pm, Day Break, 816 Beaver Dam Rd. Call Mary Purcell 732-892-1717.

Toms River Meets 1st and 3rd Mon., 9:15am, Visiting Homemaker Service Day Care, Conference Room. Call Michelle Mahieu 732-244-5565.

Toms River Meets 3rd Thurs., 2pm, Bey Lea Nursing Home, 1351 Old Freehold Rd. Call Edward Mount or Irene Barrett 732-240-0090.

Toms River Meets 2nd Tues., 6pm, Country Manor Nursing and Rehabilitation Center, 16 Whitesville Rd. Call Lilly Ballance 732-341-1600.

Toms River Meets 3rd Sat., 10am, Magnolia Gardens Assisted Living, 1935 Lakewood Rd. Call Cathy Vakulchik or Amy Palazzo 732-557-6500 ext. 0.

Tuckerton Meets 2nd Thurs., 2pm, (July, Sept., Oct., Dec.) Seacrest Village, 1001 Center Street, Tuckerton. Before attending call Robyn Ciangetti 609-296-9292 (day).

Whiting Meets 2nd Wed., 10:30am, St. Elizabeth Ann Seton Church, Parish Hall, School House Rd. Call Marion Ariemma 732-350-8688.

Ocean Alzheimer's Caregivers Support Group Support for caregivers of those afflicted with Alzheimer's or dementia. Advocacy, guest speakers, mutual sharing, phone help, literature and educational information. Meets Wed., 1:30-3:30pm, First Aid Squad Building, Colonial Drive, Manchester Township. Call Therese 732-818-1992 (day/eve) or Lynn Clair 732-780-0998.

PASSAIC

Alzheimer's Association Family Support Group *Professionally-run.* Provides support and education to caregivers of persons who are diagnosed with Alzheimer's disease or other related neurological disorders. Mutual sharing, literature and community resources.

Clifton Meets 2nd Mon., 7:30-9pm, Clifton Family Medicine, 716 Broad St. Call Diane Lesko 973-904-5000 (day).

Hawthorne Meets 3rd Thurs., 7pm, Van Dyk Park Place, (Assisted Living), 644 Goffle Rd. Call 973-648-4062.

SOMERSET

Alzheimer's Association Family Support *Professionally-run* Mutual support and education for caregivers and family members of individuals afflicted with Alzheimer's or related neurological disorders. Mutual sharing and literature.

Bridgewater Meets 1st Wed., 6pm, Harborside Healthcare Woods Edge,

875 Route 202/206 North. Call Jay Bowden or Margaret McArdle 908-526-8600.

Hillsborough Meets 1st Thurs., 7pm, Summerville Senior Living, 600 Auten Rd. Call Allison Elkow Lazicky or Peter Farewege 908-431-1300.

Somerset Meets 2nd Thurs., 6:30pm, Central New Jersey Jewish Home for the Aged, 380 DeMott Lane. Call 732-873-2000.

Alzheimer's Caregivers Support Group Support for caregivers of those afflicted with Alzheimer's or dementia. Advocacy, guest speakers, mutual sharing, phone help, literature and educational information. Meets 3rd Wed., 1-2:30pm, The Martin and Edith Stein Assisted Living Residence, Somerbrook, 350 De Mott Lane, Somerset. Call Toby Ehrlich 732-568-1155 (day). *Email:* tehrlich@steinresidence.org

SUSSEX

Alzheimer's Association Family Support Group *Professionally-run.* Support and information for those caring for someone with dementia, Alzheimer's or any form of disability. Peer counseling, guest speakers.

Newton Meets 1st Wed., 7-9pm, Sussex County Adult Day Center, 55 Mill St. Call Shelly Green-Hinton 973-579-6699 (day) or Joseph Vishak 973-579-8620 (day).

Newton Meets 4th Wed., 1pm, The Homestead, 129 Morris Turnpike, County Route 655. Call Liz Shuster or Mary Lou Schnurr 973-948-5400.

Newton *(Open to caregivers of any disability)* Meets 1st Tues., 1pm, Barn Hill Care Center, 249 High St. Call Doreen Cook 973-383-5600.

Alzheimer's Support Group *Professionally-run.* Support and information for those caring for someone with Alzheimer's. Peer counseling, guest speakers. Meets 2nd Wed., 7-9pm, Visiting Nurse Association of Saint Clares, Sparta Plaza, 191 Woodport Rd., Sparta. Call Linda Schurmann 973-729-7078 (day).

UNION

Alzheimer's Association Family Support Group Support for caregivers and family members of Alzheimer's and related disorders. Peer counseling, guest speakers, educational materials.

Berkeley Heights *Professionally-run.* Meets 3rd Thurs., 1pm, Runnells Specialized Hospital, Family Conference Room, 40 Watchung Way. Call Liz Carabuena, LSW 908-771-5828 (day).

Cranford Meets 1st Wed., 7pm, Family Resource Center, 300 North Ave. Call Ruth 908-994-7313.

Summit Meets 2nd and 4th Thurs., 7-9pm, Overlook Hospital, 99 Beauvoir Ave. Call Jack Becker 908-719-2276.

WARREN

Alzheimer's Association Family Support Group Support and education for caregivers and friends of individuals afflicted with Alzheimer's. Support, guest speakers, educational materials. Meets 2nd Tues., 7pm, Daybreak Adult Day Care Center, 443 Schooley's Mountain Rd., (Route 24), Hackettstown. Call Valerie Hart 908-852-7300 or Joyce Partington 908-852-4801 (day).

STATEWIDE

Alzheimer's Association Greater NJ chapter *Professionally-run.* Sponsors support groups throughout 14 counties in Greater NJ. Information and referral service, education, advocacy, patient and family service programs. Write: Alzheimer's Association, 400 Morris Ave., Suite 251, Denville, NJ 07834. Call Alzheimer's Helpline 1-800-883-1180 or 973-586-4300 (day). *Website:* http://www.alznj.org

Alzheimer's Association South Jersey Chapter *Professionally-run.* Sponsors support groups for caregivers of persons with Alzheimer's and related dementias in Southern Jersey. Information, referrals, education, newsletter, advocacy, patient and family service programs. (Serves Atlantic, Burlington, Camden, Cape May, Cumberland, Gloucester and Salem counties). Write: Alzheimer's Association, South Jersey Chapter, 3 Eves Dr., Suite 310, Marlton, NJ 08053. Call 856-797-1212 or 1-800-272-3900 (day). *Website:* http://www.alz.org

NATIONAL

Alzheimer's Association *National. 150 chapters. Founded 1980.* Information and assistance for caregivers of Alzheimer's patients. Quarterly newsletter and literature. Online message board. Write: Alzheimer's Assn., 225 N. Michigan Ave., Suite 1700, Chicago, IL 60601. Call 1-800-272-3900 or 312-335-8700; TDD/TTY: 312-335-8882; Fax: 312-335-1110. *Website:* http://www.alz.org *Email:* info@alz.org

ONLINE

Lewy Body Dementia Association *Founded 2000.* Online support and exchange of information for person afflicted with Lewy Body Dementia. Also discusses the problems and concerns for caring for someone with LBD. Promotes research for a cure. *Website:* http://www.lewybodydementia.org

AMYOTROPHIC LATERAL SCLEROSIS
(ALS/Lou Gehrig's Disease)

ATLANTIC

ALS Resource Group "Lou Gehrig's Disease" *Professionally-run.* Mutual support for patients and families to learn how to cope with the daily changes associated with ALS. Guest speakers and literature. Meets 1st Tues., 6-7:30pm, Holy Redeemer Health System, 6727 Delilah Rd., Egg Harbor Township. Call Stephanie Hand-Kowchak 609-909-3509 (day).

CAMDEN

ALS Resource Group "Lou Gehrig's Disease" *Professionally-run.* Mutual support for patients and families to learn how to cope with the daily changes associated with ALS. Guest speakers and literature. Meets 2nd Wed., 7-8:30pm, Kennedy Health Systems, Chapel Ave. and Cooper Landing Rd., Private Dining Room, Cherry Hill. *Website:* http://www.alsphiladelphia.org

MERCER

ALS Association *Professionally-run.* Mutual support for patients and families to learn to cope with the daily changes associated with A.L.S. Meets 1st Sat., 1-3pm, Lawrenceville Municipal Building, Rte. 206, Lawrenceville. Rap sessions, guest speakers and literature. Newsletter. For meeting information call ALS Association 1-877-434-7441 or 215-643-5434.

MIDDLESEX

A.L.S. Association *Professionally-run.* Mutual support for patients and families to learn to cope with A.L.S. Under 18 welcome. Meetings vary, Robert Wood Johnson University Hospital, New Brunswick. For meeting information call 732-235-7331.

ANEMIA

NATIONAL

Cooley's Anemia Foundation *National. 16 chapters. Founded 1954.* Offers education and networking for families affected by Cooley's anemia (thalassemia). Fund-raising for research. Newsletter, annual seminars, research grants, patient support group, patient services, chapter development guidelines. Write: Cooley's Anemia Foundation, 129-09 26th Ave., Flushing, NY 11354. Call 718-321-2873 or

1-800-522-7222; Fax: 718-321-3340. *Website:* http://www.cooleysanemia.org *Email:* info@cooleysanemia.org

APHASIA

(see also brain injury, stroke)

BERGEN

Aphasia Support Group Mutual support for persons suffering from aphasia and their families. Disseminates information and group discussions. Dues $12yr./$2 wk. Meets Fri., (except Aug.), 10:30am-noon, Kip Center, 55 Kip Ave., Rutherford. Call Dr. N. Mikula 973-523-3896 (eve) or Kip Center 201-460-1600 (day).

Chatter's Club *Professionally-run.* Support for people with aphasia and their caregivers. Group is primarily for individuals who have had a stroke, but also includes those with head injury or other brain trauma. Lecture series, social group and guest speakers. Meets Wed., 10:45-11:45am, Adler Aphasia Center, 60 West Hunter Ave., Maywood. Call Karen Tucker 201-368-8585 (day). *Email:* ktucker@adleraphasiacenter.org

UNION

Kean University Aphasia Support Group Mutual support for persons suffering from aphasia and their families. Disseminates information and group discussions. Rap sessions and guest speakers. Meetings vary, CSI, Bldg. 101, Kean University, 1000 Morris Ave., Union. Before attending call Dr. Mary Jo Santo Pietro 908-737-5409 (day).

NATIONAL

National Aphasia Association *National umbrella organization. 350 groups. Founded 1987.* Aim is to educate the public about aphasia. Provides educational information to patients & their families about coping with aphasia. Maintains list of state representatives and support groups. Write: National Aphasia Association, 7 Dey St., Suite 600, New York, NY 10007. Call 1-800-922-4622; Fax: 212-267-2812. *Website:* http://www.aphasia.org *Email:* naa@aphasia.org

ARTHRITIS

STATEWIDE

Arthritis Foundation NJ Chapter Mutual support and education for people with arthritis and their families. Self-help in arthritis, fibromyalgia, osteoporosis and lupus. Call the Arthritis Foundation State Headquarters, Iselin. Call 1-888-467-3112 or 732-283-4300 (day). *Website:* http://www.arthritis.org

BERGEN

Juvenile Arthritis Group Mutual support and education for teens with arthritis and other rheumatic conditions. Concurrent group for parents. Meets monthly, Hackensack University Medical Center, Children's Arthritis Center, Dept. of Pediatrics, 30 Prospect St., Hackensack. For meeting information call Katie Rosenthal 201-336-8241.

BURLINGTON

Arthritis Foundation NJ Chapter Mutual support and education for people with arthritis and their families. Meets 3rd Tues., 1pm, Willingboro Senior Citizen Center, Room 302, 429 JFK Way, Willingboro. Call 1-888-847-8823.

CAMDEN

Arthritis Foundation Support Group Mutual support and education for people with arthritis and their families. Meets 1st Wed., 1pm, (except Jan., Feb., July, Aug., Sept.), Virtua Health's Barry D. Brown Health Education Center, 106 Carnie Blvd., Voorhees. Call Virtua 1-888-847-8823.

CUMBERLAND

Arthritis Foundation Support Group Mutual support for people with arthritis. Meets 3rd Tues., 3:30-4:30pm, SJ Health Care, Fitness Connect, Sherman Ave. and Orchard Rd., Vineland. Before attending call 856-696-3924.

ESSEX

Arthritis Foundation NJ Chapter Mutual support and education for people with arthritis and their families. *Website:* http://www.arthritis.org
> **Montclair** Meets 3rd Fri., noon, Montclair Public Library, 50 South Fullerton Ave. Call 732-283-4300 (day).
> **Orange** Meets 2nd Mon., 10:30am, St. Mary's Life Center, 135 South Center St. Call 973-266-3000 or 1-888-467-3112 (day).

North Jersey Regional Arthritis Center Support Group *Professionally-run.* Mutual support and education for persons with arthritis and their families. Aim is to raise quality of life for those with arthritis through group discussions, educational programs, mutual sharing and guest speakers. Offers phone help, speakers' bureau and literature. Meets 2nd Mon., 2-3pm, (except July/Aug.), Verona Community Center, 880 Bloomfield Ave., Verona. For meeting information call NJRAC 1-877-973-6500.

HUDSON

Arthritis Foundation Support Group Mutual support and education for people with arthritis and their families. Meets 2nd Wed., 2:30pm, Christ Hospital, 176 Palisade Ave., Jersey City. Call Arthritis Foundation 1-888-467-3112. *Website:* http://www.arthritis.org.

North Jersey Regional Arthritis Center Support Group *Professionally-run.* Mutual support and education for persons with arthritis and their families. Aim is to raise quality of life for those with arthritis through group discussions, educational programs, mutual sharing and guest speakers. Offers phone help, speakers' bureau and literature. Meets 2nd Tues., 10:30-11:30am, Community Crossing, 488 Broadway, Bayonne. Call NJRAC 1-877-973-6500.

HUNTERDON

Arthritis Foundation NJ Chapter Mutual support and education for people with arthritis and osteoporosis, their families. *Website:* http://www.arthritis.org
> **Flemington** Open to persons with osteoporosis. Meets 2nd Mon., 1-3pm, Hunterdon Medical Center, 2100 Wescott Dr. Call 908-788-6373 or The Arthritis Foundation 1-888-467-3112 (day).
> **Whitehouse Station** Mirota Senior/Reading Municipal Center, 509 Route 523. Call for time schedule 908-534-9752 ext. 321 or Arthritis Foundation 1-888-467-3112 (day).

MERCER

Arthritis Support Group Support and education for people with all types of arthritis. Call 609-394-4000 or Arthritis Foundation 1-888-467-3112. *Website:* http://www.arthritis.org.
> **Hamilton** Meets 3rd Wed., 7pm, Robert Wood Johnson University Hospital at Hamilton, 1 Hamilton Health Place.
> **Trenton** *Professionally-run.* Meets various days, Capital Health Systems, Mercer Campus, 446 Bellevue Ave.

If you treat an individual ... as if he were what he ought to be and could be, he will become what he ought to be and could be.--Johann Wolfgang Von Goethe

MIDDLESEX

Arthritis Foundation Juvenile Arthritis Parent Support Group Mutual support and education for parents of children of juvenile arthritis. Call Arthritis Foundation 1-888-467-3112.

> **Edison** Meets 2nd Sat., 10am, North Edison Public Library, 777 Grove St.
> **Highland Park** Meets Thurs., 11am-noon, Highland Park Senior Youth Center, 220 S. 6th Ave. Call 732-819-0052.

MONMOUTH

Arthritis Foundation NJ Chapter Mutual support and education for persons with arthritis and their families. Meets 4th Thurs., 6:30pm, Wall Township Library, 2700 Allaire Rd., Wall. Call 732-449-2733.

MORRIS

North Jersey Regional Arthritis Center Support Group *Professionally-run.* Mutual support and education for persons with arthritis and their families. Aim is to raise quality of life for those with arthritis through group discussions, educational programs, mutual sharing and guest speakers. Offers phone help, speakers' bureau and literature. Call NJRAC 1-877-973-6500.

> **Rockaway** Meets various days and times, Rockaway Township Municipal Building, 65 Mt. Hope Rd., Conference Room.
> **Whippany** Meets 2nd Thurs, 10:30am-12:30pm, Morris County Library, 30 E. Hanover Ave.

PASSAIC

Arthritis Support Group *Professionally-run.* Support and education for persons (age 50+) with arthritis. Guest speakers and literature. Meets 4th Tues., 10:30-11:30am, Renaissance Subacute Care Center, 493 Black Oak Ridge Rd., Wayne. Call Joan Beloff 973-831-5167 (day) or Kathy Ferrara 973-831-5175.

North Jersey Regional Arthritis Center Support Group *Professionally-run.* Mutual support and education for persons with arthritis or fibromyalgia and their families. Aim is to raise quality of life for those with arthritis through group discussions, educational programs, mutual sharing and guest speakers. Offers phone help, speakers' bureau and literature. Meets 1st Tues., Main Memorial Library, 292 Piaget Ave., Clifton. Call NJRAC 1-877-973-6500.

SALEM

Arthritis Foundation NJ Chapter Mutual support and education for people with arthritis and their families. Meets 3rd Tues., 3:30pm, SJ Healthcare, Elmer Division, 8 West Front St., Elmer. Call 856-363-1585. *Website:* http://www.arthritis.org

SUSSEX

North Jersey Regional Arthritis Center Support Group Mutual support and education for people with arthritis and their families. Aim is to raise quality of life for those with arthritis through group discussions, educational programs, mutual sharing and guest speakers.

> **Lafayette** *Professionally-run.* Offers phone help, speakers' bureau and literature. "Lunch and Chat" group meets 1st Tues., 11:30am-1:30pm, Lafayette House. Call NJRAC 1-877-973-6500.
> **Newton** Meets 3rd Tues., 1-3pm, Newton Memorial Hospital, NJ Cafeteria Conference Room. Call NJRAC 1-877-973-6500. *Website:* http://www.arthritis.org.

UNION

North Jersey Regional Arthritis Center Support Group *Professionally-run.* Mutual support and education for persons with arthritis and their families. Aim is to raise quality of life for those with arthritis through group discussions, educational programs, mutual sharing and guest speakers. Meets 2nd Wed., (except July/Aug.), 7-8:30pm, Westfield YMCA, 220 Clark St., Westfield. Call Westfield YMCA 908-233-2700 or NJRAC 1-877-973-6500.

WARREN

Arthritis Foundation NJ Chapter Mutual support and education for people with arthritis and their families. Call the Arthritis Foundation 1-888-467-3112 (day). *Website:* http://www.arthritis.org

NATIONAL

American Juvenile Arthritis Organization *National. 50 chapters. Founded 1981.* Council of the Arthritis Foundation devoted to serving the special needs of children, teens and young adults with childhood rheumatic diseases (including juvenile rheumatoid arthritis, systemic lupus erythematosus and ankylosing spondylitis) and their families. Provides information, advocacy, educational materials, programs, conferences. Offers online support and local chapter locator.

Dues $20 (for Arthritis Fdn). Write: AJAO,1330 West Peachtree St., Suite 100, Atlanta, GA 30309. Call 404-872-7100 ext. 7538; Fax: 440-872-9559. *Website:* http://www.arthritis.org

Arthritis Foundation *National 47 chapters. Founded 1948.* Mission is to improve lives through leadership in the prevention, control and cure of arthritis and related diseases. Offers education, support and activities for people with arthritis, their families and friends. Self-help instruction programs. Land and water exercises. Provides community-based public health, public policy and nationwide research funding. Bimonthly magazine. Write: Arthritis Foundation, 1330 West Peachtree St. NW, Atlanta, GA 30309. Call 1-800-568-4045 or 404-872-7100. *Website:* http://www.arthritis.org *Email:* help@arthritis.org

BONE MARROW / STEM CELL TRANSPLANT
(see also specific illness)

BERGEN

Bone Marrow/Stem Cell Transplant Support Group *Professionally-run.* Provides mutual aid and emotional support to bone marrow or stem cell (pre- and post-) transplant patients, their family and friends. Facilitator is transplant recipient. Meetings vary, Hackensack University Medical Center, 4th Floor, Waiting Room, 20 Prospect Ave., Hackensack. Call Medical Center 201-996-5861 (day/eve).

NATIONAL

Blood & Marrow Transplant Information Network *Resource. Founded 1990.* Provides information and support for bone marrow, peripheral stem cell and cord blood transplant patients. Publishes "Blood & Marrow Transplant Newsletter," and "Bone Marrow and Blood Stem Cell Transplants: A Guide for Patients" which describes the physical and emotional aspects of marrow and stem transplantation. Also publishes a 208-page book "Autologous Stem Cell Transplant: A Handbook for Patients." Offers information on about 220 transplant programs in U.S. and Canada, a resource directory, attorney referral service and a patient-to-survivor link service. Write: BMT Information Network, 2310 Skokie Valley Rd., Suite 104, Highland Park, IL 60035. Call 847-433-3313 or 1-888-597-7674; Fax: 847-433-4599. *Website:* http://www.bmtinfonet.org *Email:* help@bmtinfonet.org

"You need to be aware of what others are doing, applaud their efforts, acknowledge their successes, and encourage them in their pursuits. When we all help one another, everybody wins."--Jim Stovall

BRAIN TUMOR

(see also specific disorder)

STATEWIDE

Acoustic Neuroma Association of NJ Support and information for pre- and post-operative patients. Quarterly meetings present programs of interest to acoustic neuroma patients and their families. Dues $20/yr. (optional). Quarterly newsletter. Ongoing programs to create public awareness. Write: ANA/NJ, Inc., 291 Nassau St., Princeton, NJ 08540. Call Wilma Ruskin 609-683-4650 (eve); Fax: 609-279-9295. *Website:* http://www.ananj.org *Email:* ananjinc@aol.com

ESSEX

Support For Children With Brain and Spinal Cord Tumors Support groups for children with brain and spinal cord tumors. Parents and siblings are welcome. Group meets monthly, 10-11am, Jewish Community Center, 769 Northfield Ave., West Orange. For meeting information Call Lissa Parsonnet, PhD 973-921-9629. *Website:* http://www.makingheadway.org *Email:* info@makingheadway.org

MIDDLESEX

Brain Tumor (Tu-Mor Helping Hands) Support Group Support and education for individuals and their families recovering from or who will be undergoing, brain tumor surgery. Guest speakers, phone help, literature. Meets 2nd Mon., 7:00pm, Robert Wood Johnson University Hospital, One Robert Wood Johnson Place, New Brunswick. Call 732-418-8110 (day).

MONMOUTH

Monmouth and Ocean County Brain Tumor Support Group Provide support for patients and family members of those affected by all types of brain tumors. Guest speakers, literature and speakers bureau. Usually meets 1st Sat., 3-4:45pm, (evenings July/Aug.), Wall Township Branch of the Monmouth County Library, 2700 Allaire Rd., Wall. For meeting information Bruce Blount 609-758-0806 or email Nancy Conn-Levin Mngioma634@aol.com *Website:* http://www.njbt.org

SOMERSET

Brain Tumor Resources And Support Center *Professionally-run.* Support for brain tumor patients and their families. Meets 1st Thurs., 7pm, St. Luke's Church, 300 Clinton Ave., North Plainfield. Call Patty Anthony 732-321-7000 ext. 68998

(day), Stan or Virginia 908-685-0917 (day). *Website:* http://www.njbt.org *Email:* info@njbt.org

UNION

Brain Tumor Support Group Mutual support for patients with brain tumors and/or their family members. Meets various days and time, Overlook Hospital, 99 Beauvoir Ave., Summit. Call Kristen Scarlett, LPC, NCC 908-522-5255 (day).

NATIONAL

Acoustic Neuroma Association *National. 53 affiliated groups. Founded 1981.* Support and information for patients who have been diagnosed with acoustic neuroma, a benign tumor affecting the 8th cranial nerve. Quarterly newsletter ($35/yr.), nationwide support group network, biennial national symposium and patient information booklets. Write: ANA, 600 Peachtree Parkway, Suite 108, Cumming, GA 30041-6899. Call 770-205-8211; Fax: 770-205-0239. *Website:* http://www.anausa.org *Email:* ANAUSA@aol.com

American Brain Tumor Association *National. Founded 1973.* Dedicated to eliminating brain tumors by funding and encouraging research and providing free patient education, materials and resource information. Pen pal program, newsletter, publications, resource listings. Support group referrals. Assistance in starting groups Write: American Brain Tumor Association, 2720 River Rd., Suite 146, Des Plaines, IL 60018. Call 847-827-9910 or 1-800-886-2282; Fax: 847-827-9918. *Website:* http://www.abta.org *Email:* info@abta.org

Brain Tumor Society *National. 5 affiliated groups. Founded 1989.* Committed to finding a cure for brain tumors through funding research, education and patient, survivor and caregiver support programs and services. Sponsors professional conferences and patient/family/healthcare provider symposiums. Strives to improve the quality of life of all those affected by a brain tumor diagnosis through psychosocial support and resources to include a national database of brain tumor support groups. Write: Brain Tumor Society, 124 Watertown St., Suite 3-H, Watertown, MA 02472-2500. Call 1-800-770-8287 or 617-924-9998; Fax: 617-924-9998. *Website:* http://www.tbts.org *Email:* info@tbts.org

Children's Brain Tumor Foundation, Inc. *National network. Founded 1988.* Provides a parent-to-parent network to link parents of a child with a brain or spinal cord tumor with another parent with similar experiences for information and support. Telephone support groups meet once a week for six weeks which gives participants a safe and supportive environment for discussing difficult issues relating to their situation. Groups are provided for parents of newly diagnosed children and for teenage and young-adult survivors. Offers free resource guide (English/Spanish), Parker's Brain Storm (a book for children), Brain Tumor Week at Camp Sunshine, newsletter, annual teleconferences (available on website) and funds research. Write: Children's Brain Tumor Foundation, 274 Madison Ave., Suite 1301, New York, NY 10016. Call 1-866-228-4673 or 212-448-9494; Fax: 212-448-1022. *Website:* http://www.cbtf.org *Email:* info@cbtf.org

Musella Foundation *National.* Provides emotional support and exchange of information for patients with various brain tumors and their families. Information on research, medication and clinical trials. Chat rooms, support groups, video library and other resources. Write: Musella Foundation, 1100 Peninsula Blvd., Hewlett, NY 11557. Call 1-888-295-4740 or 516-295-4740; Fax: 516-205-2870. *Website:* http://www.virtualtrials.com *Email:* musella@virtualtrials.com

National Brain Tumor Foundation *National. 150+ affiliated groups. Founded 1981.* Support and information for persons with brain tumors. Provides funding for research as well as client services for brain tumor patients and family members. Offers support group listings, a quarterly newsletter, information and referrals, conferences, literature and support line. Assistance in starting and maintaining support groups. Write: NBTF, 22 Battery Street, Suite 612, SF, CA 94111-5520. Call 1-800-934-2873 or 415-834-9970; Fax: 415-834-9980. *Website:* http://www.braintumor.org *Email:* nbtf@braintumor.org

ONLINE

BRAIN TRUST, The Healing Exchange *Online. Founded 1993.* Mission is to create an exchange of information and support among people affected by brain tumors and related conditions including patient-survivors, families, caregivers and health professionals. Online support groups cover a large range of brain tumors, acquired injuries and other special interests. Write: T.H.E. BRAIN TRUST, 186 Hampshire St., Cambridge, MA 02139-1320. Call 617-876-2002; Fax: 617-876-2332. *Website:* http://www.braintrust.org *Email:* info@braintrust.org

Spouses of Brain Tumor Patients *Online.* Support for spouses of brain tumor patients. Opportunity to connect with others who understand the emotions and frustrations involved with a spouse who has a brain tumor. Message board and chat room. *Website:* http://www.bradsupdates.com/care.html

Our information is always changing. New groups are started, others end, some change contact information. Call us any time for the most updated information at 1-800-367-6274

BREAST CANCER
(see also cancer, toll-free helpline)

BERGEN

ABC's (After Breast Cancer Surgery) *Professionally-run.* Support and rehabilitation for women and men who have undergone breast cancer surgery. Group discussions, therapeutic pool exercise. Meets weekly for 8 sessions, 3 times/yr. Bergen County Y, 605 Pascack Rd, Washington Township. For meeting information call ABC's Coordinator 201-666-6610 ext. 300 (day/eve).

Breast Cancer Support Group *Professionally-run.* Support group for breast cancer patients. Family and friends welcome. Meets 2nd Wed., 7-8:30pm, Hackensack University Medical Center, 20 Prospect Ave., Reception Area, Suite 400, Hackensack. Call Elaine La Gala 201-996-4942 (day).

Support Group For Breast Cancer *(SPANISH SPEAKING)* Support for women with breast cancer. Mutual sharing, educational and guest speakers. Meetings vary, Latin America Institute, 10 Banta Place, Hackensack. Call Dr. L. Puertas 201-525-1700 (day) or 201-847-1054 (eve). *Email:* lpuertas1@verizon.net

BURLINGTON

Speak Easy Breast Cancer Support Group *Professionally-run.* Mutual support and information to breast cancer survivors. Guest speakers, phone help, literature. Meets 1st Tues., 7-9pm, (except July/ Aug.), Lourdes Medical Center of Burlington County, 218A Sunset Rd., Willingboro. Call Maxine Mayer 856-662-5474 (day).

CAMDEN

Pink Ribbon Poetry Breast Cancer Support Group Support for breast cancer survivors to use poetry as a tool for reflection. Meets 1st and 3rd Thurs., 7-9pm, Virtua Memorial Hospital, Conference Center, 175 Madison Ave., Mt. Holly. Before attending for the first time call 1-888-847-8823 (day).

Women Supporting Women Through Breast Cancer *Professionally-run.* Mutual support for breast cancer patients and those currently under treatment. Meets 2nd and 4th Wed., 6:30-8pm, Virtua Health William G. Rohrer Center for Health Fitness, 2309 Evesham Rd., Voorhees. Before attending call Virtua 1-888-847-8823 (day).

ESSEX

Circle of Women *Professionally-run.* Networking group to support women diagnosed with breast cancer. Rap sessions and phone help. Meets Tues., 7-8:30pm, Mountainside Hospital, Harries Pavilion, Cancer Center, 1 Bay Ave., Montclair. Call Sara Canzoniero, LSW 973-429-6038 (day).

Primary Breast Cancer Support Group *Professionally-run.* Mutual support for women with breast cancer to share their concerns and experiences with other women facing the same illness and treatments. Meeting dates and times vary, St. Barnabas Medical Center, 94 Old Short Hills Rd., Livingston. Call Jill Kaplan, LCSW 973-322-8405 (day).

HUNTERDON

Breast Cancer Support Group *Professionally-run.* Offers support and education for women with breast cancer. Rap sessions, guest speakers, phone help, literature. Meets 3rd Thurs., 7:30-9pm, Hunterdon Regional Cancer Center, Flemington. Call 1-800-227-2345 ext. 2 (day).

MERCER

Advanced Breast Cancer Support Group *Professionally-run.* Provides support for women living with stage IV breast cancer. Share your experiences, solutions, triumphs and concerns. Meets 1st and 3rd Mon., 7:30-9pm, YWCA Princeton Library, 59 Paul Robeson Place, Princeton. Call 609-497-2100. *Website:* http://www.bcrcnj.org *Email:* bcrc@ywcaprinceton.org

Breast Cancer Support Group *Professionally-run* Mutual support and guidance for women with breast cancer. Families welcome. Rap sessions, guest speakers, phone help, literature.. Meets 1st and 2nd Tues., 6:30-8pm, The Cancer Institute of NJ, RWJU Hospital, Hamilton Campus, 2575 Klockner Road, Hamilton. Call Trish Tatrai for 1st Tues. meeting 609-584-2836 and Lois Glasser for 2nd Tues. meeting 1-800-813-4673 ext. 107.

Breast Cancer Support Group Mutual support and guidance for women with breast cancer. Families welcome. Rap sessions, guest speakers, phone help, literature. Meets alternate Wed., 1-2pm, Capital Health System at Mercer, 446 Bellevue Ave., Trenton. Call Oncology Social Worker 609-394-4228.

Breast Cancer Support Group Provides peer support to anyone diagnosed with breast cancer, at any stage of treatment or recovery. Share questions, concerns and coping strategies in a caring, understanding environment. Meets 4th Wed.,

11:45am-1pm and 3rd Tues., 7-8:30pm, YWCA Princeton, Bramwell House Living Room, 59 Paul Robeson Place, Princeton. Call 609-497-2100, Breast Cancer Helpline 609-497-2126 or 1-866-497-3507. *Website:* http://www.bcrcnj.org *Email:* bcrc@ywcaprinceton.org

Princeton Breast Institute Self-Help Discussion Group Self-help group for women in all stages of breast disease to discuss experiences and maintain positive and constructive support. Meets every other Wed., 12:30pm, Princeton Breast Institute, 842 State Rd., Princeton. Call Elle 609-924-1528 ext. 4 (day).

Young Women's Breast Cancer Support Group *Professionally-run.* Provides support to women under the age of 45 who have been diagnosed with breast cancer. Addresses issues such as fertility, dating, raising young children and recent marriage. Meets 1st Wed., 7:30-9pm, YWCA Princeton, Bramwell House Living Room, 59 Paul Robeson Place, Princeton. Call Kara Stephenson 609-497-2100 ext. 346. *Website:* http://www.bcrcnj.org *Email:* bcrc@ywcaprinceton.org

MIDDLESEX

Breast Cancer Support Group Mutual support and education for women and their family members with breast cancer. Guest speakers. Meets 1st and 3rd Mon., 7pm, Cancer Institute of NJ, 195 Little Albany St., New Brunswick. Call 732-235-6792 (day).

Voices of Healing *Professionally-run.* Helps women with breast cancer to decrease their feelings of isolation and provides a sense of purpose and belonging. Empowerment, body image and family roles are discussed. Members are encouraged to discover the strength of their own inner resources. Meets 1st Tues., 6:30-8pm, Haven Hospice, JFK Medical Center, 65 James St., Edison. Call Elaine Murphy 732-321-7769 (day).

MONMOUTH

Breast Cancer Support Group *Professionally-run.* Support, information and mutual sharing for breast cancer survivors. Rap sessions, phone help. Meets 1st Mon., 7:30-9pm, Health Awareness Center, 65 Gibson Pl., Freehold. Call Stephanie O'Neil 732-308-1850 (day).

Breast Cancer Support Group Mutual support and education for women and their family members with breast cancer. Psycho-Social workshop. Meets Tues., 2-4pm, Breast Care Center at Jersey Shore Medical Center, Ambulatory Care Pavilion, Cancer Center Conference Room, 1945 Corlies Avenue, Neptune. Before attending call Breast Care Center 1-800-560-9990.

Breast Cancer Support Group Mutual support and education for women and their family members with breast cancer. Meets for 6 week sessions, Jersey Shore Medical Center, Ambulatory Care Center, Cancer Center Conference Room, Neptune. Call 732-776-4432 (day).

Breast Cancer Support Group *Professionally-run* Mutual support and education for women and their family members with breast cancer. Meets 1st Thurs., 7:30-9pm, Riverview Medical Center, 1 Riverview Plaza, Red Bank. Call 732-530-2382 (day).

Living with Early Stage Breast Cancer Support Group *Professionally-run.* Opportunity for women diagnosed with breast cancer to obtain information, support and coping skills. Meets 2nd and 4th Tues., 7:15-9pm, Monmouth Medical Center, Comprehensive Center, 300 Second Ave., Long Branch. Must pre-register. Call Jan Tryba 732-923-7711 (day).

Living with Metastic Breast Cancer Support Group *Professionally-run.* Support for women facing the challenge of recurrent or metastic breast cancer. A place to share information and receive support. Meets 1st and 3rd Tues., 1-2:30pm, Goldsmith Wellness Center, 4th Floor, Monmouth Medical Center, 300 Second Ave., Long Branch. Must pre-register. Call Jan Tryba 732-923-7711 (day).

Partners in Healing Support Group *Professionally-run.* Mutual support for spouses/significant others of women diagnosed with breast cancer, cervical, endometrial, ovarian and uterine cancer. Meets 3rd Tues., 7:-8:30pm, Cancer Center Conference Room, Ambulatory Care Pavilion, Jersey Shore Medical Center, Neptune. Before attending call 1-800-560-9990 (day).

Younger Generation *Professionally-run.* Mutual support for individuals with breast cancer up to the age of 45. Rap sessions and guest speakers. Meets 1st Tues., 6pm, Jersey Shore Medical Center, Ambulatory Care Pavilion, Cancer Center Conference Room, 1945 Corlies Avenue, Neptune. For scheduled meeting day call Breast Care Center 1-800-560-9990.

MORRIS

Breast Cancer Support Group *Professionally-run.* Information and support to women with breast cancer. Meets 1st and 3rd Tues., 7-8:30pm, Morristown Memorial Hospital, Carol G. Simon Cancer Center, Conference Room, 100 Madison Ave., Morristown. Call Jean Marie 973-971-6514.

Together *Professionally-run.* Education and sharing for women who are or have been undergoing treatment for breast cancer. Rap sessions, guest speakers. Before attending call 973-625-6176.

> **Denville** Meets 1st and 3rd Wed., 7-8:30pm, Saint Clare's Hospital, 25 Pocono Rd., Urban 2 Conference Room.

> **Dover** Education and sharing for women who are or have been undergoing treatment for breast cancer. Rap sessions, guest speakers. Meets twice monthly, Mon., 2-3pm, Women's Health Center, St. Clare's Hospital.

OCEAN

Breast Cancer Support Group *Professionally-run.* Education and sharing for women diagnosed with breast cancer. Rap sessions and occasional guest speaker.

> **Brick** Meets 1st Mon., 7:30-9pm, Ocean Medical Center, Bridge Conference Room, 2nd Floor, 425 Jack Martin Blvd. Significant others welcome. Before attending call Judith Willbergh 732-206-8340 (day) or American Cancer Society 732-914-1000 (day).

> **Toms River** Meets last Wed., Community Medical Center, 599 Route 37. Before attending call Rose Cowen 732-557-8076 (day).

Breast Cancer Support Group *Professionally-run.* Support and education for persons afflicted with breast cancer. Meets 2nd Tues., 7-8pm, Ocean Club, 700 Route 9 South, Stafford Township. Call 609-978-3559.

PASSAIC

Breast Cancer Support Group *Professionally-run.* Offers support and education for women with breast cancer. Meets 3rd Wed., 6-8:30pm, Barnert Hospital, Ezor Conference Room, 680 Dr. Martin Luther King, Jr. Way, Paterson. Call Ivette Mora 973-977-6600 ext. 2499 (day) or Joanne Dechert 973-977-6766 (day).

Breast Cancer Support Group - Embracing Life Self-help for women coping with breast cancer.

> **Clifton** Meets Mon., 5-6pm, St. Joseph's Regional Medical Center, 3rd Floor, Suite 1, 1135 Broad St. Registration is required. Before attending call Marie Marrinan 973-569-6329.

> **Paterson** *(SPANISH)* Meets 1st and last Wed., 5-6pm, St. Joseph's Regional Medical Center, Xavier Bldg., 4th Floor, 703 Main St. Registration is required. Before attending call Victoria Pacheco 973-616-0514.

Post-Mastectomy/Lumpectomy Program *Professionally-run.* Support and exercise for women who have had breast surgery. Meets periodically in the spring and fall at the YWHA, 199 Scoles Ave., Clifton. For information call Edith Berman 973-473-3602 (eve) or American Cancer Society 973-696-1885. *Website:* http://www.cancer.org

SOMERSET

Cancer Support Groups *Professionally-run.* Provides support for cancer patients and their families. Share feelings and concerns. Education, guest speakers, buddy system and phone help. Meets various times and days, Wellness Community, 3 Crossroads Dr., Bedminster. Call Pamela Pitchell or Karen Larsen 908-658-5400 (day). *Website:* http://www.thewellnesscommunity.org/cnj

Sisters Network of Central New Jersey Mutual support for female African American breast cancer survivors. Aim is to increase awareness of the impact of breast cancer. Literature and phone help. Meets 2nd Mon., 7-8:30pm, Somerset. Call Dorothy Reed 732-246-8300 (day). *Website:* http://www.sistercentral.com *Email:* sistercentral@aol.com

SUSSEX

Breast Cancer Support Support and information for women at any stage of breast cancer. Meets 2nd Tues., 6:30pm, Sparta Health and Wellness Center, 89 Sparta Ave., Sparta. Call Community Benefits Education 973-579-8340 (day).

UNION

Breast / Gynecological Cancer Support Support for women afflicted with breast or any gynecological cancer. Meetings vary, Pathways, 79 Maple St., Summit. Pre-registration required. Before attending call 908-273-4242 ext. 154.

NATIONAL

AABCA (African American Breast Cancer Alliance) *Model. 1 group in Minnesota. Founded 1990.* Education, support group & advocacy for Black women and men with breast cancer and their families. Provides information & referrals, education and a support group for patients and survivors to discuss issues and concerns. Open to anyone interested in supporting & working with this grassroots organization. Write: AABCA, PO Box 8981, Minneapolis, MN 55408. Call 612-825-3675; Fax: 612-825-3675. *Website:* http://www.aabcainc.org *Email:* aabcainc@yahoo.com

Breast Cancer Support and Reach to Recovery Discussion Group *National.* Local outgrowth of Reach to Recovery Program which in most areas is a one-to-one visitation program but in some areas is a support group. Contact your local or state chapter of American Cancer Society at 1-800-227-2345 to determine availability of such groups and availability of trained volunteers. Click on "survivors," then click on "support programs." *Website:* http://www.cancer.org

Mothers Supporting Daughters with Breast Cancer *Model. Founded 1995.* Offers emotional support to the mothers of daughters newly diagnosed with breast cancer to help them to be better "care partners" to their daughters. Helps mothers cope with stress, learn about breast cancer treatment and promote breast cancer awareness. Literature, advocacy, phone support. Online message board. Write: MSDBC, c/o Charmayne Dierker, 21710 Bayshore Rd., Chestertown, MD 21620. Call 410-778-1982; Fax: 410-778-1411. *Website:* http://www.mothersdaughters.org *Email:* msdbc@dmv.com

SHARE: Self-Help for Women with Breast or Ovarian Cancer *(BILINGUAL) Model. 18 sites in NY Metro Area. Founded 1976. (Bilingual)* Provides support to women with breast or ovarian cancer, their families and friends. Support groups led by trained survivors. Cutting edge educational forums and wellness programs meet in various locations throughout New York City and North Brunswick, NJ. Write: SHARE, 1501 Broadway, Suite 704A, New York, NY 10036. Call 1-866-891-2392; Breast Hotline: 212-382-2111; Ovarian Hotline: 212-719-1204; Latina Hotline (in Spanish): 212-719-4454; Fax: 212-869-3431. *Website:* http://www.sharecancersupport.org

Sisters Network Inc. *National. 42 affiliated chapters. Founded 1994.* An African American breast cancer survivors organization that offers education, outreach, advocacy and support. E-newsletter, information and referrals, annual national conferences. Establishes new affiliates. Write: SNI, 8787 Woodway Dr., Suite 4206, Houston, TX 77063. Call 1-866-781-1808 or 713-781-0255; Fax: 713-780-8998. *Website:* http://www.sistersnetworkinc.org *Email:* infonet@sistersnetworkinc.org

Y-ME Nat'l Breast Cancer Organization *National. 9 affiliate groups. Founded 1978.* Information & peer support for breast cancer patients & their families during all stages of the disease. Offers 24-hour hotlines (English & Spanish), a Latino Outreach program, a Men's Match program for husbands and partners of women with breast cancer, support groups, a Teen Education program and Advocacy Network to increase funding for research, publications, wig and prosthesis bank and newsletter. Group development guidelines. Write: Y-ME, 212 W. Van Buren St., Chicago, IL 60607-3908. Call 1-800-221-2141 (English) or 1-800-986-9505 (Spanish) (24 hrs); Fax: 312-294-8598. *Website:* http://www.y-me.org/

ONLINE

FORCE (Facing Our Risk of Cancer Empowered) *Online. Founded 1999.* Support and education for women whose family history and genetic status put them at high risk of getting ovarian or breast cancer. Open to family members. Provides resources for women to determine if they are at high risk. Write: FORCE, c/o Sue Friedman, 934 N. University Dr., PMB #213, Coral Springs, FL 33071. Call 954-255-8732. *Website:* http://www.facingourrisk.org/ *Email:* info@facingourrisk.org

MaleBC *Online. Founded 1997.* Brings men together who have been diagnosed with male breast cancer so they can share experiences, gain information and support each other. On website click on "Mailing List" and scroll down to all cancers. *Website:* http://www.acor.org

CANCER
(see also breast cancer, toll-free helplines)

ATLANTIC

Adult Support Group *Professionally-run.* Adult support for persons with cancer and their families. Meets Tues., 2pm, Shore Memorial Cancer Center, 1 East New York Ave., Somers Point. Call 609-653-3585 (day).

Gilda's Club South Jersey *Professionally-run.* Emotional and social support for anyone touched by cancer. Separate support groups, workshops, lectures and social events for family members. Meetings vary, Gilda's Club, 300 Shore Rd., Linwood. Before attending call 609-926-2699. *Website:* http://www.gildasclubsouthjersey.org *Email:* erin@gildasclubsouthjersey.org

"Man to Man" Prostate Cancer Support Group An educational, information sharing and emotional support group designed to meet the challenge of living with prostate cancer for men and their partner. Meets 2nd Tues., (except June/July/Aug.), 7-9pm, Shore Memorial Hospital, Prostate Building, 2nd Floor, Brighton Ave. and Shore Rd., Somers Point. Call Burnett Watson 609-641-7907 (day/eve).

BERGEN

Cancer Care *(BILINGUAL) Professionally-run.* Various support groups for cancer patients and their families Groups also include bereavement, telephone and internet groups. Groups start periodically and run for 8 weeks. Groups meet in Ridgewood. For meeting information call 1-800-813-4673 or 201-444-6630 (day).

CARE (Cancer Alternatives Research Exchange) Mutual support for persons with cancer and their families. Explores any type of treatment that may be of benefit with a focus on integrated medicine. Donation $5. Meets 2nd Thurs., 7-10pm (except July-Aug.), Ridgewood United Methodist Church, 100 Dayton St., Ridgewood. Call Ed Van Overloop 201-391-5931 (Mon-Fri., 9am-noon). *Email:* 31evo@optonline.net

DongGueRaMee Mutual support and education for Korean patients who have cancer, as well as cancer survivors. Families welcome. Guest speakers. Meets 1st Fri., 10am-12:30pm, Korean Community Center, 15 Ver Valen St., Closter. Call Hei Young 201-594-4848 (day).

Gastrointestinal/Colorectal Cancer Mutual support for patients, families and friends affected by gastrointestinal/colorectal cancer. Meets 2nd Thurs., 10:30am-noon, Medical Plaza, 20 Prospect Ave., Hackensack. Call Kathy Sonnabend 201-996-5836 (day).

Gilda's Club Northern NJ *Professionally-run.* Emotional and social support for anyone touched by cancer. Separate support groups, workshops, lectures and social events for family members. Programs for children also. Meetings vary, Gilda's Club, 575 Main St., Hackensack. Call 201-457-1670 (day). *Website:* http://www.gildasclubnnj.org *Email:* info@gildasclubnnj.com

Leukemia Lymphoma Support *Professionally-run.* Emotional support for patients affected by leukemia, lymphoma, Hodgkin's Disease and multiple myeloma and their family and friends. Rap sessions, guest speakers. Meets Tues., 10:30am-noon, for 8 wk sessions, Cancer Center at Hackensack, Hackensack University Medical Center, Hackensack. Registration required. Before attending call Deborah Halpern 908-654-9445 (day). *Website:* http://www.LLS.org/nj *Email:* halpernd@LLS.org

Living With Cancer Mutual support for patients, families and friends who are affected by cancer. Rap sessions, guest speakers and literature. Meets 4th Thurs., 10:30am-noon, Medical Plaza, 20 Prospect Ave., Hackensack. Call Kathy Sonnabend 201-996-5836 (day).

Lung/Thoracic Cancer Mutual support for patients, families and friends affected by lung/thoracic cancer. Rap sessions, guest speakers and literature. Meets 1st Thurs., 10:30am-noon, Medical Plaza, 20 Prospect Ave., Hackensack. Call Kathy Sonnabend 201-996-5836 (day).

We can also refer callers to over 100 individuals who are seeking others to help start new support groups throughout NJ, if you don't see it, that doesn't mean it doesn't exist!
1-800-367-6274

Multiple Myeloma *Professionally-run.* Mutual support for patients, families and friends affected by multiple myeloma. Rap sessions, guest speakers and literature. Meets 3rd Thurs., 10:30am-noon, Medical Plaza, 20 Prospect Ave., Hackensack. Call Kathy Sonnabend 201-996-5836 (day).

Northern NJ Chapter Leukemia and Lymphoma Society *Professionally-run.* Emotional support for adult patients and family members where there has been a diagnosis of leukemia, lymphoma, Hodgkin's disease or multiple myeloma. Mutual sharing, guest speakers and education. Meets 10:30am, 6 week sessions, 4 times/yr., Cancer Center, Hackensack University Medical Center, Hackensack. Call Deborah Halpern, MSW 908-654-9445 (day). *Website:* http://www.LLS.org/nj *Email:* halpernd@LLS.org

On Treatment Families *Professionally-run.* Support and education for patients, parents and siblings who have cancer or serious blood disorders. Also groups for children and families who have completed treatment. Meetings vary, Hackensack University Medical Center, Reuten Clinic, Hackensack. For meeting information call Judy Solomon 201-996-5437 (day).

Prostate Cancer Support Group Support and education for people affected by prostate cancer. Families and caregivers welcome. Guest speakers, literature.
> **Hackensack** *Professionally-run.* Meets 3rd Wed., 10am-noon, Hekemian Conference Center, Hackensack University Medical Center, 30 Prospect Ave. Call Kathy Sonnabend 201-996-5836 (day).
> **Westwood** Meets 2nd Wed., 7-9pm, Pascack Valley Hospital, 250 Old Hook Rd. Call Ray 201-670-0586 or Health Information Resource 201-358-6000 (day).

Us Too *Professionally-run.* Support and education for persons diagnosed with prostate cancer and their significant others. Meets 3rd Fri., 10am-noon, Daniel and Gloria Blumenthal Cancer Center, 2nd Floor, Meeting Room, One Valley Health Plaza, Paramus. Call Janet Carlsen 201-634-5358 (day).

BURLINGTON

Living with Lung Cancer *Professionally-run.* Mutual support and encouragement for anyone with lung cancer. Meets 1st Wed., 11:30am-12:30pm, Virtua Memorial Hospital Burlington County, Conference Center, 175 Madison Ave., Mt. Holly. Before attending for the first time call Virtua 1-888-847-8823 (day).

"Man to Man" Prostate Cancer Support Group *Professionally-run.* An educational, information sharing and emotional support group designed to meet the challenge of living with prostate cancer. Meets 3rd. Tues., 7-8:30pm, Virtua

Memorial Hospital of Burlington County, Memorial Hospital Conference Room B, 175 Madison Ave., Mt. Holly. Call 1-800-227-2345 (day). *Website:* http://www.cancer.org *Email:* michelle.mcgroarty@cancer.org

CAMDEN

Cancer Adjustment Program *Professionally-run.* Mutual support for cancer patients and their families. Meets Mon., 7:30pm, 1851 Old Cuthbert Rd., Cherry Hill. Call American Cancer Society 1-800-227-2345 (day). *Website:* http://www.cancer.org *Email:* michelle.mcgroarty@cancer.org

Leukemia Society of America *(Eastern Pennsylvania Chapter) Professionally-run.* Support and education for families to help cope with the emotional and personal issues of lymphoma, leukemia and multiple myeloma. Meets 4th Thurs., 7-8:30pm, Einstein Center One, Suite 206, 9880 Bustleton Ave., Philadelphia. Free parking. Call Anne Waldman 215-456-3822 (day). *Email:* mclaughlin@lls.org

Women's Cancer Connection *Professionally-run.* Mutual support for women with ovarian, cervical or uterine cancer. Meets 1st Tues., 7-8:30pm, Virtua Health's William G. Rohrer Center for Health Fitness, 2309 Evesham Rd., Voorhees. Before attending for the first time call Virtua 1-888-847-8823 (day).

CAPE MAY

Cancer Support Group *Professionally-run.* Mutual support and education for men and women who have cancer. Separate group for spouses and significant others. Guest speakers, literature. Both groups meet 2nd and 4th Thurs., 7pm, Burdette Tomlin Memorial Hospital, Maruchi Room, Cape May Court House. Call Burdette Tomlin Hospital 609-463-2367 (day) or 609-463-2298.

ESSEX

Beyond Primary Cancer *Professionally-run.* Group provides a supportive environment to share thoughts, concerns, gain practical information and emotional support for patients coping with recurrent or metastic cancer. Meeting days vary. Before attending call Angela McCabe 973-322-2668.

Caring Arms Opportunity for men and women who have been diagnosed with cancer to come together to offer strength, experience and hope. Provides a supportive environment where persons can express feelings and concerns with others who share a common experience. Meditation offered after meeting. Meets Mon., 12:30pm, Cathedral Regional Cancer Center, Saint Michael's Medical

Center, Conference Room, Central Ave., Newark. Before attending call Joanne Rodriguez 973-877-5620 (day).

Children's Circle, The *Professionally-run.* Support and education for children of cancer patients to help them cope with the illness of a parent. Meetings vary, St. Barnabas Medical Center, Old Short Hills Rd., Livingston. For further information call Jill Kaplan 973-322-8405.

Expressive Arts Group *Professionally-run.* Support for patients who are undergoing cancer treatment. Meeting days and times vary, St. Barnabas Medical Center, 94 Old Short Hills Rd., Livingston. Call Stephanie Buck, MPS, ATR 973-322-2171 (day).

Facing the Challenge *Professionally-run.* Mutual support for anyone diagnosed with cancer. Family and caregivers welcome. Guest speakers. Meets 2nd and 4th Mon., 6:45-8:15pm, Mountainside Hospital, Harries Pavilion, Cancer Center, 1 Bay Ave., Montclair. Call Sara Canzoniero, LSW 973-429-6038 (day).

Healing Stitches Mutual support for cancer patients to gather weekly to chat, knit or crochet while interacting and creating projects. Families and caregivers welcome. Meets Wed., 2-4pm, Mountainside Hospital, Cancer Center, 1 Bay Ave., Montclair. Call Sara Canzoniero, LSW 973-429-6038 (day).

Post Treatment Support Group *Professionally-run.* Mutual support for patients after their medical treatment is completed. Meeting dates and times vary, 10 week session, St. Barnabas Medical Center, 94 Old Short Hills Rd., Livingston. Call Jill Kaplan, LCSW 973-322-8405 (day).

Us Too (Prostate Cancer Support Group) *Professionally-run.* Information and support for men with prostate cancer and their families.

> **Livingston** Meets 2nd Tues., 7-8:30pm, St. Barnabas Medical Center, Dept. of Radiation, Oncology Room 1749, Old Short Hills Rd. Call Angela McCabe 973-322-2668 (day). *Website:* http://www.sbhcs.com
>
> **Montclair** Meets 1st Thurs., (except July), 7-8:30pm, Mountainside Hospital, Harries Pavilion, Cancer Center, Conference Room, 1 Bay Ave. Before attending call Sara Canzoniero, LSW 973-429-6038 (day).

GLOUCESTER

Leukemia and Lymphoma Support Group *Professionally-run.* Emotional support, education and discussion of common issues for people with leukemia, lymphomas and related disorders, as well as for their families and loved ones. Rap sessions, guest speakers. Meets 3rd Tues., 7-9pm, Superintendent of Schools

Building, Tanyard Rd., Sewell. Call Leukemia Society 856-869-0200 or Libby Maurer 856-468-1167.

HUDSON

Cancer Adjustment Support Group *Professionally-run.* Provides emotional support and education to those diagnosed with cancer. Meets 3rd Tues., 1:30pm, Christ Hospital, Radiation/Oncology Center, 176 Palisade Ave., Jersey City. Call 201-795-8030 (day).

Cancer Support Group *Professionally-run.* Support and education for anyone with cancer age 18 and older. Meeting days and times vary, Jersey City Medical Center, 355 Grand St., Jersey City. Call Janet Richman, LCSW 201-915-2000 ext. 3178 (day).

Cancer Support Group *(BILINGUAL)* Support group for cancer patients and their family. Literature and guest speakers. Meetings vary, 3-4pm, Columbus Health Center, 1st Floor, 115 Columbus Dr., Jersey City. Call Janet Richman, LCSW 201-946-6807 (day).

HUNTERDON

Northern NJ Chapter Leukemia and Lymphoma Society *Professionally-run.* Emotional support for patients suffering from leukemia, lymphoma, Hodgkin's and multiple myeloma. Family and friends are welcome to attend. Offers mutual sharing and guest speakers. Meets 3rd Tues., 7-8:30pm, Hunterdon Regional Cancer Center, Flemington. Before attending call Deborah Halpern, MSW 908-654-9445 (day). *Website:* http://www.LLS.org/nj *Email:* halpernd@LLS.org

Us Too! Prostate Cancer Support Group *Professionally-run.* Provides support and education for those with prostate cancer and their spouse. Guest speakers, phone help and literature. Meets 2nd Thurs., 6:30-8pm, Hunterdon Regional Cancer Center, Conference Room, 2100 Westcott Dr., Flemington. Call Denise Bernard, LCSW 908-237-2337.

MERCER

Cancer Caregiver's Support Group *Professionally-run.* Support and education for family members and friends caring for a loved one with cancer. Meets 1st and 3rd Tues., 5-6:30pm, Cancer Institute of NJ at Hamilton, 2575 Klockner Rd., Hamilton. Before attending call Elsje Reiss, MSW, LCSW 609-584-2818.

Living and Loving with Chronic Illness *Professionally-run.* Confidential group offering mutual support and discussion for persons with a variety of chronic medical conditions including heart disease, neuromuscular disorders, cancer and chronic pain. Meets alternate Wed., 2pm, St. Francis Medical Center, 601 Hamilton Ave., Trenton. Call Bev Snyderman 609-599-5657 (day).

Sharing Your Journey Through Cancer *Professionally-run.* Peer-support for persons with cancer to share experiences. Families welcomed. Phone help, literature. Meets 1st and 3rd Thurs., 6:30-8pm, The Cancer Institute of NJ at Hamilton, Campus of RWJUH, 2575 Klockner Road, Conference Room, Hamilton. Call Connie Stallone, MSW,LCSW 609-584-6680 (day).

MIDDLESEX

Cancer Support Group *(BILINGUAL)* Support for cancer survivors and their loved ones to provide an opportunity to meet with others who may be experiencing similar issues. Guest speakers, literature, speakers bureau. Meets 1st Tues., 6-7:30pm, Raritan Bay Medical Center, 530 New Brunswick Ave., Perth Amboy. Call Teresa Perez 732-324-5173 (day) or Sandra Nilsson 732-324-5079 (day).

Coping With Cancer *Professionally-run.* Provides a safe environment for cancer patients and their families to share their feelings and concerns. Helps patients become educated partners in their healthcare through information on diagnosis and treatment. Meets 4th Tues., 2-3:30pm, JFK Medical Center, 65 James St., Edison. Call Mary Aloia 732-321-7769 (day).

Healing Journey - Relaxation for Cancer Patients, The *Professionally-run.* Support for those afflicted with cancer to develop relaxation and visualization skills. Families welcome. Educational and experiential group. Meets 3rd., Tues., 6-7:30pm, Haven Hospice, JFK Medical Center, 65 James St., Edison. Call Rose Slirzewski 732-321-7769 (day).

Lesbians with Cancer Support Group *Professionally-run.* Mutual support, sharing and education. Partners welcome. Meets 2nd Mon., 7pm, The Cancer Institute of NJ, 195 Little Albany St., New Brunswick. Call 732-235-6781 (day).

Living with Cancer (Staying on Track) Support Group *Professionally-run.* Mutual support for anyone who has been diagnosed with cancer, to help them gain control over their lives through better knowledge of the disease. Family and friends welcome. Meets 2nd and 4th Wed., 7pm, Cancer Institute of NJ, 195 Little Albany St., 2nd Floor Waiting Room, New Brunswick. Must register first. Call 732-235-7557 (day).

290

Northern NJ Chapter Leukemia and Lymphoma Society *Professionally-run.* Emotional support for adult patients and family members where there has been a diagnosis of leukemia, lymphoma, Hodgkin's disease or multiple myeloma. Mutual sharing, guest speakers and education. Meets 2nd Mon., 1pm, Cancer Institute of NJ, 2nd Floor Learning Room, 195 Little Albany St., New Brunswick. Before attending call 732-235-7011.

Prostate Cancer Support Group *Professionally-run.* Mutual support for men with prostate cancer to share common experiences and learn more about prostate cancer. Open to families and friends. Meets 4th Mon., (except July/Aug.), 2pm, Cancer Institute of NJ, 195 Little Albany St., New Brunswick. Call Ellen Levine 732-235-6781 (day).

STEPS (Skills To Empower People) *Professionally-run.* Educational program for cancer patients, families and friends that focuses on ways to cope with various aspects of dealing with cancer. Guest speakers, literature and newsletter. Meeting days and times vary, The Cancer Institute of NJ, 195 Little Albany St., New Brunswick. For meeting information call Nursing Education Dept. 732-235-8784 (day).

Strength For Caring *Professionally-run.* Support, education and coping skills to families caring for a loved one with cancer. Meets 4th Tues., 7pm, Cancer Institute, 2nd Floor Learning Room, 195 Little Albany St., New Brunswick. To register call 732-235-6027 or 732-235-6792 (day).

MONMOUTH

Cancer Caregivers Support Group *Professionally-run.* Mutual support for caregivers of cancer patients. Offers encouragement and coping skills. Meets 2nd Mon., 7:30-9:30pm, Riverview Medical Center, Booker Cancer Center, 1 Riverview Plaza, Red Bank. Call 732-530-2382 (day).

Colorectal Cancer Support Support for people to actively participate in healing after a cancer diagnosis. Open to friends and family. Meets 1st Wed., 7:30-9pm, Goldsmith Wellness Center, 4th Floor, Monmouth Medical Center, 300 Second Ave., Long Branch. Call Jan Tryba 732-923-7711 (day).

Inner Circle *Professionally-run.* Mutual support for cancer patients, survivors, their families and caregivers. Meets Wed., 7:30-9:30pm, Jersey Shore University Medical Center, Ambulatory Care Center, 1945 Route 33, Neptune. Call 1-888-538-8314.

Ovarian Cancer Support Group Support for women with ovarian, cervical, uterine and endometrial cancer. Meets 1st and 3rd Tues., 11:30am-1:30pm, Jersey Shore University Medical Center, Ambulatory Care Center, Cancer Conference Room, 1945 Corlies Ave., (Route 33), Neptune. Call 1-800-560-9990.

Partners in Healing Support Group *Professionally-run.* Mutual support for spouses/significant others of women diagnosed with breast cancer, cervical, endometrial, ovarian and uterine cancer. Meets 3rd Tues., 7:00-8:30pm, Cancer Center Conference Room, Ambulatory Care Pavilion, Jersey Shore Medical Center, Neptune. Before attending call 1-800-560-9990 (day).

Us Too (Prostate Cancer Support Group) Mutual support for men who have prostate cancer. Family members are welcome.

> **Long Branch** Meets 1st Thurs, 7-9pm, Monmouth Medical Center. For registration, location and directions call Cancer Services 732-923-6575.
> **Neptune** Meets 3rd Thurs., 7-9pm, Neptune Housing Authority, 19 Davis Ave., Community Room. Call Jersey Shore Cancer Center 1-888-538-8314 (day).

Young People Have Feelings Too *Professionally-run.* Support group held in a family setting for youths (age 5-17) who have an immediate family member with cancer. Meets for 8 consecutive sessions in Neptune. Before attending call 1-888-538-8314.

MORRIS

Children's Group *Professionally-run.* Provides support to children (age 6-12) dealing with family issues of cancer. Group meets for 8 week sessions. Parents group meets concurrently. For information call Brandy Johnson 973-625-6176 (day).

Head And Neck Cancer Support for any person afflicted with head and neck cancer. Meets 3rd Wed., 1:30-3pm, Carol G. Simon Cancer Center, Morristown Memorial Hospital, 100 Madison Ave., Morristown. Call Catherine Owens, LCSW 973-971-5169.

Living with Cancer *Professionally-run.* Support and information for people with cancer, their families and supportive friends to help them adjust. Meets 2nd and 4th Wed., 7-8:30pm, Saint Clare's Hospital, Urban 2 Conference Center, Pocono Rd., Denville. Call Brandy 973-625-6176 (day). *Email:* bjohnson@saintclares.org

If you are using this book past Spring 2007, please call us for information about our most recent directory. 1-800-367-6274

Lung Cancer Support Group Support for people at any stage of lung cancer. Spouses are welcome. Meets 4th Wed., 2-3:30pm, Carol G. Simon Cancer Center, Morristown Memorial Hospital, Morristown. Call Catherine Owens, LCSW 973-971-5169.

Northern NJ Chapter Leukemia and Lymphoma Society *Professionally-run.* Emotional support for adult patients and family members where there has been a diagnosis of leukemia, lymphoma, Hodgkin's disease or multiple myeloma. Mutual sharing, guest speakers and education. Meets 10:30am, 6 week sessions, 4 times/yr., Morristown Memorial Hospital, Carol G. Simon Conference Center, Morristown. Before attending call Deborah Halpern, MSW 908-654-9445 (day). *Website:* http://www.LLS.org/nj *Email:* halpernd@LLS.org

Tri-County New Voice Laryngectomee Support Group of Morris/Sussex/Warren Counties. Mutual support and social activities for laryngectomees. Also includes neck, head and or oral cancers. Family and friends are welcome. Meets 2nd Mon. (except Jan., Feb., Mar., July, Aug.), 7:15pm, Saint Clare's Hospital, Silby Hall, 25 Pocono Rd., Denville. Call Doris Rapisardi 973-316-1993 (day) or Tom Beneventine 973-694-8417 (day).

Us Too (Prostate Cancer Support Group) *Professionally-run.* Education and support for prostate cancer survivors and their supportive family members and friends.

> **Denville** Meets 2nd Tues., (except July/ Aug.), 7:30-9pm, Saint Clare's Hospital, Silby Cafeteria, 25 Pocono Rd. Before attending call Ron 973-927-0534.
> **Morristown** Meets 1st Tues., 7:30-9:30pm, Morristown Memorial Hospital, Malcolm Forbes Amphitheater, 100 Madison Ave. Call Bill Grassmyer 973-895-2135 or Catherine Owens, LCSW 973-971-5169 (day).

Woman to Woman Mutual support for women living with cancer. Meets 1st and 3rd Tues., 2-3:30pm, Chilton Memorial Hospital, Collins Pavilion, 97 West Parkway, Pompton Plains. Call 973-831-5311 (Mon.-Fri.).

OCEAN

Cancer Concern Center Support for those coping with cancer. Family and friends welcome. Yoga, meditation, wigs and phone help free of charge. Meets Wed., 6:30-9pm, 1101 Richmond Ave., Route 35 South, Point Pleasant. Call 732-701-0250.

New Beginnings Cancer Support Organization Mutual support for persons with cancer, their families and friends. Under 18 welcome. Meets Wed., 6:30-8:30pm, Leisure Park, 1400 Route 70 West, Lakewood. Call Gloria 732-255-5940.

Prostate Cancer Support Group Provides support and education for men and their families diagnosed with prostate cancer. Meets 3rd Thurs., 2pm, The Lighthouse, 591 Lakehurst Rd., Toms River. Call 1-800-621-0096 (day) or John Wuiff 732-905-3717 (day).

PASSAIC

W.A.S.O.C. (We Are Survivors of Cancer) *Professionally-run.* Support group for cancer survivors. Meets 2nd Wed., 1pm, (Sept.-June), St. Mary's Hospital, 211 Pennington Ave., Passaic. Call Center for Senior Care 973-470-3050 (day).

SOMERSET

Cancer Support Groups *Professionally-run.* Provides support for cancer patients and their families. Sharing of feelings and concerns. Education, guest speakers, buddy system and phone help. Meets various times and days, Wellness Community, 3 Crossroads Dr., Bedminster. Call Pamela Pitchell or Karen Larsen 908-658-5400 (day). *Website:* http://www.thewellnesscommunity.org/cnj

SUSSEX

Cancer Support Group *Professionally-run.* Mutual support and education for cancer patients, their families and friends. Meets last Tues., 6:30pm, Newton Memorial Hospital, Conference Room B, Newton. Call Joseph Vishak or Sue 973-579-8620 (day).

Life After Cancer Support Group *Professionally-run.* Support and education for those with cancer at any stage, their families and friends. Meets last Tues., 6:30pm, Newton Memorial Hospital, 175 High St., Newton. Call Social Work Dept. 973-579-8620.

Lymphoma Support Group *Professionally-run.* Support for patients affected by lymphoma, their families and friends. Rap sessions and guest speakers. Meets last Wed., 6:30-8pm, Sparta Cancer Center, Sparta. Before attending call Kathryn Cramer or Nina Sullivan 973-726-0005 (day). *Website:* http://www.LLS.org/nnj

"Man to Man" Prostate Cancer Support Group An educational, information sharing and emotional support group designed to meet the challenge of living with prostate cancer for men and their partner. Educational series, literature and guest speakers. Meets 3rd Tues., 6:30-8:30pm, Sparta Health and Wellness Center, 89 Sparta Ave., Sparta. Call Michele Capossela 973-331-3794 ext. 118 (day). *Email:* Michele.capossela@cancer.org

Northern NJ Chapter Leukemia and Lymphoma Society *Professionally-run.* Emotional support for adult patients and family members where there has been a diagnosis of lymphoma. Mutual sharing, guest speakers and education. Meets last Wed., 6:30-8pm, Sparta Cancer Center, 89 Sparta Ave., Sparta. Before attending call Deborah Halpern, MSW 908-654-9445 (day). *Website:* http://www.LLS.org/nj *Email:* halpernd@LLS.org

UNION

Breast / Gynecological Cancer Support Support for women afflicted with breast or any gynecological cancer. Meetings vary, Pathways, 79 Maple St., Summit. Pre-registration required. Before attending call 908-273-4242 ext. 154.

Hearts and Hands *Professionally-run.* An open drop-in cancer support group offering patients and caregivers the opportunity to support each other. Members may knit, crochet or do other crafts while meeting. Meets Thurs., 2-4pm, Overlook Hospital, 99 Beauvoir Ave., Conference Room 1, Summit. Call Lee Anne Caffrey 908-522-5349 (day) or Kristen Scarlett 908-522-5255 (day).

Insight *Professionally-run.* Support for cancer patients and their families to talk about problems and issues in dealing with cancer. Meets 3rd Thurs., 7-9pm, Jewish Community Center, 1391 Martine Ave., Scotch Plains. Call Mary Aloia 732-321-7769 (day) or JCC 908-889-8800.

NATIONAL

Cancer Care, Inc. *National. Founded 1944.* Support for cancer patients and their families. Financial assistance, information & referrals, community and professional education. On-going telephone and in-person support groups. Free counseling. Write: Cancer Care, Inc., 275 Seventh Ave., New York, NY 10001. Call 1-800-813-4673; Fax: 212-719-0263. *Website:* http://www.cancercare.org *Email:* info@cancercare.org

Candlelighters Childhood Cancer Foundation *International. 300+ groups. Founded 1970.* Support for parents of children and adolescents with cancer, their families, adult survivors of childhood cancer and the professionals working with them. Links parents, families and groups. Provides psychosocial support, educational resource materials and advocates on behalf of childhood cancer. Newsletter, youth newsletter, educational materials and publication list. Write:

Candlelighters Childhood Cancer Foundation, PO Box 498, Kensington, MD 20895-0498. Call 1-800-366-2223 or 301-962-3520; Fax: 301-962-3521. *Website:* http://www.candlelighters.org *Email:* staff@candlelighters.org

Children's Cause for Cancer Advocacy, The., Inc. *National resource. Founded 1999.* Advocacy group focused on pediatric cancer drug discovery and development, expanding resources for research and treatment and addressing needs and concerns of survivors. Collaborates with other non-profits concerned about children with cancer. Provides national forum and information resources and addresses policy issues after care and treatment. Offers newsletter, referrals and phone support. Write: The Children's Cause for Cancer Advocacy, 1010 Wayne Ave., Suite 770, Silver Spring, MD 20910. Call 301-562-2765; Fax: 301-565-9670. *Website:* http://www.childrenscause.org *Email:* questions@childrenscause.org

Colorectal Cancer Network *National. Founded 1999. 5 affiliated groups.* Support, education and advocacy for colorectal cancer survivors and their caregivers. Peer-to-peer support groups, extensive website library of online links and resources. Group development guidelines available. Write: Colorectal Cancer Network, PO Box 182, Kensington, MD 20895-0182. Call 301-879-1500; Fax: 301-879-1901. *Website:* http://www.colorectal-cancer.net *Email:* ccnetwork@colorectal-cancer.net

DES Action USA *National. Founded 1977.* Support for women who took DES during pregnancy and their children. Support groups, physician referrals, education for the public and health workers. Quarterly newsletter. Group development guidelines. Write: DES Action U.S.A., 158 S. Stanwood Rd., Columbus, OH 43209. Call 1-800-337-9288. *Website:* http://www.desaction.org *Email:* desaction@columbus.rr.com

DES Cancer Network National. *Founded 1983.* Mutual support and education for DES-exposed women, with a special focus on DES cancer issues. Provides research advocacy and medical/legal resources. Newsletter. Write: DES Cancer Network, PO Box 220465, Chantilly, VA 20153-0465. *Website:* http://www.descancer.org *Email:* desnetwrk@aol.com

IMPACC (Intestinal Multiple Polyposis And Colorectal Cancer) *National network. Founded 1986.* Support network to help patients & families dealing with familial polyposis and hereditary colon cancer. Provides information and referrals, encourages research and educates professionals & public. Phone support network, correspondence and literature. Write: IMPACC, PO Box 11, Conyngham, PA 18219. Call Ann Fagan 570-788-1818 (day) or 570-788-3712 (eve); Fax: 570-788-4046. *Email:* impacc@epix.net

International Myeloma Foundation *International network.. Helps support over 72 myeloma support groups in the US. Founded 1990.* Mission is to improve the quality of life of myeloma patients while working toward a cure. Educational and supportive programs, information packets, phone support, newsletter. Networks patients together for mutual support. Referrals to self-help groups nationwide. Guidelines offered to assist those interested in starting a group. Write: Int'l Myeloma Foundation, 12650 Riverside Dr., Suite 206, North Hollywood, CA 91607. Call 818-487-7455 or 1-800-452-2873; Fax: 818-487-7454. *Website:* http://www.myeloma.org *Email:* TheIMF@myeloma.org

Kidney Cancer Association *National. Founded 1990.* Provides information about kidney cancer to patients and doctors. Sponsors research and advocates on behalf of patients. Newsletter, information and referrals, literature, conferences. Write: Kidney Cancer Assn., 1234 Sherman, Suite 203, Evanston, IL 60202. Call 1-800-850-9132 or 847-332-1051; Fax: 847-332-2978. *Website:* http://www.kidneycancerassociation.org *Email:* office@curekidneycancer.org

Kids Konnected *National. 17 affiliated groups. Founded 1993.* Opportunity for children who have a parent with cancer, to connect with other children in similar situations for support and understanding. Groups are headed by youth leaders and co-facilitated by professionals. Hotline, Youth Leadership program, monthly meetings, information and referrals, newsletter, summer camps. Call 1-800-899-2866 or 949-582-5443 (24 hrs). *Website:* http://www.kidskonnected.org *Email:* info@kidskonnected.org

Leukemia and Lymphoma Society, The. *National. 66 chapters. Founded 1949.* Educational materials, patient financial aid, support services for patients, families and friends coping with leukemia, lymphoma, myeloma and other blood cancers. Support group meeting schedule depends on location. Patients should consult local chapter. Live help online 10 - 5 ET. Write: LLS, 1311 Mamaroneck Ave., 3rd Floor, White Plains, NY 10605. Call 1-800-955-4572 or 914-949-5213; Fax: 914-949-6691. *Website:* http://www.lls.org *Email:* infocenter@lls.org

Lymphoma Research Foundation *20 chapters. Founded 1991.* Nation's largest lymphoma-focused voluntary health organization devoted exclusively to funding lymphoma research and providing patients and healthcare professionals with critical information on the disease. Provides information and emotional support for lymphoma patients and their families. Offers free educational materials, lymphoma helpline, national buddy program, quarterly newsletter, annual patient educational forum and local seminars. Fundraises for research. Advocacy. Write: Lymphoma Research Fdn., 8800 Venice Blvd., Suite 207, Los Angeles, CA 90034. Call 310-204-7040 or 1-800-500-9976; Fax: 310-204-7043. *Website:* http://www.lymphoma.org *Email:* LRF@lymphoma.org

Man To Man Program *National. 300 affiliated groups. Founded 1990.* Support and education for men with prostate cancer to enable them to better understand their options and to make informed decisions. Phone support, information and referrals, support group meetings, education and support visitation program. Newsletter. Some chapters invite wives and partners; other chapters have wives and partners meet separately. Assistance available for starting new groups. Call American Cancer Society 1-800-227-2345. *Website:* http://www.cancer.org

Mautner Project, the National Lesbian Health Organization *Model. Several groups in Washington, DC. Founded 1990.* Mutual support for lesbians with cancer, their partners and caregivers as well as for lesbians whose family member has died (partner, parent, child, etc.) Also provides smoking cessation groups. Helps educate health professionals about working with lesbians with cancer. Educates the lesbian community about risks of cancer and prevention issues. Information and referrals, phone support, literature, newsletter, advocacy. Write: Mautner Project, National Lesbian Health Org., 1707 L St. NW, Suite 230, Washington, DC 20036. Call 1-866-628-8637 or 202-332-5536 (day), Fax: 202-332-0662. *Website:* http://www.mautnerproject.org *Email:* mautner@mautnerproject.org

National Coalition for Cancer Survivorship *National network. Founded 1986.* Grassroots network that works on behalf of persons with any type of cancer. Mission is to advocate for quality of cancer care for all Americans by leading and strengthening the survivorship movement, empowering cancer survivors and advocating for policy issues affecting survivors' quality of life. Write: NCCS , 1010 Wayne Ave., 7th Floor , Silver Spring, MD 20910. Call 1-877-622-7937 Fax: 301-565-9670 *Website:* http//:www.canceradvocacy.org *Email:* info@canceradvocacy.org

PAACT Patient Advocates for Advanced Cancer Treatment *International. 150 affiliated groups. Founded 1984.* Provides support and advocacy for prostate cancer patients, their families and the general public at risk. Information relative to the advancements in the detection, diagnosis, evaluation and treatment of prostate cancer. Information, referrals, phone help, conferences, newsletter. Group development guidelines. Write: PAACT, PO Box 141695, Grand Rapids, MI 49514-1695. Call 616-453-1477; Fax: 616-453-1846. *Website:* http://www.paactusa.org *Email:* paact@paactusa.org

People Living Through Cancer *Model. 35 groups in New Mexico. Founded 1983.* Helps cancer survivors and their loved ones make informed choices and improve the quality of life by sharing in a community of people who have "been there." Dues $35/yr. (includes subscription to journal). Conducts national training for American Indians and Alaskan natives who are interested in developing cancer survivorship programs based on a grassroots program serving Pueblo Indians. Write: People Living Through Cancer, 3939 San Pedro Blvd. NE, Suite C-8, Albuquerque, NM 87110. Call 505-242-3263; Fax: 505-242-6756. *Website:* http://www.pltc.org *Email:* pltc@pltc.org

Pregnant with Cancer Network *National. Founded 1997.* Created by three women who were diagnosed with cancer while pregnant. Mission is to let women know that they are not alone facing cancer and pregnancy. Links women together who have a similar diagnosis. Newsletter. Write: Pregnant with Cancer Network, PO Box 1243, Buffalo, NY 14420. Call 1-800-743-4471 *Website:* http://www.pregnantwithcancer.org

SHARE: Self-Help for Women with Breast or Ovarian Cancer *(BILINGUAL) Model. 18 sites in NY Metro Area. Founded 1976.* Provides support to women with breast or ovarian cancer, their families and friends. Support groups led by trained survivors. Programs in various locations throughout New York City and in North Brunswick, NJ. Write: SHARE, 1501 Broadway, Suite 704A, New York, NY 10036. Call 1-866-891-2392; Breast Hotline: 212-382-2111; Ovarian Hotline: 212-719-1204; Latina Hotline (in Spanish): 212-719-4454 (all hotlines are staffed by trained cancer survivors and available day/eve); Fax: 212-869-3431. *Website:* http://www.sharecancersupport.org

SPOHNC (Support for People with Oral & Head & Neck Cancer) *National. 37 affiliated groups. Founded 1991.* Patient-directed self-help program offering encouragement, support, acceptance and self-expression for persons with oral and head and neck cancer. Offers small group meetings, phone support, educational programs, newsletter, one-on-one support, local chapters and information and referrals. Assistance in starting groups. Membership dues $25 (includes 9 newsletters). Write: SPOHNC, PO Box 53, Locust Valley, NY 11560-0053. Call 1-800-377-0928; Fax: 516-671-8794. *Website:* http://www.spohnc.org *Email:* info@spohnc.org

ThyCa: Thyroid Cancer Survivors' Association, Inc. *National.* Support, education and communication for people with all types of thyroid cancer, as well as their caregivers. Outreach to the public for thyroid cancer awareness and early detection. Nine online support groups, local support groups, free online newsletter, free downloadable low-iodine cookbook, free regional workshops, annual international conference, free thyroid cancer awareness brochures, Thyroid Cancer Awareness Month, funding for research and educational website. Write: ThyCa: Thyroid Cancer Survivors' Association, Inc., PO Box 1545, New York, NY 10159-1545. Call 1-877-588-7904; Fax: 630-604-6078. *Website:* http://www.thyca.org *Email:* thyca@thyca.org

Us TOO International Prostate Cancer Education & Support *International. 350+ affiliated groups. Founded 1990.* Education and support provided for men and their families with fellowship, peer counseling and timely, personalized, unbiased and reliable information about prostate cancer. Monthly newsletter distributed through support groups and also on website. Write: Us Too Int'l Prostate Cancer Education & Support, 5003 Fairview Ave., Downers Grove, IL 60515-5286. Call 1-800-808-7866 or 630-795-1002 (day); Fax: 630-795-1602. *Website:* http://www.ustoo.org *Email:* ustoo@ustoo.org

ONLINE

ACOR Association of Cancer Online Resources *Online.* Provides information in over 130 online communities each related to different types of cancer, with an emphasis on rare types of cancer. Also provides contacts for caregivers. Hosts a large collection of high quality patient websites. Write: ACOR, 173 Duane St., Suite 3A, New York, NY 10013-3334. Call 212-226-5525; Fax: 212-219-3109. *Website:* http://www.acor.org

Cancer and Careers *Online.* A resource for working women with cancer, their employers, co-workers and caregivers. Offers first-hand experiences and articles for working women with cancer. Provides resource information and publications via the website. Also provides extensive information for employers, coworkers, families and caregivers. *Website:* http://www.cancerandcareers.org *Email:* ksweeney@cew.org

Group Loop *Online.* Support for teens with cancer and their parents. Weekly scheduled online support groups with professionals, discussion boards, resources, information and news about many types of cancers and their affect on teens. *Website:* http://www.grouploop.org

FORCE (Facing Our Risk of Cancer Empowered) *Online. Founded 1999.* Support and education for women whose family history and genetic status put them at high risk of getting ovarian or breast cancer. Open to family members. Provides resources for women to determine if they are at high risk. Forums, chats, bulletin boards, member profiles. Phone support network. Write: FORCE Sue Friedman, 934 N. University Dr., PMB #213, Coral Springs, FL 33071. Call 954-255-8732 or 1-866-824-7475; Fax: 954-827-2200. *Website:* http://www.facingourrisk.org/

Johns Hopkins Disease Information *Online.* Provides information and support to cancer patients and their families. Specific cancer websites include those for colon, pancreas, ovarian, gallbladder and bile duct. Also has a message board for Barrett's esophagus and non-cancerous conditions. On website select condition from drop down menu *Website:* http://www.pathology2.jhu.edu/department/patientcare.cfm

CELIAC SPRUE /
GLUTEN INTOLERANCE

BERGEN

American Celiac Society - Bergen County Chapter Phone support for people with celiac disease. Call Laurie Schlussel 201-573-0397 (day/eve).

Celiac Disease Support Group for Parents *Professionally-run.* Information, sharing, mutual support and education for parents of children with celiac disease. Families welcome. Rap sessions, guest speakers, literature and quarterly newsletter. Meets 1st Wed., 11am-noon and 1st Thurs., 6-7pm, Don Imus Pediatric Center, Hackensack University Medical Center, Room PC 347, Hackensack. Call Joseph Chan, LCSW 201-336-8845 (day).

CAMDEN

Celiac Sprue Association *(Southern New Jersey Chapter)* Mutual support and information to persons diagnosed with celiac sprue (gluten sensitive enteropathy), dermatitis herpetiformis and parents of celiac children. Guest speakers, rap sessions, literature, phone help. Annual dues $20/yr./new members/$15/yr./thereafter. Meets 1st Sun., (except July/Aug.), 2pm, West Jersey Hospital, Barry Brown Health Education Ctr., Evesham Rd. and Carnie Blvd., Voorhees. For meeting information call Patti Townsend 856-854-5508 (eve) or Bill Lucas 609-387-7139. *Website:* http://www.home.earthlink.net/~celiac9/index.html *Email:* celiac9@earthlink.net

ESSEX

ROCK (Raising Our Celiac Kids) Support for parents of children with celiac sprue. Guest speakers, literature, phone help. Activities and events for children and young adults. Meetings vary, Millburn Library, 200 Glen Ave., Millburn. For meeting information call Ellie Fried 973-912-0253 (day/eve). *Website:* http://www.celiackids.com

MIDDLESEX

Central NJ Celiac Sprue and D.H. Support Group Dietary support for persons with celiac sprue and dermatitis herpetiformis. Also Cel-Kids Network. Dues $20/yr. Meetings vary, East Brunswick Library, East Brunswick. Before attending call Diane Paley 732-679-6566 (day/eve). *Website:* http://www.csaceliacs.org

MONMOUTH

ROCKS (Raising our Celiac Kids Support) Support group for parents of children with celiac sprue. Events planned, activities for school-aged children. Meets 7-8:45pm, meetings vary, Monmouth County Library, Summers Rd., Manalapan. Call Sue 732-462-4660. *Email:* susancav@aol.com

WARREN

Celiac Sprue Association/Gluten Free 101 Support Group Support group dedicated to helping those with celiac disease and its complication, dermatitis herpetiformis, learn to live safely on the gluten free diet. Literature, speakers bureau, advocacy, social and phone help. Meets 2nd Wed., 7:30-9:30pm, Warren Hospital, Farley Education Center, Phillipsburg. Call Gary Powers 610-438-0205 (eve). *Website:* http://www.csaceliacs.org *Email:* gppowers14@earthlink.net

NATIONAL

American Celiac Society / Dietary Support Coalition *National. 78 affiliated chapters. Founded 1976.* Mutual support and information for celiac-sprue patients, families and health care professionals. Buddy system, visitation, phone help system, participation in educational efforts. Also supports dermatitis herpetiformis, Crohn's disease, lactose intolerance, & other food allergies. Newsletter. Write: American Celiac Society, c/o Annette Bentley, PO Box 23455, New Orleans, LA 70183-0455. Call Annette Bentley 504-737-3293. *Website:* http://www.americanceliacsociety.org *Email:* amerceliacsociety@yahoo.com

Celiac Disease Foundation *National. Founded 1990.* Creates awareness and provides services and support for patients and professionals seeking information about celiac disease/dermatitis herpetiformis. Free information packets. Quarterly newsletter included with annual membership. Information is available in Spanish. Write: Celiac Disease Foundation, 13251 Ventura Blvd., Suite 1, Studio City, CA 91604. Call 818-990-2354 (day); Fax: 818-990-2379. *Website:* http://www.celiac.org *Email:* cdf@celiac.org

Celiac Sprue Association/United States of America, Inc. *National. 100 chapters and 50 resource units. Founded 1969.* Provides educational materials on celiac sprue, dermatitis herpetiformis and basics for a gluten-free diet for patients, parents of children and professionals. Provides opportunities for support groups and networking with patients and professionals. Newsletter, annual conference. Group development guidelines. Write: Celiac Sprue Association USA, PO Box 31700, Omaha, NE 68131. Call 1-877-272-4272 or 402-558-0600; Fax: 402-558-1347. *Website:* http://www.csaceliac.org *Email:* celiacs@csaceliacs.org

Gluten Intolerance Group of North America *National network. 30+ affiliated groups. Founded 1974.* Mission is to increase awareness by providing accurate and up-to-date information, education and support to persons with gluten intolerance, celiac disease/dermatitis herpetiformis, their families, health care professionals and the general public. Offers news magazine ($35), information and referral, conferences, guidance to those starting groups, group development guidelines and cookbooks. Write: Gluten Intolerance Group, 15110 10th Ave. SW, Suite A, Seattle, WA 98166-1820. Call 206-246-6652; Fax: 206-246-6531. *Website:* http://www.gluten.net *Email:* info@gluten.net

CHRONIC FATIGUE SYNDROME

STATEWIDE

NJ Chronic Fatigue Syndrome Association, Inc. Support for people with chronic fatigue syndrome. All welcome. Educational series, guest speakers, speakers bureau, advocacy, social group, literature, medical conferences, phone help. Newsletter $25/yr. Support groups throughout New Jersey in Atlantic, Bergen, Mercer, Middlesex, Monmouth and Union counties. Call Lon Smith 609-219-0662. *Website:* http://www.njcfsa.org

ATLANTIC

Atlantic County Chronic Fatigue Syndrome Support Group Offers emotional support and share the latest information on chronic fatigue syndrome for those afflicted as well as their families (under 18 welcome). Doctor referrals available. Rap sessions, guest speakers, phone help. Meets 2nd Sun., 2-4pm, (except July/Aug.), Atlantic City Medical Center, Mainland Division, Jimmie Leeds Rd., Pomona. Call Betty Mc Connell 609-748-3559 (eve). *Website:* http://www.njcfsa.org *Email:* elizabethmcconn@cs.com

BERGEN

Chronic Fatigue Syndrome Association Support Group Education support and mutual assistance for patients with chronic fatigue syndrome, their family and friends and interested professionals. Meets 3rd Sun., 2pm, Pascack Valley Hospital, Old Hook Road, Auditorium, Westwood. Call Anne 201-244-5188. *Email:* AnnieLaurie617@yahoo.com

MERCER

Chronic Fatigue Syndrome Support Group of Mercer County Mutual support, education and sharing of resources for persons with chronic fatigue syndrome, their families, caregivers and friends. Literature. Some social activities. Meets 2nd Sun., 2-4pm, Robert Wood Johnson University Hospital at Hamilton, 1 Hamilton Health Place, Hamilton. For information call 609-584-5900 ext. 1.

MIDDLESEX

Chronic Fatigue Syndrome Group Support and education for chronic fatigue syndrome patients and their families. Guest speakers, rap sessions, phone help. Meets 2nd Sun., 12:30pm, Robert Wood Johnson University Hospital, Board Room, New Brunswick. Call 609-219-0662.

WARREN

Fibromyalgia and Chronic Fatigue Support Group Provides education and support for those with fibromyalgia or chronic fatigue syndrome. Meets 1st Thurs., 7pm, (except July, Aug., Sept.), Warren Hospital, 185 Roseberry St., Farley Education Center, Phillipsburg. Before attending call 908-859-6735 (day).

NATIONAL

CFIDS Association, Inc. *National. Founded 1987.* Advocacy, information and encouragement for persons with chronic fatigue immune dysfunction syndrome. Publishes the CFIDS Chronicle newsletter ($35/US; $45/Canada; $60/Overseas/Air) and Research Newsletter. Write: The CFIDS Association, PO Box 220398, Charlotte, NC 28222-0398. Call 704-365-2343 (resources). *Website:* http://www.cfids.org *Email:* cfids@cfids.org

CLEFT PALATE

MONMOUTH

Cleft Palate Support Group *Professionally-run.* Support group for parents of children with cleft palates or cleft lips providing a forum for discussing shared concerns and exploring resources. Meets 2nd Thurs., 7-8pm, Monmouth Medical Center, Long Branch. Registration required. Call Helene Henkel 732-923-7653.

NATIONAL

Cleft Palate Foundation *National network. Founded 1973.* Provides information and referrals to individuals with cleft lip and palate or other craniofacial anomalies. Referrals to local cleft palate/craniofacial teams for treatment and to local parent support groups. Free information on various aspects of clefting for parents and individuals. Write: Cleft Palate Fdn., 1504 E.

Franklin St., Suite 102, Chapel Hill, NC 27514. Call 1-800-242-5338 or 919-933-9044; Fax: 919-933-9604. *Website:* http://www.cleftline.org *Email:* info@cleftline.org

Prescription Parents, Inc. *Model. Founded 1973.* Support group for families of children with cleft lip and palate. Education for parents of newborns, presentations by professionals. Family social events, phone support network, group development guidelines. Write: Prescription Parents, Inc., PO Box 920554, Needham, MA 02492. Call 617-499-1936. *Website:* www.prescriptionparents.org

ONLINE

cleftAdvocate *Online.* Resource for educational materials, cleft/craniofacial team information, emotional support and more. Local and regional family networking for parents, kids, teens and adults. Hosts the North American Craniofacial Family Conference for individuals and families dealing with all craniofacial conditions, including acquired facial differences (trauma, illness and disease). Write: cleftAdvocate, PO Box 751112, Las Vegas, NV, 89136. Call 702-769-9264; Fax: 702-341-5351. *Website:* http://www.cleftadvocate.org *Email:* Debbie@cleftadvocate.org

Wide Smiles *Online.* Support, inspiration, information and networking for families dealing with the challenges associated with clefting. Sharing of struggles, joys and triumphs. Referrals to doctors. Write: Wide Smiles, PO Box 5153, Stockton, CA 95205-0153. Call 209-942-2812; Fax: 209-464-1497. *Website:* http://www.widesmiles.org

CYSTIC FIBROSIS

MONMOUTH

Cystic Fibrosis Parent Support Group *Professionally-run.* Support and education for parents and adult caregivers of children who have cystic fibrosis. Meetings vary, Monmouth Medical Center, Long Branch. For registration and meeting information call Carol Porter 732-222-4474 (day).

STATEWIDE

New Jersey CF Family Network Telephone network that provides mutual support for parents of children with cystic fibrosis. Up-to-date news regarding all aspects of CF including new treatments, equipment and physicians. Call Jean Gaito 973-492-3868 (day/eve) or Carol Russo 201-265-3503. *Email:* jcgaito@msn.com

NATIONAL

Cystic Fibrosis Foundation *National. 80 affiliated groups. Founded 1955.* Provides information and referrals to patients, families, caregivers and the general public. Accredits more than 115 care centers throughout the United States. Fundraising. Provides grants to researchers. Newsletter, literature, conferences. Write: Cystic Fibrosis Foundation, 6931 Arlington Rd., Bethesda, MD 20814. Call 1-800-344-4823; Fax: 301-951-6378. *Website:* http://www.cff.org *Email:* info@cff.org

DIABETES
(see also toll-free helplines)

STATEWIDE

American Diabetes Association *(Northern NJ Area Office) Professionally-run.* Support and educational programs for persons with diabetes and families, professionals and public. Referrals to local groups and education programs. Adult and youth discussion groups; fund-raising for research. Write: American Diabetes Association, 19 Schoolhouse Rd., Somerset, NJ 08873. Call 732-469-7979; *Website:* http://www.diabetes.org

CARES (Connecting Area Resources with Education and Support) Juvenile Diabetes Research Foundation *(Mid-Jersey Chapter)* Support and educational programs for parents of children with Type 1 diabetes. Buddy system and phone help. Quarterly newsletter. Referrals to local chapter support groups. Covers: Hudson, Hunterdon, Mercer, Middlesex, Morris, Somerset. Write: C.A.R.E.S., c/o Juvenile Diabetes Research Foundation, 28 Kennedy Blvd., Suite 180, East Brunswick, NJ 08816-1248. Call Deborah Gingrich 732-296-7171 ext. 10. *Website:* http://www.jdrf.org *Email:* midjersey@jdrf.org

Juvenile Diabetes Research Foundation *(Central Jersey Chapter)* Support and educational programs for parents of children with Type 1 diabetes. Referrals to local chapter support groups. Covers: Essex, Union, Monmouth, Ocean. Write: Juvenile Diabetes Research Foundation, 740 Broad St., Shrewsbury, NJ 07702. Call 732-219-6654. *Website:* http://www.jdrf.org

Juvenile Diabetes Research Foundation *(Northern NJ Chapter)* Support and educational programs for parents of children with type 1 diabetes. Referrals to local chapter support groups. Covers Bergen, Passaic, Sussex, Warren, Rockland. Write: Juvenile Diabetes Research Foundation, 560 Sylvan Ave., Englewood, NJ 07632. Call 201-568-4838. *Website:* http://www.jdrf.org

ATLANTIC

Adult Diabetes Support *Professionally-run.* Provides information and support to individuals with diabetes. Education, guest speakers and literature. Meets 2nd Mon., 6-7pm, Shore Memorial Hospital, 1 East New York Ave., Somers Point. Call Meaghan Kim 609-653-3489 (day) or Fran Jerome 609-653-4516 (day).

BERGEN

Diabetes Support for Children and Their Families *Professionally-run.* Support for children up to age 18 with diabetes. Family members welcome. Discusses nutrition, school issues, new treatments. Guest speakers, rap sessions and education. Meets 2nd Tues., 7-9pm, (except July/Aug.), 15 Essex St., Paramus. Call Leslie Schifrien, MS, RD, CDE 201-291-6000 ext. 7116 (day) or Judy Brewer 201-447-6293 (day). *Email:* j.brewer.cde@gmail.com

Diabetes Support Group of Englewood Hospital and Medical Center *Professionally-run.* Support and education for persons with diabetes, their families and significant others. Teaches members to become self-sufficient in the daily management of their diabetes. Meets 4th Tues., 7-8:30pm, Englewood Hospital and Medical Center, 350 Engle St., Englewood. Call Diabetes Educator 201-894-3335 (day).

Holy Name Hospital Diabetes Program *Professionally-run.* Provides support and education for people with diabetes and their families. Meets 1st Wed., 7:30-9pm or last Wed., 2-3:30pm, Holy Name Hospital, 718 Teaneck Rd., Teaneck. Call Community Health Services 201-227-6250 (day).

Molly Diabetes Center Support Group *Professionally-run.* Mutual support for individuals with diabetes. Guest speakers. Meets 1st Mon., (except July and Aug.), 6-7pm, Hackensack University Medical Center, Diabetes Center, 211 Essex St., Suite 101, Hackensack. Call Judith Shanberg 201-968-0585 (day).

BURLINGTON

Diabetes Friends Support and education for those who have diabetes. Guest speakers, weight management, stress management, nutrition and mutual aid. Meets 1st Tues., (except July/Aug.), 7-8:30pm, Virtua Memorial Hospital, Conference Center, 175 Madison Ave., Mt. Holly. For meeting information call 1-888-847-8823 (day).

"A journey of a thousand miles must begin with a single step." --Lao-Tsu

CAMDEN

Diabetes Friends Voorhees Support and education for people with diabetes. Guest speakers, weight management, stress management, nutrition and mutual aid. Meets 2nd Tues., (except Jan., July, Aug.), 7-8:30pm, Virtua Health's Education Center, 106 Carnie Blvd., Voorhees. Call 1-888-847-8823 (day).

Diabetes Support Group Mutual support and education for adults with diabetes. Also has children and teen groups. Meets the 1st Tues., 7-9pm, Virtua Memorial Hospital, 175 Madison Ave., Mt. Holly or 2nd Tues., 7-9pm, Virtua Health, Barry D. Brown Health Education Center, 106 Carnie Blvd., Voorhees. Call Lois J. Gerst, RN 1-888-847-8823. *Website:* http://www.virtua.org

Diabetes Support Group *Professionally-run.* Group deals with daily life challenges related to having diabetes (both type I and II). Focuses on problem-solving and improving self-image and coping skills. Meets 4th Mon., 1-2:30pm, Kennedy Center, 1099 White Horse Road, Voorhees. Call Tanya Donovan 856-566-2096 (day) or 1-800-522-1965.

Kids Club and Parents Korner Mutual support for children with diabetes to help them better deal with their disease. Also group for parents of children with diabetes. Meets 2nd Wed., (except July/Aug.), 6:30-7:30pm, Virtua Health, Barry D. Brown Health Education Center, 106 Carnie Blvd., Voorhees. Call 1-888-847-8823 (day).

Teen Diabetes Support Group Support for teens age (13-19) with diabetes. Meets 4 times/yr. Virtua Health's Barry D. Brown Health Education Center, 106 Carnie Blvd., Voorhees. Call 1-888-847-8823 (day).

CUMBERLAND

Adult Diabetes Support Group *Professionally-run.* Mutual support for adults with type I or type II diabetes, their families, friends and caregivers. Phone help, guest speakers, rap sessions. Meets 1st Wed., 2pm, South Jersey Healthcare, 1505 West Sherman Ave., Vineland. Call Cathy Giovinazzi 856-641-7542. *Email:* giovinazzic@sjhs.com

Diabetes Trendsetters *Professionally-run.* Support and education for people with Type 1 diabetes who use insulin pumps or take several injections of insulin per day. Rap sessions, guest speakers, literature and phone help. Meets 4/times/yr, South Jersey Healthcare, 1505 West Sherman Ave., Vineland. For meeting information call Cathy Giovinazzi 856-641-7542 (day).

Pediatric Diabetes Support Group *Professionally-run.* Mutual support and education for children under the age of 12 who have diabetes. Call for meeting information. Call Cathy Giovinazzi 856-641-7542 (day). *Email:* giovinazzic@sjhs.com

South Jersey Healthcare/IMPACT Program *Professionally-run.* Educational support for kids who have diabetes, their family and friends. Mutual sharing group with educational opportunities, social activities, guest speakers and literature. Meets 6 times/year, 6:45-8:30pm, Impact Center, 1669 E. Landis Ave., Vineland. For meeting day and time call Donna Errett 856-691-4467, Cathy Giovinazzi 856-641-7542 or Eileen Niedzialek 856-641-7541.

ESSEX

Adult Diabetes Group *Professionally-run.* Support for adults with any type diabetes. Guest speakers, literature, education and mutual sharing. Meets 4th Wed., 10-11:00am, Mountainside Hospital, 1 Bay Ave., Montclair. Call 973-429-6305 or 1-800-247-9580 (day).

Diabetes at Newark Beth Israel Medical Center Support Group *Professionally-run.* Support group for people of all ages with any type of diabetes offering an open format for educational and emotional concerns. Meets monthly, Newark Beth Israel Medical Center, 201 Lyons Ave., Newark. Must pre-register. Call 973-926-3218 (day).

HUDSON

Diabetes Support Group *Professionally-run.* Provides support and education for adults with diabetes. Rap sessions, guest speakers. Meets various Thurs., Meadowlands Hospital, Secaucus. Before attending call Louise or Karen 201-392-3531 (day).

Diabetes Support Group of Bayonne *Professionally-run.* Support and education for people of all ages and ethnic backgrounds with type I and type II diabetes, as well as their families. Rap sessions, guest speakers. Meets 3rd Tues., 7pm, Community Crossings, 488 Broadway, Bayonne. Call 201-858-5219 (day).

HUNTERDON

Diabetes Education Series *Professionally-run.* Support and education in a comfortable environment for those with diabetes and their families to share feelings, listen and learn. Literature, guest speakers. Meets 2nd Thurs., 7-8pm, (except July/Aug.), Diabetes Health Center, 190 Highway 31, Suite 300, Flemington. Call Alicia Dougherty 908-788-6136.

Insulin Pump Support Group *Professionally-run.* Support for anyone, including friends and family, interested in or using insulin pump therapy as a treatment for diabetes. Meets 3rd Tues., 6-7pm, Diabetes Health Center, 190 Highway 31, Suite 300, Flemington. Call 908-788-6136.

MIDDLESEX

Adults with Diabetes *Professionally-run.* Support and education for persons with diabetes, their families and friends. Meets 1st Wed., 5-6:30pm, St. Peter's University Hospital, Medical Office Building, Conference Room 2, New Brunswick. Call Fansie Connelly 732-745-8600 ext. 8704 (day).

Diabetes Support Group Support, discussion and problem solving for persons with diabetes and their families. Meets various days, 7:30-8:30pm, Raritan Bay Medical Center, Perth Amboy and Old Bridge. For meeting information call Diabetes Center 732-360-4155 (day).

Diabetes Type 2 Support Group *Professionally-run.* Support for people affected with type 2 diabetes. Meets 1st Wed., 1:30pm and 7pm; Weight management meets 2nd and 4th Wed., 1:30pm and 7pm; Insulin pump group meets 2nd Tues., 7:15pm, JFK Medical Center, Edison. Call 1-800-991-6668 (day).

Stay On Target With Our Children Pump Group *Professionally-run.* Support and education for children with diabetes on or interested in insulin pumps (ages 11 and under). Meets monthly, 6:30-7:30pm, Saint Peters University Hospital, Ground Floor, MOB Conference Rooms, New Brunswick. Call Jody 732-745-8600 ext. 6565.

Teen Support Group For Teens With Pumps *Professionally-run.* Support and education for teens with diabetes on or interested in insulin pumps. Meets once a month, Saint Peter's Medical Center, New Brunswick. For meeting information call Jody 732-745-8600 ext. 6565.

MONMOUTH

Central Jersey Chapter Juvenile Diabetes Foundation Mutual support for insulin-dependent children and their parents to discuss solutions to the problems of day-to-day living with the disease. Meets 3rd Wed., (every other month), 7-8:30pm, Jersey Shore Medical Center, 2nd Floor, Ackerman Bldg., Conference Room 4, Neptune. For meeting information call Nancy 732-219-6654 (day).

Diabetes Insulin Pump Support Group *Professionally-run.* Support and mutual aid for any person on an insulin pump or contemplating using a pump. Meets bimonthly, Monmouth Medical Center, Long Branch. Call 732-923-6990.

Diabetes Support Group *Professionally-run.* Provides mutual support and education for adults with diabetes. Families welcome. Offers an open discussion, guest speakers. Mutual support for persons with diabetes who are on insulin injections and/or insulin pump. Learn about technology, discuss issues that affect their lives, educational series, literature and guest speakers. Meets Jan., Mar., May, July, Sept. and Nov., 7-8pm, Health Awareness Center, 65 Gibson Place, Freehold. Call Suzanne Khanna 732-294-2574 (day).

Diabetes Support Group *Professionally-run.* Provides mutual support and education for adults with diabetes. Families welcome. Offers an open discussion, guest speakers.

> **Freehold** Meets 3rd Mon., 10-11am, Health Awareness Center, 65 Gibson Place. Call Suzanne 732-294-2574.
> **Holmdel** Meeting times vary. Before attending call Kathleen Illingworth 732-888-7362 (day).
> **Long Branch** Meets 3rd Wed., 7:30-9pm, Monmouth Medical Center. Call 732-923-6990 (day).

Pediatric Insulin Pump Support Group *Professionally-run.* Support group for children using an insulin pump. Families and caregivers welcome. Meets in Long Branch. For meeting information call Gaye Madigan 732-932-7790.

MORRIS

Diabetes Support Group *Professionally-run.* Mutual support for adults with diabetes and their families. Groups meet 1st and 3rd Wed., 7:30-9pm, last Thurs., 10-11am and Spanish speaking on 2nd Thurs. 10 – 11:30 am. Saint Clare's Regional Diabetes Center, 400 W. Blackwell St., Dover. Call to confirm meeting times 973-989-3603 (day).

Diabetes Type 2 Support Group *Professionally-run.* Education and support for people (age 60+) with type 2 diabetes. Meets 1st Wed., 10-11am, Chilton Memorial Hospital, Collins Pavilion, 97 West Parkway, Pompton Plains. Call Joan Beloff 973-831-5167 (day) or Kathy Ferrara 973-831-5328 (day).

Insulin Pump Support Group *Professionally-run.* Mutual support for diabetics who use an insulin pump, families and professionals are welcome. Rap sessions, phone help, literature and guest speakers. Meets last Mon., 7:30-9pm, Saint Clare's

311

Regional Diabetes Center, 400 West Blackwell St., Dover. Before attending call 973-989-3603 (day).

Pump Continuing Education Group *Professionally-run.* Support for people living with diabetes. Mutual sharing, educational and updates on current medical treatments. Meets 1st Thurs., every other month, 7-8pm, Morristown Hospital Diabetes Center, Morristown. Call Carol Lacko 973-971-5524.

Type 2 Continuing Education *Professionally-run.* Support for people living with diabetes. Mutual sharing, educational and updates on current medical treatments. Meets 3rd Wed., 7-8pm, Morristown Hospital Diabetes Center, Bldg. B, Morristown. Call Carol Lacko 973-971-5524.

OCEAN

Center for Diabetes Support Group *Professionally-run.* Support, on-going education and social interaction for adults with type I or II diabetes and their caretakers. Rap sessions, guest speakers. Meets once per month, Center for Diabetes, 731 Lacey Rd., Suite 1, Forked River. Call Kathleen Siciliano 732-349-5757.

Diabetic Support Group *Professionally-run.* Education and sharing for people with diabetes and their families. Meets 1st Thurs., 2pm, Ocean Club, 700 Route 9 South, Stafford Township. Call Ann Gioia 609-978-3491 (day). *Website:* http://www.SOCH.ORG

Parents of Children with Diabetes Support Group *Professionally-run.* Support and information for parents of children with diabetes. Literature. Meets 3rd Wed., alternate months, 7-8:30pm, Center For Diabetes Education, 731 Lacey Rd., Suite 1, Forked River. Call Kathleen Siciliano 732-349-5757 (day).

PASSAIC

Diabetes Support Group *Professionally-run.* Provides support and education for people with diabetes. Meets 2nd Tues., 7pm, Barnert Hospital, Ivor Conference Room, 680 Dr. Martin Luther King, Jr. Way, Paterson. Call Patti Keller, RN, CDE 973-977-6683.

St. Joseph's Wayne Hospital Diabetes Support *Professionally-run.* Provides support and education for those with diabetes and their families. Monthly lectures by health professionals related to diabetes. Meets 3rd Thurs., 7pm, St. Joseph's Wayne Hospital, (except June/July/Aug.), 224 Hamburg Turnpike, Wayne. Call Mary Schneider 973-720-6733 (day). *Email:* diabetes@sjwh.org.

SALEM

Adult Diabetes Support Group *Professionally-run.* Mutual support for adults with type 1 or type 11 diabetes, their families, friends and caregivers. Phone help, guest speakers and rap sessions. Meets 2nd Tues., 2-3:30pm, South Jersey Healthcare Elmer Hospital, 501 West Front St., Elmer. Call Cathy Giovinazzi 856-641-7542 (day). *Email:* giovinazzic@sjhs.com

Insulin Pump Support Group *Professionally-run.* Mutual support and education for adolescents or adults who use insulin pumps. Meetings vary, South Jersey Healthcare, Elmer. Call Cathy Giovinazzi 856-641-7543 (day).

SOMERSET

Living Well With Diabetes Support Group *Professionally-run.* Mutual support and information for adults with diabetes and for adults with type 1 or 2 diabetes. Meets quarterly, Somerset Medical Center, Somerville. For meeting information call 908-685-2846 (day).

SUSSEX

Insulin Pump Support Group *Professionally-run.* Mutual support and education for adults who use insulin pumps. Families welcome. Rap sessions, education and guest speakers. Meets 2nd Tues., (Mar., June, Sept., Dec.), 7-9pm, Newton Memorial Hospital, 175 High St., Newton. Call Community Benefits/Education 973-579-8340 (day).

Support Group for Those with Diabetes *Professionally-run.* Provides educational enrichment and emotional support for those with diabetes. Also offers rap sessions and guest speakers. Meets 1st Wed., 10am and 4th Tues., (lecture) 7pm, (Sept. Nov. Jan. and Mar.), Newton Memorial Hospital, 175 High St., Newton. Before attending call Chris Orr 973-579-8340 (day). *Email:* corr@nmhnj.org

UNION

Diabetes Support Group *Professionally-run.* Mutual support and education for persons with type II diabetes, their family and friends. Guest speakers, rap sessions. Meets 1st Tues., 7-9pm, Robert Wood Johnson University Hospital @ Rahway, Basement Education Center, 865 Stone St., Rahway. Before attending call 732-499-6166 (day).

Diabetes Support Group *Professionally-run.* Support and education for those with diabetes and their support people. Meets Mon., 7-8:30pm, Overlook Hospital, 99 Beauvoir Ave., Summit. Before attending call 908-522-5277 (Mon.-Fri., 9am-5pm).

Parents or Caregivers of Children/Adolescents with Diabetes *Professionally-run.* Support and education for parents or caregivers of children/adolescents with diabetes. Meets various days, For information call Angela Bacque' 732-499-6175 (day).

WARREN

Diabetes Support Group *Professionally-run.* Support and education for people with diabetes, their friends, family and caregivers. Usually meets last Tues., 3pm, (except Dec.), Warren Hospital, Farley Education Center, 185 Roseberry St., Phillipsburg. Before attending call Education Dept. 908-859-6777 (day). *Email:* susandanial-azer@warrenhospital.org

EATING DISORDERS
(see also overeating/overweight, toll-free helplines)

STATEWIDE

Eating Disorders Association of New Jersey *Professionally-run.* Support for persons with eating disorders, their families, friends and interested professionals. Dues $5/mtg. Membership $50/yr. Various meeting locations throughout NJ. Call 1-800-522-2230 (voice mail). *Website:* http://www.edanj.org

BERGEN

Eating Disorders Association of New Jersey *Professionally-run.* Support for persons with anorexia, bulimia or compulsive overeating and their families. Newsletter. Donation $5 per family. Meets 3rd Sat., 10-11:30am, Hackensack Medical Center, Hekemian Conference Center Building, Hackensack. Call Pia Jacangelo, ACSW 973-882-4099 (day). *Website:* http://www.edanj.org

ESSEX

Eating Disorders Association of NJ *Professionally-run.* Support group for people with anorexia, bulimia or compulsive overeating. Meets 2nd Sun., 10-11:30am, Mountainside Hospital, Main Bldg., 1st Floor, Montclair. Donation $5. Call Maureen Kritzer-Lange, MSW, LCSW 973-313-1691, Ilene Fishman, MSW, LCSW 973-509-1400 or 1-800-522-2230 (day). *Website:* http://www.edanj.org

MERCER

Eating Disorders Association of NJ *Professionally-run.* Support for people with anorexia, bulimia or compulsive overeating and their families. ($5 donation requested). Meets 1st Mon., 7:30-9pm, Princeton Theological Seminary, Stuart Hall, Room B-17, Princeton. Call Lisa Cifrese 609-252-1120 (day). *Website:* http://www.edanj.org

MIDDLESEX

Eating Disorders Association of NJ *Professionally-run.* Support group for people with anorexia, bulimia or compulsive overeating. Meets 2nd Sat., 10:30am-noon, East Brunswick Library, Civic Center Dr. and Ryder Lane, East Brunswick. Call Tina Weishaus 732-572-0461 (day), Ann Chicchi, MS, RD 732-254-7896 or 1-800-522-2230 (day). *Website:* http://www.edanj.org

MONMOUTH

Eating Disorder Support Group *Professionally-run.* Support group for people with anorexia or bulimia and their families. Under 18 welcome. Meets 4th Sat., 10:30am-noon, Riverview Medical Center, Board Room, 1 Riverview Plaza, Red Bank. Call Monmouth Psychological Associates 732-530-9029 (day) (ask for free support group) or 1-800-870-9029.

SOMERSET

Anorexia/Bulimia Family and Friend Support Group *Professionally-run.* Support and education for family and friends of those with anorexia or bulimia to help understand the disorder. Guest speakers, quarterly newsletter. Meets Tues., 7:30-9pm, Somerset Medical Center, Family Practice Conference Room, 110 Rehill Ave., Somerville. Call Angelo Gandner 908-874-7093 (day) or Eating Disorders Unit 908-685-2847 (day).

Eating Disorders Support Group *Professionally-run.* Provides mutual support for those suffering from an eating disorder. Under 18 welcome. Members share information and experiences. Meets Tues., 7:30-9pm, Somerset Medical Center, Eating Disorder Conference Room, 1st Floor, Room 197, 110 Rehill Ave., Somerville. Call Eating Disorders Unit 908-685-2847.

"Tomorrow is the most important thing in life. Comes into us at midnight very clean. It's perfect when it arrives and it puts itself in our hands. It hopes we've learned something from yesterday." --John Wayne

NATIONAL

Eating Addictions Anonymous - SANE Fellowship *National. 6 affiliated chapters.* 12-Step recovery program for persons recovering from all forms of eating and body image addictions. Includes anorexia, bulimia, binge eating, overeating, exercise bulimics, etc. Focuses on internal growth and reclaiming bodies rather than weight or appearance. Write: E.A.A., PO Box 8151, Silver Spring, MD 20907-8151. Call 202-882-6528. *Website:* http://www.eatingaddictionsanonymous.org *Email:* 12n12@tidalwave.net

Eating Disorders Anonymous *International. Founded 2000.* Fellowship of men and women who share their experience, strength and hope with each other that they may solve their common problems and help others to recover from their eating disorders. Literature, information and referrals, pen pals, phone support. Assistance in starting groups. Offers online referrals to local groups. Write: EDA, 18233 N. 16th Way, Phoenix, AZ 85022. Call 602-788-4990. *Website:* http://www.4EDA.org *Email:* info@EatingDisordersAnonymous.org

National Association of Anorexia Nervosa & Associated Disorders, Inc. *International. 300+ affiliated groups. Founded 1976.* Provides information on self-help groups, therapy, & referrals to professionals. Newsletter. Group development guidelines. Write: ANAD, PO Box 7, Highland Park, IL 60035. Call 847-831-3438 (Mon.-Fri., 9am-5pm); Fax: 847-433-4632. *Website:* http://www.anad.org

Overcomers In Christ *International. Founded 1987.* Recovery program that deals with every aspect of addiction and dysfunction (spiritual, physical, mental, emotional and social). Uses Overcomers goals which are Christ-centered. Resources, information and referrals. Assistance in starting new groups. Literature. Write: Overcomers In Christ, PO Box 34460, Omaha, NE 68134-04604. Call 402-573-0966; Fax: 402-573-0960. *Website:* http://www.OvercomersInChrist.org *Email:* OIC@OverdcomersInChrist.org

Overcomers Outreach, Inc. *International. 700 affiliated groups. Founded 1985.* 12-Step Christ-centered support group for persons with any compulsive behavior, as well as their families and friends. Uses the 12-Steps of A.A. and applies them to the Scriptures. Uses Jesus Christ as "higher power." Supplements involvement in other 12-Step groups. Newsletter, group development guidelines, conferences. Write: Overcomers Outreach, PO Box 2208, Oakhurst, CA 93644. Call 1-800-310-3001. *Website:* http://www.overcomersoutreach.org *Email:* info@overcomersoutreach.org

ECZEMA

NATIONAL

National Eczema Association for Science and Education *National network.* *Founded 1988.* Provides support for persons with atopic dermatitis as well as other forms of eczema. Promotes education and research. Offers information & referrals, networking and newsletter. Donations accepted. Write: National Eczema Association for Science & Education, 4460 Redwood Highway, Suite 16-D, San Rafael, CA 94903-1953. Call 1-800-818-7546 or 415-499-3474; Fax: 415-472-5345. *Website:* http://www.nationaleczema.org *Email:* info@nationaleczema.org

ENDOMETRIOSIS

NATIONAL

Endometriosis Association *(MULTILINGUAL) International. Founded 1980.* Offers group support to those affected by endometriosis. Educates the public and medical community about the disease. Funds and promotes research projects. Teen programs. Brochures in 29 languages. Phone support network. Online support group, crisis call listeners and e-mail support. Write: Endometriosis Assn., 8585 N. 76th Pl., Milwaukee, WI 53223. Call 1-800-992-3636 or 414-355-2200; Fax: 414-355-6065. *Website:* http://www.endometriosisassn.org *Email:* endo@EndometriosisAssn.org

Endometriosis Research Center *International. 50 support groups worldwide. Founded 1997.* Maintains and offers a vast database of materials on every aspect of endometriosis to all those interested in the disease. Support network listserv: http://groups.yahoo.com/group/erc. Write: Endometriosis Research Center, 630 Ibis Dr., Delray Beach, FL 33444. Call 1-800-239-7280 or 561-274-7442; Fax: 561-274-0931. *Email:* EndoFL@aol.com

EPILEPSY / CONVULSIVE DISORDERS
(see also specific disorder)

STATEWIDE

Epilepsy Foundation of New Jersey Support, information and referrals for people of any age with epilepsy and their families. Support groups, employment services, pharmaceutical plan, respite care, camp, family services and education. Dues $25/yr. Write: Epilepsy Foundation of NJ, 429 River View Plaza, Trenton, NJ 08611-3420. Call Trenton: 609-392-4900 (day); Westmont: 856-858-5900 (day);

Parsippany: 973-244-0850 (day); Brick:732-262-8020 (day) or 1-800-336-5843 *Website:* http://www.efnj.com

ATLANTIC

Atlantic Cape Epilepsy Support Group *Professionally-run.* Mutual support and education for persons with epilepsy or related seizure disorder. Open to parents, caregivers and other interested persons. Rap sessions. Meets 4th Sat., 10am-noon, Shore Memorial Hospital, Jenkins Room, 2nd Floor, New York Ave., Somers Point. Call Marian 609-822-8783 (day/eve) or 609-823-8023 (day). *Email:* amrein@ix.netcom.com

BERGEN

Bergen/Passaic County Epilepsy Support Group For those age 16 and over to talk with others who are afflicted directly or indirectly with epilepsy, to show them that they are not alone and educate all about the disorder. Meets 3rd Mon., 7-8:30pm, Valley Hospital, 223 N. Van Dien Ave., Conference Room "Cheel 2", Ridgewood. Call The Epilepsy Foundation 973-992-5900 (9am-5pm). *Website:* http://www.efnj.com *Email:* mjhickey@att.com

MIDDLESEX

Epilepsy Support Group Support and education for persons with epilepsy. Buddy system, guest speakers, phone help. Transportation available. Meets last Tues., 7:30pm, (except July/Aug.), Robert Wood Johnson University Hospital, Board Room, New Brunswick. Call Elizabeth Schaaf 732-418-8110.

MORRIS

Epilepsy Support Group Support for anyone with epilepsy and their families to increase understanding and awareness. Coping skills discussed. Occasional guest speakers. Meets 3rd Thurs. 7:30-9pm, Morristown Memorial Hospital, Conference Room 3, B Level, 100 Madison Ave., Morristown. Call Pat 908-464-7346 (day). *Website:* http://www.efnj.com

NATIONAL

Epilepsy Foundation *(BILINGUAL) National. 60+ affiliates. Founded 1967.* Information and support for people with epilepsy, their families and friends. Publishes "Epilepsy USA" magazine and a wide range of informational materials for people of all ages. Referrals to local affiliates (many of which have employment related programs). Information & referrals. Write: Epilepsy Fdn. , 4351 Garden City Dr., Landover, MD 20785. Call 301-459-3700, Professional Library: 1-800-332-4050, Consumer Infoline: 1-800-332-1000; Fax: 301-577-4941. *Website:* http://www.epilepsyfoundation.org *Email:* postmaster@efa.org

ONLINE

Pyridoxine Dependent Kids *Online.* Support group for parents of children with pyridoxine dependency or parents who are using B6 as an anticonvulsant. Offers public and subscribers only message boards. *Website:* http://groups.yahoo.com/group/b6children

FIBROMYALGIA

BERGEN

Arthritis Foundation Fibromyalgia Support Group *Professionally-run.* Provides support and education to people with fibromyalgia and their families by using speakers, videos, resource materials and chat sessions. Meets 1st Sun., (except July/Aug.), 1-3pm, Pascack Valley Hospital, Old Hook Rd., Westwood. Call Ralph Higdon 201-666-5018, Hospital Relations 201-358-0054 or the Arthritis Foundation 1-888-467-3112.

CAMDEN

Fibromyalgia Support Group Mutual support and education for persons diagnosed with fibromyalgia and their families. Meets 4th Mon., 7-9pm, Virtua Health's Barry D. Brown Health Education Center, 106 Carnie Blvd., Voorhees. (except Jan., May, July, Aug. and Dec.). Call 1-888-847-8823 (day).

CUMBERLAND

Arthritis Foundation Fibromyalgia Support Group Provides those with fibromyalgia and their family and friends an opportunity to discuss their problems, offer mutual support and exchange ideas to help cope with the disease. Meets 2nd Thurs., 7pm, Vineland YMCA, 1159 E. Landis Ave., Vineland. Call Susan Thau-Kiaser 856-691-0030 or Arthritis Foundation 1-888-467-3112.

MONMOUTH

Fibromyalgia Support Group of Western Monmouth County Mutual support for people suffering from fibromyalgia. Also welcome are their families, friends and professional interested in learning about the disease. Offers phone help, group sessions, rap sessions and guest speakers.

> **Manalapan** Meets 1st Thurs., 7-9pm, Manalapan Library, Symms Rd. Call Tania Kanthal 732-462-6656.
>
> **Wall** Meets 4th Thurs., 6:30pm, Wall Township Library, 2700 Allaire Rd. Call Linda 732-449-2733.

MORRIS

North Jersey Regional Arthritis Center Fibromyalgia Support Group *Professionally-run.* Provides education, support and resources for those age 16 and over who are diagnosed with fibromyalgia. Mutual sharing, guest speakers, literature. Meets 1st Thurs., 11am-noon, Atlantic Rehabilitation Institute (RIMM), 95 Mt. Kemble Ave., 3rd Floor Chapel, Morristown. Call Dr. Michael Horowitz 973-971-4515 (day).

PASSAIC

Fibromyalgia Support Group Mutual support and education for people with fibromyalgia and their families. Meets 3rd Thurs., 7-9pm, (except July/Aug.) St. Mary's Hospital, 211 Pennington Ave., Passaic. Call 973-470-3050 (day).

North Jersey Regional Arthritis Center Support Group *Professionally-run.* Mutual support and education for persons with arthritis or fibromyalgia and their families. Aim is to raise quality of life for those with arthritis through rap sessions, educational programs, guest speakers. Offers phone help and literature. Meets 1st Tues., Clifton Main Memorial Library, 292 Piaget Ave., Clifton. For information call Anne Marie Leveto 973-365-4752 or Alicia 973-470-5773.

SUSSEX

Sussex County Fibromyalgia Enlightenment, education and empowerment for persons with fibromyalgia and affiliated illnesses (including chronic fatigue syndrome, multiple chemical sensitivity, Gulf War syndrome and autoimmune diseases). Families and friends welcome. Meets 2nd Tues., 6:30-9pm, Ogdensburg First Aid Squad Building, Willis Ave., Ogdensburg. Call Rosemary O'Connor 973-827-6625 (day/eve).

WARREN

Fibromyalgia and Chronic Fatigue Support Group Provides education and support for those with fibromyalgia or chronic fatigue syndrome. Meets 1st Thurs., 7pm, (except July, Aug., Sept.), Warren Hospital, Farley Education Center, 185 Roseberry St., Phillipsburg. Before attending call Jean 908-859-6735 (day).

NATIONAL

National Fibromyalgia Association *National network.* Provides patient support and informational services, awareness outreach, physical education and research information. Assistance in starting support groups. Magazine, networking and fundraising. Write: NFA, 2200 North Glassell St., Suite A, Orange, CA 92865. Call 714-921-0150; Fax: 714-921-6920. *Website:* http://www.FMaware.org

GRAVE'S DISEASE

NATIONAL

National Graves' Disease Foundation *National. 32 affiliated groups in 25 states. Founded 1990.* Aim is to establish patient-based Graves' exclusive support groups to provide better treatment and to increase public awareness. Participates in research. Newsletter, information and referrals, phone support, national conferences, internet bulletin board and weekly online chat room. Each group has medical back-up/resource. Guidelines available in starting similar groups. Write: National Graves' Disease Fdn., c/o Dr. Nancy Patterson, PO Box 1969, Brevard, NC 28712. Call 904-278-9480. *Website:* http://www.ngdf.org

HEADACHES
(see also chronic pain)

NATIONAL

ACHE (American Council for Headache Education) Support Group *National. 23 affiliated groups. Founded 1990.* An opportunity for headache sufferers to decrease their feeling of isolation, to help them learn more about headaches and enhance their coping skills. Newsletter, information and referrals, group meetings. Assistance in starting groups. Dues $20. Write: ACHE, 19 Mantua Rd., Mt. Royal, NJ 08061. Call 1-800-255-2243 or 856-423-0258; Fax: 856-423-0082. *Website:* http://www.achenet.org *Email:* achehq@talley.com

National Headache Foundation *National. 30+ affiliated groups. Founded 1970.* Mutual support for chronic headache sufferers and their families. Education on how to deal with chronic head pain. Group meetings, phone support, email pen pals, group development guidelines. Public awareness seminars, funds research. Newsletter, brochures and information on diets. Write: Nat'l Headache Fdn., 820 N. Orleans, Suite 217, Chicago, Il 60610-3132. Call 1-888-643-5552 (day); Fax: 312-640-9049. *Website:* http://www.headaches.org *Email:* sbarron@headaches.org

ONLINE

Cluster Headaches *Online. Founded 1998.* Offers support for cluster headache sufferers and their families. Provides message boards, live chats, links and medical information. *Website:* http://www.clusterheadaches.com

OUCH (Organization for Understanding Cluster Headaches) *Online.* Offers information and support for cluster headache sufferers worldwide. Provides message board, newsletter and informative links. Supports research to improve treatments. Holds annual conference. *Website:* http://www.clusterheadaches.org

HEART DISEASE
(see also transplants, pulmonary hypertension, specific disorder, toll-free helplines)

BERGEN

Mended Hearts, Inc. Help, encouragement and education for those anticipating or recovering from heart surgery and/or other heart disease. Family and friends welcome. Professional speakers. Meets 3rd Thurs., "meet and greet" at 7pm; meeting follows, Hackensack Medical Center, Cafeteria, Hackensack. Call Barbara Cecco 201-265-9296 (day). *Email:* bobbi0530@aol.com

BURLINGTON

Zapper Club *Professionally-run.* Support group for patients with implantable defibrillators and their families. For meeting information call Laura Gebers 609-893-1200 ext. 5258 (day). *Website:* http://www.deborah.org *Email:* gebersl@deborah.org

Zipper Club Mutual support for persons coping with heart disease or heart surgery. Meets 7 times/yr., Deborah Heart and Lung Center, Browns Mills. Call Laura 609-893-1200 ext. 5258 (day/eve) *Website:* http://www.zipperclub.com *Email:* zipperclub@juno.com

CAMDEN

Heart And Soul Cardiac Support Group Mutual support and education for persons with any type of heart disease. Meets 3rd Thurs., (except July/Aug.), 7:30-8:30pm, Virtua Health, Barry D. Brown Health Education Center, 106 Carnie Blvd., Voorhees. Call 1-888-847-8823 (day).

HUDSON

Circle of Hearts *Professionally-run.* Group provides support and education for patients with heart problems as well as their spouses and families. Rap sessions, guest speakers. Meets various days, every other month, 7pm, Meadowlands Hospital, 55 Meadowlands Pkwy, Secaucus. Call Dan Lange or Louise Sallustio 201-392-3531 (day).

Women's Cardiac Support Group *Professionally-run.* Mutual support and discussion for women to share experiences and concerns regarding heart disease and other related problems. Meets 3rd Wed., 12:30-1:30pm, Meadowlands Hospital, 55 Meadowlands Parkway, Secaucus. Call Louise Sallustio or Nancy Braddell 201-392-3531 (day).

MERCER

Living and Loving with Chronic Illness *Professionally-run.* Confidential group offering mutual support and discussion for person with a variety of chronic medical conditions, including heart disease, neuromuscular disorders, cancer and chronic pain. Meets alternate Wed., 2pm, St. Francis Medical Center, 601 Hamilton Ave., Trenton. Call Bev Snyderman 609-599-5657 (day).

MIDDLESEX

Happy Hearts of Central Jersey Support and educational programs for cardiac patients and families. Outreach, newsletter. Meets 2nd Thurs., 7pm, (except June-Aug.), Robert Wood Johnson University Hospital, Auditorium, New Brunswick. Call Community Education 732-418-8110 (day).

Surviving Hearts Support Group Mutual support and education for women with heart disease or concerned about the disease. Meets 1st and 3rd Thurs., 6pm, Robert Wood Johnson University Hospital, Women's Resource Center, One Robert Wood Johnson Place, New Brunswick. Call 732-418-8105.

MONMOUTH

ICD Patient/Family Support and Education Group *Professionally-run.* Provides supportive education and mechanism for networking for patients and families having implantable cardioverter defibrillators. Rap sessions, guest speakers, phone help, literature. Meets every other month (odd number months), Jersey Shore Medical Center, Neptune. For information call 732-775-5500 ext. 5249. *Email:* nancybowe@meridianhealth.com

MORRIS

ICD Support Group *Professionally-run.* Provides education and psycho-social support to those with implantable cardioverter defibrillators as well as their significant others. Mutual sharing, guest speakers, literature and newsletter. Meets various times, Morristown Memorial Hospital, 100 Madison Ave., Morristown. Call Sheri Raquet 973-971-7939 (day) or Myra Hoffman 973-971-4261 (day).

SOMERSET

Cardiac Support Group *Professionally-run.* Support and education for any cardiac patient. Families of patients welcome. Rap sessions and guest speakers. Meets 3rd Tues., 6-7pm, Somerset Medical Center, Conference Room A and B, 110 Rehill Ave., Somerville. Call Joyce Hoffman 908-685-2814 (day).

SUSSEX

Mended Hearts Support and encouragement for heart patients and their families. Visitation, guest speakers, socials, newsletter. Meets quarterly, Newton Memorial Hospital, 175 High St., Newton. Dues $19 - $31/yr. Call Fred C. Iliff 973-383-4175 (day/eve) or Vivian Sauter 973-691-0693 (day).

UNION

Cardiac Support Group *Professionally-run.* Support and education for cardiac patients and their families. Meets 1st Mon., 7-8:30pm, Robert Wood Johnson University Hospital at Rahway, 865 Stone St., Rahway. Call Helen Peare 732-499-6073 (day).

Mended Hearts Support and encouragement for heart patients and their families. Visitation, guest speakers, socials, newsletter. Dues $19 - $31/yr. Meets 3rd Tues., 7:30pm, Springfield First Aid Squad Building, North Trivett Ave., Springfield. Call Dan Kalem 973-376-0582 (day/eve).

WARREN

Healthy Heart Self-help group for those who have heart disease. Family members and significant others welcome. Provides emotional support and education. Meets 2nd Thurs., (except Jan.), 7pm, Warren Hospital, Farley Education Center, 185 Roseberry St., Phillipsburg. Before attending call Sue Himmelreich 908-859-6700 ext. 2180 (day).

NATIONAL

Adult Congenital Heart Association *National. 25 affiliated groups. Founded 1998.* Seeks to improve the quality of life and extend the lives of adults with congenital heart defects. Education, outreach, advocacy and promotion of research. Education, outreach, advocacy and promotion of research. Online support, quarterly newsletter, regional and national conferences. Write: ACHA, 6757 Greene St., Philadelphia, PA 19119. Call 215-849-1260; Fax: 245-849-1261. *Website:* http://www.achaheart.org *Email:* info@achaheart.org

Arrhythmia Alliance (The Heart Rhythm Charity) *Founded 2004.* A network of sufferers, medical professionals, various UK based charities and related industry promoting better understanding, diagnosis, treatment and quality of life for individuals with cardiac arrhythmias. Write: Arrhythmia Alliance, PO Box 3697, Stratford upon Avon Warwickshire CV37 8YL UK. Call +44 (0) 17890450787; Fax: +44 (0) 1789 450682. *Website:* http://www.arrhythmiaalliance.org.uk *Email:* info@arrhythmiaalliance.org.uk

CHASER (Congenital Heart Anomalies-Support, Education, Resources) *National network. Founded 1992.* Opportunity for parents of children born with heart defects to network with other parents with similar needs and concerns. Education on hospitalization, surgeries, medical treatments, etc. Newsletter, information and referral, phone support. Directory of heart surgeons and facilities. Write: CHASER, 2112 N. Wilkins Rd., Swanton, OH 43558. Call Jim & Anita Myers 419-825-5575; Fax: 419-825-2880.

International Bundle Branch Block Association *National network. Organized 1979.* Provides support and information to help bundle branch block persons and families cope. Educates the public. Informal phone support system. Guidelines and assistance for starting groups. Voluntary dues $10 (more for professionals). Write: Int'l Bundle Branch Block Assn., c/o R. K. Lewis, 6631 W. 83rd St., Los Angeles, CA 90045-2875. Call 310-670-9132.

Kids With Heart National Association for Children's Heart Disorders, Inc. *National. 3 affiliated groups. Founded 1985.* Mutual support for families and adults affected by congenital or acquired heart defects. Matches persons together for support. Referrals to local support groups nationwide. Books. Assistance in starting groups. Write: Kids With Heart NACHD, Inc., 1578 Careful Dr., Green Bay, WI 54304. Call 1-800-538-5390 or 920-498-0058. *Website:* http://www.kidswithheart.org *Email:* michelle@kidswithheart.org

Little Hearts, Inc *National.* Provides support, resources, networking and hope to families affected by congenital heart defects. Provides newsletter, literature, phone support, annual picnic and advocacy. Call 1-866-435-4673; Fax: 860-635-0006. *Website:* http://www.littlehearts.org *Email:* info@littlehearts.org

Mended Hearts *National. 277 chapters. Founded 1951.* Mutual support for persons who have heart disease, their families, friends and other interested persons. Quarterly magazine. Chapter development kit. Write: Mended Hearts, 7272 Greenville Ave., Dallas, TX 75231. Call 1-888-432-7899; Fax: 214-706-5245. *Website:* http://www.mendedhearts.org *Email:* info@mendedhearts.org

National Society for MVP & Dysautonomia *National. 59 affiliated groups. Founded 1987.* Assists individuals suffering from mitral valve prolapse syndrome and dysautonomia to find support and understanding. Education on symptoms and treatment. Newsletter, literature. Write: Nat'l Soc. for MVP & Dysautonomia, 880 Montclair Rd., Suite 370, Birmingham, AL 35213. Call 205-592-5765 (day) or 1-800-541-8602; Fax: 205-592-5707. *Website:* http://www.mvprolapse.com *Email:* staff@MVProlapse.com

SADS Foundation *International. Founded 1992.* Aim is to save the lives of young persons who are predisposed to sudden death due to cardiac arrhythmia. Offers networking, newsletter, literature, advocacy, information, phone support and referrals. Write: SADS Foundation, 508 E. South Temple, Suite 20, Salt Lake City, UT 84102. Call 1-800-786-7723 or 801-531-0937; Fax: 801-531-0945. *Website:* http://www.sads.org

Society for Mitral Valve Prolapse Syndrome *International. 23 affiliated groups. Founded 1991.* Provides support and education to patients, families and friends about mitral valve prolapse syndrome. Newsletter, phone support, literature, conferences, support group meetings. Published "survival guide." Offers guidelines to start similar groups. Write: Society for MVP Syndrome, PO Box 431, Itasca, IL 60143-0431. Call 630-250-9327; Fax: 630-773-0478. *Website:* http://www.mitralvalveprolapse.com *Email:* bonnie0107@aol.com

ONLINE

Children's Cardiomyopathy Foundation *Online.* Provides support and information on pediatric cardiomyopathy. Offers website discussion forum. *Website:* http://www.childrenscardiomyopathy.org

Congenital Heart Information Network *Online.* Offers information, support and resources to families of children with congenital heart defects, acquired heart disease and adults with congenital heart defects. Also open to interested professionals. *Website:* http://www.tchin.org

Pacemaker Club *Online. Founded 2000.* Regular exchange of messages, listserv and newsgroup. Online chats. E-mail pen pal program to support new members. Offers support information, encouragement in a fun and interactive environment. Also information on local groups. *Website:* http://www.pacemakerclub.com *Email:* info@pacemakerclub.com

SVT Support *Online. Founded 2002.* E-mail list support. Mutual aid support from and for, persons with supra ventricular tachycardia or any type arrhythmia. Newsletter. *Website:* http://groups.yahoo.com/group/SVTSupport/

HEPATITIS
(see also liver disease, infectious disease)

BERGEN

Hepatitis Support Group Mutual support, education, resources and sharing for patients with hepatitis. Families welcome. Aims to promote the quality of life while living with hepatitis. Meets 2nd Tues., 6:30pm, Englewood Hospital and Medical Center, 350 Engle St., Englewood. Call Jeffrey Aber 201-894-3496 (day).

ESSEX

HC Anonymous Mutual support for persons with hepatitis C. Literature. Meets Wed., 6:30-8pm, Al-Anon Association, 384 Seventh Ave., Newark. Call Michele 973-483-7071.

HUDSON

Hepatitis C Support Group *Professionally-run.* Mutual support and education for persons with hepatitis C. Families and friends welcome. Rap sessions, guest speakers, literature. Meets 1st Mon., 7-8pm, Meadowlands Hospital Medical Center, 55 Meadowlands Parkway, Secaucus. For meeting information call 201-392-3266 (day).

MERCER

Mercer County Survivors of Liver Disease/Hepatitis Support and education for those afflicted with liver disease or hepatitis. Family, friends and professionals welcome. Lectures, guest speakers, advocacy, rap sessions and social group. Meets 1st and 3rd Sun., 7-9pm, Robert Wood Johnson at Hamilton, 1 Hamilton Place, Hamilton. Call Peggy Goodale 609-371-3401 or Tammy Leigh 609-584-6658.

INTERNATIONAL

Hepatitis B Foundation *International network.* *Founded 1991.* Mutual support and information for persons affected by hepatitis B. Dedicated to finding a cure for hepatitis B. Supports research. Advocacy, information and referrals, educational literature, conferences, confidential phone and e-mail support, newsletter. Referrals to liver specialists. Suggested donation $40. Write: Hepatitis B Foundation, 700 E. Butler Ave., Doylestown, PA 18901. Call 215-489-4900; Fax: 215-489-4920. *Website:* http://www.hepb.org *Email:* info@hepb.org

Hepatitis Foundation International *International network.* Founded 1995. Grassroots support network for persons with viral hepatitis. Provides education about the prevention, diagnosis and treatment of viral hepatitis. Phone support network and literature. Referrals to local support groups. Quarterly newsletter. Some materials available in Spanish, Mandarin and Vietnamese. Write: Hepatitis Fdn. Int'l, 504 Blick Dr., Silver Springs, MD 20904. Call 1-800-891-0707 (day). *Website:* http://www.hepfi.org *Email:* hfi@comcast.net

ONLINE

Hepatitis Neighborhood *Online.* An online educational resource to help individuals understand hepatitis, treatment options, finding support, message boards and chat rooms. *Website:* http://www.hepatitisneighborhood.com

HERPES / SEXUALLY TRANSMITTED DISEASES

(see also specific disorder, toll-free helplines)

NATIONAL

Herpes Resource Center *National network.* *85+ groups. Founded 1914.* Emotional support and education for persons with herpes. Referrals to HELP support groups, which provide a safe, confidential environment in which to obtain accurate information, & share experiences with others. Support group development guidelines. Free pamphlets (send self-addressed stamped envelope). Quarterly journal ($25). Other materials available. Write: Herpes Resource Center, PO Box 13827, Research Triangle Park, NC 27709. Call 919-361-8488 (hotline: 9am-6pm); 919-361-8486 (for starting groups); or 919-361-8400 (ASHA); Fax 919-361-8425. *Website:* http://www.ashastd.org *Email:* herpesnet@ashastd.org

"A clay pot sitting in the sun will always be a clay pot. It has to go though the white heat of the furnace to become porcelain." --Mildred White Struven

HIGH BLOOD PRESSURE

ONLINE

High Blood Pressure (Hypertension) Online Support *Online* Email list for those suffering from high blood pressure/hypertension who are looking for others suffering from the same situation. *Website:* http://curezone.com/diseases/cardiovascular/hypertensionpage.html *Email List:* http://health.groups.yahoo.com/group/hypertension

HIP REPLACEMENT

ONLINE

Totally Hip *Online.* Support to help relieve the fear of total hip replacement surgery, share experiences and offer moral as well as spiritual support to patients. Helps answer questions on hip replacement. Click on bulletin board at website for message exchange. *Website:* http://www.totallyhip.org *Email:* inda@totallyhip.org

HUMAN PAPILLOMA VIRUS
(see also toll-free helplines)

NATIONAL

HPV Resource Center *National. 15 affiliated support groups. Founded 1999.* Provides a safe, confidential environment in which to share support and experiences with others who also have the human papilloma virus (aka genital warts and cervical dysplasia). Information and referrals, bi-monthly news journal ($25/yr.), pamphlets. Assistance in starting new groups. How-to materials. Write: ASHA/HPVRC c/o Fred, PO Box 13827, Research Triangle Park, NC 27709-3827. Call 919-361-8486; Fax: 919-361-8425. *Website:* http://www.ashastd.org *Email:* hpvnet@ashastd.org

ONLINE

Club HPV *Online.* Opportunity for people with human papilloma virus (genital warts) to share experiences and information with others. *Website:* http://groups.yahoo.com/group/clubhpv

This information is always changing. New groups start, others end. Please call us for the most up-to-date information from our database. 1-800-367-6274

HUNTINGTON'S DISEASE

(see also toll-free helplines)

STATEWIDE

Huntington's Disease Society of America *Professionally-run*. Education and support for afflicted families. Fund-raising, visitation and phone help. Meets various times at various locations throughout NJ. Call HDSA 609-448-3500 (day) or Family Service Center 732-235-5993 (day). *Website:* http://www.HDSAnj.org *Email:* info@hdsanj.org

MIDDLESEX

Huntington's Disease Support Group *Professionally-run*. Support and education for persons who have Huntington's disease, caregivers, relatives and those at risk. Meets 4th Wed., 6:30pm, 667 Hoes Lane, Piscataway. Call Christine Hogan 732-235-5993 (day).

OCEAN

Huntington's Disease Support Group *Professionally-run*. Support and education for persons who have Huntington's Disease, their caregivers, relatives and those at risk. Meets 2nd Wed., 6:30-8pm, Leisure Chateau Care Center, 962 River Ave., Lakewood. Call Judy 732-370-8600.

NATIONAL

Huntington's Disease Society of America *National. 28 chapters/10 affiliates. Founded 1967.* Provides information and referrals to local chapters, support groups and social workers, as well as referrals to local health care professionals and other resources. Provides written and audiovisual materials and publishes three newsletters. Write: Huntington's Disease Soc. of America, 158 West 29th St., 7th Fl., New York, NY 10001-5300. Call 1-800-345-4372. *Website:* http://www.hdsa.org *Email:* hdsainfo@hdsa.org

INCONTINENCE

STATEWIDE

T.I.S. Group (Tri-State Incontinence Support) Provides on-going educational and emotional support. Offers networking opportunities for persons with bladder control problems. Includes children with bladder control problems and their parents. Buddy system. Write: TIS, 51 Nassau Ave., Brooklyn, NY 11222.

Call Bob Goddard 718-599-0171 (day). *Email:* support@tis-group.org

NATIONAL

Continence Restored Inc. *International. 8 affiliated groups. Founded 1984.* Forum where persons with incontinence, their families and friends can express concerns and receive assistance. Disseminates information on bladder control. Phone support. Assistance in starting groups. Write: Continence Restored, Inc., 407 Strawberry Hill Ave., Stamford, CT 06902. Call 203-348-0601; Fax: 203-348-0601. *Email:* annevyoung@aol.com

Pull-thru Network, The *International network. Founded 1988.* Support and information for families of children born with anorectal malformations (including cloaca, VATER/VACTERL, cloacal exstrophy, imperforate anus), Hirschsprung's disease and associated diagnoses. Maintains a database for personal networking. Quarterly magazine. Online discussion group. Weekly chat for members. Phone support and literature. Dues $20. Write: Pull-thru Network, 2312 Savoy St., Hoover, Al 35226-1528. Call 205-978-2930. *Website:* http://www.pullthrough.org *Email:* info@pullthrough.org

Simon Foundation for Continence *National. 500+ affiliated groups. Founded 1983.* Support and advocacy for people suffering from incontinence. Quarterly newsletter, pen pals, books, videos, group development guidelines. Write: Simon Fdn. for Continence, PO Box 835, Wilmette, IL 60091. Call 1-800-237-4666; Fax: 847-864-9758. *Website:* http://www.simonfoundation.org *Email:* cbgartley@simonfoundation.org

INFERTILITY / CHILDLESSNESS
(see also women's health, marriage, family, specific disorder, adoption, loss of a child)

STATEWIDE

Resolve of NJ *Professionally-run.* Education, support and referrals to medical, therapeutic and adoption professionals for individuals and couples experiencing infertility. Information on current medical treatments and adoption. Bi-monthly newsletter. Membership dues $55/yr. Educational meetings held monthly. Support group meetings also held throughout the NJ counties. Call 1-888-765-2810. *Website:* http://www.resolvenj.org *Email:* info@resolvenj.org

"The reality of the other person is not in what he reveals to you, but in what he cannot reveal to you. Therefore, if you would understand him, listen not to what he says but rather what he does not say." --Kahlil Gibran

ESSEX

Infertility Support Group *Professionally-run.* Offers a variety of individual and couple support groups for those struggling with the stress of infertility. Topics include male and female infertility, pregnancy loss, the use of donors, etc. Meets 2nd and 4th Wed., 7-8:30pm, St. Barnabas, IRMS, East Wing, Livingston. Register before attending. Call 973-322-5356. *Website:* http://www.sbivf.com

HUNTERDON

Resolve Peer Support Group for Infertility Mutual support for women who have suffered with infertility to share experiences and discuss ways of coping. Rap sessions, guest speakers and newsletter. Meets 1st Wed., 6-8pm, Milford. Call Debbie 908-995-2797 (day).

NATIONAL

NINE National Infertility Network Exchange *National. Founded 1988.* Support for persons and couples with impaired fertility and the professionals who serve them. Support system to help understand, cope and reach a resolution. Monthly educational meetings, newsletter, talk line and professional referral. Guidelines to assist others start a similar group. Dues $40/yr. Write: NINE, PO Box 204, East Meadow, NY 11554. Call 516-794-5772; Fax: 516-794-0008. *Website:* http://www.nine-infertility.org *Email:* NINE204@aol.com

Organization of Parents Through Surrogacy *National. Founded 1988.* Educational, support and advocacy organization for families built through surrogate parenting. Members work together to address legislative bills on surrogacy. Dues $50/ind.; $125/professionals. Write: OPTS, PO Box 611, Gurnee, IL 60031. Call 847-782-0224; Fax: 847-782-0240. *Website:* http://www.opts.com *Email:* bzager@msn.com

RESOLVE, the National Infertility Association *National. 50+ chapters. Founded 1974.* Emotional support & medical referrals for infertile couples. Support groups, education for members & public. Quarterly magazine, publications. Chapter development guidelines. Write: RESOLVE, Inc., 7910 Woodmont Ave., Suite 1350, Bethesda, MD 20814. Call 1-888-623-0744 (helpline) or 301-652-8585 (office). *Website:* http://www.resolve.org *Email:* Info@Resolve.org

Consider passing this Directory on to a student or staff member - browsing through the Directory pages can often provide helpful education as to the wide variety of groups available.

ONLINE

Fertile Thoughts *Online*. Provides support for infertile couples through chat rooms and forums. Issues include general infertility, primary vs. secondary infertility, over 35, overweight, grief, polycystic ovarian syndrome, male infertility, adoption and parenting. *Website:* http://www.fertilethoughts.net

INCIID (International Council on Infertility Information Dissemination) *Online*. Dedicated to helping infertile couples find their best family-building options, including treatment and prevention of infertility and pregnancy loss. Guidance for those seeking to adopt. Provides free in-vitro fertilization to couples in need. Offers message boards on a variety of issues including fertility after forty, men, recurrent pregnancy loss, legal and insurance-related issues, grief, alternative therapies and medical issues. *Website:* http://www.inciid.org

Parent Soup Message Boards *Online*. Offers a large variety of message boards which deal with parenting issues including infertility, pregnancy, parenting challenges, parents of disabled, pregnancy loss, newborn babies, toddlers, equipment, adoption, family issues. etc. *Website:* http://www.parentsoup.com/boards/

TASC (The American Surrogacy Center) *Online*. Cyber community of friends and acquaintances who have a personal interest or experience concerning surrogacy issues. Various email discussions and password protected bulletin boards, live chats and monthly virtual seminars. Topics include surrogate parents, egg donation, multiple miscarriages, DES daughters, sperm donation and Mayer-Rokitansky-Kustur-Hauser syndrome. *Website:* http://www.surrogacy.com *Email:* info@surrogacy.com

INFLAMMATORY BOWEL DISEASE / IRRITABLE BOWEL SYNDROME / CROHN'S / COLITIS

STATEWIDE

Crohn's and Colitis Foundation of America, Inc. (CCFA) Greater NJ Chapter *Professionally-run*. Provides support and education for persons with inflammatory bowel disease, Crohn's, ulcerative colitis and their families. Does not include irritable bowel syndrome. Fund-raising for support, education and research. Membership dues $30/yr; $25/yr. for senior citizens and students. Various meeting locations throughout NJ. Write: NJ Chapter CCFA, 45 Wilson Ave., Manalapan, NJ 07726. Call 732-786-9960 (Mon.-Fri., 9am-5pm). *Website:* http://www.ccfa.org *Email:* newjersey@ccfa.org

BERGEN

Crohn's and Colitis Support Group Support and education for people with Crohn's and colitis. Rap sessions. Meetings vary, Hackensack Hospital, Hackensack. For information call Carolyn Zorn 201-488-2668 (eve).

Inflammatory Bowel Disease Support Group for Parents *Professionally-run.* Provides support and education for parents of children with inflammatory bowel disease. Families welcome. Meets 3rd Wed., 11am-noon and 1st Thurs., 7:15-8:15pm, Don Imus Pediatric Center, Hackensack University Medical Center, Room PC 347, Hackensack. Call Joseph Chan, LCSW 201-336-8840 (day).

MERCER

Crohn's and Colitis Support Group *Professionally-run.* Support and education for people with Crohn's and colitis. Family and friends welcome. Meetings vary, Robert Wood Johnson Hospital, Hamilton. For meeting information call Bill 609-587-7215.

MIDDLESEX

Crohn's Disease and Colitis Support Group *Professionally-run.* Support and education for people with Crohn's disease and colitis. Meets last Tues., 7pm, Robert Wood Johnson Medical School, Medical Education Bldg., Room 492, New Brunswick. Call 732-235-6360.

UNION

Irritable Bowel Syndrome Support Group Support for those with IBS. Members share information, experiences, support and literature. Periodic speakers. Meeting days vary. Overlook Hospital, 99 Beauvoir Ave., Summit. For meeting information call Lynn Jacks 908-272-9484 (day).

NATIONAL

American Celiac Society / Dietary Support Coalition *National. 78 affiliated chapters. Founded 1976.* Mutual support and information for celiac-sprue patients, families and health care professionals. Buddy system, visitation, phone help system, participation in educational efforts. Also supports dermatitis herpetiformis, Crohn's disease, lactose intolerance & other food allergies. Newsletter. Write: American Celiac Society c/o Annette Bentley, PO Box 23455, New Orleans, LA 70183-0455. Call Annette Bentley 504-737-3293. *Email:* amerceliacsoc@netscape.net

Crohn's & Colitis Foundation of America *National. 42 chapters. Founded 1967.* Offers educational programs and supportive services for people with Crohn's disease or ulcerative colitis, as well as their family and friends. Funds research that seeks the cure for these illnesses. Membership benefits include newsletter, a national magazine and discounts on books. Brochures available free of charge. Dues: Ind/$30, family/$60. Write: CCFA, 386 Park Ave. South, 17th Fl., New York, NY 10016. Call 1-800-932-2423. *Website:* http://www.ccfa.org *Email:* info@ccfa.org

International Foundation for Functional Gastrointestinal Disorders *International network. Founded 1990.* Educational and research organization that provides information, assistance and support for people affected by functional gastrointestinal disorders, irritable bowel syndrome, gastroesophageal reflux disorder and bowel incontinence. Publishes quarterly journal addressing digestive disorders in adults and children. Many other fact sheets and educational publications are available. Write: IFFGD, PO Box 170864, Milwaukee, WI 53217-8076. Call 1-888-964-2001 or 414-964-1799; Fax: 414-964-7176. *Website:* http://www.iffgd.org *Email:* iffgd@iffgd.org

Irritable Bowel Syndrome Self Help Group *National. Groups in USA and Canada. Founded 1987* Mutual support for persons with irritable bowel syndrome, their families and health care professionals. Literature, advocacy and assistance in starting similar groups. Write: IBS Self-Help and Support Group, 1440 Whalley Ave., # 145, New Haven, CT 06515. *Website:* http://www.ibsgroup.org *Email:* ibs@ibsgroup.org

Reach Out for Youth with Ileitis & Colitis, Inc. *Model. 2 local groups. Founded 1979.* Provides support and education to youth and their families. Networking, literature, advocacy, information & referrals, phone support, conferences, regular group meetings and pen pals. Promotes research and sponsors fund raising activities. Write: Reach Out for Youth with Ileitis & Colitis, Inc., 84 Northgate Circle, Melville, NY 11747. Call 631-293-3102; Fax: 631-293-3101. *Website:* http://www.reachoutforyouth.org *Email:* reachoutforyouth@reachoutforyouth.org

INTERSTITIAL CYSTISIS

BERGEN

North Jersey IC Support Group Mutual support for persons with interstitial cystitis. Exchange coping skills and help answer questions to interstitial cystitis patients. Meets 4 times a yr., Englewood Hospital, Englewood. Educational series, phone help and buddy system. For meeting information call Dianne Dragotta 973-343-3687. *Website:* http://health.groups.yahoo.com/group/njicsupportgroup

CAMDEN

Camden County ICA Support and information for persons with interstitial cystitis or painful bladder and their families and friends. Rap sessions, guest speakers, phone help, National ICA newsletter ($40). Meets bi-monthly, Sat., 1-3pm, West Jersey Hospital, Voorhees. Call Linda Benecke 856-667-5842 (Mon-Fri, eve) or Virtua 1-888-847-8823.

NATIONAL

Interstitial Cystitis Association *National. Founded 1984.* Provides education, information & support for persons with interstitial cystitis & their spouses and families. Quarterly newsletter. Dues $45/yr. Write: ICA, 110 N. Washington St. #340, Rockville, MD 20850-2239. Call 1-800-435-7422 or 301-610-5300; Fax: 301-610-5308. *Website:* http://www.ichelp.org *Email:* icamail@ichelp.org

KIDNEY DISEASE
(see also transplants, specific disorder)

ESSEX

Kidney Transplant Recipient Support Group *Professionally-run.* Provides a forum for transplant recipients to discuss their common concerns and experiences after a transplant. Meets once monthly, St. Barnabas Medical Center, Old Short Hills Rd., Livingston. Call Adriane Shaw, MSW 973-322-2204 (day).

Parents' Night Out *Professionally-run. (BILINGUAL)* Support for families of young children (up to age 8) with kidney disease. Group includes families with children on dialysis, pre or post kidney transplant. Guest speakers, phone help and buddy system. Meets at St. Barnabas Medical Center, 6-8:30pm, Livingston. For meeting day and time call Joanne Hall 973-322-2249 (day) or Jenny Orsini, RN 973-322-5264 (day).

MORRIS

The Kidney Korner *Professionally-run.* Support and education for dialysis and transplant patients. Meets every other month, 7pm, Roxbury Library, Main St., Succasunna. Call 973-584-1117.

"Confront your fears, list them, get to know them, and only then will you be able to put them aside and move ahead."--Jerry Gillies

NATIONAL

American Association of Kidney Patients *National. 14 chapters. Founded 1969.* Patient organization dedicated to helping renal patients and their families deal with the physical, emotional and social impact of kidney disease. Aim is to inform and inspire patients and their families to better understand their condition, adjust more readily to their circumstances and assume more normal, productive lives. Provides education and support for kidney patients, including those with reduced kidney function, on dialysis and transplant patients. Offers various educational materials, a bimonthly and quarterly magazine, two electronic newsletters and an annual convention. Chapter development guidelines available. Write: AAKP, 3505 East Frontage Rd., Suite 315, Tampa, FL 33607. Call 1-800-749-2257 or 813-636-8100. *Website:* http://www.aakp.org *Email:* info@aakp.org

IgA Nephropathy Support Network *National network. Founded 1992.* Acts as a clearinghouse of information for persons with IgA nephropathy and a forum in which patients can express their concerns. Promotes research into the causes and cures. Information, phone support, confidential network of patients. Newsletter. Write: IgA Nephropathy Support Network, 89 Ashfield Rd., Shelburne Falls, MA 01370. Call 413-625-9339. *Website:* http://www.igansupport.org

Kidneeds *National network. Founded 1997.* Grassroots support network for parents of children with membranoproliferative glomerulonephritis type II (aka dense deposit disease), a rare kidney disorder. Provides money for research on MPGN type 2. Offers phone support, newsletter and advocacy. Write: Kidneeds, 11 Cherry Lane NE, Iowa City, IA 52240. Call 319-338-6404. *Website:* http://www.medicine.uiowa.edu/kidneeds *Email:* llanning@blue.weeg.uiowa.edu

PKD Foundation for Research in Polycystic Kidney Disease *International. 55 volunteer friends chapters. Founded 1982.* Provides emotional support and education for persons with polycystic kidney disease and their families. Promotes public awareness and funds research. Holds medical seminars and fundraisers. Conferences, phone support, newsletter, assistance in starting new groups. Write: PKD Fdn., 9221 Ward Parkway, Suite 400, Kansas City, MO, 64114-3367. Call 1-800-753-2873 or 816-931-2600; Fax: 816-931-8655. *Website:* http://www.pkdcure.org *Email:* daves@pkdcure.org

"Medicines may be necessary. Flowers lift the heart. But your smile is the best restorative of all." --Pam Brown

LARYNGECTOMY

(see also cancer)

BERGEN

Laryngectomee Association Mutual support for laryngectomees. Pre-op and post-op visitation offered. Meets 1st Thurs., 7pm, American Cancer Society, 20 Mercer St., Hackensack. Call American Cancer Society 201-343-2222 (day) or Michael Lobosco 973-956-0278 (day).

BURLINGTON

Laryngectomy Club (Nu-Voice Program) Support for laryngectomy patients and their families. Meets 2nd Thurs., 7pm, (except July/Aug.), Raphael Meadows Health Center, Woodlane Rd., Mt. Holly. Before attending call 1-800-227-2345. *Website:* http://www.cancer.org

CAMDEN

Laryngectomy Club (Nu-Voice Program) Support group for laryngectomy patients and their families. Meets 1st Tues., 7pm, American Cancer Society, 1851 Old Cuthbert Rd., Cherry Hill. Before attending call 1-800-227-2345 (day). *Website:* http://www.cancer.org

MONMOUTH

Garden State Nu-Voice Club Dedicated to the education, rehabilitation, safety and welfare of laryngectomees. Mutual support and encouragement. Meets 1st and 3rd Sat., 9:30-11am, Riverview Medical Center, Red Bank. Call James 732-257-6927 (day/eve) or American Cancer Society 732-738-6800 (8am-noon).

MORRIS

Tri-County New Voice Laryngectomee Support Group of Morris/Sussex/Warren Counties. Mutual support and social activities for laryngectomees. Also includes anyone with neck, head and /or oral cancers. Family and friends are welcome. Meets 2nd Mon., (except Jan., Feb., Mar., July, Aug.), 7:30pm, Saint Clare's Hospital, Silby Hall, 25 Pocono Rd., Denville. Call Tom Beneventine 973-694-8417 or Doris Rapisardi 973-537-3912 (day).

OCEAN

International Association of Laryngectomees Ocean County Nu-Voice Club
Self-help for people who have had a laryngectomy. Newsletter. Dues $3. Meets 1st
Mon., 10am, The Corey Building, 599 Rt. 37 West, Toms River. Call American
Cancer Society 732-914-1000 (press 3). *Website:* http://www.cancer.org

PASSAIC

Lost Chords of New Jersey Mutual support for laryngectomees. Buddy system,
peer-counseling, outreach, discussion. Meets Wed., Wayne. For meeting
information call 1-800-227-2345 (24 hr).

SOMERSET

The Miracle Voice Club *Professionally-run.* Support and encouragement for
laryngectomy patients and their families. Meets 1st Thurs., 1pm, American Cancer
Society, 600 First Ave., Raritan. Call American Cancer Society 908-725-4664 ext.
3 (day).

INTERNATIONAL

International Association of Laryngectomees *International. 200 chapters.
Founded 1952.* Acts as a bridge starting before laryngectomy surgery through
rehabilitation. Provides practical and emotional support. Newsletter. Chapter
development guidelines. Write: Int'l Assn. of Laryngectomees, PO Box 691060,
Stockton, CA 95269-1060. Call 1-866-425-3678; Fax: 209-472-0516. *Website:*
http://www.larynxlink.com *Email:* IALhq@larynxlink.com

LIFE THREATENING / CHRONIC ILLNESS
(see also specific disorder, specific disorder, toll-free helplines)

BERGEN

Healing Hope Support with a spiritual emphasis on helping those who suffer
catastrophic loss including death, divorce, serious illness, etc. Meets 1st and 3rd
Tues., 7:30 – 9pm, Cornerstone Christian Church, 495 Wycoff Ave., Wycoff. Call
Kris Pepper 201-847-8107 (eve).

MERCER

Living and Loving with Chronic Illness *Professionally-run.* Confidential group
offering mutual support and discussion for person with a variety of chronic medical
conditions, including heart disease, neuromuscular disorders, cancer and chronic

pain. Meets alternate Wed., 2pm, St. Francis Medical Center, 601 Hamilton Ave., Trenton. Call Bev Snyderman 609-599-5657 (day).

MONMOUTH

Art Therapy for Children with a Chronically Ill Loved One *Professionally-run.* Support for children (age 4 1/2-13) who have a family member with a chronic or terminal illness. Uses art therapy to help children express their feelings. Meets periodically for 7 weeks, Riverview Medical Center, 1 Riverview Plaza, Red Bank. For information call Jane Weinheimer 732-530-2382.

OCEAN

Coping *Professionally-run.* Support group for persons with a life-threatening illness, their families and friends. Rap sessions, guest speakers and phone help. Meets 2nd and 4th Mon., 7-8:30pm, Ocean Medical Center, Oncology Department, 425 Jack Martin Blvd., Brick. Call Judith Willbergh 732-206-8340 (day).

NATIONAL

Center for Attitudinal Healing, The *National. 130+ affiliates. Founded 1975.* Emotional and spiritual support programs for children, youth and adults facing their own or a family member's life-threatening illness, long-term diagnosis or bereavement. Offers group guidelines for starting a local group. Also open to anyone wishing to change their perception of their lives. Workshops and trainings. Website contains information on centers and contacts around the world. Write: Center for Attitudinal Healing, 33 Buchanan Drive, Sausalito, CA 94965. Call 415-331-6161; Fax: 415-331-4545. *Website:* http://www.healingcenter.org *Email:* home123@aol.com

Project DOCC-Delivery Of Chronic Care *International. 26 chapters. Founded 1994.* Provides education regarding the impact of chronic illness and/or disability on a family. Information, referrals, phone support, email correspondence and "how to" guides on developing a local group. Write: Project DOCC, One South Rd., Oyster Bay Cove, NY 11771 Call 1-877-773-8747; Fax: 516-498-1899. *Website:* http://www.projectdocc.org *Email:* projdocc@aol.com

Rest Ministries *National. 275 affiliated groups. Founded 1997.* Christian ministry for people who live with chronic pain or illness and their families. Quarterly magazine, daily devotionals, share and prayer email support mailing list, online chat, etc. Information and resources manual for starting groups ($15) or complete kit available. Assistance to churches in setting up support groups, teaching church awareness and training church leadership on how to outreach to the chronically ill effectively. Write: Rest Ministries, Inc., PO Box 502928, San Diego, CA 92150. Call 1-888-751-REST or 858-486-4685; Fax: 1-800-933-1078. *Website:* http://www.hopekeepers.org *Email:* rest@restministries.org

ONLINE

Ability Online Support Network *Online.* A family friendly monitored electronic message system that enables children and adolescents with disabilities or chronic illness (also parents/caregivers/siblings) to share experiences, information, encouragement, support and hope through messages. Write: Ability Online Support Network, 104-1120 Finch Ave. W., Toronto ON M3J 3H7 Canada Call 416-650-6207; Fax: 416-650-5073. *Website:* http://www.abilityonline.org *Email:* information@ablelink.org

LIVER DISEASE
(see also hepatitis, transplants, specific disorder, toll-free helplines)

STATEWIDE

American Liver Foundation (Greater NY Chapter) (Covers northern NJ counties) *Professionally-run.* Support for persons with hepatitis or any other liver disease. Advocacy, education, guest speakers, phone help and literature. Family, friends and concerned professionals welcome. Meeting day and times vary. Call 1-877-307-7507 (day). *Website:* http://www.liverfoundation.org

CAMDEN

South Jersey Liver Opportunity for persons with any liver disease, including hepatitis C, to share coping skills. Buddy system, guest speakers, phone help. Dues $5 to join; $3/mtg. Meets 2nd Tues., (except June, July, Aug., Dec.), 7-9:30pm, West Jersey Hospital, Barry Brown Health Education Center, 316 Carnie Blvd., Voorhees. Call Harry Hagar Jr. 856-983-8247 or Marlene Reid 856-468-2883. *Website:* http://www.geocities.com/SJLDSG

MERCER

Mercer County Survivors of Liver Disease/Hepatitis Support and education for those afflicted with liver disease or hepatitis. Family, friends and professionals welcome. Lectures, guest speakers, advocacy, rap sessions and social group. Meets 1st and 3rd Sun, 7-9pm, Robert Wood Johnson University Hospital, 1 Hamilton Place, Hamilton. Call Peggy Goodale 609-371-3401 (day) or Tammy Leigh 609-584-6658 (day).

NATIONAL

American Liver Foundation *National. 25 chapters. Founded 1976.* Dedicated to the prevention, treatment and cure of hepatitis and other liver diseases through research, education and advocacy. Members include patients, families, professionals and supporters. Chapters organized and operated by lay volunteers and staff. Information on liver disease. Offers guidelines for starting groups. Online local chapter locator. Write: American Liver Foundation, 75 Maiden Lane, Suite 603, New York, NY 10038-4810. Call 1-800-465-4837; Fax: 212-483-8179. *Website:* http://www.liverfoundation.org *Email:* webmail@liverfoundation.org

CLASS (Children's Liver Association for Support Services) *Model. Founded 1995.* Dedicated to addressing the emotional, educational and financial needs of families with children with liver disease or liver transplantation. Telephone hotline, newsletter, parent matching, literature and financial assistance. Supports research and educates public about organ donations. Write: CLASS, 27023 McBean Parkway, Suite 126, Valencia, CA 91355. Call 1-877-679-8256 or 661-263-9099; Fax: 661-263-9099. *Website:* http://www.classkids.org *Email:* info@classkids.org

LUPUS
(see also toll-free helplines)

STATEWIDE

Lupus Foundation of America, Inc. Support and education for persons with lupus and their families. Social activities, fund-raising, guest speakers, newsletter, phone help, literature. Information and referral, resource library, pen pals, seminars. Dues $20yr/individual; $30yr/family. Call 1-800-322-5816 (day). *Website:* http://www.lupusnj.org

> New Jersey Chapter *Professionally-run.* Monthly support group meetings of 13 branches in 14 counties (See local county listings). Professional staff, volunteers and peer counselors assist and support lupus patients and their families. Monthly newsletter to members. Provides speakers for public and professional education. Write: Lupus Foundation Of America, NJ Chapter, P.O. Box 1184, 150 Morris Ave., Ste. 102, Springfield, NJ 07081.

> South Jersey Chapter Several educational meeting locations in Southern New Jersey. Support groups in Cherry Hill and Atlantic County. Write: Lupus Foundation of America, Heritage Executive Complex, 1873 Rt. 70 East, Suite 110F, Cherry Hill, NJ 08003. *Email:* nj4lupus@aol.com

This information is constantly changing. New groups start, others end. Please call us for the most up-to-date information from our database. 1-800-367-6274.

BERGEN

Lupus Foundation of America Support and information for lupus patients and their families. Promotes education and public awareness. Dues $20yr/individual; $30yr/family. Meets 4th Mon. (except Jan., Mar., July, Aug., Oct. and Dec.), 7:30pm, Kessler Institute for Rehabilitation, Conference Room B, 4th Floor, 300 Market Street, Elmwood Park. Call 1-800-322-5816. *Website:* http://www.lupusnj.org *Email:* nj4lupus@aol.com

CAMDEN

Lupus Foundation of America Support and information for lupus patients and their families. Promotes education and public awareness. Dues $20yr/individual; $30yr/family. Meets 3rd Sun., 1:30pm, Heritage Executive Complex, 1873 Route 70 E., Conference Room, Cherry Hill. Call 856-424-0255. *Website:* http://www.lupusnj.org

HUDSON

Lupus Foundation of America Support and information for lupus patients and their families. Promotes education and public awareness. Dues $20yr/individual; $30yr/family. Meets 4th Thurs. (except Jan., July, Aug. and Dec.), 7:30pm, St. Anne's Church, 3545 Kennedy Blvd., Jersey City. Call 1-800-322-5816. *Website:* http://www.lupusnj.org *Email:* nj4lupus@aol.com

MERCER

Lupus Foundation of America Support and information for lupus patients and their families. Promotes education and public awareness. Dues $20yr/individual; $30yr/family. Meets 3rd Wed.(except Jan., July, Aug. and Dec.), 7:30pm, Mercer County Library, 2751 Brunswick Pike, Lawrenceville. Call 1-800-322-5816. *Website:* http://www.lupusnj.org *Email:* nj4lupus@aol.com

MIDDLESEX

Lupus Foundation of America Support and information for lupus patients and their families. Promotes education and public awareness. Dues $20yr/individual; $30yr/family. Meets 4th Thurs., (except Apr., July, and Aug.), 7:30pm, Metuchen Public Library, 480 Middlesex Ave., Metuchen. Call 1-800-322-5816. *Website:* http://www.lupusnj.org *Email:* nj4lupus@aol.com

MONMOUTH

Lupus Foundation of America Support and information for lupus patients and their families. Promotes education and public awareness. Dues $20yr/individual; $30yr/family. Meets 2nd Mon. (except Jan., July, Aug.), 7:30pm, Eatontown Public Library, 33 Broad St., Joyce Stillwagon Community Room, Eatontown. Call 1-800-322-5816. *Website:* http://www.lupusnj.org *Email:* nj4lupus@aol.com

MORRIS

Lupus Foundation of America Support and information for lupus patients and their families. Promotes education and public awareness. Dues $20yr/individual; $30yr/family. Meets 2nd Wed. (except Jan., Feb., July and Aug.), 7:30pm, Saint Clare's Hospital, 1st Floor Conference Room, Room C, D and E, 400 W. Blackwell St., Dover. Call 1-800-322-5816. *Website:* http://www.lupusnj.org *Email:* nj4lupus@aol.com

PASSAIC

Lupus Foundation of America Support and information for lupus patients and their families. Promotes education and public awareness. Dues $20yr/individual; $30yr/family. Meets 4th Tues. (except Jan., July, Aug. and Dec.), 7:30pm, Siena Village Senior Citizens Retirement Home, Community Room, 1000 Siena Village, Wayne. Call 1-800-322-5816. *Website:* http://www.lupusnj.org *Email:* nj4lupus@aol.com

UNION

Lupus Foundation of America *Professionally-run.* Support and information for lupus patients and their families. Promotes education and public awareness. Dues $20yr/individual, $30yr/family. Meets 2nd Sat., (except Jan., July and Aug.), 11am., Muhlenberg University Medical Center, Park Ave. and Randolph Rd., Plainfield. Call 1-800-322-5816. *Website:* http://www.lupusnj.org *Email:* nj4lupus@aol.com

NATIONAL

Lupus Foundation of America, Inc. *National* Support and education for persons with lupus and their families. Social activities, fund-raising, guest speakers, newsletter, phone help, literature. Information and referral, resource library, pen pals, seminars. Write: Lupus Foundation of American, Inc., 2000 L/ St, NW, Suite 710, Washington, DC, 20036. Call 1-800-558-0121 or 202-349-1155; Fax: 202-349-1156. Website: http://www.lupus.org

LYME DISEASE

BURLINGTON

Lyme Disease Information Group Offers emotional support and education for those with Lyme disease. Meets 1st Wed., 7-8:30pm, Burlington County Library, Cinnaminson Branch, Riverton Rd., Cinnaminson. Call Sue Huesken 856-461-3369 (day/eve).

MORRIS

Long Valley Lyme Disease Association *Professionally-run.* Support, information and networking for people with Lyme disease. Social group, educational series, advocacy. Meets 3rd Wed., 7-9pm, Our Lady Of The Mountain Church, Springtown and Schooley's Mountain Rd., Long Valley. Call Nancy Braithwaite 908-852-5937 (eve). *Email:* dabrai@comcast.net

Morristown Lyme Support Group Support and education for Lyme disease victims and their families. Meets 3rd Tues., 7pm, The Presbyterian Parish House, 65 South St., Morristown. Call Anita Glick 973-267-8858.

OCEAN

Lyme Disease Association Inc. Very active group that focuses on education, prevention and research for Lyme disease. Referrals to health professionals and other health care. For meeting information call 1-888-366-6611. *Website:* http://www.lymediseaseassociation.org or http://www.lymenet.org *Email:* lymeliter@aol.com

NATIONAL

Lyme Disease Network *National network. Founded 1991.* Support, information and referrals for victims of Lyme disease and their families. Maintains computer information system. Write: Lyme Disease Network, 43 Winton Rd., E. Brunswick, NJ 08816. *Website:* http://www.lymenet.org *Email:* carol@lymenet.org

LYMPHEDEMA

ATLANTIC

Living with Lymphedema *Professionally-run.* Support for any type of lymphedema. Families welcome. Guest speakers, education and literature. Meets

2nd Thurs., 7-8:30pm, Shore Memorial Hospital, Cancer Center, Shore Rd. and Brighton Ave., Somers Point. Call Jennifer Hay 609-653-3512 (day).

ESSEX

Saint Barnabas Lymphedema Education/Support Group *Professionally-run.* Support and education for persons with lymphedema. Offers phone help, guest speakers, literature. Family and friends are welcome. Meets 2nd Wed., 6:30-8pm (except Jul/Aug), St. Barnabas Ambulatory Care Center, 200 S. Orange Ave., Livingston. Call Rita Loew 973-322-7293 (day).

NATIONAL

National Lymphedema Network Inc. *National. Founded 1988.* Support groups and information on primary and secondary lymphedema for patients and professionals. Newsletter, telephone infoline, conferences, pen pal program, referrals to treatment centers and physicians. Assistance in starting new groups. Dues $35. Write: National Lymphedema Network, 1611 Telegraph Ave., Suite 1111, Oakland, CA 94612. Call 1-800-541-3259 (recording) or 510-208-3200; Fax: 510-208-3110. *Website:* http://www.lymphnet.org *Email:* nln@lymphnet.org

MITRAL VALVE PROLAPSE

NATIONAL

National Society For MVP & Dysautonomia *National. 59 affiliated groups. Founded 1987.* Assists individuals suffering from mitral valve prolapse and dysautonomia to find support and understanding. Education on symptoms and treatment. Newsletter, literature. Write: Nat'l Soc. for MVP & Dysautonomia, 880 Montclair Rd., Suite 370, Birmingham, AL 35213. Call 205-592-5765 (day) or 1-800-541-8602 (day); Fax: 205-592-5707. *Website:* http//www.mvprolapse.com *Email:* staff@MVProlapse.com

MULTIPLE MYELOMA
(see also cancer)

INTERNATIONAL

International Myeloma Foundation *International network. 72 groups. Founded 1990.* Goal is to improve the quality of life of myeloma patients while working toward prevention and a cure. Operates a myeloma hotline, disseminates comprehensive printed and online information about myeloma, treatment options and disease management. Seminars and workshops for the patient, community and medical professionals. Write: IMF, 12650 Riverside Dr., Suite 206, North Hollywood, CA, 91607. Call 818-487-7455 or 1-800-452-2873; Fax: 818-487-7454. *Website:* http://www.myeloma.org *Email:* TheIMF@myeloma.org

MULTIPLE SCLEROSIS
(see also disability, specific disorder, toll-free helplines)

STATEWIDE

National Multiple Sclerosis Society/Greater Delaware Valley *Serving South Jersey, Greater Delaware Valley Area, Lehigh Valley and Reading.* 18 counties benefit from local support groups, resource centers and lending library information, education programs, national research. Write: Nat'l Multiple Sclerosis Society, Greater Delaware Valley, 1 Reed St., Suite 200, Philadelphia, PA 19147. Call 1-800-548-4611. *Website:* http://www.nationalmssociety.org/pae/home *Email:* elise.mendelsohn@pae.nmss.org

National Multiple Sclerosis Society - Greater North Jersey Chapter Serves the MS community by providing local services and funding national research. Guest speakers, advocacy, respite programs, equipment loan, camperships for children, quarterly newsletter, library resource center, sessions for the newly diagnosed and so much more. 18 groups in Bergen, Essex, Hudson, Morris, Passaic, Union, Warren and Sussex counties. Call 1-800-833-0087 or 201-967-5599. Write: Nat'l Multiple Sclerosis Society, 1 Kalisa Way, Suite 205, Paramus, NJ 07652-3550. *Website:* http://www.njbnmss.org *Email:* services@njb.nmss.org

National Multiple Sclerosis Society, Mid-Jersey Chapter Sponsors support groups throughout Monmouth, Ocean, Middlesex, Mercer, Somerset and Hunterdon counties. Call 732-660-1005 (day). Write: National MS Soc. Mid-Jersey Chapter, 246 Monmouth Rd., Oakhurst, NJ 07755

BERGEN

National "Friends" M.S. Society Support group for persons with multiple sclerosis and their families. Occasional guest speakers. Meets 1st Tues., 7pm, Holy Name Hospital, Teaneck, Call Sister Mary 201-967-5599. *Website:* http://www.njbnmss.org *Email:* pat@njb.nmss.org

National MS Society C.O.P.E. (Concern Over People's Emotion) Peer support, information and socialization for persons with multiple sclerosis. Meets last Thurs., 11am-1pm, Cornell Surgical Supply, 30 New Bridge Rd., Bergenfield. Call Joan 201-837-7790. *Website:* http://www.njbnmss.org *Email:* pat@njb.nmss.org

National MS Society T.M. (Twice Monthly) Support and education for persons diagnosed with multiple sclerosis and their families and friends. Guest speakers. Meets 1st and 3rd Mon., 7pm, Trinity Presbyterian Church, 650 Pascack Rd., Paramus. Call Joe 201-797-3386. *Website:* http://www.njbnmss.org *Email:* pat@njb.nmss.org

ESSEX

National M.S. Society Support group for persons with multiple sclerosis and their families. *Website:* http://www.njbnmss.org *Email:* pat@njb.nmss.org

> **Livingston** Always a guest speaker. Meets 2nd Mon., 7pm, Livingston Library. Call Marlene 973-992-5313 or Roy 973-338-9693.
>
> **Newark** Lunch provided. Meets 3rd Thurs., noon, University of Medicine and Dentistry. Before attending call Linda 973-923-6912.
>
> **Nutley** Meets 3rd Thurs., 7pm, Vincent United Methodist Church. Call Gary 973-667-5209.

National MS Gay/Lesbian Support Group *Professionally-run.* Mutual support for gay/lesbians with multiple sclerosis. Family and friends welcome. Rap sessions. Meets 2nd Thurs., 7pm, Vincent United Methodist Church, 100 Vincent Place, Nutley. Call Laura 973-509-8567. *Website:* http://www.njbnmss.org *Email:* pat@njb.nmss.org

GLOUCESTER

Gloucester County MSAA Client Support *Professionally-run.* Provides fellowship and support to persons with multiple sclerosis. Education, guest speakers, rap sessions and socials. Meets 4th Wed., 6:30-8:30pm, Johnson Wood Library, Highland Ave., Deptford. Call Shirley 856-228-8474.

Washington-Gloucester Twp. MS Self-Help Mutual support for persons with multiple sclerosis, their families and friends. Rap sessions, guest speakers. Meets 3rd Mon., 11am-1pm, Cardinal Retirement Home, 455 Hurffville-Crosskey Rd, Sewell. Call Denise Savarese 856-627-6401 or Joyce Nealon 856-374-9273 (12-8pm). *Website:* http://www.pae.nmss.org *Email:* deeanns53@comcast.net

HUDSON

National MS Society - Hudson County Self-Help Group Mutual support and education for persons with multiple sclerosis, their families and friends. Guest speakers, phone help, social activities. Meets periodically, Jewish Hospital and

Rehabilitation Center, Jersey City. For meeting information call Christine 201-332-3417 (day). *Website:* http://www.njbnmss.org *Email:* pat@njb.nmss.org

National Multiple Sclerosis Society/Bayonne Support Group Mutual support for persons with multiple sclerosis. Rap sessions, guest speakers. Meets 4th Mon., 1pm, Jewish Community Center, 44th St. and Kennedy Blvd., Bayonne. Call Helen 201-858-3999. *Website:* http://www.njbnmss.org *Email:* pat@njb.nmss.org

HUNTERDON

MS Hunterdon Support Group Support for multiple sclerosis patients. Family and friends welcome. Discussions, exchange of coping skills, guest speakers, literature and phone help. Meets 2nd Fri., 7:30pm, (except in Jan.-Feb., July, Aug.), Our Lady of Lourdes Church, White House Station. Call Joe 908-218-0398, Joan 732-828-1263 or NMSS Chapter 732-660-1005.

MERCER

MS Support of Mercer County Support, information and open discussions on living and managing the physical and emotional aspects of multiple sclerosis. Also open to family members. Meets 4th Sun., 2-4pm, (except July/Aug.), Morris Hall, 1 Bishop's Court and Route 546, Lawrenceville. Call Brenda 609-631-8598 or Mike 609-396-4556. *Website:* http://www.nationalmssociety.org

MIDDLESEX

Metuchen Multiple Sclerosis Peer Group Mutual help for persons with multiple sclerosis. Meets 3rd Tues., (except June, July, Aug.), 10am-1pm, First Presbyterian Church, Social Center, Woodbridge Ave. and Home St., Metuchen. Call Bob 732-249-0480 (day). *Website:* http://www.nationalmssociety.org

Multiple Sclerosis "Mild Symptoms" Mutual support for persons with multiple sclerosis who have mild symptoms. Meets 3rd Wed., 7-9pm, North Brunswick Fire House, Cozzens Lane, North Brunswick. Call Heather 732-422-1391 or Susan 732-238-0864. *Website:* http://www.nationalmssociety.org

Multiple Sclerosis Support Group/Central Jersey Chapter Mutual support for people with multiple sclerosis, their families and friends. Transportation available Meets 3rd Wed., 7-9pm, (except Dec.), East Brunswick Public Library, 2 Civic Center Dr., East Brunswick.. Before attending call Elihu 732-613-5080 (day/eve). *Website:* http://www.nationalmssociety.org

MONMOUTH

Eastern Monmouth County Multiple Sclerosis Self-Help Phone support and networking for persons with multiple sclerosis and their families. Call Evelyn Wilson 732-229-2027 (day).

Multiple Sclerosis Support Group Support, information, discussions on living, managing the physical and emotional aspects of multiple sclerosis. Families welcome.

> **Freehold** *Professionally-run.* Meets 3rd Mon., 1-3pm, CentraState Hospital, Health Awareness Center, Gibson Pl. Call Michele 732-294-2505. *Website:* http://freeholdmssupport.home.comcast.net.
> **Marlboro** Meetings vary, Marlboro Public Library, Library Ct. and Wyncrest Cr. Call Lorraine 732-671-9384 or Dianne 732-536-3033.

MORRIS

Montville Multiple Sclerosis Support Group *Professionally-run.* Fellowship of persons with multiple sclerosis. Provides information, networking and a creative exchange of ideas. Under 18 welcome. Meets 2nd Thurs., 10am, Youth Center, Changebridge Rd., Montville. Call Beatrice 973-263-2855 or Roseann 973-334-8434. *Website:* http://www.njbnmss.org *Email:* pat@njb.nmss.org

M.S. Dinner Group Mutual support and social events for singles and young adults with multiple sclerosis. Phone help, rap sessions. Meets various times and days at local restaurants. For information call Marcia Lutwin 973-625-8981 (day/eve).

National Multiple Sclerosis Morristown Support Group Fellowship of M.S. patients that meet for information, networking and creative exchange of ideas. Under 18 welcome. Guest speakers, discussions, socials. Meets 1st Tues., 7pm, Presbyterian Parish House, 65 South St., Morristown. Call Anita 973-503-1141 (anytime) or Janet 973-428-1544. *Website:* http://www.njbnmss.org *Email:* pat@njb.nmss.org

OCEAN

Multiple Sclerosis Support Group *(Sponsored by MSAA)* Mutual support for multiple sclerosis patients, their families and friends. Meets 3rd Sat., 1pm, (except June/July/Aug.), Epiphany Roman Catholic Church, All Purpose Room, Thiele Rd., Brick. Before attending call Anita 732-477-1479 or Gene Van Severen 732-920-3641 (day).

Toms River Family and Friends Support Group Provides support and education for family and friends of individuals with multiple sclerosis. Rap sessions, guest speakers and phone help. Meets 4th Fri., (except July/Aug.), 7-9pm, Community Care Center, 591 Lakehurst Rd., Toms River. Call Pat 732-244-7523. *Website:* http://www.nationalmssociety.org

Toms River Support Group Provides education, rap sessions, guest speakers, phone help, support and camaraderie for people with multiple sclerosis. Meets 4th Fri., (except July/Aug.), 7-9pm, The Lighthouse, 591 Lakehurst Rd., Toms River. Call Pat 732-244-7523 or Dianne 732-892-2230. *Website:* http://www.nationalmssociety.org

PASSAIC

National MS Society Support group for persons with multiple sclerosis and their families. Guest speakers. Meets 3rd Mon., 7pm, Packanack Lake Church, 120 Lake Drive East, Wayne. Call Michael 973-628-8991. *Website:* http://www.njbnmss.org *Email:* pat@njb.nmss.org

National MS Society Squeaky Wheels Caring and sharing support group for persons with multiple sclerosis and their families. Information, advocacy. Meets 4th Wed., noon, Hillcrest Center, Macopin Rd., West Milford. Call Janice 973-728-1282 (day) or Mary 973-835-2565. *Website:* http://www.njbnmss.org *Email:* pat@njb.nmss.org

SOMERSET

Multiple Sclerosis Support Group Information and open discussions on living with and managing physical and emotional aspects of multiple sclerosis for both the person with M.S. and their significant others. Meets 4th Thurs., 7-9pm, (except July/Aug.), Summerville At Hillsborough Assisted Living Complex, 600 Auten Rd., Hillsborough. Call Wendy 908-359-4514 (day) or Doug 908-369-4609 (before 8pm). *Website:* http://www.nationalmssociety.org

SUSSEX

National Multiple Sclerosis Sparta Support Group Fellowship of M.S. patients meeting for information, networking and creative exchange of ideas. Guest speakers, discussions, socials. Meets 1st Wed., 7pm, George Inn, Vernon. Call Dawn 973-875-3461 or Paul 973-827-0096. *Website:* http://www.njbnmss.org *Email:* pat@njb.nmss.org

We can also refer callers to over 100 individuals who are seeking others to help start new support groups throughout NJ, if you don't see it, that doesn't mean it doesn't exist!
1-800-367-6274

UNION

Bridges for Life A support group representing minorities who are challenged with multiple sclerosis. Mutual support, sharing of ideas, education and guest speakers. Meets 3rd Sat., 10am-12:30pm, Steve Sampson Senior Center, 800 Anna St., Elizabeth. Call Tina Smith 908-354-1481 (day).

Multiple Sclerosis and Family Support Mutual support, sharing and encouragement for persons with multiple sclerosis, their families and friends. Children are welcome to attend. Meets Sat., (usually the 2nd), 2-4pm, Rahway Recreation Center, 3 City Hall Plaza and Milton Ave., Rahway. For information call Francine 732-396-4754 or Beth 732-388-9407.

National MS Society "But You Look So Good" Support Group Support for those who have Multiple Sclerosis. Caregivers are welcome. Mutual sharing, education, rap sessions and guest speakers. Meets 1st Tues., 7pm, Clark Municipal Building, 951 Lincoln Ave., Clark. Call Julia 908-298-9782 or Beth 732-388-9407. *Website:* http://www.njbnmss.org *Email:* pat@njb.nmss.org

WARREN

Sharing and Caring Mutual support for persons with multiple sclerosis. Guest speakers. Meets 2nd Mon., 7:30pm, Hackettstown Hospital, Willow Grove St., Hackettstown. Call Cindy 973-786-5382 or Helen 908-979-0984. *Website:* http://www.njbnmss.org *Email:* pat@njb.nmss.org

NATIONAL

Multiple Sclerosis Association of America *National. 7 regional U.S. offices/2 Canadian affiliated group. Founded 1970.* Mutual support and education for persons with multiple sclerosis. Offers phone support, information and referrals, networking program, support group meetings, MRI funding, lending library, home modification program, cooling equipment program and more. Write: MSAA, 706 Haddonfield Rd., Cherry Hill, NJ 08002. Call 1-800-532-7667; Fax: 856-488-8257. *Website:* http://www.msaa.com *Email:* msaa@msaa.com

National Multiple Sclerosis Society *National. 1700 self-help groups. Founded 1946.* Provides emotional support and information for persons with multiple sclerosis and their families and friends. Funds research. Offers information & referrals, support groups for patients & families, professional education and newsletter. Write: National MS Society Information Resource Center, 700 Broadway, Suite 810, Denver, CO 80203. Call 1-800-344-4867. *Website:* http://www.nationalmssociety.org *Email:* kimberly.koch@nmss.org

ONLINE

MS Moms (Managing Our Multiple Sclerosis) *Online.* Support for mothers living, parenting and managing with their multiple sclerosis. *Website:* http://www.msmoms.com

MUSCULAR DYSTROPHY
ESSEX

MDA General Support Group *Professionally-run.* Mutual support for individuals with muscular dystrophy. Families welcome. Sharing of information, experiences, ideas and resources. Guest speakers. Meets 2nd Tues., 7-8:30pm, Jewish Community Center Metrowest, Meeting Room M 3, 760 Northfield Ave., West Orange. Before attending call 201-843-4452 (day).

NATIONAL

Muscular Dystrophy Association *National. 200+ chapters. Founded 1950.* Provides comprehensive medical services to persons with neuromuscular disease. Supports research into the causes, cures and treatments of neuromuscular disorders. Support programs include self-help groups, phone friends, pen pals and scheduled online chat sessions. Write: MDA, 3300 E. Sunrise Dr., Tucson, AZ 85718-3299. Call 1-800-572-1717; Fax: 520-529-5454. *Website:* http://www.mdausa.org *Email:* mda@mdausa.org

Parent Project for Muscular Dystrophy Research, Inc. *International network. Founded 1994.* Support for parents of children with Duchenne and Becker muscular dystrophy. To improve the treatment, quality of life and long-term outlook for all individuals affected by DMD through research, advocacy, education and compassion. Provides user-friendly website with online forums, scientific and legislative conferences, newsletters, information on newest diagnosis, standards of care and research strategies. Write: PPMD, 158 Linwood Plaza, Fort Lee, NJ 07024. Call 1-800-714-5437 or 201-944-9985; Fax: 201-944-9987. *Website:* http://www.parentprojectmd.org *Email:* info@parentprojectmd.org

SMDI (Society for Muscular Dystrophy Information) International *International network. Founded 1983.* Purpose is to share and encourage the exchange of non-technical, neuromuscular and disability related information. Referrals to support groups via networking website. Write: SMDI, Int'l, PO Box 479, Bridgewater, NS Canada B4V 2X6. Call 902-685-3962; Fax: 902-685-3962. *Website:* http://www.societyneuromuscularinfo.org *Email:* smdi_intl@mail_auracom.com

ONLINE

OPMD Support Group for News and Research *Online.* E-mail discussion groups for persons with oculopharyngeal muscular dystrophy, their families and friends. Provides message exchange, support and information on latest research. *Website:* http://health.groups.yahoo.com/group/opmd

NEUROPATHY

BERGEN

Northern New Jersey Peripheral Neuropathy Support Group Support, to persons with peripheral neuropathy. Guest speakers, educational series, phone help, literature. Dues $15/yr. Meets 3rd Thurs., 7:30-9:30pm, (except Jan, July and Aug), Englewood Hospital, 350 Engle St., Englewood. Call Lynda Icochea 201-814-0336(eve) for meeting information. For directions to Englewood Hospital call 201-894-3000. *Email:* licochea@yahoo.com

MERCER

Peripheral Neuropathy Support Group Support for person with nerve damage as a result of neuropathy. Family and friends are welcome. Offers guest speakers, mutual sharing, educational series, rap sessions, literature and phone help. Meetings vary, Robert Wood Johnson Hospital, Hamilton Square. For meeting information call Bill 609-587-7215.

MONMOUTH

Monmouth/Ocean Neuropathy Support Group Support and information to those afflicted with neuropathy. Mutual sharing, guest speakers, literature and phone help. Dues $15 yr. Meetings vary, Rehabilitation Hospital of Tinton Falls, 2 Centre Plaza, Tinton Falls. Call Kathleen 732-449-7845 (day/eve) or 212-692-0662. *Email:* kathylutz@optonline.net

INTERNATIONAL

Neuropathy Association *International. 214 affiliated groups. Founded 1995.* Provides support, education and advocacy for persons with peripheral neuropathy. Promotes and funds research into the cause and cure. Online bulletin board, referrals to support groups and doctors. Medical surveys. Write: Neuropathy Assn. 60 E. 42nd St., Room 942, New York, NY 10165. Call 212-692-0662; Fax: 212-692-0668. *Website:* http://www.neuropathy.org *Email:* info@neuropathy.org

ONLINE

Hereditary Neuropathy with liability to Pressure Palsies *Online.* Mutual support and information for individuals to learn about HNPP, where to find help and how to manage their symptoms. E-mail support group. *Website:* http://www.hnpp.org

OSTEOPOROSIS

BERGEN

Arthritis Foundation Osteoporosis Support Group Provides those with osteoporosis, their family and friends an opportunity to discuss their problems, offer mutual respect and exchange ideas to help cope with the disease. Rap sessions, guest speakers, phone help, literature. Meetings vary, 10-11am, Pascack Valley Hospital,Auditorium, Old Hook Rd., Westwood. Registration required. Call 201-358-6000 or 845-426-5505.

ESSEX

Osteoporosis Support Group *Professionally-run.* Support and education for people with osteoporosis, their families and friends. Discussions, guest speakers and literature. Meets 2nd Thurs., 11:30am-1pm, St. Barnabas Ambulatory Care Center, Conference Room A/B, 200 S. Orange Ave., Livingston. Call Susan Allison 973-322-7830 (day). *Email:* sallison@sbhcs.com

HUNTERDON

Arthritis Foundation NJ Chapter Mutual support and education for people with arthritis, osteoporosis and their families. Meets 2nd Mon., 1-3pm, Hunterdon Medical Center, Meeting Room A and B, 2100 Wescott Drive, Flemington. Call 908-788-6373 ext. 1.

MIDDLESEX

Arthritis Foundation Support Group for Osteoporosis Mutual support and education for people with osteoporosis and their families. Meets 1st Wed., 7pm, JFK Johnson Rehab, Day Rehab Patient and Family, 65 James St., Edison. Call Arthritis Foundation 1-888-467-3112 (day).

If you are using this book past Spring 2007,
please call us for information about our most recent directory. 1-800-367-6274

MORRIS

Morris County Osteoporosis Support Group *Professionally-run.* Provides those with osteoporosis, their family and friends an opportunity to discuss their problems, offer mutual respect and exchange ideas to help cope with the disease. Meets 3rd Thurs., 10:30am-12noon, Madison YMCA, 1 Ralph Stoddard Dr., Madison. Call Angele Thompson 908-898-0055.

OCEAN

Osteoporosis Self-Help Organization Support and education for persons with osteoporosis. Meets 1st Fri., 2:30pm, The Lighthouse, Community Medical Center, 591 Lakehurst Rd., Toms River. Call Sherlynn 732-349-8239 (day/eve) or The Lighthouse 1-800-621-0096 (day).

NATIONAL

National Osteoporosis Foundation *National. 80 affiliated support groups. Founded 1987.* Dedicated to reducing the widespread prevalence of osteoporosis through programs of research, education and advocacy. Provides referrals to existing support groups, as well as free resources and materials to assist people in starting groups. Write: NOF, 1232 22nd St. NW, Washington, DC 20037-1292. Call 202-223-2226; Fax: 202-223-2237. *Website:* http://www.nof.org *Email:* jeffrey@nof.org

OSTOMY

BURLINGTON

Ostomy Association of Southern NJ Education and encouragement for ostomy patients, those with related surgery and their families. Meets 3rd Mon., 7-9pm, Virtua Memorial Hospital of Burlington County, Conference Center, 175 Madison Ave., Mt. Holly. Call Ken Aukett 856-854-3737 (10am-10pm). *Website:* http://www.ostomyburlco.org *Email:* kenaukett@uoaa.org

ESSEX

United Ostomy Associations of America Education and encouragement for ostomy patients and their families. Outreach, peer-counseling, phone help, newsletter. Meets monthly, (except July/Aug.), St. Barnabas Ambulatory Care Center, 200 S. Orange Ave., Livingston. Call Paula Von Rosendahl 973-239-1616, Harold 973-992-8241 (day) or Margaret Tretola 973-743-9550 (visitor coordinator).

HUNTERDON

Ostomy Support Group *Professionally-run.* Education and support for ostomy patients and their families. Guest speakers, lecture series and literature. Meets 3rd Tues., 7 – 9pm, Hunterdon Medical Center, 2100 Wescott Dr., Flemington. Call Beverly Phillips 908-237-5427 (day/eve).

MIDDLESEX

United Ostomy Association Education and encouragement for ostomy patients and their families. Outreach, visitation, phone help, newsletter. Dues $25/yr. Meets 1st Wed., 7pm, Magyar Reformed Church, Somerset and Division St., New Brunswick. Call 732-572-3298 (day/eve). *Email:* medicamm@aol.com

MORRIS

Morris Ostomy Association Education and encouragement for ostomy patients and their families. Provides outreach, visitation, peer-counseling, newsletter. Meets 3rd Wed., 7:30-9:00pm, Morristown Memorial Hospital, Carol G. Simon Cancer Center, Conference Room, Morristown. Call Toni Mc Tigue, MSN,RN,CWOCN 973-971-5522 (day).

OCEAN

United Ostomy Assn. Education and encouragement for ostomy patients and their families. Visitation, peer-counseling and newsletter. Dues $5/yr. Meets 4th Fri., (except July/Aug.), 7pm, Toms River Presbyterian Church, 1070 Hooper Ave., Toms River. Call Tom 732-901-9411 (day) or American Cancer Society 732-914-1000 (day/eve).

SOMERSET

United Ostomy Assn. Education and encouragement for ostomy patients and their families. Outreach visitation, guest speakers, phone help, newsletter. Meets 3rd Tues.,(except July/Aug./Dec.), 7:30pm, Somerset Medical Center, South Fuld, Conference Room C and D, 110 Rehill Ave, Somerville. Call Joyce Hoffman 908-685-2814 (day).

UNION

Ostomy Support Group *Professionally-run.* Sharing and support for any ostomate and their families with questions and concerns related to living with an ostomy. Guest speakers. Meets one Tues. every other month, 2pm, Overlook

Hospital, 99 Beauvoir Ave., Summit. Call Virginia Moriarty 908-522-2156 (day).

WARREN

United Ostomy Assn. *Professionally-run.* Education and encouragement for ostomy patients and families (under 18 welcome). Public education, visitation program, newsletter. Meets 3rd Sun., 2pm, Warren Hospital, Phillipsburg. Dues $22.50/yr. Call Leslie Washuta 908-859-6700, ext. 2186 or Pat Lafaso 908-852-2475 (eve).

NATIONAL

Pull-thru Network, The. *International network. Founded 1988.* Support and information for the families with children born with anorectal malformations (including cloaca, VATER/VACTERL, cloacal exstrophy or an imperforate anus) and Hirschsprung's disease and associated diagnoses. Maintains a database for member networking. Quarterly magazine. Online discussion group. Weekly chat for members. Phone support and literature. Dues $20. Write: The Pull-thru Network, 2312 Savoy St., Hoover, Al 35226-1528. Call 205-978-2930. *Website:* http://www.pullthrough.org *Email:* info@pullthrough.org

United Ostomy Association *National. 380 chapters. Founded 1962.* Dedicated to helping every person with an ostomy and related surgeries return to normal living. Also has support groups for parents of children with ostomies. Chapter development help, visitation program, magazine. Local group directory on website. Write: United Ostomy Assn., 19772 MacArthur Blvd., Suite 200, Irvine, CA 92612-2405. Call 1-800-826-0826 or 949-660-8624; Fax: 949-660-9262. *Website:* http://www.uoa.org *Email:* info@uoa.org

PAIN, CHRONIC
(see also specific disorder, toll-free helplines)

ATLANTIC

Atlantic Chronic Pain Support Group Mutual support for individuals dealing with a chronic pain situation. Meets Wed., 6:30-8:30pm, Bacharach Institute for Rehabilitation, Board Room, Pomona. Call Sheile Rosen, RN 609-748-5431 (day).

BURLINGTON

Reflex Sympathetic Dystrophy and Chronic Pain Support Group Support for those persons with reflex sympathetic dystrophy or chronic pain, their families and friends. Helps members maintain as normal and pain free life as possible. Guest speakers, educational programs, pen pals, rap sessions, literature, phone help, advocacy.

Holcomb Meets 4th Tues., 6-8pm, YMCA, 5001 Centerton Rd. Call Sue Holcomb 856-461-5941 (day). *Email:* auntsuzymouse@hotmail.com

Mt. Holly Meets 2nd Wed., 7-9, Virtua Hospital, 175 Madison Ave., Conference Room, 1st Floor. Call Kathy Henson 609-268-1565 (day) or Sue Holcomb 856-461-5941 (day). *Email:* bepainfree2000@aol.com

CAMDEN

American Chronic Pain Association Help and Hope Support for those suffering from chronic pain and their families. A helping hand and friendly ear for those chronic pain sufferers willing to help themselves. Rap sessions, guest speakers and literature. Meets 2nd Mon., 7-9pm, Barry D. Brown Health Education Center, 106 Carnie Blvd., Voorhees. Call Philip Elting 856-489-4383 (day/eve).

Chronic Pain Support Group *Professionally-run.* Provides support for those living with chronic pain. Meets 2nd Fri., 10:30-11:30am, New Seasons Assisted Living, 501 Laurel Oak Rd., Voorhees. Call Tanya Donovan at Elder Med 1-800-522-1965.

MERCER

American Chronic Pain Association - Help and Hope Support for people suffering from chronic pain. Offers support, education, resources and understanding to those living with chronic pain. Meets 1st and 3rd Mon., 1-3pm, University Medical Center at Princeton, Lambert House, Classroom # 4, 253 Witherspoon St., Princeton. Call Anne 609-799-4681. *Website:* http://www.theacpa.org

Living and Loving with Chronic Illness *Professionally-run.* Confidential group offering mutual support and discussion for person with a variety of chronic medical conditions, including heart disease, neuromuscular disorders, cancer and chronic pain. Meets alternate Wed., 2pm, St. Francis Medical Center, 601 Hamilton Ave., Trenton. Call Bev Snyderman 609-599-5657 (day).

MONMOUTH

Reflex Sympathetic Dystrophy/Chronic Pain Support Group Mutual support, encouragement and information for persons suffering from reflex sympathetic dystrophy or any chronic pain situation. Meets 3rd Wed., 2pm, Grace United Methodist Church, Union Beach. For information call Catherine 732-291-7357 (9-11am, 1-3pm or 7-8pm).

MORRIS

New Hope and Healing *Professionally-run.* Support for adults experiencing pain in their lives. Offers mutual support, sharing coping skills, guest speakers, education workshops, seminars and retreats. Meets in Morris County. Call Christine 973-927-4719 (day). *Email:* newhopehealing@aol.com

NATIONAL

American Chronic Pain Association, Inc. *National. 400+ affiliated chapters. Founded 1980.* Provides peer support and education for individuals with chronic pain and their families so that they may live more fully in spite of their pain. Aim is to raise awareness among health care community, policy makers and the public about issues of living with chronic pain. Workbooks for self-help recovery. Quarterly newsletter. Group development guidelines. Phone network. Outreach program to clinics. Write: American Chronic Pain Association, PO Box 850, Rocklin, CA 95677. Call 1-800-533-3231 or 916-632-0922; Fax: 916-632-3208. *Website:* http://www.theacpa.org *Email:* ACPA@pacbell.net

National Chronic Pain Outreach Association, Inc. *National network. Founded 1980.* Clearinghouse for information about chronic pain and pain management. Aims at increasing public awareness and decreasing the stigma of chronic pain. Provides kit to develop local support groups, national physician referral service and support group listings, quarterly magazine and other materials. Dues $25/yr. Write: Nat'l Chronic Pain Outreach Assn., PO Box 274, Millboro, VA 24460. Call 540-862-9437; Fax: 540-862-9485. *Website:* http://chronicpain.org *Email:* info@chronicpain.org

Rest Ministries *National. 275 affiliated groups. Founded 1997.* Christian ministry for people who live with chronic pain or illness and their families. Quarterly magazine, daily devotionals, share and prayer email support mailing list and online chat. Information and resources manual for starting groups ($15). Assistance to churches in setting up support groups, teaching church awareness and training church leadership on how to outreach to the chronically ill effectively. Write: Rest Ministries, Inc., PO Box 502928, San Diego, CA 92150. Call 1-888-751-REST or 858-486-4685; Fax: 1-800-933-1078. *Website:* http://www.restministries.org *Email:* rest@restministries.org

---

We will open the book. Its pages are blank.
We are going to put words on them ourselves.
The book is called *Opportunity* and its first chapter is every day.
--Edith Lovejoy Pierce

PARKINSON'S DISEASE
(see also toll-free helplines)

STATEWIDE

American Parkinson's Disease Association NJ Chapter Provides literature, speakers bureau, educational programs and physician referrals. Referrals to support groups. Write: NJ APDA Information and Referral Center, Robert Wood Johnson Hosp., 1 Robert Wood Johnson Place, New Brunswick, NJ 08901. Call 732-745-7520

BERGEN

Parkinson's Support Group Mutual support and exchange of information for persons with Parkinson's, families and caregivers. Pen pals, rap sessions, guest speakers and phone help.

> **Englewood** Meets Fri., 1-3pm, Englewood Southeast Center for Independent Living, 228 Grand Ave. Call Ilse Heller 201-265-4946 (day) or Pat Marshall 201-224-8816. *Email:* pkmarshall4@msn.com
> **Greater Ridgewood Area** Meets 1st Thurs., 7:30pm; Lecture series 3rd Thurs., (except July, Aug., Dec.), 7:30pm, Cedar Hill Christian Reformed Church, Cedar Hill Ave. Call Marion Arenas 201-670-0083 (day) or Gene Provost 973-875-8429 (day).
> **Haworth** Meets 1st Sat., (except July/Aug.), 1-2:30pm, 1st Congregational Church, Haworth Ave. Call Ilse Heller 201-265-4976.

BURLINGTON

Parkinson Disease Support Support for those afflicted with Parkinson's, families and friends. Meets 3rd Wed., (except Dec.), 7-8:30pm, Virtua Health and Rehab Center, 62 Richmond Ave., Mt. Holly. Call Virtua 1-888-847-8823 (day).

CAMDEN

Parkinson's Caregivers Support Group *Professionally-run.* Offers encouragement and support to those caring for a person with Parkinson's. Meets 3rd Tues., 10:00-11:30am, New Seasons Assisted Living Communities, 501 Laurel Oak Road, Voorhees. Call Tanya Donovan 1-800-522-1965 (day).

Parkinson's Disease Support Group *Professionally-run.* Mutual support to enhance the well being of persons with Parkinson's disease. To help persons cope and continue to enjoy life. Meets 3rd Tues., 10-11:00am, New Seasons Assisted Living Communities, 501 Laurel Oak Road, Voorhees. Call Tanya Donovan 1-800-522-1965 (day).

CAPE MAY

Parkinson's Support Group of Cape May County Mutual support for Parkinson's disease patients and their families. Meets 2nd Thurs., (except July/Aug.) 1pm, Victoria Commons, Town Bank Rd., North Cape May. Call Rita 609-886-2455 (day).

ESSEX

Parkinson Support Group of North Jersey Mutual support and exchange of information for persons with Parkinson's, families and caregivers. Discussions and guest speakers. Meets 3rd Sat., 10am, Mountainside Hospital, Bay Ave., Montclair. Call Arlene 973-473-4690 (day) or Skeets 973-697-1183 (day).

GLOUCESTER

Parkinson's Support Group of Southern New Jersey *Professionally-run.* Support, education and social events for Parkinson's patients and their families. Occasional guest speakers. Meets 1st Wed., 7pm, Woodbury Mews, 122 Green Ave., Woodbury. Call Diane Gruszewski 856-582-1419 (day).

HUNTERDON

Hunterdon County Parkinson's Support Group *Professionally-run.* Support for persons with Parkinson's and their caregivers. Patients and caregivers meet both together and separately. Meets 4th Fri., 1:30-3:30pm, Senior Multi-Purpose Center, Route 31 South, Flemington. Call Barbara Burgard 908-788-6401 ext. 3149 (day).

MERCER

Parkinson's Support Group of Central Delaware Valley Support and information for Parkinson's patients and families. Guest speakers, educational programs. Meets 3rd Wed. (except July/Aug., Jan. and Feb.), 1pm, Lawrenceville Presbyterian Church, 2688 Main St., Route 206, Lawrenceville. Call John Wicoff 609-737-3364 or Robert Monacci 215-493-4774. *Email:* JRWicoff@comcast.net

MIDDLESEX

Parkinson's Disease Patient and Family Support Group Mutual support and education for those with Parkinson's, their families and caregivers. Patients and caregivers meet both separately and together. Meets 3rd Thurs., 12:30pm, Robert Wood Johnson University Hospital, Auditorium, New Brunswick. Call NJ Parkinson Disease Information and Referral Center 732-745-7520.

Saint Peter's University Hospital Parkinson Group Support, education and coping skills for individuals with Parkinson's disease. Families welcome. Literature, rap sessions and guest speakers. Meets 1st Wed., 1-2:30pm, Monroe Township Office on Aging, Municipal Complex, Perrineville Rd., Monroe Township. Pre-registration required. Call Jennifer 732-521-6111 (day) Janice Dibling 732-321-7063.

Young Onset Parkinson's Patient and Family Support Group *Professionally-run.* Support and education for Parkinson's patients under 60 years old, their families or caregivers. Meets 3rd Wed., 7pm, Robert Wood Johnson Hospital, New Brunswick. Call NJ Parkinson Information and Referral Center 732-745-7520 (day). *Website:* http://www.apdaparki nson.org *Email:* njpc3@aol.com

MONMOUTH

Organization del Mal de Parkinson *(SPANISH)* Support for Hispanic families afflicted with Parkinson's disease. Rap sessions, literature, phone help and buddy system. Meetings vary, 1-3pm, 100 Lambert Way, Freehold. For meeting dates call Elena Tuero 732-780-6853 (day). *Website:* http://www.maldeparkinson.org *Email:* info@maldeparkinson.org

Parkinson's Support Group Mutual support for Parkinson's patients and their families. Guest speakers.
> **Manalapan** Meets 2nd Tues., (except Aug.), 1:30-2:30pm, Manalapan Senior Center, Route 522. Before attending call Seniors First 732-780-3013 (day).
> **Long Branch** *Professionally-run.* Meets 1st Thurs., 10-11:30am, Center for Kids and Family, 300 Second Ave. Registration required. Before attending call 732-542-1326.
> **Red Bank** Dues $1. Meets 2nd Tues., 2-3:15pm, United Methodist Church, Broad St. Before attending call Patricia Crosby 732-530-2552 (day).

MORRIS

Parkinson Disease/Caregiver Support Group *Professionally-run.* Provides emotional support and education for those diagnosed with Parkinson's disease, their family members and caregivers. Meets 3rd Mon., 1:30-3pm, Care One at Morris, 200 Mazda Brook Road, Parsippany. Call Richard Petruce, LCSW 973-627-4087 (day) or Barbara Farrell 973-377-7978. *Email:* farrellhome@patmedia.net

OCEAN

Parkinson's Support Group Support and education for patients with Parkinson's, their families and caregivers. Meets 2nd Wed., 1-2:30pm, Community Medical Center, The Lighthouse, Toms River. Call Andrea Brandsness 1-800-621-0096.

PASSAIC

Parkinson Caregivers Support Group Support for caregivers of persons afflicted with Parkinson's disease. Newsletter. Meets 3rd Wed., Athena Reform Church, Clifton. Call for times Arlene 973-473-4690.

SUSSEX

Eleanore Chaplin Memorial Parkinson Support Group Mutual support and exchange of information for persons with Parkinson's, their families and caregivers. Rap sessions, phone help and newsletter. Meets 3rd Fri., 1-2:30pm, Senior Center (Lower Level), La Bonce Dr., Franklin Boro. Call Anita Navara 973-948-3329 (eve).

UNION

Parkinson's Support Group *Professionally-run.* Support and education for patients of all ages with Parkinson's disease. Literature, buddy system and guest speakers. Meets 2nd Wed., 1-3pm, Robert Wood Johnson University Hospital at Rahway, Stone St., Rahway. Call Dr. Paul Abend 732-516-1042 (day).

The Parkinsonian Support Group In Westfield Provides support and education to persons with Parkinson's disease as well as their caregivers, including former caregivers who have lost a family member to Parkinson's. Handicapped accessible. Meets 2nd Mon. (except July/Aug./Oct.), 1:30-3pm, Presbyterian Church in Westfield, 140 Mountain Ave., Westfield. Call Church office 908-233-0301 (day).

WARREN

The Lehigh Valley Parkinson's Support Group Mutual support and encouragement for Parkinson patients, their families and friends. Guest speakers. Meets 2nd Thurs., 10:30am-noon, Hope United Church of Christ, 1031 Flexer Ave., Allentown, PA. Free physical therapy session last Thurs., 10:30am, Good Shepherd Rehab, 5th and Saint John St., Allentown, PA. Call Geraldine 610-868-3510.

NATIONAL

American Parkinson Disease Association, Inc. *National. 65 chapters. Founded 1961.* Network of 800 support groups for patients & families. Chapter development guidelines. Quarterly newsletter. Promotes research. Fifty-four information and referral centers nationwide. Also offers online booklets, referrals and support. Write: Amer. Parkinson Disease Assn., 1250 Hylan Blvd., Suite 4B, Staten Island, NY 10305. Call 718-981-8001 or 1-800-223-2732; Fax: 718-981-4399. *Website:* http://www.apdaparkinson.org

National Parkinson Foundation *National. 1000 groups. Founded 1957* Provides information, support and education for persons with Parkinson's their families and health care professionals. Funds research. Seeks to improve quality of life for both patients and their caregivers. Includes Young Onset Parkinson network. Helps to start groups Write: National Parkinson Foundation, 1501 N.W. Ninth Ave., Miami, FL 33136. Call 1-800-327-4545 or 305-547-6666 Fax: 305-243-5595. *Website:* http://www.parkinson.org *Email:* contact@parkinson.org

POLIO

STATEWIDE

Polio Network of NJ Support and information for NJ polio survivors and their families. Optional $10/yr donation. For information on support groups in your area call the Polio Network of NJ 201-845-6860 (day). *Website:* http://www.njpolio.org *Email:* NJPN10@hotmail.com

ATLANTIC

Atlantic County Post-Polio Support Group Support and information on the late effects of polio, for post-polio survivors, their families and friends. Dues $15 yr. Meets 4th Sat., (except July/Aug.), 10:00am-noon, Atlantic Township Library, Mays Landing. Before attending call Marge 609-476-2219 (day). *Email:* mdisbrow629@aol.com

BERGEN

Bergen County Polio Support Group *Professionally-run.* Support network and information on late effects of polio and polio survivors. Peer-counseling, phone network, guest speakers. Meets 1st Sat., 10:30am, Maywood Senior Center, 145 Duvier Place, Maywood. Before attending call Heather Broad 201-845-6317. *Email:* heatherbroad@earthlink.net

CAMDEN

South West Jersey Polio Support Group Support and information on the late effects of polio for post-polio survivors and their families and friends. Dues $15/yr. Meets 4th Sat., 10:30am - noon, Kennedy Conference Center, 30 E. Laurel Rd., Stratford. Call Ann 856-784-7741 (day).

MONMOUTH

Monmouth County Post-Polio Support Group Support for persons suffering from post-polio syndrome, in need of pain management or who need help controlling their lives, through meetings, referrals, discussions, guest speakers, social events and networking. Families and friends welcome. Phone help. Dues $15/yr. Meeting days and locations vary. Call Antoinette Wilczewski (President) 732-222-2650 (day), Carol Reichel 732-229-6545 or Arthur Siegfried 908-722-7212 (day). *Website:* http://www.njpolio.org

MORRIS

Morris County Polio Network Mutual support for post-polio survivors, their families and friends. Information on the late-effects of polio. Rap sessions. Newsletter. Dues $10/yr. Meets 3rd Mon., 1pm, Charlie Brown's Restaurant, Route 46 East, Denville. However in March, July, August and December meets 3rd Wed., 7pm, Zeris Inn, Route 46 East, Mountain Lakes. Call Marion Rosenstein 201-585-8125 or Vincent Avantagiato, D.C. 973-769-0075 (day). *Email:* Marion618R@msn.com

OCEAN

Ocean County Post-Polio Support Group Support and information sharing for post-polio survivors. Networking with professionals and other groups. Phone help, guest speakers, literature and buddy system. Meets 3rd Sat., 10am-noon, (Apr., Sept., Nov.), Health South, 14 Hospital Dr., Toms River. Call Susan Gato 732-864-0998 (day) or Kevin Marie Moore 732-240-4272 (day).

SOMERSET

Raritan Valley Post-Polio Support Group Support and information sharing for post-polio survivors. Networking with professionals and other groups. Phone help, speakers, monthly newsletter. Dues $10/yr. Meets 1st Sat., (Oct., Nov., Dec., Mar., Apr.), Manville Library, Manville. Call Arthur Siegfried 908-722-7212 (eve). *Website:* http://www.njpolio.org/rvppsg *Email:* rvppsg@njpolio.org

NATIONAL

Post-Polio Health International *National network. Founded 1958.* Information on late effects of polio for survivors and health professionals. International conferences. Quarterly newsletter (free to donor members who contribute $25), annual directory $8. Guidelines and workshops for support groups. Handbook on late effects ($11.50). Write: Post-Polio Health Int'l, 4207 Lindell Blvd., Suite 110, St. Louis, MO 63108. Call 314-534-0475; Fax: 314-534-5070. *Website:* http://www.post-polio.org *Email:* info@post-polio.org

POLYCYSTIC OVARIAN SYNDROME

BERGEN

Polycystic Ovarian Syndrome Association Mutual support for women of all ages who have been diagnosed or think they may have polycystic ovarian syndrome. Guest speakers. Meets once a month, Fair Lawn. Call Elyse Ganz 617-970-5522. *Email:* eganz@pcosupport.org

INTERNATIONAL

Polycystic Ovarian Syndrome Association *International. Founded 1997.* Provides emotional support and information for women with polycystic ovarian syndrome. Provides information on various treatments and diagnosis. Newsletter, phone support, literature, conferences, regional symposiums and advocacy. Online chats and e-mail lists. Assistance in starting local groups. Dues $40. Write: PCOSA, PO Box 3403, Englewood, CO 80111. *Website:* http://www.pcosupport.org *Email:* info@pcosupport.org

PSORIASIS

NATIONAL

National Psoriasis Foundation *National. Founded 1968.* Support and information for people who have psoriasis and psoriatic arthritis, their families and friends. Education to increase public awareness of these disorders. Fund-raising for research. Bi-monthly magazine. Educational booklets and physician directory. Offers online message board and chat rooms. Write: Nat'l Psoriasis Fdn., 6600 SW 92nd Ave., Suite 300, Portland or 97223. Call 503-244-7404 or 1-800-723-9166 (free packet of information); Fax: 503-245-0626. *Website:* http://www.psoriasis.org *Email:* getinfo@psoriasis.org

REFLEX SYMPATHETIC DYSTROPHY / COMPLEX REGIONAL PAIN SYNDROME

(see also chronic pain)

STATEWIDE

Reflex Sympathetic Dystrophy Syndrome Assn. Southern NJ Chapter Aims to meet the practical and emotional needs of reflex sympathetic dystrophy syndrome patients and their families. Call Jim Everett 856-456-2107 (day). *Email:* jever.92471@aol.com

BURLINGTON

Reflex Sympathetic Dystrophy and Chronic Pain Support Group 12-Step support for persons with reflex sympathetic dystrophy or chronic pain, their families and friends. Helps members maintain as normal and pain free life as possible. Guest speakers, educational programs, pen pals, rap sessions, literature, phone help, advocacy.

> **Mt. Holly** Meets 2nd Wed., 7-9pm, Virtua Hospital, 175 Madison Ave., Conference Room, 1st Floor. Call Kathy Henson 609-268-1565 (day) or Sue Holcomb 856-461-5941. *Email:* bepainfree2000@aol.com
> **Mt. Laurel** Meets 4th Tues., 6-8pm, YMCA, 5001 Centerton Rd. Call Sue Holcomb 856-461-5941 (day). *Email:* auntsuzymouse@hotmail.com

HUDSON

RSD Support Group *Professionally-run.* Self-help group for persons with reflex sympathetic dystrophy syndrome to offer support, education and information on treatments. Family members welcome. Meets 2nd Wed., (except July/Aug) 4:30-6pm, Meadowlands Hospital, Secaucus. Call Kate Waldron, PhD, RN 201-392-3180 (day).

MONMOUTH

Reflex Sympathetic Dystrophy/Chronic Pain Support Group Mutual support, encouragement and information for persons suffering from reflex sympathetic dystrophy or any chronic pain situation. Meets 3rd Wed., 2pm, Grace United Methodist Church, Union Beach. Call Catherine 732-291-7357.

PASSAIC

Moving Forward with RSD Support Group Mutual support, information and encouragement for persons with reflex sympathetic dystrophy (aka complex regional pain syndrome) and their families. Meets 4th Tues., 7:30pm, St. Joseph

Regional Medical Center, 6th fl., Room 114 CN6, Paterson. For information call Gloria 973-743-1985. *Email:* movingfrwd@aol.com

SOMERSET

Living with RSDA/CRPS, Inc. Offers education and support for persons afflicted with reflex sympathetic dystrophy (chronic regional pain syndrome). Families and friends are welcome. Meets 1st Tues., 7-9pm, Somerset Medical Center, 110 Rehill Ave., Somerville. Call 908-575-7737 (answering machine). *Website:* http://www.livingwith rsds.com *Email:* slweiner@hotmail.com

NATIONAL

Reflex Sympathetic Dystrophy Syndrome Association *National. 100 independent groups. Founded 1984.* Aims to meet the practical & emotional needs of reflex sympathetic dystrophy syndrome (aka complex regional pain syndrome) patients & their families. RSDS is a disabling disease involving nerve, skin, muscle, blood vessels & bones. The only common symptom in all patients is pain. Promotes research, educates public and professionals. Quarterly newsletter. Group development guidelines available. Write: RSDS Assoc., PO Box 502, Milford, CT 06460. Call 1-877-662-7737. *Website:* http://www.rsds.org *Email:* info@rsds.org

RESPIRATORY DISEASE / EMPHYSEMA
(see also specific disorder)
STATEWIDE

American Lung Association of New Jersey *Professionally-run.* Refers callers to regional resources for information on lung health, asthma, smoking and environment. Referrals to support groups for persons with chronic lung disorders (emphysema, chronic bronchitis, asthma, pulmonary problems, etc.). Write: Amer. Lung Association of New Jersey, 1600 Route 22 East, Union, NJ 07083. Call 908-687-9340 (day); Fax: 908-851-2625. *Website:* http://www.lungusa.org

BURLINGTON

Better Breathers Club *Professionally-run.* Support for those with lung disease and their families. Meets 1st Wed., 10am, Deborah Heart and Lung Center, 200 Trenton Rd., Browns Mills. For schedule call PCS Dept. 609-893-1200 ext. 5618 (day). *Website:* http://deborah.org *Email:* gebersl@deborah.org

Breathe Better Mutual support for patients with chronic lung disease to share problems, solutions and experiences. Families welcome. Lecture series, guest speakers and phone help. Meets 3rd Wed., 7:30-9:30pm, Lourdes Medical Center of Burlington County, 218 Sunset Rd., Willingboro. Call Linda Booth 609-387-4146 (eve) or Doris King 856-764-3019 (day).

HUDSON

Second Wind *Professionally-run*. Group provides support and education to those with any type of lung disease. Rap sessions, guest speakers. Meetings vary, 12:30-1:30pm, Meadowlands Hospital, 55 Meadowlands Pkwy, Secaucus. For meeting information call 201-392-3531 (day).

MERCER

Better Breathers Club Mutual support for people with chronic obstructive pulmonary disease, (bronchitis, emphysema, fibrosis, asthma, post-lung cancer, etc.) their family and friends. Rap sessions, guest speakers. Princeton Medical Center, 253 Witherspoon St., Princeton. For meeting times call 908-687-9340. *Website:* http://www.lungusa.com

MONMOUTH

Monmouth Easy Breathers *Professionally-run*. Opportunity for patients (age 60+) with chronic lung disease to share problems, solutions, experiences, as well as learn new treatments and research. Registration required. Meets 1st Tues., (except June, July, Aug.), 2-3:30pm, Long Branch Senior Center, 85 Second Ave., Long Branch. Before attending call 732-923-6990 (8:30am-5pm). *Website:* http://www.saintbarnabas.com

MORRIS

IPF Support Group Mutual support for patients with idiopathic pulmonary fibrosis and their caregivers. Family members welcome. Rap sessions and phone help. Meets last Wed., 7-9pm, Morristown Memorial Hospital, 100 Madison Ave., Morristown. Before attending call Barbara and John Murphy 908-276-3394 (eve). *Email:* bjmurphy0902@aol.com

Lung Talk *Professionally-run*. Support group for patients with chronic lung disease (COPD). Families welcome. Educational series, rap sessions, literature and guest speakers. Meets 3rd Fri., 2-3pm, Chilton Memorial Hospital, 97 West Parkway, Board Room, Pompton Plains. Call William McCarthy 973-831-5070 (day) or David Gourley 973-831-5069 (day). *Email:* david_gourley@chiltonmemorial.org

WARREN

Better Breathers Club *Professionally-run.* Support for those with breathing problems, their families and friends. Education, lecture series, social and guest speakers. Meets last Wed., 1-2pm, Wellness Center, 445 Marshall St., Phillipsburg. Call Judy Reed 908-859-8716 (day).

NATIONAL

Alpha 1 Association *International. 54 affiliated groups. Founded 1988.* Support, advocacy and information for persons with alpha-1 antitrypsin deficiency and their families. Networking of members through newsletter and support groups across the country. Sharing of current information on treatments and research. Newsletter, group development guidelines, educational materials and advocacy information. Write: Alpha-1 Association, 275 West St., Suite 210, Annapolis, MD 21401. Call 1-800-521-3025 or 202-887-1900; Fax: 401-216-6983. *Website:* http://www.alpha1.org *Email:* info@alpha1.org

American Lung Association *National. Founded 1904.* Refers callers to regional resources for information on lung health, smoking and environment. Local chapters can refer to support groups for persons with chronic lung disorders (emphysema, chronic bronchitis, asthma, pulmonary problems, etc.) if available. These groups use names such as "Easy Breathers," or "Family Asthma Support Group." Write: American Lung Association, 61 Broadway 6th Floor, New York, NY 10019. Call 1-800-586-4872 or 212-315-8700. *Website:* http://www.lungusa.org

Asthma and Allergy Foundation of America *National. 100+ affiliated groups and 11 chapters. Founded 1953.* Serves persons with asthma and allergic diseases through the support of research, patient and public education and advocacy. Newsletter, support/education groups. Assistance in starting and maintaining groups. Books, videos and other educational resources. Write: AAFA, 1233 20th St. NW, Suite 402, Washington, DC 20036. Call 1-800-727-8462 or 202-466-7643; Fax: 202-466-8940. *Website:* http://www.aafa.org *Email:* info@aafa.org

Coalition for Pulmonary Fibrosis *National. 35 affiliated groups. Founded 2001.* Information, education and research efforts for patients with pulmonary fibrosis. Insurance education and assistance for patients and their families. "How-to" kit for support group coordinators. Patient mentor program. Write: CPF, 1685 Branham Lane, Suite 227, San Jose, CA 95118. Call 1-888-222-8541. *Website:* http://www.coalitionforpf.org *Email:* info@coalitionforpf.org

SAY (Support for Asthmatic Youth) *National. 30 affiliated groups. Founded 1989.* Provides an atmosphere of support, reassurance and fun for children (age 9-17) with asthma and allergies. Exchanging of personal experiences and concerns. Education, information and referrals, phone support, conferences, newsletter, advocacy, literature. Write: SAY, c/o Renee Theodorakis, 1080 Glen Cove Ave., Glen Head, NY 11545. Call 516-625-5735; Fax: 516-625-2976. *Email:* ReneeTheo1@aol.com

White Lung Association *National. Founded 1979.* Educational support and advocacy for the general public, provided in part by asbestos victims and their families. Provides public education on health hazards of asbestos and the education of workers on safe work practices. Assistance provided in starting new groups. Dues $25/yr. Write: White Lung Assn., PO Box 1483, Baltimore, MD 21203. Call 410-243-5864. *Website:* http://www.whitelung.org *Email:* jfite@whitelung.org

ONLINE

COPD-Support, Inc. *Online.* Provides a variety of online self-help support programs for chronic obstructive pulmonary disease patients, caregivers and interested medical personnel. Programs include moderated mailing lists, forums, chats, a weekly newsletter, "COPD-Watch" for those living alone, "Smoke No More" for help in quitting smoking and "Let's Get Fit" exercise program. *Website:* http://copd-support.com *Email:* management@copd-support.com

EFFORTS *Online.* Support for persons afflicted with emphysema. Offers information on local support groups. Forum for sharing ideas and help in dealing with emphysema. Advocacy for research. Listserv. Write: EFFORTS, 239 NE Highway 69, Suite D, Claycomo, MO 64119. Fax: 816-413-0176. *Website:* http://www.emphysema.net/bindex.html

Huff-n-Puff *Online.* Provides support for people with any type of interstitial lung disease (including pulmonary fibrosis). Opportunity to meet others with similar conditions, experiences and knowledge. *Website:* http://www.huff-n-puff.net

SCLERODERMA

CAMDEN

Scleroderma Camden County Support Group Provides support and education to scleroderma patients, their families and friends. Rap sessions, guest speakers and literature. Meets 2nd Thurs., 1:30-3:30pm, Barry D. Brown Health Center, Virtua Hospital, 106 Carnie Blvd., Voorhees. Call Laurie Rabin 856-231-0221. *Email:* laurierabin@yahoo.com

CUMBERLAND

Vineland Scleroderma Support Group Provides support and education to scleroderma patients, their families and friends. Rap sessions, guest speakers and literature. Meets last Wed., 6-7:30pm, YMCA, Vineland. Call Tina Mullins 856-405-0758. *Email:* tinamarie31@comcast.net

GLOUCESTER

Southwest New Jersey Scleroderma Support Group Provides support and education to scleroderma patients, their families and friends. Rap sessions, guest speakers and literature. Meets 1st Tues., 7-9pm, Underwood Memorial Hospital, 1st Floor, Dining Room, Woodbury. Call Mary Nuzzo 856-582-6456. *Email:* marynuzz@msn.com

HUNTERDON

Flemington Scleroderma Support Group Provides support and education to scleroderma patients, their families and friends. Rap sessions, guest speakers and literature. Meets 4th Mon., 6:30-8pm, Hunterdon Medical Center, Flemington. Call Mary Gocek 908-284-1332. *Email:* gocekm@earthlink.net

MIDDLESEX

New Brunswick Scleroderma Support Group Provides support and education to scleroderma patients, their families and friends. Guest speakers and literature. Meets 3rd Thurs., 6:30-8pm, Robert Wood Johnson Hospital, Board Room, New Brunswick. Call Nancy Holden 732-672-1969. *Email:* nervoh_99@yahoo.com

MONMOUTH

Scleroderma Monmouth County Support Group Provides support and education to scleroderma patients, their families and friends. Meets 2nd Sat., 10-11:30am, Jersey Shore Wellness Center, Neptune. Call Marsha Niederman 732-780-5986. *Email:* m_j_niederman@comcast.net

MORRIS

Northern New Jersey Scleroderma Support Group Provides support and education to scleroderma patients, their families and friends. Meets 2nd Tues., (Jan., Mar., May, July, Sept., Nov.), 7-9pm, St. Clares Hospital, Route 46 West, Dover. Call Kitsa Jobeless 973-328-2627 (eve) or Margaret Paxos 973-584-9607 (day/eve). *Email:* munchkit@optonline.net

OCEAN

Scleroderma Ocean County Support Group Provides support and education to scleroderma patients, their families and friends. Rap sessions, guest speakers and literature. Meets 2nd Tues., (Feb., May, Aug., Nov.), 4:30-6pm, The Lighthouse Community Medical Center, Toms River. Call 908-489-3092 (day). *Email:* support@sclerodermadv.org

STATEWIDE

Scleroderma Foundation of the Delaware Valley *(Serves southern/central NJ/Delaware/Penn) Professionally-run.* Support and education for persons with scleroderma. Funds research. Seeks to increase public awareness, provides patient education and support programs. Phone support, networking, newsletter, information and referral. $25 annual membership dues, meetings are free. Several meeting locations. Write: Scleroderma Foundation, 557 Wall Rd., Spring Lake, NJ 07762. Call Pat Johnsen 732-449-7001 (day) or 1-866-675-5545 (hotline) (Mon.-Fri., 7am-9pm). *Website:* http://www.sclerodermadv.org *Email:* sfdv@sclerodermadv.org

Scleroderma Foundation of Tri-State Chapter *(Serves northern NJ, NY, CT) Professionally-run.* Promotes the welfare of scleroderma patients and their families. Provides education, support groups, phone help, referrals. Fund-raising for research. Newsletter, resource library and other educational materials. Group development guidelines. Annual dues $25. Several meeting locations in the tri-state area. Write: Scleroderma Foundation, 62 Front St., Binghamton, NY 13905. Call Rosemary Markoff 1-800-867-0885. Fax: 607-723-2039. *Website:* http://www.scleroderma.org *Email:* sdtristate@aol.com

NATIONAL

Scleroderma Foundation, Inc. *National. 135 affiliated groups. Founded 1970.* Dedicated to providing emotional support to people with scleroderma and their families. Provides scleroderma education and public awareness and funds research. Referrals to local support groups and physicians. Advocacy. Conferences. Online chat rooms. Dues $25. Write: Scleroderma Fdn., 12 Kent Way, Suite 101, Byfield, MA 01922. Call 1-800-722-4673 (HOPE) or 978-463-5843; Fax: 978-463-5809. *Website:* http://www.scleroderma.org *Email:* sfinfo@scleroderma.org

Can't find an appropriate group in your area? The Clearinghouse helps people start groups. Give us a call at 1-800-367-6274.

SCOLIOSIS
(see also specific disorder)

CUMBERLAND

Scoliosis Association of South Jersey Mutual support for people suffering from scoliosis. Family welcome. Literature, phone help, education and guest speakers. Dues $20/yr. Meets 2nd Tues., 7:30-9pm, Rehabilitation Hospital of South Jersey, 1237 West Sherman Ave., Vineland. Call Tiffany Patterson 856-981-2161 (eve). *Website:* http://www.scoliosis-assoc.org *Email:* pattersonsky81@aol.com

NATIONAL

National Scoliosis Foundation *International. 17 affiliated groups. Founded 1976.* Dedicated to helping children, parents, adults and health care providers deal with the complexities of spinal deformities such as scoliosis. Whether the issue is early detection and screening programs, treatment methods, pain management or patient care, NSF strives to promote public awareness, provide reliable information, encourage on-going research and educate and support the scoliosis community. Bi-annual newsletter, information packets, pen pals, conferences and phone support. Assistance in starting local groups. Write: Nat'l Scoliosis Fdn., 5 Cabot Pl., Stoughton, MA 02072. Call 1-800-673-6922 or 781-341-6333; Fax: 781-341-8333. *Website:* http://www.scoliosis.org *Email:* NSF@scoliosis.org

Scoliosis Association, Inc. *National. 50 chapters. Founded 1974.* Information and support network for scoliosis patients and parents of children with scoliosis. Establishes local patient and parent self-help groups. Encourages school screening programs. Supports research. Newsletter. Membership contribution $20. Guidelines for starting chapters. Write: Scoliosis Association Inc. c/o Stanley Sacks, Chair & C.E.O., PO Box 811705, Boca Raton, FL 33481-1705. Call 1-800-800-0669; Fax: 561-994-2455. *Website:* http://www.scoliosis-assoc.org

SLEEP APNEA

MERCER

AWAKE *Professionally-run.* Support and education to individuals and their families suffering from sleep apnea. Rap sessions, guest speakers, phone help. For meeting information call George Evans 609-394-4167 (day), Capital Health System Sleep Disorders Center or Robert Perro 609-278-6990 (day), Fuld Snoring and Sleep Apnea Center. *Email:* Rbrooks@chsnj.org

MORRIS

Sleep Apnea Support Group of Northwest New Jersey Support group for persons afflicted by sleep apnea. Family members welcome. Exchange information and experiences. Guest speakers, educational and mutual sharing. Meets at St. Clare's Hospital, Dover. Before attending call Sleep Center 973-989-3477 opt. # 2.

SOMERSET

Somerset County Snoozers A.W.A.K.E. Support for person afflicted with sleep apnea. Family and friends welcome. Lecture series, educational, mutual sharing, guest speakers, rap sessions and advocacy. Meet 4th Mon., 7-10pm, Somerset Medical Center, 110 Rehill Ave., Somerville. Call Loideth Huff 908-685-2450 or Medical Center 1-800-443-4605.

NATIONAL

A.W.A.K.E. (American Sleep Apnea Association) Network Groups *National. 200+ affiliated groups. Founded 1990.* Provides education, support, social interaction for persons with sleep apnea and their families and friends. Membership dues $25/year. Assistance and guidelines for starting groups ($30). Write: A.W.A.K.E. ASAA, 1424 K St., NW, Suite 302, Washington, DC 20005. Call 202-293-3650; Fax: 202-293-3656 *Website:* http://www.sleepapnea.org *Email:* asaa@sleepapnea.org

SPINA BIFIDA

(see also disability, parents of disabled children, toll-free helplines)

STATEWIDE

Spina Bifida Association Support for persons with spina bifida and their families. Peer-counseling, advocacy, newsletter, conferences, family support coordination and continence management assistance. Various meeting times and places. Also has several telephone support groups. Write: Spina Bifida Assn., 84 Park Ave., Flemington, NJ 08822. Call 908-782-7475 (9am-3pm); Fax: 908-782-6102. *Website:* http://www.sbatsr.org *Email:* info@sbatsr.org

NATIONAL

Spina Bifida Association of America *National. 62 chapters. Founded 1972.* Encourages educational and vocational development of patients with spina bifida. Newsletter, chapter development guidelines, national resource center, scholarships, film/videotapes. Write: Spina Bifida Assn. of America, 4590 MacArthur Blvd.

NW, Suite 250, Washington, DC 20007. Call 1-800-621-3141 or 202-944-3285; Fax: 202-944-3295. *Website:* http://www.sbaa.org *Email:* sbaa@sbaa.org

STROKE

(see also caregivers, disabilities, brain injury)

ATLANTIC

Bacharach Stroke Club *Professionally-run.* Support and education for stroke survivors, their families and friends. Rap sessions, social activities, guest speakers, literature, phone help. Meets last Wed., 3pm, Bacharach Institute for Rehabilitation, 61 West Jimmy Leads Rd., Pomona. Call 609-748-5420.

BERGEN

New Jersey Stroke Activity Center Support and recovery of long-term stroke survivors, sound and movement therapy, networking and socialization. Families welcome. Rap sessions, guest speakers, phone help, newsletter and speakers bureau. Call Mary Jo Schreiber 973-450-4114. *Website:* http://www.njsac.org *Email:* maryjo@njsac.org

> **Paramus** Meets 2nd and 4th Tues., 11:30am, Care One at the Cupola, 100 West Ridgewood Ave.
> **Saddle Brook** Meets 1st and 3rd Tues., Kessler Institution for Rehabilitation, 300 Market St.

Post Stroke and Disabled Adult Program *(BERGEN COUNTY RESIDENTS ONLY) Professionally-run.* Mutual support for post-stroke patients and disabled adults. Program functions include group discussions, various activities that promote physical fitness, arts and crafts, games, exercises and occasional recreational events. Meets various times and days, E. Rutherford, Englewood, Oakland, Paramus, River Vale and Maywood. Call Leo DePinto 201-336-6502 (day) or TTY 201-336-6505

Post Stroke Support Group *Professionally-run.* Mutual support for post-stroke individuals. Meets Fri., 9am-12:30pm, 228 Grand Avenue, Englewood. Before attending call Frieda Wells 201-569-4080 (day). *Email:* lyd228@aol.com

BURLINGTON

Stroke Support Group *Professionally-run.* Mutual support group for patients, family and friends. Education, sharing of ideas and exercise.

> **Mount Holly** Meets 4th Tues., 7:30-9pm, Virtua Health and Rehab Center, 62 Richmond Ave. Before attending call 1-888-847-8823 (day).

Willingboro Meets 2nd Fri., 10-11:30am, Lourdes Health System, 218 A Sunset Rd. Call 609-835-5813.

Stroke Club *Professionally-run.* Promotes the well-being of stroke patients and families through educational and social programs and sharing of concerns. Meets 4th Tues., (except Nov./Dec.), 7-9pm, Virtua Health and Rehabilitation Center, 62 Richmond Ave., Mt. Holly. Before attending call 609-267-0700 ext. 41616.

ESSEX

New Jersey Stroke Activity Center Caregivers Group Support and guidance for caregivers and family members of persons who have had a stroke. Rap sessions, guest speakers, literature, phone help, newsletter and speakers bureau. Meets 2nd and 4th Fri., 7pm, Montclair. For meeting information call Mary Jo Schreiber 973-450-4114. *Website:* http://www.njsac.org *Email:* maryjo@njsac.org

HUNTERDON

Brain Injury Support Group *Professionally-run.* Support group for people who have brain injury due to AVM's, aneurysm, tumors or stroke. Families welcome. Guest speakers and literature. Meets 2nd Thurs., 7-9pm, Hunterdon Medical Center, 2100 Wescott Dr., Flemington. Call Gwen Bartlett-Palmer 908-246-9648.

MERCER

St. Lawrence Stroke Support Group *Professionally-run.* Promotes the well-being of stroke patients and families through educational and social programs and sharing of concerns. Discussions, guest speakers. Meets 1st Wed., 6:30-8pm, St. Lawrence Rehab Center, Room 117, 2381 Lawrenceville Rd., Lawrenceville. Call Annette Murphy, MSW, LSW 609-896-9500 ext. 2591 (day).

MIDDLESEX

JFK Stroke Wives Group Support for women who are married to men who have had strokes. Mutual sharing, rap sessions and social group. Meets 3rd Tues., 7-8:30pm, JFK Hospital, James St., Edison. Call Rosemarie 732-752-2644. *Email:* crossingladynj@aol.com

Middlesex County Stroke Support Group *Professionally-run.* Promotes the well-being of stroke patients and families through educational programs and sharing of concerns. Dues $1 mtg. Meets 1st Wed., 7:15pm, JFK Rehab Institute, 65 James St., Edison. Call Frank Roche 732-969-2097 (day). *Email:* MSCstrokeclub@msn.com

Stroke Club Support Group Support and education for stroke patients, their families and friends. Guest speakers, phone help, newsletter. Members are encouraged to bring a brown bag lunch to meeting. Meets last Fri., 12:30-2pm, (except July/Aug.), Robert Wood Johnson University Hospital, Medical Education Building, Room 108 A, New Brunswick. Call Community Education 732-418-8110 (day).

MONMOUTH

New Jersey Stroke Activity Center Support and recovery of long term stroke survivors, sound and movement therapy, networking and socialization. Families welcome. Rap sessions, guest speakers, phone help, newsletter and speakers bureau. Meets 1st and 3rd Wed., 2pm, Health South Rehabilitation Hospital, 2 Centre Plaza, Tinton Falls. Call Mary Jo Schreiber 973-450-4114. *Website:* http://www.njsac.org *Email:* maryjo@njsac.org

Stroke Support Group Mutual support for stroke patients and their families. Education, guest speakers, lecture series and literature. Meetings vary, Rehabilitation Hospital of Tinton Falls, 2 Centre Plaza, Tinton Falls. Call Sharon Collins 732-460-5378 (day) or Lara Latzsch 732-460-5377 (day).

MORRIS

New Jersey Stroke Activity Center Support and recovery of long-term stroke survivors, sound and movement therapy, networking and socialization. Families welcome. Rap sessions, guest speakers, phone help, newsletter and speakers bureau. Call Mary Jo Schreiber 973-450-4114. *Website:* http://www.njsac.org *Email:* maryjo@njsac.org

> **Chester** Meets 1st and 3rd Tues., 2pm, Kessler Institute, Outpatient Building, (back of hospital), 201 Pleasant Hill Rd.
> **Parsippany** Meets 2nd and 4th Tues., 1:30pm, Care One, 100 Mazdabrook Rd.

North Jersey Stroke Discussion Group Promotes the well-being of stroke patients and families through educational programs and sharing of concerns. Meets 2nd and 4th Tues., (except July/Aug.), 1pm, Grace Episcopal Church, Library, Route 24, Madison. Call George 973-543-6386.

OCEAN

Stroke of Luck *Professionally-run.* Mutual support for stroke survivors and caregivers. Family and friends welcome. Lecture series, guest speakers and literature. Meets last Wed., Health South Rehabilitation Hospital, 14 Hospital Dr.,

Toms River. Call Marianne Krank 732-505-5022 (day) or Marianne Harms 732-286-5688 (day).

Stroke Support Group *Professionally-run.* Purpose of group is to educate and support individuals and families associated with stroke related issues. Rap sessions, guest speakers. Under 18 welcome. Meets 4th Tues. (except Dec.-Feb.), 2pm, Shore Rehab Institute, 425 Jack Martin Blvd., Brick. Call Lisa Wazeka or Tami Pindulic 732-836-4528 or 4527.

PASSAIC

Brain Injury Association Family Support Group *Professionally-run.* Support for family members and caregivers of neurologically impaired people (brain injury, aneurysm, stroke, etc). Sharing sessions, guest speakers, literature. Meets 4th Thurs., 6pm, Haledon. Call Cindy Clawson 973-427-2600 ext. 19 (day).

New Jersey Stroke Activity Center Support and recovery of long term-stroke survivors, sound and movement therapy, networking and socialization. Families welcome. Rap sessions, guest speakers, phone help, newsletter and speakers bureau. Meets 1st and 3rd Tues., 3:30pm, Care One, 493 Black Oak Ridge Rd., Wayne. Call Mary Jo Schreiber 973-450-4114. *Website:* http://www.njsac.org *Email:* maryjo@njsac.org

SOMERSET

Somerset/Hunterdon County Brain Injury Support Group Emotional support for persons with illnesses and injuries affecting the brain, their families and friends. Information, socialization, educational series and guest speakers. Meets 3rd Thurs., 6:30pm, Neurobehavioral Institute of NJ, 626 N. Thompson St., Raritan. Call Mary Liz McNamara 908-725-8877 (day). *Email:* mlmcnamara@verizonmail.com

Stroke Club of Somerset County *Professionally-run.* Mutual support for stroke patients and their families. Meets 1st Tues., 1:30-3:30pm, Somerset County Library, Vogt Dr. and North Bridge St., Bridgewater. Before attending call Sue 908-595-2378.

SUSSEX

Stroke Support Group *Professionally-run.* Offers support for persons recovering from a stroke. Caretakers welcomed. Meets 4th Tues., 7:30pm, Newton Memorial Hospital, Rehabilitation Lounge, 175 High St., Newton. Call Carolyn Matzal 973-579-8816.

UNION

The Stroke Club *Professionally-run.* Support and socialization for stroke survivors and their families. Rap sessions, guest speakers, educational series. $1 donation (optional). Meets 2nd Thurs., 12:30-2pm, Rahway Hospital, 865 Stone St., Rahway. Call Bervessa Morgan 732-381-4200 ext. 2115 (day) or Mary Raab 732-499-6012 (day).

NATIONAL / INTERNATIONAL

American Stroke Association, Division of American Heart Association *National. 1800 groups. Founded 1979.* Maintains a listing of support groups for stroke survivors, their families, friends and interested professionals. Publishes bimonthly magazine. Provides information and referrals. Write: American Stroke Association, 7272 Greenville Ave., Dallas, TX 75231-4596. Call 1-888-478-7653 (day); Fax: 214-706-5231. *Website:* http://www.StrokeAssociation.org *Email:* strokeconnection@heart.org

National Stroke Association *National. 9 chapters. Founded 1984.* Dedicated to reducing the incidence and impact of stroke through prevention, medical treatment, rehabilitation, family support and research. Professional publications, Stroke Smart magazine, information and referrals to local groups. Guidance for starting stroke clubs and groups. Write: National Stroke Association, 9707 E. Easter Lane, Suite B, Englewood, CO 80112-3747. Call 303-649-9299 or 1-800-787-6537; Fax: 303-649-1328. *Website:* http://www.stroke.org *Email:* info@stroke.org

Stroke Clubs International *International. 900+ clubs. Founded 1968.* Organization of persons who have experienced strokes, their families and friends for the purpose of mutual support, education, social and recreational activities. Provides information & assistance to Stroke Clubs (which are usually sponsored by local organizations). Newsletter, videotapes, group development guidelines. Write: Stroke Clubs Int'l, 805 12th St., Galveston, TX 77550. Call Ellis Williamson 409-762-1022.

ONLINE

The Brain Injury Information NETwork (TBINET) *Online* Various support group email lists for brain injury, stroke and other "medical" related issues. Has lists for caregivers and family and friends. *Website:* http://www.tbinet.org

We know this Directory is big and chances are we can probably find the group you're looking for quicker than you paging through it. Call us! (We're really friendly!)
1-800-367-6274

THYROID CONDITIONS
(see also specific disorder)

OCEAN

Thyroid Support Group Support for anyone affected by a thyroid problem. Mutual support, mutual sharing, guest speakers and video viewing. Meets 2nd Mon., 1-3pm, Lighthouse, 63 Lacey Rd., Whiting. Call Lighthouse 732-849-4610 or Stefanie 732-350-2904.

NATIONAL

American Foundation of Thyroid Patients *National. 6 chapters. Founded 1993.* Offers information, education and referrals to low-cost screening. Also provides newsletter, pen pals, phone support, advocacy and networking. Dues vary. Assistance offered in starting local groups. Online mailing lists and bulletin boards. Write: American Foundation of Thyroid Patients, 4322 Douglas Ave., Midland, TX 79703. *Website:* http://www.thyroidfoundation.org *Email:* thyroid@flash.net

ThyCa: Thyroid Cancer Survivors' Association, Inc. Support, education and communication for people with all types of thyroid cancer, as well as caregivers. Outreach to the public for thyroid cancer awareness and early detection. Nine online support groups, local support groups, free online newsletter, free downloadable low-iodine cookbook, free regional workshops, annual international conference, free thyroid cancer awareness brochures, Thyroid Cancer Awareness Month, funding for research and educational website. Write: ThyCa: Thyroid Cancer Survivors' Association, Inc., PO Box 1545, New York, NY 10159-1545. Call 1-877-588-7904; Fax: 630-604-6078. *Website:* http://www.thyca.org *Email:* thyca@thyca.org

Thyroid Eye Disease Charitable Trust (TEDct), The *International. 15 area helpline organizers/50 helplines nationwide. Founded 1989.* Provides information, care and support to persons affected by thyroid eye disease (aka thyroid associated ophthalmopathy or Graves' eye disease). Information and referral, literature, phone support, conferences, newsletter. Annual subscription 10 pounds. Write: TEDct, "Solstice," Sea Rd., Winchelsea Beach, East Sussex, TN36 4LH, England. Call 0845 1210406; Fax: 01797 222338. *Email:* tedct@eclipse.co.uk

> **"Always remember, there is more strength in you than you ever realized or even imagined. Certainly nothing can keep you down if you are determined to get on top of things and stay there"**
> *—Norman Vincent Peale*

TRANSPLANT RECIPIENT, ORGAN
(see also specific disorder)

ATLANTIC

Cape Atlantic Transplant Support Group *Professionally-run.* Mutual support and education for organ transplant recipients and candidates. Families welcome. Guest speakers. Meets 4th Wed., 4:30-6pm, Shore Memorial Hospital, Pitman Room, 1 East New York Ave., Somers Point. Call Kathleen 609-653-3667 (day).

ESSEX

SPK Recipient/Family Support Group Emotional support and education to kidney pancreas recipients, their families and friends. Social group, advocacy, literature, rap sessions, guest speakers. Meets various Tuesdays, 7-9pm, (except July/Aug), St. Barnabas Medical Center, 3rd Floor, East Wing, Old Short Hills Rd., Livingston. Before attending call Marcia Krupit 973-322-8461 (day).

Transplant Patient and Family Support Group Emotional support and education for all kidney transplant recipients, their families and friends. Social group, advocacy, rap sessions, guest speakers, literature. Usually meets once a month, St. Barnabas Medical Center, Old Short Hills Rd., , 3rd Floor, Board Room, East Wing, Livingston. For information call Adriane Shaw 973-322-2204 (day).

MERCER

Circle of Hope Mutual support for recipients of organ transplants. Guest speakers, advocacy, literature and phone help. Meets 3rd Wed., (except July/Aug.), 7:30-9pm, Robert Wood Johnson University Hospital at Hamilton, One Hamilton Health Place, Hamilton. Call Chaplain Jeff Pierfy 609-631-6980 (day). *Email:* jpierfy@rwjuhh.net

MIDDLESEX

Kidney and Pancreas Support Group *Professionally-run.* Mutual support for pre- and post- kidney and pancreas transplant patients. Family and relatives welcome. Guest speakers, literature, educational series and social group. Meets 3rd Mon., 7pm, Robert Wood Johnson University Hospital, 1 Robert Wood Johnson Place, Board Room, New Brunswick. Call 732-235-8987 (day).

Second Chance Mutual support for heart transplant patients and their families. Meets 1st Thurs., 2pm, Robert Wood Johnson's Hospital, Conference Room, 1 Robert Wood Johnson Place, New Brunswick. Call 732-418-8110.

MONMOUTH

Central Jersey Transplant Lifeline Support for persons who have had or are waiting for, an organ transplant. Open to family and friends or anyone interested in organ donations. Rap sessions, mutual sharing and phone help. Meets 2nd Tues., 7-9pm, Firehouse, Little Silver. Call Virginia O'Keefe 732-450-1271.

MORRIS

Organ Transplant Recipient Support Group Provides mutual support and education to persons who have undergone an organ transplant or are considering having one. Family and friends welcome. Meets 1st Sat., 10-11:30am, Denville Library, Meeting Room, 121 Diamond Spring Rd., Denville. Call Barbara 973-335-7112 (day/eve).

OCEAN

PRE/POST Transplant Support Group Provides support to pre/post transplant recipients. Family or friends welcome. Meets 2nd Thurs., 7-8:30pm, MCOC, 425 Jack Martin Blvd., Conference Room C, Brick. Call Kathy Stritmatter 732-262-0959.

UNION

Donor Family Support Group *Professionally-run.* Bereavement support for families of organ and tissue donors. Information about transplantation and donation process. Meetings vary. The Sharing Network, 841 Mountain Ave., Springfield. For meeting information call Mary Ellen McGlynn 973-379-4535 (day). *Website:* http://www.sharenj.org *Email:* mmcglynn@sharenj.org

INTERNATIONAL

Second Wind Lung Transplant Association, Inc. *International network. Founded 1995.* Developed by transplant patients. Opportunity for persons who have undergone or who will undergo, lung transplants to share their stories on a web page. Newsletter available. Write: Second Wind Lung Transplant Assn., PO Box 1915, Largo, FL 33779. Call 1-888-855-9463 or 727-397-3497; Fax: 727-397-3609. *Website:* http://www.2ndwind.org *Email:* heering@2ndwind.org

TRIO Transplant Recipients International Organization *International. 43 chapters. Founded 1983.* Works to improve the quality of life of transplant candidates, recipients, donors and their families. Offers information online on finding local chapters. Write: TRIO, 2100 M St., NW, Suite 170-353, Washington, DC 20037. Call 1-800-874-6386. *Website:* http://www.trioweb.org

TRIGEMINAL NEURALGIA / TIC DOULOUREUX
(see also chronic pain)

MORRIS

Trigeminal Neuralgia Association Support group for persons suffering from trigeminal neuralgia, their families and friends. Meets 2 times yr., Community Presbyterian Church, 220 West Main St., Chester. For meeting times and dates call Barbara Noffke 908-876-3268.

OCEAN

The Toms River NJ TNA Support Group Offers support, encouragement and information to those afflicted with trigeminal neuralgia. Under 18 welcome. Rap sessions, guest speakers, literature, newsletter. Meets quarterly, (Dec., March, June and Sept.), Lighthouse, Route 37 East, Toms River. For meeting information call John Lanzer 732-657-8614 (day/eve).

NATIONAL

Trigeminal Neuralgia Association *National. 86+ groups. Founded 1990.* Provides information, mutual support and encouragement to persons with trigeminal neuralgia and related facial pain disorders. Families are welcome. Helps to reduce the isolation of those affected. Phone support, educational information, patient advocacy. Write: TNA, 2801 SW Archer Rd., Gainesville, FL 32608. Call 1-800-923-3608 or 352-376-9955; Fax: 352-376-8688. *Website:* http://www.tna-support.org *Email:* tnanational@tna-support.org

VACCINE

HUNTERDON

Alliance for Informed Choice in Vaccinations Support group of parents concerned about the safety of vaccines and the right to informed consent. Literature, advocacy and phone help. Professionals welcome to attend. Meetings vary. Call Renee Foster 1-800-613-9925 (answering machine). *Email:* njaicv@aol.com

OCEAN

HANDIN Health and Natural Decisions for Immunity Network Provides support, research aid and information on the freedom of vaccine choice. Mutual sharing, guest speakers, literature. Dues $3/family. Telephone support network. For information call Cathy Millet 732-892-4852. *Email:* handin@comcast.net

NATIONAL

National Vaccine Information Center *National. 20 affiliated groups. Founded 1982.* Support, information and advocacy group for parents whose children were adversely affected by vaccines. Advocates for safety reforms in the mass vaccination system and safer vaccines. Promotes education for parents and professionals. Various literature. Dues $25/yr. Write: NVIC, 421 E. Church St., Vienna, VA 22180. Call 703-938-DPT3; Fax: 703-938-5768. *Website:* http://www.nvic.org *Email:* Kathi@nvic.org

WOMEN'S HEALTH
(see also specific disorder, toll-free helplines)

BURLINGTON

Midpoint *Professionally-run.* Support and discussion for women to share their feelings, fears and concerns in coping with menopause and mid-life issues. Phone help, speakers. Meets 4th Wed., 7:30-9:30pm, (except July/Aug.), Lourdes Medical Center of Burlington County, Wellness Center, 218 A Sunset Rd., Willingboro. Call Hospital 609-835-5813 or Lorraine 856-663-7862 (eve).

MONMOUTH

Abrazos Latina Support *(SPANISH) Professionally-run.* Provides support and education for women regarding health, family and emotional issues. Meets 2nd Fri., 10am, Brookdale Learning Center, 213 Broadway, Room 19, Long Branch. Call Xiomara Pino, CSW 732-923-7138.

NATIONAL

Black Women's Health Imperative *International. 15 chapters. Founded 1981.* Grassroots organization aimed at improving the health of Black women by providing wellness education, services, self-help group development, leadership development, health information and advocacy. Assists in the development of new local affiliate groups. Self-help brochure, quarterly newsletter and annual news magazine. Membership dues vary. Write: Black Women's Health Imperative, 600

Pennsylvania Ave., SE, Suite 310, Washington, DC 20003. Call 202-548-4000 Fax: 202-543-9743 *Website:* http://www.blackwomenshealth.org *Email:* nbwhp@nbwhp.org

DES Action U.S.A. *National. Founded 1977.* Support for women who were prescribed DES during pregnancy and their children. Provides physician referrals and education for the public and health workers. Quarterly newsletter. Write: DES-Action U.S.A., 158 Standwood Rd., Columbus, OH 43209. Call 1-800-337-9288 Fax: 510-465-4815 *Website:* http://www.desaction.org *Email:* desaction@columbus.rr.com

DES Cancer Network *National. Founded 1983.* Mutual support and education for DES-exposed women, with a special focus on DES cancer issues. Provides research advocacy and medical/legal resources. Newsletter ($25). Annual conferences. Write: DES Cancer Network, PO Box 220465, Chantilly, VA 20153-0465. *Website:* http://www.descancer.org *Email:* desnetwrk@aol.com

International Premature Ovarian Foundation *National network. 8 affiliated groups. Founded 1995.* Mutual support for women who have prematurely entered menopause. Information and referrals, phone support, literature. Assistance in starting groups. Write: Catherine Corp, PO Box 23643, Alexandria, VA 22304. Call 703-913-4787 *Website:* http://www.pofsupport.org *Email:* info@pofsupport.org

National Latina Health Organization *(BILINGUAL) National network. Founded 1986.* Works toward bilingual access to quality health care through self-empowerment, educational programs, health advocacy, outreach and developing public policy specifically aimed at Latinas. Information & referrals, phone support, literature. Self-help facilitator trainings. Conducts school-based youth programs. Write: Nat'l Latina Health Org., PO Box 7567, Oakland, CA 94601. Call 510-534-1362 Fax: 510-534-1364 *Website:* http://www.latinahealth.org *Email:*NLHO@latinahealth.org

ONLINE

Mullerian Anomalies of the Uterus *Online* Support and information for those with Mullerian anomalies of the uterus such as bicornuate, septate, unicornauate, hypoplastic and didelphys uteria. Weekly chat, email list and message board. *Website:* http://health.groups.yahoo.com/group/MullerianAnomalies/

Postpartum Hemorrhage Survivors *Online* Email list for women who are supporting each other after a postpartum hemorrhage and hysterectomy. *Website:* http://health.groups.yahoo.com/group/pph-survivors/

It is raining still... Maybe it is not one of those showers that is here one minute and gone the next, as I had so boldly assumed.

Maybe none of them are.

After all, life in itself is a chain of rainy days. But there are times when not all of us have umbrellas to walk under. Those are the times when *we need* people who are willing to lend their umbrellas to a wet stranger on a rainy day.

I think I'll go for a walk with my umbrella.

--Sun-Young Park

MENTAL HEALTH

ANXIETY ATTACKS / PHOBIAS / AGORAPHOBIA
(see also mental health general, mental health consumers, toll-free helplines)

STATEWIDE

GROW A mutual self-help group to prevent and recover from depression, anxiety and other mental health problems. Caring and sharing community to attain emotional maturity, personal responsibility and recovery. Meets in various counties in NJ. Write: GROW Center, 206 University Blvd., Glassboro, NJ 08028. Call 856-881-2008.

BERGEN

Recovery, Inc. Self-help method of will training. Offers techniques for controlling temperamental behavior and changing attitudes toward nervous symptoms, anxiety, depression and fears. Call 201-612-8153. *Website:* http://www.recovery-inc.com
> **Hasbrouck Heights** Meets Wed., 8pm, First Reformed Church, Washington Place and Burton Ave.
> **Ridgewood** Meets Fri., 1:30pm, Christ Church, Cottage Place and Franklin Ave.

BURLINGTON

GROW A mutual self-help group to prevent and recover from depression, anxiety and other mental health problems. Caring and sharing community to attain emotional maturity, personal responsibility and recovery. Meets Tues., 7pm, Family Services, Pat le Bon Room, 770 Woodlane Rd., Mt. Holly. Before attending call Brenda 856-881-2008.

Recovery, Inc. Self-help method of will training. Offers techniques for controlling temperamental behavior and changing attitudes toward nervous symptoms, anxiety, depression and fears. Call 215-332-0722. *Website:* http://www.recovery-inc.com
> **Marlton** Meets Mon., 8pm and Thurs., 7pm, Prince of Peace Lutheran Church, 61 Route 70 East.
> **Westampton** Meets Tues., 7pm, Hampton Hospital, Cafeteria, Rancocas Rd. and Route 295.

We can also refer callers to over 100 individuals who are seeking others to help start new support groups throughout NJ, if you don't see it, that doesn't mean it doesn't exist!
1-800-367-6274.

CAMDEN

DBSA of Camden County: New Beginnings Support Group Mutual support, encouragement and education for persons with depression, bipolar disorder, anxiety, panic, OCD, or other mental health issues. Provides a caring, empathetic place to listen and share successes. Meets Mon., 7-9pm, (families welcome 1st and 3rd Mon.) and Wed., 11am-1pm, Holy Trinity Lutheran Church, 214 N. Warwick Rd., Magnolia. Call Gary 856-227-5678 (day/eve) or Maribel 856-232-3181. For family group call Karen 856-451-1240.

Depression / Anxiety Support Group For anyone suffering from anxiety and/or depression to support one another in an effort to remain healthy, to share common problems and concerns. Under 18 welcome. Rap sessions, phone help, literature. Meets 3rd Mon., 7:15-9pm, Marie Fleche Library, White Horse Pike, Berlin. Call Nancy 856-768-1258 (eve) or Rhonda 856-768-2030 (day/eve).

Recovery, Inc. Self-help method of will training. Offers techniques for controlling temperamental behavior and changing attitudes toward nervous symptoms, anxiety, depression and fears. Meets Sat., 11:30am, Starting Point, 215 Highland Ave., Westmont. Call 215-332-0722. *Website:* http://www.recovery-inc.com

South Jersey Social Anxiety/Phobia Group Support, education and social activities for people suffering from anxiety disorders. Provides a cognitive behavioral approach to social anxiety. Newsletter. Meets for 10 week sessions, 4 times yr., Kennedy Memorial Hospital, 2201 Chapel Ave., Cherry Hill. For meeting information call Sam 267-738-7694 (eve) or Lynn 215-285-5403 (eve).

CUMBERLAND

GROW A mutual self-help group to prevent and recover from depression, anxiety and other mental health problems. Caring and sharing community to attain emotional maturity, personal responsibility and recovery. Meets Thurs., 7pm, Church of Christian/Missionary Alliance, Main Rd. and Harding Ave., Board Room, Vineland. Before attending call Daniel 856-881-2008.

ESSEX

Recovery, Inc. Self-help method of will training. Offers techniques for controlling temperamental behavior and changing attitudes toward nervous symptoms, anxiety, depression and fears. Meets Tues., 8pm, Prospect Presbyterian Church, 646 Prospect St., Maplewood. Call 201-612-8153. *Website:* http://www.recovery-inc.com

GLOUCESTER

GROW A mutual self-help group to prevent and recover from depression, anxiety and other mental health problems. A caring and sharing community to attain emotional maturity, personal responsibility and recovery. Meets Mon., 7pm, Grow Center, 206 University Blvd., Glassboro. Before attending call Brenda 856-881-2008.

Recovery, Inc. Self-help method of will training. Offers techniques for controlling temperamental behavior and changing attitudes toward nervous symptoms, anxiety, depression and fears. Families welcome. Meets Fri., 10-11am, James Johnson Library, 670 Ward Dr., Deptford. Call Barry Stockinger, Sr. 856-848-8715. *Website:* http://www.recovery-inc.com

MERCER

GROW A mutual self-help group to prevent and recover from depression, anxiety and other mental health problems. Caring and sharing community to attain emotional maturity, personal responsibility and recovery. Meets Tues., 5:45pm, Reach Out/Speak Out, 121 North Broad St., Trenton. Before attending call Denise 609-989-0255.

New Perspectives Mutual support for persons with depression, bipolar disorder, anxiety, or panic attacks. Meets every other Mon., 7:30pm, Unitarian Universalist Church, Washington Crossing. Call David Hughes 609-818-0177 (eve). *E-mail:* David.Hughes419@att.net

P.U.S.H. (Phobics Using Self-Help) Mutual support and encouragement for persons suffering from agoraphobia or panic attacks. Donation $1/week. Meets Mon., 7pm, Mercerville. For information call P.U.S.H. 609-291-0095.

MIDDLESEX

Overcomer's Outreach Christian 12-Step. Fellowship to overcome any type of addiction or compulsive behavior, anxiety, depression, or loneliness using God's word as a basis of recovery. Discussion, bible study, prayer, phone help. Meets Mon., 7:30-9:15pm, Metuchen Assembly of God, Rose and Whitman St., Metuchen. Call Janet 732-388-2856 (eve).

If you are using this book past Spring 2007, please call us for information about our most recent directory. 1-800-367-6274

MONMOUTH

GROW A mutual self-help group to prevent and recover from depression, anxiety and other mental health problems. Caring and sharing community to attain emotional maturity, personal responsibility and recovery.

> **Freehold** Meets Wed., 7pm, 11 Spring St. Before attending call Nancy 732-350-4800.
>
> **Ocean Grove** Meets Thurs., 6:45pm, St. Paul's Methodist Church, 80 Enbury St., Stokes Room. Before attending call Margo 732-206-1138.

MORRIS

Anxiety Support Group Mutual support and encouragement to people suffering from anxiety and phobias. Meets Mon., 7-8:30pm, United Methodist Church, 903 South Beverwyck Rd., Parsippany. Call Flora 973-257-7023. *E-mail:* sbuchert@verizon.net

OCEAN

GROW A mutual self-help group to prevent and recover from depression, anxiety and other mental health problems. Caring and sharing community to attain emotional maturity, personal responsibility and recovery.

> **Brick** Meets Tues., 6:30pm, Brick Presbyterian Church, 111 Drum Point Rd. Before attending call Caroline 732-899-7540.
>
> **Manchester** Meets Thurs., 7:30pm, Redeemer Lutheran Church, 2309 Route 70. Before attending call Nancy 732-350-4800.
>
> **Toms River** Meets Thurs., noon, Presbyterian Church of Toms River, River Room, Hooper Ave. and Chestnut St. Before attending call Lisa 732-350-4800.
>
> **Toms River** Meets Mon., 7pm, S&F Plaza, Unit 6, 2008 Route 37 East. Before attending call Nancy 732-350-4800.

P.H.O.B.I.A. (People Helping Others Become Independent Again) Support group for people with panic attacks, anxiety, phobias, depression and agoraphobia. Families welcome. Guest speakers, literature and phone help. Meets Wed., 7-9pm, St. Stephen's Church, Route 9, Waretown. Call Cathy 609-971-9110. *Website:* http://www.members.tripod.com/~phobiagroup/index.html *Email:* phobia@verizon.net

Recovery, Inc. Self-help method of will training. Offers techniques for controlling temperamental behavior and changing attitudes toward nervous symptoms, anxiety, depression and fears. Meets Mon., 7:30pm, Presbyterian Church of Toms River,

Hoopers Ave. and Chestnut St., Toms River. Call 201-612-8153. *Website:* http://www.recovery-inc.com

SOMERSET

P.A.C.T. (Phobics With Anxiety Coping Together) Self-help group for persons with panic attacks and/or agoraphobia. Meets Mon., 7-8:30pm, Somerset Medical Center, 110 Rehill Ave., Somerville. Call Diane 908-393-2719 (2-6pm), Violet 908-369-3892 or Marti 908-218-8919.

Recovery, Inc. Self-help method of will training. Offers techniques for controlling temperamental behavior and changing attitudes toward nervous symptoms, anxiety, depression and fears. Meets Thurs., 7:30pm, Richard Hall Community Mental Health Center, 500 N. Bridge St. and Vogt Dr., Bridgewater. Call 201-612-8153. *Website:* http://www.recovery-inc.com

UNION

Recovery, Inc. Offers techniques for controlling temperamental behavior and changing attitudes toward nervous symptoms, anxiety, depression and fears. Call 201-612-8153. *Website:* http://www.recovery-inc.com
> **Summit** Meets Wed., 7:45pm, Central Presbyterian Center, Morris Ave. and Maple St., (parking lot entrance).
> **Westfield** Meets Fri., 8pm, Union County Community Services Building, 300 North Ave. East, 2nd Floor, Conference Room.

NATIONAL

ABIL (Agoraphobics Building Independent Lives), Inc. *National. 15+ groups/contacts. Founded 1986.* Mutual support, encouragement, hope, goal setting and education for persons with agoraphobia, anxiety, or panic-related disorders, their families and friends. Write: ABIL, Inc., 400 West 32nd St., Richmond, VA 23225. Call 804-353-3964; Fax: 804-353-3687. *Website:* http://www.anxietysupport.org *Email:* answers@anxietysupport.org

Agoraphobics In Motion *National. 7 groups. Founded 1983.* Self-help group using specific behavioral and cognitive techniques to help people recover from anxiety disorders. Group development guidelines ($2.50). Write: AIM, 1719 Crooks, Royal Oak, MI 48067-1306. Call 248-547-0400. *Website:* http://www.aim-hg.org *Email:* anny@ameritech.net

Anxiety Disorders Association of America *National network. Founded 1980.* Promotes the welfare of people with phobias and related anxiety disorders.

An organization for consumers, health care professionals and other concerned individuals. Publishes national membership directory, self-help group directory, ADAA Reporter, newsletter. Offers development guidelines to those interested in starting a group. Write: ADAA, 8730 Georgia Ave., Suite 600, Silver Spring, MD 20910. Call 240-485-1001; Fax: 240-485-1035. *Website:* http://www.adaa.org

GROW in America *International. 143 groups. Founded in 1957.* 12-Step. Mutual help group offering friendship, community, education and leadership. Focused on recovery and personal growth. Open to all, including those with mental health issues, problems in living, depression, anxiety, grief, fears, etc. Write: GROW in America, PO Box 3667, Champaign, IL 61826. Call 1-888-741-4760. *Email:* growil@sbcglobal.net

International Paruresis Association, Inc. *International network. 35 affiliated groups. Founded 1996.* Provides emotional support and information for persons with paruresis (shy or bashful bladder). Supports research to develop effective treatments. Information, referrals, literature, phone support, workshops, conferences and advocacy. Assistance in starting similar groups. Write: Int'l Paruresis Association, PO Box 65111, Baltimore, MD 21209. Call 1-800-247-3864. *Website:* http://www.paruresis.org *Email:* ssoifer@ssw.umaryland.edu

Open Door Outreach, Inc. *Model. 4 groups in MN. Founded 1986.* Provides support and information on anxiety disorders. Offers strategies in anxiety management. Open to families and friends. Literature, information referrals, phone support, pen pals, conferences and newsletter. Assistance in starting local groups. Write: Open Door Outreach, Inc., c/o Judith Bemis, 608 Russell Ave. S, Minneapolis, MN 55405. Call 612-377-2467 (eve); Fax: 612-928-6716. *Website:* http://www.anxietysupport.net *Email:* jbemis608@yahoo.com

Recovery, Inc. *International. 640 groups. Founded 1937.* Mental health self-help organization that offers weekly group meetings for people suffering from various emotional and mental conditions. Principles parallel those found in cognitive-behavioral therapy. Write: Recovery, Inc., 802 N. Dearborn St., Chicago, IL 60610. Call 312-337-5661; Fax: 312-337-5756. *Website:* http://www.recovery-inc.com *Email:* inquiries@recovery-inc.org

ONLINE

Alt.Support.Shyness.FAQ *Online. Founded 1994.* Support for shyness. Offers information on understanding shyness, tackling shyness, job hunting, overcoming shyness and assertiveness. Includes shyness/dating, children with shyness and general self-help. Message board and newsgroup. *Website:* http://members.aol.com/cybernettr/shyness.html

Panic Survivor *Online.* Support group for persons who suffer from anxiety, panic attacks, social anxiety, generalized anxiety, post traumatic stress disorder, obsessive compulsive disorder, hypochondria, or any other form of anxiety. Focus is on recovery, day-to-day survival, with a "can do" attitude. *Website:* http://panicsurvivor.com/

"Taking Flight" Fear of Flying Support *Online.* Mutual help group, created by and for fearful fliers for their own recovery. Message boards, information and a variety of resources. *Website:* http://www.takingflight.us *Email:* info@takingflight.us

DEPRESSION / MANIC-DEPRESSION/ POST-PARTUM DEPRESSION

STATEWIDE

DBSA (Depression and Bipolar Support Alliance) of NJ *17 chapters throughout New Jersey.* Education and support for persons with depression or bipolar depression disorder, their families and friends. Peer support groups and educational programs. Write: DBSA (Depression and Bipolar Support Alliance) of NJ, 21 North 3rd St., 1st Floor, Surf City, NJ 08008. Call 609-494-3211.

GROW Mutual self-help group to prevent and recover from depression, anxiety and other mental health problems. Caring and sharing community to attain emotional maturity, personal responsibility and recovery. Meets in various counties in NJ. Write: GROW Center, 206 University Blvd., Glassboro, NJ 08028. Call 856-881-2008.

ATLANTIC

DBSA (Depression and Bipolar Support Alliance) Support and education for persons suffering from depression or bipolar depression. Share experiences, feelings, information and strategies for living with depression or bipolar depression. Meets Wed., 7-9pm, Presbyterian Church Annex, (located between the Church and Bank of America Building), 111 Route 50, Mays Landing. Call Tammie, Marty or Mike 609-665-0258. *Email:* dbsaatlanticco@aol.com

Can't find an appropriate group in your area? The Clearinghouse helps people start groups. Give us a call at 1-800-367-6274.

BERGEN

DBSA (Depression and Bipolar Support Alliance) Mutual support for persons with bipolar or unipolar disorders. Families and friends welcome. Phone help, guest speakers, rap sessions and literature. Donation $1. Meets Thurs., 7:15pm, Bergen Regional Medical Center, 230 E. Ridgewood Ave., Psych Pavilion, Room E007, Paramus. Call Cecily 973-423-4394 or 201-387-0091. *Website:* http://www.dbsabergennj.org/ *Email:* bergendmda@aol.com

POKIBID (Parents of Kids with Bipolar Disorder) Support for parents of bipolar children up to the age of 18. Meets in Madison, Livingston and Paramus. For meeting information call Amy 908-522-0369. *Website:* http://www.pokibid.org *Email:* AmySharak@comcast.net

Recovery, Inc. Self-help method of will training. Offers techniques for controlling temperamental behavior and changing attitudes toward nervous symptoms, anxiety, depression and fears. Call 201-612-8153. *Website:* http://www.recovery-inc.com
> **Hasbrouck Heights** Meets Wed., 8pm, First Reformed Church, Washington Place and Burton Ave.
> **Ridgewood** Meets Fri., 1:30pm, Christ Church, Cottage Place and Franklin Ave.

BURLINGTON

DBSA (Depression and Bipolar Support Alliance) Support group for parents of children with bipolar disorder and individuals with depressive or bipolar disorder. Rap sessions and education series. Meets 2nd Tues. and 4th Wed., 7pm, Virtua Memorial Hospital, Conference Room C, Mt. Holly. Call Natalie 609-702-1520 (eve). *Website:* http://www.moodgarden.org/burlington.htm *Email:* nataliedewmoore@hotmail.com

GROW A mutual self-help group to prevent and recover from depression, anxiety and other mental health problems. Caring and sharing community to attain emotional maturity, personal responsibility and recovery. Meets Tues., 7pm, Family Services, Pat le Bon Room, 770 Woodlane Rd., Mt. Holly. Before attending call Brenda 856-881-2008.

Postpartum Depression Support Group Mutual support and education for women experiencing postpartum depression. Babies are welcome. Meets 2nd Thurs. in Mt. Holly. For meeting information call Virtua Health 1-888-847-8823.

Recovery, Inc. Self-help method of will training. Offers techniques for controlling temperamental behavior and changing attitudes toward nervous symptoms, anxiety, depression and fears. Call 215-332-0722. *Website:* http://www.recovery-inc.com

> **Marlton** Meets Mon., 8pm and Thurs., 7pm, Prince of Peace Lutheran Church, 61 Route 70 East.

> **Westampton** Meets Tues., 7pm, Hampton Hospital, Cafeteria, Rancocas Rd.

CAMDEN

DBSA of Camden County: New Beginnings Support Group Mutual support, encouragement and education for persons with depression, bipolar disorder, anxiety, panic, OCD or other mental health issues. Provides a caring, empathetic place to listen and share successes. Meets Mon., 7-9pm, (families welcome 1st and 3rd Mon.) and Wed., 11am-1pm, Holy Trinity Lutheran Church, 214 N. Warwick Rd., Magnolia. Call Gary 856-227-5678 (day/eve) or Maribel 856-232-3181. For family group call Karen 856-451-1240.

Depression / Anxiety Support Group For anyone suffering from anxiety and/or depression to support one another in an effort to remain healthy and share common problems and concerns. Under 18 welcome. Rap sessions, phone help, literature. Meets 3rd Mon., 7:15-9pm, Marie Fleche Library, Berlin. Call Nancy 856-768-1258 (eve) or Rhonda 856-768-2030 (day). *Email:* smartteach@msn.com

Manic-Depressives Anonymous Self-help group to guide manic-depressives, depressives, their families and friends. Rap sessions. Meets Wed., 8-9pm, Stratford. Call Jackie 856-667-3485 (day).

Pink and Blues DBSA Group (Gay/Lesbian) A gay, lesbian, bisexual and transgender support group for those with depression, bipolar disorder, schizophrenia, or any other mental illness. Meets Wed., 7pm, St. Luke's and the Epiphany Church, 330 S. 13th St., Philadelphia, PA. Call Mark Davis 215-546-0300 ext. 3301 (day) or 215-627-0424 (eve). *E-mail:* mark.davis@phila.gov

Postpartum Depression Support Group Mutual support and education for women experiencing postpartum depression. Babies are welcome. Meets Thurs., 10:30am-noon, Virtua Health, Barry D. Brown Health Education Center, 106 Carnie Blvd., Voorhees. Call 1-888-847-8823 (day).

Recovery, Inc. Self-help method of will training. Offers techniques for controlling temperamental behavior and changing attitudes toward nervous symptoms, anxiety, depression and fears. Meets Sat., 11:30am, Starting Point, 215 Highland Ave., Westmont. Call 215-332-0722. *Website:* http://www.recovery-inc.com

CUMBERLAND

Depression Support Group Mutual support for persons suffering from depression or any other mental illness. Provides a safe and comfortable environment where persons can share with others who also suffer from depression. Meets Wed., 7pm in Millville. For meeting information call 856-825-3521 (after 10am).

GROW A mutual self-help group to prevent and recover from depression, anxiety and other mental health problems. Caring and sharing community to attain emotional maturity, personal responsibility and recovery. Meets Thurs., 7pm, Church of Christian/Missionary Alliance, Main Rd. and Harding Ave., Board Room, Vineland. Before attending call Daniel 856-881-2008.

ESSEX

Comfort Zone, The Provides mutual support for people suffering from depression and manic-depression. Meets the 2nd and 4th Fri., noon-1:30pm, Mental Health Association of Essex County, 33 South Fullerton Ave., Montclair. Call Mary Ann Forster-King 973-509-9777 (day).

DBSA (Depression and Bipolar Support Alliance) Mutual support and sharing of information for individuals diagnosed with depression or bipolar disorder. Family members welcome. Rap sessions, guest speakers, educational programs, literature, phone help and e-mail.

> **Montclair** Meets Mon. and Thurs., 7:15-9pm, First Congregational Church, 40 South Fullerton Ave. (Crescent St. entrance) Call Margo Atwell 973-744-5230 or Tom B. 201-998-5751. *Website:* http://www.dbsanewjersey.org/essexcounty *Email:* margoatwell@msn.com

> **Newark** Meets Fri., 7-8:30pm, University of Medicine and Dentistry of NJ, Behavioral Health Sciences Building, 183 South Orange Ave., Level B Conference Room. Call Kevin 973-848-1859 (day/eve). *Website:* http://www.dbsanewjersey.org/essexcounty/newark.htm *Email:* newarksupportgroup@hotmail.com

POKIBID (Parents of Kids with Bipolar Disorder) Support for parents of bipolar children up to the age of 18. Meets in Madison, Livingston and Paramus. For meeting information call Amy 908-522-0369. *Website:* http://www.pokibid.org *Email:* AmySharak@comcast.net

Postpartum Depression Support Group *Professionally-run.* Support group for pregnant and new mothers experiencing anxiety and/or depression. Meets Tues., 10-11:30am, Ambulatory Care Center, South Orange Ave., Livingston. Call Dr. Lauren Meisels, PhD. 973-762-4147.

Recovery, Inc. Self-help method of will training. Offers techniques for controlling temperamental behavior and changing attitudes toward nervous symptoms, anxiety, depression and fears. Meets Tues., 8pm, Prospect Presbyterian Church, 646 Prospect St., Maplewood. Call 201-612-8153. *Website:* http://www.recovery-inc.com

GLOUCESTER

DBSA (Depression and Bipolar Support Alliance) Mutual support and sharing of information for individuals diagnosed with depression or bipolar disorder. Rap sessions, guest speakers, educational programs, literature, phone help and e-mail. Meets 1st and 3rd Thurs., 7:30-9pm, Church of Jesus Christ of Latter Day Saints, 259 Lambs Rd., Pitman. Call Ralph 856-264-4239. *Website:* http://www.dbsagc.org *Email:* brclement@snip.net

GROW A mutual self-help group to prevent and recover from depression, anxiety and other mental health problems. A caring and sharing community to attain emotional maturity, personal responsibility and recovery. Meets Mon., 7pm, Grow Center, 206 University Blvd., Glassboro. Before attending call Brenda 856-881-2008.

Recovery, Inc. Self-help method of will training. Offers techniques for controlling temperamental behavior and changing attitudes toward nervous symptoms, anxiety, depression and fears. Families welcome. Meets Fri., 10-11am, James Johnson Library, 670 Ward Dr., Deptford. Call Barry Stockinger, Sr. 856-848-8715. *Website:* http://www.recovery-inc.com

HUDSON

DBSA (Depression and Bipolar Support Alliance) Mutual support for persons with depression and bipolar depression. Meets 2nd and 4th Mon., 6-7pm, Hudson County Self-Help Center, 3000 Kennedy Blvd., Suite 305, Jersey City. Call Debbie or Carol 201-420-8013.

DBSA (Depression and Bipolar Support Alliance) Mutual support for persons with depression and bipolar depression. Meets Fri. 7pm, Community Mental Health Center, 597 Broadway, Bayonne. Call 201-384-8051.

Postpartum Depression *Professionally-run.* Support for new mothers and their families. Meetings vary, Meadowlands Hospital, 55 Meadowlands Parkway, Secaucus. Call Kate Waldron 201-392-3180 (day).

HUNTERDON

Postpartum Depression Support Group *Professionally-run.* Mutual support and education for women experiencing postpartum depression. Babies welcome. Meets 1st and 3rd Fri., 10:30-11:30am, Hunterdon Medical Center, 2100 Westcott Dr., Flemington. Before attending call Jean Jamele, RN 908-788-6634 (day).

MERCER

DBSA (Depression and Bipolar Support Alliance) An informal forum for education, support and socialization among patients diagnosed with depression, bipolar disorder, or related disorders. Families, friends and interested others welcome. Meets Tues., 7:30-9:30pm, Lambert House, 253 Witherspoon and Franklin St., Room 1 and 2, Princeton. Call 1-888-226-6437. *Website:* http://www.moodgarden.org/princeton.htm *Email:* mcman@mcmanweb.com

GROW A mutual self-help group to prevent and recover from depression, anxiety and other mental health problems. Meets Tues., 5:45pm, Reach Out/Speak Out, 121 North Broad Street, Trenton. Before attending call Denise 609-989-0255.

New Perspectives Mutual support for persons with depression, bipolar disorder, anxiety, or panic attacks. Meets every other Mon., 7:30pm, Unitarian Universalist Church, Washington Crossing. Call David Hughes 609-818-0177 (eve). *Email:* David.Hughes419@att.net

Pregnancy and Postpartum Support Group *Professionally-run.* Support for pregnant and new mothers adjusting to emotional issues such as blues, depression and anxiety. Meets 3rd Sat., 10:30am-noon, 60 Mt. Lucas Rd., Princeton. Pre-registration required. Before attending call Joyce 609-683-1000.

MIDDLESEX

DBSA (Depression Bipolar Support Alliance) Support and information for manic-depressive/depressive sufferers. Meets Fri., 7:30pm, Robert Wood Johnson University Hospital, Auditorium, Main Floor, New Brunswick. Call 1-888-226-6437. *Website:* http://www.moodgarden.org/middlesex.htm *Email:* dbsamsex@hotmail.com

MONMOUTH

DBSA (Depression and Bipolar Support Alliance) Support for persons affected by depression and manic depression. Families and interested professionals are welcome. Guest speakers, phone help and mutual sharing. Meets at St. Mary's Church, Route 34 and Phalanx Rd., Colts Neck. Before attending call Rick 732-919-7739 (eve) or Tony Katz 609-812-9646 (after 9pm). *Website:* http://www.moodgarden.org/coltsneck.htm *Email:* rcallen@monmouth.com or Antwon82763@aol.com

GROW A mutual self-help group to prevent and recover from depression, anxiety and other mental health problems. Caring and sharing community to attain emotional maturity, personal responsibility and recovery.

> **Freehold** Meets Wed., 7pm, 11 Spring St. Before attending call Nancy 732-350-4800.
> **Ocean Grove** Meets Thurs., 6:45pm, St. Paul's Methodist Church, 80 Enbury St., Stokes Room. Before attending call Margo 732-206-1138.

MORRIS

DBSA (Depression and Bipolar Support Alliance) Education and support for persons with depression or bipolar disorder, their families and friends. Peer support groups and educational programs.

> **Morristown** Rap group meets Tues., 7:30-9pm; Lecture/educational series meets last Wed., 7:30pm (call for schedules Nov./Dec.), (suggested donation $3), Morristown Unitarian Fellowship, 21 Normandy Heights Rd. Call Linda 973-994-1143 (day/eve) or 908-447-2826 (for weather cancellations). *Website:* http://www.dbsanewjersey.org/morristownarea *Email:* lsbl@panix.com
> **Succasunna** Meets 1st and 3rd Thurs., 7:15-9pm, Temple Shalom, 215 South Hillside Ave. Call Bonnie 973-361-5456 or Ann Kays 973-927-3810 (day). *Website:* http://www.dbsanewjersey.org/succasunna2 *Email:* bonnie@therosenthals.net

POKIBID (Parents of Kids with Bipolar Disorder) Support for parents of bipolar children up to the age of 18. Meets in Madison, Livingston and Paramus. For meeting information call Amy 908-522-0369. *Website:* http://www.pokibid.org *Email:* AmySharak@comcast.net

Consider passing this Directory on to a student or staff member - browsing through the Directory pages can often provide helpful education as to the wide variety of groups available.

Postpartum Support Group *Professionally-run.* Provides support for new mothers experiencing postpartum depression. Meets 1st and 3rd Tues., 7-8pm, Saint Clare's Behavioral Health Center, 50 Morris Ave., Denville. Before attending call 1-888-626-2111 (ask for mom's support group).

OCEAN

DBSA (Depression and Bipolar Support Alliance) An informal forum for education, support and socialization among patients diagnosed with depression, bipolar disorder, or related disorders, their families, friends and interested others.

> **Brant Beach** Meetings vary, St. Francis Community Center, Seniors' Luncheon Room, 47th and Long Beach Blvd. Call Salvina 609-494-3211; for families and friends call Catherine 609-494-3931. *Website:* http://www.dbsanewjersey.org/LBI *Email:* sivan710@comcast.net

> **Toms River** Meets Fri., 7:30-9:30pm, Community Medical Center, 99 Route 37 West, Auditorium B. Call 1-888-226-6437. *Website:* http://www.moodgarden.org/ocean.htm *Email:* dbsamsex@hotmail.com

GROW A mutual self-help group to prevent and recover from depression, anxiety and other mental health problems. Caring and sharing community to attain emotional maturity, personal responsibility and recovery.

> **Brick** Meets Tues., 6:30pm, Brick Presbyterian Church, 11 Drum Point Rd. Before attending call Caroline 732-899-7540.

> **Manchester** Meets Thurs., 7:30pm, Redeemer Lutheran Church, 2309 Route 70. Call Nancy 732-350-4800.

> **Toms River** Meets Thurs., noon, Presbyterian Church of Toms River, River Room, Hooper Ave. and Chestnut St. Before attending call Lisa 732-350-4800.

> **Toms River** Meets Mon., 7pm, S&F Plaza, Unit 6, 2008 Route 37 East. Call Nancy 732-350-4800.

Recovery, Inc. Self-help method of will training. Offers techniques for controlling temperamental behavior and changing attitudes toward nervous symptoms, anxiety, depression and fears. Meets Mon., 7:30pm, Presbyterian Church of Toms River, Hoopers Ave. and Chestnut St., Toms River. Call 201-612-8153. *Website:* http://www.recovery-inc.com

SOMERSET

Recovery, Inc. Self-help method of will training. Offers techniques for controlling temperamental behavior and changing attitudes toward nervous symptoms, anxiety, depression and fears. Meets Thurs., 7:30pm, Richard Hall Community Mental

Health Center, 500 N. Bridge St. and Vogt Dr., Bridgewater. Call 201-612-8153. *Website:* http://www.recovery-inc.com

SUSSEX

DBSA (Depression and Bipolar Support Alliance) Sussex County Support and education for persons suffering from depression or bipolar depression. Rap sessions and guest speakers. Family and friends welcome. Meets Wed., 7:30-9pm, Redeemer Lutheran Church, 37 Newton-Sparta Rd., Newton. Call Dan 973-948-6999 or Jean 973-383-3808. *Website:* http://www.scdbsa.org *Email:* dan@dancarter.net

People Suffering from Depression Provides support and education for anyone suffering from depression. Rap sessions, guest speakers. Meets 2nd and 4th Mon., 10:30am-noon, 16 Allamuchy Trail, Cranberry Lake. Call Betty 973-347-3873.

UNION

DBSA (Depression and Bipolar Support Alliance) Education and support for persons with depression or bipolar disorder (manic depression), their families and friends. Rap sessions. Meets 1st and 3rd Thurs., 7:30-9pm, Overlook Hospital, Conference Room # 1 and 4th Sat., 1-3pm, First Floor, Conference Room # 2, Summit. Call Theldora Hawkins 908-233-7074 (day/eve). *Website:* http://www.dbsanewjersey.org/essexcounty

Recovery, Inc. Self-help method of will training. Offers techniques for controlling temperamental behavior and changing attitudes toward nervous symptoms, anxiety, depression and fears. Call 201-612-8153. *Website:* http://www.recovery-inc.com
> **Summit** Meets Wed., 7:45pm, Central Presbyterian Center, Morris Ave. and Maple St., (parking lot entrance).
> **Westfield** Meets Fri., 8pm, Union County Community Services Building, 300 North Ave. East, 2nd Floor, Conference Room, (rear parking lot entrance).

NATIONAL

Dep-Anon *National. Founded 1999.* 12-Step. Fellowship of men, women and children whose lives have been affected by a family member's depression. Members share hope, strength and experience in order to grow emotionally and spiritually. Write: Dep-Anon, PO Box 17414, Louisville, KY 40217. Call Hugh S. 502-569-1989. *Website:* http://www.depressedanon.com *Email:* depanon@ka.net

Depressed Anonymous *International. 50 affiliated groups. Founded 1985.* 12-Step program to help depressed persons believe & hope they can feel better. Newsletter, phone support, information & referrals, workshops, conferences and seminars. Information packet. Assistance starting a similar group. Write: D.A.P., Box 17414, Louisville, KY 40217. Call Hugh 502-569-1989. *Website:* http://www.depressedanon.com *Email:* depanon@ka.net

Depression After Delivery *National. Founded 1985.* Support and information for women who have suffered from postpartum depression. Volunteer phone support in most states, some local support groups, newsletter, group development guidelines. *Website:* http://www.depressionafterdelivery.com

Depression and Bipolar Support Alliance *National. 400+ affiliated groups. Founded 1986.* Mutual support and information for persons with depressive and manic-depressive illness and their families. Public education on the nature of depressive illnesses. Advocacy for research and improved access to care. Annual conference, chapter development guidelines and quarterly newsletter. Write: DBSA, 730 N. Franklin, Suite 501, Chicago, IL 60610, Call 1-800-826-3632 or 312-642-0049; Fax: 312-642-7243. *Website:* http://www.dbsalliance.org

DRADA (Depression & Related Affective Disorders Association) *International. 73 affiliated groups. Founded 1986.* Aims to alleviate the suffering arising from depression and manic-depression by assisting self-help groups. Provides education, information and supports research. Also offers newsletter, literature, phone support. Assistance in starting new groups, training for group leaders and peer support programs. Young People's Outreach Project. Write: DRADA, 2330 West Joppa Rd., Foxleigh Bldg., Suite 100, Lutherville, MD 21093. Call 410-583-2919 or 1-888-288-1104; Fax: 410-583-2964. *Website:* http://www.drada.org *Email:* drada@jhmi.edu

GROW in America *International. 143 groups. Founded in 1957.* Groups in Illinois, New Jersey, Rhode Island. 12-Step group that offers mutual help, friendship, community, education and leadership. Focused on recovery and personal growth. Open to all, including those with mental health issues, problems in living, depression, anxiety, grief, fears, etc. Write: GROW in America, Box 3667, Champaign, IL 61826. Call 217-352-6989; Fax: 217-352-8530. *Email:* growil@sbcglobal.net

"A man doesn't realize how much he can stand until he is put to the test. You can stand far more than you think you can. You are much stronger than you think you are."--Martin Niemoller

MDSG-NY (Mood Disorders Support Group, Inc.) *Model. 2 affiliated groups in New York. Founded 1981.* Support & education for people with manic-depression or depression & their families & friends. Guest lectures, newsletter and rap groups. Write: MDSG, Inc., PO Box 30377, New York, NY 10011. Call 212-533-6374; Fax: 212-675-0218. *Website:* http://www.mdsg.org *Email:* info@mdsg.org

Postpartum Support International *International. 400+ members; support networks in 38 states; 25 countries. Founded 1987.* To increase the awareness of the emotional changes women often experience during pregnancy and after the birth of a baby. Information on diagnosis & treatment of postpartum depression. Provides education, advocacy and annual conference. Encourages formation of support groups. Helps strengthen existing groups. Phone support, referrals, literature and newsletter. Write: Postpartum Support International, 927 N. Kellogg Ave., Santa Barbara, CA 93111. Call 805-967-7636; Fax: 805-967-0608. *Website:* http://www.postpartum.net *Email:* psioffice@earthlink.net

Recovery, Inc. *International. 640 groups. Founded 1937.* Mental health self-help organization that offers weekly group meetings for people suffering from various emotional and mental conditions. Teaches people how to change the thoughts, reactions and behaviors that cause their physical and emotional symptoms. Write: Recovery, Inc., 802 N. Dearborn St., Chicago, IL 60610. Call 312-337-5661; Fax: 312-337-5756. *Website:* http://www.recovery-inc.org *Email:* inquiries@recovery-inc.com

ONLINE

BPSO (Bipolar Significant Others Bulletin Board) *Online.* Provides support and information for families and friends of persons with bipolar disorder. Opportunity to communicate online with others in similar situations. Website offers chat, forums, Email list and over 3000 web pages of information. *Website:* http://www.bipolarworld.net/ *Email:* bipolarworld@yahoo.com

Child & Adolescent Bipolar Foundation *Online.* Site provides information posted by members to provide support to families of children or teens with bipolar disorder. Offers message boards, support group information, community center and general information. *Website:* http://www.bpkids.org

Conduct Disorders Parent Message Board *Online.* Support for parents living with a child with one of the many behavior disorders including attention deficit hyperactivity disorder, oppositional defiance disorder, conduct disorder, depression and substance abuse. Parents with children of all ages welcome. *Website:* http://www.conductdisorders.com

MENTAL HEALTH CONSUMERS

(see also other mental health sections)

STATEWIDE

COMHCO (Coalition Of Mental Health Consumer Organizations) Information, support and advocacy on mental health issues. Speakers, workshops. Membership $5/yr. For meeting time and location, call Annette Wright 973-778-8810 (after 1pm). *E-mail:* comhco@aol.com

Consumer Connections Support Network Regional support group meetings for consumers who work in mental health/social services. Groups focus on work-related issues only. Write: Consumer Connections - MHA in NJ, 88 Pompton Ave., Verona, NJ 07044. Call Penny Grande 973-571-4100 (day); Fax: 973-857-1777. *Website:* http://www.mhanj.org

CSP (Collaborative Support Programs) of NJ, Inc. Assists statewide in the development and networking of mental health consumer/psychiatric survivor groups. Workshops, quarterly newsletter, conferences, system advocacy, funding of consumer-run self-help centers, community services, technical assistance and supportive housing. Brochures available. Write: CSP, 11 Spring St., Freehold, NJ 07728. Call 1-800-227-3729 or 732-780-1175 (Mon.-Fri., 9am-5pm); Fax: 732-780-8977. *Website:* http://www.cspnj.org/comencorp.com

NAMI CARE (Consumers Advocating Recovery through Empowerment) Support for anyone afflicted with any type of psychiatric disorder. Follows a national model, based upon shared insights and empathy. Groups are affiliated with local NAMI family groups for education and advocacy. Offers trained peer facilitators. Help in forming CARE groups. Call Jay Yudof, NAMI NJ Consumer Outreach Liaison 1-866-464-3267. *Website:* http://www.naminj.org *Email:* jyudof@hotmail.com

ATLANTIC

Gay, Lesbian, Transgendered, Bisexual Support Group Mutual support for persons with mental illness who are struggling with their own sexual identity. Goal is to share feelings and discuss barriers to a healthy relationship in a non-judgmental, caring atmosphere. Guest speakers, social activities, phone help, advocacy, literature and educational series. Meets 1st Sun., 1-2pm (social hour); 2-4pm (support group), ICE Self-Help Center, 611 Doughty Rd., Pleasantville. Call Leslie 609-272-0928.

ICE Self-Help Center Provides an environment of support and empowerment that provides wellness. Offers self-help groups and recreational activities for mental health consumers. For information call ICE Self-Help Center 609-272-0928.

BERGEN

For Us/By Us *Consumer-run.* Self-help center that brings together consumers of mental health services. Center provides support, socializing, recreational activities and advocacy. Open Mon., Wed., Thurs. and Fri., 3-7pm and Sun., 1-5pm, For Us/By Us Self-Help/Drop In Center, 40 North Van Brunt St., Room 22, 2nd Floor, Englewood. Call 201-541-1221.

On Our Own Self-Help Center Offers support groups, socializing, recreational activities and advocacy to bring together consumers of mental health services. Open Mon-Fri., 12-7pm; Sat and Sun., 1-5pm. Support group meets 1st and 3rd Thurs., 6-8:30pm, On Our Own Self-Help Center, 179 Main St., Suite A, Hackensack. Call 201-489-8402, Center Non-Emergency Rap Line 201-342-3856 or Judy Banes 973-340-2346 (day).

BURLINGTON

RITE Center (Realizing Independence Through Empowerment), The Consumer-run and managed self-help center that provide opportunities for sharing, recreation and advocacy. Offers rap sessions, literature, socialization and outside activities. Open Tues. and Wed., 3:30-6:30pm; Fri., 2-6pm; Sat., noon-4pm, 112 W. Broad St., Burlington. Call 609-747-0697.

Riverbank Self-Help Center Provides self-help, mutual support, advocacy and social activities for mental health consumers. Open Wed., 5-9pm, every other Fri., 6:30-9pm and Sun., 2-6pm, Riverbank Self-Help Center, 114 Delaware Ave., Burlington. Call 609-239-1786. *Email:* riverhelps@juno.com

CAMDEN

Donald Mays Self-Help Center, The *Consumer-run.* Center offers support, recreational activities and advocacy for mental health consumers. Open Mon., Wed., Fri., 3-8pm and Sat., noon-4pm, 1 Colby Ave., Stratford. For information call 856-346-9043.

Pink and Blues DBSA Group (Gay/Lesbian) A gay, lesbian, bisexual and transgender support group for those with depression, bipolar disorder, schizophrenia, or any other mental illness. Meets Wed., 7pm, St. Luke's and the Epiphany Church, 330 S. 13th St., Philadelphia, PA. Call Mark Davis 215-546-0300 ext. 3301 (day) or 215-627-0424 (eve). *Email:* mark.davis@phila.gov

CAPE MAY

The C.A.P.E. Consumer-run. Self-help center providing mutual support, advocacy, social and recreational activities for mental health consumers. Located at 4410 Pacific Ave., Wildwood. For meeting information call 609-523-7100.

CUMBERLAND

New Horizons *Consumer-run.* Self-help center providing mutual support, socializing, recreational activities and advocacy for mental health care consumers. Located at 739 Wood St., Vineland. For information call 856-696-8921.

ESSEX

East Essex Self-Help Center *(Formerly Pleasant Moments Self-Help Center)* Consumer-run self-help center offers support, discussions, computers, speakers, socializing and self-help groups for mental health consumers. Open Mon., Tues. and Wed., 3-7:30pm, East Essex Self-Help Center, 570 Belleville Ave., (entrance on Franklin Ave.), Belleville. For information call 973-450-0347.

Spirituality Group Support for mental health consumers fostering an awareness of spirituality and a sense that we are a part of a much larger powerful entity. Offers mutual sharing, education, rap sessions, social, phone help and advocacy. Meets Thurs., 5-6pm, Where Peaceful Waters Flow, 47 Cleveland St., Orange. Call Celine 973-746-3244 (eve) or Jacqueline 973-676-0658 (day).

Thursdays *Professionally-run.* Drop-in center that provides mutual support for mental health care consumers. Opportunity to socialize, guest speakers and trips. Meets Thurs., 6:30-9pm, MHA of Essex, 33 South Fullerton Ave., Montclair. Call Judi Fiederer 973-509-9777.

Where Peaceful Waters Flow *Consumer-run.* Self-help center that offers support and advocacy for mental health consumers. Provides resources, socialization, rap sessions, recreational activities, literature and phone help. Open Mon., Tues., Wed., 3-7pm and Sat., 10am-3pm, Where Peaceful Waters Flow, 47 Cleveland St., Orange. Call 973-762-7469.

GLOUCESTER

Up Your Alley Self-Help Center Self-help center run by and for consumers of mental health services that provides socialization, support, advocacy, rap sessions and guest speakers. Open Mon.-Wed., 4-8pm and Sat., noon-4pm, located at 13A Curtis Ave., Woodbury. Call 856-853-6828. *E-mail:* gloucestershc@snip.net

HUDSON

Hudson County Self-Help Center *Professionally-run.* Provides socialization, recreation and advocacy for mental health consumers. Open Mon., Tues., Wed., Fri., 3-7pm; and Sat. 1-5pm, Hudson County Self-Help Center, 3000 Kennedy Blvd., Suite 305, Jersey City. Call 201-420-8013.

Schizophrenics Anonymous Fellowship for persons diagnosed with any schizophrenia-related disorder. Focuses on recovery, using a 6-step program, along with medication and professional help. Meets 1st and 3rd Tues., 4:30pm, Hudson County Self-Help Center, 3000 Kennedy Blvd., Suite 305, Jersey City. Call Anthony or Barbara 201-420-8013 (eve).

HUNTERDON

Getting Together Self-Help Center Drop-in center for mental health consumers and drop-in center. Educational series, support groups, social and advocacy. Open Sun., noon-4pm; Tues., 4-7pm; Wed., 2-6pm; Fri., 4-8pm and Sat., 5-8pm, 162A Route 31 N., Flemington. Call Juliette or Eileen 908-806-8202 (day/eve). *Email:* outreach31@earthlink.net

NAMI CARE (Consumers Advocating Recovery through Empowerment) Peer based mutual support group for anyone diagnosed with a mental illness. Program is designed to help peers share experiences in a positive, supportive and understanding atmosphere. Opportunity to learn from each other in a safe and confidential environment. Rap sessions and literature. Meets 2nd and 5th Thurs., 7:30-9pm, Getting Together Self-Help Center, 162A Route 31 North, Flemington. Call Walter 908-638-8024. *Email:* dudzinski@net-lynx.com

MERCER

NAMI CARE (Consumers Advocating Recovery through Empowerment) Self-help group run by and for consumers. Meets 2nd and 4th Mon., 6-7 pm, NAMI Mercer Office, Lawrenceville. Call 609-799-8994 (day). *Website:* http://www.namimercer.org *Email:* home@namimercer.org

Reachout/Speakout *Consumer-run.* Offers mutual support and socialization for mental health consumers. Advocacy, education, social activities and referrals. Center open various days. Support group meeting held Tues., 5-8pm, Reachout-Speakout Self-Help Center, 121 North Broad St., Trenton. Call Self-Help Center 609-989-0255.

MIDDLESEX

CAMHOP-NJ (Chinese Mental Health Self-Help Group) *(BILINGUAL) Professionally-run.* Mutual support group for families and individuals of Chinese origin with mental illnesses. Meets 3rd Tues., 7-8:45pm, Stelton Baptist Church, 334 Plainfield Ave., Edison. Call Maggie Luo 732-940-0991 (day). *Website:* http://www.naminj.org/programs/camhop/camhop.html   *Email:* namichinesegroup@yahoo.com

Member To Member Rap Group Support and confidential discussion of concerns for mental health consumers. Meets Wed., 4pm and Thurs., 4:30pm, Self Help Center of New Brunswick, 96 Bayard St., Lower Level, Suite B-17, New Brunswick. Call Self-Help Center 732-296-0303 (day). *Website:* http://www.cspnj.org *Email:* newbrunswickshc@snip.net

Rap Group Offers a safe supportive environment for consumers to express and share their feelings about mental health issues. Meets Wed. and Thurs., 3-7pm; Sat., 1-5pm, Self-Help Center of New Brunswick, 96 Bayard St., Lower Level, B-17, New Brunswick. Call 732-296-0303 (day) or Carey 732-656-9288 (eve). *Email:* newbrunswickshc@attglobal.net

Schizophrenics Anonymous Mutual support for persons with schizophrenia or schizophrenia related disorders. Guest speakers, literature. Meets 1st and 3rd Tues., 4pm, Self-Help Center of New Brunswick, 96 Bayard St., Lower Level, Suite B-17, New Brunswick. Call Integrated Case Management Services 732-235-6184 (day), Self-Help Center 732-296-0303 (day) or Attila 732-220-1671 (eve).

Self-Help Center of New Brunswick Self-help center offers socialization and support for adults with a mental health issue or other special needs. Handicapped accessible. Open Wed. and Thurs., 3-7pm; Sat., 1-5pm, 96 Bayard St., Lower Level, Suite B17, New Brunswick. Call The Center 732-296-0303. *Website:* http://www.cspnj.com

MONMOUTH

C.A.R.E. Center (Consumer Advocacy Recreation Exchange) Self-help center for mental health consumers to provide support and socialization.

Open Sun.-Sat. (closed Tues.), noon, CARE Center, 700 Mattison Ave., Asbury Park. Call Irene 732-409-5499 (day).

Freehold Self-Help Center Support group for mental health consumers and drop-in center. Consumer resource center, rap sessions, social, educational and employment resources for persons with disabilities. Open Thurs., 5-9pm; Fri., 3-9pm and Sat., 1-7pm, 17 Bannard St., Freehold. Call 732-625-9485.

NAMI CARE (Consumers Advocating Recovery through Empowerment) Support and advocacy group for mental health consumers. Meets 3rd Tues., 7-8:45pm, Lutheran Church of the Good Shepherd, 112 Middletown Rd., Holmdel. Call Jay 732-531-7624. *Email:* jyudof@hotmail.com

MORRIS

CAP (Consumer Advocacy Program) Advocacy group for mental health consumers and drop-in center. Consumer resource center group meets last Tues., 10am-2pm, Mental Health Association, 100 Route 46 E., Bldg. C, Mountain Lakes. Call Christa Utz 973-334-3496 (day).

M.O.M.M.I.E.S. Group, The (Mothers Overcoming Medical Mental Illnesses Eternal Support) A support group for mothers with illnesses who have children of all ages. Rap sessions, education, guest speakers, newsletter, literature, buddy system and phone help. Meets Fri., 6-7pm, St. Clare's Hospital, 130 Powerville Rd., Community Room, Boonton Township. Call Kim-Marie De Lauro 973-257-9585 (day).

Morris Self-Help Center Socialization for mental health consumers. Handicapped accessible. Drop-in center. Open Mon., Tues., Wed. and Fri., 3-7pm; Sat. and Sun., 1-5pm, Self-Help Center, 1259 Route 46 East, Bldg. 4 D, Parisppany. Call 973-334-2470.

Schizophrenics Anonymous Fellowship, support, information for persons with schizophrenia or related disorders. Focuses upon recovery, using a 6-step program, along with medication and professional help. Meets the 1st and 3rd Wed., 7pm, Mental Health Association, 100 Route 46 E., Bldg. C, Mountain Lakes. Call Christa Utz 973-334-3496.

"Take the first step in faith. You don't have to see the whole staircase, just take the first step." --Martin Luther King Jr.

OCEAN

Brighter Days Self-Help Mutual Aid Center Mutual support and discussion for mental health consumers. Rap sessions, socials and special celebrations. Open Tues., Wed., Thurs., 4-8pm and Sat., 1-4pm, S and F Plaza, 2008 Route 37 West, Suite 6, Toms River. Call Mental Health Association 732-905-1132 (day) or Brighter Days 732-270-6061.

PASSAIC

Social Connections Self-help center that provides support for mental health consumers. Rap groups, social activities and meeting new friends. Meets various times and days, Vanderhoef House, 1 Westervelt Ave., Weaslebrook Park, Clifton. Call Annette Wright 973-778-8810. *Email:* comhco@aol.com

Wellness Support Club *Consumer-run.* Rap sessions, mutual sharing and phone help. Meets twice monthly, Mental Health Association, 404 Clifton Ave., Clifton. Before attending call Denise 973-478-4444 ext. 17 (day).

SALEM

NAMI CARE (Consumers Advocating Recovery through Empowerment) Support and advocacy group for mental health consumers. Meets 2nd and 4th Wed., 7-8:30pm, First Baptist Church, 117 S. Main St., Woodstown. Call Kathleen Chance 856-299-4012.

New Dimensions Socialization for mental health consumers. Handicapped accessible. Arts, crafts, mental health education, lending library. Open Tues., Wed., Thurs. and Sat., 5-9pm; and Sun., 1-4pm, 316A Merion Ave., Carneys Point. Call 856-351-9100 (day).

SOMERSET

Freedom Trail Self-Help Center Socializing, advocacy and support for mental health consumers. Open Mon. and Wed., 9am-2pm and Thurs. and Sat., 6-11pm, Third Reformed Church, 10 W. Somerset St., Raritan. Call Rose-Marie DeVito 908-722-5778 (above hours).

SUSSEX

A Way To Freedom 12-Step. A place where mental health consumers can support each other. Advocacy, education, socialization and recreation. Phone help, food

412

bank and part time consumer employment opportunities. Meets Mon., Wed. and Fri., 3-7pm; Sat., noon-4pm, 69 Water St., Newton. Call Ann Lovell or Betty 973-300-0830.

UNION

Esperanza (Hope) *(SPANISH) Professionally-run.* Mutual support, social and recreational activities for Latino mental health consumers to provide positive interpersonal relationships. Self-help center open Mon. and Thurs., 9am-1pm, 60 Prince St., Elizabeth. Call Anne Portas 973-571-4100.

New Beginnings Self-Help Center Support for mental health consumers to establish a social network to share experiences, resource information, encouragement and companionship. Recreational and social activities, self-help group discussions. Open Mon., Wed., Thurs., Fri., 3-8pm and Sun., 2-7pm, New Beginnings Self-Help Center, 60 Prince St., Basement, Elizabeth. Call Joyce Haberer or Kenneth Quigley 908-352-7830 (day).

Youth Partnership Group Adult supervised activities for youth (age 13-21) with complex emotional, mental health, or behavioral issues to help them express what they have been through and share concerns. Rap sessions. Meets 2nd and 4th Wed., 6:30-8:30pm, Family Support Organization, 137 Elmer St., Westfield. Call Kathy Wagner 908-789-7625 (day).

WARREN

Better Future Self-Help Center Self-help drop-in center for persons with a mental illness and/or clinical depression. Various support groups are offered. Open Mon.-Fri., 5-9pm and Sat., 1pm, 21 West Washington Ave., Washington. Call 908-835-1180.

NATIONAL

CONTAC (Consumer Organization And Networking Technical Assistance Center) *Resource.* Center for mental health consumers and consumer-run organizations nationwide that promotes self-help, recovery and empowerment. Provides technical assistance for organizing and maintaining self-help groups. Conducts leadership training. Listserv, electronic library, on-line peer support. Call 1-888-825-8324 or 304-345-7312; Fax: 304-345-7303. Write: CONTAC, P.O. Box 11000, Charleston, WV 25339. *Website:* http://www.contac.org *Email:* usacontac@contac.org

National Mental Health Consumers Self-Help Clearinghouse *National.* *Founded 1986.* Provides information and recovery-oriented services for mental health consumers. Provides assistance in self and system advocacy, on-site consultations, training and educational events. Assistance in starting groups. Also provides technical assistance to consumer-run groups. Maintains a database of consumer support and advocacy groups. Write: Nat'l MH Consumers Self-Help Clearinghouse, 1211 Chestnut St., Suite 1207, Philadelphia, PA 19107-4103. Call 1-800-553-4539; Fax: 215-636-6312; TTY/TDD: 215-751-9655. *Website:* http://www.mhselfhelp.org

Schizophrenics Anonymous *International.* *150+ groups.* *Founded 1985.* Organized and run by people with a schizophrenia-related disorder. Focuses on recovery, using a 6-step program, along with medication and professional help. Weekly meetings and newsletters. Provides assistance in starting and maintaining groups. Write: S.A. Nat'l Schizophrenia Foundation, 403 Seymour St., Suite 202, Lansing, MI 48933. Call 517-485-7168 or Consumer Line: 1-800-482-9534; Fax: 517-485-7180. *Website:* http:/www.nsfoundation.org *Email:* sareferrals@nsfoundation.org

Well Mind Association of Greater Washington *Model.* *1 group in Maryland.* *Founded 1967.* Holistic medical information clearinghouse with an emphasis on mental health. Provides education about mental illness as principally a metabolic or biochemical disorder. Explores the connection between mental illness & environmental, biological & physiological factors. Write: Well Mind Association, PO Box 312, Ashton, MD 20861-0312. Call 301-774-6617; Fax: 301-774-6617. *Website:* http://ourworld.compuserve.com/homepages/WMIND/

ONLINE

BPD WORLD *Online.* Support for individuals with borderline personality disorder. Other topics include information on depression, self-harm, schizophrenia, or any other mental health problem. Offers forums and live chat room with peer volunteers. *Website:* http://www.bpdworld.org

MENTAL HEALTH FAMILY SUPPORT
(see also mental health consumers, general mental health, toll-free helplines)

STATEWIDE

NAMI NJ (National Alliance on Mental Illness of New Jersey) Dedicated to improving the quality of life for people with mental illness and their families; provides self-help groups, education and advocacy. An array of public education and mental illness awareness activities creates understanding and eradicate the stigma associated with mental illness. For referral information and advocacy call 732-940-0991 (day) or 1-866-626-4437. *Website:* http://www.naminj.org *E-mail:* naminj@optonline.net

ATLANTIC

Intensive Family Support Services *Professionally-run.* Education and support for families dealing with a mentally ill family member. Guest speakers. Meets 2nd Thurs., 10:30am and 4th Thurs., 5:30pm, Mental Health Association, 1147 North New Rd., Absecon. Call 609-272-1700 ext. 301 (day). *Website:* http://www.mhaac.info *Email:* cgromadzyn@mhanj.org

NAMI Atlantic County Support and advocacy for families of persons with chronic psychiatric disorders. Offers a 12 week "Family-to-Family" education series. Support group meets 1st Tues., 7:30pm, Pleasantville Presbyterian Church, 1311 S. Main St., Pleasantville. Call Gary 609-748-9558 (eve) or Gail 609-927-0215 (eve). *Email:* nami844@aol.com

Parents Supporting Parents Provides education and social support to parents/caregivers who have children struggling with emotional and/or behavioral difficulties. Guest speakers and literature. Meets 1st & 3rd Wed., 6:30-8:30pm, Atlantic County Family Support Organization, 2312 New Rd., Northfield. Call Andrea Burleigh 609-485-0575 ext. 105 (day).

BERGEN

Family Support Organization of Bergen County Provides support, advocacy and education to families and caregivers of children with complex emotional and behavioral challenges. Rap sessions and literature. Meets Mon. and Wed., 7-8:30pm, Family Support Organization of Bergen County, 0-108 29th St., Fair Lawn. Call Lynne Bolson, MSW 201-796-6209 ext. 102 (day). *Website:* http://www.fsobergen.org

Intensive Family Support Service *Professionally-run.* Support, education and advocacy for family members of the mentally ill. Meets Wed., 7pm, in Oradell. Family Education Workshops meets 3 times/yr., Paramus. Call Nadine Venezia 201-646-0333 (day). *Website:* http://www.cbhcare.com

"Sometimes when you think you are done, it is just the edge of beginning. Probably that's why we decide we're done. It's getting too scary. We are touching down onto something real. It is beyond the point when you think you are done that often something strong comes out."--Natalie Goldberg

NAMI Bergen County Support, education, advocacy, information and referral for families of the mentally ill. Newsletter. Membership $20/yr. Meets 1st Mon., 8pm, Community Services Building, (Museum Building), 327 Ridgewood Ave., Paramus. Call 201-635-9595 (day). *Website:* http://www.namibergen.org *Email:* namibergen@namibergen.org

NAMI En Espanol of Bergen County *(SPANISH)* Advocacy and support for family and friends of the mentally ill. Meets 3rd Fri., 6:30-8pm, Universidad Luterana, 10 Banta Pl., Hackensack. Before attending call Martha Silva 1-888-803-3413. *Website:* http://www.naminj.org *Email:* naminjenespanol@msn.com

NAMI Family Organization of Bergen County *Professionally-run.* Provides support, information, education and advocacy to families of the mentally ill. Membership $30/single, $35/couple. Guest speakers. Meets 1st Wed., 7-9pm, Care Plus Mental Health Center Inc., 610 Valley Health Plaza, Paramus. Call 201-797-3579 (day).

SMG ~ CAN Connections *Professionally-run.* Provides support and education for parents and professionals involved with a selectively mute child. Rap sessions, guest speakers, literature and phone help. Dues $45/yr. Meets 3rd Mon., 12:45-2:30pm, Manito School, 111 Manito Ave., Oakland. Call Gail Kervatt 973-208-1848 (day/eve). *Email:* kervatt@optonline.net

BURLINGTON

Intensive Family Support Services *Professionally-run.* Support, information and advocacy for family members and caregivers of an adult mentally ill relative. Meets 3rd Thurs., 1-3pm, Riverbank Building, Catholic Charities, 114 Delaware Ave., Burlington or 1st Wed., 6-7:30pm, Virtua Memorial Hospital of Burlington County, 175 Madison Ave., Mt. Holly. Call Emmanuel Estacio 609-386-8653 (day).

NAMI Burlington FACE (Family And Consumer Exchange) Mutual support for families and friends of the mentally ill. Education, information and referrals. Dues $25 (includes newsletter). Meets 2nd and 4th Mon., 7:30pm, First Presbyterian Church, Moorestown. Call Lucille Klein 609-877-4260, Larry Joyce 856-461-3339 (day) or 609-914-0933 (office). *Email:* NAMIFACENJ@aol.com

We know this Directory is big and chances are we can probably find the group you're looking for quicker than you paging through it. Call us! (We're really friendly!)
1-800-367-6274

CAMDEN

DBSA of Camden County: New Beginnings Support Group Mutual support, encouragement and education for persons with depression, bipolar disorder, anxiety, panic, OCD, or other mental health issues. Provides a caring, empathetic place to listen and share successes. Meets Mon., 7-9pm, (families welcome 1st and 3rd Mon.) and Wed., 11am-1pm, Holy Trinity Lutheran Church, 214 N. Warwick Rd., Magnolia. Call Gary 856-227-5678 (day/eve) or Maribel 856-232-3181. For family group call Karen 856-451-1240.

Grandparents Raising Grandchildren Support and education for women and men who are caring for their grandchildren struggling with emotional, behavioral and mental challenges. Guest speakers, literature, social, advocacy and buddy system. Meets 2nd and 4th Mon., 6:30-8:30pm, Holy Trinity Lutheran Church, 325 South Whitehorse Pike, Audubon. Call Marge Varneke 856-547-1620 (eve) or Susan A. Doherty-Funke 856-662-2600 (day).

Lean On Me Mutual support for parents/caregivers of children with emotional, behavioral and mental health issues. Share experiences, resources, rap sessions, guest speakers, literature and phone help. Meets 2nd and 4th Wed., 10:30am-noon, Camden County Family Support Organization, 23 West Park Ave., Suite 103-104, Merchantville. Call Susan A. Doherty-Funke 856-662-2600 (day) or 856-261-0233 (eve). *Email:* kbirmingham@camdenfso.org

NAMI of Camden County Mutual support for families and friends of the mentally ill. Advocacy, phone help and guest speakers. Meets 2nd and 4th Tues., 7pm, Steininger Behavioral Care Services, 19 East Ormond Ave., Cherry Hill. Call Barbara 856-783-2518 (day).

Transitions Mutual support for parents/caregivers of children with mental, behavioral and emotional challenges. Rap sessions, guest speakers, literature and phone help. Meets 2nd and 4th Thurs., 7-9pm, Camden County Family Support Organization, 23 West Park Ave., Suite 103-104, Merchantville. Call Susan A. Doherty-Funke 856-662-2600 (day) or 856-261-0233 (eve).

CAPE MAY

Atlantic Cape Support Organization Provides education and social support to parents/caregivers who have children struggling with emotional and/or behavioral difficulties. Guest speakers and literature. Meets 1st & 3rd Wed., 6:30-8:30pm, Atlantic County Family Support Organization, 2312 New Rd., Northfield. Call Andrea Burleigh 609-485-0575 ext. 105 (day).

IFSS Family Support Group Support and advocacy for families and friends of the mentally ill. Rap sessions and guest speakers. Meets 2nd Thurs., 6:30-8:30pm, Cape Counseling Center, 217 N. Main St., Suite 202, Cape May Courthouse. Call Samantha Knocke 609-463-0014 ext. 17.

Parents Supporting Parents Support, education and advocacy for parents/caregivers of children with emotional and behavioral challenges. Rap sessions, guest speakers, buddy system, literature, speakers' bureau, newsletter and phone help. Meets 4th Tues., 6:30-8:30pm, Atlantic Cape Family Support Organization, 303 Courthouse-Dennisville Rd., Ste. 2, Cape May Court House. Call Andrea Burleigh or Sondra Dublinsky 609-485-0575 (day). *Website:* http://www.famsupport.org *Email:* sdublinsky@famsupport.org

CUMBERLAND

Intensive Family Support Services *Professionally-run.* Information, support and advocacy for family members and caregivers of an adult with major mental illness. Guest speakers and phone help. Meets Thurs., 10am-noon or 2nd, 4th and 5th Tues., 7-9pm, Cumberland County Guidance Center, 2038 Carmel Rd., Millville. Call Diana White 856-825-6810 ext. 286 or Daniel Rickets 856-825-6810 ext. 278 (day).

NAMI Cumberland County *Professionally-run.* Support for families and friends of the mentally ill. Mutual sharing, education, advocacy, literature, phone help, guest speakers. Dues $23/yr. Meets 3rd Wed., 7:15pm, 1st Presbyterian Church, 8th and Landis Ave., Vineland. Call 856-691-9234 or 856-794-9987.

ESSEX

Family Resource Center, The *Professionally-run.* Support for family members and significant others of persons with chronic mental/emotional illness. Groups for parents of adults with mental illness. Groups for siblings and adult offspring meet on a time limited basis. Children and adolescents who have a mentally ill family member attend Kids Cope in age appropriate groups at various locations. Meets various times and days. Call 973-509-9777 (day). *Website:* http://www.mhaessex.org

NAMI Essex County Group helps families of the mentally ill by sharing ideas and experiences in a caring atmosphere. Guest speakers, phone help, newsletter. Dues $25/yr. single, $30/yr. family. Meets 4th Mon., 7:30pm, 33 S. Fullerton Ave., Montclair. Call Katie 973-983-9236 (day).

418

Women Coping with a Depressed Family Member Support for women to share their feelings, helplessness, anger, guilt and fear with others who understand dealing with a depressed family member. Groups start periodically and run for 6 weeks. Meets various days, 7:30-9pm, Linda and Rudy Slucker NCJW Center for Women, 513 West Mt. Pleasant Ave., Suite 325, Livingston. Registration fee $45. Call Center for Women 973-994-4994 (day).

GLOUCESTER

NAMI Gloucester County Mutual support and education for families and friends of persons with mental illness. Advocacy, phone help, literature, professional speakers. Dues $30/yr. Meets 2nd Wed., 6:30pm, Newpoint Behavioral Health, 1070 Main St., Sewell. Call Domenica Grant 856-423-1217 or Lucille Nelson 856-845-8137 *Website:* http://community.nj.com/cc/NAMIgloucestercounty

HUDSON

NAMI Hudson County Advocacy and support for family and friends of the mentally ill. Meets 2nd Tues., 6:30-9pm, (except Aug.), 3040 Kennedy Blvd., (entrance on Huron Ave., behind St. John's Church), Jersey City. Before attending call Martha Silva 201-861-0614 or 1-888-803-3413. *Email:* NamiHudson@msn.com

NAMI NJ en Espanol of Hudson County *(SPANISH)* Advocacy and support for family and friends of the mentally ill. Meets 1st Wed., (except Aug.), 6:30-8pm, Catholic Community Service Office, 2201 Bergenline Ave., 2nd Floor, Union City. Call Martha Silva 1-888-803-3413. *Email:* naminjenespanol@msn.com

HUNTERDON

Families of Mentally Ill Opportunity for families of persons with mental illness to share experiences. Rap sessions, mutual sharing, psycho-education and encouragement. Meets 4th Wed., 6:30-8:30pm, Hunterdon Medical Center, 2100 Wescott Dr., 5th Floor, Conference Room, Flemington. Call Cris Maglione 908-788-6401 ext. 3006 or Elaine Howe 908-788-6401 ext. 3029.

Family Support Group Provides support, information and education for families of children and adults with mental illness. Meets 1st and 3rd Mon., 7-8:30pm, Clinton Presbyterian Church, Center St., Clinton. Call Walt Dudzinski 908-638-8034.

MERCER

IFSS Families of Young Adults Group *Professionally-run.* Support for families who have an adult, ages 18-25, with a mental illness. Guest speakers, phone help, literature. Meets Wed., 5:30-7pm, NAMI Mercer, Lawrence Commons, 3371 Brunswick Pike, Suite 124, Lawrenceville. Call Nick 609-396-6788 ext. 236 or Amy ext. 287.

IFSS Family Support Group *Professionally-run.* Support for family members and caregivers of any adult with a mental illness. Guest speakers, phone help, literature. Meets Mon., 5:30-7pm, Lawrence Road Presbyterian Church, 1039 Lawrence Rd., Lawrenceville. Call Nick 609-396-6788 ext. 236 or Amy ext. 287 (day).

NAMI C.A.R.E.S. Kids Support for caregivers of children and adolescents with brain disorders. Families are welcome. Meets 1st Wed., 7:30-9pm, Lawrence Commons, 3371 Brunswick Pike, Suite 124, Lawrenceville. Also 3rd Sat. (call for time and location). Call Linda Mc Grath 609-799-8994 (day). *Website:* http://www.namimercer.org *Email:* home@namimercer.org

NAMI Hunterdon County Support and advocacy for the mentally ill, their families and friends. Dues $30/yr. Meets 2nd Wed., 7pm, Getting Together Center, 162 Route 31, Flemington. Call Walt Dudzinski 908-638-8034.

NAMI Mercer County *Professionally-run.* Mutual support, education and advocacy for families and friends of the mentally ill. Dues $38/yr per family/associate member. Meets 3rd Tues., 7:30pm, Lawrenceville Library, Darrah Lane, Lawrenceville. Call 609-799-8994. *Website:* http://www.namimercer.org *Email:* home@namimercer.org

MIDDLESEX

CAMHOP-NJ (Chinese Mental Health Self-Help Group) *(BILINGUAL) Professionally-run.* Mutual support group for families and individuals of Chinese origin with mental illnesses. Meets 3rd Tues., 7-8:45pm, Stelton Baptist Church, 334 Plainfield Ave., Edison. Call Maggie Luo or Aruna Rao 732-940-0991 (day). *Website:* http://www.naminj.org/programs/camhop/camhop.htm. *Email:* namichinesegroup@yahoo.com

Family Support Organization of Middlesex County Support for parents raising a child with emotional and behavioral challenges. Meets Mon., 6:30-8:30pm (for parents of children 13 and above) and Thurs., 6-8pm, (for parents of children age 12 and under), Family Support Organization of Middlesex County, 1950 Route 27, Suite D, North Brunswick. Call Bobbie Locke, Bryn Schain or Lirie Mulaj 732-940-2837 (day). *Website:* http://www.njfamily.org

NAMI Middlesex County For families of the mentally ill and consumers to promote improved quality of life for people with severe mental illness. Dues $25/person and $35/family/yr. Education and advocacy program meets 1st Mon., 7pm, University Behavioral Mental Health Center, Room D 201, 671 Hoes Lane, Piscataway. Coping meeting meets 2nd Thurs., 7pm, IFSS, 1440 How Lane, Suite 2 A, North Brunswick. Call Dorothy Goldstein 732-846-9517 or Carol Piekarski 732-297-4959 (eve). *Website:* http://www.naminj.org

NAMI NJ en Espanol of Middlesex County *(SPANISH) Professionally-run.* Support and advocacy for families of those with a mental illness. Meets 3rd Thurs., 6:30-8pm, Christian Centers Ministry, 299 Barclay St., Perth Amboy. Call Ms. Betzaida Aponte 732-940-0991. *Email:* namiespanol@optonline.net

MONMOUTH

Family Support Group Support group for family members of patients age (18+) with a psychiatric diagnosis. Meets twice a month, 6-7:30pm, Community Connections, 75 N. Bath and Second Ave., Long Branch. Registration required. Call Ron Collier 732-923-5226.

Monmouth Family and Friends Group *Professionally-run.* Mutual help and support group for families and friends of adult psychiatrically disabled. Discussions, learning and advocacy for improved services. Educational workshops. Meets 1st and 3rd Tues., noon-1:30pm; or 2nd and 4th Tues., 7:30-9pm, Mental Health Association, 59 Broad St., Eatontown. Call 732-542-6422 (day). *Website:* http://www.mentalhealthmonmouth.org *Email:* mhamonmouth@verizon.net

NAMI Greater Monmouth Support, education and advocacy for the families of the mentally ill. Guest speakers, literature and mutual sharing. Optional membership dues. Meets 3rd Tues., 7pm, Lutheran Church of the Good Shepherd, 112 Middletown Rd., Holmdel. Call 732-449-2356.

Parent Support Group Mutual support for parents with children experiencing emotional and behavioral problems. Childcare and limited transportation. Rap sessions, guest speakers, literature, phone help and newsletter. Call 732-571-3272 (day).

> **Eatontown** Meets Thurs., 7-9pm, Family Based Services Association, 11 White St.

Eatontown *(SPANISH)* Meets Wed., 7-9pm, Family Based Services Association, 11 White St. Call Ana Salgado 732-713-9027 (day).
Howell Meets Wed., 7-9pm, Church of the Master, 110 Salem Hill Rd.
Keansburg Meets Tues., 7-9pm, First United Methodist Church, 21 Church St.

Shore Family and Friends for Mental Health *Professionally-run.* Mutual support and education for families and friends of individuals with mental illness. Meets 1st and 3rd Tues., 7:30-9pm, Jersey Shore Medical Center, Rosa Pavilion, 1945 Hwy. 33, Neptune. Call Linda Ballin, RNC 732-776-4777 (day) or Dennis Broschart, LCSW 732-776-4176 (day). *Email:* lballin@meridianhealth.com

MORRIS

Concerned Families for the Mentally Ill Mutual support, education and advocacy for families and friends of the mentally ill. Meets 2nd and 4th Mon., 7:30pm, Presbyterian Church, Parish House, Room 4, Morristown. Call Karen Donofrio 973-334-3496 ext. 107 (day).

IFSS Family Support Group *Professionally-run.* Support and education for family members or caretakers of individuals with a mental illness. Meets Wed., 7-8pm, Saint Clare's Behavioral Health Center, 50 Morris Ave., Room 320, Denville. Call 973-625-7131 (day).

IFSS Parent Support Group Education and support for parents of adults with depression or bipolar illness. Meets 4th Thurs., 7pm, Saint Clare's Behavioral Health Center, 50 Morris Ave., Room 320, Denville. Call 973-625-7095 (day).

Kids Cope *Professionally-run.* Support for children (age 3-17) whose lives have been impacted by a family member with a mental illness. Children groups are separated into different age groups. Groups provide mutual sharing, art and games to encourage social interaction. 9 week sessions. Meets at St. Clare's Behavioral Health Center, 50 Morris Ave., Room 320, Denville. Call 973-625-7069.

NAMI Concerned Families of Greystone *Professionally-run.* Advocacy and support for family and friends of the mentally ill. Provides literature, advocacy, guest speakers and mutual sharing. Dues $5/yr. Meets 4th Tues., (except July/Aug.), 6:30-8:30pm, Greystone Hospital, Central Ave., Main Building, Boardroom, Greystone Park. Call Dorothy Thaller 973-386-1845.

NAMI Morris County Support and advocacy for families of persons with chronic psychiatric disorders. Educational series. Meets 3rd Mon., 7:30pm, St.

Francis Residential, Community Room, 122 Diamond Spring Rd., Denville. Call Eileen Griffith 908-879-5687.

Parents Connecting Mutual support for parents of children with juvenile bipolar, anxiety and other mood disorders. Families welcome. Rap sessions and guest speakers. Meets 1st & 3rd Mon., 7:15-9pm, Redeemer Lutheran Church, 203 Eyland Ave. & Unneberg Ave., Succasunna. Call 973-927-0383. *Email:* parentsconnecting@yahoo.com

OCEAN

Family Support Family Group designed for parents to network together to offer support and information. Rap sessions and guest speakers. Meets 4th Tues., 7-9pm, Ocean County Family Support Organization, 44 Washington St., Suite 2A, Toms River. Call Maria Cruz 732-281-5770 (day).

NAMI Ocean County *Professionally-run.* Support, education, socialization, advocacy, coping and support for families and friends of the mentally ill. Dues $23/yr (can be waived). Meets 2nd Wed., 6:30pm (speaker) and 8-9pm (group), Ocean County Complex, Hooper Ave. and Madison Ave., 2nd Level Cafeteria, Toms River. Call Mary 732-886-7461 (day).

PASSAIC

Family Circle Support Group *Professionally-run.* Mutual support for families living with a mentally ill relative. An opportunity to share their experiences with others. Guest speakers. Meets 2nd and 4th Wed., 7-8:30pm, Mental Health Association, 404 Clifton Ave., Clifton. Call Anabel Lago 973-478-4444 ext. 13.

Family Support Organization of Passaic County *(BILINGUAL)* Support for parents raising a child with emotional and behavioral challenges. Group will meet in April, 2006. Meets at Family Support Organization of Passaic County, 1 Ottilio Terrace, Totowa. For meeting information call 973-720-0010.

NAMI - Families In Quest *Professionally-run.* For families and friends of the mentally ill. Mutual support, advocacy and exchange of information. Meets 1st Tues., 7:30pm, Mental Health Association, 2nd Floor, 404 Clifton Ave., Clifton. Call 973-478-4444 (day) or Edward 973-773-5112.

NAMI NJ en Espanol of Passaic County *(SPANISH)* Mutual support for Latino families of persons with mental illness. Meets 3rd Tues., 6:30-8pm, St. Mary's Hospital, 211 Pennington Ave., Passaic. Call Beatriz Amador 201-348-9159 or 1-888-803-3413.

SALEM

NAMI Salem County Mutual sharing, understanding, discussion of problems and education for families of the mentally ill. All welcome. (Dues $15/yr - not mandatory). Meets 1st Wed., 7pm, Union Presbyterian Church, Carneys Point. Call Virginia 856-769-2492 (day/eve) or Brittany 856-582-4551. *Email:* saullnami@aol.com

SOMERSET

Intensive Family Support Service Group Mutual support, psycho-education and advocacy for families and friends of the mentally ill. Guest speakers. Meets 4th Wed., 7-9:00pm, United Reformed Church, 100 W. Main St., Somerville. Call Linda Newton 908-722-4300 ext. 619 (day). *Website:* http://www.nj.easterseals.com *Email:* lnewton@nj.easter-seals.org

Mental Health Awareness Group *Professionally-run.* Support for families and friends who have a loved one who is diagnosed with a mental illness. Meets Sun., 1-2pm, Dave's Place, Carrier Clinic, 252 Rt. 601, Belle Mead. Call Community Relations Dept. 908-281-1513 (day). *Website:* http://www.carrier.org

NAMI Somerset County Education, advocacy and mutual support for families of persons with mental illness. Dues $25/yr. Meets 1st Thurs., Business meeting, 7pm and Coping meeting, 7:30pm, Richard Hall Mental Health Center, Bridgewater. Call Sonja Peterson 908-781-2071 (day) or Helen Campbell 908-359-0321.

SAMHAJ Support for South Asians Mutual support for South Asian (Indians, Pakistanis, Bangladeshi, Sri Lankan) families affected by mental illness. Educational series, guest speakers and literature. Meets 1st Thurs., 7-9pm, 84 Cortelyou Lane, Somerset. Call Aruna Rao 732-940-0991 (day).

SUSSEX

NAMI Sussex County Support for families dealing with a loved one's mental illness. Dues $25/yr. Meets 1st Mon., 7pm, Newton Memorial Hospital, Sussex House, Meeting Room, Newton. Call Jane Blackburn 973-875-7802.

UNION

Family Support Group *Professionally-run.* Provides support, information and education for families of adults with mental illness. Meets 1st and 3rd Wed., 7:30pm, Mental Health Association in NJ, 109 South Ave. West, Cranford.

Call Joyce Benz 908-497-1921 ext. 12 (day). *Website:* www.mhanj.org *Email:* jbenz@mhanj.org

Family Support Organization of Union County Support for parents raising a child with emotional and behavioral challenges. Meets 3rd Tues., 6:30-8:30pm, (also separate youth group meets 2nd and 4th Wed.). Family Support Organization of Union County, 137 Elmer St., Westfield. Before attending call 908-789-7625. *Website:* http://www.fso-union.org

NAMI NJ en Espanol Union County *(SPANISH)* Education, advocacy and support for families of persons with mental illness. Meets 4th Thurs., 7:30-9:30pm, Osceola Presbyterian Church, 1689 Raritan Rd., Clark. Call 908-233-1628.

NAMI Union County Provides education, information, support for persons suffering from mental illness. Dues $30/yr. Meets 4th Tues., 7:30-9:30pm, Osceola Presbyterian Church, 1689 Raritan Rd., Clark. Call NAMI Union 908-233-1628. *Email:* nami.union.nj@nami.org

Sibling Support Group *Professionally-run.* Support, for siblings of adults with mental illness. Meets 2nd Wed., 7:30-9pm, Mental Health Association in NJ, 109 South Avenue West, Cranford. Call Joyce Benz 908-497-1921 ext. 12 (day). *Website:* www.mhanj.org *Email:* jbenz@mhanj.org

Spouse and Partner Support Group Support, information and education for spouses of people with mental illness. Meets 4th Wed., 7:30-9pm, Mental Health Association, 109 South Ave. West, Cranford. Call Joyce Benz 908-497-1921 ext. 12 (day). *Website:* www.mhanj.org *Email:* jbenz@mhanj.org

WARREN

Family Support Group *Professionally-run.* Support for family members of adults or youths with a mental illness. Meets Wed., 7-8:30pm, Family Guidance Center, 128 Maple Ave., Hackettstown. Call Elaine Chichester 908-689-1000 (day).

IFSS Family Support Group *Professionally-run.* Provides support for families and friends of the mentally ill. Meets 2nd and 4th Tues., 7-8:30pm, Family Guidance Center, 492 Route 57 West, Washington. Call Suzette 908-689-1000 (day).

NAMI Warren County Mutual support and advocacy for families and friends of the mentally ill. Dues $25/yr. (can be waived). Meets 1st Wed., 7:30-9pm, St. Joseph Church, 200 Carlton Ave., Washington. Call 908-859-4368 (day/eve). *Email:* NAMI_Warren_county@NAMI.org

NATIONAL

Attachment Disorder Network *National network. Founded 1997.* Support and information for parents and professionals dealing with children with attachment issues and reactive attachment disorder. Newsletter, phone support and referrals. Dues $25 (includes newsletter). Write: ADN, PO Box 4104, Overland Park, KS 66204. Call 847-855-8676. *Website:* http://www.radzebra.org *Email:* info@radzebra.org

Federation of Families for Children's Mental Health *National. 137 affiliated groups. Founded 1989.* Parent-run organization focused on the needs of children and youth with emotional, behavioral or mental disorders and their families. Guidelines available to help start similar groups. Provides information and advocacy, newsletter, conferences. Local support group information available at website. Write: Federation of Families for Children's Mental Health, 1101 King St., Suite 420, Alexandria, VA 22314. Call Sandra Spencer 703-684-7710; Fax: 703-836-1040. *Website:* http://www.ffcmh.org *Email:* ffcmh@ffcmh.org

National Alliance for the Mentally Ill (NAMI) *National. 1200+ affiliates. Founded 1979.* Grassroots, self-help groups for family members affected by serious mental illness. Also has some groups for consumers. Focuses on education, advocacy, research and support. Quarterly newsletter. Write: NAMI, c/o Colonial Place Three, 2107 Wilson Blvd., Suite 300, Arlington, VA 22201-3042. Call 1-800-950-6264 (helpline) or 703-524-7600 (day); Fax: 703-524-9094. *Website:* http://www.nami.org

Relatives Project, The *National. 3 affiliated groups. Founded 1994.* Offers self-help groups for families and friends of persons with mental or emotional problems. Helps families and friends deal with troublesome relationships. Teaches coping skills and techniques to manage stress in order to create a peaceful domestic environment. Assistance in starting new groups. Write: Relatives Project, c/o Phyllis Berning, Abraham A. Low Institute, 550 Frontage Rd., Suite 2797, Northfield, IL 60093. Call 847-441-0445; Fax: 847-441-0446. *Website:* http://lowinstitute.org *Email:* lowinstitute@aol.com

Schizophrenia Society of Canada (French & English). *National. 110 societies. Founded 1979.* Information, support and advocacy for families and friends of persons with schizophrenia. Public awareness campaigns, advocacy and fund-raising. Newsletters. Guidelines and assistance for starting self-help groups. Write: Schizophrenia Society of Canada, 50 Acadia Ave., Suite 205, Markham, Ontario, L3R 0B3, Canada. Call 905-415-2007; Fax: 905-415-2337. *Website:* http://www.schizophrenia.ca *Email:* info@schizophrenia.ca

Selective Mutism Foundation Inc *National. Founded 1992.* Mutual support for parents of children with selective mutism, a psychiatric anxiety disorder, in which children are unable to speak in social situations. Also open to adults who have, or have outgrown the disorder. Provides information and online support. Write: Selective Mutism Foundation, c/o Carolyn Miller, PO Box 13133, Sissonville, WV 25360. *Website:* http://www.selectivemutismfoundation.org *Email:* sue@selectivemutismfoundation.org

ONLINE

Attachment Disorder Support Group *Online.* Provides an interactive supportive website for parents, families, friends and professionals concerned with a child's troublesome behavior. Offers message forum, e-mail listserv, live chat room, general information, educational material and helpful links. *Website:* http://adsg.syix.com

BPD Central *Online.* Provides links to online groups for persons dealing with a loved one with borderline personality disorder. Several mailing lists given for parents, siblings, grandparents and others close to someone with BPD and one group for persons with BPD themselves. *Website:* http://www.bpdcentral.com

Conduct Disorders Parent Message Board *Online* Support for parents living with a child with one of the many behavior disorders including attention deficit hyperactivity disorder, oppositional defiance disorder, conduct disorder, depression and substance abuse. Parents with children of all ages welcome. *Website:* http://www.conductdisorders.com

Helen's World of BPD Resources *Online.* Support for family, friends and loved ones of those with borderline personality disorder. Links to hundreds of helpful text and information. *Website:* http://www.bpdresources.com

North American Society for Childhood Onset Schizophrenia (NASCOS) *Online Founded 2004.* Provides families of children with childhood-onset schizophrenia (onset before age 13) with access to information, discussion forum and email list as well as geographical locator in order to find other members in your region. Families and caregivers of older patients, whose onset was during childhood, as well as interested professionals, are welcome to join. Write: NASCOS, 88 Briarwood Drive E., Berkeley Heights, NJ 07922. *Website:* http://www.nascos.org; *Email:* info@nascos.org

Selective Mutism Group *Online.* Devoted to educating and promoting awareness on selective mutism and other related childhood anxiety disorders. Online support group for parents, teachers and professionals dealing with selective mutism. *Website:* http://selectivemutism.org *Email:* sminfo@selectivemutism.org

MENTAL HEALTH GENERAL
(see also mental health consumers, specific disorder, toll-free helplines)

STATEWIDE

GROW A mutual self-help group to prevent and recover from depression, anxiety and other mental health problems. Caring and sharing community to attain emotional maturity, personal responsibility and recovery. Meets in various counties in NJ. Write: GROW Center, 206 University Blvd., Glassboro, NJ 08028. Call 856-881-2008.

BERGEN

Emotions Anonymous 12-Step. Fellowship sharing experiences, hopes and strengths in order to gain better emotional health. Deals with anxiety, fears, anger, depression, etc. Donation $2/mtg. Meets Tues., 7:45pm; Wed., 11:30am; Thurs., 7:30pm and Sat. 10:30am, Zion Lutheran Parish House, (next to church), 159 2nd Ave., Westwood. Call Lea 201-666-1009.

Recovery, Inc. Self-help method of will training. Offers techniques for controlling temperamental behavior and changing attitudes toward nervous symptoms, anxiety, depression and fears. Call 201-612-8153. *Website:* http://www.recovery-inc.com
> **Hasbrouck Heights** Meets Wed., 8pm, First Reformed Church, Washington Place and Burton Ave.
> **Ridgewood** Meets Fri., 1:30pm, Christ Church, Cottage Place and Franklin Ave.

BURLINGTON

Grow A mutual self-help group to prevent and recover from depression, anxiety and other mental health problems. Caring and sharing community to attain emotional maturity, personal responsibility and recovery. Meets Tues., 7pm, Family Services, 770 Woodlane Rd., Pat le Bon Room, Mt. Holly. Before attending call Brenda 856-881-2008.

Recovery, Inc. Self-help method of will training. Offers techniques for controlling temperamental behavior and changing attitudes toward nervous symptoms, anxiety, depression and fears. Call 215-332-0722. *Website:* http://www.recovery-inc.com

Marlton Meets Mon., 8pm and Thurs., 7pm, Prince of Peace Lutheran Church, 61 Route 70 East.

Westampton Meets Tues., 7pm, Hampton Hospital, Cafeteria, Rancocas Rd. and Route 295.

CAMDEN

DBSA of Camden County: New Beginnings Support Group Mutual support, encouragement and education for persons with depression, bipolar disorder, anxiety, panic, OCD, or other mental health issues. Provides a caring, empathetic place to listen and share successes. Meets Mon., 7-9pm, (families welcome on 1st and 3rd Mon.) and Wed., 11am-1pm, Holy Trinity Lutheran Church, 214 N. Warwick Rd., Magnolia. Call Gary 856-227-5678 (day/eve) or Maribel 856-232-3181. For family group call Karen 856-451-1240.

Recovery, Inc. Self-help method of will training. Offers techniques for controlling temperamental behavior and changing attitudes toward nervous symptoms, anxiety, depression and fears. Meets Sat., 11:30am, Starting Point, 215 Highland Ave., Westmont. Call 215-332-0722. *Website:* http://www.recovery-inc.com

CUMBERLAND

Grow A mutual self-help group to prevent and recover from depression, anxiety and other mental health problems. Caring and sharing community to attain emotional maturity, personal responsibility and recovery. Meets Thurs., 7pm, Church of Christian/Missionary Alliance, Board Room, Main Rd. and Harding Ave., Vineland. Before attending call Daniel 856-881-2008.

ESSEX

Recovery, Inc. Self-help method of will training. Offers techniques for controlling temperamental behavior and changing attitudes toward nervous symptoms, anxiety, depression and fears. Meets Tues., 8pm, Prospect Presbyterian Church, 646 Prospect St., Maplewood. Call 201-612-8153. *Website:* http://www.recovery-inc.com

Women and Self-Esteem Mutual support for women who are having issues about their self-esteem. Group starts periodically and runs for 6 weeks. Registration fee $45. Meets at Linda and Rudy Slucker NCJW Center for Women, Suite 325, Livingston. Call Project GRO 973-994-4994. *Website:* http://www.centerforwomennj.org *Email:* centerforwomen@ncjwessex.org

GLOUCESTER

Grow A mutual self-help group to prevent and recover from depression, anxiety and other mental health problems. A caring and sharing community to attain emotional maturity, personal responsibility and recovery. Meets Mon., 7pm, Grow Center, 206 University Blvd., Glassboro. Before attending call Brenda 856-881-2008.

Recovery, Inc. Self-help method of will training. Offers techniques for controlling temperamental behavior and changing attitudes toward nervous symptoms, anxiety, depression and fears. Families welcome. Meets Fri., 10-11am, James Johnson Library, 670 Ward Dr., Deptford. Call Barry Stockinger, Sr. 856-848-8715. *Website:* http://www.recovery-inc.com

MERCER

Grow A mutual self-help group to prevent and recover from depression, anxiety and other mental health problems. Caring and sharing community to attain emotional maturity, personal responsibility and recovery. Meets Tues., 5:45pm, Reach Out/Speak Out, 121 North Broad St., Trenton. Before attending call Denise 609-989-0255.

MIDDLESEX

Emotions Anonymous 12-Step. Fellowship sharing experiences, hopes and strengths with each other in order to gain better emotional health. Phone help. Donation. Meets Wed., 8:15pm, Community Presbyterian Church, 75 Glenville Rd. at Blvd. of the Eagles, Edison. Call Paul 908-685-1335 (day/eve) or Carolyn 732-723-1960 (day).

Rap Group Offering a safe supportive environment for consumers to express and share their feelings about mental health issues. Meets Wed. and Thurs., 3-7pm; Sat., 1-5pm, Self-Help Center of New Brunswick, 96 Bayard St., Lower Level, New Brunswick. Call 732-296-0303 (day) or Carey 732-656-9288 (eve). *Email:* newbrunswickshc@attglobal.net

MONMOUTH

Emotions Anonymous Fellowship sharing experiences, hopes and strengths, following the 12-Step program, in order to gain better emotional health. Dues $1 week. Meets Sat., noon, Port Monmouth. Call Chris or Lillian 732-495-7453 (day). *E-mail:* graye22@netzero.net

Grow A mutual self-help group to prevent and recover from depression, anxiety and other mental health problems. Caring and sharing community to attain emotional maturity, personal responsibility and recovery.

> **Freehold** Meets Wed., 7pm, 11 Spring St. Before attending call Nancy 732-350-4800.
>
> **Ocean Grove** Meets Thurs., 6:45pm, St. Paul's Methodist Church, 80 Embry St., Stokes Room. Before attending call Margo 732-206-1138.

Youth Partnership Group Peer support and advocacy to empower youth (age 13-21) with emotional or behavioral challenges. Rap sessions, guest speakers, literature, phone help and newsletter. Meets Tues., 7-9:30pm, Family Based Services Association, 11 White St., Eatontown. Call Dori Erickson 732-571-3272.

OCEAN

Anger Management for Children *Professionally-run.* Support for children (age 7-16) dealing with various types of anger. Educational series. Meetings vary, Center for Kids and Family, 591 Lakehurst Rd., Toms River. Call Michele 732-505-5437 (day).

GROW A mutual self-help group to prevent and recover from depression, anxiety and other mental health problems. Caring and sharing community to attain emotional maturity, personal responsibility and recovery.

> **Brick** Meets Tues., 6:30pm, Brick Presbyterian Church, 111 Drum Point Rd. Before attending call Caroline 732-899-7540.
>
> **Manchester** Meets Thurs., 7:30pm, Redeemer Lutheran Church, 2309 Route 70. Before attending call Nancy 732-350-4800.
>
> **Toms River** Meets Thurs., noon, Presbyterian Church of Toms River, River Room, Hooper Ave. and Chestnut St. Before attending call Lisa 732-350-4800.
>
> **Toms River** Meets Mon., 7pm, S&F Plaza, Unit 6, 2008 Route 37 East. Before attending call Nancy 732-350-4800.

Recovery, Inc. Self-help method of will training. Offers techniques for controlling temperamental behavior and changing attitudes toward nervous symptoms, anxiety, depression and fears. Meets Mon., 7:30pm, Presbyterian Church of Toms River, Hoopers Ave. and Chestnut St., Toms River. Call 201-612-8153. *Website:* http://www.recovery-inc.com

If you are using this book past Spring 2007, please call us for information about our most recent directory. 1-800-367-6274

SOMERSET

Recovery, Inc. Self-help method of will training. Offers techniques for controlling temperamental behavior and changing attitudes toward nervous symptoms, anxiety, depression and fears. Meets Thurs., 7:30pm, Richard Hall Community Mental Health Center, 500 N. Bridge St. and Vogt Dr., Bridgewater. Call 201-612-8153. *Website:* http://www.recovery-inc.com

UNION

Recovery, Inc. Self-help method of will training. Offers techniques for controlling temperamental behavior and changing attitudes toward nervous symptoms, anxiety, depression and fears. Call 201-612-8153. *Website:* http://www.recovery-inc.com

> **Summit** Meets Wed., 7:45pm, Central Presbyterian Center, Morris Ave. and Maple St., (parking lot entrance).
>
> **Westfield** Meets Fri., 8pm, Union County Community Services Building, 300 North Ave. East, 2nd Floor, Conference Room, (parking lot entrance).

WARREN

Emotions Anonymous 12-Step. Fellowship sharing experiences, hopes and strengths in order to gain better emotional health. Deals with anxiety, fears, anger, depression, etc. Meets Sat., 2pm, Washington. Call Joan 908-689-6381 (eve).

NATIONAL

C.A.I.R. (Changing Attitudes In Recovery) *Model. 30 groups. Founded 1990.* Self-help "family" sharing a common commitment to gain healthy esteem. Includes persons with relationship problems, addictions, mental illness, etc. Offers new techniques and tools that lead to better self-esteem. Assistance in starting groups. Handbook ($9.95), audio tapes, leader's manual. Write: CAIR, c/o Psych. Assoc. Press, 706 13th St., Modesto, CA 95354. Call 209-577-1667; Fax: 209-577-3805. *Website:* http://www.cairforyou.com

Emotions Anonymous *International. 1000 chapters. Founded 1971.* Fellowship for people experiencing emotional difficulties. Uses the 12-Step program sharing experiences, strengths and hopes in order to improve emotional health. Books and literature available to new and existing groups. Guidelines available to help start a similar group. Write: E.A., PO Box 4245, St. Paul, MN 55104-0245. Call 651-647-9712; Fax: 651-647-1593. *Website:* http://www.emotionsanonymous.org *Email:* info@emotionsanomymous.org

GROW in America *International. 143 groups. Founded in 1957.* 12-Step. Mutual help group offering friendship, community, education and leadership. Focuses on recovery and personal growth. Open to all, including those with mental health issues, problems in living, depression, anxiety, grief, fears, etc. Write: GROW in America, PO Box 3667, Champaign, IL 61826. Call 1-888-741-4769. *Email:* growil@sbcglobal.net

HE/SHE Anonymous *National. Founded 1997.* 12-Step. Fellowship that helps members recover from any addictive or abusive behavior. Helps members stay emotionally sober. Groups for adults and adolescents. Deals with any addiction, compulsion, abusive behavior, or dysfunction. Write: HE/SHE World Service, PO Box 1752, Keene, NH 03431. Call 802-447-4736; Fax: 775-255-4287. *Website:* http://www.berks.com/12step *Email:* heshe@together.net

International Association for Clear Thinking *International. 100 chapters. Founded 1970.* Support for people interested in living their lives more effectively and satisfactorily. Uses principles of clear thinking and self-counseling. Offers group handbook, chapter development kit, audio tapes, facilitator leadership training and self-help materials. Write: IACT, PO Box 1011, Appleton, WI 54912. Call 920-739-8311; Fax: 920-582-9783.

Pathways To Peace *International. 11 groups. Founded 1998.* Self-help program for anger management. Offers peer support, education, workbook ($17.95) and assists with starting groups. Write: Pathways To Peace, PO Box 259, Cassadaga, NY 14718. Call 1-800-775-4212 or 716-595-3886. *Website:* http://www.pathwaystopeaceinc.com/index.htm#1 *Email:* transfrm@netsync.net

Recovery, Inc. *International. 640 groups. Founded 1937.* Offers weekly group meetings for people suffering from various emotional and mental conditions. Principles parallel those found in cognitive-behavioral therapy. Teaches people how to change the thoughts, reactions and behaviors that cause their physical and emotional symptoms. Write: Recovery, Inc., 802 N. Dearborn St., Chicago, IL 60610. Call 312-337-5661; Fax: 312-337-5756. *Website:* http://www.recovery-inc.com *Email:* inquiries@recovery-inc.org

ONLINE

Anger Management Live Chat *Online.* Message board. Offers support and understanding. *Website:* http://www.angermgmt.com

---

We can also refer callers to over 100 individuals who are seeking others to help start new support groups throughout NJ, if you don't see it, that doesn't mean it doesn't exist! **1-800-367-6274**

OBSESSIVE COMPULSIVE DISORDER

STATEWIDE

NJ Affiliate of the OCF, Inc. Mutual support for anyone concerned with obsessive compulsive disorder. Provides newsletter 4 times/yr, referrals to professionals, speakers bureau, fund-raising, education, socials, support group network, phone help and literature. Provides assistance in starting new groups. Call Ina Spero 732-828-0099 or Dr. Allen Weg 732-390-6694. *Website:* http://www.njocf.org *Email:* julina@patmedia.net

BURLINGTON

OCD Support Group Support for persons who suffer from obsessive compulsive disorders. Family members and friends are welcome to attend. Meets 2nd and 4th Mon., 7:30-9:30pm, Virtua West Hospital, Howe Room, 90 Brick Rd., Marlton. Call Betty 856-751-1957. *Email:* bettybeach@earthlink.net

CAMDEN

DBSA of Camden County: New Beginnings Support Group Mutual support, encouragement and education for persons with depression, bipolar disorder, anxiety, panic, OCD, or other mental health issues. Provides a caring, empathetic place to listen and share successes. Meets Mon., 7-9pm, (families welcome 1st and 3rd Mon.) and Wed., 11am-1pm, Holy Trinity Lutheran Church, 214 N. Warwick Rd., Magnolia. Call Gary 856-227-5678 (day/eve) or Maribel 856-232-3181. For family group call Karen 856-451-1240.

ESSEX

Obsessive-Compulsive Support Group Support for persons with obsessive compulsive disorder. Meets 1st and 3rd Thurs., 8-10pm, Mountainside Hospital, Schering-Plough Conference Room 3, Montclair. Call Nancy 973-472-8215 (eve).

GLOUCESTER

OCD Families Support Group Mutual support and coping skills for families and friends of children and adolescents who suffer from obsessive compulsive disorder. Rap sessions. Meets 1st Sun., 6:30-7:30pm, Underwood Memorial Hospital, Medical Arts Building, Suite 14, 509 North Broad St., Woodbury. Call Rich Bellamente 856-853-2011 (day).

MIDDLESEX

Central NJ Affiliate of the Obsessive Compulsive Foundation Support for any persons concerned with OCD. Meets 2nd Mon., (Mar., June, Sept., Dec.), 7-9pm, Robert Wood Johnson Hospital, Medical Education Building, New Brunswick. For meeting information call Ina Spero 732-828-0099.

Rutgers OCD Support Group *Professionally-run.* Group provides support and education for individuals with obsessive compulsive disorder, their families and friends. Donation $1. Meets 1st and 3rd Wed., 7-8:30pm, Rutgers University, 797 Hoes Lane West, Piscataway. Call 732-445-5384 (day).

MONMOUTH

Obsessive Compulsive Anonymous 12-Step. Provides mutual support for individuals recovering from obsessive compulsive disorder. Literature, phone help and buddy system. Must have a desire to recover from OCD to attend meetings. Meets Sun., 7-8pm, First Presbyterian Church of Matawan, 883 Highway 34 and Franklin St., Matawan. Call Matt C. 732-331-6494 (eve).

Obsessive Compulsive Anonymous 12-Step. Fellowship for persons affected by obsessive compulsive disorder. Offers mutual sharing, rap sessions and stories from the big book. Meets Wed., 8-9:15pm, Prince of Peace Lutheran Church, E. Aldrich Rd., Howell Twp. Call Ron 848-702-5044 (day/eve). *Email:* RonnyHugs@aol.com

MORRIS

OCD Support Group Mutual support for persons with obsessive compulsive disorder. Family welcome. Opportunity to discuss techniques and solutions to overcome the disorder. Rap sessions, phone help and literature. Meets Wed., 7:45pm, Saint Clare's Hospital, Boonton. Call Diane Walker 862-268-6397.

SOMERSET

Obsessive - Compulsive Disorder Support Group *Professionally-run.* Support, education and coping skills for persons suffering with, or recovering from obsessive compulsive disorder (including trichotillomania). Families welcome. Meets 3rd Thurs., 7:30pm, Somerset Medical Center, Hamilton Wing, Conference Room, Somerville. Call Joseph Donnellan, M.D. 908-725-5595 (day).

While it's no substitution for talking to our staff, you can call evenings or weekends! Leave a message and we will get back to you the next workday. ***1-800-367-6274***

OCD Support Group Mutual support for children and adolescents (under age 18) and their families. Meets 2nd Wed., 7-8:30pm, Richard Hall Community Mental Health Center, 500 North Bridge St., Bridgewater. Call Barbara 908-229-1367. *Email:* OCDhelp4kids@yahoo.com

UNION

Obsessive Compulsive Anonymous 12-Step. Provides relief or recovery from obsessive compulsive disorder. Offers support by sharing experience, strength and hope. Must have obsessive compulsive disorder to attend meetings. Donations optional. Meets Mon., 7:45-9:15pm, Diamond Hill United Methodist Church, Diamond Hill Rd., Berkley Heights. Call Jim 201-941-8143. *Website:* http://hometown.aol.com/west24th/index.html

NATIONAL

Obsessive-Compulsive Anonymous *National. 50 affiliated groups. Founded 1988.* 12-Step self-help group for people with obsessive-compulsive disorders. Assistance and guidelines available for starting groups. Write: O.C.A., PO Box 215, New Hyde Park, NY 11040. Call 516-739-0662. *Website:* http://members.aol.com/west24th/index.html

Obsessive-Compulsive Foundation, Inc. *International. 9 chapters. Founded 1986.* Support and education for people with obsessive-compulsive and related disorders, their families, friends and professionals. Online chat room. Write: OCF, PO Box 9573, New Haven, CT 06535. Call 203-401-2070; Fax: 203-401-2076. *Website:* http://www.ocfoundation.org *Email:* info@ocfoundation.org

Trichotillomania Learning Center *International. Founded 1991.* Information and support to patients, families and professionals about trichotillomania (compulsive hair pulling). Newsletter, information and referrals, annual retreat, conferences, phone support, pen pals and literature. Assistance in starting similar groups. Write: TLC, 303 Potrero St., Suite 51, Santa Cruz, CA 95060. Call 831-457-1004; Fax: 831-426-4383. *Website:* http://www.trich.org *Email:* trichster@aol.com

ONLINE

OCD and Parenting List *Online.* Mutual support and information for parents of children with obsessive-compulsive disorder through an e-mail discussion group. Professional advisors respond to questions. Also has an extensive listing of web links. *Website:* http://health.groups.yahoo.com/group/ocdandparenting/ *Email:* louisharkins@yahoo.com

MISCELLANEOUS

AGING / OLDER PERSONS
(see also caregivers, toll-free helplines)

STATEWIDE

AARP A membership organization for people age 50 and over. Provides information, resources, advocacy and newsletter. Offers a wide range of benefits and services. National membership $12.50/yr. Write: AARP - NJ State Office, 101 Buckingham Rd., Princeton, NJ 08550. Call 1-866-542-8165 (Mon.-Fri., 9am-5pm). *Website:* http://www.aarp.org/nj

DOROT/University Without Walls Telephone Support Teleconference support groups for persons age 59+ who are coping with vision loss, caregiving, aging issues, etc. There is a $10 registration fee and $15 tuition per support group. Scholarships are available. Write: DOROT, 171 W. 85th St., NY, NY 10024. For more information call DOROT 1-877-819-9147. *Website:* http://www.dorotusa.org

BERGEN

Coping with Life Changes *Professionally-run.* Support to help deal with the problems of getting older and the changes that occur. Meets Weds., 10:45-11:45am, 228 Grand Ave., Englewood. Members must be age 55+. Before attending call Frieda Wells 201-569-4080 (day). *Email:* lyd228@aol.com

Family Issues *Professionally-run.* Self-help group designed to support seniors with interpersonal relationship problems. Opportunity for members to share feelings and experiences. Meets Tues., 1:15pm, Southeast Senior Center for Independent Living, 228 Grand Ave., Englewood. Call Gail Farina, SW 201-569-4080 (Tues. or Thurs.).

Transitions Discussions *Professionally-run.* Support for seniors age 60+ to discuss problems of aging, relocation, loss of spouse, friends, health, relationships and children.
> **Midland Park** Meets Mon., 12:30-2pm, Northwest Senior Center. Call 201-445-5690 (day).
> **Wallington** Meets Mon., 10-11:30am, Wallington Senior Center, 24 Union Blvd. Call 973-777-5815 (day).

CAMDEN

Adjustment to Later Life Changes *Professionally-run.* Support group for men and women age 70+ to enhance coping skills for later life changes. Meets 2nd Tues., 10:30am-noon, Kennedy Center at Voorhees, 1099 White Horse Rd., Voorhees. Call Tanya 856-566-2096 or 1-800-522-1965.

ESSEX

Single in the Suburbs Mutual support for women of any age who are living alone. Group starts periodically and runs for 6 weeks. Registration fee $45. Meets at Linda and Rudy Slucker NCJW Center for Women, Livingston. Call Project GRO 973-994-4994. *Website:* http://www.centerforwomennj.org *Email:* centerforwomen@ncjwessex.org

GLOUCESTER

Families of the Frail Elderly *Professionally-run.* Support for families with elders in nursing homes. Literature and buddy system. Meets 3rd Tues., 7-8:30pm, Kennedy Health Care Center, 535 Egg Harbor Rd., Sewell. Call Ruth Aspell 856-582-3186 (day).

OCEAN

Gay and Lesbian Senior Support Group Mutual support for lesbian and gay seniors age 50+ to share common concerns and challenges to reduce sense of isolation. Meets 2nd and 4th Thurs., 5-6:30pm, The Lighthouse, 599 Route 37 West, Toms River. Call 1-800-621-0096 (day).

Senior Support Group *Professionally-run.* Mutual support to share experiences, coping skills and topics of interest for the elderly. Social and guest speakers. Call Rita Sason or Carol Powell 732-363-8010 (day).

> **Brick** Meets Thurs., 10-11:30am, Temple Beth Or, 200 Van Zile Rd.
> **Lakewood** Meets Wed., 1-2:30pm, Jewish Family and Children's Services, 301 Madison Ave.

UNION

Older Women's League (Voice of Middle and Older Women) Education and advocacy focusing on the critical issues facing women as they age. Literature. Dues $35/yr. Meetings vary. Call Teresa 908-862-5454 ext. 124 (day).

NATIONAL

AARP *National. 4000 chapters. Founded 1958.* Organization for people age 50 and older. Addresses needs and interests through information and education, advocacy and community service which are provided by a network of local chapters and experienced volunteers throughout the country. Offers members a wide range of special benefits and services, including "Modern Maturity" magazine and the monthly "Bulletin." Write: AARP, 601 E St., NW, Washington, DC 20049. Call 1-800-687-2277 *Website:* http://www.aarp.org

DOROT/University Without Walls Telephone Support Teleconference support groups for a variety of topics are available. Registration fee $10 and $15 tuition per support group. Scholarships are available. Groups for coping with vision loss, care giving, aging issues, etc. Write: DOROT, 171 W. 85th St., NY, NY, 10024. For more information call DOROT 1-877-819-9147. *Website:* http://www.dorotusa.org

Gray Panthers *National. 47 chapters. Founded 1970.* Multigenerational education and advocacy movement/organization which works to bring about fundamental social changes including a national health care system, elimination of all forms of discrimination and economic justice. Dues $20/US; $35/Org.; $40/Int'l. Write: Gray Panthers, 733 15th St., NW, Suite 437, Washington, DC 20005. Call 1-800-280-5362 or 202-737-6637 Fax: 202-737-1160 *Website:* http://www.graypanthers.org *Email:* info@graypanthers.org

Older Women's League *National. 60+ chapters. Founded 1980.* Membership organization that advocates on behalf of various economic & social issues for midlife & older women (social security, pension rights, employment, caregiver support, elder abuse, etc.). Newsletter, chapter development guidelines. Dues $25/yr. Write: OWL, 1750 New York Ave., NW, #350, Washington, DC 20006. Call 1-800-825-3695 or 202-783-6686; Fax: 202-628-0458 *Website:* http://www.owl-national.org *Email:* owlinfo@owl-national.org

ACCIDENT VICTIMS
(see also trauma)

NATIONAL

ACCESS (AirCraft Casualty Emotional Support Services) *National network. Founded 1996.* Matches persons who have lost a loved one in an aircraft-related tragedy to volunteers who previously experienced a similar loss. Goal is to help fill the void that occurs when the emergency and disaster relief organizations disband, the initial shock subsides and the natural grieving process intensifies.

Offers guidelines to help start a similar group. Persons communicate through email or by phone. Online newsletter. Write: ACCESS, 1202 Lexington Ave., #335, New York, NY, 10028. Call 1-877-227-6435. *Website:* http://www.accesshelp.org *Email:* info@accesshelp.org

Wings of Light, Inc. *National. 3 support networks. Founded 1995.* Support & information network for individuals whose lives have been touched by aviation accidents. Separate networks for airplane accident survivors; families & friends of persons killed in airplane accidents; and persons involved in the rescue, recovery and investigation of crashes. Information and referrals, phone support. Write: Wings of Light, PMB 448, 16845 N. 29th Ave., Suite 1, Phoenix, AZ 85053. Call 623-516-1115. *Website:* http://www.wingsoflight.org

ONLINE

CRASH Foundation (Citizens for Reliable And Safe Highways) *Online.* Dedicated to providing immediate compassionate support to truck crash survivors and families of truck crash victims. Referrals to grief counseling, medical services and truck crash experts. Phone support, conferences, advocacy, First Response Program and survivors' network. Write: CRASH, PO Box 14380, Washington, DC 20044-4380. Call 1-888-353-4572; Fax: 202-232-4661. *Website:* http://www.trucksafety.org/ *Email:* crash@trucksafety.org

ARTISTIC CREATIVITY

CAPE MAY

ARTS Anonymous (Artists Recovering through the Twelve Steps) A spiritual program based on the 12-Steps and 12-tradtions of AA. The only requirement for membership is a desire to fulfill creative potential. Meets Thurs., 9:30 am, Cape May County Library, Lower Cape Branch, 2600 Bayshore Rd., Villas. Call Don T. 718-251-3828. *Website:* http://www.artsanonymous.org *Email:* artseasternregion@yahoo.com

MONMOUTH

ARTS Anonymous (Artists Recovering Through the Twelve Steps) A spiritual program based on the 12-Steps and 12-tradtions of AA. The only requirement for membership is a desire to fulfill creative potential. Meets Fri., 10:30 am, Monmouth Beach Cultural Center, 128 Ocean Ave., Rte. 36, Monmouth Park. Call Don T. 718-251-3828. *Website:* http://www.artsanonymous.org *Email:* artseasternregion@yahoo.com

INTERNATIONAL

ARTS Anonymous (Artists Recovering through the Twelve Steps) *International. 150 affiliated groups. Founded 1984.* A spiritual program based on the 12-Steps and 12-traditions of A.A. The only requirement for membership is a desire to fulfill creative potential. Retreats, literature. Meeting start-up guidelines. Include self-addressed stamped envelope. (For requests outside of NY/NJ/CT area, include $2 with name of nearby cities). Write: ARTS Anonymous, PO Box 230175, New York, NY 10023. Call for NY/NJ/CT group information call 212-873-7075. *Website:* http://www.artsanonymous.org *Email:* artseasternregion@yahoo.com

CAREGIVERS /
FAMILIES OF NURSING HOME RESIDENTS
(see also Alzheimer's, toll-free helplines)

STATEWIDE

DOROT/University Without Walls Telephone Support Teleconference support groups for persons age 59+ who are coping with vision loss, care giving, aging issues, etc. Write: DOROT, 171 W. 85th St., NY, NY 10024. For more information call DOROT 1-877-819-9147. *Website:* http://www.dorotusa.org

BERGEN

ARC Adult Reach Center *Professionally-run.* Provides emotional support, information and referrals for caregivers. Guest speakers. Meets 2nd Wed., 7:30pm, (except Aug.), and 4th Thurs., 11:00 am, JCC on the Palisades, 411 E. Clinton Ave., Tenafly. Call Vivian Green Korner 201-569-7900 ext. 461 (day). *Website:* jcconthepalisades.org *Email:* Vkorner@jcconthepalisades.org

Caregiver Support Group *Professionally-run.* Provides mutual support for people caring for an ill relative (age 60+). Meets Tues., 10-11am, Northwest Senior Center, 46-50 Center St., Midland Park. Call Sheila Brogan 201-447-5695 (Tues./Wed., 9am-3pm).

Caregivers Family Support Group *Professionally-run.* Support for caregivers and family members of persons with Alzheimer's or related disorders. Meets 3rd Thurs., 1:30-3pm, Bergen County Dept. of Health, Senior Care Center, Room 208, 327 E. Ridgewood Ave., Paramus. Call first if requesting professional supervision on frail family member. Call Diana Shapiro 201-634-2822 (day).

Caregivers of the Disabled or Elderly *Professionally-run.* Mutual support, sharing of coping skills and education for persons who are caregivers of elderly or disabled adults. Meets 1st Wed., 1:30pm, Day-A-Way, Holy Name Hospital, Community Services Building, 725 Teaneck Rd., Teaneck. Call Ann Marie Cecere, LCSW 201-833-3757 (afternoon).

Sandwich Generation *Professionally-run.* Support and information for caregivers of the elderly. Peer counseling, guest speakers. Meets 3rd Thurs., 7pm, Northern Valley Adult Day Center, 2 Park Ave., Dumont. Call Nancy Bortinger 201-384-7734 (day).

Well Spouse Group Self-help for spouses or partners of persons with any type of illness or chronic disability. Meets 2nd and 4th Tues., 3:30, Nyack Hospital, Nyack, NY. Call Jeanmarie Grahn 845-634-6885 (day). *Email:* norina_osborne@prodigy.net

BURLINGTON

Caregiver Support Group *Professionally-run.* Support and education for caregivers of older adults. Family, friends and professionals are welcome to attend. Guest speakers, literature and mutual sharing. Meets last Thurs., 7-8:30pm, Senior Care of Delran, 8008 Route 130 N, Building B, Suite 300, Delran. Call Janine Brown 856-461-1700 (day).

CAMDEN

Caregivers of Seniors Support Group *Professionally-run.* Mutual support for family members and caregivers of seniors. Education, discussions, respite and resource information. Meets 3rd Thurs., 7-8:30pm, Virtua Health and Rehab Center, 62 Richmond Ave., Mt. Holly. Before attending call Virtua 1-888-847-8823 (day).

Promised Partners Support Group *Professionally-run.* Support for any caregiver focused on their ongoing needs. Rap sessions, guest speakers, literature and mutual sharing. Meets last Mon., (except July/Aug.), 7pm, Promise Adult Day Health Center, 1149 Marlkress Rd., Cherry Hill. Call Kathy Licardo or Dan Keashen 856-751-4884 (day).

Senior Care of Voorhees Caregiver Support Group *Professionally-run.* Offers information and support for families or caregivers of any senior. Mutual sharing, education and guest speakers. Meets last Thurs., 6-7pm, Senior Care at Voorhees, 1000 Voorhees Dr., Voorhees. Call Joanne Lemay 856-784-4000 (day).

Well Spouse Foundation Support for a spouse or partner who care for a chronically-ill spouse (MS, Parkinson's, emphysema, diabetes, etc.) to share common feelings and concerns. Meets 2nd Thurs., 7:30pm, Kennedy Memorial Hospital, Chapel Ave. and Cooper Landing Rd., Cherry Hill. Call Judy Baumbach 609-654-5618 (eve). *Email:* JEBaumbach@JUNO.com

CAPE MAY

Caring for You, Caring for Me *Professionally-run.* Support for those who provide care for family or friends. Discussion, activities, speakers and refreshments. Meets 1st Tues., 1-3pm and 3rd Wed., Burdette Tomlin Memorial Hospital, Maruchi Room, Two Stone Harbor Blvd., Cape May Courthouse. Call Bonnie Kratzer, RN 609-463-4043 (day).

ESSEX

Senior Care and Activities Center Support Group *Professionally-run.* Support, education and training for caregivers. Also various special activities series. Meets 1st Tues., 2-3pm or 1st Mon., 7-9pm, Senior Care and Activities Center, 110 Greenwood Ave., Montclair. Call Fran Moravick or Colleen Beach 973-783-5589 (day). *Website:* http://www.scac.org *Email:* sencareclub@monmouth.com

Women Dealing with Aging Parents Discussion group for women experiencing problems with aging parents. Group starts periodically and runs for 6 weeks. Registration fee $45. Meets at NCJW Center for Women, Livingston. Call Project GRO 973-994-4994 (day). *Website:* http://www.centerforwomennj.org *Email:* centerforwomen@ncjwessex.org

GLOUCESTER

Circle of Caring *Professionally-run.* Promotes the well-being of caregivers through emotional support and information. Families welcome. Phone help, guest speakers and literature. Meets last Fri., 10am-noon, County Offices at Five Points, 211 County House Rd., Sewell. Call 856-232-4646 ext. 4931 (day).

Support Group for Caregivers of the Elderly *Professionally-run.* Promotes the well-being of caregivers through emotional support and information. Assists with coping skills and problems with loss. Rap sessions, phone help, literature, occasional guest speakers. Meets 1st Wed., 1-2:30pm, New Seasons Assisted Living, 600 Medical Center Dr., Sewell. Call Tanya 1-800-522-1965.

HUDSON

Take Care: Caregivers Support Group *Professionally-run.* Support and education for caregivers. Families welcome. Literature available. Meets 4th Tues., 11am-noon, Community Crossing, 488 Broadway, Bayonne. Call Mary Scullin 201-339-5319 (day).

HUNTERDON

Caregivers Support Group *Professionally-run.* Support for family caregivers of the frail elderly. Meets 1st Thurs. and 2nd Tues., 1-3pm; also meets 4th Tues. and 3rd Wed., 7-9pm, Hunterdon Medical Center, 4th Floor, Conference Room, 2100 Westcott Drive, Flemington. Call 908-788-6401 ext. 3149.

MERCER

Caregiver Support Group *Professionally-run.* Support for those caring for an older adult. Any type of care, including Alzheimer's, Parkinson's, stroke, heart, COPD or other illnesses of aging. Meets 2nd Mon., 1-2pm, Princeton Senior Resource Center, Suzanne Patterson Building, (behind Borough Hall), 45 Stockton St., Princeton. Call Susan Hoskins 609-924-7108 (day).

Caregivers Support Group *Professionally-run.* Provides support and education for caregivers who are caring for family members or friends with a serious chronic disease. On-going and short term groups. For meeting day, time and location call Barbara Stender 609-396-6788 ext. 241 (day). *Email:* bstender@gtbhc.org.

Children of Aging Parents *Professionally-run.* Information, education and peer support for adult children who are caring for aging parents near or far. Literature and guest speakers Meets 3rd Wed., 4:30-6pm, Princeton Senior Resource Center, Suzanne Patterson Bldg., (behind Borough Hall), 45 Stockton St., Princeton. Call Susan Hoskins 609-924-7108 (day).

MIDDLESEX

Alzheimer's Association Family Support Group *Professionally-run.* Mutual support and understanding for spouses of persons with any type of memory loss (Alzheimer's, Parkinson's, vascular disease, stroke, head injury, dementia, etc.). Meets 1st Mon., 9:30am, COPSA Institute for Alzheimer's disease, North Bldg., University Behavioral Health Center at Piscataway, 667 Hoes Lane, Piscataway. Call Mary Catherine Lundquist 732-235-2858 (day).

EARS (Educate, Advocate, Reduce Stress) For Caregivers *Professionally-run.* Mutual support for caregivers of the elderly. Rap sessions, guest speakers, educational series and phone help. Meets 2nd Wed., 1-3pm, Metroplex Corporate Center, 100 Metroplex Dr., Suite 200, (off Plainfield Ave.), Edison. Call Susan Schwartz 1-866-300-3277 (day).

Spouses Caregiver Support Group *Professionally-run.* Mutual support for elderly persons caring for a spouse. Meets 2nd Thurs., 1:30-3pm, St. Peter's Adult Daycare Center, Pondview Plaza, 200 Overlook Dr., Monroe. Call Stephanie Fitzsimmons 1-800-269-7508 ext. 8662 (day).

Strength For Caring Provides support and education to families coping with the emotional strain of caring for a loved one with cancer. Offers literature and mutual sharing. Meets 4th Tues., Cancer Institute of NJ, 195 Little Albany St., New Brunswick. Registration required. Call Brenda Bly 732-235-6027.

MONMOUTH

Parkinson's Disease Support Group *Professionally-run.* Support group for patients and caregivers. Provides mutual support, education and information. Meets 1st Thurs., 10-11:30am, SCAN Learning Center, Monmouth Mall, Eatontown. Must register before attending. Call 732-542-1326. *Website:* http://www.saintbarnabas.com

Well Spouse Association Provides peer-to-peer emotional support for spousal caregivers or significant others who care for a chronically ill or disabled spouse. Quarterly newsletter. Dues $25/yr. Meets 2nd Tues., 7pm, Freehold. Call Donna 732-580-4119 or 1-800-838-0879 (day). *Website:* http://www.wellspouse.org *Email:* info@wellspouse.org

MORRIS

Caregivers Support Group *Professionally-run.* Support and sharing of experiences for persons who are caring for the elderly. Rap sessions, guest speakers and educational series. Meets 1st Thurs., 5:30-7:30pm, Morris View Nursing Home, 540 W. Hanover Rd., Morris Plains. Call Carolann Roberto 973-326-7288 (day).

Evening Caregivers Support Group *Professionally-run.* To provide support, information and education to caregivers of dependent adults. Mutual sharing sessions. Meets 2nd Wed., 7-9pm, Time Out Adult Care Center, 4 Division Ave., Madison. Call Ellen Brody 973-822-8006 (day). *Website:* http://www.fsmc.org

Your Aging Parent and You *Professionally-run.* Support and education for those caring for their aging parents. Mutual sharing, education, guest speakers, literature. Fee $15. Meets evenings for 5 week sessions, 2 times per year, Chilton Memorial Hospital, 97 West Parkway, Pompton Plains. Call Joan Beloff 973-831-5167 (day). *Email:* joan-beloff@chiltonmemorial.org

OCEAN

Caregiver Support Group *Professionally-run.* Provide caregivers with a place to share problems and solutions with others in the same circumstance. Families welcome. Lecture series, rap sessions and guest speakers. Meets 4th Tues., 10-11am, Wellsprings, 515 State Highway 70, Lakewood. Call Rita Sason or Carol Powell 732-363-8010 (day). *Email:* ocjf@optonline.net

Caregiver Support Group *Professionally-run.* Mutual support for adult children (age 50+) dealing with an aging parent. Literature available. Meets 4th Mon., 7pm, Adult Day Care Center, 591 Lakehurst Rd., Toms River. Call Lisa 732-505-9420 (day).

Well Spouse Support Group Mutual help with a focus on how well spouses of ill or disabled can help one another. Rap sessions and guest speakers. Meets last Wed., 7:30-9pm, Southern Education of Ocean County College, Conference Room, 195 Cedar Bridge Rd., Manahawkin. Call Vivian 609-660-1529 (eve). *Website:* http://www.wellspouseassociation.org *Email:* justdoitviv@aol.com

PASSAIC

Caregivers Support Group *Professionally-run.* Mutual support for individuals and families who are the primary caregiver of anyone with any type of dementia. Rap sessions, guest speakers. Lunch provided. Meets last Tues., 11am-12:30pm, Daughters of Miriam, 155 Hazel St., Rothenberg Bldg., Clifton. Call 973-253-5709 (day).

SALEM

Caregivers Support Group *Professionally-run.* Support through discussions, education, sharing and referrals for caregivers of the aged or disabled at home. Guest speakers. Meets 3rd Wed., 4:30-6pm, Fenwick Plaza, Broadway and Walnut St., Salem. Call Melinda Lodge 856-878-6035 (day).

We can also refer callers to over 100 individuals who are seeking others to help start new support groups throughout NJ, if you don't see it, that doesn't mean it doesn't exist!
1-800-367-6274

SOMERSET

F.A.R.E. (Friends And Relatives of the Elderly) *Professionally-run.* Mutual support for emotional and practical concerns facing those taking care of an elderly or disabled person. Call Respite Care 908-766-0180 (day). *Website:* http://www.visitingnurse.org

> **Basking Ridge** Meets 4th Mon., 1:30pm, Somerset Hills Adult Day Center, 510 Mt. Airy Rd.
>
> **Bridgewater** Meets 2nd Wed., 7pm, Arbor Glen, 100 Monroe St.

SUSSEX

Caregiver/Alzheimer's Support Group *Professionally-run.* Support and information for those caring for someone with dementia, Alzheimer's or any type of disability. Peer counseling, guest speakers. Meets 1st Wed., 7-9pm, Sussex County Adult Day Center, 55 Mill St., Newton. Call Shelly Green-Hinton 973-579-6699 (day) or Joseph Vishak 973-579-8620 (day).

UNION

Caregivers Support Mutual sharing and support for caregivers of the elderly. Meetings vary, Muhlenberg Regional Medical Center, Adult Day Health Center, Park Ave and Randolph Rd., Plainfield. For information call MRMC Adult Day Health Center 908-668-2328.

Caretakers of the Elderly Support Group Mutual support for people responsible for caring for an elderly family member. Assists through group discussions. Meets 1st Mon., 8pm, St. Helen's Parish Center, 1600 Rahway Ave., Westfield. Call Marilyn Ryan 908-232-1867 (day).

C.O.O.P. (Children Of Older Parents) Mutual support for adult children of elderly persons. Guest speakers and phone help. Meets last Wed., 7pm, Cranford Community Center, Walnut Ave., Cranford. Call Jo D'Arcangelo 908-276-9206 (day) or Reggi Bleemer 908-272-6731. *Email:* regmel@aol.com

Engel Center Support Group *Professionally-run.* Support group for caregivers of the elderly. Sharing of information and experiences. Meets 2nd Wed., noon - 1:30pm (lunch served), 505 South Ave. East, Cranford. Call Hazel Garlic 908-497-3944 or 908-497-3945 (day).

P.R.E.P. (People Responsible for Elderly Persons) *Professionally-run.* Mutual support and education for caregivers of elderly people. Meets 3rd Wed.,

7-9pm, SAGE Eldercare, 290 Broad St., Summit. Call Ellen McNally 908-598-5509 (day). *Website:* http://www.sageeldercare.org *Email:* emcnally@sageeldercare.org

NATIONAL

CAPS (Children of Aging Parents) *National. 65 groups. Founded 1977.* Non-profit membership organization dedicated to the needs of caregivers of the elderly. National network of support. Offers information, referral and counseling. Write: CAPS, PO Box 7250, Penndel, PA 19047-7250. Call 1-800-227-7294 or 215-945-6900. *Website:* http://www.CAPS4caregivers.org *Email:* admin@caps4caregivers.org

DOROT/University Without Walls Telephone Support Teleconference support groups for a variety of topics are available. Registration fee $10 and $15 tuition per support group. Groups for coping with vision loss, care giving, aging issues, etc. Write: DOROT, 171 W. 85th St., NY, NY, 10024. For more information call DOROT 1-877-819-9147. *Website:* http://www.dorotusa.org

ElderCare Rights Alliance *Statewide model. Founded 1972.* Promotes the principles of justice and dignity in the long-term care system through education, advocacy and action. Provides individual advocacy, crime victim support, family caregiver training, nursing home resident and family action councils, community education, legislative advocacy and volunteer resources. Advocates for the rights and safety of elders and adults with disabilities living in nursing homes. Write: ElderCare Rights Alliance, 2626 E. 82nd St., Suite 230 Bloomington, MN 55425. Call 952-854-7304; Fax: 952-854-8535. *Website:* http://www.eldercarerights.org *Email:* kkelso@eldercarerights.org

National Family Caregivers Association *National. Founded 1992.* Dedicated to improving the quality of life for family caregivers through support and validation, education and information, public awareness and advocacy. Information and referrals, quarterly newsletter, resources and literature. Write: National Family Caregivers Association, 10400 Connecticut Ave., Suite 500, Kensington, MD 20895-3944. Call 301-942-6430 or 1-800-896-3650; Fax: 301-942-2302. *Website:* http://www.thefamilycaregiver.org *Email:* info@thefamilycaregiver.org

Well Spouse Association *International. 50+ affiliated groups. Founded 1988.* Provides emotional support and information to the well spouses and children of the chronically ill. Informs educators, human service professionals and the public about the needs of spousal caregivers. Quarterly newsletter. Guidelines and assistance available for starting new groups. Write: Well Spouse Association, 63 West Main St., Suite H, Freehold, NJ 07728. Call 1-800-838-0879 or 732-577-8899;

Fax: 732-577-8644. *Website:* http://www.wellspouse.org *Email:* info@wellspouse.org

ONLINE

ElderCare Online *Online. Founded 1997.* Provides daily support for caregivers. Biweekly email newsletter that includes articles, news releases, self-care tips, etc. Online chats and message online message boards covering a broad range of topics. Some chat rooms are run by authors and professionals. Offers software for medical planners, taxes, etc. *Website:* http://www.ec-online.net *Email:* rich@ec-online.net

Family Caregiver Alliance *Online.* Unmoderated listserv for caregivers to share strategies, information, education, support and ideas with each other. Write: Family Caregiver Alliance,180 Montgomery St., Suite 1100, San Francisco, CA, 07857. Call 1-800-445-8106; Fax: 415-434-3508. *Website:* http://www.caregiver.org *Email:* info@caregiver.org

CRIME VICTIMS / OFFENDERS
(see also trauma, spouse abuse, sexual abuse and toll-free helplines)

STATEWIDE

MADD (Mothers Against Drunk Driving) Mission is to stop drunk driving. Offers support for the victims of this violent crime and prevent underage drinking. Has 11 chapter locations in NJ. Call 609-585-7233 (day) or the victim hotline 1-800-448-6233 (day). *Website:* http://www.madd.org/nj *Email:* maddnj@erols.com

BERGEN

END DWI Support for victims of drunk driving crashes in Bergen/Hudson counties. Aims to prevent drunk driving crashes. Helps victims through the court system. Phone support. Regular membership dues $20/individual; $35/family; $10/senior citizens; free for victims. Meets 1st Thurs., Bogota. Call 201-525-5414 (day). *Website:* http://www.enddwi.com *Email:* enddwi@mindspring.com

BURLINGTON

Helping Hand Grief Support Group Support for someone bereaving the loss of a loved one (including death of a child, loss to homicide or suicide) through education, encouragement, counseling and understanding. Families welcome. Meets 1st and 3rd Mon., 7-9pm, (10 week sessions), Fellowship Alliance Chapel,

(Log house in back of church), 199 Church Rd., Medford. Call Wanda and George Stein 609-953-7333 ext. 309 (day/eve).

ESSEX

Prisoners Resource Center *(ESSEX COUNTY RESIDENTS ONLY)* Provides support for ex-offenders and their families. Assists ex-offenders with resolving issues of re-entry, employment, educational and vocational opportunities, counseling, detoxification programs, resume writing and family crisis intervention. Provides support for prisoners and ex-offenders and their families. Offers information, advocacy, employment assistance, detoxification programs and crisis intervention. Meets Mon., 10am, 972 Broad St., Newark. Call Prisoners Resource Center 973-643-2205 (day).

RAP (Reality After Prison) Group *Professionally-run.* Rap group for ex-offenders to discuss issues relating to re-entry struggles and living healthy lives in the community. Guest speakers and literature. Meets 2nd Wed., 5-7pm, 155 Washington St., Newark. Call 1-800-433-0254 (day).

HUDSON

Keeping It Real Community Outreach Mutual support program to aid females in their transition from incarceration or addiction to productive lifestyles. Meetings vary, Jersey City. Call Marsha 201-433-9113 (eve); Fax 201-433-8295.

MONMOUTH

Parents United *Professionally-run.* Support group for the non-offending parent and perpetrator of sexual abuse, incest or rape. Slight fee required (sliding scale). Meets various times in Red Bank. Before attending call Judith Loder 732-758-0094 (day).

PASSAIC

Life Support Discussion Spiritual group to help victims of violence reclaim their lives. Goal is to reach out to all victims (including sexual assault, domestic violence, families of incarcerated and homicide victims) to provide words of encouragement to help them become survivors; then advocates. Meets alternate Sat., 4-6pm, Paterson. For meeting information call Elizabeth 973-881-2500.

R.I.D. (Remove Intoxicated Drivers) Aims to remove intoxicated drivers from the road. Network for crash victims, families and friends. Newsletter. Membership dues $20/yr. (can be waived). Meets 1st Wed., 8pm, in Wayne area. For meeting information call Lorraine Roy 973-696-2245 (day).

UNION

Outmate Outreach Support, discussions and sharing of information for wives and girlfriends of prison inmates. Meets 3rd Sat., 9-11am, Resurrection Temple Church, 1229 Spruce St., Roselle. Call Reverend Holmes 908-620-0470 (day) or 908-456-3928 (eve).

Homicide Survivors *Professionally-run.* Provides support to family members and friends of homicide victims. Rap sessions, guest speakers. Meets 3rd Mon., (except July/Aug.), 7:30-9pm, Rahway Hospital, Rahway. Call Elaine O'Neal 908-527-4596 (day).

NATIONAL

C.A.S.A. (Cleptomaniacs And Shoplifters Anonymous) *Model. Founded 1992.* Secular support group for recovering shoplifters, cleptomaniacs and other persons suffering from dishonesty related to fraud, stealing or cheating. Pen pals, information and referrals, phone support. Assistance in starting similar groups. Include self-addressed stamped envelope. Offers online chat room and e-group. Write: C.A.S.A., c/o Terry S., PO Box 250008, Franklin, MI 48025. Call 248-358-8508. *Website:* http://www.shopliftersanonymous.com *Email:* info@shopliftersanonymous.com

Criminals & Gangmembers Anonymous, Inc. *Founded 1996.* 12-Step group for criminals and gang members who have a sincere desire to find relief from their addiction to all forms of criminality. For those with a desire for peace within themselves and a wish to live in harmony with others. Online chat room. Write: Criminals & Gangmembers Anonymous, PO Box 255867, Sacramento, CA 95865-5867. Call 916-973-8603. *Website:* http://www.cga-anon.com *Email:* Martha2CGA@aol.com

MADD (Mothers Against Drunk Driving) *National. 600+ chapters. Founded 1980.* The mission of MADD is to stop drunken driving, support victims of this violent crime and prevent underage drinking. Newsletter, chapter development guidelines. Write: MADD , 511 E. John Carpenter Freeway, Suite 700 , Irving, TX 75062-8187. Call 214-744-6233; 1-800-GET-MADD (general information); 1-877-MADD-HELP (victim hotline); Fax: 972-869-2206. *Website:* http://www.madd.org

Molesters Anonymous *Founded 1985.* Provides support with anonymity & confidentiality for men who molest children. Use of "thought stoppage" technique & buddy system. Groups are initiated by a professional but become member-run. Group development manual $9.95. Write: Jerry Goffman, PhD, 1040 S. Mt. Vernon Ave., G-306, Colton, CA 92324. Call Dr. Jerry Goffman 909-355-1100; Fax: 909-370-0438. *Email:* jerrygoffman@hotmail.com

National Organization for Victim Assistance *National. 2300 members. Founded 1975.* Support and advocacy for victims and survivors of violent crimes and disaster. Newsletter, information and referrals, phone help, conferences, crisis response training, group development guidelines. Referrals to local self-help groups. Dues $35/ind; $125/org. Write: NOVA, 510 King St., Suite 424, Alexandria, VA 22314. Call 703-535-6682 or 1-800-879-6682 (victim referral line); Fax: 703-535-5500. *Website:* http://www.try-nova.org *Email:* nova@try-nova.org

National Organization of Parents of Murdered Children *National. 300 chapters and contact persons. Founded 1978.* Provides self-help groups to support persons who survived the violent death of someone close. Newsletter and guidelines for starting local chapters. Court accompaniment also provided in many areas. Parole Block Program and Second Opinion Service also available. Write: NOPMC, 100 E. 8th St., B-41, Cincinnati, OH 45202. Call 1-888-818-7662 or 513-721-5683 (office); Fax: 513-345-4489. *Website:* http://www.pomc.com *Email:* NatlPOMC@aol.com

RID (Remove Intoxicated Drivers) *National. 152 chapters in 41 states. Founded 1978.* Citizens' project organized to advocate against drunk driving, educate the public, reform legislation and aid victims of drunk driving. Newsletter. Chapter information kit ($20). For descriptive pamphlet send self-addressed stamped envelope. Write: RID, c/o Doris Aiken, PO Box 520, Schenectady, NY 12301. Call 518-372-0034 or 518-393-HELP; Fax: 518-370-4917. *Website:* http://www.rid-usa.org *Email:* RIDUSA@netzero.net

ONLINE

Families-of-Inmates *Online. Founded 1998.* Email list for people with loved ones in jail or prison, who "support each other through the rough times." Offers public and subscribers only chat rooms. *Website:* http://groups.yahoo.com/group/Families-of-inmates

Prison Talk *Online* support for families of inmates. Also offers support to the incarcerated. Offers advocacy, education and mutual support. *Website:* http://www.prisontalk.com/forums/

CULTS

STATEWIDE

Cult Information Service Public education about destructive mind control cults. Mutual support for families and friends of cult members and teenagers involved. Group meets in Teaneck. Helps cult members return to society. Write: Cult Information Service, PO Box 867, Teaneck, NJ 07666. Call 201-833-1212 (day) or 201-833-0817.

NATIONAL

reFOCUS (recovering FOrmer CUltists Support) *National network. Founded 1984.* Support for former members of closed, high demand groups, relationships or cults. Referrals to other former cult members by group and/or area, support groups, therapists and services. Literature, free internet newsletter, recovery workshops, conferences. Write: reFOCUS, PO Box 2180, Flagler Beach, FL 32136. Call 386-439-7541; Fax: 386-439-7537. *Website:* http://www.refocus.org *Email:* torefocus@aol.com

EMPLOYMENT / RETIREMENT
(see also women,aging, toll-free helplines)

BERGEN

Employment Peer Support Provides support to those that are unemployed. Meets Mon., 8pm, Church of the Presentation, 271 West Saddle River Rd., Upper Saddle River. Call 201-327-1313.

Job Support Group *Professionally-run.* Exchange of job hunting experience, "hands-on" skills of resume development, networking, interviewing and prayer support. Meets Thurs., 7:30-9pm, 228 Vittorio Court, Park Ridge. Call Bob Miller 201-391-0657 (day/eve). *Email:* RJMiller@aol.com

Professional Service Group *Professionally-run.* Mutual support to help unemployed and underemployed professional-level job seekers develop leads, learn effective job search techniques and network. Meets various times, NJ State Employment Service, 60 State St., Hackensack. Call Bruce Lauber 201-996-8950 ext. 16 (day); Fax: 201-996-8884. *Website:* http://wnjpin.net

We are constantly updating this information. If you do not see what you are looking for call us at 1-800-367-6274.

ESSEX

Job Seekers of Montclair Mutual support and education for people seeking a new job or in career transitions. Meets Wed., 7:30pm, St. Luke's Church, Dining Hall, 73 S. Fullerton Ave., Montclair. Call 973-783-3442. *Website:* http://www.jobseekersofmontclair.org

MERCER

Jobseekers Education, support and networking for unemployed people and those who are changing jobs or careers. Meets Tues., 7:30pm, Trinity Church, 33 Mercer St., Princeton. Call the church office 609-924-2277 (day). *Website:* http://www.trinityprinceton.org (click on "Job Seekers")

MORRIS

Professional Services Group *Professionally-run.* Self-help organization sponsored by the New Jersey Department of Labor, for professional-level job seekers. Meets Wed., 9am, (new member orientation Wed., 1pm), Dover Employment Service, 107 Bassett Highway, Dover. Call 973-361-1034 (9am-4pm) or Cindy 973-361-9050. *Website:* http://www.wnjpin.net

SOMERSET

JANUS Bereavement Group *Professionally-run.* Support and education for anyone who has experienced a loss such as a job, retirement, relocation, separation/divorce or death. Helps individuals accept and adjust to the loss. Meets 2nd Tues., 7:30-9pm, Bridgewater Baptist Church, 324 Milltown Rd. Bridgewater. Call Barbara Ronca, LCSW 908-218-9062 (Mon.-Fri., 9am-3pm).

Somerset Hills YMCA - Career Forum Mutual support for individuals seeking a career/job change, early retirement. For those who are under-employed or unemployed. Meets Tues., 7:30pm, Somerset Hills YMCA, 140 Mt. Airy Rd., Basking Ridge. Call 908-766-7898 (day).

SUSSEX

OLL Job Networking Group Provides job seeking skills, strategies, networking contacts, leads, referrals, tips and techniques to aid in job search. For those who are unemployed, underemployed or concerned about current job. Guest speakers and phone help. Meets 2nd Wed., 6:30pm, Our Lady of the Lake Parish, 294 Sparta Ave., Conference Room, Sparta. Call Frank 973-300-1010 (day). *Website:* http://www.ourladyofthelake.org *Email:* frank@iresinic.com

NATIONAL

9 to 5, National Association of Working Women *National. 24 chapters. Founded 1973.* Support, advocacy and legislative assistance on issues that affect women who work. Job problem counselors can advise women on how to make changes on their jobs. Dues $25/yr. Group development guidelines. Write: 9 to 5, National Assn. of Working Women, 501 Pulliam St. SW, # 344, Atlanta, GA 30312. Call Job Problem Hotline 1-800-522-0925 or 404-222-0001. *Website:* http://www.9to5.org *Email:* Hotline9to5@hotmail.org

Business & Professional Women/USA *National. 2800 chapters. Founded 1919.* Organization comprised of working women, to promote workplace equity and provide networking opportunities. Lobbying efforts, tri-annual magazine, periodic publications, resource center and grassroots community action projects. Annual national convention. Local group information available online. Write: Business & Prof. Women/USA, 1900 M St., NW, Suite 310, Washington, DC 20036. Call 202-293-1100; Fax: 202-861-0298. *Website:* http://www.bpwusa.org *Email:* memberservices@bpwusa.org

Employment Support Center *Model. 1 group in Washington, DC. Founded 1984.* Provides technical assistance for self-help groups for the unemployed, underemployed and persons in job transition. Provides leadership training for groups. Sets up new groups and coalitions of job clubs with training and materials. Newsletter. Extensive network of group leaders, employment professionals, job seekers. Provides job bank, consultations, network meetings & programs, small business seminars, self-help & job search sessions. Provides assistance in starting new groups. "Self-Help Bridge to Employment" manual ($25 prepaid). Dues $50. Write: ESC, 1556 Wisconsin Ave. NW, Washington, DC 20007. Call 202-628-2919. *Website:* http://www.angelfire.com/biz/jobclubs *Email:* jobclubs@hotmail.com

FOOD
(see also toll-free helplines)

ONLINE

S.T.O.P. (Safe Tables Our Priority) *Online. Founded 1993.* Offers support, education and advocacy for victims and family of victims of food borne infectious diseases, (E.coli, salmonella listeria, shigella, vibrio and many others).   Phone and online networking, newsletter and annual meeting. *Website:* http://www.safetables.org *Email:* mail@safetables.org

HAZARDOUS WASTE
(see also toll-free helplines)

NATIONAL

Center for Health, Environment & Justice *National. 10,000 groups. Founded 1981.* Grassroots environmental crisis center, providing information and networking for people affected by toxic waste. Assists in organizing self-help groups and provides scientific and technical backup. Conferences, information and referrals. Newsletters. Write: Center for Health, Environment, & Justice, PO Box 6806, Falls Church, VA 22040-6806. Call 703-237-2249; Fax: 703-237-8389. *Website:* http://www.chej.org *Email:* chej@chej.org

HOUSING

STATEWIDE

New Jersey Tenants Organization Works for pro-tenant state legislation. Helps organize local tenants associations. Gives legal guidance to members and fights for rights for tenants. Membership dues $22/yr. Meets once a year in alternating towns. Call Bonnie Shapiro 201-342-3775 (day). *Website:* http://www.njto.org *Email:* info@njto.org

LANDMINE SURVIVORS
(see also disabilities, general)

INTERNATIONAL

Landmine Survivors Network *International network. Founded 1997.* Created by and for landmine survivors. Links victims in mine-affected countries to a range of rehabilitative services. Provides peer counseling and direct assistance. Promotes social and economic reintegration. Strives to protect future generations from the scourge of landmines. Maintains database of medical facilities, prosthetic clinics and rehabilitation projects who work with landmine survivors and their families. Provides active support network online. Write: Landmine Survivors Network, 1420 K St. NW, Suite 300, Washington, DC 20005. Call 202-464-0007. *Website:* http://www.landminesurvivors.org *Email:* info@landminesurvivors.org

We know this Directory is big and chances are we can probably find the group you're looking for quicker than you paging through it. Call us! (We're really friendly!)
1-800-367-6274

LIGHTNING / SHOCK

INTERNATIONAL

Lightning Strike & Electric Shock Survivors Int'l, Inc. *International network. Founded 1989.* Mutual support for survivors of lightning or electric shock, their families and families of non-survivors. Studies the long-term after-effects. Information and referrals, phone support, annual conferences, help in starting support groups. Newsletter. Books and tapes available. Write: LS & ESSI Inc., PO Box 1156, Jacksonville, NC 28541-1156. Call Steve Marshburn, Sr. 910-346-4708; Fax: 910-346-4708. *Website:* http://www.lightning-strike.org *Email:* lightning1@ec.rr.com

MEN'S ISSUES
(see also separation / divorce)

ESSEX

Men With No Name Provides a safe place for men to speak, be heard and talk about men's issues. Meets alternate Thurs., 8-10pm, in members' homes in Essex County. Call Jotham 973-763-4054 or George 973-746-9482.

MIDDLESEX

Men's Group Offers mutual support for men. Opportunity for men to discuss issues that are important in their lives. Meets twice a month in various members' homes in Southern Middlesex County. Call Frank Foulkes 609-655-0059 (eve).

MORRIS

Men-To-Men Mutual support for men in transition. Topics include divorce, anger, parenting, health, aging, relationships, etc. Offers networking, phone support and guest speakers. Dues $10 per meeting. Meets Wed., Xavier Center, St. Elizabeth College, Convent Station. Before attending call Dale Leffler 732-494-8198. *Website:* http://www.men-to-men.themenscenter.com

SOMERSET

Men Mentoring Men A men's center dedicated to the sharing of a man's unique experience in a complex world through organizing and facilitating peer led men's discussion groups. Rap sessions, speaker's bureau, guest speakers, literature. Suggested donation $15/mtg. Meets twice a month, 7:30pm, 125 West End. Ave., Somerville. Call Richard Horowitz or Jerry Zipkin 908-707-0774.

Website: http://www.menmentoringmen.org *Email:* questions@mthree.org

NATIONAL

Bald-Headed Men of America *National. 6 affiliated groups. Founded 1973.* Self-help group instilling pride in being bald. Offers opportunity to exchange feelings and experiences through group discussions which may lead to acceptance of being bald. "We believe the best cure for baldness is to promote a positive mental attitude...with humor." Annual conference usually in Sept., newsletter. Write: Bald Headed Men of Amer., 102 Bald Dr., Morehead City, NC 28557. Call 252-726-1855; *Website:* http://www.members.aol.com/baldusa/ *Email:* jcapps4102@aol.com

NORM (National Organization of Restoring Men) *International. 20 affiliated groups. Founded 1989.* (Meetings for MEN ONLY; information for all) Provides a safe environment in which men can, without fear of being ridiculed, share their concerns about circumcision/restoration and their desire to be intact & whole again. Confidential discussions of goals and methods of foreskin restoration. Information and referrals, phone support, assistance in starting new groups. Write: NORM, c/o R. Wayne Griffiths, 3205 Northwood Dr., #209, Concord, CA 94520-4506. Call 925-827-4077. *Website:* http://www.norm.org *Email:* waynerobb@aol.com

ONLINE

National Men's Resource Center. *Online. Founded 1982.* Thousands of onsite men's book reviews and covers, men's resources and hyperlinks to hundreds of men's issues, events, periodicals and groups. Educational and volunteer website serves a diverse men's community (men's rights, mythopoetic, pro-feminist, recovery, re-evaluation counseling and religious). Provides information on men's issues regarding positive changes in male roles and relationships (including abuse, aging, circumcision, divorce, fathers, health, isolation, kid stuff, mid-life, multicultural, prostate, sexuality, spirituality, transition, violence, work, etc). *Website:* http://www.menstuff.org *Email:* info@menstuff.org

MESSINESS / COMPULSIVE SAVING

BERGEN

Clutterers Anonymous Support for persons who have a problem with clutter. Opportunity to share experience, strength and hope with one another in the hope of solving this common problem and helping each other to recover. Meets Mon., 7:30pm, Bogart Memorial Reformed Church, 311 Larch Ave. and West Fort Lee Rd., Bogota. Call Laraine 201-836-5149.

BURLINGTON

Clutterers Anonymous Support for persons who have a problem with clutter. Opportunity to share experience, strength and hope with one another in the hope of solving this common problem and helping each other to recover. Meets 1st and 3rd Mon., 7:30pm, Virtua Hospital, Route 73, Marlton. Call Elaine 1-866-800-3881.

ESSEX

Clutterers Anonymous Support to help overcome compulsive saving, pack ratting, procrastination and cluttering. Donation. Meets Mon., 7:30pm, 21 Dodd Street, Bloomfield. Call Aloma 973-748-0423 (day).

MIDDLESEX

Clutterers Anonymous Support for persons who have a problem with clutter. Opportunity to share experience, strength and hope with one another in the hope of solving this common problem and helping each other to recover. Meets Sun., 5pm, St. Luke's Episcopal Church, Parish Hall, Middlesex and Oak Ave., Metuchen. Call Aileen 609-875-1001.

MORRIS

Clutter Club *Professionally-run.* Support and discussion group for individuals struggling with issues relating to clutter. Rap sessions, literature and educational series. Meets 2nd Thurs., (except Aug.), 7:30-9pm, Sages Pages Fine Books, 250 Main St., Madison. Call Ellen Kazanoff 908-403-6217 (day). *Email:* clean.slate@att.net

PASSAIC

Clutterers Anonymous 12 Step. Support for persons who have a problem with clutter. Opportunity to share experience, strength and hope with one another in the hope of solving this common problem and helping each other to recover. Meets Thurs., 6pm, St. Michael's Episcopal Church, 1219 Ratzer Rd., Room 1, Wayne. Call Peter 908-875-3881.

Be gentle to all and stern with yourself.
--St. Teresa of Avila

UNION

Clutter Club *Professionally-run.* Mutual support for persons who have a problem with clutter. Rap sessions, literature, phone help, newsletter and buddy system. Meets 3rd Mon., 7:30-9pm, Barnes and Noble, Raritan Rd., Clark. Call Jamie 1-866-294-9900. *Email:* jamie@jamienovak.com

NATIONAL

Clutterers Anonymous *National. 59 affiliated chapters.* 12-Step 12-tradition fellowship of individuals who share experience, strength and hope with each other that they may solve their common problem with clutter and help others recover. Fellowship is based on suggestion, interchange of experience, rotation of leadership and service. The only requirement for membership is a desire to eliminate clutter and bring order into one's life. Write: CLA WSO, PO Box 91413, Los Angeles, CA 90009. Call 310-281-6084 Recorded Meeting Information Line. *Website:* http://www.clutterersanonymous.net *Email:* clawso@hotmail.com

Clutterless Recovery Groups Inc. *National. 6 affiliated groups. Founded 2000.* Support for those persons that find it difficult to discard unwanted possessions. Group uses psychological principles to change behavior. Provides newsletter, literature, information, referrals, conferences, pen pals and group meeting locations. Also offers online networking. Offers information on starting similar groups ($15 includes 3-ring binder with CD and hardcopy brochure). Write: Clutterless, 2421 S. Conway Ave., #764, Mission, TX, 78572. Call 956-580-4870 or 512-351-4058. *Website:* http://www.clutterless.org *Email:* director@clutterless.org

Messies Anonymous *(MULTILINGUAL) National. 100 groups. Founded 1981.* 12-Step. Group that aims to improve the quality of life of disorganized homemakers. Provides motivation and a program for change to help members improve self-image as control of house and life is obtained. Optional donation at meetings. Online newsletter: "The Organizer Lady." Interactive online group. Write: Messies Anonymous, c/o Nest Builders, PO Box 343566, Homestead, FL 33034-0566. Call Sandra 305-271-8404; Fax: 786-243-2793. *Website:* http://www.messies.com *Email:* nestbuilder@earthlink.net

ONLINE

Messies Anonymous *Online.* Offers many different support groups surrounding the issue of "messiness" and clutter. Groups for singles, spirituality, parents, teachers, family and friends, those with ADD/ADHD and hoarders. *Website:* http://www.messies.com/selfhelp.htm

NEAR DEATH EXPERIENCE

NATIONAL

International Association for Near-Death Studies *National. 35 affiliated groups. Founded 1981.* Support group for anyone who has had a near-death experience, their families and the professionals working with them. Write: IANDS, PO Box 502, E. Windsor Hill, CT 06028-0502. Call 860-882-1211; Fax: 860-882-1212. *Website:* http://www.iands.org *Email:* services@iands.org

NETWORKING FOR ILL / DISABLED

STATEWIDE

C.U.S.A. Correspondence support group for persons of all faiths with any type of disability or chronic illness. Catholic in founding but open to all. Emphasis on spiritual values and mutual support. Through "group letters" members find close relationships, understanding and courage. Dues $20/yr. (can be waived). Write: CUSA, 176 West 8th St., Bayonne, NJ 07002; *Email:* ams4@juno.com *Website:* http://www.cusan.org

NATIONAL

MUMS National Parent-to-Parent Network *National. 61 affiliated groups. Founded 1979.* Mutual support and networking for parents or care providers of children with any disability, rare disorder, chromosomal abnormality or health condition using a database of over 19,000 families from 60 countries, covering 3400 disorders, very rare syndromes or undiagnosed conditions. Referrals to support groups and provides assistance in starting groups. Newsletter ($15/parents - $25/professionals). Matching services $5. Other literature available. Write: MUMS Nat'l Parent-to-Parent Network, 150 Custer Ct., Green Bay, WI 54301-1243. Call 1-877-336-5333 (parents only) or 920-336-5333 (day); Fax: 920-339-0995. *Website:* http://www.netnet.net/mums/ *Email:* mums@netnet.net

PATIENT'S RIGHTS

MODEL

New England Patients' Rights Group *Model. Founded 1993.* Mutual support for health care consumers, many of whom are suffering because of deficiencies or negligence in the system. Advocates for consumer empowerment, quality, accurate information, informed consent, insurance needs, patients' rights and protection. Newsletter. Write: New England Patients Rights Group, PO Box 141,

461

Norwood, MA 02062. Call 781-769-5720; Fax: 781-769-0882. *Email:* NEPRG@verizon.net

POLICE OFFICERS

ESSEX

Wounded Officers Support Group of NJ *Professionally-run.* Provides support to officers who were wounded in the line of duty. Meets 3rd Wed., 9:30-11:30am, Fraternal Order of Police Building, Lodge # 12, 51 Rector St., 2nd Floor Conference Room, Newark. Call Joe Orgo or Fred Mitchell 1-866-267-2267 (day).

PREJUDICE / RACISM

NATIONAL

Recovering Racists Network *National. Groups in CA, MO and MI. Founded 1997.* Mutual support to help people overcome their everyday racism and prejudice. Anti-racism training, high school Race Awareness Program, online support, information and referral. Assistance in helping others to start similar groups. Write: RRN, c/o John McKenzie, 517 Loon Dr., Petaluma, CA 94954. Call 707-789-9505 or 415-577-8331. *Website:* http://www.rrnet.org *Email:* info@rrnet.org

PROSTITION / SEX INDUSTRY

MODEL

PRIDE (from PRostitution to Independence, Dignity & Equality) *Model. One group in Minnesota. Founded 1978.* Provides PRIDE support groups and other services to assist women and children in escaping the sex industry (including prostitution, pornography and stripping). Write: PRIDE, Family & Children Service, 4123 E. Lake St., Minneapolis, MN 55406. Call 612-729-0340. *Website:* http://www.fcsmn.org/pride/

SELF-ABUSE / SELF-MUTILATION

MORRIS

BSSI (Breaking the Silence of Self-Injury) Christian-based group to provide support for those who cut, burn or harm their body as a way of coping with overwhelming emotions, thoughts and circumstances. Purpose is to realize that a life can be lived without self-injurious behavior. Meets 1st and 3rd Fri., 7:15-9pm,

Living Praise Church, Room 205, 37 Vreeland Rd., Florham Park. Call Vicki Duffy 973-983-1250 (day) or 973-224-4144 (eve). *Website:* http://www.endallthepain.com *Email:* vicki@endallthepain.com

NATIONAL

Inspiration Support Group *Model.* Support for people who self-injure themselves by cutting or other injury to the body without the intention of ending their life. Helps members recognize "triggers," control their thoughts and solve their problems. Manual and CD with exercises and education materials available. Consultation on group development guidelines ($65 postpaid). Write: Safe In Canada, 611 Wonderland Rd N., Suite 224, London, Ontario, Canada N6H-5N7. Call 519-657-6570. *Website:* http://www.safeincanada.ca *Email:* bjthom_6@yahoo.ca

Self Mutilators Anonymous *National. 10 affiliated groups.* 12-Step fellowship of men and women who share their experiences, strength and hope with each other, that they may solve their common problem and help others recover from physical self-mutilation. Online meeting. *Website:* http://www.selfmutilatorsanonymous.org

ONLINE

Secret Shame: Self Injury Information & Support *Online.* Extensive information resource on self-injury and self-abuse. Resources for how to deal with self-abuse and the self-abuse of family or friends. Offers web board and separate email lists for self-injurers, their family and friends. (Email lists are named BUS for "bodies under siege" and are located in the right hand column). *Web Board:* http://buslist.org *Website:* http://www.selfharm.net

SEXUALITY

STATEWIDE

Gay and Lesbian Political Action and Support Group Provides opportunity for individuals in isolated areas to be politically active and establish support groups where they are needed. Write: GLPASC, PO Box 11406, New Brunswick, NJ 08906-1406. For information call 732-744-1370 (day). *Website:* http://www.gaypasg.org *Email:* gaypasg@att.net

Lambda Families of New Jersey Provides support, advocacy and education for gay and lesbian parents, their families and prospective parents. Social activities, quarterly newsletter. Membership dues $20/yr. Write: Lambda Families

quarterly newsletter. Membership dues $20/yr. Write: Lambda Families of NJ, PO Box 4385, Maplewood, NJ, 07040. For further information call 973-763-8511 (day/eve). *Website:* http://www.lambdafamiliesofnj.org *Email:* info@lambdafamiliesofnj.org

ATLANTIC

Gay, Lesbian, Transgendered, Bisexual Support Group Mutual support for persons with mental illness who are struggling with their own sexual identity. Goal is to share feelings and discuss barriers to a healthy relationship in a non-judgmental, caring atmosphere. Guest speakers, social activities, phone help, advocacy, literature and educational series. Meets 1st Sun., 1-2pm (social hour); 2-4pm (support group), ICE Self-Help Center, 611 Doughty Rd., Pleasantville. Call Leslie 609-272-0928.

BERGEN

P-FLAG (Parents, Families and Friends of Lesbians and Gays) Support and discussion groups to help people understand and accept homosexuality. Educates society and advocates for full human rights for all, regardless of sexual orientation. Speakers, newsletter, phone help. Membership dues $30/yr (includes monthly newsletter). All welcome. Meets 3rd Tues., 8pm, (7:30pm newcomers), Washington Twp. Call 201-287-0318 (eve). *Website:* http://www.pflag-bergennj.org *Email:* info@pflag-bergennj.org

Straight Spouse Support Network Supports anyone whose current or former partner/spouse is gay, lesbian, transgender or bisexual. Mutual sharing, rap sessions, resources, phone help, regular email correspondence and newsletter (3 times/yr). Donations accepted. Meets 2nd Fri., 6:30-9pm, 61 North Bayard Lane, Mahwah. Call Kathryn Callori 201-825-7512 (eve). *Website:* http://www.ssnetwk.org. *Email:* SSSNNJ@aol.com

CAMDEN

South Jersey Lesbians of Color Discussion and social support group for lesbians of color (age 21+) in Southern New Jersey. Rap sessions, socials and guest speakers. Dues $3 per meeting. Meets 3rd Fri., 7:30-9:30pm, The Starting Point, 215 Highland Ave., Suite C, Westmont. Call Stephanie 856-465-6186 (eve). *Email:* SJLOC-owner@yahoogroups.com

Can't find an appropriate group in your area? The Clearinghouse helps people start groups. Give us a call at 1-800-367-6274.

CAPE MAY

Gables of Cape May County Provides support to gays, lesbians and bisexuals, as well as their family and friends. Rap sessions, guest speakers, newsletter. Dues $20/yr. Meets 1st and 3rd Mon., Cape May. Call 609-861-1848 (answer machine). *Website:* http://www.gablescapemay.com *Email:* gables00@email.com

ESSEX

Dignity Organization of lesbian, gay and bisexual Catholics, their family and friends. Socials and rap sessions. Meets 1st and 3rd Sun., 4pm, St. George's Episcopal Church, 550 Ridgewood Rd., Maplewood. Call 973-857-4040 (day). *Email:* dignitymetronj@msn.com

GALY-NJ (Gay And Lesbian Youth in New Jersey) Mutual support for self-identified lesbian, gay or bisexual adolescents (ages 16-21). Meets weekly in Essex County. For information call Gay Activist Alliance in Morris County 973-285-1595 (eve).

P-FLAG (Parents, Families and Friends of Lesbians and Gays) Support and discussion group to help people understand and accept homosexuality. Educates society and advocates for full human rights for all, regardless of sexual orientation. Speakers, newsletter, phone help. All welcome. Membership dues $25/single; $35/family. Meets 2nd Sun., 2:30-4:30pm (newcomers 1:30pm), South Orange. Call P-FLAG hotline 973-267-8414. *Website:* www.pflagnorthjersey.org

HUDSON

GLITZ (Girls Living In the Transgender Zone) *(HUDSON COUNTY RESIDENTS ONLY)* Peer support for women dealing with transgender issues. Rap sessions, guest speakers, literature and phone help. Meets Tues., 6:30-8:30pm, Jersey City. Call Coy or Joanne 201-963-4779.

MERCER

"First and Third" *Professionally-run.* Educational and social support for gay, lesbian, bisexual and transgender youth. Rap sessions, phone help, guest speakers and mutual sharing. Meets 1st and 3rd Sat., 2:30-4:30pm, 21 Wiggins St., Princeton. Call Corrine 609-683-5155 ext. 17 (day). *Website:* http://www.hitops.org *Email:* corrine@hitops.org

While it's no substitution for talking to our staff, you can call evenings or weekends! Leave a message and we will get back to you the next workday. **1-800-367-6274**

465

MIDDLESEX

Lesbian/Bisexual Women in Heterosexual Marriages Support for lesbian/bisexual women who are married to men to deal with feelings of loneliness, guilt and depression. Rap sessions. Meets 3rd Wed., 7:30pm, The Pride Center of NJ, 1048 Livingston Ave., North Brunswick. For meeting information call 732-846-2232. *Website:* http://www.pridecenter.org *Email:* info@pridecenter.org

Lesbians and Gay Men of New Brunswick Social and educational group for lesbian women and gay men. Guest speakers, social activities. Meetings $2 donation. Meets 2nd and 4th Tues., 8pm, The Pride Center, 1048 Livingston Ave., North Brunswick. Call 732-846-2232. *Website:* http://www.pridecenter.org *Email:* njrj@aol.com

Men's Coming Out Rap Group Assists men dealing with issues pertaining to coming out. Dues $2. Meets Wed., 7:30-9pm, The Pride Center, 1048 Livingston Ave., North Brunswick. Call Gary P. 732-846-2232 (day). *Website:* http://www.pridecenter.org *Email:* info@pridecenter.org

Orthodykes - NJ *Professionally-run.* Mutual support for Orthodox Jewish lesbians as they attempt to integrate these two identities. Rap sessions and newsletter. Dues $3. Meets 1st Sun., 7:30-8:30pm, Pride Center of NJ, 1048 North Brunswick Ave., North Brunswick. Call Elissa 732-650-1010 (mailbox # 5). *Email:* info@njhav.org

OWLs (Older Wilder Lesbians) Group of mature lesbians who meet for support and socialization. Meets 3rd Fri., 8pm, The Pride Center, 1048 Livingston Ave., North Brunswick. Call 732-846-2232 (day). *Website:* http://www.pridecenter.org *Email:* info@pridecenter.org

Together We Can Support and social group for the lesbian, gay, bisexual, transgender and intersex community age (18+). Provides a safe, honest, open and supportive setting for people dealing with all types of issues. Meets Tues., 7-8:30pm, The Pride Center of NJ, 1048 Livingston Ave., North Brunswick. Call Patricia Hepp, MSW 732-846-2232 or Robert Lord-Taylor, PhD. 732-220-9137. *Website:* http://www.pridecenter.org *Email:* info@pridecenter.org

Under the Rainbow Support and socials for lesbian, gay, bisexual, transgendered, intersexed and questioning young adults (age 18-25). Meets 1st Wed., 7:30-9pm, The Pride Center, 1048 Livingston Ave., North Brunswick. Call 732-846-2232. *Website:* http://www.pridecenter.org *Email:* info@pridecenter.org

Youth Drop-In Center Support and socials for lesbian, gay, bisexual, transgendered, intersexed and questioning youth (age 17 and under) and their allies. Meets 2nd and 4th Sat., Pride Center, 1048 Livingston Ave., North Brunswick. Call 732-846-2232. *Website:* http://www.pridecenter.org *Email:* info@pridecenter.org

Women's Peer Support Group Social discussion and support for women. Meets 2nd and 4th Thurs., 7:30pm, The Pride Center, 1048 Livingston Ave., North Brunswick. Call 732-846-2232. *Website:* http://www.pridecenter.org *Email:* info@pridecenter.org

MORRIS

Gay Activist Alliance in Morris County Educates the lesbian and gay community through speakers and programs, socials, political involvement. Monthly newsletter, speakers' bureau. Publishes resource book. Membership $40/yr. Dues $4/member; $6/non-member. Meets Mon., 8:30pm, (7:30pm separate discussion groups for men/women), Morristown Unitarian Fellowship, 21 Normandy Heights Rd., Morristown. Call Helpline 973-285-1595 (leave message). *Website:* http://www.gaamc.org *Email:* info@gaamc.org

OCEAN

Gay and Lesbian Senior Support Group Mutual support for lesbian and gay seniors (age 50+) to share common concerns and challenges to reduce sense of isolation. Meets 2nd and 4th Thurs., 5-6:30pm, The Lighthouse, 599 Route 37 West, Toms River. Call 1-800-621-0096 (day).

P-FLAG (Parents, Families and Friends of Lesbians and Gays) *Jersey Shore Chapter* Support and discussion group to help people understand and accept variance in sexual orientation and gender identity. Speakers, literature and phone help. All welcome. Meets 2nd Wed., 7-9pm, United Church of Christ, 1681 Ridgeway Rd., (Route 571), Toms River. Call 732-408-1745 (day). *Website:* http://www.jerseyshorepflag.org *Email:* jerseyshorepflag@yahoo.com

SOMERSET

Transit Fellowship of transsexual men and women who share their experience, strength and hope with each other, that they may solve their common problems and help others heal from the effects of gender identity conflicts. Offers an informal support group. Meets Sun., 1pm, in Bridgewater. For directions call Dr. Aviva Sinvany Nubel 908-722-9884 (day). *Email:* avivanubel@yahoo.com *Website:* http://www.tgdoctor.com

NATIONAL

COLAGE (Children Of Lesbians And Gays Everywhere) *International. 40 affiliated groups. Founded 1990.* Mission is to connect and empower people to make the world better for children of lesbian, gay, bisexual and transgender parents. Information and referrals, conferences, pen pals, literature, newsletter. Various online programs. Write: COLAGE, 3543 18th St., Suite 1, San Francisco, CA 94110. Call 415-861-5437; Fax: 415-255-8345. *Website:* http://www.colage.org *Email:* colage@colage.org

COURAGE *International. Over 95 groups. Founded 1980.* Provides spiritual support and fellowship for men and women with same-sex attractions who are striving to live chaste lives in accordance with the Roman Catholic Church's teachings. The companion group, EnCourage, is for families and friends of persons with same-sex attractions. Newsletter, phone help, conferences, assistance in starting groups. Write: COURAGE, c/o St. John the Baptist, 210 W. 31st St., New York, NY 10001. Call 212-268-1010. *Website:* http://www.couragerc.net *Email:* NYCourage@aol.com

Dignity/USA *National. 50 chapters. Founded 1969.* Organization of gay, lesbian, bisexual & transgendered Catholics, their families and friends. Concerned with spiritual development, feminism, education & advocacy. Newsletter and chapter development guidelines. Write: Dignity/USA, 1500 Massachusetts Ave., NW, #08, Washington, DC 20005. Call 1-800-877-8797; Fax: 202-429-9808. *Website:* http://www.dignityusa.org *Email:* info@dignityusa.org

Family Pride Coalition *National. 160+ local groups. Founded 1979.* Support, education and advocacy for gay, lesbian and transgendered parents and prospective parents and their families. Information and referrals, phone support, family events, literature. Newsletter. Assistance in starting groups. Write: Family Pride Coalition, PO Box 65327, Washington, DC 20035-5327. Call 202-331-5015; Fax: 202-331-0080. *Website:* http://www.familypride.org *Email:* info@familypride.org

Homosexuals Anonymous *National. 55 chapters. Founded 1980.* Christian fellowship of men and women who have chosen to help each other to live free from homosexuality. Group support through weekly meetings. Online groups. Write: Homosexuals Anonymous, PO Box 7881, Reading, PA 19603. Call 610-779-2500 or 1-800-288-HAFS. *Website:* http://members.aol.com/hawebpage

International Foundation for Gender Education *International. Founded 1987.* Support and educational services for and about gender variant persons (including transsexuals, cross-dressers, intersex, androgynes, non-gendered and multi-gendered persons). Services include referrals to local support groups and to medical and psychological professionals. Speakers program, publication of "Transgender Tapestry" magazine, synchronicity bookstore and national outreach. Write: IFGE, PO Box 540229, Waltham, MA, 02454-0229. Call 781-899-2212; Fax: 781-899-5703. *Website:* http://www.ifge.org *Email:* info@ifge.org

National Gay & Lesbian Task Force *National. Founded 1973.* Advocates and organizes for the rights of gay, lesbian, bisexual and transgendered people. Technical assistance for state and local organizers. Write: National Gay & Lesbian Task Force, 1325 Massachusetts Ave., NW, Suite 600, Washington, DC 20005. Call 202-393-5177; Fax: 202-393-2241; TDD/TTY: 202-393-2284. *Website:* http://www.thetaskforce.org *Email:* ngltf@ngltf.org

P-FLAG (Parents, Families and Friends of Lesbians and Gays) *International. 490 chapters worldwide. Founded 1981.* Helps families understand and accept gay, lesbian, bisexual and transgendered family members. Offers help in strengthening families, support groups for families & friends, educational outreach, newsletter, chapter development guidelines, grassroots advocacy, information and referrals. Also has a Transgender Network. Write: P-FLAG, 1726 M Street, NW, Suite 400, Washington, DC 20036. Call 202-467-8180 or 216-691-4357; Fax: 202-467-8194. *Website:* http://www.pflag.org *Email:* info@pflag.org

Rainbow Room *Model. Founded 1979.* Adult-facilitated support group for gay, lesbian, bisexual, transgender and questioning youth (age 13-21). Provides a safe space for youth to talk about the issues that affect their daily lives. Write: Rainbow Room, c/o Hartford Gay & Lesbian Health Collective, PO Box 2094, Hartford, CT 06145-2094. Call 860-278-4163; Fax: 860-278-5995. *Email:* info@hglhc.org

Renaissance Transgender Association, Inc. *National. 6 chapters and 6 affiliates. Founded 1987.* Mutual support for both transvestites and transsexuals. Provides education about transgender issues for the public and the transgender community. Networking with other support groups, information and referrals, phone support, pen pals. Assistance in starting new groups. Write: Renaissance Transgender Association, 987 Old Eagle School Rd., Suite 719, Wayne, PA 19087. Call 610-975-9119; Fax: 610-971-0144. *Website:* http://www.ren.org *Email:* info@ren.org

Straight Spouse Network *International network. 75 groups & 61 state/country contacts. Founded 1992.* Confidential personal support network of current or former heterosexual spouses or partners of gay, lesbian, bisexual or transgender mates. Helps straight spouses or partners cope constructively with the coming-out crisis and assists spouses, mixed-orientation couples and their children build bridges of understanding. Resource information, referrals and newsletter.

Guideline available for starting new groups. Numerous confidential internet lists. Write: SSN, 8215 Terrace Dr., El Cerrito, CA 94530-3058. Call 510-525-0200. *Website:* http://www.straightspouse.org

SHORT / TALL
(see also specific disorder)

STATEWIDE

Little People of America - Garden State Chapter Mutual support for short-statured people (infants - adults) and parents of short-statured children. Guest speakers, social get-togethers and fund-raisers. Spring and Fall regional conferences and national conventions. Dues $50/yr. per household. Call Helen Finkle 732-780-3827 or Robin Thibault 973-822-3665 (day/eve). *Website:* http://www.lpaonline.org

NATIONAL

Growth Hormone Deficiency Support Network *National network. Founded 1989.* Network and exchange of information for families of children with growth hormone deficiency disorders. Information and referrals, phone support, pen pals, conferences, literature, annual convention and membership newsletter ($30/yr). Write: Growth Hormone Deficiency Support Network, c/o MAGIC Foundation, 6645 W. North Ave., Oak Park, IL 60302. Call 1-800-3-MAGIC-3 or 708-383-0808; Fax: 708-383-0899. *Website:* http://www.magicfoundation.org *Email:* mary@magicfoundation.org

Human Growth Foundation *National. 31 chapters. Founded 1965.* Local groups provide members the opportunity to meet other parents of children with growth-related disorders. Monthly & quarterly newsletter. Parent-to-parent support and networking program. Annual conference. Also offers online support list for parents and adults. Write: Human Growth Foundation, 997 Glen Cove Ave., Glen Head, NY 11545-1564. Call 516-671-4041 or 1-800-451-6434; Fax: 516-671-4055. *Website:* http://www.hgfound.org *Email:* hgf1@hgfound.org

MAGIC Foundation for Children's Growth *National network. Founded 1989.* Provides public education and networking for families of children with growth-related disorders. Includes 11 divisions including growth hormone deficiency, congenital adrenal hyperplasia, Turner's syndrome, precocious puberty, McCune Albright syndrome, panhypopituitarism, adult growth hormone deficiency, Russell Silver Syndrome, thyroid disorders, chronic renal insufficiencies and septo optic dysplasia. Information & referrals, phone support, pen pals, annual convention and conferences. Newsletters for children and adults. Write: The MAGIC Foundation for Children's Growth, 6645 W. North Ave, Oak Park, IL. 60302. Call 1-800-362-4423; Fax: 708-383-0899. *Website:* http://www.magicfoundation.org *Email:* mary@magicfoundation.org

Little People of America *(BILINGUAL) National. 68 chapters. Founded 1957.* Provides mutual support to people of short stature (4'10" and under) and their families. Information on physical and developmental concerns, employment, education and disability rights, medical issues, adaptive devices, etc. Newsletter. Provides educational scholarships and medical assistance grants, access to medical advisory board, assistance in adoption. Local, regional and national conferences and athletic events. Online chat room, listserv. Dues $50/year; $10/seniors; $500/lifetime. Write: LPA, 5289 NE Elam Young Parkway, Suite F-100, Hillsboro OR 97124-6440. Call 1-888-572-2001. *Website:* http://www.lpaonline.org *Email:* info@lpaonline.org

Tall Clubs International *International. 65+ groups. Founded 1938.* Social support for tall persons, (men at least 6'2", women at least 5'10"). Also advocacy for clothing & other special needs of tall people. Skywriters and TALLrific for persons under 21. Group development guidelines, information & referrals, conferences, newsletters and social gatherings. Write: Tall Clubs International, PO Box 1811, Cincinnati, OH 45201. Call 1-888-468-2552. *Website:* http://www.tall.org

SINGLES
(see also separation / divorce, widowhood)

CAMDEN

Friendly Singles Fifty Plus Club, Inc. Provides social activities for singles, age 50 and over. Barbeques, house parties, bus trips, dances, hay rides, weenie roasts. Dues $20/yr. Dances $7/members; $8/non-members. Meets Fri., 8-11pm, VFW, Chestnut Ave., Berlin. Call Lori 856-228-1039 (day).

ESSEX

Single in the Suburbs Mutual support for single women. Groups start periodically and run for 6 weeks. Registration fee $45. Meets at Linda and Rudy Slucker NCJW Center for Women, 513 West Mount Pleasant Ave., Suite 325, Livingston. Call Project GRO 973-994-4994. *Website:* http://www.centerforwomennj.org *Email:* centerforwomen@ncjwessex.org

GLOUCESTER

Joyful Singles Provides a safe environment where singles over the age of 35 can find trust, support, significance and purpose through discussions, encouragement, accountability and prayer. Meets Thurs., 7-8:30pm, Hope House, Lincoln Ave., Pitman. Call JoAnne 856-863-0401 or Jim 856-256-0940.

SOMERSET

Single Senior Women Support for women (age 60+) who are divorced, separated, widowed, never married or have a spouse who is ill. Recreational activities. Meets 2nd and 4th Thurs., 10am-noon, Office on Aging, 92 East Main St., Somerville. Call Erin 908-704-6339 (day).

SPEECH / STUTTERING
(see also specific disorder, toll-free helplines)

STATEWIDE

Toastmasters International Mutual help for people to improve speaking skills, express themselves more effectively and to gain confidence. For those who are hesitant to speak before an audience. Membership fees. Monthly magazine. For location of the nearest group check their website: http://www.toastmasters.org

BERGEN

Speak Easy International Foundation, Inc. Self-help group for people who stutter. Must have speech dysfunction or phobia. Phone network, peer-counseling, newsletter, yearly conference. Dues $80/yr. Meets alternate Tues., 7:30pm, Cerebral Palsy Center, Fair Lawn. Call Bob 201-262-0895.

Toastmasters International Mutual support for people to improve speaking skills, express themselves more effectively and to gain confidence. For those who are hesitant to speak before an audience.

> **Haworth – Valley Chapter** Dues $70 (includes workbook and monthly magazine). Meets 1st and 3rd Mon., 8-10pm, First Congregational United Church of Christ, 276 Haworth Ave. Call Don Kaufman 201-784-0826 (eve).
> **Ramsey – Park Chapter** Dues $44/yr. Meets 2nd and 4th Fri., 7:15pm, Ramsey Library, 30 Wyckoff Ave. Call Frank Lomonaco 201-337-5496 (day/eve). *Website:* http://www.geocities.com/parkvped
> **Rutherford** Dues $24/semi-yearly. Meets Sat. (except July and Aug.), 9-11am, Rutherford Public Library, Park Ave. and Chestnut St. Call

Sylvia Schaja 973-773-4998 (day). *Website:* http://www.toastmaster.org *Email:* fairleighearlybirds@yahoo.com

CAMDEN

National Stuttering Association - New Jersey Division To provide support to and promote fluency for stutterers. Meets 2nd and 4th Thurs., 7-9pm, John F. Kennedy Hospital, Stratford. Call Kathy Filer 609-706-4098. *Website:* http://www.nsastutter.org *Email:* katfiler@aol.com

CAPE MAY

Toastmasters International *Boardwalk Chapter* - Support and education to improve communication, leadership, social and public speaking skills. Dues $56/yr.; $21 initiation. Meets 1st and 3rd Wed., Chatterbox Restaurant, Ninth and Central Ave., Ocean City. Call Ted Armstrong or Karol Armstrong 856-691-7748 (day) or Rich Catando 609-652-9169 (day). *Website:* http://www.boardwalktoastmasters.org *Email:* armstrong@tedkarol.com

ESSEX

Speak Easy Toastmasters Club Provides mutual support and a positive learning environment in order for members to develop communication and leadership skills. Meets 1st and 3rd Thurs., 12:30-1:30pm, Formosa Plastics Corp., Training Room, 9 Peach Tree Hill Rd., Livingston. Call Prokopis 973-716-7284 (day). *Website:* http://www.27.brinkster.com/njtoastmasters/

MERCER

First Amendment of Princeton Meets to practice air-flow speech technique to overcome stuttering. Under 18 welcome. Prior speech therapy required. Meets odd Mon., 7:30pm, Princeton Medical Center, Merwick Unit, Rt. 206, Princeton. Call Elliot Dennis 609-275-3806 (day/eve). *Email:* elliotdennis@yahoo.com

UNION

Summit Toastmasters Support and education to improve communication, leadership, social and public speaking skills. Guest speakers and speakers' bureau. Dues $34 twice a year. Meets Wed., 8-10pm, St. John's Church, 587 Springfield Ave., Summit. Call Kevin Moulton 1-877-854-5014 (day). *Website:* http://www.summittoastmasters.com *Email:* info@summittoastmaters.com

NATIONAL

International Foundation for Stutterers, Inc. *International. 6 chapters. Founded 1980.* Aims to eliminate stuttering through speech therapy in conjunction with self-help groups. Education for public & professionals about stuttering & self-help. Newsletter, speakers, phone help system, guidelines on forming self-help groups. Write: Int'l Foundation for Stutterers, 304 Hampshire Dr., Plainsboro, NJ 08536. Call Elliot Dennis 609-275-3806 (eve). *Email:* elliotdennis@yahoo.com

National Stuttering Association *National 80 groups. Founded 1977.* Provides information about stuttering. Self-help chapter meetings provide supportive environment where people who stutter can learn to communicate more effectively. Network of groups. Referrals, advocacy, monthly newsletter, group development guidelines. Dues $35; $20 (senior, student, low income). Write: National Stuttering Association, 119 West 40th St., 14th Floor, New York, NY 10018. Call 1-800-364-1677; Fax: 212-944-8244. *Website:* http://www.WeStutter.org *Email:* info@WeStutter.org

Speak Easy International Foundation, Inc. *International. 6 chapters. Founded 1977.* Self-help group for adult and adolescent stutterers. Must have speech dysfunction or phobia. Phone network, peer counseling, newsletter. Offers assistance in starting new groups. Annual national symposium and Fall retreat. Dues $80/yr. Write: Speak Easy Int'l, c/o Bob Gathman, 233 Concord Dr., Paramus, NJ 07652. Call Bob 201-262-0895. *Email:* speakezusa@juno.com

Toastmasters International *International. 10,000 chapters. Founded 1924.* Mutual help for people to improve speaking and leadership skills, to express themselves more effectively and to gain confidence. For those who are hesitant to speak before an audience. Leadership training. Membership fees. Monthly magazine. Write: Toastmasters Int'l, PO Box 9052, Mission Viejo, CA 92690-7052. Call 949-858-8255; Fax: 949-858-1207. *Website:* http://www.toastmasters.org *Email:* tminfo@toastmasters.org

U.S. Society for Augmentative & Alternative Communication *National. 30 affiliated groups. Founded in 1986.* Addresses the needs of persons who are severely speech impaired or unable to speak. Works to improve services and products. Dues $63 (includes newsletter). Information and referrals, conferences, advocacy, literature, networking. Write: USSAAC, 15 West 72nd St., Suite 10-B, New York, NY 10023. Call 917-743-4640. *Website:* http://ussaac.org *Email:* info@ussaac.org

If someone listens or stretches out a hand or whispers a kind word of encouragement or attempts to understand a lonely person, extraordinary things begin to happen. Loretta Girzatlis

ONLINE

Latetalkers *Online.* Email group to discuss developmental speech delays caused by apraxia, dyspraxia, phonological disorders, autism spectrum disorders, learning disabilities or other causes. Aim is to help children attain intelligible speech. Open to families, speech language pathologists, medical professionals, students and educators. *Website:* http://groups.yahoo.com/group/latetalkers

SPIRITUALITY / MEDITATION

ESSEX

Spiritual Sisters With a Purpose *(WOMEN ONLY)* A spiritual support group to help members lift each other up and find a purpose to connect their spirits to a higher power. Meets 4th Sat., 5-7pm, 827 So. 14th St., Newark. Before attending call Deborah 973-596-0896 (eve) or Yvonne 973-313-9329 (eve). *Email:* millard43@msn.com

Spirituality Group Support for mental health consumers fostering an awareness of spirituality and a sense of being a part of a much larger powerful entity. Offers mutual sharing, education, rap sessions, social, phone help and advocacy. Meets Thurs., 5-6pm, Where Peaceful Waters Flow, 3-5 Vose Ave., 2nd Floor, South Orange. Call Celine or Jacqueline 973-762-7469 (eve).

TRAUMA
(see also specific disorder / event)

ONLINE

Gift From Within *Online. (WOMEN ONLY)* Offers a one-on-one email/pen pal support network for women with post traumatic stress disorder. Female victims of specific trauma are matched with survivors of similar traumas. *Website:* http://www.giftfromwithin.org *Email:* joyceb3955@aol.com

Trauma Anonymous *Online.* Provides information on trauma and post-traumatic stress disorder. Information on symptoms and treatment. Chat rooms for veterans, victims of domestic violence and survivors of sexual abuse. Message board for victims. *Website:* http://www.bein.com/trauma/index.html

"Trauma survivors... they become thrivers, and they become teachers. They can go back and remember various things, and answer all those questions we have. They have hope, and they have sense, and the ability to care about other people... to look into the eyes of others who have gone through the things that they have gone through, and to be at peace with that, and to show that they did it." Dr. Charles R. Figley

VETERANS / MILITARY
(see also toll-free helplines)

STATEWIDE

Vet Center Support Groups *Professionally-run. Four Veteran Centers.* Support groups and related services for both combat veterans of all wars (Iraq, Afghan, Vietnam, WWII) and their families to deal with PTSD and other readjustment issues. Write: Ann Talmage, Newark Vet Center, 2 Broad St., Suite 703, Bloomfield, NJ 07003. For group types and times, contact the closest center: Newark (Essex) 973-748-0980 Jersey City (Hudson) 201-748-4467; Trenton (Mercer) 609-989-2260; Ventnor (Atlantic) 609-487-8387. *Website:* http://www.va.gov/rcs *Email:* ann.talmage@med.va.gov

HUDSON

M.A.C.A.N. (Marine, Army, Coast Guard, Air Force, Navy) Mutual support for anyone who has a loved one serving in the military. Family and friends welcome. Rap sessions, guest speakers and phone help. Meetings vary, Community Crossing, 488 Broadway, Bayonne. Before attending call Ronnie Lehman 201-339-8055 (day/eve).

HUNTERDON

Balkan Military Support Group Informal support network for Hunterdon County families and friends of American troops in Bosnia and staging areas. For information call 908-782-6722. *Email:* nhnn@hotmail.com

East Amwell Operation Desert Shield Support Groups Mutual support for soldiers who served in the Gulf and their families. For meeting information call Teddie 908-782-6722.

MIDDLESEX

Army and Air National Guard Family Support Offers support for any family member of military personnel. Mutual support to discuss or share any issues of concern. Family member does not have to be on active duty. For meeting information call 732-937-6290.

> **We are all dependent on one another,**
> **every soul of us on earth.**
> **-- George Bernard Shaw**

NATIONAL

Blinded Veterans Association *National. 55 regional groups. Founded 1945.* Information, support and outreach to blinded veterans, including those who were blinded in combat and those suffering from age-related macular degeneration and other eye diseases. Help in obtaining prosthetic devices and accessing the latest technological advances to assist the blind. Information on benefits and rehabilitation programs. Quarterly newsletter. Regional meetings. Write: BVA, 477 H St., NW, Washington, DC 20001 Call 202-371-8880 or 1-800-669-7079; Fax: 202-371-8258. *Website:* http://www.bva.org *Email:* bva@bva.org

EX-POSE (Ex-Partners of Servicemembers for Equality) *National membership. Founded 1981.* Lobbies for changes in military divorce laws. Disseminates information concerning military divorce. Lawyer referral. Quarterly newsletter. Publishes "Guide for Military Separation & Divorce." Membership dues $15. Write: EX-POSE, PO Box 11191, Alexandria, VA 22312. Call 703-941-5844 (day); Fax: 703-212-6951. *Website:* http://www.ex-pose.org *Email:* ex-pose@juno.com

National Gulf War Resource Center, Inc. *National. 61 affiliated groups. Founded 1995.* Supports the efforts of grassroots organizations that assist veterans affected by the Persian Gulf War illnesses. Conducts research into the causes of Gulf War syndrome. Information & referrals, media assistance, provides congressional testimony, advocacy, literature, self-help guides. Write: National Gulf War Resource Center, 8605 Cameron St., Suite 400, Silver Spring, MD 20910. Call 1-800-882-1316 ext. 162 or 301-585-4000 ext. 162; Fax: 301-585-3180. *Website:* http://www.ngwrc.org *Email:* srobinson@ngwrc.org

Paralyzed Veterans of America *National. Chapters nationwide. Founded 1946.* To ensure that spinal cord injured or diseased veterans achieve the highest quality of life possible. Membership is available solely to individuals who are American citizens who suffer from spinal cord dysfunction as a result of trauma or disease. Must have served on active duty and had anything other than dishonorable discharge. Write: PVA, 801 18th St. NW, Washington, DC 20006. Call 202-872-1300. *Website:* http://www.pva.org *Email:* info@pva.org

Society of Military Widows *National. 27 chapters. Founded 1968.* Support & assistance for widows/widowers of members of all U.S. uniformed services. Help in coping with adjustment to life on their own. Promotes public awareness. Bi-monthly magazine/journal. Dues $12. Chapter development guidelines. Online listing on local chapters. Write: Society of Military Widows, 5535 Hempstead Way, Springfield, VA 22151. Call 253-750-1342 or 1-800-842-3451 (press 5). *Website:* http://www.militarywidows.org *Email:* h.grant@naus.org

TAPS (Tragedy Assistance Program for Survivors) *National network.* Provides support for persons who have lost a loved one while serving in any armed forces Also TAPS youth programs. Write: TAPS, 1621 Connecticut Ave. NW, Suite 300, Washington, DC 20009. Call 1-800-959-8277 or 202-588-8277; Fax: 202-588-0784. *Website:* http://www.taps.org *Email:* info@taps.org

Vietnam Veterans of America, Inc. *National. 600 chapters. Founded 1978.* Devoted to the needs and concerns of Vietnam era veterans and their families. Provides leadership and advocacy in all areas that have an impact on veterans, with an emphasis on Agent Orange related problems and post traumatic stress disorder. Bimonthly newspaper. Write: VVA, 8605 Cameron St., Suite 400, Silver Spring, MD 20910-3710. Call 1-800-882-1316 or 301-585-4000; Fax: 301-585-0519. *Website:* http://www.vva.org

ONLINE

Kathy's Military Links *Online resource.* Lists about 150 online sites for family members of military. In addition to many online groups for wives, mothers and girlfriends of those in the military, other listed groups address special situations, such as pregnant marine wives or interracial military marriages. *Website:* http://geocities.com/kathysmilitarylinks/mom.html

Marine Moms *Online.* Email discussion forum. Offers support, information, questions, answers and chat room. There is also a forum for dads. *Website:* http://mmo.proboards10.com/index.cgi

Soldier Moms *Online.* Support group for moms with adult children in any branch of the military service. Opportunity to share news, pain, joy and encouragement. *Website:* http://www.geocities.com/soldiermoms/

Support4militarywives *Online.* Support for military wives. Provides online chat room and some useful links. *Website:* http://www.groups.yahoo.com/group/support4militarywives/

WOMEN'S ISSUES
(see also toll-free helplines)

STATEWIDE

N.O.W. - N.J. (National Organization for Women of N.J.) Political advocacy for women's equality in society. Dedicated to eliminating sexism and racism. Political advocacy for reproductive rights, older women's rights, homemakers rights, women in the work force, lesbian rights, etc. Dues $35/yr. Write: N.O.W - NJ, 110 W. State St., Trenton, NJ 08608-1102. Call 609-393-0156 (day). *Website:* http://www.nownj.org *Email:* NOW-NJ@nownj.org

CAMDEN

Hispanic Women's Resource Center *(BILINGUAL)* Support to meet the needs of Latina women. Offers support to displaced homemakers. Job readiness, job counseling, job training a variety of support groups and referrals. Meetings vary. Call Altie 856-365-7393 (day). *Email:* hfcwrc123@aol.com

ESSEX

Project G.R.O. Various support groups dealing with women's issues (including marriage, separation/divorce, women living alone, parenting, self-esteem, aging parents, widows, singles, etc). Groups start periodically and run for 6 weeks. Registration fee $45. Meets at Linda and Rudy Slucker NCJW Center for Women, 513 West Mt. Pleasant Ave., Suite 325, Livingston. Call Project Gro 973-994-4994. *Website:* http://www.centerforwomennj.org *Email:* centerforwomen@ncjwessex.org

Women Adjusting to a New Country and Culture To help women connect with others facing the challenge of a new and different culture. Topics covered language difficulties and seeing children think, dress and behave in a new way. Group meets periodically and runs for 6 weeks. Meets 7:30-9pm, Linda and Rudy Slucker NCJW Center for Women, 513 West Mt. Pleasant Ave., Suite 325, Livingston. Call Center for Women 973-994-4994 (day).

Women Coping With Loneliness Support for women's concerns about their feelings of loneliness. Group meets periodically for 6 weeks. Registration fee $45. Meets various days, Linda and Rudy Slucker NCJW Center for Women, 513 West Mt. Pleasant Ave., Livingston. Call Center for Women 973-994-4994. *Website:* http://www.centerforwomennj.org *Email:* centerforwomen@ncjwessex.org

GLOUCESTER

Center for People in Transition *Professionally-run.* Assists displaced homemakers to become emotionally and economically self-sufficient through life skills training, career decision making, education or vocational training and supportive services. Evening divorce and bereavement support groups for men and women. For information call 856-415-2222 (Mon.-Fri.). *Email:* peopleintransition@gccnj.edu

Women's Co-Dependent/God-Dependent Safe place where women are free to talk, feel, trust God and one another for any dysfunction, past or present or co-dependent issues that effects them. Educational series. Meets Wed., (except Aug.), 7-8:30pm, St. John's United Methodist Church, 149 Ganttown Rd., Turnersville. Call Rosemary 856-869-0084 (eve). *Website:* http://www.addvicinc.org *Email:* AddVicInc.@aol.com

HUDSON

Women's Project Groups *Professionally-run.* Education, support, workshops and groups to help women on subjects such as assertiveness, separation/divorce, self-esteem, relaxation, parenting, along with stress management. Meets various days and times, Christ Hospital, 176 Palisade Ave., Jersey City. Call Michele Bernstein 201-795-8375 ext. 8416 (day).

HUNTERDON

Career and Life Planning Center *Professionally-run.* Offers support and assistance to displaced homemakers. Education, mutual sharing, guest speakers, literature, newsletter. Meets various days, both days and evenings, Educational Services Commission, Sandhill School Campus, 215 Rt. 31, Flemington. Call Denise Brown Kahney 908-788-1453 (day). *Website:* http://www.dhnnj.org/DHN2/index.htm *Email:* dbrownkahney@hcesc.com

MERCER

Latinas Unidas *(SPANISH) Professionally-run.* Support and education for Latina women. Rap sessions, guest speakers, phone help, information, referrals and short term counseling. Lunch, transportation and child care provided on Fridays. Meets Mon.-Fri., in the Trenton area. Call 609-396-3040 (day) or 609-396-8291 ext. 14 *Email:* cweeast@ywcatrenton.org

MIDDLESEX

Women Helping Women in Metuchen Offers various self-help support groups for women dealing with such issues as separation and divorce, self-esteem, mid-life, exploring your marriage and co-dependency. Groups meet weekly and run for 10 weeks. Dues $8/wk members; $10/wk non-members. Meets various days and times, Metuchen. Call Women Helping Women in Metuchen 732-549-6000 (day). *Website:* http://www.whwnj.com *Email:* helpline@whwnj.com

If you are using this book past Spring 2007, please call us for information about our most recent directory. 1-800-367-6274

MONMOUTH

Women's Support Group Helps women who are displaced homemakers (facing the loss of their primary source of income due to separation, divorce, disability or death of spouse). Issues addressed include self-sufficiency, career development, assertiveness, self-esteem, divorce, separation, widowhood and other related topics. Groups are set-up as needed in Asbury Park, Long Branch, Bayshore and Lincroft. Call Robin Vogel 732-495-4496 (day) or Mary Ann O'Brien 732-229-8675.

MORRIS

Familias en Paz *Professionally-run. (BILINGUAL)* Support group for Latino women who want to improve their personal life through education, insight and self-empowerment. Discusses issues such as domestic abuse, relationships and other issues of interest to women. Education, advocacy, guest speakers, literature and buddy system. Meets Mon., 7-9pm, Sister Catherine Health Center, 400 West Blackwell St., Dover. Call Alberto Olarte 973-625-7035 (day) or 201-919-4742 (eve) (after 9pm). *Email:* user9398@optonline.net

Morris County National Organization For Women Goals are to bring women into full participation in the mainstream of American society. Dues $15-35/yr. Meets 1st Tues., 7:30-9pm, Morris Plains. Call 973-285-1200 (day).

SUSSEX

Women's Self Enhancement Support Group *Professionally-run.* Support for women who want to make improvements in their personal lives. Meets Tues., (except June/July/Aug.), 7:30-9:30pm, Partnership for Social Services Family Center, 48 Wyker Rd., Franklin. Call Dr. Thomasina Gebhard 973-827-4702 (day).

UNION

Older Women's League (Voice of Mid-Life and Older Women) Education and advocacy focusing on the critical issues facing women as they age. Literature. Dues $35/yr. Meetings vary. Call Teresa 908-862-5454 ext. 124 (day).

WARREN

Transitions Center for Displaced Homemakers *Professionally-run.* Provides support services, vocational counseling and career training for displaced homemakers. For women who have lost their primary source of income due to divorce, separation, death or disability of her spouse. Meets various times, 108 East Washington Ave., Rt. 57, Washington. Call 908-835-2624 (day/eve).

481

NATIONAL

Business & Professional Women/USA *National. 2800 chapters. Founded 1919.* Organization comprised of working women, to promote workplace equity and provide networking opportunities. Lobbying efforts, tri-annual magazine, periodic publications, resource center and grassroots community action projects. Annual national convention. Local group information available online. Write: Business & Prof. Women/USA, 1900 M St., NW, Suite 310, Washington, DC 20036. Fax: 202-861-0298. *Website:* http://www.bpwusa.org *Email:* memberservices@bpwusa.org

Love-N-Addiction *International. 85 chapters. Founded 1986.* Explores how loving can become an addiction. Builds a healthy support system to aid in the recovery from addictive love into healthy love. Uses ideas from book "Women Who Love Too Much" by Robin Norwood. Chapter development guidelines ($15). Write: Love-N-Addiction, PO Box 759, Willimantic, CT 06226. Call Carolyn Meister 860-423-2344 (will return call collect or leave mailing address).

National Organization for Women *National. 500 chapters. Founded 1966.* NOW is an action organization that seeks social, political, economic and legal equity between women and men through grassroots organizing, lobbying, litigation, protests and demonstrations. Educational meetings, national newsletter. Chapter development guidelines. Write: NOW, 1100 H Street NW, Suite 300, Washington, DC 20005. Call 202-628-8669 202-331-9002; Fax: 202-785-8576. *Website:* http://www.now.org *Email:* now@now.org

Older Women's League *National. 60+ chapters. Founded 1980.* Membership organization that advocates on behalf of various economic & social issues for midlife & older women (social security, pension rights, employment, caregiver support, elder abuse, etc.). Newsletter, chapter development guidelines. Dues $25/yr. Write: OWL, 1750 New York Ave., NW, #350, Washington, DC 20006. Call 202-783-6686 or 1-800-825-3695; Fax: 202-628-0458. *Website:* http://www.owl-national.org *Email:* owlinfo@owl-national.org

SOWN (Supportive Older Women's Network) *Model. 50 groups in Philadelphia area. Founded 1982.* Helps women (60+) cope with their specialized aging concerns. Support groups, leadership training, consultation, telephone support, outreach and networking. Newsletter. Write: SOWN, 2805 N. 47th St., Philadelphia, PA 19131. Call 215-477-6000; Fax: 215-477-6555. *Website:* http://www.sown.org *Email:* info@sown.org

WORKAHOLICS

INTERNATIONAL

Workaholics Anonymous World Service Organization, Inc. *International. 30+ groups. Founded 1983.* 12-Step fellowship for men and women who feel their work lives have gotten out of control. Write: Workaholics Anonymous, PO Box 289, Menlo Park, CA 94026-0289. Call 510-273-9253. *Website:* http://www.workaholics-anonymous.org *Email:* wso@workaholics-anonymous.org

YOUTH / STUDENTS
(see also toll-free helplines)

CUMBERLAND

Pink Roses, Inc. Mutual support for young women age (12-18) to make better choices by sharing feelings, thoughts, problems and experiences. Families welcome. Rap sessions, guest speakers, literature, phone help and buddy system. Dues $1/mtg. Meets 2nd Mon., 6:30-8:30pm, Bridgeton. Call Janice 856-455-2099.

ESSEX

NULITES *Professionally-run.* Teen school-to-work program that provides leadership development, educational enrichment, cultural enhancement and exposure, community service and youth advocacy for teens. Employment readiness training. Meets Mon.-Fri., 3:30-5:30pm, Urban League of Essex County, 508 Central Ave., Newark. Call 973-624-9535 ext. 105 (day). *Website:* http://www.ulec.org *Email:* info@ulec.org

UNION

Youth Partnership Group Adult supervised activities for youth (age 13-21) with complex emotional, mental health or behavioral issues to help them express what they have been through and share concerns. Rap sessions. Meets 2nd and 4th Wed., 6:30-8:30pm, Family Support Organization, 137 Elmer St., Westfield. Call Kathy Wagner 908-789-7625 (day).

NATIONAL

SADD (Students Against Destructive Decisions) *National. 10,000 groups. Founded 1981.* Provides prevention and intervention tools to eliminate impaired driving, end underage drinking, drug abuse and other destructive

483

decisions. Offers community awareness programs, literature, sponsors SADD chapters. Group development guidelines. Write: SADD, PO Box 800, Marlboro, MA 01752, Call 1-877-723-3462 or 508-481-3568; Fax: 508-481-5759. *Website:* http://www.sadd.org *Email:* info@sadd.org

ONLINE

Pregnant Teen Support *Online* Email list support group for teens 12-20 years old who are facing an unplanned, unexpected or unwanted pregnancy. *Website:* http://health.groups.yahoo.com/group/Pregnant_Teen_Support

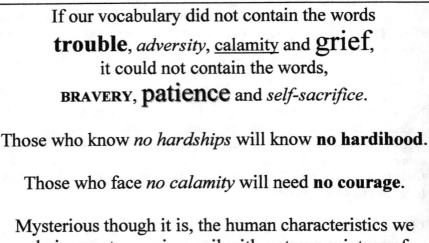

If our vocabulary did not contain the words
trouble, *adversity*, calamity and grief,
it could not contain the words,
BRAVERY, patience and *self-sacrifice*.

Those who know *no hardships* will know **no hardihood**.

Those who face *no calamity* will need **no courage**.

Mysterious though it is, the human characteristics we admire most grow in a soil with a strong mixture of trouble.

--Dale Turner

RARE ILLNESS

49XXXXY SYNDROME

49XXXXY *National network.* *Founded 1990.* Mutual support and networking for families affected by 49XXXXY disorder. Information, pen pals, phone support and newsletter. Write: 49XXXXY c/o Elise Watzka, 870 Miranda Green, Palo Alto, CA 94306. Call 650-941-2408. *Website:* http://klinefeltersyndrome.org/49er.htm *Email:* epwatzka@iname.com

AARSKOG SYNDROME

Aarskog Syndrome Parents Support Group *International network.* *Founded 1993.* Mutual support, networking and sharing of ideas for families of children and adults affected with Aarskog syndrome. Pen pal club, e-mail addresses and contact pages with mailing addresses for support via correspondence. Write: Aarskog Syndrome Family Support Group, c/o Shannon Caranci, 62 Robin Hill Lane, Levittown, PA 19055. Call Shannon Caranci 215-943-7131. *Email:* shannonfaith49@msn.com

ACIDEMIA

Organic Acidemia Association, Inc. *International.* *Founded 1982.* Support, information and networking for families affected by organic acidemia and related disorders. Advocates for newborn screening. Dues $25/yr. Internet listserv, family conferences, research information (http://www.mmaresearch.com)and tri-annual newsletter. Write: Organic Acidemia Association, c/o Kathy Stagni, 13210 35th Ave. North, Plymouth, MN 55441. Call 763-559-1797; TTY/TDD: 763-694-0017. *Website:* http://www.oaanews.org/ *Email:* oaanews@aol.com

ACID MALTASE DEFICIENCY (POMPE DISEASE)

Acid Maltase Deficiency Association *International network.* *Founded 1995.* Support and information for persons affected by Pompe disease (acid maltase deficiency). Newsletter, literature, information and referrals and phone support. Supports research into the cause and cure. Write: AMDA, PO Box 700248, San Antonio, TX 78270. Call 210-494-6144; Fax: 210-490-7161. *Website:* http://www.amda-pompe.org *Email:* tianrama@aol.com

485

ACNE SCARS

Acne Scar Support Group *Model. Founded 2001.* Goal is to share results from scar-revision procedures and to offer information about results for those interested in scar-revision. Offers a support group, phone support and e-mail pen pals. Write: Acne Scar Support Group, 5500 Friendship Blvd., Apt. 821, Chevy Chase, MD 20815-7258. Call Greg 301-718-0952. *Website:* http://www.geocities.com/grege20815/washdcacnescarsupportgrp.html *Email:* gregestrada@verizon.net

ADDISON'S/ADRENAL DISEASE

CAMDEN

Addison's Support Group Mutual support and information for those with Addison's disease. Rap sessions, literature, phone help and guest speakers. Meets Sat., 4 times/yr., St. Pius Parish Center, Kresson Rd., Cherry Hill. Call Janice Judge 856-354-6029 (day/eve) or Susanne Mee 856-764-6583 (day). *Email:* JanPT@aol.com

NATIONAL

National Adrenal Diseases Foundation *National. 29 affiliated groups. Founded 1984.* Dedicated to serving the needs of those with adrenal diseases and their families, especially through information, education and support. Quarterly newsletters, pamphlets and group development guidelines. Write: NADF, 505 Northern Blvd., Suite 200, Great Neck, NY 11021. Call 516-487-4992. *Website:* http://medhelp.org/nadf *Email:* nadfmail@aol.com

AGENESIS OF THE CORPUS CALLOSUM

ACC Network, The *International network. Founded 1989.* Helps individuals with agenesis (or other anomaly) of the corpus callosum, their families and professionals. Helps identify others who are experiencing similar issues to share information and support. Phone support, information, newsletter and referrals. Coordinates listserv, an electronic discussion group on the internet. Write: ACC Network, c/o University of Maine, 5749 Merrill Hall, Rm. 118, Orono, ME 04469-5749. Call 207-581-3119; TTY/TDD: 207-581-3120 *Email:* UM-ACC@maine.edu

Consider passing this Directory on to a student or staff member - browsing through the Directory pages can often provide helpful education as to the wide variety of groups available.

AICARDI SYNDROME / INFANTILE SPASMS
(see also epilepsy/seizure disorders)

Aicardi Syndrome Newsletter, Inc. *International network. 5 regional chapters. Founded 1983.* Support for families with children with Aicardi syndrome, a rare seizure disorder that affects primarily females and is characterized by seizures and retinal lesions. Information and referrals, resources, research projects. Biennial conferences, phone support network, research group, newsletters. Dues $25/year. Write: Aicardi Syndrome Newsletter, Inc., c/o Denise Park Parsons, 1510 Polo Fields Ct., Louisville, KY 40245. Call 502-244-9152. *Website:* http://www.aicardisyndrome.org *Email:* aicnews@aol.com

Infantile Spasms List *Online. Founded 1998.* Support and information for parents and caregivers of children with infantile spasms. Opportunity to discuss their children, treatment options and offer each other emotional support. Professionals welcomed. *Website:* http://health.groups.yahoo.com/group/infantilespasms

ALAGILLE SYNDROME

Alagille Syndrome Alliance *National network. Founded 1993.* Support network for anyone who cares about people with Alagille syndrome, a rare, multi-symptom, genetic disorder. Disseminates information. Aims to increase awareness in health professionals. Newsletter, phone support, information and referrals, medical advisory board. Write: Alagille Syndrome Alliance, c/o Cindy L. Hahn, 10500 S.W. Starr Dr., Tualatin OR 97062. Call 503-885-0455. *Website:* http://www.alagille.org *Email:* alagille@earthlink.net

ALBINISM

NOAH (National Organization for Albinism & Hypopigmentation) *National. Local chapters and contact people. Founded 1982.* Support and information for individuals with albinism (a lack of melanin pigment) their families and interested professionals. Encourages research leading to improved diagnosis and treatment. Newsletter, online community and regional gatherings, chapter development guidelines and a national conference. Dues $20/ind.; $25/family. Write: NOAH, PO Box 959, East Hampstead, NH 03826-0959. Call 1-800-473-2310 or 603-887-2310; Fax: 1-800-648-2310. *Website:* http://www.albinism.org/ *Email:* info@albinism.org

Can't find an appropriate group in your area? The Clearinghouse helps people start groups. Give us a call at 1-800-367-6274.

ALOPECIA AREATA

MIDDLESEX

Alopecia Support Group Mutual support and encouragement for persons with alopecia and their families. Meets 3rd Tues., 7pm, Bristol Myers Sqibb Children's Hospital, (meeting room varies), 1 Robert Wood Johnson Pl., New Brunswick. For meeting room location or further information call Carol 732-322-3993 or 732-418-8110 (hospital).

NATIONAL

National Alopecia Areata Foundation *National. Founded 1981.* Support network for people with alopecia areata, totalis and universalis. Goals are to set up support groups around the country, educate the public and fundraise for research. Offers quarterly newsletter and support group guidelines. Write: National Alopecia Areata Foundation, 14 Mitchell Blvd., San Rafael, CA 94903. Call 415-472-3780; Fax: 415-472-5343. *Website:* http://www.naaf.org *Email:* info@naaf.org

ALSTROM SYNDROME

Alstrom Syndrome International *International network. 4 affiliated groups (Canada, France, Brazil and UK). Founded 1995.* Provides support and networking for families affected by Alstrom syndrome. Supports medical research initiatives to more fully understand the complexities of Alstrom syndrome and develop better therapies for Alstrom patients. Publishes a quarterly newsletter. Provides information resources to families, educators, researchers and physicians. Write: Alstrom Syndrome Int'l, 14 Whitney Farm Rd., Mount Desert, ME 04660. Call 1-800-371-3628 or 207-288-6385; Fax: 207-244-7678. *Website:* http://www.jax.org/alstrom *Email:* jdm@jax.org

ALVEOLAR CAPILLARY DYSPLASIA

Alveolar Capillary Dysplasia Association *International network. Founded 1996.* Mutual support for families who have lost a child to alveolar capillary dysplasia (ACD), a congenital lung disorder. Aim is to share information while offering a supportive environment to share fears and concerns. Encourages research into cause and cure. Literature, networking, information newsletter and referrals. Write: ACDA, c/o Steve & Donna Hanson, 5902 Marcie Court, Garland TX 75044-4958. *Website:* http://www.acd-association.com *Email:* sdesj@verizon.net

AMYLOIDOSIS
(see also neurological disorders)

Amyloidosis Network International *International network.* Information and support for persons affected by amyloidosis, an accumulation of abnormal proteins. Networks individuals together for support. Provides education to the public and professionals about the disease. Write: Amyloidosis Network International, Inc., 7118 Cole Creek Dr., Houston, TX 77092-1421. Call 1-888-269-5643.

Amyloidosis Support Network Inc. *International. 19 regional support groups. Founded 1999.* Provides mutual support for persons with amyloidosis and their families through networking and resource information. Committed to increasing the rate of early detection of amyloidosis, thereby improving survivability and quality of life. Aims to increase the awareness among the public and professional communities, as well as linking patients/families to further experienced medical and emotional support resources. Write: Amyloidosis Support Network, Inc., 1490 Herndon Lane, Marietta, GA 30062. Call 1-800-689-1238 ext. 27 or 770-977-1500; Fax: 678-560-7280. *Website:* http://www.amyloidosis.org *Email:* info@amyloidosis.org

ANDROGEN INSENSITIVITY

AISSG-USA (Androgen Insensitivity Syndrome Support Group) *Founded 1995.* Provides information and support to people affected by androgen insensitivity syndrome (AIS) and related conditions. Includes adults with the condition, parents of AIS children and professionals working with AIS patients. Information and referrals, phone support, regional and national support group meetings, literature, advocacy and newsletters. Write: AISSG-USA, PO Box 2148, Duncan, OK 73534-2148. *Website:* http://www.medhelp.org/www/ais *Email:* aissgusa@hotmail.com

ANENCEPHALY

ONLINE

Anencephaly Support Foundation *Online. Founded 1992.* Provides support for families who have had a baby born with anencephaly or couples who are continuing a pregnancy after being diagnosed with an anencephalic infant. Information and resources for parents and professionals. Phone support, member discussion board, chat room, pregnancy message board. Registration required. Write: Anencephaly Support Fdn., 20311 Sienna Pines Court, Spring, TX 77379. *Website:* http://www.asfhelp.com

ANGELMAN SYNDROME

Angelman Syndrome Foundation, Inc. *National network. Founded 1992.* Mission is to advance the awareness and treatment of Angelman syndrome through education, information, research and support for individuals with Angelman syndrome, their families and other concerned persons. Write: Angelman Syndrome Foundation, 3015 E. New York St., Suite A2265, Aurora, IL 60504. Call 1-800-432-6435 or 630-978-4245; Fax: 630-978-7408. *Website:* http://www.angelman.org *Email:* info@angelman.org

ANKYLOSING SPONDYLITIS

Spondylitis Association of America *International network. 25 affiliated groups. Founded 1983.* Provides research, advocacy, support and education for patients, families, friends and health professionals concerned with ankylosing spondylitis and related diseases (reactive arthritis/Reiter's syndrome, psoriatic arthritis and inflammatory bowel disease). Offers publications, videotapes and newsletter. Guidelines available to start support groups. Write: Spondylitis Association of America, PO Box 5872, Sherman Oaks, CA 91413. Call 1-800-777-8189 or 818-981-1616 (in CA); Fax: 818-981-9826. *Website:* http://www.spondylitis.org *Email:* info@spondylitis.org

ONLINE

KickAS.org *Online.* Support and information for persons with ankylosing spondylitis and related disorders. Provides inspiration, friendship and humor. Message board. Separate forums for affected persons, families, friends and affected teens. *Website:* http://www.kickas.org

ANORCHIDISM

STATEWIDE

Anorchidism Support Group - USA Provides information and support for families and persons affected by anorchidism (absence of the testes) whether congenital or acquired. Dues $30 yr. Newsletter, information and referrals, phone support, pen pals and literature. Write: Anorchidism Support Group - USA, c/o Marianne Bittle, 4 Funny Bone Court, Sicklerville, NJ 08081. Call 856-740-1748 (eve). *Email:* asg.uk@virgin.net

We know this Directory is big and chances are we can probably find the group you're looking for quicker than you paging through it. Call us! (We're really friendly!)
1-800-367-6274

INTERNATIONAL

Anorchidism Support Group *International network. Founded 1995.* Information and support for families and persons affected by anorchidism (absence of the testes) whether congenital or acquired (aka testicular regression syndrome, anorchia, vanishing testes syndrome or absent testes). Newsletter. Provide information and support via phone, letter or e-mail. An information leaflet available on request. Write: ASG, PO Box 3025, Romford, Essex RM3 8GX, England. Call 44(0)1708 372597 (will return phone calls outside of UK. Please allow for time difference when phoning). *Website:* http://freespace.virgin.net/asg.uk *Email:* asg.uk@virgin.net

ANORECTAL MALFORMATIONS

Pull-thru Network, The. *International. 2 affiliated groups. Founded 1988.* Support and information for the families with children born with anorectal malformations (including cloaca, VATER/VACTERL, cloacal exstrophy or an imperforate anus) and Hirschsprung's disease and the associated diagnoses. Maintains a database for member networking. Weekly chat for members. Phone support and literature. Dues $20-$31. Write: The Pull-Thru Network, 2312 Savoy St., Hoover, AL 35226-1528. Call 205-978-2930. *Website:* http://www.pullthrough.org *Email:* info@pullthrough.org

ANOSMIA / PAROSMIA

Anosmia *Online. Founded 1999.* Provides mailing list and resources for people with anosmia (lacking the sense of smell). *Website:* http://groups.yahoo.com/group/anosmia

Congenital Anosmia Forums *Online* Forum for persons who suffer from congenital anosmia (born without a sense of smell). Provides support and information. *Website:* http://www.anosmia.net/

Parosmia Smelling Disorder Online *Online* Provides mutual support and information for persons who have distortions of their smell. *Website:* http://health.groups.yahoo.com/group/parosmia/

APERT SYNDROME

Apert Syndrome Pen Pals *National network. Founded 1992.* Group correspondence program for persons with Apert syndrome to share experiences. Information and referrals, pen pals, phone help. Write: Apert Syndrome Pen Pals, PO Box 115, Providence, RI 02901. Call 401-454-0704 (after 4:30pm).

APRAXIA
(see also speech)

BERGEN

Apraxia Network of Bergen County Support for parents and caregivers of children with apraxia. Mutual sharing, socials, guest speakers, literature and education. Suggested donation $10/yr. Meets 4 times/yr., River Edge. Call Jeanne 201-741-4035. *Email:* jbmistletoe@optonline.net

NATIONAL

Apraxia Kids *(A program of The Childhood Apraxia of Speech Association) National. Founded 2000.* Information and support for parents of children with apraxia of speech, a motor speech disorder. Provides encouragement for parents to start support groups. Education, newsletter, literature, conferences, information, listserv, message boards, e-mail and help desk referrals to self-help groups nationwide. Write: Apraxia Kids, 1151 Freeport Rd., #243, Pittsburgh, PA 15238. *Website:* http://www.apraxia-kids.org *Email:* helpdesk@apraxia-kids.org

ARNOLD-CHIARI MALFORMATION

World Arnold Chiari Malformation Association Online. *International. 3400+ members. Founded 1996.* Provides information, support and understanding to persons concerned with Arnold Chiari malformation. Separate adult and children's online support groups. Write: WACMA, c/o Bernard Meyer, 31 Newton Woods Rd., Newtown Square, PA 19073. Call 610-353-4737. *Website:* http://www.pressenter.com/~wacma *Email:* chip@pressenter.com

ARTERIO VENOUS MALFORMATION/ BRAIN ANEURYSM
(see also brain injury)

HUNTERDON

Brain Injury Support Group *Professionally-run.* Support group for people who have brain injury due to AVM's, aneurysm, tumors or stroke. Families welcome. Guest speakers and literature. Meets 2nd Thurs., 7-9pm, Hunterdon Medical Center, 2100 Wescott Dr., Flemington. Call Gwen Bartlett-Palmer 908-246-9648.

While it's no substitution for talking to our staff, you can call evenings or weekends! Leave a message and we will get back to you the next workday. ***1-800-367-6274***

MIDDLESEX

Kathleen McCriskin Brain AVM/Aneurysm Support Group *Professionally-run.* Provides mutual support and encouragement for persons with brain aneurysms, arterio-venous malformations (AVM) or subarachnoid hemorrhage. Rap sessions, guest speakers. Meets 4th Wed., (except July/Aug.), 7:30pm, JFK Medical Center, Neuroscience Conference Room, 65 James St., Edison. Call Nancy Di Pinto 732-321-7000 ext. 68973.

ARTHROGRYPOSIS

ONLINE

Adults with AMC *Online. 178 members. Founded 2001.* Offers support for adults with arthrogryposis to come together and communicate with others affected by AMC. *Website:* http://groups.yahoo.com/group/amc_adults/

Arthrogryposis Support Group *Online. 184 members. Founded 2000.* Offers an online support group for children, adults and family members of people with arthrogryposis. *Website:* http://groups.yahoo.com/group/arthrogryposissupportgroup/

ASHERMAN'S SYNDROME

ONLINE

Asherman's Syndrome Online Community *Online.* Community of women worldwide who have been diagnosed with Asherman's syndrome (aka intrauterine or uterine synechiae). Provides support by sharing of information and knowledge. *Website:* http://www.ashermans.org *Email:* ashermansbook@yahoo.com

ATAXIA

BERGEN

North Jersey Ataxia Self Help Group Mutual support for people with hereditary ataxia, their families and friends. Information, rap sessions, guest speakers, phone help. Meets 3rd Wed., 7:30-10pm, Children's Therapy Center, 30th St. and Berkshire Rd., Fair Lawn. Call Hortense Oberndorf 201-797-6657 (day/eve).

If you are using this book past Spring 2007, please call us for information about our most recent directory. 1-800-367-6274

NATIONAL

A-T Children's Project *Online. Founded 1993. (BILINGUAL)* Enables families of children affected by ataxia telangiectasia to seek information and share thoughts with other families. Family online forum. Information, workshops. Write: A-T Children's Project, 668 S. Military Trail, Deerfield Beach, FL 33442. Call 954-481-6611 or 1-800-5-HELP-AT. *Website:* http://www.atcp.org *Email:* info@atcp.org

National Ataxia Foundation *International. 73 groups. Founded 1957.* Assists families with ataxia. Provides education for professionals and the public. Encourages prevention of ataxia through genetic counseling. Newsletter, information and referral, assistance in starting support groups. Group development guidelines. Write: Nat'l Ataxia Foundation, c/o Michael Parent, 2600 Fernbrook Lane, Suite 119, Minneapolis, MN 55447. Call 763-553-0020; Fax: 763-553-0167. *Website:* http://www.ataxia.org *Email:* naf@ataxia.org

AUTOIMMUNE DISORDERS
(see also specific disorder)

OCEAN

Autoimmune Information Network Mutual support for patients with any one of over 85 autoimmune diseases. Family members welcome. Rap sessions, literature, phone help, advocacy, guest speakers and buddy system. Meets 4th Sun., 1-3pm, Ocean Medical Center, Conference Room C, 425 Jack Martin Blvd., Brick. Call Barbara Yodice 732-262-0450 (day/eve).

NATIONAL

American Autoimmune Related Diseases Assn., Inc. *National. 2 affiliated groups. Founded 1991.* Mutual support and education for patients with any type of autoimmune disease. Advocacy, referrals to support groups, literature, conferences. Quarterly newsletter. Supports research, physician symposium. Assistance in starting groups. Dues/newsletter subscription $24. Write: American Autoimmune Related Diseases Assn., 22100 Gratiot Ave., East Detroit, MI 48021-2227. Call 586-776-3900; Fax: 586-776-3903. *Website:* http://www.aarda.org *Email:* aarda@aarda.org

BARTH SYNDROME

Barth Syndrome Foundation, The *International. Founded 2000. (MULTILINGUAL)* Offers support to families and individuals affected by Barth syndrome, a rare genetic disorder characterized by neutropenia, cardiomyopathy, muscle weakness and failure to thrive. Provides information, outreach, newsletter, referrals, pen pals and biennial conference. Supports awareness and research. Peer-to-peer mentoring program. Write: The Barth Syndrome Foundation, PO Box 974, Perry, FL 32348. Call 850-223-1128 (Voice/Fax). *Website:* http://www.barthsyndrome.org *Email:* inifo@barthsyndrome.org

BATTEN DISEASE

Batten Disease Support and Research Association *International. 20 affiliated groups. Founded 1987.* Emotional support for persons with Batten disease. Information and referrals, support group meetings, phone support, conferences, newsletter. Assistance provided for starting new groups. Write: Batten Disease Support & Research Assn., 120 Humphries Dr., Suite 2, Reynoldsburg, OH 43068. Call 1-800-448-4570. *Website:* http://www.bdsra.org *Email:* bdsra1@bdsra.org

BECKWITH-WIEDEMANN SYNDROME

Beckwith Wiedemann Family Forum *Online. 334 members. Founded 2000. (MULTILINGUAL)* Promotes support and exchange of information among families affected by Beckwith Weidmann syndrome (BWS). Open to anyone interested in BWS. Family chat forum (http://groups.yahoo.com/group/bwschat/) *Website:* http://www.geocities.com/beckwith_wiedemann/

Beckwith-Wiedemann Support Network *Online. Founded 1989.* Support and information for parents of children with Beckwith-Wiedemann syndrome or isolated hemihypertrophy and interested medical professionals. Newsletter, parent directory, informational brochures, chat rooms and message boards. Write: Beckwith-Wiedemann Support Network, c/o Susan Fettes, President, 2711 Colony Rd., Ann Arbor, MI 48104. *Website:* http://www.beckwith-wiedemann.org *Email:* beckwithbrowning@earthlink.net

BEHCET'S SYNDROME

American Behcet's Disease Association *National network. Founded 1978.* Mutual support and information for Behcet's patients, their families and professionals. Newsletter (transcribed on tape for visually impaired), information and referrals, phone support, pen pals, conferences, medical advisory board.

495

Pamphlets, literature, press kit. Write: ABDA, PO Box 19952, Amarillo, TX, 79114. Call 1-800-723-4238 (11am-4pm). *Website:* http://www.behcets.com

BELL'S PALSY / FACIAL PARALYSIS
(see also neurological disorders)

Bell's Palsy Research Foundation *National network. Founded 1995.* Provides information, support and referrals for treatment and rehabilitation to persons diagnosed with Bell's Palsy and other forms of facial paralysis due to acoustic neuroma, Ramsey-Hunt syndrome, pregnancy-induced palsy or Lyme disease. Provides referrals, phone support and advocacy. Write: Bell's Palsy Research Foundation, 9713 Lookout Pl., Montgomery Village, MD 20886. Call 301-330-3223. *Website:* http://www.bellspalsy.com *Email:* DrTargan@erols.com

BENIGN ESSENTIAL BLEPHAROSPASM

MONMOUTH

Benign Essential Blepharospasm Support Group Mutual support and understanding for persons with benign essential blepharospasm (BEB). Meetings vary, Ocean Township. Call Bonnie O'Rourke 732-922-4429 (day/eve). *Website:* http://www.blepharospasm.org *Email:* tombor@worldnet.att.net

NATIONAL

Benign Essential Blepharospasm Research Foundation, Inc. *National. 170 groups. Founded 1981.* Provides information and emotional support to persons with benign essential blepharospasm (BEB). Networks people together with similar symptoms. Doctor referrals, education. Supports research. Bimonthly newsletter. Local group development guidelines. Voluntary contributions. Write: B.E.B. Foundation, PO Box 12468, Beaumont, TX 77726-2468. Call 409-832-0788; Fax: 409-832-0890. *Website:* http://www.blepharospasm.org *Email:* bebrf@sbcglobal.net

BLADDER EXSTROPHY

Association for the Bladder Exstrophy Community *International network. Founded 1991.* Mutual support for persons affected by bladder exstrophy including parents of children with bladder exstrophy, adults, healthcare professionals and others interested in exstrophy. Informal pen pal program, conferences, advocacy, directory of members. Informal kids e-mail exchange. Dues $25/yr. Write: ABC, PO Box 10152, Fort Irwin, CA 92310. Call Karen Moseley 1-866-300-2222. *Website:* http://www.bladderexstrophy.com/ *Email:* admin@bladderexstrophy.com

496

BLEPHAROPHIMOSIS / PTOSIS / EPICANTHUS INVERSUS

BPEI Family Network *National network. Founded 1994.* Provides information and support to families affected by blepharophimosis, ptosis, epicanthus inversus. Phone support, online group. Write: BPEI Family Network, SE 820 Meadow Vale Dr., Pullman, WA 99163. Call 509-332-6628. *Website:* http://freespace.virgin.net/andy.bowles/ *Email:* lschauble@gocougs.wsu.edu

BRACHIAL PLEXUS INJURY / ERB'S PALSY

Brachial Plexus Palsy Foundation, The *International. 4 affiliated groups. Founded 1994.* Education and support for families affected by brachial plexus palsy, a condition caused by injury. Information on treatment. Newsletter, phone support, information and referral. Guidelines for starting similar group. Fundraising. Write: Brachial Plexus Palsy Foundation, 210 Springhaven Circle, Royersford, PA 19468. Call 610-792-4234; Fax: 610-948-0678. *Website:* http://www.brachialplexuspalsyfoundation.org *Email:* contact@brachialplexuspalsyfoundation.org

Erb's Place *Online. International network. 39 groups.* Provides support and information for persons affected by Erb's palsy (aka brachial plexus injury). Live chat on Wednesday evenings. Message board, listserv, family matching. Information on local groups. Provides assistance in starting local groups. Write: National Brachial Plexus/Erb's Palsy Assn., Inc., PO Box 23, Larsen, WI 54947. *Website:* http://www.nbpepa.org *Email:* erbspalsy@usa.net

BRONCHIECTASIS

ONLINE

Bronchiectasis Chat Group *Online.* E-mail support group for people who have bronchiectasis and their relatives. To join the online chat room send an email to address. *Email:* bronchiectasis-subscribe@yahoogroups.com

CANAVAN DISEASE
(see also leukodystrophy)

Canavan Foundation *International. Founded 1992.* Provides information and education for persons affected by Canavan disease. Offers literature, phone support, conferences and advocacy. Supports research. Online support available. Write: Canavan Foundation, 450 West End Ave., New York, NY 10024. Call

212-873-4640   or   1-877-422-6282;   Fax: 212-873-7892.   *Website:* http://www.canavanfoundation.org

CARDIOFACIOCUTANEOUS SYNDROME

CFC International *International network. Founded 1991.* Mutual support for parents of children with cardiofaciocutaneous syndrome. Strives to find and disseminate information on CFC syndrome. Offers newsletter, information, referrals, online listserv and phone support. Medical advisors. International clinic and family conferences every two years. Write: CFC International, c/o Brenda Conger, 183 Brown Rd., Vestal, NY, 13850. Call 607-772-9666 (eve). *Website:* http://www.cfcsyndrome.org *Email:* bconger@cfcsyndrome.org

CAVERNOUS ANGIOMA

Angioma Alliance *Online. Founded 2002. (MULTILINGUAL)* Support and information for any person affected by cavernous angioma of the brain and spine. Educational materials, support via a community forum, listserv, chats and contact information for research studies. Site available in Spanish and in a limited way, in Portuguese. Hosts annual national family conferences. Works to increase physician and public awareness of the illness. Call 1-866-432-5226. *Website:* http://www.angiomaalliance.org *Email:* info@angiomaalliance.org

CEREBROCOSTOMANDIBULAR SYNDROME

Cerebrocostomandibular Syndrome Support Group *National network. Founded 1998.* Provides support and guidance to families of children with cerebrocostomandibular syndrome, characterized by a recessed lower mandible and rib anomalies. Exchange of messages through email. Guidelines and help available for starting new groups. Call 609-239-7831; Fax: 609-239-6916. Write: Tara Montague, 7 Primrose Dr., Burlington, NJ 08016. *Email:* tmontague@comcast.net

CHARCOT-MARIE-TOOTH DISEASE / PERONEAL MUSCULAR ATROPHY / HEREDITARY MOTOR SENSORY NEUROPATHY

Charcot Marie Tooth Association *National. 25 affiliated groups. Founded 1983.* Information & support for patients & families affected by Charcot-Marie-Tooth disorders (also known as peroneal muscular atrophy or hereditary motor sensory neuropathy). Referrals, newsletter, phone help, support groups, conferences. Assistance starting similar groups. Write: CMT Association, 2700 Chestnut Pkwy,

Chester, PA 19013. Call Pat Dreibelbis 1-800-606-2682 or 610-499-9264; Fax: 610-499-9267. *Website:* http://www.charcot-marie-tooth.org *Email:* cmtassoc@aol.com

Hereditary Neuropathy Foundation *International network. Founded 2000.* Sharing and caring for those with Charcot-Marie-Tooth disease (also known as peroneal muscular dystrophy or hereditary motor sensory neuropathy). Information for patients and professionals. Write: Hereditary Neuropathy Foundation, PO Box 287103, New York, NY 10128. Call 917-648-6971. *Website:* http://www.hnf-cure.org *Email:* info@hereditaryneuropathy.org

CHARGE SYNDROME

CHARGE Syndrome Foundation, Inc. *International network. Founded 1993.* Networking of families affected by CHARGE Syndrome (coloboma of the eye, cranial nerve abnormalities, characteristic ears and other problems). Publications include CHARGE Syndrome Brochure, New Parent Packet (12+ pages), "CHARGE Syndrome: A Management Manual for Parents" (270 pgs)and conference papers. Membership ($15/families; $20/professionals; $30/organizations) includes quarterly newsletter and parent-to-parent support. Conferences in odd years (e.g. 2005). Write: CHARGE Syndrome Foundation, Inc., c/o Marion A. Norbury, 409 Vandiver Dr., Ste. 5-104, Columbia, MO 65202-1563. Call 573-499-4694 (Voice/Fax) or Families Only 1-800-442-7604. *Website:* http://www.chargesyndrome *Email:* marion@chargesyndrome.org

CHEMICAL HYPERSENSITIVITY / ENVIRONMENTAL ILLNESS

H.E.A.L. (Human Ecology Action League, Inc.) *National. 40+ chapters. Founded 1977.* Education and information for persons concerned about the health effects of environmental exposures. Quarterly newsletter. Other publications include information sheets, resource list, directories, reading list and book "Fragrance and Health." Referrals to local and regional chapters and support services. Dues $26/US; $32/Canada; $38/Int'l. Write: HEAL, PO Box 509, Stockbridge, GA 30281. Call 770-389-4519; Fax: 770-389-4520. *Website:* http://members.aol.com/HEALNatnl/index.html *Email:* HEALNatnl@aol.com

National Center for Environmental Health Strategies *National network. Founded 1986.* Fosters the development of creative solutions to environmental health problems with a focus on indoor air quality, chemical and electrical sensitivities and environmental disabilities. Clearinghouse and technical services, educational materials, workshops, community outreach, policy development, research, support and advocacy for persons injured by chemical/environment exposures. Special projects on school-related exposures and Gulf War veterans. Books and publications, newsletter. Focus on access and accommodation rights. Free information packets. Write: NCEHS, 1100 Rural Ave., Voorhees, NJ 08043. Call Mary Lamielle 856-429-5358. *Website:* http://www.ncehs.org *Email:* mary@ncehs.org or ncehs@ncehs.org

CHROMOSOME DISORDERS

4P- Support Group *International. Founded 1984.* Provides support and information to families of children with chromosome 4 conditions. Offers phone support and biographies on other children with these conditions. Quarterly newsletter. Write: 4P- Support Group, c/o Larry Bentley, Exec. Dir., PO Box 1676, Gresham or 97030. Call 503-661-1855. *Website:* http://www.4p-supportgroup.org

Chromosome 18 Registry & Research Society *International network. Founded 1990.* Provides support and education concerning disorders of chromosome 18. Encourages and conducts research into areas that impact families. Links affected families and their physicians to the research community. Newsletter, phone support, information and referrals, annual conference. Dues $20/US Int'l/$25. Write: Chromosome 18 Registry & Research Society, c/o Gloria Ellwanger, 7155 Oakridge Dr., San Antonio, TX 78229. Call 210-657-4968. *Website:* http://www.chromosome18.org *Email:* office@chromosome18.org

Chromosome 9P- Network *International network. Founded 1983.* Provides information, parent-to-parent networking and technical support to parents of children with 9P- and other deletions of 9P, ring 9, mosaic, translocations, inverted 9p, etc. Facilitates research to further understand monosomy 9P. Information, referrals, phone support and yearly conferences. Write: Chromosome 9P- Network, PO Box 54, Stanley, ID 83278. *Website:* http://www.9pminus.org

Chromosome 22 Central *International network. Founded 1996.* Networking and support for parents of children with any chromosome disorder. Supports research. Offers literature, phone support, newsletter and pen pals. bulletin boards. Write: Chromosome 22 Central, 237 Kent Ave., Timmins, Ontario, Canada P4N 3C2. Call 705-268-3099; TDD/TTY: 705-267-3374. *Website:* http://www.c22c.org *Email:* a815@c22c.org

Chromosome Deletion Outreach *National network. Founded 1992.* Provides support and information for families having a child diagnosed with any type of rare chromosome disorder. Dues $25 year/family for mailed newsletter. Electronic version only $10/annually. Write: CDO, PO Box 724, Boca Raton, FL 33429-0724. Call 561-395-4252; Fax: 561-395-4252. *Website:* http://www.chromodisorder.org *Email:* info@chromodisorder.org

Disorders of Chromosome 16 Foundation *International network. Founded 1998.* Provides support and information to families of children affected by any chromosome 16 disorder, including partial trisomy 16 and unbalanced translocations. Information and referrals, phone support, literature. Write: DOC16, 1327 Marcy St., Iowa City, IA 52240. Call Alex or Dan Schaeffel at 319-354-5478. *Website:* http://www.trisomy16.org *Email:* danalex@avalon.net

National Center for Chromosome Inversions *National network. Founded 1992.* Mutual support for families affected by chromosome inversions. Information and referrals, phone support, pen pal program. Write: National Center for Chromosome Inversions, 282 SE Anastasia St., Lake City, FL 32025-1730. Call 386-752-1548 (Voice/Fax). *Email:* ncfci@msn.com

CLUB FOOT

Clubfoot Mailing List *Online. 420 members. Founded 1998.* Support group for parents of children with clubfoot/feet, persons with clubfoot/feet or anyone needing support on this topic. Goal is to provide support, friendship and encouragement. Operates through an e-mail mailing list. Must subscribe to list to join group. *Website:* http://health.groups.yahoo.com/group/clubfoot/

COBALAMIN, METABOLISM, INBORN ERRORS OF

Cobalamin Network, The *International network. Founded 1985.* Emotional support and information for families of children affected by inborn errors of cobalamin metabolism. Referrals to pediatric metabolic practitioners. Write: Cobalamin Network, PO Box 174, Thetford Center, VT 05075. Call 802-785-4029, 802-785-3112 or 985-798-5631. *Email:* SueBee18@valley.net

COCKAYNE SYNDROME / CACHETIC DWARFISM
(see also growth disorders, short / tall)

Share & Care Cockayne Syndrome *Network International network. Founded 1981. (BILINGUAL)* Mutual support and networking for families affected by Cockayne syndrome (cachectic dwarfism). Sharing of information between families and professionals. Maintains registry of families. Information, referrals, newsletter and phone support. Write: Share & Care Cockayne Syndrome Network, PO Box 828, Waterford VA, 20197. Call 540-882-3380. *Website:* http://www.cockayne-syndrome.org *Email:* JackieClark@aol.com

We can also refer callers to over 100 individuals who are seeking others to help start new support groups throughout NJ, if you don't see it, that doesn't mean it doesn't exist!
1-800-367-6274

COFFIN-LOWRY SYNDROME

Coffin-Lowry Syndrome Foundation, The *International network. Founded 1991.* Serves as a clearinghouse for information on Coffin-Lowry syndrome. Forum for exchanging experiences, advice and information with other CLS families. Seeks to become a visible group in the medical, scientific, educational and professional communities in order to facilitate referrals of newly diagnosed individuals and to encourage medical and behavioral research. Maintains mailing list of families and professionals. Provides newsletter, family support and informational packet. Write: The CLS Foundation, c/o Mary Hoffman, 3045 255th Ave., S.E., Sammamish, WA 98075. Call 425-427-0939 (after 5:30pm). *Website:* http://clsf.info *Email:* clsfoundation@yahoo.com

COGAN'S SYNDROME

Cogan's Contact Network *National network. Founded 1989.* Mutual support and sharing of experiences and strategies for persons with Cogan's syndrome. Aim is to help people understand this rare disorder that affects hearing, eyes, balance, etc. Networking, pen pals, literature. online dues $12/yr. Written membership $20/yr. Write: YUPPA/Cogan's Contact, PO Box 145, Freehold, NJ 07728-0145. Call Anthony 732-761-9809. *Email:* uscogans@juno.com

COHEN SYNDROME / PEPPER SYNDROME

Cohen Syndrome Support Group *International network. Founded 1996.* Information and support for families of children with Cohen syndrome (aka Pepper syndrome), a rare, genetic disorder. Parent-to-parent networking, information, newsletter and booklet. Write: Cohen Syndrome Support Group, 21 Tudor Ave, Bebington Wirral, CH63 3EJ UK. Call 0151 334 4297. *Website:* http://www.cafamily.org.uk/Direct/c48.html

CONGENITAL ADRENAL HYPERPLASIA SYNDROME

CARES Foundation Inc. *International. 25 regional support groups. Founded 2001.* Goal is to educate the public and professionals about all types of congenital adrenal hyperplasia, the symptoms, diagnostic protocol, treatment, genetic frequency and the necessity for early intervention through newborn screening. Offers information and support to affected individuals and their families. Write: CARES Foundation, 189 Main St., Milburn, NJ 07041. Call 1-866-227-3737 or 973-912-3895; Fax: 973-912-8890. *Website:* http://www.caresfoundation.org *Email:* info@caresfoundation.org

Congenital Adrenal Hyperplasia *National network. Founded 1989.* Offers educational and emotional support to families of children with congenital adrenal hyperplasia. Provides information and referrals, kids program, phone support, annual convention, networking and a quarterly newsletter. Assistance in starting new groups. Write: CAH Division of MAGIC Foundation, c/o Mary Andrews, 6645 W. North Ave., Oak Park, IL 60302. Call 1-800-362-4423; Fax: 708-383-0899. *Website:* http://www.magicfoundation.org *Email:* mary@magicfoundation.org

CONGENITAL CENTRAL HYPOVENTILATION / ONDINE'S CURSE

WARREN

CCHS Family Network Support for families of children with congenital central hypoventilation syndrome (under 18 welcome). Phone help, advocacy, pen pals and literature. Family conference every 2 years, otherwise communicate via phone, letters and quarterly newsletters. Call Desiree Cougle 908-852-2082 (day/eve); Fax: 908-850-9537. *Website:* http://www.cchs.org

NATIONAL

CCHS Network *Online. International network. Founded 1990.* Mutual support for families caring for a child who has congenital central hypoventilation syndrome (aka Ondine's curse). Provides information and referrals, family newsletter, physician directory and equipment information. Facilitates and supports CCHS research. Holds family educational conferences every three years. Provides online referrals to local support groups. Write: CCHS Network, c/o Mary Vanderlaan, 71 Maple St., Oneonta, NY 13820. *Website:* http://www.cchsnetwork.org *Email:* vanderlaanm@hartwick.edu

CONGENITAL CYTOMEGALOVIRUS DISEASE

National Congenital Cytomegalovirus Disease Registry *National network. Founded 1990.* Parent support network that provides support to families of children with congenital cytomegalovirus disease (CMV). Information, referrals, newsletter and literature. Write: Nat'l Congenital Cytomegalovirus Disease Registry, c/o Feigin Ctr., Suite 1150, MC3-2371, Houston, TX 77030-2399. Call Carol Griesser, RN 832-824-4387; Fax: 832-825-4347. *Website:* http://www.bcm.tmc.edu/pedi/infect/cmv *Email:* cmv@bcm.tmc.edu

CONJOINED TWINS

Conjoined Twins International *International network. Founded 1996.* Support for conjoined twins, their families and professionals. Offers peer support, professional counseling, crisis intervention, telephone helpline, pen pal network, videos, information and referrals. Provides peer counseling and a speakers' bureau. Registry of affected families and membership directory. Write: Conjoined Twins International, PO Box 10895, Prescott, AZ 86304-0895. Call 928-445-2777. *Website:* http://www.conjoinedtwinsint.com *Email:* dwdegeraty@myexcel.com

CORNELIA DE LANGE SYNDROME

Cornelia de Lange Syndrome Foundation, Inc. *National. 2500+ member families. Founded 1981.* Provides support and education to families affected by Cornelia de Lange syndrome. Supports research. Newsletter. Family album available for networking and mutual support. Annual meetings. Professional network. Write: Cornelia de Lange Syndrome Foundation, 302 West Main St., Suite 100, Avon, CT 06001. Call 1-800-223-8355 or 860-676-8166; Fax: 860-676-8337. *Website:* http://cdlsusa.org *Email:* info@cdlsusa.org

CORTICO-BASAL GANGLIONIC DEGENERATION

CBGD Support Network *Online. 455 members. Founded 1998.* Support for anyone affected by corticobasal ganglionic degeneration (a rare neurological disorder characterized by cell loss in the brain). Offers education, information and newsletter. Networks members together for emotional support. Write: CBGD Support Network, c/o Theresa Roberts, 1941 Stevely Ave., Long Beach, CA 90815. *Website:* http://health.groups.yahoo.com/group/cbgd_support

COSTELLO SYNDROME

International Costello Syndrome Support Group *International network. Founded 1996.* Mutual support for parents of children with Costello syndrome, a very rare disorder. Information and referrals, literature, phone support, pen pals, online chat room, newsletter. Write: Int'l Costello Syndrome Support Group, c/o Colin & Cath Stone, 90 Parkfield Rd. North, New Moston, M40 3RQ, United Kingdom. Call +44 161 682 2479. *Website:* http://www.costellokids.org.uk *Email:* c.stone8@ntlworld.com

We know this Directory is big and chances are we can probably find the group you're looking for quicker than you paging through it. Call us! (We're really friendly!)
1-800-367-6274

CRANIOPHARYNGIOMA

(see also brain tumor)

Craniopharyngioma Internet Support Group *Online. Founded 1996.* Mutual support for adults and parents of children who have or had a craniopharyngioma, a rare brain tumor. Opportunity to exchange information and ideas, offer and receive help and network with other parents. Open to professionals. *Website:* http://www.braintrust.org/cranio/

CREUTZFELDT-JAKOB DISEASE

STATEWIDE

CJD Foundation Information and support to family members and friends of victims of Creutzfeldt-Jakob disease. Phone help, speakers bureau, literature. Call Marie Kassai 201-791-8425 (eve). *Email:* mariek43@optonline.net

NATIONAL

Creutzfeldt-Jakob Disease Foundation, Inc. *National network. Founded 1993.* Provides support to families who have a loved one with or have lost a loved one to, Creutzfeldt-Jakob disease. Seeks to promote research, education and awareness of this disease. Write: Creutzfeldt-Jakob Disease Foundation, PO Box 5312, Akron, OH 44334. Call 1-800-659-1991. *Website:* http://www.cjdfoundation.org *Email:* wanda@cjdfoundation.org

ONLINE

CJD Voice *Online.* Provides information and emotional support to persons who have a loved one with or lost someone to Creutzfeldt-Jakob disease, a fatal brain-deteriorating disorder. Advocacy. E-mail discussion group, message board and scheduled chat room sessions. *Website:* http://www.cjdvoice.org *Email:* dek@provalue.net

CRI DU CHAT / (5P) SYNDROME

5P- Society *International network. Founded 1987.* Support organization for families having a child with 5P- syndrome (aka cri du chat), a genetic disorder characterized by a high-pitched cry. Listing of families in U.S. & Canada. Newsletter. Annual meeting. International chat room (Sun. & Thurs). Write: 5P-Society, PO Box 268, Lakewood, CA 90714-0268. Call 1-888-970-0777; Fax: 562-920-5240. *Website:* http://www.fivepminus.org *Email:* director@fivepminus.org

CROUZON SYNDROME

ONLINE

Crouzon Support Network *Online.* Support group for individuals and families who are dealing with Crouzon syndrome and other craniofacial anomalies. A place to share experience, mutual support, inspiration and information. *Website:* http://health.groups.yahoo.com/group/crouzons

CUSHING'S DISEASE
(see also pituitary disorders)

Cushing's Help and Support *International.* *Founded 2000.* Support and information for persons with Cushing's disease. Offers support to family and friends. Offers message boards, literature, chat room, guest speakers, annual national conference, pen pals, phone support network and advocacy. Write: Cushing's Help and Support, 13222 Point Pleasant Dr., Fairfax, VA 22033-3515. Call 1-877-825-0128; Fax: 703-378-8517. *Website:* http://www.cushings-help.com *Email:* CushingsSupport@aol.com

Cushing's Support and Research Foundation, Inc. *International.* *Founded 1995.* Provides information and support to patients with Cushing's disease. Offers newsletter and networking so patients can contact others with Cushing's disease. Write: Cushing's Support & Research Fdn., 65 East India Row, 22B, Boston, MA 02110. *Website:* http://www.CSRF.net *Email:* cushinfo@csrf.net

CUTIS LAXA

Cutis Laxa Internationale *International.* *Founded 2001.* Support group for those afflicted with any type of cutis laxa, a rare, genetic disorder. Provides networking between those afflicted, promotes research and advocacy. Dues $27/yr. Write: Cutis Laxa Internationale, 35 route des Chaignes, 17740 Sainte Marie de Re, France. Call 33 (0)5 46 55 00 59. *Website:* http://www.orpha.net/nestasso/cutislax *Email:* mcjlboiteux@aol.com

CYSTINOSIS

ONLINE

Cystinosis Research Network *Online.* *Founded 1996.* Dedicated to supporting and advocating for continued research, providing family support and education programs. Professionals and caregivers are welcome to join. Promotes and supports research that will lead to a better understanding, improved treatments and a cure for cystinosis. Aims to improve the awareness and education of cystinosis to be utilized as a resource for families and public. Support group, networking, newsletter and family conferences. Write: Cystinosis Research Network, 10 Pine Ave., Burlington, MA 01803. Call 1-866-276-3669 or 781-229-6182; Fax: 781-229-6030. *Website:* http://www.cystinosis.org *Email:* CRN@cystinosis.org

CYSTINURIA
(see also kidney)

Cystinuria Support Network *International network. Founded 1994.* Provides support and an opportunity for sharing information for persons with cystinuria, a kidney disorder that causes kidney stones. Information and referrals, newsletter. Write: Cystinuria Support Network, 21001 NE 36th St., Sammamish, WA 98074. Call 425-868-2996 (eve). *Website:* http://www.cystinuria.com *Email:* cystinuria@aol.com

DANCING EYE SYNDROME / KINSBOURNE SYNDROME / OPSOCLONUS / MYOCLONIC ENCEPHALOPATHY

Dancing Eye Syndrome *International network. Founded 1988.* Support and information for families of children with dancing eye syndrome (aka Kinsbourne syndrome, opsoclonus myoclonus or myoclonic encephalopathy of infants), a disorder consisting of loss of balance, irregular eye movements and muscle jerking. Newsletter, phone help. Write: Dancing Eye Syndrome, c/o J. Stanton-Roberts, 78, Quantock Rd., W. Sussex BN13 2HQ, England. Call 01903-532383 (Voice/Fax). *Website:* http://www.dancingeyes.org.uk *Email:* support@dancingeyes.org.uk

Opsoclonus-Myoclonus Support Network *National network. Founded 1994.* Networking for parents of children with opsoclonus-myoclonus syndrome through phone and online messages. Doctor referrals, consultation. Literature, current research information. Write: Opsoclonus-Myoclonus Support Network, 725 North St., Jim Thorpe, PA 18229. Call 570-325-3302. *Website:* http://www.geocities.com/opso-myoclonus *Email:* sandragreenberg@hotmail.com

DANDY WALKER SYNDROME

Dandy-Walker Syndrome Network *International network. Founded 1993.* Provides mutual support, information and networking for families affected by Dandy-Walker syndrome. Phone support. Write: Dandy-Walker Syndrome Network, c/o Desiree Fleming, 5030 142nd Path, Apple Valley, MN 55124. Call 952-423-4008.

DEGOS DISEASE /
MALIGNANT ATROPHIC PAPULOSIS

ONLINE

Degos Patients Support Network *Online.* Support and information for persons with Degos disease (aka malignant atrophic papulosis or Kohlmeier-Degos disease), an extremely rare thrombotic vasculopathy affecting people of all ages all over the world. Message board for patients and their families and caregivers. Secure section with access to discussion forum and other information for medical professionals only. *Website:* http://www.degosdisease.com *Email:* judith@degosdisease.com

DENTATORUBRAL PALLIDOLUYSIAN ATROPHY

DRPLA Network *International network. Founded 1999.* Support and information for persons affected by dentatorubral pallidoluysian atrophy, a rare genetic disorder that leads to physical and cognitive problems. Phone support, pen pals, online and e-mail discussions. Write: DRPLA, c/o Frank J. Marone, Ph.D., 1426 46th Ave., San Francisco, CA 94122-2903. Call 415-753-5695 or 1-800-499-7803. *Email:* bmsca@juno.com

DERCUM'S DISEASE

Dercum's Disease *Online. Founded 1998.* Support for persons with Dercum's disease (aka adiposis dolorsa), characterized by fatty lipomas under the skin that cause pain. Aim is to eradicate the pain and suffering of Dercum's disease through finding the cause and cure. Forum for personal stories links to support groups and medical articles. *Website:* http://www.dercum.org *Email:* dercum@dercum.org

DIABETES INSIPIDUS

Diabetes Insipidus Foundation, Inc. *International network. Founded 1996. (MULTILINGUAL)* Support for families and professionals coping with neurogenic/central, nephrogenic, gestagenic and dipsogenic/polydipsic diabetes insipidus. Provides information and referrals, phone support and advocacy. Website includes articles (English, French and Spanish). Message board and 24 hour chat room. Newsletter. Write: Diabetes Insipidus Fdn. Inc., 5203 New Prospect Dr., Ellicott City, MD 21043. Call Mary Evans-Lee 706-323-7576; Fax: 410-247-5584. *Website:* http://www.diabetesinsipidus.org *Email:* info@diabetesinsipidus.org

DUBOWITZ SYNDROME

NE Dubowitz Syndrome Support *Model. 1 group in Rhode Island. Founded 1997.* Information, education, support and networking for parents of children with Dubowitz syndrome and concerned professionals. Information on assistive technology and educational issues. Referrals, pen pals, advocacy, information on geneticists. Write: NE Dubowitz Syndrome Support, c/o Sharon Terzian, 106 Verndale St., Warwick, RI 02889. Call 401-737-3138. *Website:* http://www.dubowitzsyndrome.net *Email:* dubowitzsyndrome@netzero.net

DYSAUTONOMIA

Dysautonomia Foundation, Inc., The *International. 13 chapters. Founded 1951.* Provides peer support, information and referrals for families affected by familial dysautonomia. Raises funds for medical and clinical research, as well as for public awareness. Newsletter. Write: Dysautonomia Foundation, 315 West 39th St., Suite 701, New York, NY 10018. Call 212-279-1066; Fax: 212-279-2066. *Website:* http://www.familialdysautonomia.org *Email:* info@familialdysautonomia.org

National Dysautonomia Research Foundation *National network. Founded 1996.* Provides support, educational material and medical referrals for persons who have dysautonomia (a disorder of the autonomic nervous system). Networking, literature, advocacy, phone support and conferences. Encourages research. online email and discussion support forum, groups and free downloadable online Patient Handbook. Write: NDRF, 1407 West Fourth St., Suite 160, Red Wing, MN 55066-2108. Call 651-267-0525 (day); Fax: 651-267-0524. *Website:* http://www.ndrf.org *Email:* ndrf@ndrf.org

National Society For MVP & Dysautonomia *National. 59 affiliated groups. Founded 1987.* Assists individuals suffering from mitral valve prolapse and dysautonomia to find support and understanding. Education on symptoms and treatment. Newsletter, literature. Write: Nat'l Soc. for MVP & Dysautonomia, 880 Montclair Rd., Suite 370, Birmingham, AL 35213. Call 205-592-5765 (day) or 1-800-541-8602 (day); Fax: 205-592-5707. *Website:* http//www.mvprolapse.com *Email:* staff@MVProlapse.com

DYSTONIA

ESSEX

Heart of NJ Dystonia Support and Action Group Mutual support, education and the opportunity to interact with others with dystonia. Families welcome. Rap sessions, lecture series, guest speakers and phone help. Meets 3-4 times a year,

Cranes Mill Retirement Community, West Caldwell. For meeting information call Lois or Norman Gebeloff 973-228-2765 (day/eve). *Email:* norman23@comcast.net

NATIONAL

Dystonia Medical Research Foundation *International. 110 chapters. Founded 1976.* Provides education, awareness and support groups for persons with dystonia. Fundraises for research. Newsletter, information, referrals to local groups. Also offers guidelines for starting similar groups. Write: Dystonia Med. Research Fdn., 1 E. Wacker Dr., Suite 2430, Chicago, IL 60601-1905. Call 312-755-0198; Fax: 312-803-0138. *Website:* http://www.dystonia-foundation.org/ *Email:* dystonia@dystonia-foundation.org

DYSTROPHIC EPIDERMOLYSIS BULLOSA

DEBRA (Dystrophic Epidermolysis Bullosa Research Association) of America *National. 14 chapters. Founded 1980.* Support and information for families affected by epidermolysis bullosa. Promotes research, provides education for patients, families and professionals, pen pals, phone network, information and referrals, newsletter, regional conferences. Write: DEBRA of America, 5 W. 36th St., Room 404, New York, NY 10018-7179. Call 212-868-1573 or 1-866-332-7276; Fax: 212-868-9296. *Website:* http://www.debra.org *Email:* staff@debra.org

EAR ANOMALIES

ONLINE

Atresia-Microtia Group *Online. 500+ members.* Forum for people and parents of children, with aural atresia and/or microtia. Issues addressed include emotional support, hearing aids, ear reconstruction and insurance. *Website:* http://health.groups.yahoo.com/group/AtresiaMicrotia/ *Email:* AtresiaMicrotia-owner@yahoogroups.com

ECTODERMAL DYSPLASIAS SYNDROME

National Foundation for Ectodermal Dysplasias *National network. Founded 1981.* Distributes information on ectodermal dysplasia syndrome and treatments. Provides support programs for families and funds research projects. Quarterly newsletter. Annual family conference and regional conferences, dental implant program and scholarship opportunities. Directory of members for informal contacts among families. Write: National Foundation for Ectodermal Dysplasias, 410 E.

Main St., Box 114, Mascoutah, IL 62258-0114. Call 618-566-2020; Fax: 618-566-4718. *Website:* http://www.nfed.org *Email:* info@nfed.org

EHLERS DANLOS SYNDROME

Ehlers-Danlos National Foundation *National. 35 local groups. Founded 1985.* Provides resources for Ehlers-Danlos syndrome patients, families and health care professionals. Mission is to disseminate accurate information, to provide a network of support and communication and to foster and support research. Online message boards for EDNF members. Write: EDNF, 3200 Wilshire Blvd., Suite 1601, South Tower, Los Angeles, CA 90010. Call 213-368-3800; Fax: 213-427-0057. *Website:* http://www.ednf.org *Email:* staff@ednf.org

ELLIS VAN CREVELD SYNDROME / CHRONDROECTODERMAL DYSPLASIA
(see also growth disorders, short / tall)

Ellis Van Creveld Support Group *International network. Founded 1997.* Provides support and information for families affected by Ellis Van Creveld syndrome (aka chondroectodermal dysplasia), an extremely rare form of dwarfism. Networks families together for support. Literature, advocacy, information and referrals, phone support. Connects with medical community to find ways to save the lives of infants born with this genetic disorder. Write: Ellis Van Creveld Support Group, 17 Bridlewood Trail, Honeoye Falls, NY 14472. Call 585-624-8277. *Email:* PattiMO44@aol.com

ENCEPHALITIS

NATIONAL

Encephalitis Information Resource *International network. Founded 1994.* Provides support and information for persons with encephalitis (inflammation of the brain) and their families. Links individuals together for mutual support. Aims to educate public and professionals about the condition. Information and referrals, newsletter, computer networking. Write: Encephalitis Information Resource, 7B Saville St., Malton, North Yorkshire, YO17 7LL UK. Call +44 (0) 653 699 599. *Website:* http://www.encephalitis.info *Email:* mail@encephalitis.info

ONLINE

Encephalitis Global *Online.* Provides support and information for encephalitis survivors, caregivers and loved ones and for interested persons. Includes a guide for newly diagnosed persons, links, downloadable information pamphlet, group

511

discussions and live chats. *Website:* http://www.encephalitisglobal.com *Email:* EncephalitisGlobal@shaw.ca

EOSINOPHILIA-MYALGIA SYNDROME

National Eosinophilia Myalgia Syndrome Network *National network. Founded 1993.* Mutual support for persons with eosinophilia myalgia syndrome (EMS) caused by using L-tryptophan and their families. Information and support through online support groups, phone contacts and newsletter. Medical and legal information, advocacy, literature and conferences. Write: National EMS Network c/o Jann Heston, 155 Delaware Ave., Lexington, OH 44904-1212. Call 419-884-8177. *Website:* http://www.nemsn.org *Email:* nemsn-2005@earthlink.net

ERYTHROMELALGIA

TEA (The Erythromelalgia Association) *International network. Founded 1999.* Provides support and information to those diagnosed with erythromelalgia. Offers education to increase awareness of this rare condition within the medical profession and the general public. Fundraises to promote research into the causes, diagnostic methods and treatments. Write: TEA, 24 Pickering Lane, Wethersfield, CT 06109. Call 860-529-5261. *Website:* http://www.erythromelalgia.org *Email:* membership@erythromelalgia.org

ESSENTIAL TREMOR
(see also neurological disorders)

International Essential Tremor Foundation *International. 72 affiliated groups. Founded 1989.* Provides information and support for persons affected by essential tremor. Information and referrals, literature, research updates. Quarterly newsletter. Dues $25. Write: Int'l Tremor Fdn., PO Box 14005, Lenexa, KS 66285. Call 1-888-387-3667 or 913-341-3880; Fax: 913-341-1296. *Website:* http://www.essentialtremor.org/ *Email:* STAFF@essentialtremor.org

FABRY DISEASE

Fabry Support & Information Group *National network. Founded 1996.* Dedicated to dispensing information and encouraging mutual self-help as a means of emotional support to Fabry patients and family members. Information and referrals, newsletters, networking of members, discussion page. Write: FSIG, PO Box 510, Concordia, MO 64020. Call 660-463-1355; Fax: 660-463-1356. *Website:* http://www.fabry.org *Email:* info@fabry.org

FACIAL DISFIGUREMENT
(see also specific disorders, burn victims, accidents)

AboutFace USA *National. Founded 1991.* Provides emotional support and information to persons with facial differences and their families. Network database of 900+ families who have similar concerns. Promotes public education and awareness. Also has cleft advocate program which provides on line parent-patient support network. Newsletter, information and referrals. Write: AboutFace USA, PO Box 969, Batavia, IL 60510-0969. Call 1-888-486-1209. *Website:* http://www.aboutfaceusa.org *Email:* info@aboutfaceusa.org

Forward Face *Model. 1 group in New York. Founded 1978.* Mutual support for people with craniofacial disfigurement and their families. Strongly advocates educating members and the public in the quest for understanding and acceptance. Liaison with medical personnel. Newsletter. Videotapes. Dues $30. Teen/young adult support group: The Inner Faces. Write: Forward Face, 317 E. 34th St., 9th Floor, Suite 901A, New York, NY 10016. *Website:* http://www.forwardface.org *Email:* camille@forwardface.org

Let's Face It *National. Founded 1987.* Information and support network of people with facial disfigurement, their families and the professionals caring for them. Free annual 40-page resource list with over 200 listings. One-page updates issued twice per year (available on website.) For resource booklet send 9" x 12" self-addressed envelope with a note about yourself. Write: Let's Face It, PO 29972, Bellingham, WA 98228-1972. Call Betsy Wilson 360-676-7325. *Website:* http://www.faceit.org *Email:* letsfaceit@faceit.org

FACIOSCAPULOHUMERAL DISEASE / LANDOUZY-DEJERINE
(see also muscular dystrophy)

FSH Society, Inc. *National network. Founded 1991.* Support, information, education, networking and advocacy for individuals with facioscapulohumeral disease (aka Landouzy-Dejerine muscular dystrophy). Funds research. Newsletter, support group meetings, conferences, literature. Write: FSH Society, 3 Westwood Rd., Lexington, MA 02420 USA. Call Carol Perez 781-860-0501 (day); Fax: 781-860-0599. *Website:* http://www.fshsociety.org *Email:* info@fshsociety.org

FACTOR V LEIDEN / THROMBOPHILIA

Factor V Leiden Mailing List and Digest *Online.* Mailing list that offers support and information for persons affected by Factor V Leiden (thrombophilia), a hereditary blood coagulation disorder. Daily digest (condensed version of the mailing list) also available. *Website:* http://www.fvleiden.org

FATTY OXIDATION DISORDER

(see also metabolic disorders)

FOD Family Support Group *International network. Founded 1991.* Opportunity for families dealing with fatty oxidation disorders (i.e. MCAD, LCHAD, VLCAD, SCAD, etc.) to network with others dealing with these rare, genetic, metabolic disorders. Information and referrals, phone support, e-mail list. Write: FOD Family Support Group, c/o Deb & Dan Gould, 1559 New Garden Rd., 2E, Greensboro, NC 27410. Call 336-547-8682; Fax: 336-292-0536. *Website:* http://www.fodsupport.org *Email:* deb@fodsupport.org

FETAL ALCOHOL SYNDROME/DRUG-AFFECTED

Family Empowerment Network *National network. Founded 1992.* Support, education, advocacy and training for families of children and adults with fetal alcohol syndrome (FAS) or fetal alcohol effects and interested professionals. Annual family retreats, newsletter. FAS resources, referrals for diagnosis and therapies. Networks families together for support. Assistance in starting support groups. Write: FEN, 777 S. Mills St., Madison, WI 53715. Call 1-800-462-5254 or 608-262-6590; Fax: 608-263-5813. *Website:* http://www.fammed.wisc.edu/fen *Email:* fen@fammed.wisc.edu

Fetal Alcohol Syndrome Family Resource Institute *International. Founded 1990.* Grassroots coalition of families and professionals concerned with fetal alcohol syndrome/effects. Educational programs, brochures, information packets. Regional representatives being identified. Support group meetings. Advocacy, information & referrals, phone support, conferences. Write: FAS Family Resource Institute, PO Box 2525, Lynnwood, WA 98036. Call 1-800-999-3429 (in WA) or 253-531-2878 (outside WA); Fax: 425-640-9155. *Website:* http://fetalalcoholsyndrome.org *Email:* vicky@fetalalcoholsyndrome.org

FG SYNDROME

FG Syndrome Homepage *Online.* Support network for persons interested in FG syndrome, a multiple congenital genetic anomaly. Newsletter, listserv, conferences, fundraising and general family support. *Website:* http://www.fg-syndrome.org *Email:* info@fg-syndrome.org

FIBRODYSPLASIA OSSIFICANS PROGRESSIVA

International Fibrodysplasia Ossificans Progressiva Assn. *International network. Founded 1988.* Serves as a support network for families dealing with fibrodysplasia ossificans progressiva (FOP). Supports education, communication and medical research. Newsletter. Write: Int'l FOP Association, Box 196217, Winter Springs, FL 32719-6217. Call 407-365-4194; Fax: 407-365-3213. *Website:* http://www.ifopa.org *Email:* together@ifopa.org

FLOATING HARBOR SYNDROME

Floating Harbor Syndrome Support Group *National network. Founded 1999.* Provides mutual support and networking for parents of children with Floating Harbor syndrome. Newsletter, literature, phone support. Pictures of children with Floating Harbor syndrome available online. Write: Floating Harbor Syndrome Support Group, c/o Deana Swanson, 160 Guild NE, Grand Rapids, MI 49505. Call 616-447-9175.*Website:* http://www.geocities.com/floatingharbor@sbcglobal.net/floating_harbor.html *Email:* jdswanson@sbcglobal.net

FRAGILE X SYNDROME

STATEWIDE

Fragile X Association Organization of parents and professionals dedicated to improving the lives of individuals and families affected by fragile X syndrome. For information on fragile-x call Jennifer Keenan 856-985-3257. *Website:* http://www.fragilexnj.org *Email:* sjkeenan@worldnet.att.net

INTERNATIONAL

FRAXA Research Foundation *International. 30 affiliated groups. Founded 1994.* Information and support on fragile-X syndrome. Funds medical research investigator-initiated grants and postdoctoral fellowships. Newsletter, literature. Some chapters have support group meetings. Guidelines available on starting similar groups. Write: FRAXA Research Fdn., 45 Pleasant St., Newburyport, MA 01950. Call 978-462-1866; Fax: 978-463-9985. *Website:* http://www.fraxa.org *Email:* kclappFRAXA@comcast.net

National Fragile X Foundation, The *International. 55 groups. Founded 1984.* Mission includes phone and email support, promoting awareness, education, research and legislative advocacy regarding fragile X syndrome, a hereditary condition which is the most common known cause of inherited mental impairment.

Services also include a quarterly journal, research grants, local, national and international conferences and educational resources (books and videotapes for a fee). Write: National Fragile X Foundation, PO Box 190488, San Francisco, CA 94119-0488. Call 1-800-688-8765; Fax: 925-938-9315. *Website:* http://www.FragileX.org *Email:* NATLFX@FragileX.org

FREEMAN-SHELDON

Freeman-Sheldon Parent Support Group *International network. Founded 1982.* Provides emotional support for parents of children with Freeman-Sheldon syndrome and for adults with this syndrome. Sharing of helpful medical literature. Provides information on growth and development of individuals affected. Participates in research projects. Members network by phone, mail and through a members-only listserv. Newsletter. Write: Freeman-Sheldon Parent Support Group, 509 E. Northmont Way, Salt Lake City, UT 84103. Call 801-364-7060. *Website:* http://www.fspsg.org *Email:* fspsg@mail.burgoyne.com

GALACTOSEMIA

Parents of Galactosemic Children, Inc. *National network. Founded 1985.* Information and mutual support for parents of galactosemic children. Newsletter, literature, pen pals, conferences and phone support, online message board. Write: Parents of Galactosemic Children, c/o Evelyn Rice, 885 Del Sol St., Sparks, NV 89436. Call 775-626-0885. *Website:* http://www.galactosemia.org *Email:* mesameadow@aol.com

GASTROESOPHAGEAL REFLUX

PAGER (Pediatric/Adolescent Gastroesophageal Reflux Association) *National network. Founded 1992.* Offers support and information for parents whose children suffer from gastroesophageal reflux, an inappropriate backwash of stomach contents into the esophagus that affects seven million children and 50 million adults. Educates the public on this disorder. Newsletter, literature, telephone support network. Helps new chapters start when leaders are identified. Extensive free information is available via website and mail. Dues $25/yr. Write: PAGER, PO Box 486, Buckeystown, MD 21717. Call 301-601-9541. *Website:* http://www.reflux.org *Email:* gergroup@aol.com

GASTROINTESTINAL MOTILITY DISORDERS

Association of Gastrointestinal Motility Disorders, Inc. *International network. Founded 1991.* Support and education for persons affected by digestive motility disorders. Serves as educational resource and information base for medical professionals. Physician referrals, video tapes, large variety of educational materials, networking support, symposiums and several publications. Dues $35/US; $42/Int'l (can be waived). Write: AGMD International Corp. Headquarters, 11 North St., Lexington, MA 02420. Call 781-861-3874; Fax: 781-861-7834. *Website:* http://www.agmd-gimotility.org *Email:* gimotility@msn.com

GAUCHER DISEASE

National Gaucher Foundation *National. 2 chapters. Founded 1984.* Provides information and assistance for those affected by Gaucher disease. Provides education and outreach to increase public awareness. Operates the Gaucher Disease Family Support Network. Quarterly newsletter, phone support, medical board. Guidelines to help start similar groups. Write: National Gaucher Foundation, 61 General Early Dr., Harpers Ferry, WV 25425. Call 1-800-428-2437; Fax: 304-725-6429. *Website:* http://www.gaucherdisease.org *Email:* ngf@gaucherdisease.org

GENETIC DISORDERS
(see also specific disorder)

Genetic Alliance, The *International network. Founded 1986.* Consortium of support groups, professional organizations, industry and governmental agencies dedicated to helping individuals and families affected by genetic disorders. Information and referrals to support groups and genetic services. Offers assistance in starting a similar group. Write: Genetic Alliance, 4301 Connecticut Ave. NW, Suite 404, Washington, DC 20008. Call 1-800-336-4363 or 202-966-5557; Fax: 202-966-8553. *Website:* http://www.geneticalliance.org *Email:* information@geneticalliance.org

GLYCOGEN STORAGE DISEASE

Association For Glycogen Storage Disease *U.S. & Canadian network. 3 affiliated groups. Founded 1979.* Mutual support and information sharing among parents of children with glycogen storage disease. Newsletter, phone support, conference. Offers online support. Write: Association for Glycogen Storage Disease, PO Box 896, Durant, IA 52747. Call 563-785-6038; Fax: 563-785-6038. *Website:* http://www.agsdus.org *Email:* maryc@agsdus.org

GOLDENHAR SYNDROME

Goldenhar Syndrome Support Network *International network. Founded 1998.* Support and information for individuals and their families affected by Goldenhar syndrome. Information and referrals, newsletter, literature, pen pals and advocacy.

Online mailing list. Write: Goldenhar Syndrome Support Network, c/o Barb Miles, 9325 163 Street, Edmonton, AB T5R 2P4, Canada. *Website:* http://www.goldenharsyndrome.org *Email:* support@goldenharsyndrome.org

GORLIN SYNDROME /
NEVOID BASAL CELL SYNDROME /
BASAL CELL CARCINOMA NEVUS SYNDROME

Basal Cell Carcinoma Nevus Syndrome Life Support Network *National network.* Provides support services to patients, families and medical professionals dealing with the many manifestations of basal cell carcinoma, (aka Gorlin syndrome or nevoid basal cell syndrome). Offers online forum, quarterly newsletter, annual retreat and conference and periodic regional meetings. Write: BCCNS Life Support Network, c/o Sheila LaRosa, PO Box 321, Burton, OH 44021. Call 1-866-834-1895; Fax: 440-635-0267. *Website:* http://www.bccns.org *Email:* info@bccns.org

Gorlin Syndrome Group, The *International network. 3 affiliated groups. Founded 1992.* Provides support and information for individuals with Gorlin syndrome (aka nevoid basal cell carcinoma) and their families. Helpline, newsletter, meetings, networking. Write: The Gorlin Syndrome Group Margaret Costello, 11 Blackberry Way, Penwortham, Preston, Lancashire PR1 9LQ England. Call +440 1772517624. *Website:* http:// www.gorlingroup.co.uk *Email:* info@gorlingroup.co.uk

GRANULOMATOUS, CHRONIC

Chronic Granulomatous Disease Assn. Inc. *International network. Founded 1982.* Support & information for persons with chronic granulomatous disease, their families. Networks patients with similar CGD-related illnesses. Support through correspondence and phone. International registry of patients. Referrals to physicians. Write: CGD Assn., 2616 Monterey Rd., San Marino, CA 91108. Call 626-441-4118. *Website:* http://www.cgdassociation.org *Email:* cgda@socal.rr.com

GUILLAIN-BARRE SYNDROME/
CHRONIC INFLAMMATORY DEMYELINATING
POLYNEUROPATHY

GBS/CIDP Foundation International *International. 160 chapters. Founded 1980.* Emotional support, hospital visitation and education for people affected by Guillain-Barre syndrome, chronic inflammatory demyelinating polyneuropathy (CIDP)and its variants. Promotes support, education and research. Newsletter, pen pals, phone network, online chat room. Group development guidelines and international symposium. Write: Guillain-Barre Syndrome Foundation, PO Box 262, Wynnewood, PA 19096, Call 610-667-0131; Fax: 610-667-7036. *Website:* http://www.gbsfi.com *Email:* info@gbsfi.com

HALLERVORDEN-SPATZ SYNDROME / NEURODEGENERATION WITH BRAIN IRON ACCUMULATION

Neurodegeneration with Brain Iron Accumulation Association *International network. Founded 1996.* Provides emotional support to families affected by neurodegeneration with brain iron accumulation (NBIA). NBLA (formerly Hallervorden-Spatz syndrome) is a rare, progressive neurological disorder, resulting in iron deposits in the brain that causes loss of muscle control. Aim is to educate the public on this disorder. Supports and monitors research. Newsletter, literature, phone support network, pen pals, advocacy efforts. Write: NBIA Disorders Assn., 2082 Monaco Ct., El Cajon, CA 92019-4235. Call 619-588-2315; Fax: 619-588-4093. *Website:* http://www.NBIAdisorders.org *Email:* info@NBIAdisorders.org

HELLP SYNDROME

HELLP Syndrome Society, The *International network. Founded 1996.* Mutual support, networking and information for persons affected by HELLP syndrome (hemolysis, elevated liver enzymes and low platelet count). This syndrome affects pregnant mothers and is usually in tandem with pre-eclampsia. Brochure, newsletter. Write: The HELLP Syndrome Society, PO Box 44, Bethany, WV 26032. *Website:* http://www.hellpsyndrome.org

HEMANGIOMA

Hemangioma Support System *National network. Founded 1990.* Provides parent-to-parent support for families with children affected by hemangiomas. Write: Hemangioma Support System, c/o Cynthia Schumerth, 1484 Sand Acres Dr., DePere, WI 54115. Call 920-336-9399 (after 8:30pm).

NOVA (National Organization of Vascular Anomalies) Provides support for patients and their families in the diagnosis of hemangioma and vascular malformations. Networks families together for support. Offers videos, doctor referrals, free medical conferences, educational and support materials. online newsletter. Write: NOVA, PO Box 0358, Findlay, OH 45840. Call 419-425-1593. *Website:* http://www.novanews.org *Email:* hemangnews@msn.com

HEMIFACIAL SPASM

Hemifacial Spasm Association *Online. Founded 2001.* A support community of individuals who had or continue to suffer from hemifacial spasm (HFS) and are eager to provide information, understanding and support to other individuals and their families when coping with hemifacial spasm. *Website:* http://www.hfs-assn.org *Email:* info@hfs-assn.org

HEMIHYPERTROPHY

Hemihypertrophy Support & Information Page *Online.* Support and information for persons with hemihypertrophy, a rare condition in which one side of the body grows faster than the other. Mailing list, chat room. *Website:* http://www.geocities.com/HotSprings/Spa/6112.index.html

HEMIPLEGIA

CHASA (Children's Hemiplegia And Stroke Association) *National network. Founded 1996.* Provides support and information for families of children who are diagnosed with hemiplegia or have had a pediatric stroke. Local support group information available. Also provides online email support groups, networking, advocacy, phone support, annual family retreat, medical conference and matching with other families. Write: CHASA, 4101 W. Green Oaks, Suite 305, PMB 149, Arlington, TX 76016. Call 817-492-4325. *Website:* http://www.chasa.org or http://www.hemikids.org *Email:* info437@chasa.org

HEMOCHROMATOSIS / IRON OVERLOAD

Iron Overload Diseases Assoc., Inc. *International network. Founded 1981.* A clearinghouse of support and information for hemochromatosis and other iron overload disease patients, their families and physicians. Encourages research and public awareness. Bi-monthly newsletter "Ironic Blood." Membership dues $50/yr. Write: Iron Overload Diseases Association, 433 Westwind Dr., N. Palm Beach, FL 33408. Call 561-840-8512 or 561-840-8513; Fax: 561-842-9881. *Website:* http://www.ironoverload.org *Email:* iod@ironoverload.org

HEMOPHILIA

STATEWIDE

Hemophilia Association of New Jersey *Professionally-run.* Self-help support for persons with hemophilia and their families. Provides information and referrals, advocacy, group meetings, educational seminars, phone networking, peer counseling, guest speakers, financial assistance and vocational counseling. Dues $20/yr. Write: Hemophilia Association of New Jersey, 197 Route 18 South, Suite 206 North, E. Brunswick, NJ 08816. Call Julie Frenkel 732-249-6000 (day). *Website:* http://www.hanj.org *Email:* hemnj@comcast.net

NATIONAL

National Hemophilia Foundation *National. 47 chapters. Founded 1948.* Dedicated to finding better treatments and cures for bleeding and clotting disorders and to preventing the complications of these disorders through education, advocacy and research. Write: National Hemophilia Foundation, 116 W. 32nd St., 11th Floor, New York, NY 10001. Call 1-800-424-2634; Fax: 212-328-3777. *Website:* http://www.hemophilia.org *Email:* info@hemophilia.org

HEREDITARY HEMORRHAGIC TELANGIECTASIA / OSLER-WEBER-RENDU SYNDROME

HHT Foundation International, Inc *International. Founded 1991.* Mutual support and education for persons interested in hereditary hemorrhagic telangiectasia (aka Osler-Weber-Rendu syndrome). Supports clinical and genetic research. Counseling and advice for patients. Referrals to appropriate treatment centers. Annual conference. Newsletters. Aims to protect all members under the Right To Privacy Act. Dues $45/yr. Write: HHT Fdn. Int'l, PO Box 329, Monkton, MD 21111. Call 1-800-448-6389 (U.S.) 410-357-9932 (International); Fax: 410-357-9931. *Website:* http://www.hht.org *Email:* hhtinfo@hht.org

HEREDITARY SPASTIC PARAPLEGIA

Spastic Paraplegia Foundation, Inc. *National. Founded 2002.* Offers support and information to those affected by primary lateral sclerosis and hereditary spastic paraplegia. Support research. Offers regional and email support groups, an online chat group, newsletter and information. Write: Spastic Paraplegia Foundation, Inc., 209 Park Rd, Chelmsford, MA 01824. Call 703-495-9261. *Website:* http://www.sp-foundation.org

HERMANSKY-PUDLAK SYNDROME/ CHEDIAK HIGASHI SYNDROME

Hermansky-Pudlak Syndrome Network *International network. 2 affiliated groups. Founded 1992.* Mutual support and education for families affected by Hermansky-Pudlak syndrome and Chediak Higashi syndrome. Networks families together for support. Newsletter, annual conference. Supports research. Write: Hermansky-Pudlak Syndrome Network, c/o Donna Jean Appell, 1 South Rd., Oyster Bay, NY 11771-1905. Call 1-800-789-9HPS (voice/fax) or 516-922-3440; Fax: 516-922-4022. *Website:* http://www.hpsnetwork.org *Email:* hpsnet@worldnet.att.net

HIDRADENITIS SUPPURATIVA

Hidradenitis Suppurativa Webring *Online.* Chat room and message board for persons affected by hidradenitis suppurativa, a disease of the sweat glands, that causes painful boil-type lesions. *Website:* http://health.yahoo.com/clubs/hidradenitis

HIP REPLACEMENT
(see also specific disorder)

Totally Hip *Online.* Support to help relieve the fear of total hip replacement surgery, share experiences and offer moral as well as spiritual support to patients. Helps answer questions on hip replacement. Click on bulletin board at website for message exchange. *Website:* http://www.totallyhip.org *Email:* Linda@totallyhip.org

HISTIOCYTOSIS-X

Histiocytosis Association of America *International. network. Founded 1985.* Mutual support and information for parents & patients with this group of rare disorders. Includes hemophagocytic lymphohistiocytosis, pulmonary eosinophilic granuloma, histiocytosis and familial erythrophagocytic lymphohistiocytosis. Provides parent-patient directory to facilitate networking and communication. Write: Histiocytosis Assn. of America, 72 E. Holly Ave., Suite 101, Pitman, NJ 08071. Call Jeff & Sally Toughill 856-589-6606; Fax: 856-589-6614. *Website:* http://www.histio.org *Email:* association@histio.org

HYDROCEPHALUS

Hydrocephalus Association *National network. Founded 1984.* Provides support, education and advocacy for people with hydrocephalus and their families. Provides a wealth of resource materials on hydrocephalus for all age groups, quarterly newsletter, directory of neurosurgeons, bi-annual national conference and scholarships for young adults. Write: Hydrocephalus Assn., 870 Market St., Suite 705, San Francisco, CA 94102. Call 1-888-598-3789 or 415-732-7040; Fax: 415-732-7044. *Website:* http://www.hydroassoc.org *Email:* info@hydroassoc.org

Guardians of Hydrocephalus Research Foundation *National network. Founded 1977.* Information and referral service to persons affected by hydrocephalus. Phone networking for parents of children with hydrocephalus. Referrals to doctors, newsletter, literature and books for children and adults with hydrocephalus (in English and Spanish). Write: Guardians of Hydrocephalus Research Foundation, 2618 Ave. Z, Brooklyn, NY 11235. Call Marie Fischetti 718-743-4473; Fax: 718-743-1171. *Website:* http://ghrf.homestead.com/ghrf.html *Email:* ghrf2618@aol.com

National Hydrocephalus Foundation *National and international network. Founded 1979.* Mission is to establish and facilitate a communication network, provide informational and educational assistance for individuals and families affected by hydrocephalus, increase public awareness, promote and support research on the cause, prevention and treatment of hydrocephalus. Guidelines to help start support groups available. Write: National Hydrocephalus Foundation, 12413 Centralia Rd., Lakewood, CA 90715-1623. Call 1-888-857-3434 or 562-924-6666 (voice/Fax). *Website:* http://nhfonline.org *Email:* hydrobrat@Earthlink.net

HYPERACUSIS / SENSITIVE HEARING

Hyperacusis Network, The *International network. Founded 1991.* Mutual support and sharing of information and education for individuals and their families with hyperacusis & recruitment (hypersensitive hearing). Promotes research into cause and cure. Newsletter, information and referrals, phone support, pen pals. Write: Hyperacusis Network, PO Box 8007, Green Bay, WI 54302. Call 920-468-4663 (eve); Fax: 920-468-0168. *Website:* http://www.hyperacusis.net *Email:* earhelp@yahoo.com

HYPOPARATHYROIDISM
(see also pituitary disorders)

Hypoparathyroidism Association Inc. *(MULTILINGUAL) International network. 1900 members from 59 countries. Founded 1994.* Dedicated to improving the lives of people with all forms of hypoparathyroidism, a rare medical disorder. Guidelines available for starting similar groups. Promotes awareness of this disorder through quarterly newsletter and website. Online newsletter, member gallery, online forum, chat room and extensive compilation of links and various articles. Write: Hypoparathyroidism Association, Inc., c/o James E. Sanders, 2835 Salmon, Idaho Falls, ID 83406. Call 208-524-3857. *Website:* http://www.hypoparathyroidism.org *Email:* hpth@hypoparathyroidism.org

HYPOPHOSPHATASIA

Hypophosphatasia Division *International network.* *Founded 1990.* Provides support for families affected by hypophosphatasia. Newsletters, updated medical information, phone support, annual conventions. online assistance available for finding or forming local support groups. Dues $30/yr. Write: Hypophosphatasia Division, c/o MAGIC Foundation, 6645 West North Ave., Oak Park, IL 60302. Call 1-800-362-4423; Fax: 708-383-0899. *Website:* http://www.magicfoundation.org *Email:* mary@magicfoundation.org

ICHTHYOSIS

F.I.R.S.T. (Foundation for Ichthyosis & Related Skin Types) *National network.* *Founded 1981.* Provides support for people with ichthyosis through networking with others. Public and professional education. Supports research on treatment and current advocacy issues. Quarterly newsletter, publications, bi-annual conference. Dues $40; Int'l/$50. Write: FIRST, 1601 S. Valley Forge Rd., Suite 10, Lansdale, PA 19446. Call 1-800-545-3286 or 215-631-1411; Fax: 215-631-1413. *Website:* http://www.scalyskin.org *Email:* info@scalyskin.org

IDIOPATHIC THROMBOCYTOPENIC PURPURA

Platelet Disorder Support Association *Founded 1998.* Provides information and support to persons who have idiopathic thrombocytopenic purpura (ITP) and related blood disorders. Members regularly exchange messages. Support meetings, conferences, advocacy, newsletter and written material. online support for women with ITP who are or thinking about, becoming pregnant. Write: PDSA, c/o Joan Young, President, 133 Rollins Ave., Suite 5, Rockville, MD 20852. Call 1-877-528-3538. *Website:* http://www.pdsa.org *Email:* pdsa@pdsa.org

IMMUNE DEFICIENCY

Immune Deficiency Foundation *National.* *Founded 1980.* Provides support and education for families affected by primary immune deficiency diseases. Newsletter, handbook, videotape and educational materials for public and medical professionals. Networks individuals and family members affected by immune deficiency. Scholarships and fellowship program. Group development guidelines. Write: Immune Deficiency Fdn., 40 W. Chesapeake Ave., Suite 308, Towson, MD 21204. Call 1-800-296-4433. *Website:* http://www.primaryimmune.org *Email:* idf@primaryimmune.org

SCID Mailing Group *Online.. Founded 1997.* online self-help group for families afflicted with severe combined immune deficiency or who have lost a child

524

to this very rare genetic disorder which results in severe infections. Provides opportunity for families to share information and resources with one another. *Website:* http://www.scid.net *Email:* SCIDemail@scid.net

INCONTINENTIA PIGMENTI

Incontinentia Pigmenti International Foundation *International network. Founded 1995.* Dedicated to research, family support and physician awareness on incontinentia pigmenti. Maintains international database of patients. Write: Incontinentia Pigmenti Int'l Fdn., 30 East 72nd St., 16th Fl., New York, NY 10021. Call 212-452-1231; Fax: 212-452-1406. *Website:* http://www.imgen.bcm.tmc.edu/IPIF *Email:* ipif@ipif.org

INFECTIOUS ILLNESS, GENERAL

PKIDs (Parents of Kids with Infectious Diseases) *National network. Founded 1996.* Provides informational and educational support for parents of children with chronic viral infectious diseases, with an emphasis on HIV and hepatitis B and C. Opportunity for parents, children and teens to share information and experiences. Newsletter, literature, advocacy, pen pals, phone support. Supports research. online email list, support group and other resources. Write: PKIDS, PO Box 5666, Vancouver, WA 98668. Call 1-877-557-5437 or 360-695-0293; Fax: 360-695-6941. *Website:* http://www.pkids.org *Email:* pkids@pkids.org

INTESTINAL MULTIPLE POLYPOSIS

IMPACC (Intestinal Multiple Polyposis And Colorectal Cancer) *National network. Founded 1986.* Support network to help patients and families dealing with familial polyposis and hereditary colon cancer. Information and referrals, encourages research and educates professionals & public. Phone support network, correspondence and literature. Write: IMPACC, PO Box 11, Conyngham, PA 18219. Call Ann Fagan 570-788-1818 (day) or 570-788-3712 (eve); Fax: 570-788-4046. *Email:* impacc@epix.net

INVERTED DUPLICATION 15

IDEAS (IsoDicentric 15 Exchange, Advocacy & Support) *International network. Founded 1994.* Support, information and advocacy for people affected by inverted duplication 15. Information and referrals, phone support, literature, newsletter. Write: IDEAS, c/o Paul Rivard, PO Box 4616, Manchester, NH, 03108. Call 503-253-2872 (day)

JOSEPH DISEASE

International Joseph Diseases Foundation, Inc. *International network. Founded 1977.* Support network for patients, families and health care professionals concerned about Joseph disease. Offers information, referrals to DNA marker test sites and other services. Newsletter. Dues $15/yr. Write: Int'l Joseph Disease Fdn., PO Box 994268, Redding, CA 96099. Call 530-246-4722. *Website:* http://www.ijdf.net *Email:* MJD@ijdf.net

JOUBERT SYNDROME

Joubert Syndrome Foundation & Related Cerebellar Disorders *International network. 7 chapters. Founded 1992.* Sharing of knowledge, experience and emotional support for parents of children with Joubert syndrome and related cerebellar disorders. Aims to educate physicians and support team. Group offers a newsletter and a biennial conference. Write: Joubert Syndrome Foundation, 6931 South Carlinda Ave., Columbia, MD 21046. Call 410-997-8084 or 410-992-9184; Fax: 410-992-9184. *Website:* http://www.joubertsyndrome.org *Email:* joubertduquette@comcast.net

KABUKI SYNDROME / NIIKAWAKUROKI SYNDROME

Kabuki Syndrome Network *International network. Founded 1997.* Provides mutual support and information for families affected by Kabuki syndrome (aka Niikawakuroki syndrome). Coordinates family directory. Literature, phone support, pen pals, newsletter. Write: Kabuki Syndrome Network, c/o Dean & Margot Schmiedge, 8060 Struthers Cr., Regina, Saskatchewan, Canada S4Y 1J3. Call Margot and Dean Schmiedge 306-543-8715. *Website:* http://www.kabukisyndrome.com *Email:* margot@kabukisyndrome.com

KALLMANN'S SYNDROME / HYPOGONADOTROPHIC HYPOGONADISM

HYPOHH (Helping You to be Positive about Hypogonadotrophic Hypogonadism) *Online.* Provides information, support, forum and encouragement to persons suffering from Kallmann's syndrome and other forms of hypogonadotrophic hypogonadism. Open to families and friends. *Website:* http://www.hypohh.net/ *Email:* mark@hypohh.net

Kallmann's Syndrome *Online* Support group for people with Kallmann's syndrome, their families and medical professionals. Diverse resources, photo gallery, weekly surveys and various discussions. *Website:* http://health.yahoo.com/ency/healthwise/shc29kal *Email:* hypohh@fsmail.net

KAWASAKI DISEASE

Kawasaki Families' Network *Online. Founded 1996.* Provides a means of circulating information and support for families affected by Kawasaki disease, an inflammatory illness which primarily threatens the cardiovascular system. Members can exchange messages online through an e-mail listserv. Write: Kawasaki Families' Network, c/o Vickie Machado, 46-111 Nahewai Place, Kaneohe, HI 96744. Call 808-525-8053. *Email:* vicki.machado@verizon.net

KENNEDY'S DISEASE / SPINAL BULBAR MUSCULAR ATROPHY

Kennedy's Disease Association, Inc. *National network. Founded 2000.* Mutual support and information for persons with Kennedy's disease (aka spinal and bulbar muscular atrophy), their families and caregivers. Opportunity to share personal experiences to help alleviate the feeling of aloneness and to engender hope and a positive attitude. Sharing of information regarding diagnosis, treatment and current research. online chat room every two weeks. Write: KDA, Inc, PO Box 1105, Coarsegold, CA 93614-1105. Call 559-658-5950. *Website:* http://www.kennedysdisease.org *Email:* info@kennedysdisease.org

KLINEFELTER SYNDROME

Klinefelter Syndrome and Associates *National network. 4 affiliated groups. Founded 1990.* Mission is to educate, encourage research and foster treatment and cures for symptoms of sex chromosome variations. These include, but are not limited to XXY, XXX, XYY, XXXY, XXXXXY, XXYY, etc. Brochures are available that describe basic symptoms, diagnoses and treatments. Newsletter ($25/US; $27/Canada; $30/Int'l (in US funds). Write: Klinefelter Syndrome and Associates, 11 Keats Court, Coto de Caza, CA 92679. Call 1-888-999-9428; Fax: 949-858-3443. *Website:* http://www.genetic.org *Email:* help1@genetic.org

Klinefelter Syndrome Support Group *Online.* Provides e-mail list to chat with others, information on variations of the disorder, conferences and information on local support group meetings. *Website:* http://www.efeltersyndrome.org

Consider passing this Directory on to a student or staff member - browsing through the Directory pages can often provide helpful education as to the wide variety of groups available.

KLIPPEL FEIL SYNDROME

KFS Circle of Friends, The *International network. Founded 1996.* Provides information on Klippel-Feil syndrome, a rare, congenital disorder primarily comprised of cervical-spine fusion, renal abnormalities and scoliosis. Networks families together for emotional support. Support and information provided mainly online, but literature and pen pals are also available. Write: The KFS Circle of Friends, 877 Charlotte St., Fredericton, NB E3B 1M7 Canada. *Website:* http://members.fortunecity.com/bethc/kfs.html *Email:* bethc@rogers.com

KLIPPEL-TRENAUNAY

Klippel-Trenaunay Support Group *National network. Founded 1986.* Provides mutual support and sharing of experiences among families of children with KT and adults with KT. Newsletter, phone support, meetings every two years. online mailing list. Write: KT Support Group, 5404 Dundee Rd., Edina, MN 55436. Call 952-925-2596. *Website:* http://www.k-t.org *Email:* ktnewmembers@yahoo.com

LEAD POISONING

United Parents Against Lead *National. 12 affiliated groups.* Coalition of self-help groups run by and for parents of lead poisoned children. Members support one another through resource referral, education and advocacy efforts. Aim is to end the continuing threat of lead poisoning. Offers newsletter and literature. Helps parents interested in starting new chapters. Write: UPAL, PO Box 24773, Richmond, VA 23224. Call 804-714-1618 804-714-0798 *Website:* http://www.upal.org *Email:* UPAL@juno.com

LEUKODYSTROPHY

United Leukodystrophy Foundation, Inc. *National network. Founded 1982.* Provides information and resources for leukodystrophy patients and their families. Communication network among families. Promotes research, public and professional awareness. Quarterly newsletter. National conference. Dues $25/family; $50/professional. Write: United Leukodystrophy Fdn., 2304 Highland Dr., Sycamore, IL 60178. Call 815-895-3211 or 1-800-728-5483; Fax: 815-895-2432. *Website:* http://www.ulf.org *Email:* ulf@tbcnet.com

This information is constantly changing. New groups start, others end. Please call us for the most up-to-date information from our database. 1-800-367-6274

LISSENCEPHALY /
NEURONAL MIGRATION DISORDERS

Lissencephaly Network, The *International network. Founded 1991.* Support for families affected by lissencephaly or other neuronal migration disorders as well as physicians & therapists. Helps relieve the stress of caring for an ill child. Research updates, newsletter, database of affected children. Networking of parents. Write: Lissencephaly Network, c/o Dianna Fitzgerald, 10408 Bitterroot Ct., Ft. Wayne, IN 46804. Call 260-432-4310; Fax: 260-436-7374. *Website:* http://www.lissencephaly.org *Email:* LissencephalyOne@aol.com

LOIN PAIN HEMATURIA SYNDROME

Hearts and Hands *Model. 1 group in NC. Founded 1993.* Emotional, spiritual and educational support for persons with either rare or undiagnosed illnesses and their families. Also has a registry for loin pain hematuria syndrome. Write: Hearts and Hands, c/o Winoka Plummer, 1648 Oliver's Crossing Circle, Winston-Salem, NC 27127. Call 336-785-7612. *Website:* ttp://www.geocities.com/hotsprings/spa/2464/index.html

LOWE SYNDROME

Lowe Syndrome Association *International network. Founded 1983.* For parents, friends, professionals and others who are interested in Lowe syndrome. Provides medical and educational information and online discussion. Supports medical research. Offers booklet, newsletter. International conference. Dues $15 (can be waived if parents are in need). Write: Lowe Syndrome Association, 18919 Voss Rd., Dallas, TX 75287. Call 612-869-5693; Fax: 612-866-3222. *Website:* http://www.lowesyndrome.org *Email:* info@lowesyndrome.org

LYMPHANGIOLEIOMYOMATOSIS

LAM Foundation, The *International network. Founded 1995.* Provides support and hope for women and their families who have LAM (lymphangioleiomyomatosis), a rare lung disorder affecting only women, where smooth muscle cells grow throughout the lungs. Fund-raising activities to fund clinical and basic research and education through conferences. One newsletter for general distribution and one solely for LAM patients. Patient directory. Listserv and advocacy program. Write: The LAM Foundation, c/o Sue Byrnes, 10105 Beacon Hills Dr., Cincinnati, OH 45241. Call 513-777-6889; Fax: 513-777-4109. *Website:* http://lam.uc.edu/ *Email:* lam@one.net

MALIGNANT HYPERTHERMIA

Malignant Hyperthermia Assn. of the U.S. *National network. Founded 1981.* Education and support for malignant hyperthermia-susceptible patients and their physicians. Information for health care professionals and MH-susceptible patients. Conducts limited research. Newsletter, literature, regional conferences. Write: MHAUS, 11 E. State St., PO Box 1069, Sherburne, NY 13460. Call 1-800-644-9737 or 607-674-7901; Fax: 607-674-7910. *Website:* http://www.mhaus.org *Email:* info@mhaus.org

MANNOSIDOSIS / GLYCOPROTEIN STORAGE DISEASE

International Society for Mannosidosis & Related Diseases *International network. Founded 1999.* Provides emotional support for families affected by any glycoprotein storage disease. Offers educational resources for medical community. Promotes research to develop treatments. Phone support, literature, pen pals, information and referrals, newsletter, advocacy. online message boards, chat rooms and e-mail discussions. Write: International Society for Mannosidosis & Related Diseases, Inc., 1030 Saxon Hill Dr., Cockeysville, MD 21214. Call 410-628-9991. *Website:* http://www.mannosidosis.org *Email:* info@mannosidosis.org

MAPLE SYRUP URINE DISEASE

Maple Syrup Urine Disease Family Support Group *National network. Founded 1982.* Opportunity for support and personal contact for those with maple syrup urine disease and their families. Provides information on MSUD. Aims to strengthen the liaison between families and professionals. Encourages research and newborn screening for MSUD. Newsletter ($10/yr), phone support, conferences, advocacy. Write: MSUD Family Support Group, c/o Sandra Bulcher, 82 Ravine Rd., Powell, OH 43065. Call 740-548-4475. *Website:* http://www.msud-support.org *Email:* dbulcher@aol.com

MARFAN SYNDROME

National Marfan Foundation *National network. 100+ chapters, support groups and telephone contact persons. Founded 1981.* Provides information on Marfan syndrome and related connective tissue disorders to patients, families and physicians. Provides a means for patients and relatives to share experiences and support one another. Research, conference, newsletter, publications. Write: Nat'l Marfan Fdn., 22 Manhasset Ave., Port Washington, NY 11050.

Call   1-800-862-7326or   516-883-8712;   Fax: 516-883-8040.   *Website:* http://www.marfan.org *Email:* staff@marfan.org

MARINESCO-SJOGREN SYNDROME

Mariensco-Sjogren Syndrome Support Group *National network. Founded 2000.* Support for families affected by Marinesco-Sjogren syndrome (MSS), a rare, genetic disorder characterized by ataxia, cataracts, small stature and retardation. Write: MSS Support Group, 1640 Crystal View Circle, Newbury Park, CA 91320. Call   805-499-7410.   *Website:*   http://www.marinesco-sjogren.org   *Email:* mss@marinesco-sjogren.org

MASTOCYTOSIS
(see also myeloproliferative disease, cancer)

Mastocytosis Society, The *International network. Founded 1994.* Mutual support through a newsletter for persons with mastocytosis (a proliferation of mast cells), their families, friends and professionals working with them. E-mail discussion group for patients and researchers. Fundraising for research, phone support. Write: TMS, c/o Rita Barlow, PO Box 284, Russell, MA 01071. Call 413-862-4556. *Website:* http://www.tmsforacure.org *Email:* jbar5@verizon.net

MCCUNE-ALBRIGHT SYNDROME

McCune-Albright Syndrome/Fibrous Dysplasia Division *International network. Founded 1990.* Provides support for families of McCune-Albright syndrome patients. Newsletters, updated medical information, phone support, annual conventions. Dues $30/yr. Write: McCune-Albright Syndrome/Fibrous Dysplasia Division, c/o MAGIC Foundation, 6645 West North Ave., Oak Park, IL 60302. Call   1-800-362-4423;   Fax: 708-383-0899.   *Website:* http://www.magicfoundation.org *Email:* mary@magicfondation.org

MEMBRANOPROLIFERATIVE GLOMERULONEPHRITIS TYPE II
(see also kidney)

Kidneeds *National network. Founded 1997.* Grassroots support network for parents of children with membranoproliferative glomerulonephritis (MPGN) type II (aka dense deposit disease), a rare kidney disorder. Provides money for research on MPGN type II. Phone support, newsletter and advocacy. Write: Kidneeds, 11 Cherry Lane NE, Iowa City, IA 52240. Call 319-338-6404 (Voice/Fax). *Website:* http://www.medicine.uiowa.edu/kidneeds *Email:* llanning@blue.weeg.uiowa.edu

MENKES KINKY HAIR SYNDROME /
STEELY HAIR DISEASE

Menkes Kinky Hair Syndrome *Online. Founded 1999.* Support and information for others affected with Menkes kinky hair syndrome related to deficient levels of copper in the cells. Also known as Kinky Hair disease and Steely Hair disease. Message boards and chat rooms. *Website:* http://groups.yahoo.com/group/menkes_kinky_hair/ *Email:* menkes_kinky_hair-subscribe@yahoogroups.com

METABOLIC DISORDERS
(see also specific disorder)

CDG Family Network Foundation *International network. Founded 1996.* Support for parents of children diagnosed with congenital disorders of glycosylation, an inherited metabolic disease affecting all body parts, especially the central and peripheral nervous systems. Support is attained primarily online, but the group also provides information and referrals, bi-annual newsletter, phone support and advocacy. Bulletin board for families to interact with questions, comments and updates. Write: CDG Family Network, c/o Cynthia Wren-Gray, President, PO Box 860847, Plano, TX, 75074. Call 1-800-250-5273; Fax: 903-640-8254. *Website:* http://www.cdgs.com *Email:* cdgaware@aol.com

CLIMB - National Information and Advice Centre for Metabolic Disease *International Network.* Supplies information on over 700 metabolic conditions and offers long-term support. Provides a family support network, newsletter, phone support, pen pals, annual conference, befriender network. Write: CLIMB – Nat'l Info. & Advice Ctr. For Metabolic Disease Climb Building, 176 Nantwich Rd., Crewe, CW2 6BG UK. Call 0044 870 77 00 326 (day); Fax: 0044 870 77 00 327. *Website:* http://www.climb.org.uk *Email:* info@climb.org.uk

Purine Research Society *Model. Founded 1986.* Support for persons affected by purine metabolic disorders caused by a defective gene resulting in the production of an enzyme with too little to too much catalytic activity. Purine metabolic diseases include gout, purine autism, Lesch-Nyhan syndrome, ADA deficiency and others. Funds research to find the defective enzyme responsible for purine autism, the largest single sub-group of autism. Offers online information on diagnosis, purine restricted diet, referrals. Write: Purine Research Society, c/o Tahma Metz, 5424 Beech Ave., Bethesda, MD 20814. Call Tahma Metz 301-530-0354; Fax: 301-564-9597. *Website:* http://www.PurineResearchSociety.org *Email:* purine@erols.com

METATROPIC DYSPLASIA DWARFISM
(see also growth disorders, short/tall)

Metatropic Dysplasia Dwarf Registry *National network. Founded 1980.* Support and information for persons affected by metatropic dwarfism. Networks families and shares information. Offers phone support, information and referrals, limited literature. Write: Metatropic Dysplasia Dwarf Registry, 3393 Geneva Dr., Santa Clara, CA 95051. Call 408-244-6354; Fax: 408-296-6317. *Website:* http://www.lpbayarea.org/metatrophic *Email:* figone@netgate.net

MILLER'S SYNDROME

Foundation for Nager and Miller Syndromes *International network. Founded 1989.* Networking for families that are affected by Nager or Miller syndromes. Provides referrals, library of information, phone support, newsletter, brochures and scholarships for Camp About Face. Write: FNMS, c/o De De Van Quill, 13210 South East 342nd St., Auburn, WA 98092. Call 1-800-507-3667 or 253-333-1483; Fax: 253-288-7679. *Website:* http://www.fnms.net *Email:* ddfnms@aol.com

MITOCHONDRIAL DISORDERS

United Mitochondrial Disease Foundation *National network. 9 chapters. Founded 1995.* Promotes research and education for the diagnosis, treatment and cure of mitochondrial disorders and provides support to affected individuals and families. Chapter and support groups, networking for families affected by mitochondrial disease, a genetic, degenerative disease. Quarterly newsletter, information and referrals, library of medical publications, patient registry, phone help and annual symposium are available. Awards research grants. Write: UMDF, 8085 Saltsburg Rd., Suite 201, Pittsburgh, PA 15239. Call 412-793-8077; Fax: 412-793-6477. *Website:* http://www.umdf.org *Email:* info@umdf.org

MOEBIUS SYNDROME

Moebius Syndrome Foundation *International network. Founded 1994.* Communication and support network for persons with Moebius syndrome (a paralysis of the 6th and 7th cranial nerves) and their families. Information, education. Fund raising for research. Newsletter, phone support, informal meetings, national conference. Help with starting groups. Write: Moebius Syndrome Fdn., PO Box 147, Pilot Grove, MO 65276. Call Vicki McCarrell 660-834-3406 (eve) or 660-882-5576 ext. 120 (day) 660-834-3407. *Website:* http://www.moebiussyndrome.com *Email:* vickimc@iland.net

MOTILITY DISORDERS
(see also specific disorder)

Asociation of Gastrointestinal Motility Disorders, Inc. *International network.* *Founded 1991.* Support and education for persons affected by digestive motility disorders. Serves as an educational resource and information base for medical professionals. Physician referrals, video tapes, large variety of educational materials, networking support, symposiums and several publications. Dues $35/US; 42/Int'l (can be waived). Write: AGMD International Corp Headquarters, 11 North St., Lexington, MA 02420. Call 781-861-3874; Fax: 781-861-7834. *Website:* http://www.agmd-gimotility.org *Email:* gimotility@msn.com

MUCOLIPIDOSIS TYPE 4

ML4 Foundation *National network.* *Founded 1983.* Support network for families of children diagnosed with mucolipidosis type 4, a genetic disorder characterized by variable psychomotor retardation that primarily affects Ashkenazi Jews. Supports fund-raising for research. Information and referrals, phone support. Write: ML4 Fdn., 719 E. 17th St., Brooklyn, NY 11230. Call 718-434-5067; Fax: 718-859-7371. *Website:* http://www.ml4.org *Email:* ml4www@aol.com

MUCOPOLYSACCHARIDOSES / MUCOLIPIDOSES
MORQUIO'S SYNDROME

International Morquio Support Group, The *International network.* *Founded 1999.* Provides support and education for families of children with Morquio Type A. Helps educate health care professionals about this lysosomal storage disease. Funds research. Maintains database of families. Referrals to physicians and medical information. Pen pals, phone support, conferences, newsletter. online guestbook and helpful links. Write: Morquio Support Group, PO Box 64184, Tucson, AZ 85728-4184. Call 520-744-2531; Fax: 520-744-2535. *Website:* http://www.morquio.com *Email:* mbs85705@yahoo.com

National MPS Society *National.* *Founded 1974.* Support for families with mucopolysaccharidoses and mucolipidoses. Support groups, public education, fund-raising for research, parent referral service for networking. Quarterly newsletter and phone support network. Write: Nat'l MPS Soc., c/o Barbara Wedehase, PO Box 736, Bangor, ME 04402-0736. Call 207-947-1445; Fax: 207-990-3074. *Website:* http://www.mpssociety.org *Email:* info@mpssociety.org

MULTIPLE ENDOCRINE NEOPLASIA /
WERNER SYNDROME / ADENOMATOSIS

Multiple Endocrine Neoplasia Society *International network. 21 affiliated groups. Founded 1995.* Mutual support to persons afflicted with familial multiple endocrine neoplasia type 1 (aka Wermer syndrome or adenomatosis)and their families. MEN1 affects the endocrine glands. Literature, information and referrals, phone support and pen pals. Access to doctors and current research. Dues $10/yr. Write: MENS, Box 100, Meota, SK, Canada S0M 1X0. Call 306-892-2080; Fax: 306-892-2587. *Website:* http://www.mensociety.net *Email:* mensociety@sasktel.net

Pheochromocytoma Information Group *Online.* Offers support and information for persons with pheochromocytoma or multiple endocrine neoplasia syndrome. *Website:* http://www.pheochromocytoma.org

MULTIPLE HEREDITARY EXOSTOSES

MHE and Me: A Support Group for Kids with MHE *Online. (A member of The MHE Coalition) Founded 1999.* Provides peers and a supportive community to children suffering from multiple hereditary exostoses (a genetic disorder in which benign cartilage-capped bone tumors grow from growth plates of long bones or surface of flat bones). Develops information and literature to assist children and their families in dealing with the disease. Advocacy, information and referrals, phone and email support. Write: MHE and Me, c/o Susan Wynn, 14 Stony Brook Dr., Pine Island NY 10969. Call 845-258-6058. *Website:* http://www.mheandme.com *Email:* mheandme@yahoo.com

MHE Coalition, The *Online. 4 affiliated groups. Founded 2000.* Support and information for persons and their families affected by multiple hereditary exostosis, a skeletal disorder characterized by the formation of abnormal bony growths. Promotes and encourages research to find the cause, treatment and cure. Newsletter, networking, literature, advocacy, online groups, information and referrals, phone support, pen pals. Write: MHE Coalition, 8838 Holly Lane, Olmsted Falls, OH 44138. Call Chele Zelina, President 440-235-6325 (eve). *Website:* http://www.mhecoalition.com *Email:* CheleZ1@aol.com

MULLERIAN ANOMALIES

Mullerian Anomalies of the Uterus *Online* Support and information for those with mullerian anomalies of the uterus such as bicornuate, septate, unicornauate, hypoplastic and didelphys uteria. Weekly chat, email list and message board. *Website:* http://health.groups.yahoo.com/group/MullerianAnomalies/

MYASTHENIA GRAVIS

OCEAN

Myasthenia Gravis Support Group Support and education for patients with myasthenia gravis. Families, friend and caregivers welcome. Guest speakers, buddy system and phone help. Meets 3rd Sun., 1pm, Ocean Medical Center, 425 Jack Martin Blvd., Brick. Call Barbara Yodice 732-262-0450. *Email:* autoimmunehelp@aol.com

STATEWIDE

Myasthenia Gravis Foundation - Garden State Chapter Public and professional education about MG, patient support, fund-raising for research, phone help, peer-counseling, outreach, professional speakers. State newsletter. Monthly board meetings. Area representatives in most counties. Membership dues $20/yr (Can be waived). Quarterly meetings in various locations throughout NJ. Write: Myasthenia Gravis Foundation, P.O. Box 4258, Wayne, NJ 07474-4258. Call 1-800-437-4949 (in NJ); 973-835-4444 (day); Fax: 973-835-4452. *Website:* http://www.webspan.net/~gsmg/

NATIONAL

Myasthenia Gravis Foundation of America, Inc. *National. 33 chapters. Founded 1952.* Promotes research and education into myasthenia gravis, a chronic neuromuscular disease. Provides supportive services for patients and families. Information and referral. Newsletter, support groups, various web-based services, annual and scientific meetings. Write: Myasthenia Gravis Fdn., 1821 University Ave. W., Suite S256, St. Paul, MN, 55104. Call 1-800-541-5454 or 651-917-6256; Fax: 651-917-1835. *Website:* http://www.myasthenia.org *Email:* mgfa@myasthenia.org

ONLINE

Myasthenia Gravis Patient-To-Patient *Online.* Offers support and chat rooms where members can share problems, solutions and support. *Website:* http://pages.prodigy.net/stanley.way/myasthenia/patient.htm *Email:* Stanley.way@prodigy.net

"Man never made any material as resilient as the human spirit."
--Bern Williams

MYCOSIS FUNGOIDES

Mycosis Fungoides UK *Online.* Support for any person affected by mycosis fungoides. Provides chat room and message board. Offers medical information links and support. *Website:* http://groups.msn.com/MycosisFungoidesUK

MYELODYSOKASTIC SYNDROMES

Aplastic Anemia and MDS Int'l Foundation, Inc. *International. Founded 1983.* Provides emotional support and support groups worldwide for persons with aplastic anemia, myelodysplastic syndromes, paroxysmal nocturnal demoglobinuria and other bone marrow failure diseases. Financially supports research. Offers free educational materials, information about current research and clinical trials and financial assistance. Write: Aplastic Anemia and MDS Int'l Foundation, Inc., PO Box 613, Annapolis, MD 21404. Call 1-800-747-2820 or 410-867-0242; Fax: 410-867-0240. *Website:* http://www.aamds.org *Email:* help@aamds.org
ONLINE

Myelodysplastic Syndromes Foundation *Online.* Unmoderated forums for patients and professionals dealing with myelodysplastic syndromes, a group of bone marrow diseases. Also has referrals to treatment centers. *Website:* http://www.mds-foundation.org *Email:* patientliaison@mds-foundation.org

MYELOPROLIFERATIVE DISEASE
(see also specific disorder, cancer)

MPD-Net *Online. Founded 1989.* Support network where persons with myeloproliferative disease can share their experiences and problems. Supports research. Publishes materials pertaining to MPD. Professional involvement. Newsletter, phone support, conferences, information and referrals. online listserv with 1800 members with MPD who exchange emails about their disease. Write: MPD-Net, c/o Joyce Niblack, 115 E. 72nd St., New York, NY 10021. *Website:* http://www.mpdinfo.org *Email:* JNiblack@mpdinfo.org

MYOSITIS

Myositis Association, The *International network. 65 groups. Founded 1993.* Dedicated to serving those with polymyositis, dermatomyositis, juvenile myositis and inclusion body myositis. Provides education and support. Also serves as a clearinghouse between patients and scientists. Area meetings available. Annual conference. Guidelines available for starting similar groups. Fundraising for research. Dues $35. Write: The Myositis Assn., 1233 20th St., NW, #402,

Washington DC, 20036. Call 202-887-0088 (day); Fax: 202-466-8940. *Website:* http://www.myositis.org *Email:* tma@myositis.org

MYOTONIA CONGENITA FORUM

Myotonia Congenita *Online.* Forum for people with myotonia congenita as well as their friends and families. Opportunity to ask questions and share tips for living with myotonia congenita. *Email:* jan@accessfitness.com *Website:* http://www.accessfitness.com/myotoniacongenita.html

MYOTUBULAR MYOPATHY

Myotubular Myopathy Resource Group *International network. Founded 1993.* Information for patients, parents and doctors regarding myotubular myopathy, a family of three rare muscle disorders usually causing low muscle tone and diminished respiratory capacity. Exchanging of successes with other affected families. Phone support, information and referrals, literature. Write: Myotubular Myopathy Resource Group, c/o Pam Scoggin, 2602 Quaker Dr., Texas City, TX 77590. Call 409-945-8569. *Website:* http://www.mtmrg.org *Email:* gscoggin@aol.com

NAGER SYNDROME

Foundation for Nager and Miller Syndromes *International. Founded 1989.* Networking for families that are affected by Nager or Miller syndromes. Provides referrals, library of information, phone support, newsletter, brochures and scholarships for Camp About Face. Write: FNMS, c/o De De Van Quill, 13210 South East 342nd St., Auburn, WA 98092. Call 1-800-507-3667 or 253-333-1483; Fax: 253-288-7679. *Website:* http://www.fnms.net *Email:* ddfnms@aol.com

NAIL PATELLA SYNDROME

Nail Patella Syndrome Networking/Support Group *International network. Founded 1995.* Support network for persons with nail patella syndrome to exchange information. Links to a research study and other NPS-related sites. Provides information and online chat. Write: NPS Networking/Support Group, 67 Woodlake Dr., Holland PA 18966. *Website:* http://hometown.aol.com/PACALI/npspage.html *Email:* PACALI@aol.com

If you are using this book past Spring 2007, please call us for information about our most recent directory. 1-800-367-6274

NARCOLEPSY

Narcolepsy Network *National. 100 affiliated support groups. Founded 1986.* Support & education for persons with narcolepsy & other sleep disorders, their families & interested others. Helps with coping skills, family & community problems. Provides advocacy & education, supports research. Newsletter, conferences, phone support & group development guidelines. Dues $35. Write: Narcolepsy Network, 631B Ten Rod Road, North Kingstown, RI 02852. Call 1-888-292-6522; Fax: 513-891-3836. *Website:* http://www.narcolepsynetwork.org *Email:* narnet@narcolepysnetwork.org

NECROTIZING FASCIITIS / FLESH EATING BACTERIA

National Necrotizing Fasciitis Foundation *Online. Founded 1997.* Provides education and support for persons affected by necrotizing fasciitis (aka flesh-eating bacteria). Aim is to educate public and advocate for research. Provides literature, phone support, newsletter, pen pals, conferences and information and referrals. Publishes "Surviving the Flesh-Eating Bacteria: Understanding, Preventing, Treating And Living With the Effects of Necrotizing Fasciitis." *Website:* http://www.nnff.com

NEMALINE MYOPATHY, CONGENITAL

Nemaline Myopathy Foundation *National network. Founded 1991.* Grassroots group that offers newsletter that networks families affected by pediatric/adolescent nemaline myopathy for support and information. Pen pals, literature, phone support, information and referrals. Write: NMN, c/o Krystyn Plymell, 12265 S. Albervan St., Olathe, KS 66062-5940. Call 913-768-7767. *Website:* http://www.davidmcd.btinternet.co.uk *Email:* kplymell@amli.com

NEUROCARDIOGENIC SYNCOPE
(see also dysautonomia)

Neurocardiogenic Syncope Fainting List *Online.* Support and understanding for those suffering from neurocardiogenic syncope, dysautonomia, orthostatic hypotension, neurally mediated hypotension, low blood pressure and other diseases that can cause fainting, heat sensitivity, nausea or dizziness. Open to families and friends. Sharing of stories, struggles, triumphs and information. *Website:* http://health.groups.yahoo.com/group/neurocardiogenicsyncope-fainting

We can also refer callers to over 100 individuals who are seeking others to help start new support groups throughout NJ, if you don't see it, that doesn't mean it doesn't exist! 1-800-367-6274

NEUROFIBROMATOSIS
(see also specific disorder)

Children's Tumor Foundation *National. 50 chapters. Founded 1978.* For patients with neurofibromatosis & their families. Promotes & supports research into the causes of and cure for, NF. Provides information, assistance & education. Dues $50/year. Quarterly newsletter. Professional grants awarded for research. Write: Children's Tumor Foundation, 95 Pine St., 16th Floor, New York, NY 10005. Call 1-800-323-7938 or 212-344-6633; Fax: 212-747-0004. *Website:* http://www.ctf.org *Email:* info@ctf.org

Neurofibromatosis, Inc. *National. 8 groups. Founded 1988.* Dedicated to individuals and families affected by the neurofibromatoses (NF-1 & NF-2) through education, support and clinical and research programs. Offers newsletter, networking, videotapes, printed materials, information and referrals, phone support. Assistance in starting groups. Write: Neurofibromatosis, Inc., PO Box 18246, Minneapolis, MN 55418. Call 301-918-4600 or 1-800-942-6825 (patient inquiries); Fax: 301-918-0009. *Website:* http://www.nfinc.org *Email:* NFInfo@nfinc.org

NEUROLOGICAL DISORDERS

Brain Talk MGH Neurology WebForums *Online.* Provides both unmoderated message boards and chat rooms for specific neurological disorders including amyloidosis, arachnoiditis, Bell's palsy, cerebellar ataxia, congenital fiber type disproportion, CFS leak, DeMorsiers syndrome, erythromelalgia, meningitis, meralgia paresthetic, Norrie disease, periodic paralysis, phantom limb pain, Romberg disorder, Syndenhams chorea, rare neurological disorders and thoracic outlet syndrome, plus many, many more. *Website:* http://www.braintalk.org

NEUTROPENIA

Neutropenia Support Association, Inc. *International. Serves 30 countries. Founded 1989.* Information and support for persons with neutropenia, their families and the medical community. Aims to increase awareness, support research and disseminate literature. Support group meetings. Write: Neutropenia Support Assoc. Inc., PO Box 243, 971 Corydon Ave., Winnipeg, Manitoba R3M 3S7 Canada. Call 204-489-8454 or 1-800-663-8876. *Website:* http://www.neutropenia.ca *Email:* stevens@neutropenia.ca

NEVUS, CONGENITAL / NEUROCUTANEOUS MELANOSIS

Nevus Network *(MULTILINGUAL) International network. Founded 1983.* Provides a network of support and information for people with a large brown birthmark called a giant congenital nevus and/or an associated condition, neurocutaneous melanosis. Write: Nevus Network PO Box 305, West Salem, OH 44287. Call 419-853-4525 or 405-377-3403. *Website:* http://www.nevusnetwork.org *Email:* info@nevusnetwork.org

Nevus Outreach, Inc. *International network.* Dedicated to improving awareness and providing support for people affected by congenital pigmented nevi and finding a cure. Website, literature, 24-hour support hotline, international conferences. Write: Nevus Outreach, Inc., 1601 Madison Blvd., Bartlesville, OK 74006. Call 918-331-0595 or 1-877-426-3887 (hotline). *Website:* http://www.nevus.org

NIEMANN PICK DISEASE

National Niemann-Pick Disease Foundation, Inc. *International network. Founded 1992.* Provides support for families affected by Niemann-Pick disease type A, B and C. Promotes and supports research. Provides newsletter, family directory, networking, family conference, phone support, information and referrals. Guidelines available to help start similar groups. Dues $20. Write: National Niemann-Pick Disease Foundation,, PO Box 49, 401B Madison Ave., Fort Atkinson, WI 53538. Call 920-563-0930; Fax: 920-563-0931. *Website:* http://www.nnpdf.org *Email:* nnpdf@idcnet.com

NONKETOTIC HYPERGLYCINEMIA
(see also metabolic disorders)

NKH International Family Network *International network. Founded 1995.* Support and networking for parents of children with nonketotic hyperglycinemia (NKH), an inherited metabolic disorder. Newsletter, online network, discussion board, information and referrals, phone support. Dues $15. Write: NKH Int'l Family Network, 172 Makalley Ln., Tazewell, TN 37879. Call 423-626-6718. *Email:* burkenkh@communicomm.com

NOONAN SYNDROME

Noonan Syndrome Support Group *International network. Founded 1996.* Provides information for persons with Noonan syndrome, their families and interested others. Networks individuals together for peer support. Write: Noonan Syndrome Support Group, PO Box 145, Upperco, MD 21155.

Call 1-888-686-2224 or 410-374-5245. *Website:* http://www.noonansyndrome.org *Email:* Wandar@bellatlantic.net

NYSTAGMUS

American Nystagmus Network *National network.* Founded 1999. Network of persons affected by nystagmus, an involuntary, rapid movement of the eyeball. Open to parents of affected children, adults with nystagmus and interested professionals. Provides general information. Promotes research into cause and cure. E-mail discussion group, discussion board and biannual newsletter and conferences. Write: American Nystagmus Network, Inc., 303-D Beltline Place #321, Decatur, Alabama 35603. *Website:* http://www.nystagmus.org *Email:* webmaster@nystagmus.org

ODOR (BODY / BREATH)

NARA (Not A Rose Association) *Model. 1 group in GA. Founded 1998.* Mutual support for persons suffering from "odorous" conditions of the body, breath or unknown sources. Offers coping skills. Write: NARA, 5227 Selene Dr., Stone Mountain, GA 30088. Call Bobbie 770-879-5922. *Email:* annhenry99@yahoo.com

OPITZ-G/BBB SYNDROME

Opitz G/BBB Family Network *International. Founded 1994.* Support, encouragement, education and sharing of successes and ideas for families affected by Opitz-G/BBB syndrome. Maintains database of members. Referrals to other families. Family conferences. Write: Opitz Family Network, PO Box 515, Grand Lake, CO 80447. Call 970-627-8935; Fax: 970-627-8818. *Website:* http://www.opitznet.org *Email:* opitznet@mac.com

OSTEOGENESIS IMPERFECTA

ESSEX

NJ Osteogenesis Imperfecta Support Group Purpose is to share information and support and improve the quality of life for people affected by O.I. Rap sessions, guest speakers and phone help. Information and referrals. For meeting information call Rosemarie or JoAnn 201-489-9232 (day). *Email:* RDKOIF@verizon.net

NATIONAL

Osteogenesis Imperfecta Foundation *National. 24 affiliated support groups. Founded 1970.* Support and resources for families dealing with osteogenesis imperfecta. Provides information for medical professionals. Supports research. Literature, quarterly newsletter. Phone support network. Write: O.I. Fdn., 804 W. Diamond Ave., Suite 210, Gaithersburg, MD 20878. Call 1-800-981-2663 or 301-947-0083; Fax: 301-947-0456. *Website:* http://www.oif.org *Email:* bonelink@oif.org

OSTEONECROSIS / AVASCULAR NECROSIS

ON/AVN Support Group International Association, Inc. *Online.* Support for persons who suffer from ostenecrosis (aka avascular necrosis). Goal is to educate the world and offer emotional support to both those with ON/AVN and their families. Provides information and referral and newsletter. Also has special section for youth with ON/AVN. Open to other chronic bone, joint or muscular conditions and persons with joint replacements. Write: ON/AVN Support Group Int'l Assn., 8500 Henry Ave., Box 118, Philadelphia, PA, 19128. *Website:* http://www.osteonecrosisavnsupport.org *Email:* avninfo@osteonecrosisavnsupport.org

Osteonecrosis Self-Help Group Listserv *Online* Designed as an open forum for those having experience with the chronic bone disorder, osteonecrosis (aka avascular necrosis). All are welcome to join in and share successes and frustrations in getting diagnosed and treated. Exchange of coping skills dealing with this "on again off again" chronic disease. *Website:*http://health.groups.yahoo.com/group/osteonecrosis/

OXALOSIS & HYPEROXALURIA

Oxalosis and Hyperoxaluria Foundation *National network. Founded 1989.* Provides support and current information for patients, families and medical professionals in the field of primary hyperoxaluria and oxalate stone disease. Educates the public, supports research. Yearly dues $25/ind; $50/prof; $100/business. Write: OHF, 201 E. 19th St., #12E, New York, NY 10003. Call 1-800-643-8699; Fax: 212-777-0471. *Website:* http://www.ohf.org *Email:* info@ohf.org

PAGET'S DISEASE

National Association for the Relief of Paget's Disease *Model. 5 regional groups in UK. 2500 member network. Founded 1973.* Offers support to persons with Paget's disease. Aim is to raise awareness of this disorder through newsletter and publications. Sponsors research. Guidelines available for starting similar groups. Write: Nat'l Assn. for the Relief of Paget's Disease, 323 Manchester Rd., Walkden, Worsley, Manchester M28 3HH, UK. Call 44- 0161-799-4646.

Website: http:www.paget.org.uk *Email:* director@paget.org.uk

PANHYPOPITUITARISM

Panhypopituitarism Division *International network. Founded 1990.* Provides support for families affected by panhypopituitarism. Newsletters, updated medical information, phone support, annual conventions and Kids Program. online assistance available for finding or forming local support groups. Dues start at $30 (overseas is more). Write: Panhypopituitarism Division, c/o MAGIC Foundation, 6645 W. North Ave., Oak Park, IL 60302. Call 1-800-362-4423; Fax: 708-383-0899. *Website:* http://www.magicfoundation.org *Email:* mary@magicfoundation.org

PANNICULITIS

Erythema Nodosum Support Group *Online. Founded 2003.* Mutual support of erythema nodosum and pyoderma gangreblosum patients and available resources. Website: http://health.groups.yahoo.com/group/erythema_nodosum_group/

Panniculitis *Online.* Support for persons afflicted with any form of panniculitis (Weber Christian, erythema nodosum, mesenteric panniculitis, erythema induratum, lupus panniculitis, subcutaneous sarcoid, etc.) Offers message boards, information and chat rooms. *Website:* http://groups.yahoo.com/group/Panniculitis

PAPILLOMATOSIS

STATEWIDE

Recurrent Respiratory Papillomatosis Foundation National network. *Founded 1992.* Networking for families affected by recurrent respiratory papillomatosis interested professionals are welcome. Newsletter, phone support. Write: RRPF, P.O. Box 6643, Lawrenceville, NJ 08648-0643. Call Bill Stern 609-530-1443; Fax: 609-530-1912. *Website:* http://www.rrpf.org *Email:* bills@rrpf.org

NATIONAL

American Laryngeal Papilloma Foundation *National network. Founded 1991.* Assists those afflicted with laryngeal papillomatosis. Sharing of experiences and information through networking. Seeks to provide financial aid to needy families and affected persons. Vitamin supplement program. National registry. Newsletter, phone support, information, referrals, exhibits and conferences. Write: ALPF, 489

Ft. Mill Lane, Spring Hill, FL 34609-9678. Call 352-686-8583 (voice/fax). *Website:* http://www.alpf.org *Email:* alpf@atlantic.net

Recurrent Respiratory Papillomatosis Foundation *National network. Founded 1992.* Networking for families affected by recurrent respiratory papillomatosis (RRP) and interested professionals. Newsletter, phone support. online support and referrals to local support groups. Write: RRPF, PO Box 6643, Lawrenceville, NJ 08648-0643. Call Bill Stern 609-530-1443; Fax: 609-530-1912. *Website:* http://www.rrpf.org *Email:* bills@rrpf.org

PARRY-ROMBERG SYNDROME / PROGRESSIVE FACIAL HEMIATROPHY
(see also neurological disorders)

Romberg's Connection, The *Online. Founded 1997.* Offers mutual support for persons affected by Parry-Romberg's syndrome (aka progressive facial hemiatrophy or Romberg's syndrome), their families and friends. Parry Romberg syndrome is a rare disorder causing atrophy to usually one-half of the face. Aim is to locate affected persons and offer strength, hope, courage and friendship. Communication is through a group mailing list and via mail. There are some face-to-face meetings. *Website:* http://www.geocities.com/HotSprings/1018/ *Email:* rombergs@hotmail.com

PEMPHIGUS

International Pemphigus Foundation *National network. 16 affiliated groups. Founded 1994.* Provides support and information on pemphigus and related autoimmune blistering diseases for patients, families, friends and the medical community. Offers listserv, literature, newsletter, information and referrals, advocacy and phone and online support groups. Write: Int'l Pemphigus Fdn., 150 River Park Dr., Suite 208, Sacramento, CA 95815. Call 916-922-1298; Fax: 916-922-1458. *Website:* http://www.pemphigus.org *Email:* pemphigus@pemphigus.org

PERIODIC PARALYSIS / NON-DYSTROPHIC MYOTONIAS
(see also neurological disorders)

Periodic Paralysis Association *Online.* Provides information and support to individuals with periodic paralysis and non-dystrophic myotonias (disorders characterized by episodic paralysis and weakness), their families and health care professionals. Offers links to online specialist referrals, private e-mail listserv, Ask-the-experts, online newsletter and patient advocacy. Write: Periodic Paralysis Association, 1124 Royal Oak Dr, Monrovia, CA 91016. Call 626-303-3244; Fax:

626-337-1966. *Website:* http://www.periodicparalysis.org *Email:* info@periodicparalysis.org

PETERS' ANOMALY

Peter's Anomaly Support Group *Online.* Support for families of children with Peter's anomaly. Offers message board and forum. Also many useful links. *Website:* http://www.petersanomaly.org *Email:* rmcginn66@yahoo.com

PEUTZ JEGHERS SYNDROME

Peutz Jeghers Syndrome *Online 188 members worldwide. Founded 2000.* Provides information for individuals with Peutz Jeghers syndrome and their families. Provides peer support, matching individuals and their families and medical referrals. Must subscribe to view the archives. *Website:* http://www.peutz-jeghers.com *Email:* pj4steph@aol.com

PHEOCHROMOCYTOMA / MULTIPLE ENDOCRINE HEOPLASIA SYNDROME

Pheochromocytoma Information Group *Online.* Offers support and information for persons with pheochromocytoma or multiple endocrine neoplasia syndrome. *Website:* http://www.pheochromocytoma.org

PIERRE ROBIN SYNDROME/SEQUENCE

Pierre Robin Network *National network. Founded 1999.* Support and education for individuals, parents, caregivers and professionals dealing with Pierre Robin syndrome or sequence. Literature, newsletter, information, advocacy. Online e-mail group and bulletin board. Outreach committee comprised of families worldwide available to correspond via mail, phone, in person or e-mail. Write: Pierre Robin Network, PO Box 3274, Quincy, IL 62305. Fax: 217-224-0292. *Website:* http://www.pierrerobin.org *Email:* info@pierrerobin.org

PINK DISEASE / MERCURY TOXICITY

Pink Disease Support Group *International network. Founded 1989.* Support group for people affected by Pink disease (babyhood mercury toxicity) and their relatives. Provides information, support and newsletters by mail and email. Online chat group. Dues $15 yr. (Australia) or $25 (int'l). Write: Pink Disease Support Group, PO Box 134, Gilgandra NSW, Australia 2827. *Website:* http://www.users.bigpond.com/difarnsworth/ *Email:* difarnsworth@bigpond.com

PITUITARY DISORDERS
(see also specific disorder)

Pituitary Network Association *International network. Founded 1992.* Mutual support for persons with all types of pituitary disorders and diseases. Promotes early diagnosis, medical and public awareness and continued research to find a cure. Newsletter, information and referrals, phone support, resource guide, patient conferences. Write: PNA, PO Box 1958, Thousand Oaks, CA 91358. Call 805-499-9973; Fax: 805-480-0633. *Website:* http://www.pituitary.org *Email:* PNA@pituitary.org

PITYRIASIS RUBRA PILARIS

Pityriasis Rubra Pilaris Support Group *Online. Founded 1997.* An international forum for persons affected by pityriasis rubra pilaris (PRP), a rare and chronic skin disorder that often appears suddenly. Symptoms may include reddish-orange patches on the skin, severe flaking, itching and thickening of the skin. Offers a caring forum where people can share information, personal experiences and treatment options. Spouses, partners, families and friends are welcome. *Website:* http://www.prp-support.org *Email:* prp-l@tip.net.au or rgreene@temple.edu

PORPHYRIA

American Porphyria Foundation *National network. Founded 1981.* Mutual support and information for porphyria patients. Supports research, provides education to the public, patients and physicians and networks porphyria patients & support groups. Quarterly newsletter, pen pal program, phone network. Group development guidelines available. Donation $35/yr. Write: America Porphyria Foundation, PO Box 22712, Houston, TX 77227. Call 713-266-9617; Fax: 713-871-1788. *Website:* http://www.porphyriafoundation.com *Email:* porphyrus@aol.com

Canadian Porphyria Foundation, Inc. *National. Founded 1988.* Dedicated to improving the quality of life for people affected by porphyria, a group of rare genetic disorders characterized by disturbances of porphyria metabolism. Offers programs of awareness, education, service, advocacy and support. Promotes awareness of porphyria through educational literature, articles, newsletters, information and referrals. Offers support groups and advocacy. Encourages and supports research. Assistance in starting groups. Write: Canadian Porphyria Fdn., Inc., PO Box 1206, Neepawa, Manitoba, Canada R0J 1H0. Call 1-866-476-2801 or 204-476-2800; Fax: 204-476-2800. *Website:* http://www.cpf-inc.ca *Email:* porphyria@cpf-inc.ca

PRADER-WILLI SYNDROME

STATEWIDE

Parents of Prader-Willi Syndrome Children *Professionally-run*. Parents meet twice a year to provide support and education. This uncommon birth defect results in initial hypotonia, hypogenitalism and central nervous system performance dysfunction which includes an insatiable appetite leading to obesity if not controlled. Write: Parents of Prader-Willi Syndrome Children, c/o Douglas Taylor, 16 Gettysburg Way, Lincoln Park, NJ 07035. Call Douglas Taylor 973-628-6945 (eve). *Website:* http://www.pwsausa.org/nj *Email:* pwsa.nj@gmail.com

Prader-Willi Syndrome Association *National. 38 chapters. Founded 1975.* Support and education for anyone impacted by Prader-Willi syndrome. Bi-monthly newsletter. Membership dues $35. Many publications available. Chapter development kits available. Write: Prader-Willi Syndrome Assn., 5700 Midnight Pass Rd., Suite 6, Sarasota, FL 34242. Call 1-800-926-4797 or 941-312-0400; Fax: 941-312-0142. *Website:* http://www.pwsausa.org *Email:* national@pwsausa.org

PRECOCIOUS PUBERTY

Precocious Puberty Support Network *National network. Founded 1989.* Network and exchange of information for children who are experiencing precocious puberty and their families. Newsletter ($30/yr). Write: Precocious Puberty Support Network, c/o MAGIC Foundation, 6645 W. North Ave, Oak Park, IL 60302. Call 1-800-362-4423 or 708-383-0808; Fax: 708-383-0899. *Website:* http://www.magicfoundation.org *Email:* mary@magicfoundation.org

PRIMARY LATERAL SCLEROSIS / HEREDITARY SPASTIC PARAPLEGIA

Spastic Paraplegia Foundation, Inc. *National. Founded 2002.* Offers support and information to those affected by primary lateral sclerosis and hereditary spastic paraplegia. Supports research. Offers regional and email support groups, an online chat group, newsletter and information. Write: Spastic Paraplegia Foundation, Inc., 209 Park Rd, Chelmsford, MA 01824. Call 703-495-9261. *Website:* http://www.sp-foundation.org

PLS Friends *Online.* Opportunity for persons with primary lateral sclerosis, a progressive neuromuscular disease, to share information and support via an online discussion group. Fosters support and an exchange of ideas among PLS patients, their relatives, caregivers and health care professionals.

Must   subscribe   to   join   online   groups   at: http://groups.yahoo.com/group/PLS-FRIENDS/join   *Website:* http://www.geocities.com/freyerse/ *Email:* jreyerse@shaw.ca

PROGRESSIVE OSSEOUS HETEROPLASIA

Progressive Osseous Heteroplasia Association *National network. Founded 1995.* Support network for patients and families affected by progressive osseous heteroplasia. Fundraising for research. Write: Progressive Osseous Heteroplasia Assn., 33 Stonehearth Square, Indian Head Park, IL 60525. Call 708-246-9410; Fax: 708-246-9410.   *Website:*   http://www.pohdisease.org   *Email:* poha@comcast.net

PROGRESSIVE SUPRANUCLEAR PALSY

Society for Progressive Supranuclear Palsy, Inc. *International network. 75 affiliated groups. Founded 1990.* Provides support for patients with progressive supranuclear palsy and their families. Advocacy. Offers newsletter, information and referrals, phone support, conferences, listserv, educational materials and assistance in starting support groups. Write: SPSP, Inc., 1838 Greene Tree Rd., Suite 515, Baltimore, MD 21208. Call 1-800-457-4777; Fax: 410-785-7009. *Website:* http://www.psp.org *Email:* quintilian@psp.org

PROSTATE PROBLEMS

Man To Man Program *National. 300 affiliated groups. Founded 1990.* Support and education for men with prostate cancer to enable them to better understand their options and to make informed decisions. Phone support, information and referrals, support group meetings, education and support visitation program. Newsletter. Some chapters invite wives and partners; other chapters have wives and partners meet separately. Assistance available for starting new groups. Call American Cancer Society 1-800-227-2345. *Website:* http://www.cancer.org

PAACT (Patient Advocates for Advanced Cancer Treatment) *International. 150 affiliated groups. Founded 1984.* Provides support and advocacy for prostate cancer patients, their families and the general public at risk. Information relative to the advancements in the detection, diagnosis, evaluation and treatment of prostate cancer. Information, referrals, phone help, conferences, newsletters. Group development guidelines. Write: PAACT, PO Box 141695, Grand Rapids, MI 49514-1695.   Call   616-453-1477;   Fax: 616-453-1846.   *Website:* http://www.paactusa.org *Email:* paact@paactusa.org

US TOO International, Inc. *International. 350+ affiliated groups. Founded 1990.* Mutual support, information and education for prostate cancer patients, their families and friends. Provides newsletter, information, phone support, assistance in starting new groups. Write: US TOO International, Inc., 5003 Fairview Ave., Downers Grove, IL 60515-5286. Call 1-800-808-7866 or 630-795-1002 (day); Fax: 630-795-1602. *Website:* http://www.ustoo.org *Email:* ustoo@ustoo.org

Male Chronic Pelvic Pain Network *Online.* Support and information for men affected by male chronic pelvic pain syndrome (aka chronic prostatitis, interstitial cystitis and pelvic myoneuropathy). Exchange of information forum. *Website:* http://www.chronicprostatitis.com

PROTEUS SYNDROME

Proteus Syndrome Foundation *International network. Founded 1991.* Provides education and support for families or children with Proteus syndrome. Supports research into cause and cure of this disorder. Newsletter, pen pals, literature and database of families. Fundraising. Write: Proteus Syndrome Fdn., 4915 Dry Stone Dr., Colorado Springs, CO 80918. Call Kim Hoag 719-264-8445 (day) or Barbara King 901-756-9375 (day). *Website:* http://www.proteus-syndrome.org *Email:* kimkhoag@adelphia.net

PROXIMAL FEMORAL FOCAL DEFICIENCY / MYOTONIC DYSTROPHY TYPE 2
(see also muscular dystrophy)

Proximal Femoral Focal Deficiency Virtual Support Group *Online.* Information and support for parents of children with proximal femoral focal deficiency (PFFD). Sharing of information, strength and encouragement. *Website:* http://www.pffdvs.org *Email:* pffdvsg@nls.net

PROXIMAL MYOTONIC MYOPATHY

PROMM *Online. 77 members. Founded 2001.* An e-mail discussion group for people with proximal myotonic myopathy (aka myotonic dystrophy type 2), a rare form of muscular dystrophy. Open to families, friends and professionals associated with them. Discussion centered on symptomology, adaptation and variant manifestation. *Website:* http://groups.yahoo.com/group/PROMM *Email:* kili1247@yahoo.com

We know this Directory is big and chances are we can probably find the group you're looking for quicker than you paging through it. Call us! (We're really friendly!)
1-800-367-6274

PSEUDOTUMOR CEREBRI

Pseudotumor Cerebri Support Network *Online International network. Founded 1995.* Mutual support and education for persons with pseudotumor cerebri. Newsletter, information and referrals, pen pals. PTC Primer: Living With Pseudotumor Cerebri. *Website:* http://www.pseudotumorcerebri.com

PSEUDOXANTHOMA ELASTICUM

STATEWIDE

NY-NJ Chapter of PXE International Promotes support, education, advocacy and research for those with pseudoxanthoma elasticum and their families. Patient tissue registry, listserv and email connection. Guest speakers, pen pals, phone help, literature. Meets quarterly in various locations. Call Judy Roller 732-297-7055. *Website:* http://wwwpxe.org *Email:* jroller123@aol.com

NATIONAL / INTERNATIONAL

National Association for Pseudoxanthoma Elasticum *National network. Founded 1988.* Support, education, research and advocacy for persons with PXE, their families, interested others and professionals. Newsletter, information & referrals, phone support. Donations appreciated. Write: NAPE, 8764 Manchester Rd. # 200, St. Louis, MO 63144-2724. Call 314-962-0100 (Voice/Fax); Fax: 314-962-0100. *Website:* http://www.pxenape.org *Email:* napestlouis@sbcglobal.net

PXE International, Inc. *International. 50 affiliated groups. Founded 1995.* Initiates, funds and manages research, supports patients and educates clinicians. Write: PXE International, Inc., 4301 Connecticut Ave. NW, Suite 404, Washington, DC 20008-2369. Call 202-362-9599; Fax: 202-966-8553. *Website:* http://www.pxe.org *Email:* info@pxe.org

PSORIASIS

National Psoriasis Foundation *National. Founded 1968.* Support and information for people who have psoriasis and psoriatic arthritis, their families and friends. Education to increase public awareness of these disorders. Fund-raising for research. Bi-monthly magazine. Educational booklets and physician directory. Offers message board and chat rooms. Write: Nat'l Psoriasis Fdn., 6600 SW 92nd Ave., Suite 300, Portland OR 97223. Call 503-244-7404 or 1-800-723-9166 (free packet of information); Fax: 503-245-0626. *Website:* http://www.psoriasis.org *Email:* getinfo@psoriasis.org

PULMONARY HYPERTENSION
(see also heart disease)

BERGEN

Pulmonary Hypertension Association Support for patients with primary or secondary pulmonary hypertension and their families. Meets various times. Dues $15/yr. Call 1-800-748-7274 (day). *Website:* http://www.phassociation.org *Email:* pha@phassociation.org

NATIONAL

Pulmonary Hypertension Association *National network. Founded 1990.* Support & information for patients with pulmonary hypertension (a cardiovascular disease), their families & medical professionals. Encourages research, promotes awareness and provides resource referrals. Networking, phone help, pen pals, assistance in starting groups. Membership $15 (includes 2 newsletters). Write: Pulmonary Hypertension Association, 850 Sligo Ave., Suite 800, Silver Spring, MD 20910. Call 1-800-748-7274 or 301-565-3004; Fax: 301-565-3994. *Website:* http://www.phassociation.org *Email:* pha@phassociation.org

RARE DISORDERS, GENERAL

BERGEN

Northern Lights (NORD North Jersey Support Group) Provides phone support, information and advocacy for adults and children with rare disorders, their families and friends. Call Linda 973-503-0682. *Email:* northernlights@alumnae.mtholyoke.edu

NATIONAL

Hearts and Hands *Model. 1 group in NC. Founded 1993.* Emotional, spiritual and educational support for persons with either a rare or undiagnosed illness and their families. Also has a registry for loin pain hematuria syndrome. Write: Hearts and Hands, c/o Winoka Plummer, 1648 Oliver's Crossing Circle, Winston-Salem, NC 27127. Call 336-785-7612. *Website:* http://www.geocities.com/hotsprings/spa/2464/index.html

National Organization for Rare Disorders *National network. Founded 1983.* Information and networking for persons with any type of rare disorder. Literature, information and referrals. Advocacy for orphan diseases. Networks persons or families with the same disorder for support. Guidelines available for starting similar

552

groups. Write: NORD, PO Box 1968, Danbury, CT 06813. Call 1-800-999-6673 or 203-744-0100; Fax: 203-798-2291. *Website:* http://www.rarediseases.org *Email:* orphan@rarediseases.org

RAYNAUD'S DISEASE

Raynaud's Association, Inc. *National. Founded 1992.* Mutual support to help Raynaud's sufferers cope with day-to-day activities to maintain or improve their quality of life. Aims to increase awareness of the disease among public and medical communities. Assists in supporting treatment research efforts. Newsletter, information and referrals, special event meetings and literature. Dues $20 (optional). Write: Raynaud's Association, 94 Mercer Ave., Hartsdale, NY 10530. Call Lynn Wunderman 1-800-280-8055; Fax: 914-946-4685. *Website:* http://www.raynauds.org *Email:* Lynn@raynauds.org

REFLEX ANOXIC SEIZURE DISORDER / STEPHENSION SEIZURE / WHITE BREATH HOLDING / PALLID INFANTILE SYNCOPE

STARS (Syncope Trust And Reflex Anoxic Seizures) *International network. Founded 1993.* Network of parents and sufferers of syncope and reflex anoxic seizure (characterized by temporary heart stoppage and a seizure-like response to any unexpected stimuli), also known as Stephenson's seizure, white breath holding or pallid infantile syncope. Information, education, video. Supports research. Write: STARS, PO Box 175, Stratford-Upon-Avon, Warwickshire, CV37 8YD, UK. Call +44(0)17894 50564 or 0 800 0286362 (UK Only); Fax: 011-44 01789 4505682 (UK). *Website:* http://www.stars.org.uk *Email:* trudie@stars.org.uk

RESTLESS LEGS SYNDROME

Restless Legs Syndrome Foundation *National network. 92 affiliated groups. Founded 1993.* Promotes awareness and information about restless legs syndrome. Offers network of support and educational groups nationwide. Publishes a free information booklet and a quarterly newsletter. Write: RLS Foundation, 819 2nd St. SW, Rochester, MN 55902-2985. Call 507-287-6465 or 1-877-463-6757 (to request information); Fax: 507-287-6312. *Website:* http://www.rls.org *Email:* rlsfoundation@rls.org

I get by with a little help from my friends.
John Lennon

RETT SYNDROME

International Rett Syndrome Association *International. 17 affiliated groups. Founded 1985.* For parents, interested professionals and others concerned with Rett syndrome. Provides information and referral, peer support among parents and funds research. Quarterly newsletter. Dues $30/ind; $35/family; $40/int'l. Write: IRSA, 9121 Piscataway Rd., Suite 2B, Clinton, MD 20735-2561. Call 1-800-818-7388 or 301-856-3334; Fax: 301-856-3336. *Website:* http://www.rettsyndrome.org *Email:* irsa@rettsyndrome.org

REYE'S SYNDROME

National Reye's Syndrome Foundation *National. 4 affiliated chapters, 189 representatives in 45 states. Founded 1974.* Devoted to spreading awareness of Reye's syndrome, a disease affecting the liver and brain. It affects persons of all ages and races. Provides support, information and referrals. Encourages research. Representatives are usually a parent, sibling or survivor, but are open to any interested person. Write: National Reye's Syndrome Foundation, PO Box 829, Bryan, OH 43506. Call 1-800-233-7393; Fax: 419-636-9897. *Website:* http://www.reyessyndrome.org *Email:* nrsf@reyessyndrome.org

ROBINOW SYNDROME / FETAL FACE SYNDROME
(see also growth disorders, short/tall)

Robinow Syndrome Foundation *National network. Founded 1994.* Aim is to locate, educate and support persons affected by Robinow syndrome, (also known as fetal face syndrome) a very rare, genetic dwarfing syndrome. Online support and newsletter, bi-annual conventions, family networking. Write: Robinow Syndrome Fdn., c/o Karla Kruger, PO Box 1072, Anoka, MN 55303. Call Karla Kruger 763-434-1152 (Voice/Fax); Fax: 763-434-1152. *Website:* http://www.robinow.org *Email:* kmkruger@comcast.net

ROSACEA

Rosacea Support Group *Online.* Email support group for rosacea sufferers, their family and friends. *Website:* http://health.groups.yahoo.com/group/rosacea-support

RUBINSTEIN-TAYBI SYNDROME

Rubinstein-Taybi Parent Group *National network. 350 member families. Founded 1984.* Mutual support, information & sharing for parents of children with Rubinstein-Taybi syndrome. Information, phone contact, parent contact list, chat room and listserv. Write: Rubinstein-Taybi Parent Group, c/o Garry & Lorrie Baxter, PO Box 146, Smith Center, KS 66967. Call 1-888-447-2989. *Website:* http://www.rubinstein-taybi.org *Email:* lbaxter@ruraltel.net

RUSSELL-SILVER SYNDROME

Russell-Silver Syndrome Support Network *National network. Founded 1989.* Network and exchange of information for parents of children with Russell-Silver syndrome. Information and referrals, phone support, pen pals, conferences, annual convention, literature. Newsletter $30/yr. Write: Russell-Silver Syndrome Support Network, c/o MAGIC Foundation, 6645 W. North Ave., Oak Park, IL 60302. Call 1-800-362-4423; TTY/TDD: 708-383-0808; Fax: 708-383-0899. *Website:* http://www.magicfoundation.org *Email:* mary@magicfoundation.org

SARCOIDOSIS

MIDDLESEX

Central New Jersey Sarcoidosis Support Group Mutual support for sarcoid patients and their families. Provides telephone support, networking, literature and educational workshops and lectures. Meets 4th Tues., 7:30-9pm, East Brunswick Library, Ryders Lane and Civic Center Dr., E. Brunswick. Call Sondra 732-699-0733. *Website:* http://www.nsrc-global.net

NATIONAL

National Sarcoidosis Resource Center *International network. 2 affiliated groups. Founded 1992.* Mutual support for sarcoid patients and their families. Provides telephone support, networking, workshops & lectures, literature and education. Maintains national database, encourages research, provides support and physician referrals, resource guide. Online support and referrals to local support groups. Dues $25/yr. Write: National Sarcoidosis Resource Center, PO Box 1593, Piscataway, NJ 08855-1593. Call 732-699-0733 (day/eve); Fax: 732-699-0882. *Website:* http://www.nsrc-global.net *Email:* nsrc@nsrc-global.net

Sarcoid Networking Association *National network. 3 chapters. Founded 1992.* Provides support and education for sarcoidosis patients, their families and friends through newsletter, correspondence, phone and e-mail. Publishes Sarcoidosis Networking. Provides information on local groups. Offers seminars, conferences, research, advocacy and meetings. Assistance in starting new groups. Write: Sarcoid Networking Assn., 6424 151st Ave. East, Sumner, WA 98390-2601. Call 253-826-7737 or 253-891-2106. *Website:* http://www.sarcoidosisnetwork.org *Email:* sarcoidosis_network@prodigy.net

SELECTIVE MUTISM

BERGEN

SMG ~ CAN Connections *Professionally-run*. Provides support and education for parents and professionals involved with a selectively mute child. Rap sessions, guest speakers, literature and phone help. Dues $45/yr. Meets 3rd Mon., 12:45-2:30pm, Manito School, 111 Manito Ave., Oakland. Call Gail Kervatt 973-208-1848 (day/eve). *Email:* kervatt@optonline.net

NATIONAL

Selective Mutism Foundation Inc *National. Founded 1991.* Mutual support for parents of children with selective mutism, a psychiatric anxiety disorder in which children are unable to speak in social situations. Also open to adults who have or have outgrown, the disorder. Provides information and online support. Parent packets for families to complete for research participation. Write: Selective Mutism Fdn., Inc., c/o Carolyn Miller, PO Box 13133, Sissonville, WV 25360. *Website:* http://www.selectivemutismfoundation.org   *Email:* sue@selectivemutismfoundation.org

Selective Mutism Group, The *Online.* Devoted to educating and promoting awareness on selective mutism and other related childhood anxiety disorders. online support group for parents, teachers and professionals dealing with selective mutism.   *Website:*   http://www.selectivemutism.org   *Email:* sminfo@selectivemutism.org

SEMANTIC-PRAGMATIC DISORDER

Semantic-Pragmatic Disorder Forum *Online.* Opportunity for persons affected by semantic-pragmatic disorder, a communication disorder and their families. SPD is characterized by problems in processing the meaning of language. *Website:* http://forums.delphiforums.com/pragma/start

SEPTO OPTIC DYSPLASIA /
OPTIC NERVE HYPOPLASIA / DEMORSIER SYNDROME

Septo Optic Dysplasia Division *National network. Founded 1989.* Provides public education and networking for families of children with septo-optic dysplasia. Information and referrals, phone support, pen pals, annual convention and conferences. Write: Septo Optic Dysplasia Division, c/o The MAGIC Fdn., 6645 W. North Ave. Oak Park, IL 60302. Call 1-800-362-4423; Fax: 708-383-0899. *Website:* http://www.magicfoundation.org *Email:* mary@magicfoundation.org

Focus Families *Online.* E-mail support group for parents of children with septo-optic dysplasia and optic nerve hypoplasia (aka deMorsier syndrome). Opportunity to share experiences. Online newsletter, annual conference. *Website:* http://www.focusfamilies.org/focus/ *Email:* Support@focusfamilies.org

SHINGLES

STATEWIDE

Shingles Telephone Support Group Telephone network to provide support and encouragement to people suffering with shingles. Contact Laura 732-928-7696 (day/early eve) or Barbara 201-447-5978 (day).

SHWACHMAN-DIAMOND SYNDROME

Shwachman-Diamond Syndrome Foundation *National network. Founded 1994.* Patient advocacy organization whose goals are to educate and support research towards a cure and improve medical management of symptoms. Links families together for emotional support. Distributes current medical information through professional, medical advisory board. Write: Shwachman-Diamond Syndrome Foundation, 710 Brassie Drive, Grand Junction, CO 81506. Call 1-877-737-4685 (day) or 614-939-2324; Fax: 970-255-8293. *Website:* http://www.shwachman-diamond.org *Email:* 4sskids@shwachman-diamond.org

SICKLE CELL DISEASE

Sickle Cell Disease Association of America, Inc. *National. 60 chapters. Founded 1971.* Education for the public & professionals about sickle cell disease. Support & information for persons affected by the disease. Supports research. Quarterly newsletter, chapter development guidelines, phone network, videos. Online network, research updates and forum. Write: Sickle Cell Disease Association of America, 16 S. Calvert St., Suite 600, Baltimore, MD 21202. Call 1-800-421-8453; Fax: 410-528-1495. *Website:* http://www.sicklecelldisease.org

SJOGREN'S SYNDROME

OCEAN

Sjogren's Syndrome Support Group Support for persons afflicted with Sjogren's syndrome. Meetings vary, Pine Beach. Call Cinde 732-914-1019 (day). *Website:* http://www.sjogrens.org

NATIONAL

Sjogren's Syndrome Foundation, Inc. *National. 78 groups. Founded 1983.* Information & education for Sjogren's syndrome patients, families, health professionals & the public. Opportunities for patients to share ways of coping. Stimulates research for treatments & cures. Newsletter "Moisture Seekers," chapter development assistance, video tapes, annual symposium. Sjogren's handbook. Write: Sjogren's Syndrome Foundation, Inc., 8120 Woodmont Ave., Suite 530, Bethesda, MD 10814. Call 301-718-0300; Fax: 301-718-0322. *Website:* http://www.sjogrens.org

SMITH-LEMLI-OPITZ

Smith-Lemli-Opitz Advocacy & Exchange *International network. Founded 1988.* Network of families with children with Smith-Lemli-Opitz (RSH) syndrome. Exchange of information, sharing of similar experiences and correspondence between families. Provides education to medical community, new parents and others. Phone support. Newsletter. Dues $10/yr. Write: Smith-Lemli-Opitz Advocacy & Exchange, 2650 Valley Forge Dr., Boothwyn, PA 19061. Call 610-485-9663. *Email:* bhook@comcast.net

SMITH-MAGENIS SYNDROME

PRISMS (Parents & Researchers Interested in Smith-Magenis) *International network. Founded 1993.* Parent-to-parent program offering support, advocacy and education for families affected by Smith-Magenis syndrome. Information, referrals, literature, phone support and newsletter. Dues $30. Write: PRISMS, Inc, PO Box 741914, Dallas, TX 75374-1914. Call 972-231-0035. *Website:* http://www.prisms.org *Email:* info@prisms.org

SOTOS SYNDROME

Sotos Syndrome Support Association *International network. Founded 1984.* Provides information and mutual support for families of children with Sotos syndrome. Newsletter, information & referrals, phone support, pen pals, annual conferences. Write: SSSA, PO Box 4626, Wheaton, IL 60189. Call 1-888-246-7772. *Website:* http://www.well.com/user/sssa *Email:* sssa@well.com

SPASMODIC DYSPHONIA

National Spasmodic Dysphonia Association *National. 35 affiliated support groups. Founded 1990.* Dedicated to advancing medical research into the causes of and treatments for spasmodic dysphonia Promotes physician and public awareness of the disorder through outreach and sponsoring support activities for people with SD and their families through educational materials, annual symposiums, support groups and on-line resources. Offers assistance in starting similar groups. Newsletter. Write: Nat'l Spasmodic Dysphonia Assn., 300 Park Blvd., Suite 350, Itasca, IL 60143. Call 1-800-795-6732. *Website:* http://www.dysphonia.org *Email:* kkuman@dysphonia.org

Spasmodic Dysphonia Support Group of New York *Model. Founded 1987.* Provides members with the latest information regarding spasmodic dysphonia, as well as providing emotional and practical support. Offers workshops and discussions. Encourages education for the public and physicians. Guest speakers, information and referrals. Write: Spasmodic Dysphonia Support Group of NY, c/o A. Simons, 67-33 152 St., Flushing, NY 11367. Call 718-793-2442. *Website:* http://www.dystonia.org

SPASMODIC TORTICOLLIS

National Spasmodic Torticollis Association *National. 75 chapters. Founded 1983.* Advocacy group providing information and support to spasmodic torticollis patients and their families. Network of support groups and volunteers on-call to talk with other patients. Quarterly magazine, annual symposium. Educates the public and medical community. Supports research. Email support. Write: NSTA, 9920 Talbert Ave., Fountain Valley, CA 92708. Call 1-800-487-8385 or 714-378-7837; Fax: 714-378-7830. *Website:* http://www.torticollis.org *Email:* NSTAmail@aol.com

SPINAL MUSCULAR ATROPHY

Families of S.M.A. *International. 29 chapters. Founded 1984. (Multilingual)* Funding of research, support and networking for families affected by spinal muscular atrophy types I, II, III, adult onset and Kennedy's. Educational resources, group development guidelines, quarterly newsletter, pen pals, phone support and videotapes. Write: Families of SMA, PO Box 196, Libertyville, IL 60048-0196. Call 1-800-886-1762 or 847-367-7620; Fax: 847-367-7623. *Website:* http://www.fsma.org *Email:* sma@fsma.org

STEVENS JOHNSON SYNDROME / TOXIC EDPIDERMAL NECROLYSIS

Stevens Johnson Syndrome Foundation *International network. Founded 1995.* Provides information on adverse allergic drug reactions to the public and medical communities. Aim is to quicken diagnoses in order to avoid permanent damage in patients. Literature, phone support, information and referrals. Write: Stevens

Johnson Syndrome Foundation, PO Box 350333, Westminster, CO 80035. Call 303-635-1241. *Website:* http://www.sjsupport.org *Email:* sjsupport@aol.com

STICKLER SYNDROME

Stickler Involved People *International network. Founded 1995.* Network that offers support and education for persons affected by Stickler syndrome. This genetic disorder affects connective tissues, including the joints, eyes, palate, heart and hearing. Phone support, information and referrals, annual conference, literature and newsletter. Online listserv. Write: SIP, 15 Angelina, Augusta, KS 67010. Call 316-775-2993. *Website:* http://www.sticklers.org *Email:* sip@sticklers.org

STREP, GROUP B

Canadian Strep B Foundation *International network. Founded 2003.* Educates the public about group B streptococcal infections during pregnancy. Information and referrals, advocacy and phone support. Group development guidelines available. Write: The Canadian Strep B Foundation, c/o Patricia Normand President, PO Box 598, Prevost, Quebec JOR 1TO. Call 1-877-873-7424 or 450-224-7718. *Website:* http://www.strepb.ca *Email:* info@strepb.ca

STURGE-WEBER SYNDROME / PORT WINE STAIN / KLIPPEL-TRENAUNAY SYNDROME

Sturge-Weber Foundation, The *International network. Members in 50 states and internationally. Founded 1987.* Mutual support network for families and professionals involved with port wine stains, Sturge-Weber syndrome or Klippel Trenaunay syndrome. Disseminates information, funds and facilitates research. Newsletter, monthly e-news, phone support, pen pals, active email support group and bulletin board. Educational materials for schools, parents and clinicians. Biennial conference. Write: Sturge-Weber Foundation, PO Box 418, Mt. Freedom, NJ 07970. Call 1-800-627-5482 or 973-895-4445; Fax: 973-895-4846. *Website:* http://www.sturgeweber.com *Email:* swf@sturgeweber.com

SYRINGOMYELIA / CHIARI MALFORMATION

American Syringomyelia Alliance Project *International network. Founded 1988.* Support, networking and information for people affected by syringomyelia and chiari malformation and their families and friends. Newsletter, phone support, pen pals, conferences. Also offers online message boards and chat rooms. Write: ASAP, PO Box 1586, Longview, TX 75606-1586. Call 903-236-7079 or 1-800-272-7282; Fax: 903-757-7456. *Website:* http://www.asap.org *Email:* info@asap.org

TAKAYASU'S ARTERITIS

Takayasu's Arteritis Association *Model. Founded 1995.* Education and support for persons with Takayasu's arteritis (an inflammation of the large elastic arteries and aorta), their families and health professionals. Network program, information, phone and on-line support, literature, newsletters, research conferences and resources. Write: Takayasu's Arteritis Association, 2030 County Line Rd., Suite 199, Huntingdon Valley, PA 19006. Call 1-800-575-9390, Access Code 00. *Website:* http://www.takayasus.org *Email:* admin@takayaus.org

TAY-SACHS DISEASE / CANAVAN DISEASE

National Tay-Sachs and Allied Diseases Association *(BILINGUAL) International. 5 affiliated groups. Founded 1957.* Dedicated to the treatment and prevention of Tay-Sachs, Canavan and related genetic diseases. Provides information and support services to individuals of all ages and families affected by these disorders as well caregivers and the public at large. The strategies for achieving these goals include public and professional education, research, genetic screening, support services (i.e. peer support group for parents, grandparents and extended family members)and advocacy. Translations available in Spanish, Russian, Hebrew and French. Write: National Tay-Sachs & Allied Diseases Association, 2001 Beacon St., Suite 204, Boston, MA 02135. Call 1-800-906-8723 or 617-277-4463; Fax: 617-277-0134. *Website:* http://www.ntsad.org *Email:* info@ntsad.org

TEMPOROMANDIBULAR JOINT DYSFUNCTION (TMJ)

TMJ Association *International. Founded 1986.* Developed by two patients suffering from temporomandibular joint dysfunction (diseases and disorders that cause pain and dysfunction in and around the temporomandibular or jaw joint). Write: TMJ Association, PO Box 26770, Milwaukee, WI 53226-0770. Call 414-259-3223; Fax: 414-259-8112. *Website:* http://www.tmj.org *Email:* info@tmj.org

TOURETTE SYNDROME

STATEWIDE

Tourette Syndrome Association of NJ, Inc. Mission is to support the needs of families of persons with Tourette syndrome, as well as adults with TS. Offers advocacy for persons with Tourette Syndrome. Provides education to the public and professionals. Offers peer-counseling and a quarterly children's group. Support group meetings in Atlantic, Bergen, Burlington, Mercer, Middlesex, Monmouth, Morris and Somerset Counties. Write: TSA of NJ, Inc., 50 Division St., Suite 205, Somerville, NJ 08876. Call 732-972-4459. *Website:* http://www.tsanj.org

NATIONAL

Tourette Syndrome Association *National. 45 chapters. Founded 1972.* Dedicated to identifying the cause, finding the current controlling the effects of Tourette syndrome through education, research and service. Provides support services to families and professionals to enable patients to achieve optimum development. Chapter development guidelines, newsletter. Dues $45. Write: Tourette Syndrome Assn., 42-40 Bell Blvd., Bayside, NY 11361-2820. Call 718-224-2999 or 1-888-486-8738; Fax: 718-279-9596. *Website:* http://www.tsa-usa.org *Email:* ts@tsa-usa.org

TRACHEO ESOPHAGEAL FISTULA / ESOPHAGAL ATRESIA

EA/TEF Child and Family Support Connection, Inc. *International. 6 chapters. Founded 1993.* Dedicated to providing educational resources and emotional and practical support for families of children with esophageal atresia and tracheoesophageal fistula. Offers newsletter, family directory for phone networking, information, lending library, educational brochures and literature. Sunshine program sends birthday greetings and gifts to hospitalized children. Assistance starting similar groups. Online listing of local support groups. Write: EA/TEF Child and Family Support Connection, 111 West Jackson Blvd., Suite 1145, Chicago, IL 60604-3502. Call 312-987-9085; Fax: 312-987-9086. *Website:* http://www.eatef.org *Email:* info@eatef.org

TEF/VATER Support Network *International. 6 groups. Founded 1992.* Offers support & encouragement for parents of children with tracheo esophageal fistula, esophageal atresia and VATER. Aims to bring current information to parents and the medical community. Newsletter, information & referrals, phone support. Write: TEF/VATER Support Network, c/o Greg & Terri Burke, 15301 Grey Fox Rd., Upper Marlboro, MD 20772. Call 301-952-6837; Fax: 301-952-9152. *Website:* http://www.tefvater.org *Email:* tefvater@ix.netcom.com

TRACHEOSTOMY

Aaron's Tracheostomy Page *Online. Founded 1998.* Mutual support and information sharing for persons who have or anticipate having, a tracheostomy. Open to parents of children, patients, families, caregivers and professionals. Through a listserv, members are given a chance to support each other, ask questions and offer coping tips. Write: Trachties, 102 Morene Ave.,Waxahachie, TX 75165. *Website:* http://www.tracheostomy.com

TRANSVERSE MYELITIS

Transverse Myelitis Association Offers support and education to persons with transverse myelitis and other neuroimmunologic diseases of the central nervous system (e.g. acute disseminated encephalomyelitis, optic neuritis and neuromyelitis optica, Devic's disease)and their families. Networks families together for support. Provides research literature, newsletter and membership directory. Investigates, advocates for and supports research and treatment efforts. Provides a support forum for communication. Bulletin board. Assists in the development of local support groups. Fundraises for research. Conducts symposiums and workshops. Write: Transverse Myelitis Assn., c/o Sandy Siegel, 1787 Sutter Parkway, Powell, OH 43065-8806. Call 614-766-1806. *Website:* http://www.myelitis.org *Email:* ssiegel@myelitis.org

TREACHER COLLINS SYNDROME

Treacher Collins Foundation *National network. Founded 1988.* Support for families, individuals & professionals affected by Treacher Collins syndrome and related disorders. Provides networking, educational materials, newsletter, information & referrals, phone support, resource list, bibliography and central library, videos and booklets. online resources and newsletter. Write: Treacher Collins Fdn., PO Box 683, Norwich, VT 05055. *Website:* http://www.treachercollinsfnd.org/ *Email:* hopecharkins@hotmail.com

TRIPLE-X SYNDROME / 47,XXX SYNDROME

Triple X Support Group *International network. Founded 1997.* Provides support, resources and informational materials to parents of children with triple X syndrome (aka trisomy X or 47,XXX syndrome). Networks parents together for support. Write: Triple X Support Group, c/o Helen Clements, 32 Francemary Rd, Brockley, London, England SE4 1JS. Call (020)86909445. *Website:* http://www.triplo-x.org *Email:* helenclements@hotmail.com

TRISOMY

STATEWIDE

S.O.F.T. (Support Organization For Trisomy) Support for families of children with trisomy 18 and 13 and related disorders. Education about trisomy, implications to families and community. Meets various times and locations.

Call Colleen Frazier 609-567-4151, Pat O'Toole 215-663-9652 or Kathleen Johnson 215-489-2678.

NATIONAL

SOFT (Support Organization For Trisomy) *National. 50 chapters. Founded 1979.* Support and education for families of children with trisomy 18 and 13 and related genetic disorders (including trisomy 9). Education for professionals. Quarterly newsletter. Pen pal program, phone network. Regional gatherings. Annual international conference, booklets. online information on finding a local support group. Dues $25. Write: SOFT, c/o Barbara Van Herreweghe, 2982 S. Union St., Rochester, NY 14624. Call Barbara Van Herreweghe 585-594-4621 or 1-800-716-SOFT (for families); Fax: 585-594-1957. *Website:* http://www.trisomy.org *Email:* barbsoft@rochester.rr.com

TUBE FEEDING

Oley Foundation, Inc. *National. 70 affiliated groups. Founded 1983.* Provides information and psychosocial support for home nutrition support (intravenous or tube-feeding) patients, their families, caregivers and professionals. Programs include bi-monthly newsletter, national network of volunteers providing patient support, annual summer conference, regional meetings, patient-to-patient networking and information clearinghouse. Write: Oley Foundation, c/o Albany Medical Center, 214 HUN Memorial, MC-28, Albany, NY 12208. Call 1-800-776-6539 (day) or 518-262-5079; Fax: 518-262-5528. *Website:* http://www.oley.org *Email:* BishopJ@mail.amc.edu

TUBEROUS SCLEROSIS

Tuberous Sclerosis Alliance *National. Staff/volunteer area representatives. Founded 1974.* Dedicated to finding a cure for tuberous sclerosis while improving the lives of those affected. Provides research, support and education among individuals, families and the helping professions. Newsletter, peer-networking programs, conferences, information. Write: Tuberous Sclerosis Alliance, 801 Roeder Rd., Suite 750, Silver Spring, MD 20910-4467. Call 301-562-9890 or 1-800-225-6872; Fax: 301-562-9870. *Website:* http://www.tsalliance.org *Email:* info@tsalliance.org

TURNER'S SYNDROME

Turner's Syndrome Society *National. 15 chapters. Founded 1981.* Provides support and education to Turner's syndrome patients and their families. Tapes, publications, referral to U.S. & Canadian groups. Quarterly newsletter. Pen pal program, chapter development guidelines, annual conference. Write: Turner's Syndrome Society, 21 Blackthorn Ave., Toronto, Ontario M6N 3H4, Canada. Call 1-800-465-6744 or 416-781-2086; Fax: 416-781-7245. *Website:* http://www.turnersyndrome.ca *Email:* tssincan@web.net

Turner Syndrome Society of the U.S. *National. 20 chapters. Founded 1987.* Self-help for women, girls, & their families affected by Turner syndrome. Increases public awareness about the disorder. Quarterly newsletter, chapter development assistance, advocacy, education, annual conference. Write: Turner Syndrome Society U.S., 14450 TC Jester, Suite 260, Houston, TX 77014. Call 1-800-365-9944 or 832-249-9988; Fax: 832-249-99876. *Website:* http://www.turnersyndrome.org *Email:* tssus@turnersyndrome.org

Turner Syndrome Support Network *National network. Founded 1989.* Network and exchange of information for parents of children with Turner's syndrome. Information and referrals, phone support, pen pals, conferences, literature. Annual convention. Newsletter ($30/yr). Write: Turner Syndrome Support Network, c/o MAGIC Foundation, 6645 W. North Ave., Oak Park, IL 60302. Call 1-800-362-4423, TTY/TDD: 708-383-0899; Fax: 709-383-0899. *Website:* http://www.magicfoundation.org *Email:* mary@magicfoundation.org

TWIN TO TWIN TRANSFUSION SYNDROME

Twin to Twin Transfusion Syndrome Foundation *(MULTILINGUAL) International. Founded 1989.* Dedicated to providing immediate and lifesaving educational, emotional and financial support for families, medical professionals and caregivers before, during and after pregnancy with twin to twin transfusion syndrome. Dedicated to saving the babies, improving their future health and care, furthering medical research, providing neonatal intensive care, special needs and bereavement support. Pen pals, newsletter, literature, phone support, visitation, conferences. Guidelines for professionals on multiple birth loss during pregnancy. Help in starting new chapters. International registry. Website in many languages. Write: TTTS, 411 Longbeach Parkway, Bay Village, OH 44140. Call 1-800-815-9211 or 440-899-8887. *Website:* http://www.tttsoundation.org *Email:* info@tttsfoundation.org

UNDIAGNOSED ILLNESS

Hearts and Hands *Model. 1 group in NC. Founded 1993.* Emotional, spiritual and educational support for persons with either a rare or undiagnosed illness and their families. Also has a registry for loin pain hematuria syndrome. Write: Hearts and Hands, c/o Winoka Plummer, 1648 Oliver's Crossing Circle, Winston-Salem, NC

27127.   Call   336-785-7612.   *Website:*
http://www.geocities.com/hotsprings/spa/2464/index.html

UREA CYCLE DISORDERS

National Urea Cycle Disorders Foundation *National network. Founded 1989.* Links families, friends and professionals who are dedicated to the identification, treatment and cure of urea cycle disorders, a genetic disorder causing an enzyme deficiency in the urea cycle. Networks families together for support, educates professionals and public and supports research. Phone support, literature and newsletter. Dues $35. Write: National Urea Cycle Disorders Foundation, 4841 Hill St., La Canada, CA 91011. Call 1-800-386-8233; Fax: 818-952-2184. *Website:* http://www.nucdf.org *Email:* info@nucdf.org

ASA Kids *Online.* Opportunity for parents of children with argininosuccinic aciduria to come together for support and information. Discussion board, stories on affected   children   and   links.   *Website:* http://www.geocities.com/oliphint4/index.html

T.R.U.E. Kids (Transplanted to Resolve Urea-cycle Enzyme-deficiency) *Online.* Mutual support and information for families of transplanted children with urea cycle disorder. *Website:* http://www.geocities.com/paulajoe123/

Urea Cycle Disorder Discussion Board *Online.* Opportunity for parents caring for a child with a urea cycle disorder to discuss concerns and ideas. Goal is to increase awareness of urea cycle disorders in order to improve diagnosis. *Website:* http://www.2endure.com

VATER ASSOCIATION

TEF/VATER Support Network *International. 6 groups. Founded 1992.* Offers support & encouragement for parents of children with tracheo esophageal fistula, esophageal atresia and VATER. Newsletter, information & referrals, phone support. Write: TEF/VATER Support Network, c/o Greg & Terri Burke, 15301 Grey Fox Rd., Upper Marlboro, MD 20772. Call 301-952-6837; Fax: 301-952-9152. *Website:* http://www.tefvater.org *Email:* tefvater@ix.netcom.com

VATER Connection, Inc, The. *International network. Founded 1996.* Provides information and support to families whose children have VATER Association (Vertebrae problems, Anal anomalies, Trachea problems, Esophagus problems, Radius and/or Renal problems). Newsletter. Bi-annual conferences, online bulletin board. Write: The VATER Connection, Inc., 1722 Yucca Lane, Emporia, KS 66801. Call 620-342-6954 (day/eve). *Website:* http://www.vaterconnection.org

VELO-CARDIO-FACIAL SYNDROME / SHPRINTZEN SYNDROME / 22Q11 DELETION SYNDROME

Northeast VCFS Support Group *National network. Founded 1996.* Support and resource network for families coping with velo-cardio-facial syndrome (aka Shprintzen syndrome, 22q11 deletion syndrome). Provides information and referrals, literature, conferences and assistance in starting local groups. Listserv. Write: Northeast VCFS Support Group, c/o Maureen Anderson, 2 Lansing Dr., Salem, NH 03079. Call 603-898-6332 (Voice/Fax); TTY/TDD: 603-898-6332. *Email:* mladja@aol.com

VENTILATOR USERS

International Ventilator Users Network *International network. Founded 1987.* Information sharing between ventilator users and health care professionals experienced in home mechanical ventilation. Annual directory ($8). Quarterly newsletter (free for membership dues of $25). Write: IVUN, 4207 Lindell Blvd., Suite 110, St. Louis, MO 63108. Call 314-534-0475; Fax: 314-534-5070. *Website:* http://www.post-polio.org/ivun *Email:* info@post-polio.org

VESTIBULAR DISORDERS
(see also deaf, hard-of-hearing)

Vestibular Disorders Association *International. 125 independent groups. Founded 1983.* Information, referrals & support for people affected by disorders caused by inner ear problems. Public education, group development assistance, quarterly newsletter, library of resources, support network. Distributes several videotapes and publishes 70 documents, including full-length books on Meniere's disease and benign paroxysmal positional vertigo (BPPV). Write: Vestibular Disorders Association, PO Box 13305, Portland OR 97213. Call 1-800-837-8428 or 503-229-7705; Fax: 503-229-8064. *Website:* http://www.vestibular.org *Email:* veda@vestibular.org

VITILIGO

American Vitiligo Research Foundation *National. 22+ groups. Founded 1995.* Aim is to raise the awareness, educate and support not only the patients but family members as well so that patients can live with acceptance. Networking, literature, newsletter, information & referrals, phone help, conferences, billboards and public services announcements. Write: American Vitiligo Research Foundation, PO Box 7540, Clearwater, FL 33758. Call 727-461-3899; Fax: 727-461-4796. *Website:* http://www.avrf.org *Email:* vitiligo@avrf.org

Vitiligo Support International, Inc. *Online. Founded 2000* Provides social support, information and resources to person affected by vitiligo. Active message boards, chats and international physician referral. Includes "just for kids" page. *Website:* http://www.vitiligosupport.org *Email:* info@vitiligosupport.org

VON HIPPEL LINDAU

VHL Family Alliance *(MULTILINGUAL) International network. 28 US chapters, 11 foreign affiliates. Founded 1993.* Opportunity for families affected by Von Hippel Lindau to share their knowledge and experiences with each other & the medical community. Goal is to improve diagnosis, treatment & quality of life for VHL families. Newsletter, phone support and education, tissue bank and handbook. Literature available in Spanish, German, French, Japanese, Dutch and other languages. Funds research. Assistance in starting local chapters. Write: VHL Family Alliance, 171 Clinton Rd., Brookline, MA 02445-5815. Call 1-800-767-4845 or 617-277-5667; Fax: 858-712-8712. *Website:* http://www.vhl.org *Email:* info@vhl.org

VOMITING, CYCLIC

Cyclic Vomiting Syndrome Assn. *International. 30+ affiliated groups. Founded 1993.* Mutual support and information for families and professionals dealing with cyclic vomiting syndrome. Networking, phone support, educational materials and research support. Newsletter. Write: CVSA, c/o Debra Waites, 3585 Cedar Hill Rd. NW, Canal Winchester, OH 43110. Call 614-837-2586; Fax: 614-837-2586. *Website:* http://www.cvsaonline.org *Email:* waitesd@cvsaonline.org

VULVAR DISORDERS

National Vulvodynia Association, Inc. *National. 100 affiliated groups. Founded 1994.* Provides information and support to women with vulvodynia. Educates health care professionals and the public about this condition. Newsletter, literature, information and referrals, phone support and advocacy. Write: NVA, PO Box 4491, Silver Spring, MD 20914-4491. Call 301-649-2236; Fax: 301-299-3999. *Website:* http://www.nva.org *Email:* mate@nva.org

WAGR SYNDROME

International WAGR Syndrome Association *International network. 3 affiliated groups. Founded 2000.* Provides information and support to persons with WAGR Syndrome or aniridia and their families, physicians, teachers. Literature, free bi-annual newsletter, networking, information and referral and phone support. Encourages research. Email group. Write: International WAGR Syndrome

Association, 2063 Regina Ave., Lincoln Park, MI 48146. Call 210-481-9288. *Website:* http://www.wagr.org

WALDENSTROM'S MACROGLOBULINEMIA

International Waldenstrom's Macroglobulinemia Foundation *International. 30 affiliated groups. Founded 1994.* Provides support and information to persons with Waldenstrom's macroglobulinemia, their families and caregivers. Information and referrals, phone support, conferences, newsletter and literature. Regular support group meetings. Provides assistance in starting new groups. Write: Int'l Waldenstrom's Macroglobulinemia Fdn., 3932D Swift Rd., Sarasota, FL 34231. Call 941-927-4963; Fax: 941-927-4467. *Website:* http://www.iwmf.com *Email:* info@iwmf.com

WEGENER'S GRANULOMATOSIS

Wegener's Granulomatosis Association *National. 35 affiliated groups. Founded 1986.* Emotional support and information for patients with life-threatening, uncommon Wegener's granulomatosis and related vascular illnesses. Educates families, friends and general public about the devastating effects of Wegener's, its symptoms and treatment. Dues $25/US; $30/Int'l (which includes bimonthly newsletter). Write: Wegener's Granulomatosis Association, PO Box 28660, Kansas City, MO 64188-8660. Call 1-800-277-9474; Fax: 816-436-8211. *Website:* http://www.wgassociaton.org *Email:* wga@wgassociation.org

WILLIAM'S SYNDROME

Williams Syndrome Association *National network. 16 chapters. Founded 1982.* Purpose is to encourage research related to Williams syndrome, find and support families with Williams syndrome and share information among parents and professionals regarding educational, medical and behavioral experiences. Newsletter. Write: Williams Syndrome Assn., PO Box 297, Clawson, MI 48017-0297. Call 248-244-2229; Fax: 248-244-2230. *Website:* http://www.williams-syndrome.org *Email:* info@williams-syndrome.org

WILSON'S DISEASE

Wilson's Disease Association *International network. Founded 1979.* Provides information and referrals about Wilson's disease, a genetic disorder that causes excessive amounts of copper accumulation in the body, affecting the liver and brain. Provides mutual support and aid for those affected by the disease & their families. Promotes research into treatment & cure. Quarterly newsletter. Provides phone support network. Offers e-mail group. Write: Wilson's Disease Association,

1802 Brookside Dr., Wooster, OH 44691. Call 1-888-264-1450 or 330-264-1450. *Website:* http://www.wilsonsdisease.org *Email:* mary.graper@wilsonsdisease.org

WORSTER-DROUGHT

(see also cerebral palsy)

Worster Drought Syndrome Support Group *Model.* Provides support and information for families of children with Worster-Drought, a form of cerebral palsy. Offers phone support in the United Kingdom. Pen pals, networking of families, literature and newsletter. Write: Worster-Drought Syndrome, c/o Contact a Family, 209-211 City Road, London EC1V 1JN, UK. Call 020 7383 3555; Fax: 020 7383 0259. *Website:* http://www.wdssg.org.uk/ *Email:* national.contact@wdssg.org.uk

XERODERMA PIGMENTOSUM

Xeroderma Pigmentosum Society *International network. Founded 1995.* Provides sharing of support, information and coping skills for families affected by xeroderma pigmentosum. Quarterly informational newsletter. Promotes research into finding a cure. Information and referrals, phone support, conferences, literature, advocacy in community, education and protection. Free window tinting on homes of patients. Camp Sundown for patients of all ages and their families. Write: XP Soc., 437 Snydertown Rd., Craryville, NY 12521. Call 518-851-2612 or 1-877-XPS-CURE. *Website:* http://www.xps.org *Email:* caren@xps.org

X-LINKED HYOPHOSPHATEMIA / FAMILIAL HYPOPHOSPHATEMIC RICKETS / VITAMIN D RESISTANT RICKETS

XLH Network *Online. Founded 1996.* Support and information for individuals and families affected by X-linked hypophosphatemia (aka X-linked hypophosphatemic rickets, familial hypophosphatemic rickets or vitamin D resistant rickets). Also open to those affected by similar disorders including autosomal dominant hypophosphatemic rickets and tumor-induced osteomalacia. Open to interested professionals dedicated to understanding in terms of support, research and developing new treatments. Exchanges and disseminated information. Offers an online brochure, members listserv. Write: XLH Network, c/o Joan Reed, 4562 Stoneledge Lane, Manlius, NY 13104. *Website:* http://www.xlhnetwork.org *Email:* joan@xlhnetwork.org

This information is constantly changing. New groups start, others end. Please call us for the most up-to-date information from our database. 1-800-367-6274.

MENTAL HEALTH RESOURCES

MENTAL HEALTH ADMINISTRATORS

Offers assistance and advocacy for mental health consumers and families when they are experiencing difficulties with the mental health system. Also provides referrals to mental health providers by county.

ATLANTIC	Sally Williams 609-645-7700 ext. 4307
BERGEN	Michele Hart-Loughlin 201-634-2751
BURLINGTON	Gary Miller 609-265-5610
CAMDEN	Chuck Steinmetz 856-663-3998
CAPE MAY	Pat Devaney 609-465-1055
CUMBERLAND	Ethan Aronoff 856-453-7804
ESSEX	Joseph Scarpelli 973-228-8021
GLOUCESTER	Kathleen Spinosi 856-384-6870
HUDSON	Jim Gallagher 201-271-4344
HUNTERDON	Pamela Pontrelli 908-788-1253
MERCER	Marc A. Celentana, PhD 609-989-6574.
MIDDLESEX	Lori Dillon 732-745-4518.
MONMOUTH	Charles D. Brown 732-431-7200
MORRIS	Laurie Becker 973-285-6852
OCEAN	Jill Perez 732-506-5374
PASSAIC	Francine Vince 973-225-3700
SALEM	Dr. Isaac A. Young 856-339-8618
SOMERSET	Pam Mastro 908-704-6302
SUSSEX	Joseph Stapleton 973-948-6000
UNION	James Eddleton 908-527-4846
WARREN	Shannon Brennan 908-475-6331

COMMUNITY HEALTH LAW PROJECT

Promotes protecting the rights of persons with any disability. Community Health Law represents low income individuals who are disabled physically, mentally and/or who are elderly and are unable to afford private attorneys. Offers counseling referrals, advocacy, training, education, etc. *Website:* http://www.chlp.org

CAMDEN	856-858-9500
ESSEX	973-680-5599; TTY/TDD 973-680-1116
MERCER	609-392-5553
MONMOUTH	732-502-0059
UNION	908-355-8282

EMPLOYMENT / VOCATIONAL TRAINING

BERGEN

Friendship House Non-profit rehabilitation. Comprehensive pre-vocational training and employment support for adults and adolescents with all types of disabilities. Offers a personalized plan considering a persons specific needs. Traditional and supportive employment programs. Sliding fee scale, Medicaid. Call 201-488-2121. *Website:* http://www.njfriendshiphouse.com

INTENSIVE FAMILY SUPPORT PROGRAMS

Intensive Family Support Services Offers supportive activities statewide to assist families with a mentally ill relative. Families are offered a variety of services based on the individuals need. Services are available to any family, free of charge. Psycho education, single family consultations, family support, respite, advocacy and referrals. Call 1-866-626-4437.

HOUSING FOR MENTAL HEALTH CONSUMERS

CAMDEN

Steininger Behavioral Care Services Provides housing units to consumers who have achieved a high degree of self-reliance. Residences are designed as long-term, stable places to live. Case managers assist residents with daily living skills. Rent collected under Federal Section 8. Call 856-428-1300.

HUDSON

SERV Behavioral Health System Human services for adults, children and seniors. Services include group homes and supervised apartments for adults and seniors with chronic psychiatric problems and for those with a substance addiction and psychiatric problem. Call 1-800-987-7378 or 609-406-0100 (Mon.-Fri.,9am-4pm). *Website:* http://www.servbhs.org

MERCER

SERV Centers of NJ Offers group homes and supervised apartments for adults with chronic psychiatric problems and for those with a substance addiction and psychiatric problem. Also a residential service for children, adolescents and adults with developmental disabilities. Call 1-800-987-7378 (Mon.-Fri., 9am-4pm). *Website:* http://www.servbhs.org

Greater Trenton Behavioral Healthcare Homeless Outreach A case manager provides linkage to mental health services, medical, entitlements and housing. Case management, nursing assessments, psychiatric evaluations and medication management services are provided every Mon. night at The Rescue Mission. Call 609-396-6788 ext. 232/284 or 1-888-866-9565.

On My Own Supportive Housing Program Assists persons with mental illness to choose, find, get and keep their own place to live, through continuous support services with daily living skills and short term crisis stabilization. Call 609-890-2527.

MIDDLESEX

Service Centers of New Jersey Offers group homes and supervised apartments for adults and seniors with chronic psychiatric problems and for those with a substance addiction and psychiatric problem. Call 1-800-987-7378. *Website:* http://www.servbhs.org

MORRIS

Continuum of Care Provides assistance, support and skills teaching to the adult psychiatric community enabling successful, independent living in the community for each consumer in an environment of their choice. Supervised housing and supported community living. Call 973-401-2121.

PASSAIC

Service Center Offers group homes and supervised apartments for adults and seniors with chronic psychiatric problems and for those with a substance addiction and psychiatric problem. Call 1-800-987-7378 (Mon.-Fri., 9am-4pm). *Website:* http://www.servghs.org

UNION

Service Center Offers group homes and supervised apartments for adults and seniors with chronic psychiatric problems and for those with a substance addiction and psychiatric problem. Also a residential service for children, adolescents and adults with disabilities. Call 1-800-987-7378 (Mon.-Fri., 9am-4pm). *Website:* http://www.servbhs.org

Diversified Children's Services Offers group homes foster care and day programming for adolescents with an emotional or behavioral problem. Call 908-276-3359.

MENTAL HEALTH ASSOCIATIONS

STATEWIDE

Mental Health Association in New Jersey Helps mental health consumers and their families explore services available in their community. Also advocates for needed services. Write: MHA of NJ, 88 Pompton Ave., Verona, NJ, 07044. Call 973-571-4100; Fax: 973-857-1777. *Website:* http://www.mhanj.org *Email:* info@mhanj.org

ATLANTIC	609-272-1700
CAMDEN	856-966-6767
ESSEX	973-509-9777
HUDSON	201-653-4700
MERCER	609-656-0110
MONMOUTH	732-542-6422
MORRIS	973-334-3496
OCEAN	732-905-1132
PASSAIC	973-478-4444
UNION	908-272-0300

MENTAL HEALTH OUTPATIENT SERVICES

STATEWIDE

Catholic Charities Trenton, Mercer Outpatient Services Provides a wide range of services for anyone with a mental illness, substance abuse concerns, individual, group, couples and families welcome. Call 1-800-360-7711.

ATLANTIC

Mental Health Outpatient Program Provides treatment and a variety of mental health services. Offers counseling for anxiety, depression, grief, life transitions, parenting, eating disorders, child behavioral issues. Sign language interpreters can be arranged. Sliding scale fees are charged accordingly. Call Jewish Family Services 609-822-1108.

BERGEN

Latin America Institute Youth and Family Community Program An intensive youth, family and community intervention. Anger and behavioral management, mentoring, addiction assessment and treatment programs for teens. Call 201-525-1700. *Email:* lpuertas1@verizon.net

Mental Health Care Plus NJ Inc. Offers outpatient services for anyone experiencing difficulty handling life's challenges. Addictions, behavioral issues, eating disorders, chronic and debilitating mental health, attention deficit, adolescent issues, social limitations, etc. Fees based on sliding scale. Call 201-265-8200. *Website:* http://www.careplusnj.org

HUDSON

Outpatient Services Jersey City Medical Center Offers adult and children programs. Consultations, addiction, grief, men's domestic violence program. Call 201-915-2272 (24 hr).

HUNTERDON

Hunterdon Behavioral Health Outpatient Services Offers a full range of behavioral health needs. Treats depression, anxiety, relationship problems, family conflict, parenting issues, chronic pain, vocational problems, abuse victims and male and female issues. Sliding scale fee. Call Behavioral Health 908-788-6401.

575

MERCER

Delaware House Mental Health Services Provides psychiatric treatment and a variety of mental health services including residential services, supportive housing, partial care, vocational services and supported employment. Offers counseling, advocacy, medical coordination, family support, Riverbank Self-Help Center and Riverbank transportation. Sliding scale fees are charged accordingly in addition to Medicaid and Medicare. Call Delaware House 609-267-9339.

Bermingham Clinic Outpatient Services *(MULTILINGUAL)* Services include counseling for children, adults, families, groups, MICA treatment, psychiatric medication monitoring on a planned or emergency basis. Spanish and American Sign Language. Call 609-396-8877 Mon. and Tues., 9-6pm; Wed., 9-9pm; Thurs., noon-8pm; Fri. 8:50am-5pm. For referral information call 1-888-866-9565.

MONMOUTH

Monmouth Medical Outpatient Services Offers confidential outpatient services for adults and children. Individual and family services available. Medication and substance abuse counseling. Adults are offered support in anxiety, depression, schizophrenia, personality disorders, psychosis, substance abuse, AIDS counseling, grief and loss, etc. Sliding scale fees. Call 732-923-6500.

MORRIS

Saint Clare's Behavioral Health Outpatient Offers a wide variety of services for the mental health consumer. Individual, marital, family and group therapy. Case management, medication monitoring, psychosocial rehabilitation and residential services for discharged psychiatric patients. Fee based on sliding scale. Call 973-401-2121.

Saint Clare's Continuum of Care Provides assistance, support and skills teaching to the adult psychiatric community enabling successful, independent living in the community for each consumer in an environment of their choice. Supervised housing and supported community living. For more information call 973-401-2121.

OCEAN

Saint Barnabas Outpatient Services Offers outpatient programs to adults. Geriatrtric services also available. MICA and evening programs available. Call Behavioral Health 1-800-300-0628.

PASSAIC

Barnert Hospital Mental Health Outpatient Services Provides treatment and a variety of mental health services. Offers counseling for anxiety, depression, grief, life transitions, parenting, eating disorders, child behavioral issues, juvenile sexual behavioral, crisis intervention, etc. Sign language interpreters available. Sliding scale fees are charged accordingly. Call Barnert Community Counseling Service 973-977-6660; TTY/TDD: 973-977-6690.

Clifton Behavioral Health Care/SERV Centers Offers outpatient individual, couples, family and group psychotherapy. Located in Clifton. Sliding scale fee. Call 1-800-987-7378. *Website:* http://www.servbhs.org

SALEM

Mental Health Outpatient Healthcare Commons Offers assistance to anyone who has an emotional problem, mental disorder, or is under stress. Individual, group and family counseling. Child adolescents and adult outpatient services available based on a sliding scale. Call 856-299-3200 ext. O. *Website:* http://www.hcommons.com

UNION

Trinitas Adult Outpatient Services Multicultural services for persons with a mental illness or severe psychological distress. Offers assistance in anxiety, depression, panic, suicidal intention, schizophrenia, bipolar, sex offender evaluations and treatment, domestic violence perpetrators, life transitions and medication management. Sliding scale fee. Call Trinitas 908-994-7557.

WARREN

Warren County Family Services Mental Health Outpatient Provides treatment and a variety of mental health services. Offers counseling for families, individuals and group therapy. Information and referrals. Helps with life crisis such as birth, death, marriage, difficult children, violence and adults dealing with childhood sexual abuse. Substance abuse treatment available. Sliding scale fees. Call Family Guidance Center of Warren County 908-689-1000.

Consider passing this Directory on to a student or staff member - browsing through the Directory pages can often provide helpful education as to the wide variety of groups available.

MENTAL HEALTH PACT TEAMS

Community based program for adults with a serious and persistent mental illness. There are strict registration criteria, e.g., previous hospitalization is required.

ATLANTIC	609-407-0042
BERGEN	201-398-9110
BURLINGTON	609-261-6627
CAMDEN	856-428-7632
CAPE MAY	609-463-8990
CUMBERLAND	856-691-8579
ESSEX	973-466-1300
GLOUCESTER	856-251-1414
HUDSON	201-653-3980
HUNTERDON	908-835-8660
MERCER	609-394-5285
MIDDLESEX	732-257-6100
MONMOUTH	732-842-2000 ext. 4301 or 4302
MORRIS / SUSSEX	1-888-626-2111 or 973-625-7084
OCEAN	732-349-0515
PASSAIC	973-470-3056 press 9 after connecting
SALEM	856-691-8579
SOMERSET	908-704-8252
UNION	908-352-0242
WARREN	908-835-8660

PARTIAL CARE PROGRAMS

HUDSON, MERCER, MIDDLESEX

ADAPT A partial care program for adults working to recover from and cope with mental illness. Individualized guidance toward the development skills needed to live and work successfully in the community. Sliding scale fees. Call 1-800-987-7378.

YOUTH SERVICES

BERGEN

CompCare For Adolescents and Their Families Therapeutic after-school program for children (age 11-17), who are in need of intensive structured therapy. Addresses serious emotional problems. Offers group, individual, art and family therapy. Transportation and many other services are provided. Sliding scale fee. Call CompCare 201-646-0333. *Website:* http://www.cbhcare.com *Email:* mmiddleman@cbhcare.com

BURLINGTON

Capital Academy An innovative residential treatment facility for severely emotionally disturbed children (age 15-18), who have been abused or neglected. A variety of services are provided. Call 609-434-1003.

MORRIS

Saint Clares Children's Services Adolescent services, parenting workshops, special needs groups for parents. School consultations, for Child Study Teams and guidance counselors provided at no charge. All other services are on a sliding scale. Call 973-401-2121.

LOCAL COMMUNITY HELPLINES

These helplines provide information and referrals to local services and agencies. Many also provide crisis intervention and listening services. Some publish directories of local community services.

ATLANTIC

Contact 856-795-2155 (24 hr.) Information and referral, active listening and reassurance calls to shut-ins. Serves Atlantic and Cape May Counties. Sponsored in part by United Way. *Email:* contact-c-a@excite.com

Intergenerational Services Dial 211 (24 hr.) (may not be available from public or cell phones or from some larger workplace phone systems) or 1-888-426-9243. Provides information and referral services to local services and agencies.

BERGEN

Community Resource Council 201-343-4900 (9am-5pm). Information and referral services, crisis intervention. Youth helpline 1-866-FOR-R-YOUTH.

First Call For Help Dial 211 (24 hr) (211 is not available from public phones, some cell phones or from some larger workplace phone systems) or 1-800-435-7555 or 973-331-3663 (Mon.-Fri., 8:30am-5pm). Provides information and referral for local services and agencies. *Website:* http://www.firstcall.org *Email:* help@firstcall.org

BURLINGTON

Contact of Burlington County Dial 211 (24 hr) (may not be available from public or cell phones or from some larger workplace phone systems); 609-871-4700, 609-267-8500 or 856-234-8888; Kids Line: 609-261-2220; Teen Line: 609-871-1433; Pet Friends for grieving pet owners: 856-234-4688. Provides crisis intervention, information and referral, rape care and sexual assault services, reassurance "care calls." All services are free. *Website:* http://www.contactburlco.org *Email:* contact333@contactburlco.org

CAMDEN

Contact Community Helpline 1-877-266-8222 (South Jersey only) (24 hr crisis); 856-795-4980 (reassurance calls to elderly and hearing impaired shut-ins (Mon.-Fri., 9am-4:30pm). Provides information, referrals and listening services. Sponsored by United Way. *Website:* http://www.contacthelplines.org *Email:* info@contacthelplines.org

First Call For Help Dial 211 (may not be available from public or cell phones or from some larger workplace phone systems), 1-800-331-7272 (South Jersey only) or 856-663-2255 (8am-4:30pm). Will take calls after 4:30pm for emergencies. Information and referrals. Sponsored by UOSS Community Information Systems. *Website:* http://www.infonet.org

CAPE MAY

Contact 856-795-2155 (24 hr.) Information and referral, active listening and reassurance calls to shut-ins. Serves Atlantic and Cape May Counties. Sponsored in part by United Way. *Email:* contact-c-a@excite.com

First Call For Help 609-729-2255 (Mon.-Fri., 8:30am-4:30pm). Information and referrals to local services and agencies. Serves Cape May County. Sponsored by United Way.

CUMBERLAND

Contact of Gloucester County 1-877-266-8222 (South Jersey only) (24 hr). Listening, information and referrals. Serves Gloucester, Salem and Cumberland Counties. Sponsored by Contact USA. *Website:* http://www.contacthelplines.org *Email:* info@contacthelplines.org

ESSEX

Contact We Care 908-232-2880 (24 hr). Information and referrals, crisis and suicide helpline, listening. Covers Union/Essex/Middlesex/Somerset counties.

First Call for Help Dial 211 (24 hr) (may not be available from public or cell phones or from some larger workplace phone systems) or 1-800-435-7555 (Mon.-Fri., 8:30am-5pm). Information and referrals to local services and agencies. *Website:* http://www.firstcall.org *Email:* help@firstcall.org

GLOUCESTER

CONTACT Community Helpline 1-877-266-8222 (South Jersey only) (24 hr). Crisis counseling; reassurance calls 856-795-4980 (Mon.-Fri., 9am-4:30pm). Provides information, referrals and listening services. Sponsored by United Way. *Website:* http://www.contacthelplines.org *Email:* info@contacthelplines.org

First Call For Help Dial 211 (24 hr) (may not be available from public or cell phones or from some larger workplace phones) or 1-800-648-0132. Information, referrals, active listening, crisis counseling and referrals for homeless. Serves Gloucester County. Funded by United Way.

HUDSON

First Call for Help of Essex and West Hudson *(BILINGUAL)* Dial 211 (24 hr) (may not be available from public or cell phones or from some larger workplace phone systems) or 1-800-435-7555 (Mon.-Fri., 8:30am-5pm). Information and referrals to local services and agencies. *Website:* http://www.firstcall.org *Email:* help@firstcall.org

581

HUNTERDON

Hunterdon Helpline Dial 211 (24 hr) (may not be available from public or cell phones or from some larger workplace phone systems); 1-800-272-4630, 908-735-4357 or 908-782-4357; TDD also available. Information and referrals, friendly visits and assurance calls offered to the elderly. Suicide prevention hotline. Assistance for the homeless and hungry. Provides information for Hunterdon County Links Transport Service. Professional and volunteer run. Serves Hunterdon, Monmouth and Somerset Counties. Sponsored by United Way. *Website:* http//helplinehc.org

MERCER

Contact of Mercer County 609-896-2120 (24 hr) Crisis counseling, listening, information and referrals. Kids Line: 609-896-4434. *Website:* http://www.contactofmercer.org *Email:* contactofmercer@verizon.net

Info Line of Central Jersey Dial 211 (24 hr) (may not be available from public or cell phones or from some larger workplace phone systems) or 1-888-908-4636. Provides information and referral to local services and agencies. Serves Mercer County. Sponsored by United Way of Greater Mercer.

Mercer County Hispanic Association (SPANISH) 609-392-2446 (Mon.-Fri., 8:30am-3pm) Information and referrals, assistance with job searches, youth services, women's issues and housing.

MIDDLESEX

Contact We Care 908-232-2880 (24 hr) Information and referrals, crisis and suicidal helpline, listening. Covers Union/Essex/Middlesex/Somerset counties.

Info Line of Central Jersey *(BILINGUAL)* Dial 211 (24 hr) (may not be available from public or cell phones or from some larger workplace phone systems) 1-888-908-4636 (Voice/TDD). Provides information and referral to local services and agencies. *Website:* http://www.info-line.org *Email:* help@info-line.org

MONMOUTH

Monmouth Helpline Dial 211 (24 hr) (may not be available from public or cell phones or from some larger workplace phone systems) or 1-800-272-4630 (24 hr). Provides information and referrals to local services and agencies. Serves Monmouth, Somerset and Hunterdon.

MORRIS

First Call For Help Dial 211 (24 hr) (may not be available from public phones, some cell phones or from some larger workplace phone systems), 1-800-435-7555 or 973-331-3663 (Mon.-Fri., 8:30am-5pm). Provides information and referral for local services and agencies. *Website:* http://www.211firstcall.org *Email:* info@211firstcall.org

Peer-to-Peer Support Line 1-877-760-4987 (5–10 pm) Non-crisis peer counseling for mental health consumers. Provides support, information and resources.

OCEAN

Contact of Ocean County Dial 211 (24 hr) (may not be available from public or cell phones or from some larger workplace phone systems) or 732-240-6100. Information and referrals, listening service. Serves Ocean County. *Website:* http://www.contactocean.org *Email:* contactofoceanco@aol.com

PASSAIC

First Call For Help Dial 211 (24 hr) (may not be available from public or cell phones or from some larger workplace phone systems), 1-800-435-7555 or 973-331-3663 (Mon.-Fri., 8:30am-5pm). Provides information and referral for local services and agencies. *Website:* http://www.firstcall.org *Email:* help@firstcall.org

SALEM

Contact Community Services 1-877-266-8222 (South Jersey only) (24 hr crisis counseling); 856-795-4980 (reassurance calls to elderly and hearing impaired shut-in) (Mon.-Fri., 9am-4:30pm). Provides information, referrals and listening services. Sponsored by United Way. *Website:* http://www.contacthelplines.org *Email:* info@contacthelplines.org

SOMERSET

Contact We Care 908-232-2880 (24 hr); TDD: 908-232-3333 (7am-11pm). Information and referrals, crisis and suicidal helpline, listening. Covers Union/Essex/Middlesex/Somerset counties.

Somerset Helpline Dial 211 (24 hr) (may not be available from public or cell phones or from some larger workplace phone systems). Provides information and referrals to local and regional services and agencies. Serves Somerset County. Sponsored by United Way of Somerset County.

SUSSEX

Sussex County Helpline Dial 211 (24 hr) (may not be available from public or cell phones or from some larger workplace phone systems) or 973-209-4357. Confidential listening, information and referrals. Serves Sussex County. Funded by United Way.

UNION

Contact We Care 908-232-2880 (24 hr). Information and referrals, crisis and suicidal helpline, listening. Covers Union/Essex/Middlesex/Somerset counties. *Website:* http://www.contactwecare.org *Email:* contactw@bellatlantic.net

First Call For Help Dial 211 (24 hr) (may not be available from public or cell phone, also from some larger work place numbers) or 908-353-7171, press 0 (Mon.-Fri., 9am-5pm). Provides information and referral to local services and agencies. *Website:* http://www.unioncountynj.org

WARREN

First Call for Help Dial 211 (24 hr) (may not be available from public or cell phones or from some larger workplace phone systems) (24 hr), 908-454-4850 or 1-877-661-4357. Information and referrals. Central Holiday Intake (meals on holidays). Information on housing for persons with AIDS. Serves Warren County. Funded in part by United Way. Fax (908)454-2968. *Website:* http://www.norwescap.org

PSYCHIATRIC EMERGENCIES

The psychiatric emergency services listed below provide crisis/suicide intervention with trained professionals. Some counties provide mobile crisis services. All are available 24 hours a day. Hotlines should be contacted only in case of real mental health emergencies.

ATLANTIC
Atlantic City Medical Ctr. 609-344-1118

BERGEN
Psychiatric Emergency Screening Program 201-262-4357

BURLINGTON
Screening Crisis Intervention Program 609-835-6180

CAMDEN
Steininger Center 856-541-2222
Kennedy Memorial Hospital 856-428-4357

CAPE MAY
Burdette Tomlin Hospital 609-465-5999

CUMBERLAND
Cumberland County Guidance Center 856-455-5555

ESSEX
East Orange General Hospital 973-672-9685
Newark Beth Israel Hospital 973-926-7416
UMDNJ 973-623-2323

GLOUCESTER
CMHC of Gloucester County 856-845-9100

HUDSON
Jersey City Medical Center 201-915-2210
Bayonne Hospital 201-858-5286

HUNTERDON
Hunterdon Medical 908-788-6400

MERCER
Helene Fuld Medical Center 609-394-6086

MIDDLESEX
UMDNJ 732-235-5700

MONMOUTH
Monmouth Medical Center 732-923-6999
CentraState Medical Center 732-780-6023
Riverview Medical Center 732-219-5325

MORRIS
Saint Clare's Health Services 973-625-0280
Morristown Memorial Hospital 973-540-0100
Chilton Memorial Hospital 973-831-5078

OCEAN
Kimball Medical Center 732-886-4474

PASSAIC
Chilton Memorial Hospital 973-831-5078
St. Mary's 973-470-3025
Barnert Hospital 973-977-6996

SALEM
Salem County Healthcare Common 856-299-3001

SOMERSET
Richard Hall CMHC 908-526-4100

SUSSEX
Newton Memorial Hospital 973-383-0973

UNION
Trinitas 908-994-7131
Mulenburg 908-668-2599

WARREN
Warren Crisis Line 908-454-5141

Strange is our situation here upon earth.

Each of us comes for a short visit, not knowing why, yet sometimes seeming to divine a purpose.

From the standpoint of daily life, however, there is one thing we do know:

That man is here for the sake of other men.

Unknown

TOLL-FREE HELPLINES

The following toll-free numbers may be a helpful, cost-free resource for persons seeking additional information on a particular subject. These non-profit agencies provide information and referrals, literature and other services.

ADOPTION / FOSTER CARE

Foster and Adoptive Family Services *(New Jersey)* 1-800-222-0047 (Mon.-Fri., 9am-6pm); Provides training, offers support services and answers questions on becoming a foster or adoptive parent. Offers scholarships to foster and adoptive youth, holiday toy drive and fostering wishes for children. Sponsored by Division of Youth and Family Services. Fax: 609-520-1515 *Website:* http://www.FAFSonline.org. *Email:* mawrachow@FAFSonline.org.

National Adoption Center 1-800-TO-ADOPT (1-800-862-3678). Provides information on adoption agencies and support groups. Offers network for matching parents and children with special needs. Fax: 215-735-9410. *Website:* http://www.adopt.org/adopt *Email:* NAC@adopt.org

National Adoption Information Clearinghouse 1-888-251-0075. Provides professionals and the general public information on all aspects of the adoption process. Offers literature and referrals. Sponsored by US Dept. of Health and Human Services. *Website:* http://www.naic.acf.hhs.gov

NJ Adopt *(New Jersey)* 1-800-992-3678. Information on the adoption process and training. Serves NJ. Sponsored by Div. of Family Services. *Website:* http://www.njadopt.org

AGING / SENIOR CITIZENS

Alliance for Aging Research 1-800-639-2421. Citizen advocate organization that strives to improve the health and independence of older Americans through public and private research. Promotes healthy aging among people of all ages. Provides statistics on the health and well-being of older persons. Conducts information campaigns. *Website:* http://www.agingresearch.org

Eldercare Locator 1-800-677-1116 (Mon.-Fri., 9am-8pm ET). Provides information for families & friends of the elderly (60+). Makes referrals to area agencies on aging for information on insurance, Medicaid, taxes, respite care, etc. Information for disabled also provided on these subjects. *Website:* http://www.eldercare.gov

Freedom Eldercare *(New Jersey)* 1-866-737-3336 (24 hr). Free information and referral service to assist individuals in navigating the complex healthcare system. Specialists represent the fields of nursing, social work and geriatric care management. *Website:* http://www.freedomeldercare.com

Lifeline Programs *(New Jersey)* 1-800-792-9745 (Mon.-Fri., 8:30am-5pm). Recorded information on pharmaceutical and utility benefits for qualified seniors and the disabled.

National Council on the Aging 1-800-424-9046; Fax: 202-479-0735. Information to the aged, families and professionals. *Website:* http://www.ncoa.org

National Institute on Aging 1-800-222-2225 (Voice/TDD); TDD/TTY 1-800-222-4225; Fax: 301-495-3334. Provides publications on topics of interest to older adults, doctors, nurses, social activities directors, health educators and the public. Sponsored by federal government. *Website:* http://www.nia.nih.gov *Email:* niaic@jbs1.com

NJ Ease *(New Jersey)* 1-877-222-3737 (Mon.-Fri., 8:30am-5pm) Fax: 973-285-6883. Provides information to seniors, disabled, veterans and their caregivers on available local benefits and programs. Information on housing options, nursing homes, elder abuse issues, assisted living facilities, transportation, nutrition, caregivers, insurance, healthcare, long-term care, social activities, volunteer opportunities and care management.

Senior Citizen Information and Referral *(New Jersey)* 1-800-792-8820 (Mon.-Fri., 8:30am-5pm). Provides information and referrals to services for senior citizens 60+ and their caregivers. Addresses elder abuse issues. Makes referrals to local offices on aging statewide. Sponsored by NJ Department of Health and Senior Services. *Website:* http://www.state.nj.us/health/senior

AIDS

AIDS Info *(BILINGUAL)* 1-800-448-0440 or 301-519-0459 (ET) TDD/TTY 1-888-480-3739; Fax: 301-519-6616. Resource information on clinical trials for AIDS and HIV+ patients. Information about current treatments and prevention techniques. Provides live online assistance. *Website:* http://aidsinfo.nih.gov *Email:* contactus@aidsinfo.nih.gov

CDC National Prevention Information Network *(BILINGUAL)* 1-800-458-523 (Mon.-Fri., 9am-8pm). Provides information on resources and support groups, educational materials and business and labor responses to AIDS, sexually transmitted diseases and tuberculosis, via touch tone phone. Many different service and publications offered. *Website:* http://www.cdcnpin.org *Email:* info@cdcnpin.org

CDC National STD/AIDS Hotline *(BILINGUAL)* English: 1-800-342-2437 or 1-800-227-8922 (24 hour ET); Spanish: 1-800-344-7432; Herpes Hotline: 919-361-8488 (Mon.-Fri., 9am-6pm); TDD/TTY: 1-800-243-7889 (Mon.-Fri., 10am-10pm). Provides education and research about sexually transmitted diseases. Information on minor and major sexually transmitted disease infections (including yeast, AIDS, cancroids, herpes, genital warts, syphilis and gonorrhea). Referrals, information on prevention, free pamphlets. *Website:* http://www.ashastd.org *Email:* hivnet@ashastd.org

Gay Men's Health Crisis *(BILINGUAL)* 1-800-243-7692. Provides information and referrals for persons affected by AIDS (including gay men, lesbian women, bisexuals, transgendered, straight and immigrants). *Website:* http://www.gmhc.org *Email:* lynns@gmhc.org

New Jersey AIDS/STD Hotline *(New Jersey)* 1-800-624-2377; TTY: 973-926-8008 (24 hr); Fax: 973-643-2537. Information and referral on AIDS/Sexually Transmitted Diseases. Counseling, treatment information. Referrals to testing locations. Sponsored by NJ Department of Health.

Project Inform *(BILINGUAL)* 1-800-822-7422 (Mon.-Fri., 10am-4pm PT). Provides information about experimental drugs, treatment of AIDS, volunteer training programs. Quarterly newsletter, journal. *Website:* http://www.projectinform.org *Email:* info@projectinform.org

Sister Connect *(New Jersey)* 1-800-747-1108 (Mon.-Fri., 9am-5pm). Peer support program that provides information, referrals and peer support to the community and women living with HIV/AIDS. Sponsored by NJ Women and AIDS Network. *Website:* www.njwan.org *Email:* office@njwan.org

TEEN AIDSline *(New Jersey)* 1-800-618-8336 (Mon./Wed./Thurs., 4:30-9:30pm). Provides information and referrals to teens regarding HIV/AIDS and related issues. Confidential. *Website:* http://www.TeenAIDSonline.com *Email:* TeenAIDSline@acsnj.org

ALCOHOL

Addictions Hotline of NJ 1-800-238-2333 (voice/TDD) (24 hr.) Crisis counseling, information and referrals for all kinds of drug and alcohol related issues (both prescription and illegal drugs).

Community Recovery *(New Jersey)* 1-800-292-8262. Offers services for veterans who are experiencing problems with drugs or alcohol. Offers a wide variety of services throughout the state.

National Association for Children of Alcoholics 1-888-554-2627. Advocates for children and families affected by alcoholism and other drug dependencies. Helps children hurt by parental alcohol and drug abuse. Newsletter, advocacy, policy making, literature, videos, educational materials. *Website:* http://www.nacoa.org *Email:* nacoa@nacoa.org

National Clearinghouse for Alcohol and Drug Information *(BILINGUAL)* 1-800-729-6686 or 301-468-2600; Spanish: 1-877-767-8432; TDD/TTY: 1-800-487-4889; Fax: 301-468-6433. Information on alcohol, tobacco, drug abuse and prevention. Referrals to treatment centers, research, groups, drugs in the work place, community programs, AIDS and drug abuse. *Website:* http://www.health.org *Email:* info@health.org

National Council on Alcoholism & Drug Dependence 1-800-622-2255 (24 hr). Provides information on counseling and treatment services for alcohol or drug abuse. Prevention and education programs. Newsletter. *Website:* http://www.ncadd.org *Email:* national@mcadd.org

National Organization on Fetal Alcohol Syndrome 1-800-666-6327. Provides information and referrals on fetal alcohol syndrome. *Website:* http://www.nofas.org

ALZHEIMER'S DISEASE

Alzheimer's Disease Education & Referral Center 1-800-438-4380 or 301-495-3311; Fax: 301-495-3334. Provides information and publications on Alzheimer's disease to health and service professionals, patients and their families, caregivers and public. Sponsored by Nat'l Inst. on Aging. *Website:* http://www.alzheimers.org *Email:* adear@alzheimers.org

Alzheimer's Disease Helpline *(New Jersey)* 1-800-424-2494. Information, counseling, referrals and support for Alzheimer's and related disorders. Also offers assistance for caregivers.

American Health Assistance Foundation 1-800-437-2423 (Mon.-Fri., 9am-5pm). Provides educational information and funds research for Alzheimer's disease, glaucoma, heart disease and macular degeneration. *Website:* http://www.ahaf.org

ATTORNEY

Legal Services of New Jersey *(BILINGUAL)* *(New Jersey)* 1-888-576-5529 or 732-572-9100 (Mon.-Fri., 9am-4:30pm). Provides free legal advice over the phone for low income persons for civil cases (housing, landlord, tenant, public assistance and entitlements, family law and domestic violence, consumer law and bankruptcy, employment law, immigration, etc). *Website:* http://www.lsnj.org

National Organization of Social Security Claimant's Reps 1-800-431-2804. Provides referrals to social security lawyers who assist claimants in getting social security. *Website:* http://www.nosscr.org

BLIND

American Foundation for the Blind 1-800-232-5463 (Mon.-Fri., 8:30am-4:30pm); TDD/TTY: 212-502-7662. Clearinghouse of information and referrals for the blind. Catalog of publications available. *Website:* http://www.afb.org *Email:* afbinfo@AFB.net

American Health Assistance Foundation 1-800-437-2423 (Mon.-Fri., 9am-5pm). Provides educational information and funds research for Alzheimer's disease, glaucoma, heart disease and macular degeneration. *Website:* http://www.ahaf.org

Braille Institute 1-800-272-4553 (Mon.-Fri., 8:30am-5pm). Provides publications, cassettes and free books for visually impaired children. Free Braille calendar. Referrals to resources. Tapes on vision loss available to companies and organizations. *Website:* http://www.brailleinstitute.org *Email:* info@brailleinstitute.org

DB-Link (National Information Clearinghouse on Children Who Are Deaf/Blind) 1-800-438-9376; TDD/TTY: 1-800-854-7013. Information & referral on education, health, employment, technology, communication and recreation for children who are deaf/blind. Newsletter. *Website:* http://www.dblink.org *Email:* dblink@tr.wou.edu

Glaucoma Research Foundation 1-800-826-6693 or 415-986-3162 (Mon.-Fri., 8:30am-5pm PT). Phone support network for persons with glaucoma. Free literature. Funds research. *Website:* http://www.glaucoma.org *Email:* info@glaucoma.org

Guide Dog Foundation 1-800-548-4337; Fax: 631-361-5192. Provides seeing eye dogs to the blind free of charge. *Website:* http://www.guidedog.org

591

Guiding Eyes for the Blind 1-800-942-0149 or 914-245-4024; Fax: 914-962-1403. Dedicated to enriching the lives of blind and visually impaired men and women by providing them with guide dogs free of charge. *Website:* http://www.guiding-eyes.org *Email:* info@guidingeyes.org

Hadley School for the Blind 1-800-323-4238 or 847-441-8111; TDD/TTY: 847-446-4111. Provides free distance education to blind and visually impaired persons using Braille materials, large print or audio-cassettes. *Website:* http://www.hadley.edu *Email:* info@Hadley.edu

Library of Congress National Library Blind & Physically Handicapped 1-800-424-8567; TDD/TTY: 202-707-0744; Fax: 202-707-0712. Refers callers to libraries that have information on books on tapes and in Braille available for qualified blind or handicapped persons who can't read standard print. *Website:* http://www.loc.gov/nls *Email:* nls@loc.gov

New Jersey Library for the Blind and Handicapped *(BILINGUAL) (New Jersey)* English: 1-800-792-8322; Spanish: 1-800-582-5945; TDD: 1-877-882-5593 (Mon.-Fri., 9am-4:30pm; Sat., 9am-3pm) Fax: 609-530-6384. Information on provision of recorded materials, large print, Braille, radio reading service. Deaf and hard of hearing awareness program offers over 700 videos, books on hearing loss and deafness. Assistive devices such as TTYs, baby cry signalers, bed vibrators, closed captioned decoders and assistive listening devices. Sign language interpreting services for library events. Sponsored by Bureau of State Library, Thomas Edison State College. *Website:* http://www.njlbh.org *Email:* njlbh@njstatelib.org

NJ Commission for the Blind and Visually Impaired *(New Jersey)* 1-877-685-8878 (Mon.-Fri., 9am-5pm) (voice mail). Information and referral for persons with a visual impairment re: educational, social, occupational and vocational services. *Website:* http://www.cbvi.nj.gov

Prevent Blindness America 1-800-331-2020 (Mon.-Fri. 8:30am-5pm ET); Fax: 847-843-8458. Fights vision loss through research, education and direct services. Provides referrals to local services. Offers literature on vision, eye health and safety. *Website:* http://www.preventblindness.org *Email:* info@preventblindness.org

Recording For The Blind and Dyslexic 1-866-732-3585 (Mon.-Fri., 8:30am-4:30pm). Information on free cassettes, recorded textbooks and consumer publications to eligible handicapped persons. (Information on volunteer programs for recording tapes.) Membership dues $100/1st year; $35 subsequent years.

Worldwide services. Fax: 609-987-8116. *Website:* http://www.rfbd.org *Email:* custserv@rfbd.org

Research to Prevent Blindness 1-800-621-0026 or 212-752-4333. Provides publications and information on various eye diseases including macular degeneration, cataracts, glaucoma, diabetic retinopathy, corneal disease, retinitis pigmentosa, amblyopia/strabismus, uveitis, as well as general information. Funds research. *Website:* http://www.rpbusa.org

Retinitis Pigmentosa International 1-800-344-4877. Provides support and information for persons affected by retinitis pigmentosa and their families. Supports research. *Website:* http://www.rpinternational.org *Email:* RPInt@pacbell.net

BRAIN TUMOR

Pediatric Brain Tumor Foundation 1-800-253-6530 or 828-665-6891; Fax: 828-665-6894. Provides support and education concerning pediatric brain tumors. Seeks to find the cause and cure by supporting research. Encourages interaction among affected families for emotional support. *Website:* http://www.pbtfus.org *Email:* aalexander@pbtfus.org

BUSINESS

SCORE (Service Corps Of Retired Executives) 1-800-634-0245. Provides counseling for starting or maintaining businesses. *Website:* http://www.score.org

U.S. Small Business Administration 1-800-827-5722. Provides information, training and literature on starting and financing small businesses. *Website:* http://www.sba.gov

CANCER

ALCASE (Alliance for Lung Cancer Advocacy, Support & Education) 1-800-298-2436; Fax: 360-735-1305. Operates a national "phone buddies" program, comprehensive helpline and many other additional services for persons with lung cancer and their families. *Website:* http://www.alcase.org *Email:* info@alcase.org

AMC Cancer Information and Counseling Line 1-800-525-3777 (Mon.-Fri., 8:30-5pm MT). Provides current medical information and counseling for cancer issues. *Website:* http://www.amc.org

593

American Cancer Society *(MULTILINGUAL)* 1-800-227-2345 (24 hr). Provides information on issues related to cancer (services, transportation, encouragement and support). Spanish and English speaking. *Website:* http://www.cancer.org

Anderson Network 1-800-345-6324 (Mon.-Fri., 8am-5pm CT); Fax: 713-745-5231. Matches cancer patients with others with exact diagnosis for support. *Website:* http://www.mdanderson.org

Cancer Care, Inc. 1-800-813-4673 (Mon.-Fri., 9am-5pm) or 201-444-6630. Free counseling for cancer patients and their families. Financial assistance, information and referrals, community and professional education. Teleconference programs. On-going telephone and in-person support groups. *Website:* http://www.cancercare.org *Email:* info@cancercare.org

Cancer Hope Network 1-877-467-3638. One-on-one support offered to cancer patients and their families undergoing cancer treatment from trained volunteers who have survived cancer themselves. *Website:* http://www.cancerhopenetwork.org *Email:* info@cancerhopenetwork.org

Cancer Information Service *(BILINGUAL)* 1-800-422-6237. Provides information about cancer and cancer-related resources to patients, the public and health professionals. Offers one-on-one smoking cessation counseling and literature. Free publications. Sponsored by National Cancer Institute. *Website:* http://www.cancer.gov

Cancer Research Institute 1-800-99-CANCER or 212-688-7515; Fax: 212-832-9376. Provides general cancer resource information. Supports leading-edge research aimed at developing immunologic methods of preventing, treating and curing cancer. *Website:* http://www.cancerreseaarch.org *Email:* info@cancerresearch.org

CureSearch 1-800-458-6223; Fax: 626-447-6359. Advocates for the needs of children with cancer and their families. Information, newsletter. *Website:* http://www.curesearch.org Email: celia.leon@curesearch.org

Dana Farber Cancer Institute Family Studies Cancer Risk Line 1-800-828-6622. Information on familial cancers. *Website:* http://www.partners.org

Gilda Radner Familial Ovarian Cancer Registry 1-800-682-7426 (Mon.-Fri., 9am-5:30pm ET). Information on the warning signs of cancer, diagnostic tests and family history. Sponsored by Roswell Park Cancer Inst. *Website:* http://www.ovariancancer.com

Gynecologic Cancer Foundation 1-800-444-4441. Makes referrals to physicians who specialize in the treatment of gynecological cancer. Referrals to doctors, brochures, literature. Online resources. *Website:* http://www.wcn.org *Email:* gcs@sba.com

Hereditary Cancer Institute 1-800-648-8133 or 402-280-2942 (Mon.-Fri., 8am-4:30pm CT). Studies family-linked cancer. Provides counseling, information on clinical trials, cancer and hereditary factors. *Website:* http://www.medicine.creighton.edu/HCI *Email:* tinley@creighton.edu

International Myeloma Foundation 1-800-452-2873; Fax: 818-487-7454. Provides information, seminars, grants and newsletter on myeloma. *Website:* http://www.myeloma.org *Email:* info@myeloma.org

Locks of Love 1-888-896-1588 or 561-963-1677; Fax: 561-963-9914. Provides custom hairpieces to financially disadvantaged children with long-term medical hair loss. Uses donated hair. *Website:* http://www.locksoflove.org/ *Email:* info@locksoflove.org

Look Good, Feel Better 1-800-227-2345. Helps cancer patients improve their appearance during treatment. Free workshops across the country. *Website:* http://www.cancer.org

Ovarian Cancer Research Fund 1-800-873-9569; Fax: 212-947-5652. Dedicated to advancing and supporting laboratory and clinical research that promotes the development of new therapies and techniques for early detection, screening and treatment of ovarian cancer. *Website:* http://www.ocrf.org

Patient Advocate Foundation 1-800-532-5274 or 757-873-6668; Fax: 757-873-8999. Provides education and legal counseling to cancer patients (relative to a diagnosis) concerning managed care, discrimination, insurance and financial issues. *Website:* http://www.patientadvocate.org *Email:* help@patientadvocate.org

R.A. Bloch Cancer Foundation Cancer Hotline 1-800-433-0464. Networks persons with cancer and home volunteers with same type of cancer. Free books about cancer. *Website:* http://www.blochcancer.org *Email:* hotline@hrbloch.com

Skin Cancer Foundation 1-800-754-6490 (Mon.-Fri., 9am-5pm ET). Provides free packets of information on skin cancer and treatment. *Website:* http://www.skincancer.org *Email:* info@skincancer.org

S. Koman Breast Cancer Foundation 1-800-462-9273 (Mon.-Fri., 9am-4:30pm). Information on breast cancer and breast health. *Website:* http://www.komen.org/

CAREERS

Careers Hotline *(New Jersey)* 1-800-222-1309 (Mon.-Fri., 8:30am-4:30pm); Fax 609-292-6692. Provides descriptions and outlooks on various careers. Has information on New Jersey vocational schools, national colleges, graduate school programs and New Jersey day care centers. Publishes a sample resume and information on job interviews. Not a job search agency. Sponsored by NJ Dept. of Labor. *Website:* http://www.wnjpin.net/coei *Email:* lseidel@dol.state.nj.us

National Job Corps Information Line *(BILINGUAL)* 1-800-733-5627 (24 hr) Referrals to job corps training for persons 16-24. Helps persons to earn high school equivalency diplomas.

CHARITY / SERVICE ORGANIZATIONS

AmVets 1-800-244-6350. Makes referrals to used clothing collection agencies and provides pick-up information.

Goodwill Industries 1-800-741-0186 or 301-530-6500. Provides employment and training services for people with disabilities and other disadvantaging conditions (welfare dependency, illiteracy, criminal history, homeless).

Volunteers of America 1-800-899-0089 or 703-341-5000. Provides local human services programs and opportunities for individual and community involvement in volunteer programs that deal with social problems. Also has Retiree Volunteer Coalition.

Volunteers of American of Delaware Valley 1-800-281-4354 or 856-854-7466 Provides local human service programs and opportunities for individual and community involvement in volunteer programs that deal with social problems. Also has Retiree Volunteer Coalition.

CHILD ABUSE

American Humane Association 1-800-227-4645. Mission is to protect children and animals from abuse, neglect and cruelty. Advocates on behalf of children (fire arms, capital/corporal punishment, child protective services, medical neglect, etc) and animals. *Website:* http://www.americanhumane.org

Child Help USA Hotline *(BILINGUAL)* 1-800-422-4453 (24 hr) or 480-922-8212 Fax: 480-922-7061. General information on child abuse and related issues Referrals to local agencies for child abuse reporting. Crisis counseling. *Website* http://www.childhelpusa.org/

Child Abuse Hotline *(New Jersey)* 1-800-792-8610 (24 hr); TDD: 1-800-835-5510 (24 hr); Fax: 609-588-2997. Accepts reports of child abuse or neglect. Emergency response for children at risk. Anonymous if callers prefer. Sponsored by Division of Youth and Family Services, Trenton.

National Clearinghouse on Child Abuse and Neglect 1-800-394-3366 (Mon.-Fri., 8:30am-5:30pm). Provides information on all aspects of child maltreatment. *Website:* http://www.nccanch.acf.hhs.gov *Email:* nccanch@caliber.com

Prevent Child Abuse America 1-800-244-5373. Through automated system, caller can request literature on a large variety of topics including: neglect, adult survivors of child abuse, discipline, sexual abuse, etc. Information will be sent via mail. *Website:* http://www.preventchildabuse.org *Email:* info@preventchildabuse.org

Project Child Find *(New Jersey)* 1-800-322-8174; TDD: 609-984-8432 (Mon.-Fri., 8:15am-4:15pm). Information and referrals for children, from birth to 21 years, with any developmental delay. Sponsored by Dept. of Education. *Website:* http://www.state.nj/education

U.S. Customs Service 1-800-232-5378. Will take reports on child pornography on the internet. Aim is to stop this form of child sexual abuse. *Email:* c3@customs.treas.gov.

CHILD CARE

Healthy Families *(New Jersey)* 1-800-244-5373. For any new parent who feels alone, frightened or overwhelmed. Offers support, education, links to health care and assists in helping to meet family needs. Stays with parents as their child grows. Services are free and will work with persons to help them to be the best parent they can be.

National Association for Family Child Care *(BILINGUAL)* 1-800-359-3817 (Mon.-Fri. 8am-5pm MT). Provides information and training for in-home care providers. Newsletter.

National Child Care Information Center 1-800-616-2242 (Mon., Tues., Thurs., Fri., 8:30am-5:30pm; Wed. 8:30am-8pm ET). Provides information to enhance and promote quality child care. *Website:* http://www.nccic.org *Email:* info@nccic.org

Registered Family Day Care Line *(New Jersey)* 1-800-332-9227 (Mon.-Fri., 9am-5pm). Callers can obtain the telephone number of their local Child Care

Resource and Referral System to get information about various child care options and subsidized child care services. Caregivers can also learn how to become a registered family day care provider. Provides information on how to evaluate the child care environment to make an informed decision on the selection process.

CHILD SUPPORT

New Jersey Child Support Information *(New Jersey)* 1-800-621-5437 (for existing cases); 1-877-NJ KIDS 1 (customer service). Provides information on child support issues and problems. *Website:* http://www.njchildsupport.org

CHOLESTEROL

UAB Eat Right 1-800-231-3438 (Mon.-Fri., 8am-4pm ET). Provides information on nutrition & related topics (weight loss & cholesterol). Sponsored by Nutrition Info. Svcs.

COMPLAINTS

Directors Action Line *(New Jersey)* 1-800-331-3937 (Mon.-Fri., 9am-5pm). Responds to concerns and questions about the Division of Youth and Family Service and its services. Also answers questions regarding DYFS and refers callers to other assistance if needed.

Long Term Care Systems *(New Jersey)* 1-800-792-9770 (Mon.-Fri., 8:45am-4:45pm) (answering machine other times), Fax: 609-633-9060. Complaint line for hospitals, nursing homes, residential care facilities and assisted living. Sponsored by State Facilities. *Website:* http://www.state.nj.us.health

CONSUMER

FDA Consumer Affairs 1-888-463-6332 (Mon.-Fri., 10am-4pm); Fax: 301-443-1726. Information on any FDA-regulated product (food and drugs). Has information on rare illnesses, starting businesses, freedom of information act, health and medical issues. Free literature. Referrals to toll-free numbers. Assists in emergency situations. *Website:* http://www.fda.gov

National Do Not Call Registry 1-888-382-1222. An opportunity to limit the telemarketing calls that are received. The registry was created to offer consumers a choice regarding telemarketing calls. *Website:* http://www.donotcall.gov

New Jersey Division of Consumer Affairs *(New Jersey)* 1-800-242-5846 or 973-504-6200 (8:30am-5pm). Takes complaints against businesses, advisory and professional boards, health clubs, home repairs, car dealerships and charities. Information on Lemon Law (automobiles), weights and measures, legalized games of chance, Bureau of Securities, etc. *Website:* http://www.njconsumeraffairs.com *Email:* AskConsumerAffairs@lps.state.nj.us

Opt Out 1-888-567-8688. Removes your name and address from all mailing lists offered by the main consumer credit reporting agencies (Trans Union, Experian, Equifax and Innovis) which advertise and send out new charge card offers. When writing include your first, middle and last name (including Jr., Sr., etc), current address, previous address (if you've moved in the last six months), social security number, date of birth and signature.

Toy Safety Hotline 1-877-486-9723. Provides information on toy safety. Brochures. Information on best selling age-appropriate toys. *Website:* http://www.toy-tia.org

U.S. Consumer Product Safety Commission *(BILINGUAL)* 1-800-638-2772; TDD/TTY: 1-800-638-8270; Fax: 301-504-0124. Computer operated recorded information on product safety. Takes reports on unsafe products. *Website:* http://www.cpsc.gov *Email:* info@cpsc.gov

CREDIT COUNSELING

Consumer Credit Counseling Services 1-800-388-2227. With touch-tone phone, callers can find out about credit counseling services in their local areas. Sponsored by the Nat'l Foundation for Consumer Credit. *Website:* http://www.nfcc.org

CRIME VICTIMS

Consumer Response Center 1-877-382-4357. Assistance for people who are victims of fraud. Complaints are shared with law enforcement agencies. Does not resolve individual disputes. Sponsored by Federal Trade Commission. *Website:* http://www.ftc.gov

Fight Crime Invest in Kids 1-800-245-6476 (9am-6pm ET) or 202-776-0027; Fax: 202-776-0110. Aim is to provide access to educational child care and after-school programs in order to prevent crime. *Website:* http://www.fightcrime.org/ *Email:* information@fightcrime.org

GAINS Center 1-800-311-4246 option 2; Fax: 518-439-7612. Provides information on services for people with co-occurring mental health and substance abuse disorders who come in contact with the justice system. Provides technical assistance, needs assessment and literature to communities. *Website:* http://www.gainsctr.com *Email:* gains@prainc.com

Juvenile Justice Clearinghouse 1-800-851-3420 (Mon.-Fri., 8:30am-7pm); Fax: 410-792-4358. Information and referrals regarding juvenile justice programs and department of justice.

National Criminal Justice Referral Service 1-800-851-3420 (Mon.-Fri., 9:55am-6:01pm). Provides information on all aspects of the criminal justice system and support for victims. *Website:* http://www.ncjrs.org

National Center for Victims of Crime 1-800-394-2255. Provides information, referrals and advocacy to crime victims nationwide. An affiliate to the National Crime Victim Bar Association which provides referrals to file civil suit against perpetrators and other responsible individuals. Also operates Stalking Resource Center which provides training and technical assistance on the issue of stalking. *Website:* http://www.ncvc.org *Email:* gethelp@ncvc.org

National Institute of Corrections 1-800-995-6423 ext. 70147 or 202-307-0147 (Mon.-Fri., 8am-5pm). Provides information and technical assistance re: mentally ill persons in prison. *Website:* http://www.nicic.org *Email:* aault@bob.gov

NJ Bias Crime Victims' Support Service *(New Jersey)* 1-800-277-2427 or 609-896-8967. Makes referrals to law enforcement agencies, advocacy groups and mental health professionals for victims of bias crimes. *Website:* http://www.njbiascrime.org

Stalking *(New Jersey)* 1-800-572-7233 (24 hr). Support and information for anyone with a restraining order, who is being stalked in New Jersey. Sponsored by the Prevention of Violence Against Women.

Victims of Crime Compensation Board *(New Jersey)* 1-800-242-0804 (24 hr); Fax: 973-648-7031. Provides counseling, information on compensation and referrals for victims of violent crimes. Can help in emergency situations for qualified persons. Otherwise leave message. Sponsored by Victims of Crimes Compensation Board. *Website:* http://www.state.nj.us/victim *Email:* njvictims@yahoo.com

We Tip Hotlines *(BILINGUAL)* 1-800-782-7463 (general); 1-800-873-7283 (felony). Takes reports on crimes or felonies.

CYSTIC FIBROSIS

Children's Organ Transplant Association 1-800-366-2682 (Mon.-Fri., 8am-5pm ET); Fax: 812-336-8885. Provides public education on organ transplants. Assists families in fund-raising for transplant and transplant-related expenses. Assistance for all children and adults with cystic fibrosis who are U.S. citizens in need of an organ transplant. *Website:* http://www.cota.org *Email:* cota@cota.org

Cystic Fibrosis Foundation 1-800-344-4823 (Mon.-Fri., 8:30am-5:30pm); Pharmacy: 1-800-541-4959. Provides information, brochures, insurance information, pharmaceutical services and updates on research. *Website:* http://www.cff.org *Email:* info@cff.org

DEAF

ASHA Hearing & Speech Helpline *(BILINGUAL)* 1-800-638-8255 (Voice/TDD) (Mon.-Fri., 8:30am-5pm ET). Information on speech, hearing and language disabilities. Referrals to ASHA certified clinics. Database of information on listening devices. Sponsored by American Speech Language & Hearing Assn. *Website:* http://www.asha.org *Email:* actioncenter@asha.org

Better Hearing Institute 1-800-327-9355 or 703-684-3391 (Mon.-Fri., 9am-5pm ET); Fax: 703-684-6048. Information & literature on any hearing-related issue. *Website:* http://www.betterhearing.org *Email:* mail@betterhearing.org

Captioned Media Program 1-800-237-6213 (Mon.-Fri., 8:30am-5pm ET); TDD/TTY: 1-800-237-6819; Fax: 1-800-538-5636. Provides free loan program for open captioned media for the deaf or hearing-impaired. Also provides captioned materials for family members and professionals who work with hard-of-hearing. Sponsored by US Dept. of Education. *Website:* http://www.cfv.org *Email:* info@cfv.org

DB-Link (National Information Clearinghouse for Children Who Are Deaf/Blind) 1-800-438-9376 (Voice); TDD/TTY: 1-800-854-7013. Information & referral on education, health, employment, technology, communication and recreation for children who are deaf-blind. Newsletter. All services are free of charge. *Website:* http://www.tr.wou.edu/dblink *Email:* dblink@tr.wou.edu

Dial-A-Hearing Screening Test 1-800-222-3277 (Mon.-Fri., 9am-5pm ET). Offers over the phone hearing screening for anyone (age 14+). Provides hearing information and referral services. *Email:* dahst@aol.com

Division of Deaf and Hard of Hearing *(New Jersey)* 1-800-792-8339 (Voice/TTY) or 609-984-7281 (Mon.-Fri., 8:30-4:30pm) Information and referral for the deaf and hard of hearing. Interpreter referral service. Sensitivity training available for the public. *Website:* http://www.state.nj.us/humanservices/ddhh/index.html *Email:* Brian.shomo@dhs.state.nj

Hearing Aid 1-800-521-5247 or 734-522-7200 (Mon.-Fri., 8am-5pm ET). Provides general literature on hearing aids & hearing loss. Referrals to hearing instrument specialists. Leave name and address and information will be mailed. Sponsored by Int'l Hearing Society. *Website:* http://www.ihsinfo.org *Email:* amarkey@ihsinfo.org

Hearing Aid Assistance to the Aged and Disabled (HAAAD) *(New Jersey)* 1-800-792-9745 (Mon.-Fri., 8:30am-5pm); Fax: 609-588-7122 Provides a $100 reimbursement to eligible persons who purchase a hearing aid. Sponsored by NJ State Dept. of Health, Div. of Senior Affairs.

HEAR Now 1-800-648-4327 (Mon.-Fri., 8am-5pm). Helps financially needy individuals obtain hearing aids.

John Tracy Clinic for Preschool Deaf Children 1-800-522-4582 (Mon.-Fri., 8am-4pm PT); Fax: 213-749-1651. Information and support for parents and preschool deaf children. Free correspondence course for parents. *Website:* http://www.jtc.org

National Cued Speech Association 1-800-459-3529 (Voice/TDD). Encourages and supports the use of cued speech for communication, language development and literacy. Networking, literature, advocacy, information and referrals, phone support, conferences and family camps. *Website:* http://www.cuedspeech.org *Email:* cuedspeech.com

National Institute on Deafness & Other Communication Disorders 1-800-241-1044; TDD/TTY: 1-800-241-1055; Fax: 301-770-8977. Referrals to national agencies on hearing, speech, language, smell, taste, voice and balance disorders. Publishes fact sheets, brochures, information packets and newsletters. *Website:* http://www.nidcd.nih.gov *Email:* nidcdinfo@nidcd.nih.gov

New Jersey Library for the Blind and Handicapped *(New Jersey)* *(BILINGUAL)* English: 1-800-792-8322; Spanish: 1-800-582-5945; TDD: 1-877-882-5593 (Mon.-Fri., 9am-4:30pm; Sat., 9am-3pm) Fax: 609-530-6384 Information on provision of recorded materials, large print, Braille, radio reading service. Deaf and hard of hearing awareness program offers over 700 videos, books on hearing loss and deafness. Assistive devices such as: TTYs, baby cry signalers, bed vibrators, closed captioned decoders and assistive listening devices. Sign language interpreting services for library events. Sponsored by Bureau of State Library, Thomas Edison State College. *Website:* http://www.njstatelib.org *Email:* njlbh@njstatelib.org

DENTAL

Dental Care for Handicapped 1-888-471-6334. Information on free dental care for qualified elderly, disabled or chronically ill patients. Services include dentures, crowns or other significant dental work. *Website:* http://www.nfdh.org

DEPRESSION

National Institute of Mental Health Information Line *(BILINGUAL)* 1-800-421-4211 (publications). Phone system that takes orders for free brochures on depression, anxiety, etc. *Website:* http://www.nimh.nih.gov

Speak Up When You're Down *(New Jersey)* 1-800-328-3838 (24 hr). Resources for anyone experiencing postpartum depression, their families and friends. *Website:* http://www.njspeakup.gov

DIABETES

National Diabetes Education Program *(BILINGUAL)* 1-800-438-5383 or 1-800-860-8747. Provides educational information on diabetes. Publishes "Do Your Level Best" kit and diabetes kit to public and health care professionals. Sponsored by National Inst. of Diabetics, Digestive & Kidney Diseases and Ctr. for Diabetes Control & Prevention.

National Institute of Diabetes & Digestive & Kidney Diseases 1-800-891-5390 (kidney); 1-800-860-8747 (diabetes); 1-800-891-5389 (digestive diseases). Provides referrals and literature on a broad range of subjects concerning diabetes, digestive disorders, kidney disease, metabolic and endocrine disorders, hematological diseases and urologic disorders. *Website:* http://www.niddk.nih.gov *Email:* nkudic@info.niddk.nih.gov

DISABILITY

Abledata 1-800-227-0216. Provides information, publications and consumer reviews of all types of assistive technologies for persons with disabilities. Sponsored by Nat'l Inst. on Disability & Rehab Research and U.S. Dept. of Education. *Website:* http://www.abledata.com/

603

Access Board *(BILINGUAL)* 1-800-872-2253 or 202-272-0080. Advocates for accessibility. Provides publications and forms to press charges against agencies that are not accessible.

ADA Technical Assistance Line *(BILINGUAL)* 1-800-514-0301 (Mon., Tues., Wed., Fri., 9:30am-5:30pm; Thurs., 12:30-5pm); TDD/TTY: 1-800-514-0383. Provides free publications on the American Disabilities Act. A new publication will be available each month in a limited supply. *Website:* http://www.ada.gov

Assistive Technology Advocacy Center Buy or sell equipment (Back In Action): 1-800-554-2626; Information and funding assistance: 1-800-342-5832 (Voice) (Mon.-Fri., 8:30am-4:30pm). Maintains listing of used equipment available for sale. Information on assistive technology. Catalog of equipment published quarterly ($6).

Canine Companions for Independence 1-800-572-2275. Trains dogs to assist people with physical and developmental disabilities. Also has opportunities for people interested in volunteering to raise puppies. *Website:* http://www.cci.org

Childcare Plus 1-800-235-4122. Information and referrals to families of children (birth to 5) with disabilities. Inclusion training for professionals. *Website:* http://www.ccplus.org *Email:* ccplus@ruralinstitute.umt.edu

Disabled American Veterans 1-877-426-2838. Provides free, professional assistance to veterans and their families in obtaining benefits and services earned through military service and provided by the department of Veterans Affairs and other agencies of the government. Guidelines for developing chapters. *Website:* http://www.dav.org *Email:* feedback@davmail.org

Disabled and Alone 1-800-995-0066 or 212-532-6740; Fax: 212-532-3588. Helps families and caretakers of disabled persons make lifetime plans for the care of their loved one after they are gone. One time membership fee. *Website:* http://www.disabledandalone.org *Email:* info@disabledandalone.org

Division of Disability Services *(New Jersey)* 1-888-285-3036; TDD: 609-292-1210; Fax: 609-292-1233. Information and referral services for persons of all ages with disabilities. Serves as the chief link between state government and the county offices on disabilities. Publishes a statewide directory of disability services. *Website:* http://www.state.nj.us/humanservices/dds

Easter Seals National Headquarters Disability Helpline *(BILINGUAL)* 1-800-221-6827 (Mon.-Fri., 8:30am-5pm CT). Provides disability resource packets for children and adults with disabilities. Online directory available. *Website:* http://www.easterseals.com

Families and Advocates Partnership for Education 1-888-248-0822 (Mon. Fri., 8am 5:30pm); TDD/TTY: 952-838-0190. Support and education for families of children with any disability. Advocates for the Individuals with Disabilities Education Act. Literature, training sessions, information and referrals. *Website:* http://www.fape.org *Email:* fape@pacer.org

Family Support Center of New Jersey *(New Jersey)* 1-800-372-6510 or 732-528-8080 (Mon.-Fri., 8am-5pm); Fax: 732-528-4744. Information and referral agency offering services to individuals with a disability or families who live with a family member with special needs. Also works with professionals who service this community. A support network for parents is also available through the center. *Website:* http://www.familysupportnj.com *Email:* fsc@familysupportnj.com

Friends' Health Connection *(BILINGUAL)* 1-800-483-7436. A communication support network that connects patients and caregivers with any disorder, illness or handicap. Members are networked with each other based on health problem, symptoms, lifestyle, interests, occupation, location and other criteria and communicate via letters, phone and e-mail. It is intended for emotional support, not for romantic purposes. Also provides educational, therapeutic and recreational programs. Dues $9.95/yr. *Website:* http://www.friendshealthconnection.org *Email:* info@friendshealthconnection.org

HEATH Resource Center 1-800-544-3284 (Voice/TDD); Fax: 202-973-0908. Information and referrals on post-secondary education & adult training programs for people with disabilities. Sponsored by U.S. Dept. of Education. *Website:* http://www.heath.gwu.edu *Email:* askheath@heath.gwu.edu

Job Accommodation Network 1-800-526-7234 or 1-800-232-9675 (Voice/TDD) (Mon.-Thurs., 8am-8pm, Fri., 8am-7pm ET); Fax: 304-293-5407. Information on accommodations for people with disabilities. Sponsored Office of Disability Employment Policy and Dept. of the Labor. *Website:* http://www.jan.wvu.edu *Email:* jan@jan.icdi.wvu.edu

Library of Congress National Library Blind & Physically Handicapped 1-800-424-8567 (Mon.-Fri., 8:30-5pm ET); TDD/TTY: 202-707-0744; Fax: 202-707-0712. Refers callers to libraries that have information on books on tapes and in Braille available for qualified blind or handicapped persons who can't read standard print. *Website:* http://www.loc.gov/nls *Email:* nls@loc.gov

Lifeline Programs 1-800-792-9745 (Mon.-Fri., 8:30am-5pm). Recorded information on pharmaceutical and utility benefits for qualified seniors and the disabled.

National Accessible Apartment Clearinghouse 1-800-421-1221; Fax 703-518-6191. Maintains a database of over 46,000 accessible apartment nationwide. Helps people with disabilities find accessible apartments. Owners and managers may also use this service to register their accessible units. *Website* http://www.naahq.org

National Council on Independent Living 1-877-525-3400 or 703-525-3406 TDD/TTY: 703-525-4153; Fax: 703-525-3409. Provides information and referral to independent living centers. *Website:* http://www.ncil.org *Email:* ncil@ncil.org

National Dissemination Center for Children with Disabilities *(BILINGUAL)* 1-800-695-0285 (Mon.-Fri., 9am-5pm); TDD/TTY: 1-800-695-0285 or 202-884-8200; Fax: 202-884-8441. Provides information on disabilities with a special focus on children (birth to age 22). Services include information, referrals technical assistance to parents, educators, caregivers and advocates. Referrals to support groups. Publications available for a small fee. *Email:* nichcy@aed.org

National Institute for Rehab Engineering 1-800-736-2216 (day). Provide information, advice and referrals to people with all types of disabilities about assistive technology equipment. Aim is to help people with disabilities to be more independent and self-sufficient. *Website:* http://www.theofficenet/nire

New Jersey Library for the Blind and Handicapped *(New Jersey) (BILINGUAL)* English: 1-800-792-8322; Spanish: 1-800-582-5945; TDD 1-877-882-5593 (Mon.-Fri., 9am-4:30pm; Sat., 9am-3pm); Fax: 609-530-6384 Information on provision of recorded materials, large print, Braille, radio reading service. Deaf and hard-of-hearing awareness program offers over 700 videos, book on hearing loss and deafness. Assistive devices such as TTYs, baby cry signalers bed vibrators, closed captioned decoders and assistive listening devices. Sign language interpreting services for library events. Sponsored by Bureau of State Library, Thomas Edison State College. *Email:* njlbh@njstatelib.org *Website* http://www.njlbh.org

NJ Protection and Advocacy, Inc. *(New Jersey)* 1-800-922-7233 or 609-292-9742 (Mon.-Fri., 9am-5pm); TTY: 609-633-7106 Fax: 609-777-0187 Provides legal assistance and advocacy services to citizens of New Jersey with any type of disability (both physical and mental). Information and referral services educational programs, technical assistance and training. *Website* http://www.njpanda.org *Email:* jprioli@njpanda.org

NJ WINS (Work Incentive Programs) *(New Jersey)* 1-877-659-4672 or 1-888-322-1918. Enables social security administration beneficiaries with disabilities make informed choices about work and assist them in exploring work incentives that are available. *Website:* http://www.njwins.org *Email:* njwins@cpof-nj.org

Northeast ADA and IT Center *(BILINGUAL)* 1-800-949-4232 (Voice, TDD and Spanish). Fax: (607)255-2763. Provides free technical assistance to employers, individuals with disabilities, state and local government agencies and others in the implementation of the Americans with Disabilities Act. They also provide free training workshops and awareness programs. *Website:* http://www.northeastada.org *Email:* northeastada@cornell.edu

Project Child Find *(New Jersey)* 1-800-322-8174; TDD: 609-984-8432 (Mon.-Fri., 8:15am-4:15pm). Information and referrals for children, from birth to 21 years, with any developmental delay. Sponsored by Dept. of Education.

Rural Institute on Disabilities 1-800-732-0323 (Mon.-Fri., 8am-5pm MT); Fax: 406-243-4730. Provides assistance for disabled children and adults who live in rural areas. Technological services, early intervention and services for the elderly. Conducts research, rural transportation, employment and health promotion for disabled. *Email:* rural@uralinstitute.umt.edu

SNAP (Special Needs Advocate for Parents) 1-888-310-9889 or 973-236-9887; Fax: 973-236-9874. Support for parents of children with special needs. Referrals to educational advocates, support groups, attorneys, other resources. Assistance with estate planning. Newsletter, speakers' bureau. Interactive bulletin boards. *Website:* http://www.snapinfo.org *Email:* info@snapinfo.org

State Interagency Coordinating Council, The *(New Jersey)* 1-877-909-7422. Early intervention for infants and toddlers with disabilities. Offers support to enhance the capacity of families to meet the development and health needs of children birth to age three. Also promotes collaborative partnerships among families and the community.

Through the Looking Glass 1-800-644-2666 or 510-848-1112 (Mon.-Fri., 8:30-5pm); TDD/TTY: 1-800-804-1616; Fax: 510-848-4445. Information & referrals for disabled parents or parents of disabled children. Newsletter, phone support. *Website:* http://www.lookingglass.org *Email:* tlg@lookingglass.org

U.S. Equal Employment Opportunity Commission *(MULTILINGUAL)* 1-800-669-4000; TDD/TTY: 1-800-669-6820. Information, speakers, technical assistance, training and referrals re: enforcing ADA and prohibiting discrimination in employment of disabled persons. *Website:* http://www.eeoc.gov

Value Options *(New Jersey)* 1-877-652-7624 (24 hr) or 609-689-6205; TTD 1-866-896-6975. Provides comprehensive information on all emotional, behavioral and mental health services for children up to the age of 18 and their families.

DISCRIMINATION

Equal Employment Opportunity 1-800-669-4000 (Mon.-Fri., 8am-4:30pm) Investigates allegations of discrimination due to race, creed, age, religion, gender or disabilities. Sponsored by Federal Government.

Office for Civil Rights 1-800-368-1019 (Mon.-Fri., 8:30am-5:30pm). Refers people who feel they have been discriminated against. Sponsored by the Dept. of Health and Human Services. *Website:* http://www.ed.gov/offices/ocr

DOMESTIC VIOLENCE

National Domestic Abuse Helpline for Men 1-888-7-HELPLINE (Crisis line) or 207-683-5758 (Non-crisis). Crisis line and referral services for battered men. *Website:* http://www.noexcuse4abuse.org *Email:* help@noexcuse4abuse.org

National Domestic Violence Hotline 1-800-799-7233; TDD/TTY 1-800-787-3224. Information and referrals for victims of domestic violence. *Website:* http://www.ndvh.org

NJ Domestic Violence Hotline *(New Jersey)* 1-800-572-7233 (24 hr) Information and referrals for victims or perpetrators of domestic violence. *Website* http://www.womanspace.org

DOWN SYNDROME

National Down Syndrome Society 1-800-221-4602 or 212-460-9330 (Mon.-Fri. 9am-5pm ET); Fax: 212-979-2873. Information and referral. Free packets to new parents, information on education, support groups, medical research, newsletter phone support, information on conferences. *Website:* http://www.ndss.org *Email:* info@ndss.org

If you are using this book past Spring 2007, please call us for information about our most recent directory. 1-800-367-6274

DRUG ABUSE

Addictions Hotline of NJ 1-800-238-2333 (voice/TDD) (24 hr.) Crisis counseling, information and referrals for all kinds of drug and alcohol related issues (both prescription and illegal drugs).

American Council for Drug Education *(BILINGUAL)* 1-800-488-3784. Provides general information on drug abuse and treatment. Brochures. Referrals to crisis counseling. Publications. Affiliated with Phoenix House.

Community Recovery *(New Jersey)* 1-800-292-8262. Offers services for veterans who are experiencing problems with drugs or alcohol. The program offers a wide variety of services throughout the state.

Drug Policy Information Clearinghouse 1-800-666-3332; Fax: 301-519-5212 (Mon.-Fri., 10am-6pm). Sends out information on drug abuse and publications on national drug policies. *Website:* http://www.whitehousedrugpolicy.gov *Email:* ondcp@ncjrs.org

National Association for Children of Alcoholics 1-888-554-2627. Advocates for children and families affected by alcoholism and other drug dependencies. Helps children hurt by parental alcohol and drug abuse. Newsletter, advocacy, policy making, literature, videos, educational materials. *Website:* http://www.nacoa.org *Email:* nacoa@nacoa.org

National Clearinghouse for Alcohol and Drug Information *(BILINGUAL)* 1-800-729-6686 or 301-468-2600; Spanish: 1-877-767-8432; TDD/TTY: 1-800-487-4889; Fax: 301-468-6433. Information on alcohol, tobacco and drug abuse and prevention. Referrals to treatment centers, research, groups, drugs in the work place, community programs, AIDS and drug abuse. *Website:* http://www.health.org *Email:* info@health.org

National Helpline *(BILINGUAL)* 1-800-662-4357 or 1-800-729-6686 (24 hr). Referrals to substance abuse treatment centers. Sponsored by Phoenix House. *Website:* http://www.health.org

National Council on Alcoholism & Drug Dependence 1-800-622-2255. Provides information on counseling and treatment services for alcohol or drug abuse. Prevention and education programs. Newsletter. *Email:* national@mcadd.org *Website:* http://www.ncadd.org

National Inhalant Prevention Center 1-800-269-4237. Provides information and referrals to persons concerned about inhalants. Literature, training and technical assistance. Conducts national inhalant and poisons awareness week. Quarterly newsletter. *Website:* http://www.inhalants.org *Email:* nipc@io.com

National PRIDE (Parents' Resource Institute for Drug Education) 1-800-668-9277. Trains youth volunteers on how to conduct drug prevention education.

DWARFISM

Little People's Research Fund 1-800-232-5773 or 410-747-1100 (Mon.-Fri., 9am-5pm ET). Referrals (primarily research) and literature on dwarfism. Networks parents together. *Website:* http://www.iprf.org

DYSLEXIA / LEARNING DISABILITIES

Recording For The Blind and Dyslexic *(New Jersey)* 1-866-732-3585 (Mon.-Fri., 8:30am-4:30pm). Fax: (609)987-8116. Information on free cassettes and recorded textbooks and consumer publications to eligible handicapped persons. Information on volunteer programs for recording tapes. Membership dues $100/1st year; $35/subsequent years. Worldwide services. *Website:* http://www.rfbd.org *Email:* custserv@rfbd.org

International Dyslexia Association 1-800-222-3123 or 410-296-0232 (Mon.-Fri., 8:30am-4:30pm). Provides information and referrals for persons with dyslexia. *Website:* http://www.interdys.org *Email:* info@interdys.org
National Center for Learning Disabilities 1-888-575-7373; Fax: 212-545-9665. Provides information and referrals for learning disabled adults and children. *Website:* http://www.ld.org

EATING DISORDERS

Eat Right Hotline 1-800-231-3438. Provides information on all aspects of nutrition, exercise and diet. Nutritionist can answer questions or have information mailed to you. Will research questions.

National Eating Disorders Association 1-800-931-2237. Provides information on local professional services and support groups nationwide for persons with eating disorders. Free literature, training, conferences. *Website:* http://www.nationaleatingdisorders.org *Email:* info@NationalEatingDisorders.org

New Jersey Eating Disorders Helpline *(New Jersey)* 1-800-624-2268 (Mon.-Fri., 10am-5pm); Fax: 973-740-0702. Provides information and referrals for dealing with all types of eating disorders. Feel free to leave a message and your call will be returned. *Website:* http://www.edhelp.com *Email:* livctr@aol.com

EDUCATION

Federal Student Aid Information Center 1-800-433-3243 (Mon-Fri, 8am-midnight; Sat. 9am-6pm ET). Information available regarding student aid. Sponsored by U.S. Dept. of Education. *Website:* http://www.fafsa.ed.gov

Goodwill Industries 1-800-741-0186 or 301-530-6500. Provides employment and training services for people with disabilities and other disadvantaging conditions (welfare dependency, illiteracy, criminal history, homeless) . *Website:* http://www.goodwill.org

HESAA Hotline, The *(New Jersey)* 1-800-792-8670, TDD: 609-588-2526; Fax: 609-588-2228 (Mon.-Fri., 9am-5pm). Information on colleges and universities, adult evening and Vo-Tech education, financial aid. *Website:* http://www.HESAA.org

National Job Corps Information Line *(BILINGUAL)* 1-877-872-5627 (24 hr). Referrals to job corps training for persons 16-24. Helps persons to earn high school equivalency diplomas. *Website:* http://www.doleta.gov

ENERGY / UTILITIES

Energy Efficiency and Renewable Energy Clearinghouse 1-877-337-3463 (Mon.-Fri., 9am-5:30pm); Fax: 360-956-2214. Free information on energy efficiency & renewable energy. Answers technical questions. Provides referral to other organizations. Sponsored by Dept. of Energy. *Website:* http://www.eere.energy.gov (publications)

Lifeline Utility Assistance Program *(New Jersey)* 1-800-792-9745 (Mon.-Fri., 8:30am-5pm). Utility assistance to residents of NJ who are 65+ years old or who are 18 and older and receive Social Security Disability and meet the income eligibility guidelines. Recipients may receive up to $150.

NJ Weatherization and Home Energy Assistance Program *(New Jersey)* 1-800-510-3102. Provides home weatherization and insulation and heating and cooling assistance to eligible New Jersey residents.

ENVIRONMENTAL

American Public Information on Environment 1-800-320-2743 (Mon.-Fri. 8:30am-5pm CT). Information, education and aid to families with environmental concerns. *Website:* http://www.americanpie.org *Email:* info@americanpie.org

Chemical Information Referral Center 1-800-424-9300. Takes reports on emergency chemical or other hazardous spills. *Website:* http://www.chemtrec.org

EPA (Environmental Protection Agency) 1-800-426-4791. Provides information on safe drinking water and policy regulations on a variety of environmental concerns. *Website:* http://www.epa.gov/safewater *Email:* sdwa@epa.gov

Indoor Air Quality Info Clearinghouse 1-800-438-4318 (Mon.-Fri., 9am-5pm ET); Fax: 703-356-5386. Provides information and referral on indoor air quality pollutants and sources, health effects, control methods, commercial building operations and maintenance. Sponsored by the EPA. *Website:* http://www.epa.gov/iaq/ *Email:* iaqinfo@aol.com

National Lead Information Center & Clearinghouse *(BILINGUAL,* 1-800-424-5323. Provides information on lead-based paint for the home and safe work practices for renovating. Distributes EPA literature. *Website:* http://www.epa.gov/lead *Email:* hotline.lead@epamail.epa.gov

EPILEPSY

Epilepsy Information Service 1-800-642-0500. Answers general questions on epilepsy. Free literature. Conducts workshops, conferences. *Website:* http://www.WFUBMC.edu

EYE CARE

Eye Care America Seniors: 1-800-222-3937; Glaucoma: 1-800-391-3937; Diabetes Eye Care: 1-800-272-3937; Children: 1-877-887-6327 (Mon.-Fri. 8am-4pm PT); Fax: 415-561-8567. Assists financially disadvantaged persons (children & seniors) in obtaining medical eye care. Sponsored by American Academy of Ophthalmology Fdn. *Website:* http://www.aao.org

FACIAL DISFIGUREMENT

Children's Craniofacial Association 1-800-535-3643 (24 hr); Provides information and support for children with craniofacial disfigurement and their families. Makes referrals to doctors and support groups. Disseminates educational booklets. Information on free medical clinics, Cher's Family Retreat, advocacy. *Website:* http://www.ccakids.com

FACES: The National Craniofacial Assn. 1-800-332-2373 (Mon.-Fri. 9am-5pm ET). Dedicated to assisting children and adults with craniofacial disorders resulting from disease, accident or birth. Financial assistance, referrals to support groups, newsletter, information & referrals to services and medical professionals. Fax: 423-267-3124   *Website:*   http://www.faces-cranio.org   *Email:* faces@mindspring.com

FOOD HANDLING / FOOD CO-OP

America's Second Harvest 1-800-771-2303. Provides hunger relief through a network of over 200 food banks and food-rescue programs. *Website:* http://www.secondharvest.org

Center for Food Safety and Applied Nutrition 1-888-723-3366 (Mon.-Fri., 10am-4pm). Provides information on food safety, cosmetics and colors, seafood and women's nutritional health. Sponsored by FDA. *Website:* http://www.cfsan.fda.gov

Meat and Poultry Hotline 1-800-535-4555 (Mon.-Fri., 10am-4pm ET). Answers safe handling questions. Information on food handling. Helps persons understand labels on meat and poultry. Will answer questions about safe handling procedures. Sponsored by US Dept of Agriculture. *Website:* http://www.fsis.usda.gov *Email:* mphotline.fsis@usda.gov

Safe Tables Our Priority (S.T.O.P.) 1-800-863-7867. Support, education and advocacy for victims and families of victims of food borne infectious diseases, (E-coli, salmonella listeria, shigella, vibrio vulnificus and many others). Phone and online networking, newsletter and annual meeting. *Website:* http://www.safetables.org *Email:* mail@safetables.org

FOOT CARE

Foot Care Information Center 1-800-366-8227. Provides literature and referrals on foot care and podiatric medicine. Sponsored by American Podiatric Medical Association. Referrals to podiatrist. *Website:* http://www.apma.org

The greatest good you can do for another is not just share your riches, but to reveal to him, his own.
Benjamin Disraeli

GAMBLING

Council on Compulsive Gambling of New Jersey *(New Jersey)* 1-800-426-253'
(24 hr) or 609-588-5515; Fax: 609-588-5665. Information to help compulsiv
gamblers. Referrals to self-help groups, in-patient treatment programs, counselin
services, free evaluations for the compulsive gambler. Speakers' bureau. *Website*
http://www.800gambler.org *Email:* ccgnj@800gambler.org

National Council on Problem Gambling 1-800-522-4700 or 202-547-9204; Fax
202-547-9206. Information, referrals to support groups and counseling fo
compulsive   gamblers.   *Website:*   http://www.ncpgambling.org   *Emai*
ncpg@erols.com

HEALTH

Alliance for Informed Choice on Vaccinations *(New Jersey)* 1-800-613-9925. T
address the concerns about the safety of vaccines and the right to informed consen
Literature, advocacy and phone help.

American Dietetic Association *(BILINGUAL)* 1-800-366-1655 (Mon.-Fri
10am-5pm ET). Information on diet. Referrals to dietitians. Brochures sometime
available. Sponsored by National Center for Nutrition & Dietetics. *Website*
http://www.eatright.org
American Board of Medical Specialties 1-866-275-2267 or 847-491-9091; Fax
847-328-3596. Will tell you if your physician is board certified. *Website*
http://www.abms.org

American Health Assistance Foundation 1-800-437-2423 (Mon.-Fri., 9am-5pm
Provides educational information and funds research for Alzheimer's disease
glaucoma, heart disease and macular degeneration. *Website:* http://www.ahaf.org

American Running Association 1-800-776-2732 or 301-913-9517 (Mon.-Fri
9am-5pm). Information on aerobic sports. Referrals to sports medicine clinic
podiatrists and orthopedists. *Website:* http://www.americanrunning.org/ *Emai*
run@americanrunning.org

Center for Human Genetics at Duke University Medical Cente
1-800-283-4316. Provides information on disorders currently under study by th
Center for Human Genetics. These include: Alzheimer's, ALS, autism, attentio
deficit disorder, Asperger syndrome, Charcot Marie Tooth disease, chia
malformation, syringomyelia, cardiovascular disease, essential tremo
facioscapulohumeral   muscular   dystrophies,   familial   focal   segment
glomerulosclerosis, spastic paraparesis, glaucoma, benign intraepithelia

614

dyskeratosis, limb-girdle muscular dystrophy, multiple sclerosis, neural tube defects, Parkinson's, sickle cell disease, trichotillomania and tuberculosis. See website for complete list. *Website:* http://www.chg.duke.edu/

Centers for Disease Control and Prevention 1-800-311-3435. Provides information over the phone on specific diseases. *Website:* http://www.cdc.gov *Email:* inquiry@edc.gov

Eat Right Hotline 1-800-231-3438 (CT). Provides information on all aspects of nutrition, exercise and diet. Nutritionist can answer questions or have information mailed to you. Will research questions.

FDA Office on Orphan Product Development 1-800-300-7469. Provides referrals for persons who need a rare orphan drug. *Website:* http://www.fda.gov/orphan

Genetic Alliance Information 1-800-336-4363 (Mon.-Fri., 9am-6pm ET). Non-profit coalition of consumer advocates, health professionals, researchers and policy makers that provides individuals and families with quality genetics resources so that they may make quality healthcare decisions. Directs the public and health professionals to information, support resources, research findings and referrals. *Website:* http://www.geneticalliance.org *Email:* info@geneticalliance.org

Health Information *(New Jersey)* 1-800-367-6543 (Mon.-Fri., 8:30am-6pm) Assistance by professionals who route callers to the appropriate department for information. Information on VA Hospitals, health certificates, shots required for overseas, etc. Sponsored by Dept. of Health and Senior Services. *Website:* http://www.state.nj.us/health

March of Dimes 1-888-663-4637. Dedicated to decreasing the incidence of birth defects, infant mortality, low birth weight and lack of prenatal care. Provides information, referrals and literature. *Website:* http://www.marchofdimes.com

Medicare + Choice Helpline Assistant *(BILINGUAL)* 1-800-MEDICARE (633-4273). Provides information on Medicare, Medigap and health plan options. Publications, audiotapes. Sponsored by federal government. *Website:* http://www.medicare.gov

Minority Health Resource Center 1-800-444-6472 (Mon.-Fri., 9am-5pm ET); TDD/TTY: 301-230-7199; Fax: 301-230-7198. Federally-funded library service that provides information and referral to sources on health problems for minorities. *Website:* http://www.omhrc.gov

National Center on Complementary & Alternative Medicine 1-888-644-6226 or 301-519-3153; TDD/TTY: 1-866-464-3615; Fax: 1-866-464-3616. Provides information on clinical trials and current research projects conducted on alternative medicine. *Website:* http://www.nccam.nih.gov *Email:* info@nccam.nih.gov

National Health Information Center 1-800-336-4797 or 301-565-4167 (Mon.-Fri., 9-5:30pm ET); 301-468-5960 (publications); Fax: 301-984-4256. Helps the public and health professionals locate health information through identification of health, information resources, information and referral systems. Distributes publications and directories on good health and disease prevention topics. *Website:* http://www.healthfinder.gov *Email:* info@nhic.org

National Immunizations Information Hotline *(BILINGUAL)* 1-800-232-2522; Spanish: 1-800-232-0233; TDD/TTY: 1-800-243-7889; Fax: 1-800-232-3299. Information and referrals on immunizations for infants, adults and health care professionals. *Website:* http://www.cdc.gov/nip *Email:* nipinfo@cdc.gov

National Institute of Allergy & Infectious Disease 1-800-243-7644 (Mon.-Fri., 8:30-5pm ET). Provides information on clinical trials being conducted on allergic and infectious diseases. Main focus is on AIDS and HIV+. *Website:* http://www.niaid.nih.gov/hivelinic

National Institute for Occupational Safety and Health 1-800-356-4674 or 513-533-8326; Fax: 1-888-232-3299. Information on all aspects of occupational health and safety. *Website:* http://www.cdc.gov/niosh *Email:* eidtechinfo@cdc.gov (for publications)

National Library of Medicine 1-888-346-3656. Provides information and referrals to help callers research health questions. *Website:* http://www.nlm.nih.gov *Email:* custserv@nlm.nih.gov

National Reference Center for Bioethics Literature 1-800-633-3849 (Mon.-Fri., 9am-5pm). Provides information via e-mail, websites or mail on bioethical topics. Will do limited searches on special topics. *Website:* http://bioethic.georgetown.edu *Email:* bioethics@georgetown.edu

National Women's Health Information Center *(BILINGUAL)* 1-800-994-9662 (Mon.-Fri., 9am-6pm); TDD/TTY: 1-888-220-5546 (English/Spanish). Provides information and referrals for all women's health questions and any questions on breast feeding. *Website:* http://www.4woman.gov *Email:* 4woman@soza.com

National Women's Health Resource Center 1-877-986-9472. Provides information on women's health issues. Dedicated to helping women make informed decisions about their health. *Website:* http://www.healthywomen.org *Email:* info@healthwomen.org

NJ Family Health line *(New Jersey)* 1-800-328-3838 (24 hr). Provides information and referral to programs on family planning, pre-natal care, child health, pediatric HIV infection and special child health care. Information on WIC program which provide nutritional assistance for qualified women with children up to age of 5 years. Sponsored by United Way.

NORD (National Organization for Rare Disorders) 1-800-999-6673 or 203-744-0100 (in Connecticut) (Mon.-Fri., 9am-5pm). Information and networking for persons with rare disorders. Literature. *Website:* http://www.rarediseases.org *Email:* orphan@rarediseases.org

"Su Familia" Health Helpline *(BILINGUAL)* 1-866-783-2645 (9am-5pm ET). Provides confidential health information to Hispanic patients and their families. Provides bilingual fact sheets for a wide variety of health topics. Sponsored by the Nat'l Alliance for Hispanic Health. *Website:* http://www.hispanichealth.org

To Your Health *(New Jersey)* 1-888-838-3180. Provides educational materials and information to residents of New Jersey within the managed care system. Helps the consumer understand their rights under commercial and government sponsored managed care programs. *Website:* http://www.chlp.org

Visiting Nurse Association of America 1-888-866-8773 or 617-737-3200; Fax: 617-737-1144. Referrals to local Visiting Nurse Associations. *Website:* http://www.vnaa.org *Email:* vnaa@vnaa.org

UAB Eat Right 1-800-231-3438 (Mon.-Fri., 8am-4pm CT). Information on nutrition & related topics (weight loss & cholesterol). Sponsored by Nutrition Info. Svcs.

HEART

American Heart Association *(BILINGUAL)* 1-800-242-8721 (Mon.-Fri., 6am-midnight; Sat, 8am-10pm ET). Information on heart health and support groups. *Website:* http://www.americanheart.org

Arrhythmogenic Right Ventricular Dysplasia Registry 1-800-483-2662. Provides information on ARVD. A nurse coordinator will answer questions and help with diagnosis. Raises funds for research. Offers referrals to doctors conducting studies. *Website:* http://www.arvd.org

Cardiac Arrhythmias Research and Education Foundation, Inc. 1-800-404-9500 or 949-752-2273 (Mon.-Fri., 9am-5pm); Fax: 949-752-9119. Support, education and registry for individuals and families affected by long QT syndrome and other genetic arrhythmias. Helps to create community forums for mutual support. *Website:* http://www.longqt.org *Email:* care@longqt.org

NIH National Heart, Lung & Blood Inst. Helpline 1-800-575-9355. Provides recorded information on the prevention and treatment of high blood pressure and high blood cholesterol.

Texas Heart Institute Heart Information Service 1-800-292-2221. Answers cardiovascular questions via phone, mail or e-mail. Literature on aneurisms, cholesterol and heart transplants, stroke patients, women and heart disease. Information on support groups. *Website:* http://www.texasheartinstitute.org *Email:* his@heart.thi.tmc.edu

HOMOSEXUALITY

Gay & Lesbian National Hotline 1-888-843-4564 (Mon.-Fri., 4pm-midnight; Sat., noon-5pm ET). Provides information and referrals for gays, lesbians, transgendered and persons with questions about their sexuality. Information, referrals and peer counseling. *Website:* http://www.glnh.org *Email:* glnh@glnh.org

HOSPITAL

Hill Burton Hotline 1-800-638-0742 or 301-443-5656 (Mon.-Fri., 9am-5pm). Information about free hospital care for eligible low income persons. Directories of medical centers that are part of Hill Burton program throughout US. *Website:* http://www.hrsa.gov/osp/dfcr *Email:* dfcrcomm@hrsa.gov

National Association of Hospital Hospitality Houses 1-800-542-9730. Makes referrals to hospital hospitality housing that provide lodging for families of hospital patients and/or hospital outpatients. *Website:* http://www.nahhh.org

Shriner's Hospital 1-800-237-5055 or 813-281-0300 (Mon.-Fri., 8am-5pm). Information on free hospital care available to children under the age of 18 needing treatment for burns, spinal cord injury, cleft palate or orthopedic care. *Website:* http://www.shrinershq.org

HOSPICE

Children's Hospice International 1-800-242-4453 (Mon.-Fri., 9am-5pm ET); or 703-684-0330 (volunteer info). Refers patients to hospices & specialists in their areas. Bibliography, manuals. *Website:* http://www.chionline.org *Email:* info@chionline.com

Hospice Education Institute 1-800-331-1620 or 207-255-8800; Fax: 207-255-8008. Provides information and referrals regarding hospice care. *Website:* http://www.hospiceworld.org *Email:* hospiceall@aol.com

Hospice Foundation of America 1-800-854-3402; Fax: 202-638-5312. Provides education and information on hospice care. Sponsors research. Offers teleconference series "Living with Grief" for bereaved families. Audiotapes for clergy. *Website:* http://www.hospicefoundation.org

National Hospice & Palliative Care Organization *(BILINGUAL)* 1-800-658-8898 (Mon.-Fri., 9am-5pm ET). Information for hospice care for terminally ill persons. Referrals to hospice programs nationwide. *Website:* http://www.nhpco.org *Email:* nhpco_info@nhpco.org

HOUSING

Community Connections 1-800-998-9999; TDD/TTY: 1-800-483-2209. Provides information about housing and community development, homeless prevention, first-time homebuyer programs, veterans and low-income housing and HUD. *Website:* http://www.com.org

Housing and Mortgage Finance Agency *(New Jersey)* 1-800-654-6873 (Mon.-Fri., 8am-5pm). Information on mortgages available to first time home buyers and buyers in targeted areas. Offers low down payment and low interest rate mortgages.

National Accessible Apartment Clearinghouse 1-800-421-1221; Fax: 703-518-6191. Maintains a database of over 46,000 accessible apartments nationwide. Helps people with disabilities find accessible apartments. Owners and managers may also use this service to register their accessible units. *Website:* http://www.naahq.org

Public Housing Drug Elimination Support Center 1-800-955-2232 (Mon.-Fri., 9-5pm); Fax: 301-585-6271. Has information and publications on public housing, welfare to work program and drug prevention (drug use and violence in public housing). Sponsored by US Dept of HUD, Public & Indian Housing Info & Resource Center. *Website:* http://www.hud.gov

IMMUNE DEFICIENCY

Jeffrey Modell Foundation 1-800-533-3844 (24 hr). Provides information on specific primary immune deficiency diseases. Referrals to major medical centers, psychiatric and social support services. Information on insurance reimbursement.

IMMIGRATION

Immigration and Naturalization Services 1-800-375-5283; TDD/TTY: 1-800-767-1833 (Mon.-Fri., 8am-10am & 4pm-6pm). Comprehensive information for immigrants including naturalization processes, adjustment of status for permanent residency, travel documents. Also has information on international services and border patrols. *Website:* http://www.uscis.gov/graphics/index.htm

IMPOTENCE

Impotence Information Center 1-800-843-4315 (Mon.-Fri., 9-4:30pm). Provides free information about the causes and treatments of impotence. This includes brochures and a list of local physicians who treat impotence. *Website:* http://www.americanmedicalsystems.com

INCONTINENCE

Incontinence Information Center 1-800-843-4315 (Mon-Fri, 9-4:30pm CT). Provides free information about the causes and treatments of incontinence. This information consists of brochures and a list of physicians who treat incontinence within the caller's geographic area. *Website:* http://www.americanmedicalsystems.com

National Association for Continence *(BILINGUAL)* 1-800-252-3337 or 843-377-0900 (Mon.-Fri., 8am-5pm ET); Fax: 843-377-0905. Clearinghouse of information on incontinence. Physician locater service. *Website:* http://www.nafc.org *Email:* lbrown@nafc.org

INSURANCE

Hurricane Insurance Information Center 1-800-942-4242 (24 hours). Provides general information on hurricane insurance. *Website:* http://www.iii.org

Insurance Information Institute 1-800-331-9146. Provides information on home and auto insurance. Also provides hints and literature on preventing theft and accidents. Has information on organizations which have information on health and life insurance. *Website:* http://www.iii.org

New Jersey Family Care Hotline *(New Jersey)* *(MULTILINGUAL)* 1-800-701-0710; TTY: 1-800-701-0720 Provides information on health insurance to uninsured children and teens up to age 18. *Website:* http://www.njfamilycare.org

KIDNEY DISEASE

American Kidney Fund *(BILINGUAL)* 1-800-638-8299; Spanish: 1-866-300-2900 (Mon.-Fri., 9am-5pm ET). Provides information, referrals and financial assistance to kidney patients. *Website:* http://www.kidneyfund.org

Kidney and Urology Foundation of America *(BILINGUAL)* 1-800-633-6628. Dedicated to helping persons afflicted with any debilitating kidney, urologic or related diseases. Offers education, information, health fairs, grants, patient scholarships, physician referrals, fellowship and Pediatric Enrichment program. *Website:* http://www.kidneyurology.org *Email:* info@kidneyurology.org

National Institute of Diabetes & Digestive & Kidney Diseases 1-800-891-5390 (kidney); 1-800-860-8747 (diabetes); 1-800-891-5389 (digestive diseases). Provides referrals and literature on a broad range of subjects concerning diabetes, digestive disorders, kidney disease, metabolic and endocrine disorders, hematological diseases, urologic disorders. *Website:* http://www.niddk.nih.gov/

National Kidney Foundation *(BILINGUAL)* 1-800-622-9010 or 212-889-2210; Fax: 212-689-9261 (Mon.-Fri., 8:30am-5:30pm ET). Provides education and research information on kidney disease. Referrals to local affiliates. *Website:* http://www.kidney.org

LEGISLATION / GOVERNMENT

League of Women Voters *(New Jersey)* 1-800-792-8683 (Mon.-Fri., 9am-4:30pm); Fax: 609-599-3993 Provides information regarding voting, New Jersey Government and election information. Membership $50/yr. *Website:* http://www.lwvnj.org *Email:* contact@lwvnj.org

Legislative Information and Bill Room *(New Jersey)* 1-800-792-8630; TDD: 1-800-257-7490 Fax: 609-777-2440 (Mon.-Fri., 8:30am-5pm) Information on the status of bills, calendar and roster. Referrals. Sponsored by NJ Office of Legislative

Services. *Website:* http://www.njleg.state.nj.us *Email:* leginfo@njleg.org (legislative matters only).

Project Vote Smart 1-888-868-3762 or 406-859-8683. Non-partisan information about all elected officials and candidates for federal, state and local gubernatorial offices. *Website:* http://www.vote-smart.org

U.S. Government Federal Information Center *(BILINGUAL)* 1-800-688-9889 (Mon.-Fri., 8am-8pm ET); TDD/TTY: 1-800-326-2996. Information about federal government programs and agencies including patents, taxes, jobs, social security, rules and regulations, passports, visas, dept. of states and veteran affairs. *Website:* http://www.firstgov.gov

LEPROSY

American Leprosy Missions 1-800-543-3135 (Mon.-Fri., 8am-5pm ET). Provides information on projects & programs that fight leprosy in 23 countries. *Website:* http://www.leprosy.org *Email:* amlep@leprosy.org

LIFE-THREATENING ILLNESS

Catastrophic Illness in Children Relief Fund *(New Jersey)* 1-800-335-3863. Provides financial assistance to families of children 21 and under who have experienced an illness or condition which is not covered by insurance or any State or Federal program. For medical bills which exceed 10% over the family income.

Friends of Karen *(NJ, NY, CT)* 1-800-637-2774 (Mon.-Fri, 9am-5pm). Dedicated to helping families with children affected by life-threatening illnesses. Provides emotional and financial assistance in the NY metropolitan area. Information packets available.

Medical Escrow Society 1-800-422-1314 (24 hr). Provides information on obtaining advance cash from life insurance policies for persons with a life threatening illness or who are over age 65. *Website:* http://www.lifeassets.net

Partnership For Caring 1-800-658-8898 (Mon-Fri., 9am-5pm) or 202-296-8071 or 1-800-406-8345 (emergencies). Provides information and education concerning end-of-life issues. Includes caregiver questions. *Website:* http://www.partnershipforcaring.org *Email:* pfc@partnershipforcaring.org

> Advice is like snow; the softer it falls, the longer it dwells upon,
> and the deeper it sinks into the mind.
> *Samuel Taylor Coleridge*

LITERACY

Literacy Volunteers of New Jersey, Inc. *(New Jersey)* 1-800-848-0048 (Mon.-Fri., 9am-4pm) or 1-800-228-8813 (24 hr. outside of NJ). Refers callers who read below 5th grade level and persons for whom English is a second language to LVA programs statewide. Also has information on other adult education programs. Refers potential volunteers to LVA training programs. *Website:* http://www.nifl.gov *Email:* ed4lvnj@aol.com

LUNG DISEASE

Allergy & Asthma Network - Mothers of Asthmatics *(BILINGUAL)* 1-800-878-4403; Fax: 703-573-7794. Provides emotional support and patient education resources for persons with asthma and allergies. Newsletter. *Website:* http://www.aanma.org *Email:* info@aanma.org

National Jewish Lung Line 1-800-222-5864 (Mon.-Fri., 10am-6:30pm). Information & referrals. Registered nurses answer questions on all types of lung diseases. Referrals to doctors, free literature. *Website:* http://www.njc.org *Email:* lungline@njc.org

Office on Smoking and Health 1-800-232-1311 or 770-488-5705 (Mon.-Fri., 8-4pm ET). Provides information on the affects of tobacco on health, how to stop smoking, second hand smoke and other current topics relating to tobacco. Sponsored by Federal Government. *Website:* http://www.cdc.gov/tobacco *Email:* tobaccoinfo@cdc.gov

LYME DISEASE

American Lyme Disease Foundation 1-800-876-5963 or 914-277-6970; Fax: 914-277-6974. Information on Lyme disease. Referrals to doctors. Brochures. *Website:* http://www.aldf.com *Email:* Inquire@aldf.com

Lyme Disease *(New Jersey)* 1-800-792-8831 (Mon.-Fri., 8am-5pm). Provides NJ residents with information about Lyme disease. Sponsored by the NJ Dept. of Health. *Website:* http://www.state.nj.us/health/ed/f_lyme.htm

National Lyme Disease Foundation 1-800-886-5963. Provides information and referrals for Lyme disease. Education, literature, advocacy. Need touch-tone phone.

Consider passing this Directory on to a student or staff member - browsing through the Directory pages can often provide helpful education as to the wide variety of groups available.

MARROW TRANSPLANT

Caitlin Raymond International Bone Marrow Registry 1-800-726-2824 or 508-334-8969; Fax: 508-334-8972. Comprehensive international resource for patients and physicians conducting a search for unrelated bone marrow or cord blood donor. *Website:* http://www.crir.org *Email:* info@CRIR.org

National BMT LINK 1-800-546-5268. Provides information and referral for bone marrow and stem cell transplants for patients, family and professionals. Referrals to support groups. Peer-support, online phone support groups, information on becoming a donor and educational booklets. *Website:* http://www.nbmtlink.org

National Marrow Donor Program 1-800-627-7692, 1-800-654-1247 or 1-800-526-7809 (Mon.-Fri., 8am-6pm CT). Provides information on bone marrow and stem cell transplants and information on becoming a marrow donor. Maintains computerized databank of available tissue-typed marrow donors nationwide. Provides patient advocacy to assist patients through the donor search and transplant process. *Website:* http://www.marrow.org

MENINGITIS

Meningitis Foundation 1-800-668-1129; 317-595-6383 or Admin 317-595-6395 (Mon.-Fri., 8am-5pm); Fax: 317-595-6370. Support for persons with spinal meningitis and their families. Provides information, education and supports research. Live chat rooms. *Website:* http://www.musa.org *Email:* support@musa.org

MENTAL HEALTH

Compeer 1-800-836-0475. Provides volunteer "friends" for children and adults who receive mental health treatment. *Website:* http://www.compeer.org *Email:* compeerp@rochester.rr.com

Family Support Resources *(New Jersey)* 1-866-626-4437 (24 hr). Automated information line that provides local NJ contacts for Intensive Family Support Services and National Alliance for the Mentally Ill groups. Sponsored by NAMI-NJ.

National Alliance for Research on Schizophrenia & Depression 1-800-829-8289. Provides information on schizophrenia, depression and bipolar disorder. Has information on research being conducted on these disorders. Newsletter, literature, brochures. *Website:* http://www.narsad.org

624

National Institute of Mental Health Information Line 1-800-647-2642 or 301-443-4513. Provides information and literature on anxiety, phobias, obsessive-compulsive and depression. Leave name and mailing address and they will mail literature to you. *Website:* http://www.nimh.nih.gov

National Mental Health Association 1-800-969-6642 (Mon.-Fri., 9am-5pm); TDD/TTY: 1-800-433-5959. Provides free information on over 200 mental health topics including bipolar disorder, depression, bereavement, post-traumatic stress disorder and warning signs of mental illness. Referrals to local mental health services. Distributes free national directory of local mental health associations and offers low-cost materials. Advocates to remove stigma of mental illness and for mental health benefits parity. *Website:* http://www.nmha.org *Email:* infoctr@nmha.org

National Mental Health Services Knowledge Exchange Network *(BILINGUAL)* 1-800-789-2647. Makes referrals to many mental health organizations nationwide. *Website:* http://www.mentalhealth.samhsa.gov *Email:* ken@mentalhealth.org

NIMH Anxiety Information Line 1-888-826-9438 or 301-443-4513. Provides literature on anxiety, depression and medications. Leave name and mailing address and they will mail literature to you. *Website:* http://www.nimh.nih.gov

NJ Mental Health Cares Helpline *(New Jersey)* 1-866-202-4357; TTY 877-294-4356. Provides information and referral to all public mental health services in New Jersey. Answers questions regarding mental health and illness. Staffed by mental health professionals.

NJ Psychological Association *(New Jersey)* 1-800-281-6572 or 973-243-9800 (Mon.-Fri., 8:30am-4:30pm). Fax: 973-243-9818. Provides referrals to psychologists in your area by specialty, language, etc. *Website:* http://www.psychologynj.org *Email:* NJPA@psychologynj.org

State Division of Mental Health Helpline *(New Jersey)* 1-800-382-6717 (Mon.-Fri., 8:30am-5pm). Provides information on state mental health services and takes any complaints about them. *Website:* http://www.state.nj.us/humanservices/dmhs *Email:* dmhsmail@dhs.state.nj.us

Summit Hospital *(Serves NJ/NY/CT)* 1-800-753-5223 (24 hr); 908-522-7000. Information on drug or psychiatric problems. Referrals to community mental health centers. Sponsored by Summit Oaks Hospital.

TARA 1-888-482-7227 or 212-966-6514; Fax: 212-966-6895. Education and advocacy organization. Provides information on borderline personality to families, consumers and providers. Referrals to clinicians, treatment programs and self-help groups. BPD Journal, speakers bureau. Professional conferences, advocacy. *Website:* http://www.tara4bpd.org *Email:* taraapd@aol.com

Value Options *(New Jersey)* 1-877-652-7624 (24 hr) or 609-689-6205; TDD: 866-896-6975 Provides comprehensive information on all emotional, behavioral and mental health services for children up to the age of 18 and their families.

MENTAL RETARDATION

American Association on Mental Retardation 1-800-424-3688 (Mon-Fri, 9am-5pm ET). Provides general information on mental retardation. *Website:* http://www.aamr.org *Email:* anam@aamr.org

Rehab Res. Training Center on Aging with Developmental Disabilities 1-800-996-8845 or 312-413-1520; TDD/TTY: 312-413-0453; Fax: 312-996-6942. Aim is to promote independence, productivity, inclusion and self-determination of older adults with mental retardation. Provides training, technical assistance and materials to patients, families and professionals.

METABLOLIC DISORDERS

National Institute of Diabetes & Digestive & Kidney Diseases 1-800-891-5390 (kidney); 1-800-860-8747 (diabetes); 1-800-891-5389 (digestive diseases). Provides referrals and literature on a broad range of subjects concerning diabetes, digestive disorders, kidney disease, metabolic and endocrine disorders, hematological diseases, urologic disorders. *Website:* http://www.niddk.nih.gov *Email:* nkudic@info.niddk.nih.gov

NIH Osteoporosis & Related Bone Diseases Resource Center *(MULTILINGUAL)* 1-800-624-2663 or 202-223-0344; TDD/TTY: 202-466-4315; Fax: 202-293-2356. Provides written information to patients, professionals and the public with resources and information on metabolic bone diseases such as osteoporosis, Paget's disease, osteogenesis imperfecta and primary hyperparathyroidism. Annotated bibliography on current research to professionals. *Website:* http://www.osteo.org *Email:* osteoinfo@osteo.org

World Life Foundation 1-800-289-5433; Fax: 817-285-0216. Provides support, research, information and referrals for persons interested in rare metabolic disorders. Provides air transportation for ambulatory patients who need non-emergency treatment.

MILITARY / VETERANS

Army Community Service/Family Support *(New Jersey)* 1-800-877-2380. Military affiliated only. Family advocacy, parent education, employment readiness, relocation assistance, support groups and a wide variety of resources.

Community Recovery *(New Jersey)* 1-800-292-8262. Offers services for veterans who are experiencing problems with drugs or alcohol. The program offers a wide variety of services throughout the state.

Department of Veterans Affairs 1-800-827-1000 (Mon.-Fri., 8-4pm); TDD/TTY: 800-829-4833. Provides comprehensive information on available programs and services for veterans including pensions, vocational rehab, survivor's benefits, presidential memorial certificates, education programs, home loan programs for dependents. Special programs for disabled, homeless, minority and women veterans. *Website:* http://www.va.gov/

Disabled American Veterans 1-877-426-2838. Provides free, professional assistance to veterans and their families in obtaining benefits and services earned through military service and provided by the department of Veteran Affairs and other agencies of the government. Guidelines for developing chapters. *Website:* http://www.dav.org *Email:* feedback@davmail.org

Disabled Veterans Assistance Line 1-800-378-4559 (24 hr hotline). Provides assistance and referrals for returning disabled service members, recently medically retired service members and spouses of disabled service members. Supports veterans of Operation Iraqi Freedom, Operation Enduring Freedom, as well as all disabled veterans of other conflicts, campaigns or wars and disabled children. *Website:* http://www.donhr.navy.mil

National Veterans Service Fund, Inc. 1-800-521-0198 or 570-603-9740 (9am-4pm, Mon.-Fri. ET); Fax: 570-603-9741. Provides social services for Vietnam and Persian Gulf War veterans and their families, focusing on those with disabled children. Publications. Also offers online bulletin board. *Website:* http://www.vvnw.org

Paralyzed Vets of America 1-800-424-8200 (Mon.-Fri., 8:30am-5pm ET); 202-872-1300 Ext. 622. Information, referral and advocacy for disabled, paralyzed vets. *Website:* http://www.pva.org

VA Special Issues Helpline 1-800-749-8387. Refers Gulf war veterans and veterans affected by Agent Orange with medical problems to local VA medical centers. Other special issues addressed.

Veterans Counseling Hotline *(New Jersey)* 1-866-838-7654 or 1-866-VETS-NJ-4 (24 hr). Provides peer support, clinical assessment and case management, family resources and referral to a comprehensive mental health network of providers if necessary. Developed by the NJ Department of Military and Veterans Affairs.

Veterans of the Vietnam War, Inc. 1-800-843-8626 (hotline) (Mon.-Fri., 8-4pm) or 570-603-9740 (general information). Veterans in Conflict with the Law Program: 1-800-843-8626. Membership organization open to all veterans and their supporters. Educates public about post-traumatic stress disorder, veteran health issues, Agent Orange and POW/MIA issues. Maintains a Find-a-Vet locator service. Publishes newsletter. Works with homeless veterans and incarcerated vets. *Website:* http://www.vvnw.org *Email:* vvnwnatl@epix.net

MISSING PEOPLE

Child Find of America Hotline 1-800-426-5678; Admin: 845-255-1848 (Mon.-Fri., 9am-5pm ET); Fax: 845-255-5706. Helps parents to locate children. Helps lost children who need assistance. Also offers support services. All services are free. *Website:* http://www.childfindofamerica.org *Email:* childfindamerica@aol.com

National Center for Missing Adults 1-800-690-3463. Operates as the national clearinghouse for missing adults, providing services and coordination between various government agencies, law enforcement, media and most importantly - the families of missing adults.

National Center for Missing & Exploited Children 1-800-843-5678 (24 hr); Admin: 703-274-3900. Information re: missing and exploited youth. Helps parents locate missing children. *Website:* http://www.missingkids.com

Vanished Children Alliance 1-800-826-4743 (24 hr); Admin: 408-296-1113 (day); Fax: 408-296-1117. Provides emotional support and technical assistance to families of missing children. Case management, search assistance, information & referral and family reunification program. *Website:* http://www.vca.org *Email:* info@vca.org

MULTIPLE SCLEROSIS

Multiple Sclerosis Foundation 1-800-441-7055 or 1-888-673-6287; Fax: 954-938-8708 (Mon.-Fri., 9am-7pm). (ET) Support services for those diagnosed with multiple sclerosis. Grants for research, information and referrals on traditional and alternative treatments. Online doctors forum. Newsletter. Phone support. *Website:* http://www.msfocus.org *Email:* support@msfocus.org

MUSCULAR DYSTROPHY

Muscular Dystrophy Family Foundation, Inc. 1-800-544-1213 (Mon.-Thurs., 8:30am-5pm; Fri., 8:30am-4pm) or 317-443-2054 (eve); Fax: 317-923-6334. Provides services, resources, home medical equipment and adaptive devices to help people with muscular dystrophy and their families. Provides comprehensive direct services. *Website:* http://www.mdff.org *Email:* mdff@mdff.org

NEUROLOGICAL IMPAIRMENT

National Institute of Neurological Disorders 1-800-352-9424; Fax: 301-402-2186 (Mon.-Fri., 8:30-5pm). Provides information on neurological disorders and stroke. Sponsored by NIH. *Website:* http://www.ninds.nih.gov

NICOTINE HELPLINE

NJ Quitline *(New Jersey)* 1-866-657-8677; TDD: 1-866-257-2971 (Mon.-Fri. 8am-8pm; Sat., 11am-5pm) Information and counseling for anyone who has a nicotine addiction. Serves all of New Jersey. Sponsored by NJ State 1998 Master Settlement. *Website:* http://www.nj.quitline.com

Office on Smoking and Health 1-800-232-1311 or info specialists: 770-488-5705 (Mon.-Fri., 8-4pm ET). Provides information on the affects of tobacco on health, how to stop smoking, second hand smoke and other current topics relating to tobacco. Sponsored by Federal Government. *Website:* http://www.cdc.gov/tobacco *Email:* tobaccoinfo@cdc.gov

ORGAN DONATION

Children's Organ Transplant Association 1-800-366-2682 (Mon.-Fri., 8am-5pm ET); Fax: 812-336-8885. Provides public education on organ transplants. Assists families in fund-raising for transplant and transplant-related expenses. Assistance for all children and adults with cystic fibrosis who are U.S. citizens in need of an organ transplant. *Website:* http://www.cota.org *Email:* cota@cota.org

Living Bank - National Organ & Transplant Registry 1-800-528-2971 *(BILINGUAL).* Provides donor cards, educational materials and referrals to medical schools for persons wishing to donate their bodies after death. *Website:* http://www.livingbank.org *Email:* info@livingbank.org

Minority Organ Tissue Transplant Education Program 1-800-393-2839. Provides educational information on preventative measures and organ transplants. Referrals to physicians. *Website:* http://www.nationalmottep.org

National Foundation for Transplants 1-800-489-3863 or 901-684-1697 (Mon.-Fri., 8:30am-4:30pm CT). Provides support services, financial assistance and advocacy to adult and child organ and bone marrow transplant candidates and recipients. Assists in fund-raising activities. *Website:* http://www.transplants.org *Email:* jhill@transplants.org

New Jersey Organ and Tissue Sharing Network *(New Jersey)* 1-800-742-7365, 1-800-541-0075 (24 hr donor referral line) or 973-379-4535 (Mon.-Fri., 8:30am-5pm). Federally-designated, state-certified procurement organization responsible for recovering organs and tissues for NJ residents in need of transplants. Issues donors cards. *Website:* http://www.sharenj.org *Email:* tsn@sharenj.org

OSTEOPOROSIS

NIH Osteoporosis & Related Bone Diseases Resource Center *(MULTILINGUAL)* 1-800-624-2663 or 202-223-0344; TDD/TTY: 202-466-4315; Fax: 202-293-2356. Provides written information to patients, professionals and the public with resources and information on metabolic bone diseases such as osteoporosis, Paget's disease, osteogenesis imperfecta and primary hyperparathyroidism. Annotated bibliography on current research to professionals. *Website:* http://www.osteo.org *Email:* osteoinfo@osteo.org

Osteoporosis Helpline 1-888-934-2663 (Mon.-Fri., 9am-5pm ET). Provides general information and fact sheets on the symptoms, causes and treatment of osteoporosis. Offers referrals to osteoporosis specialists. *Email:* toneyourbones@uab.edu

PAGET'S

NIH Osteoporosis & Related Bone Diseases Resource Center *(MULTILINGUAL)* 1-800-624-2663 or 202-223-0344; TDD/TTY: 202-466-4315; Fax: 202-293-2356. Provides written information to patients, professionals and the public with resources and information on metabolic bone diseases such as osteoporosis, Paget's disease, osteogenesis imperfecta and primary hyperparathyroidism. Annotated bibliography on current research to professionals. *Website:* http://www.osteo.org *Email:* osteoinfo@osteo.org

Paget's Foundation 1-800-237-2438 or 212-509-5335; Fax: 212-509-8492 (Mon.-Fri., 9am-5pm). Information, brochures, patient's guide, doctor referrals, professional packets and newsletter on Paget's disease of the bone, as well as primary hyperparathyroidism. *Website:* http://www.paget.org *Email:* pagetfdn@aol.com

PARENTING

Healthy Families *(New Jersey)* 1-800-244-5373 For any new parent who feels alone, frightened or overwhelmed. Offers support, education, links to health care and assistance in helping to meet the family needs. Stays with person as child grows. Services are free and will work with person to be the best parent they can be.

Kinship Navigator Program *(New Jersey) (BILINGUAL)* 1-877-816-3211 Information and referrals for a wide range of services designed for caregivers of sisters, brothers or grandchildren. Support group referrals, child care resources, respite, educational issues, custody, medical resources and other legal issues.

PARKINSON'S

National Parkinson's Foundation 1-800-327-4545; Florida 1-800-433-7022; Miami 305-547-6666 (Mon.-Fri., 8:30am-5pm); Fax: 305-243-4403. Professional will answer any question on Parkinson disease. *Website:* http://www.parkinson.org *Email:* mailbox@parkinson.org

Parkinson's Disease Foundation, Inc. 1-800-457-6676. Provides Parkinson's disease research, patient education and advocacy for increased federal funding for individuals with Parkinson's, their families and caregivers. *Website:* http://www.pdf.org *Email:* info@pdf.org

PEDICULOSIS

National Pediculosis Association 1-800-446-4672; TTY/TDD: 780-449-6487; Fax: 781-449-8129. Provides information and materials concerning head lice. Books, videos and literature. *Website:* http://www.headlice.org *Email:* npa@headlice.org

PESTICIDES

National Pesticide Information Center 1-800-858-7378 (6:30am-4:30pm PT). Information on most aspects of pesticides. (No information related to antimicrobials i.e. water purifiers, disinfectants, etc.) Brochures available by calling or going to website. Sponsored by EPA. *Website:* http://www.npic.orst.edu *Email:* npic@ace.orst.edu

PET LOSS SUPPORT

PetFriends *(New Jersey)* 1-800-404-7387 (24 hr). Compassionate phone support, information and referrals to people who have lost or anticipate losing, a pet through death or other separation.

Pet Loss Support Hotline 1-800-565-1526. Offers a non-judgmental outlet for people to express their feelings and concerns when faced with difficult times regarding their pets. Staffed by veterinary students with grief training.

POISON

New Jersey Poison Control Centers *(New Jersey)* 1-800-222-1222 (24 hr). Emergency helpline that provides information on medication errors, drug overdoses, food poisoning, food safety, etc.

POLICE OFFICERS

Cop-to-Cop *(New Jersey)* 1-866-267-2267 (24 hr). Serves active and retired policemen and their families. Retired officers and mental health professionals offer callers support. Provides support and referrals to counseling and mental health, substance abuse, partial care and inpatient treatment.

PRESCRIPTIONS, LOW COST

PAAD (Pharmaceutical Assistance) *(New Jersey)* 1-800-792-9745 (8am-5pm). Financial assistance to the aged (65 or older) or disabled to help pay for medications. Hearing aid assistance also offered. Sponsored by NJ State Pharmaceutical Assistance Program

Pharmaceutical Patient Assistance Directory Line 1-800-762-4636. Mails a directory of various pharmaceutical assistance programs for persons who cannot afford prescriptions on their own. Leave name and address on answering machine. *Website:* http://www.phrma.org

Rx4NJ (A Partnership for Prescription Assistance) *(New Jersey)* 1-888-793-6765. Information on specific types of discounted or free prescription medications. A no-cost service of NJ pharmaceutical companies. Call or visit their website to answer a few questions. *Website:* http://www.rx4nj.org

PREGNANCY / CHILDBIRTH

Antiepileptic Drug Pregnancy Registry *(MULTILINGUAL)* 1-888-233-2334 (8:30am-5:00pm ET). Registry of women who are taking antiepileptic drugs and who are pregnant. Helps to determine which medications are associated with increased risks. Physicians are encouraged to refer women. *Website:* http://www.aedpregnancyregistry.org

Family Helpline *(New Jersey)* *(MULTILINGUAL)* 1-800-843-5437 *(24 hr)*. Confidential and untraceable help for teens to talk about all the options available. Refers caller to a local, confidential assistance. *Website:* http://www.pa-of-nj.org

National Abortion Federation 1-800-772-9100 (Mon.-Fri., 8am-10pm; Sat.-Sun., 9am-5pm). Information and referrals regarding abortions. Financial aid. *Website:* http://www.prochoice.org

National Hispanic Prenatal Helpline *(BILINGUAL)* 1-800-504-7081 (9am-6pm). Provides health information on pregnancy, referral to healthcare centers and doctors. Sponsored by the Nat'l Alliance for Hispanic Health. *Website:* http://www.hispanichealth.org *Email:* mcontreni@hispanichealth.org

National Life Center, Inc. 1-800-848-5683. Provides counseling and information for pregnant women. Referrals to testing sites, baby clothes and formula. *Website:* http://www.nationallifecenter.com

New Jersey Safe Haven Infant Protection Act 1-877-839-2339. Offers a safe haven for a person to voluntarily relinquish their infant under 30 days old. Completely confidential. Also answers questions from the public and offers support to those considering giving up or abandoning their infant.

OTIS (Organization of Teratology Information Services) *(MULTILINGUAL)* 1-866-626-6847 (Mon.-Fri., 8:30am-4pm PT). Provides local referrals to agencies that provide information concerning prenatal drug, medication, chemical and other potentially harmful exposures. Literature. *Website:* http://www.otispregnancy.org/*Email:* bdefects@ucsd.edu

Planned Parenthood *(BILINGUAL)* 1-800-230-7526 (Mon.-Fri., 8:30am-5pm). Referrals to neighborhood planned parenthood clinics nationwide. *Website:* http://www.plannedparenthood.org/

Pregnancy Hotline 1-800-848-5683 (24 hr); Fax: 856-848-2380. Free, confidential information for pregnant women, shelters for women and girls, baby clothes, adoption referrals. *Website:* http://www.nationallifecenter.com *Email:* nlc1stway@snip.net

Pregnancy Hotline 1-800-238-4269 (24 hour). Information and counseling to pregnant women. Referrals to free pregnancy test facilities, foster and adoption centers. Sponsored by Bethany Christian Services. *Website:* http://www.bethany.org

Safe Place for Newborns/Newborn Lifeline Network 1-877-440-2229 (24 hour). Provides referrals to locations where mothers can safely and anonymously take their babies to be placed for adoption. *Website:* http://www.safeplacefornewsborns.com *Email:* safeplace@safeplacefornewborns.com

PROSTATE

Prostatitis Foundation 1-888-891-4200; Fax: 309-325-7184. Provides support and education to men with prostatitis. Encourages research funding. Information and referrals. Newsletter $1. *Website:* http://www.prostatitis.org

PROSTITUTION

HIPS Hotline 1-800-676-4477. Provides crisis peer counseling and support for persons involved in or affected by, the sex industry. Counseling and information provided for sex workers and their families in a non-judgmental, supportive atmosphere. *Website:* http://www.hips.org

PSYCHIATRIST/PSYCHOLOGIST

New Jersey Psychiatric Association *(New Jersey)* 1-800-345-0143 or 908-685-0650 (Mon.-Thurs., 9am-1pm); Fax: 908-725-8610. Provides referrals to psychiatrists. Lists by language, geographical areas, problems. Information packets available. *Website:* http://www.psychnj.org *Email:* psychnjoptonline.net

NJ Psychological Association *(New Jersey)* 1-800-281-6572 or 973-243-9800 (Mon.-Fri., 8:30am-4:30pm). Provides referrals to psychologists in your area by specialty, language, etc. Fax: 973-243-9818. *Website:* http://www.psychologynj.org *Email:* NJPA@psychologynj.org

Therapist Network *(New Jersey)* 1-800-843-7274 or 908-232-0957. Makes referrals to local mental health associations, mental health professionals and other resources.

RADIATION

National Association of Radiation Survivors 1-800-798-5102. Provides general information for persons exposed to ionizing radiation from the development, production, testing, use or storage of nuclear weapons and nuclear waste. Advocacy, research and public education. *Website:* http://www.radiationsurvivors.org/ *Email:* nars@radiationsurvivors.org

RAPE

New Jersey Coalition Against Sexual Assault *(New Jersey)* 1-800-601-7200 (24 hr). Information and referral. Provides information on services for sexual assault victims and their families. Calls are automatically routed to the caller's local county information services. *Website:* http://www.njcasa.org

RAINN (Rape, Abuse and Incest National Network) 1-800-656-4673 (24 hour). Provides support and confidential crisis counseling for victims of sexual assault. Callers are automatically routed to the crisis center nearest to them. *Email:* info@rainn.org *Website:* http://www.rainn.org

REHABILITATION

American Medical Rehabilitation Providers Association 1-800-368-3513 or 1-888-346-4624. Refers callers to rehabilitation hospitals or centers.

Center for Rehab Technologies 1-800-726-9119 or 404-894-0240; Fax: 404-894-9320. Provides information on products, technology, resources and services for persons with disabilities. *Website:* http://www.assistivetech.net *Email:* zena.rubin@arch.gatech.edu

National Rehabilitation Information Center 1-800-346-2742 or 301-459-5900; TDD/TTY: 301-459-5984; Fax: 301-459-5900. Library and information center on disability and rehabilitation of all types. Sponsored by U.S. Dept of Education. *Website:* http://www.naric.com *Email:* naricinfo@heitechservices.com

REYE'S SYNDROME

National Reye's Syndrome 1-800-233-7393 (Mon.-Fri., 8am-5pm ET). Guidance to families affected by Reye's syndrome. Helps increase public awareness. Fundraising. *Website:* http://www.reyessyndrome.org *Email:* nrsf@reyessyndrome.org

ROSACEA

National Rosacea Society 1-888-662-5874. Information and educational materials on rosacea. A chronic, acne-like condition of the facial skin. *Website:* http://www.rosacea.org

RUNAWAYS

National Runaway Switchboard 1-800-621-4000 (24 hour). Provides crisis intervention, information and referrals for runaways re: shelter, counseling, food pantries and transportation. Suicide & crisis counseling. Greyhound bus tickets available for qualifying kids. Parents are welcome to call for assistance. *Website:* http://www.nrscrisisline.org *Email:* info@nrscrisisline.org

National Youth Crisis Hotline 1-800-448-4663 (24 hour). Crisis hotline and information & referral for runaways or youth (17 and younger) with other problems and their parents. Sponsored by Youth Development International.

RURAL ISSUES

Rural Information Center 1-800-633-7701. Information on rural issues. Provides brief database searches for free. *Website:* http://www.nalusda.gov/ric *Email:* ric@nal.usda.gov

SCLERODERMA

Scleroderma Research Foundation 1-800-441-2873. Provides referrals to doctors and clinics nationwide that treat scleroderma. Conducts research into the cause and cure of scleroderma. *Website:* http://www.srfcure.org

SELF ABUSE

SAFE (Self-Abuse Finally Ends) Alternative Info Line 1-800-366-8288. Provides recorded information on dealing with self-abuse and self-mutilation and treatment options. *Website:* http://www.selfinjury.com

SEXUALLY TRANSMITTED DISEASES

CDC National Prevention Information Network *(BILINGUAL)* 1-800-458-5231 (Mon.-Fri., 9am-8pm ET); TDD/TTY: 1-800-243-7012; Fax: 1-888-282-7681. Provides information on resources and support groups, educational materials and business and labor responses to AIDS, sexually transmitted diseases and tuberculosis, via touch tone phone. Many different services, publications offered. *Website:* http://www.cdcnpin.org *Email:* info@cdcnpin.org

CDC National STD/AIDS Hotline *(BILINGUAL)* English: 1-800-342-2437 or 1-800-227-8922 (24 hr); Spanish: 1-800-344-7432 (Mon.-Fri., 10am-10pm); Herpes Hotline: 919-361-8488 (Mon.-Fri., 9am-6pm ET); TDD/TTY: 1-800-243-7889. Education and research about sexually transmitted diseases. Information on minor and major sexually transmitted disease (including yeast, AIDS, chancroid, herpes, genital warts, syphilis and gonorrhea). Referrals, information on prevention, free pamphlets. *Website:* http://www.ashastd.org *Email:* hivnet@ashastd.org

SOCIAL SECURITY

National Organization of Social Security Claimant's Reps 1-800-431-2804 (voice mail). Provides referrals to social security lawyers who assist claimants in getting social security.

NJ WINS (Work Incentive Programs) *(New Jersey)* 1-877-659-4672 or 1-888-322-1918. Enables social security administration beneficiaries with disabilities to make informed choices about work and assist them in exploring work incentives that are available. *Website:* http://www.njwins.org *Email:* njwins@cpof-nj.org

Social Security 1-800-772-1213. Provides information on all aspects of social security, supplemental security income and Medicare. Can speak with a person or use touch-tone phone to hear messages *Website:* http://www.socialsecurity.gov

SPINAL CORD INJURY

Christopher and Dana Reeve Paralysis Resource Center *(BILINGUAL)* 1-800-539-7309 Information and referrals. Publishes a free book Paralysis Resource for consumers. Available in English or Spanish. *Website:* http://www.paralysis.org *Email:* info@paralysis.org

Foundation for Spinal Cord Injury Prevention, Care and Cure 1-800-342-0330. Dedicated to the prevention, care and cure of spinal cord injuries through public awareness, education and funding research. Free counseling for victims and their families. Networking of patients and families. *Website:* http://www.fscip.org/ *Email:* info@fscip.org

National Spinal Cord Injury Hotline *(BILINGUAL)* 1-800-962-9629 (Mon.-Fri., 9am-5pm ET--24 hour for new injuries), 301-582-6959 (resource center); Fax: 410-448-6627. Information, referral and peer support for spinal cord injured persons & their families. *Website:* http://www.spinalcord.org *Email:* scihotline@aol.com

Paralyzed Vets of America 1-800-424-8200 (Mon.-Fri., 8:30am-5pm ET); TDD/TTY: 202-872-1300 Ext. 622. Information, referral and advocacy for disabilities, paralyzed vets. *Website:* http://www.pva.org

STUTTERING

Stuttering Foundation of America 1-800-992-9392 or 1-800-967-7700 (24 hr). Information and referrals for stutterers and those who treat stutterers. Phone support, conferences. Maintains a nationwide referral list of speech pathologist that specialize in stuttering. *Website:* http://www.stutteringhelp.org *Email:* info@stutteringhelp.org

SUDDEN INFANT DEATH SYNDROME (SIDS)

American SIDS Institute 1-800-232-7437 or 770-426-8746 (24 hr). Dedicated to the prevention of sudden infant death syndrome. Promotes infant health through research. Education and support for families. *Website:* http://www.sids.org *Email:* prevent@sids.org

First Candle/SIDS Alliance 1-800-221-7437 or 410-653-8226; Fax: 410-653-8709. Information for parents looking for ways to help their infants thrive. Also for parents who have lost an infant to SIDS. Information on medical research, referrals to local support groups, referrals to community services, education. *Website:* http://www.firstcandle.org *Email:* sidshq@charm.net

SUICIDE PREVENTION

1-800-SUICIDE *(BILINGUAL)* 1-800-784-2433 (24 hr); 1-800-273-8255 (Crisis) Spanish: 1-800-442-4673; Admin: 202-237-2280. National suicide prevention line that routes callers to a local or regional suicide crisis hotline. *Website:* http://www.suicidology.org *Email:* info@suicidology.org

SURGERY

American Society of Plastic Surgeons 1-800-635-0635. Referrals to plastic surgeons. Information on particular plastic surgeons as to their particular qualifications. *Website:* http://www.plasticsurgery.org

Facial Plastic Surgery Information Service 1-800-332-3223. Makes referrals to board certified plastic surgeons. *Website:* http://www.plasticsurgery.org

TAX INFORMATION

IRS Federal Tax Information 1-800-829-1040 (24 hr). Provides information regarding federal tax questions, problems and refund information (30 day waiting period for written requests.) *Website:* http://www.irs.gov

NJ Tax Talk *(New Jersey)* 1-800-323-4400 or 609-292-6400 (Mon-Fri, 8:30am-4:30pm). Provides status of refunds and at certain times of the year status of Homestead Rebate applications, order forms and publication or listen to recorded tax topics. *Website:* http://www.state.nj.us/treasury/taxation

TRANSPORTATION

ACCESS LINK *(New Jersey)* 1-800-955-2321; TTY: 1-800-955-6765. Provides people with disabilities paratransit service comparable to the local bus service. Specifically for people whose disability prevents them from using existing local bus service.

Air Ambulance Central 1-800-262-8526 or 1-800-843-8418. Will fly patients from anywhere for needed medical services. *Email:* airmedusa@aol.com

Angel Flight 1-877-247-5433 (24 hr). Provides referrals to 1200 volunteer pilots who will fly needy patients for medical care. *Website:* http://www.angelflightne.org

Miracle Flights for Kids 1-800-359-1711 (Mon.-Thurs., 7:30am-6pm PT). Arranges airplane travel for children and adults with healthcare problems. Need doctor's note and 16 days notice. *Website:* http://www.miracleflights.org

National Patient Travel Center 1-800-296-1217 (Mon.-Fri., 10:30am-12:30pm). Information and referral for persons who need cost effective transportation for specialized treatment after an illness or accident. Fax: 757-318-9107 *Website:* http://www.patienttravel.org

NJ Transit Accessible Services *(New Jersey)* 1-800-772-2222 (northern NJ); 1-800-582-5946 (southern NJ) (6am-midnight, 7 days/wk for rail/bus schedule); TTY: 1-800-772-2287. For information on accessible services, stations and schedules. Reserves lift equipment bus for state and interstate use. *Website:* http://www.njtransit.com Sponsored by NJ Transit.

World Life Foundation 1-800-289-5433; Fax: 817-285-0216. Provides support, research, information and referrals for persons interested in rare metabolic disorders. Provides air transportation for ambulatory patients who need non-emergency treatment.

TRAUMA / DISASTERS

American Red Cross 1-866-438-4636 (Mon.-Fri., 8am-5pm ET). Provides disaster relief, emergency, health, safety and community services. *Website:* http://www.redcross.org

American Trauma Society 1-800-556-7890 or 301-420-4189 (Mon.-Fri., 8:30am-4:30pm ET); Fax: 301-420-0617. Provides referrals and educational materials on the prevention of physical traumas. *Website:* http://www.amtrauma.org *Email:* info@amtrauma.org

Think First Foundation/National Injury Prevention 1-800-844-6556 or 847-290-8600; Fax: 847-290-9005. Aims to prevent brain, spinal cord and other traumatic injuries through education and training. Information for children and teens. *Website:* http://www.thinkfirst.org *Email:* thinkfirst@thinkfirst.org

UROLOGIC DISEASE

American Foundation for Urologic Disease 1-800-828-7866 (Mon.-Fri., 8:30am-5pm); 1-800-242-2383 (booklets). Educational information for patients and others interested about urological diseases. *Website:* http://www.afud.org/

Kidney and Urology Foundation of America *(BILINGUAL)* 1-800-633-6628. Dedicated to helping persons afflicted with any debilitating kidney, urologic and related diseases. Offers education, information, health fairs, grants, patient scholarships, physician referrals, fellowship and Pediatric Enrichment program. *Website:* http://www.kidneyurology.org *Email:* info@kidneyurology.org

National Institute of Diabetes & Digestive & Kidney Diseases 1-800-891-5390 (kidney); 1-800-860-8747 (diabetes); 1-800-891-5389 (digestive diseases). Provides referrals and literature on a broad range of subjects concerning diabetes, digestive disorders, kidney disease, metabolic and endocrine disorders, hematological diseases, urologic disorders. *Website:* http://www.niddk.nih.gov *Email:* nkudic@info.niddk.nih.gov

VACCINATIONS

Alliance for Informed Choice on Vaccinations 1-800-613-9925. Addresses the concerns about the safety of vaccines and the right to informed consent. Literature, advocacy and phone help.

VARICELLO ZOSTER DISEASE

VZV Info Line 1-800-472-8478. Provides recorded information on varicello zoster virus. Free packets of information available for chicken pox, shingles and post-herpetic neuralgia. *Website:* http://www.vzvfoundation.org

WELFARE

Division of Family Development *(New Jersey)* 1-800-792-9773 (Mon.-Fri., 8am-4:30pm) Information on welfare and food stamps. Sponsored by Dept. of Human Services.

Goodwill Industries 1-800-741-0186 or 301-530-6500. Provides employment and training services for people with disabilities and other disadvantaging conditions (welfare dependency, illiteracy, criminal history, homeless). *Website:* http://www.goodwill.org

WISH GRANTING FOR ILL CHILDREN

Believe in Tomorrow Foundation 1-800-933-5470. Provides programs and services for children with life threatening illnesses. Fax: 410-744-1984 *Website:* http://www.believeintomorrow.org

Children's Wish Foundation Int'l 1-800-323-9474 (Mon.-Fri., 8:50am-5pm ET); Fax: 770-393-0683. Grants wishes to terminally ill children up to age of 18. *Website:* http://www.childrenswish.org *Email:* wish@childrenswish.org

Dream Factory 1-800-456-7556. Grants dreams for children with a life threatening or critical chronic illness. *Website:* http://www.dreamfactoryinc.com *Email:* info@dreamfactoryinc.com

Give Kids the World Foundation 1-800-995-5437 or 407-396-1114. Offers a 51-acre, non-profit resort for use by children with life-threatening illnesses whose one wish is to visit Central Florida's best-loved attractions. *Website:* http://www.gktw.org

Make-A-Wish Foundation 1-800-722-9474. Grants wishes to children with serious illnesses or life threatening medical conditions. *Website:* http://www.wish.org

Special Wish Foundation 1-800-486-9474 (Mon.-Fri., 9am-4:30pm ET). Grants wishes to children with terminal illnesses or life threatening disorders. *Website:* http://www.spwish.org *Email:* spwish@coil.com

Starlight Children's Foundation 1-800-274-7827 (9am-5pm, Mon.-Fri. PT). Grants wishes for seriously ill children. Also provides a variety of in-hospital services that focus on distraction entertainment. *Website:* http://www.starlight.org *Email:* info@starlight.org

WOMEN'S HELPLINE

National Women's Health Information Center *(BILINGUAL)* 1-800-994-9662 (Mon.-Fri., 9am-6pm); TDD/TTY: 1-888-220-5546. Provides information and referrals for all women's health questions and any questions on breast feeding. *Website:* http://www.4woman.gov *Email:* 4woman@soza.com

National Women's Health Resource Center *(New Jersey)* 1-877-986-9472 (Mon.-Fri., 9am-5pm). Information and resources about health concerns. By talking with staff, consumers will learn the key questions and issues to discuss with their physicians/health care professionals.

North American Menopause Society 1-800-774-5342. Provides free packet of information on menopause. Referrals to clinicians and discussions groups. *Website:* http://www.menopause.org

Endometriosis Helpline *(BILINGUAL)* 1-800-370-2943. Offers information on cause, treatment options, clinical trials, conducts research and offers referrals. *Website:* http://www.nichd.nih.gov *Email:* NICHDClearinghouse@mail.nih.gov

Women's Referral Central *(New Jersey)* 1-800-322-8092 (24 hr). Information and referrals on any issues concerning women. Education, homelessness, child support, custody, personal growth, domestic violence, etc.

WORLD TRADE CENTER

Cop-to-Cop *(New Jersey)* 1-866-267-2267 (24 hr). Serves active and retired law enforcement officers and their families. Retired officers and mental health professionals offer callers support. Provides peer support and referrals to counseling and mental health, substance abuse, partial care and inpatient treatment.

NJ Disaster Mental Health Helpline *(New Jersey)* 1-877-294-4357 (Mon.-Fri., 9am-5pm). Offers assistance and counseling to those affected by 9-11.

We know this Directory is big and chances are we can probably find the information you're looking for quicker than you paging through it. Call us! (We're really friendly!)
1-800-367-6274

YOUTH

Action, Parent and Teen Support 1-800-367-8336 (24 hr). Provides referrals to all types of agencies and services for troubled teens and their parents. *Email:* actionprogram@aol.com

Children's Defense Fund 1-800-233-1200 (Mon.-Fri., 9am-5pm CT). Advocacy for children who cannot speak for themselves. Emphasis on low income and disabled children. Develops prevention programs to help children. Training seminars to develop Confident Kids Support Groups. *Website:* http://www.childrensdefense.org *Email:* dcfinfo@childrensdefense.org

FACES (For All Children Experiencing Stress) *(New Jersey)* 1-877-653-2237 Information for teens coping with anxiety, stress, peer pressure and other issues that can be overwhelming. Monitored bulletin boards and chat rooms for kids, teens and parents. *Website:* http://www.NJFACES.org

Girl's and Boy's Town National Hotline *(BILINGUAL)* 1-800-448-3000 (24 hr); TDD/TTY: 1-800-448-1833. Provides crisis intervention, information & referrals for general population. Free, confidential. Short-term crisis intervention. Works with children and families. *Website:* http://www.girlsandboystown.org

National Youth Crisis Hotline 1-800-448-4663. Crisis hotline and information & referral for runaways or youth (17 and younger) with other problems and their parents. Sponsored by Youth Development International

NineLine 1-800-999-9999 (24 hr) or 212-613-0300. Nationwide crisis/suicide hotline. Referrals for youth or parents regarding drugs, domestic violence, homelessness, runaways, etc. Message relays, reports of abuse. Helps parents with problems with their kids. If all counselors are busy, stay on line & one will be with you as soon as possible. Sponsored by Nine Line/Covenant House. *Website:* http://www.covenanthouse.org/

Safe Sitter 1-800-255-4089. Trains adolescents 11-13 on how to be effective baby sitters. *Website:* http://www.safesitter.org *Email:* safesitter@safesitter.org

Consider passing this Directory on to a student or novice staff member - their simply browsing through the Directory pages can often provide truly helpful education as to the wide variety of groups available

Joy, happiness ... we do not question. They are beyond question, maybe. A matter of being.

But pain forces us to think, and to make connections ... to discover what has been happening to cause it.

And, curiously enough, pain draws us to other human beings in a significant way, whereas joy or happiness to some extent, isolates.

--May Sarton

NATIONAL/LOCAL CLEARINGHOUSES

SELF-HELP CLEARINGHOUSES

To locate a support group for your concern, review the list of Self-Help Clearinghouses, to see if there is one that serves your community. Our clearinghouse can provide information on other clearinghouse services both nationally and internationally. Give us a call 1-800-367-6274 (NJ only) or 973-326-6789. Self-help clearinghouses assist in the finding and forming of local groups. Some clearinghouses also provide training workshops, distribute "how-to" materials, publish directories and offer newsletters.

NATIONAL

American Self-Help Clearinghouse Maintains database of national self-help headquarters and model one-of-a-kind groups. Referrals to self-help clearinghouses nationwide. Offers assistance to persons interested in starting new groups. Director: Ed Madara. Write: American Self-Help Clearinghouse, 100 E. Hanover Ave., Suite 202, Cedar Knolls, NJ 07927-2020. Call 973-326-6789; Fax: 973-326-9467. *Website:* http://www.selfhelpgroups.org *E-mail:* ashc@cybernex.net

National Self-Help Clearinghouse *Founded 1976.* Provides information and referral to self-help groups and regional self-help clearinghouses. Encourages and conducts training of professionals about self-help. Carries out research activities, publishes manuals and training materials. Write: National Self-Help Clearinghouse, c/o CUNY, Graduate School and University Center, 365 Fifth Ave., Suite 3300, New York, NY 10016. Call 212-817-1822. *Website:* http://www.selfhelpweb.org *E-mail:* ajgartner@gc.cuny.edu

CONNECTICUT

Connecticut Self-Help Support Network *Founded 1981.* Information and referrals to support groups. Provides technical assistance in starting and maintaining groups. Group leadership training, educational workshops and conferences. Publishes directory of self-help groups, newsletter and other publications. Write: Connecticut SHSN, c/o Susan Zimmerman, LCSW, The Consultation Center, 389 Whitney Ave., New Haven, CT 06511. Call 203-624-6982; Fax: 203-562-6355. *Website:* http://www.theconsultationcenter.org *E-mail:* info@theconsultationcenter.org (attention: self-help)

NEW YORK

Institute for Human Services/HELPLINE *(Steuben, Allegany and Chemung Counties). Founded 1984.* Information and referrals to local services and agencies, as well as local support groups. Provides assistance to new and existing self-help groups. Also acts as 24-hour crisis and referral line. Newsletter, information and referral. Write: Institute for Human Services, 6666 County Rd. Il, Bath, NY 14810-7722. Call 1-800-346-2211 (in NY); Admin. 607-776-9467; Helpline 607-776-9604; Fax: 607-776-9482. *Website:* http://www.ihsnet.org *E-mail:* helpline@ihsnet.org

Long Island Self-Help Clearinghouse Provides referrals to local support groups. Assistance to new and existing groups. Coordinator: Eileen Giannetti. Write: Long Island Self-Help Clearinghouse, c/o NY College of Osteopathic Medicine, NY Institute of Technology, Northern Blvd. Old Westbury, NY 11568. Call 516-626-1721. Fax: 516-686-7890. *E-mail:* egiannet@nyit.edu

Mental Health Association of Monroe County Provides information and referrals to local support groups. Assistance in starting new groups, training workshops and how-to materials. Consultation to existing groups, directory of local groups published online. Write: MHA, 339 East Ave., Suite 201, Rochester, NY 14604. Call Debra Sponable 585-325-3145 ext. 18; Fax: 585-325-3188. *Website:* http://www.mharochester.org

National Self-Help Clearinghouse *Founded 1976.* Provides information and referrals to self-help groups and regional self-help clearinghouses. Encourages and conducts training of professionals about self-help. Carries out research activities. Publishes manuals and training materials. Write: National Self-Help Clearinghouse, c/o CUNY, Graduate School and University Center, 365 Fifth Ave., Suite 3300, New York, NY 10016. Call 212-817-1822. *Website:* http://www.selfhelpweb.org *E-mail:* info@selfhelpweb.org

New York City Self Help Center Information and referrals to support groups in the five boroughs (Manhattan, Bronx, Staten Island, Queens and Brooklyn). Assistance to new and developing groups. Write: NYC Self-Help Center, 850 7th Ave., Suite 1201, New York, NY 10019. Call 212-586-5770; Fax: 212-399-2475.

Niagara Self-Help Clearinghouse *(Niagara County). Founded 1985.* Information and referrals to local support groups. Provides technical assistance to new groups. Networks with other community resources. Helps with new group development and holds group leader training. Directory of self-help groups, mental health video/book library. Write: Niagara Self-Help Clearinghouse, c/o MHA in Niagara County, 36 Pine St., Lockport, NY 14094. Call 716-433-3780 ext 12; Fax: 716-433-3847. *Website:* http://www.mhanc.com

Self-Help Clearinghouse of Cattaraugus County Provides information and referrals to local support groups in Cattaraugus County. Offers assistance in starting new groups. Provides assistance with utility payments, disaster funding and assistance, various health and safety training classes, monthly blood drives and military emergency service (24 hr). Write: Self-Help Clearinghouse of Cattaraugus County, c/o American Red Cross, Greater Buffalo Chapter, 452 N. Barry St., Olean, NY 14760-2612. Call 716-372-5800.

Self-Help Clearinghouse *(Rockland County) Founded 1951.* Information and referrals concerning self-help groups. Provides consultation and assistance to new groups that are forming. Publishes newsletter, self-help group directory ($3). Offers assistance starting support groups. Write: Self-Help Clearinghouse, c/o MHA of Rockland County Inc., 20 Squadron Blvd., New City, NY 10956. Call 845-639-7400 ext. 22; Fax: 845-639-7419. *Website:* http://www.mharockland.org *E-mail:* lhilton@mharockland.org

Self-Help Resource Center *(Broome County) Founded 1998.* Information and referrals to local self-help groups. Maintains an updated database and publishes a directory of local self-help groups. Presents free consumer conferences designed to educate public about psychiatric diagnoses and self-help methods for symptom management. Presents ongoing workshop series which offers a variety of topics including artistic expression, community involvement, leadership and wellness. Assistance provided to start support groups. Write: Self-Help Resource Center, c/o MHA, 82 Oak St., Binghamton, NY 13905. Call 607-771-8888; Fax: 607-771-8892. *Website:* http://www.yourmha.com *E-mail:* lise.fiato@yourmha.com

Westchester Self-Help Clearinghouse *Founded 1979.* A central resource for mutual support groups. Provides information and referrals to mutual support groups in Westchester County. Assists in the formation of new groups. Provides community education and publishes a directory of self-help groups every other year. Phone networks for newly widowed men and women; and newly separated women. Director: Lenore Rosenbaum, MS. Write: Westchester Self-Help Clearinghouse, 845 N. Broadway, White Plains, NY 10603. Call 914-761-0600 ext. 308; Fax: 914-761-5859. *E-mail:* lrosenbaum@wjcs.com

PENNSYLVANIA

Mutual Support Group Clearinghouse *Founded 1997.* Provides referral information on self-help groups in the central Susquehanna Valley region. Also provides technical assistance to new and existing groups. Workshops, newsletter, directory of regional self-help groups. Write: Mutual Support Group Clearinghouse, c/o MHA, 37 W. Main St., Suite 206, Bloomsburg, PA 17815. Call 1-800-874-8363 or 570-784-9583; Fax: 570-784-3220. *Website:* http://www.mhacsv.org

Self-Help Information Network Exchange (SHINE) *(Lackawanna County)* Provides information and referrals to support groups in northeastern Pennsylvania. Sponsors workshops and special events for self-help advocates. Brochure. Community resource library. Write: SHINE, 538 Spruce St., Suite 420, Scranton, PA 18503. Call 570-961-1234 (24 hr); Admin: 570-347-5616; Fax: 570-341-5816. *Website:* http://www.vacnepa.org *E-mail:* shine@vacnepa.org

---

When you plant lettuce, if it does not grow well, you don't blame the lettuce. You look for reasons it is not doing well. It may need fertilizer, or more water, or less sun. You never blame the lettuce.

Yet if we have problems with our friends or our family, we blame the other person. But if we know how to take care of them, they will grow well, like the lettuce.

Blaming has no positive effect at all, nor does trying to persuade using reason and argument. That is my experience. If you understand, and you show that you understand, you can love, and the situation will change.

--Thich Nhat Hahn

INDEX

E

F

L

M

Although every effort was made to assess accuracy in this directory, group contact information does change on a daily basis. So if you were unable to find the appropriate group, give us a call. Also if you have a group listed in our directory and would like to update your information, please call **1-800-367-6274**, more easily remembered as **1-800-F.O.R.-M.A.S.H.** (Mutual Aid Self-Help).

Celebrating 25 Years of Service

Since its official start on Jan. 1, 1981, your **Self-Help Group Clearinghouse** has worked hard to meet its mission of increasing the awareness, utilization, development and understanding of Mutual Aid Self-Help groups in order to help reduce emotional suffering and isolation of people who face any of a broad spectrum of stressful life problems. This has been done, in part, by:

* Developing Needed New Groups
Since 1981, has helped courageous and dedicated individuals to develop over 1,050 new volunteer-run self-help groups in New Jersey.

* Helping People to Find Groups
The Clearinghouse helps about 10,000 callers a year through toll-free phone service, and aided many more through its annual Directory and website. The Clearinghouse has identified over 4,500 local group meetings within the state and over 1,100 national, online, and model groups outside NJ.

* Increased Recognition of the Value of Self-Help Groups
Through its education and outreach efforts, the Clearinghouse has increased awareness of self-help groups at state and national levels. We make numerous presentations to professional organizations each year

CLEARINGHOUSE FIRSTS

* First Statewide Self-Help Clearinghouse in the country.

* First Toll-free Accessible Self-Help Information Phone Service

* On-Line Support Group Meetings
The Clearinghouse helped pioneer some of the first on-line mutual help message boards and self-help group meetings in the early 1980's.

Current Clearinghouse Staff:
Barbara J. White, State Consultation & Training Services Coordinator
Nicole Klem, Information & Referral Services Supervisor
Wendy Rodenbaugh, Information & Referral Services Assistant
Jeanne Rohach, Assistant Trainer & Group Facilitator
Ed Madara, Program Administrator
and approximately **18 dedicated volunteers** whose contributions make the Clearinghouse services truly possible.